Dawn Farough '96

FAMI

AN INTRODUCTION

SECOND EDITION

FAMILIES IN CANADIAN SOCIETY

AN INTRODUCTION

MAUREEN BAKER
McGill University

JANET DRYDEN
Consulting Editor

McGRAW-HILL RYERSON LIMITED
Toronto Montreal New York Auckland Bogotá Caracas Lisbon London Madrid Mexico Milan New Delhi Paris San Juan Singapore Sydney Tokyo

FAMILIES IN CANADIAN SOCIETY: AN INTRODUCTION, *Second Edition*

ISBN 0-07-551366-8

4 5 6 7 8 9 10 W 2 1 0 9 8 7 6 5

Printed and bound in Canada

Care has been taken to trace the ownership of copyright material contained in this text. The publishers will gladly take any information that will enable them to rectify any reference or credit in subsequent editions.

Canadian Cataloguing in Publication Data

Baker, Maureen
Families in Canadian society

2nd ed.
Includes bibliographical references and index.
ISBN 0-07-551366-8

1, Family—Canada. I. Title

HQ560.B35 1993 306.85'0971 C92-095095-7

PUBLISHER: JANICE MATTHEWS
ASSOCIATE EDITOR: NANCY SAUNDERCOOK
SENIOR SUPERVISING EDITOR: CAROL ALTILIA
PERMISSIONS EDITOR: JACQUELINE RUSSELL
COPY EDITOR: GERALDINE KIKUTA
COVER AND INTERIOR DESIGN: MATTHEWS COMMUNICATIONS DESIGN
COVER IMAGE: "JOYOUS MOTHERHOOD" BY CECIL YOUNGFOX

This book was manufactured in Canada using acid-free and recycled paper.

Contents

Figures and Tables

Chapter 1

Chapter 2

Chapter 3

Chapter 4

Chapter 5

Chapter 6

Chapter 7

CHAPTER 8

CHAPTER 9

Preface

Over the past few decades, Canadians have experienced rapid social change in family life. Living arrangements, child care patterns, family law, sexual attitudes and practices, reproductive technologies, parent/adolescent relations, women's work lives, and household labour are all in a state of flux. This book is designed to introduce students to these changes, to place them within a historical, cultural, and theoretical context, and to help students develop their capacity to probe into social issues in a critical way.

In using this text, students will gain an understanding of Canadian social, demographic, economic, legal, and cultural trends relating to family life. This book should also create an awareness of the similarities and differences between family life in Canada and other countries, as well as among different ethnic and cultural groups within our country. In addition to contributing to theoretical and empirical knowledge about family life, this text should assist students in developing an awareness of their own family situations and relationships. Students should also learn to critically review news reports and journal articles and may further develop their own informed opinions about controversial social issues.

This textbook is intended to expand the student's knowledge of changing family life in Canada. At the same time, however, it is anticipated that the student will develop analytical and cognitive skills valuable in other social science courses at the college or university level.

Each chapter of the book follows a different stage in the family life cycle[1] and contains a discussion of developmental or specific tasks, historical background, cross-cultural perspectives, social issues, and some projections about future trends relevant to that particular stage in the family life cycle. Throughout these chapters, students are familiarized with theories and studies that should help them to see these topics within a social science framework.

Several approaches to family studies are used in this text. First of all, the family life cycle provides the organizational framework for each chapter. This means that the family is seen as an ever-changing unit in which relationships and interaction vary depending on the stage of development. This approach may roughly parallel people's lives and therefore may be a familiar way of looking at families. Before

---

[1] The stages followed are those set out by Carter and McGoldrick in *The Changing Family Life Cycle: A Framework for Family Therapy (1988).*

marriage, for example, a young person's relationships with extended family members, attitudes toward family life, and major preoccupations or developmental tasks may differ considerably from a young couple with infant children. Similarly, as the children grow older, they place different demands on their parents that affect the relationships between the parents, among parents and their children, and between family members and those outside the household. Childless couples may organize their lives in quite diverse ways because they do not have the same responsibilities and pressures.

The assumption behind the family life cycle approach is that living through the various stages —singleness, the early adjustments of married life, years of married life or a possible divorce, childrearing, children's development of independence in adolescence, child-launching, growing old with the same partner or premature bereavement, having grandchildren or being together all day with a retired marital partner—changes people's behaviour and attitudes. The life cycle approach assumes that people grow and develop by living through these stages and that families have similar experiences at the same stage.

One advantage of the family life cycle approach is that families are seen as continually changing groups in which relationships and behaviour evolve to fit the new circumstances of family members. A disadvantage is that the approach assumes that all people experience each of these stages, and that all family members experience them at the same time. In fact, we know that some people never marry, while others remain childless or divorce. Some people remarry and begin new families while children from their previous marriages are cared for by their former spouses. Although there may be "typical" stages that many people pass through within a particular culture, not everyone experiences these stages or experiences them in the same way.

At each typical stage in the family life cycle, historical and cross-cultural material relating to that stage is introduced to show how that particular stage of family life has changed over time, and how it varies among cultural and ethnic groups. Several contemporary issues related to each stage are also presented to encourage more in-depth analysis, classroom discussion, or further research.

Each chapter ends with a prediction of future trends in family behaviour and research within that particular stage of the life cycle and a suggestion of possible future issues. It is expected that the analysis and discussion of these social issues will provide students with the cognitive and research skills necessary to evaluate social science issues as they arise in the future.

Key concepts are printed in bold type and are defined in the glossary at the end. The book also contains current statistics on family trends, articles reprinted from other sources such as books and newspapers, questions at the end of each chapter to promote critical thinking skills and discussion, and some suggestions for further reading.

I would like to thank several individuals who assisted me in preparing this book. In the School Division of McGraw-Hill Ryerson, Nancy Saundercook, Associate Editor, and Janice Matthews, Publisher, guided the book through its various stages of development. Various reviewers offered additional comments that helped me to revise the manuscript. I would like to acknowledge Gloria Baxter, Board of Education for the City of Scarborough; Nancy McGregor, R.S. McLaughlin Collegiate and Vocational Institute, Oshawa, ON; John Kaposy, Metropolitan Separate School Board; and Tracy Williams-Shreve. David Tippin, my husband, provided valuable moral support and, as usual, kept the household functioning while I was preoccupied with preparing the manuscript.

Most of all, I would like to thank Janet Dryden from Peterborough County Board of Education, and emphasize the significant contribution she has made as consulting editor of this book. With the greatest of tact, Janet critically reviewed each page of the first edition and suggested improvements for the second edition. Her teaching experience with OAC Family Studies and knowledge of the interests and concerns of both teachers and students in the field played an important role in the creation of the second edition.

Maureen Baker, Ph.D.

McGill University

1

Introduction to Family Studies

UNDERSTANDING FAMILY LIFE

The Importance of Family Life

Throughout childhood and adolescence, most people live with one or both of their parents as part of a family group. Although young people are influenced by friends, teachers, extracurricular activities, part-time jobs, what they read, and what they see on television, their family experiences usually establish their attitudes, their relationships, their lifestyles, and their aspirations for the future. Whether or not we admire our parents' way of life, we cannot deny its importance in forming our attitudes and future behaviour. Furthermore, throughout our lives, many of us rely on our families more than friends or neighbours to provide us with emotional and financial support, even when we live far away from them.

Despite human individuality, social scientists have found patterns in personal and family behaviour. This should not be surprising, however, as we are not permitted to behave any way we want to either within our families or in the outside world. For one thing, legal requirements govern our personal behaviour and family life. For example, we need a licence from our provincial government before we can marry legally, and we are not permitted to marry certain categories of relatives. We are obliged to register the births of children and provide these children with first and surnames. As parents, we are required to feed and clothe our children and provide them with the necessities of life. We must support them financially and provide them with a formal education until they are old enough to work legally for pay. Furthermore, we are responsible if our children misbehave or become involved in delinquent acts. How and why these laws develop over time and how they vary in different cultures could be analyzed within the field of family studies.

In addition to legal requirements, there are also social expectations of behaviour placed upon us by our relatives, friends, neighbours, teachers, and employers that govern our actions. Expectations about how we should behave in certain situations as well as traditional patterns of behaviour are called **social norms.** We can ignore these norms, but we face certain consequences if we do. There are many examples of behavioural expectations relating to family life. As children, we are taught to respect our parents and to abide by their house rules and guidelines. Before we leave school, our parents usually expect us to have acquired enough formal education and life skills to find a job that will enable us to become self-supporting. By the time we reach our mid to late teens, we are usually expected to show some interest in the opposite sex and, later, to marry and produce children. After marriage, we are expected to remain monogamous and reproduce only with our spouses. After bearing children, we are encouraged to make some personal and financial sacrifices in order to raise them to adulthood. The exact details of social expectations vary by historical time period, country, region, cultural group, and neighbourhood, as does the reaction to those who step outside these majority norms. How children learn behavioural standards or norms and what happens to those who do not conform to such expectations could also be the subject of analysis in family studies.

Personal Experience and Social Science

Because all of us have first-hand knowledge of some form of family life, it is possible to discuss the subject matter of family studies with greater personal interest and intensity than other subjects. Yet, studying family life from a social science perspective means that different ways of behaving can be identified, systematically analyzed, compared, and explained within the context of the culture and the era. Patterns in human behaviour are identifiable because behaviour is influenced by a number of social and cultural factors, such as people's income, education, and occupation; their religious upbringing; their racial or **ethnic origin**; and the wider cultural values and practices in their society.

Within social science, stages in the family life cycle can be studied in other societies, among ethnic and cultural groups within our own country, and during different periods of history. Social scientists also look for relationships between various family types and other **social institutions** such as the economy, legal and educational systems, or political structures.

When studying families from a social science perspective, our personal assumptions about what constitutes "normal behaviour" need to be questioned. This is partly to compare our assumptions with research findings about how people behave in other cultures and historical time periods. But we also need to question our assumptions to see if they accurately describe family life in Canada today. After all, if we generalize from our own experiences, we may discover that these experiences are not typical. Family life differs according to people's cultural and religious background, family structure, family income, occupation, and education. While some of these differences may be subtle, others are more obvious.

We cannot assume that all people live the same way; nor should we judge other people's behaviour by our own standards. Our prejudices should be set aside so that we can more accurately describe and explain social and cultural trends in family life.

Before any topic can be systematically analyzed, it is important to define clearly all relevant terms. Only if we have the same understanding of definitions can we make comparisons of how families are similar or different in varying time periods, **social classes**, or cultural groups.

DEFINING FAMILY AND HOUSEHOLD

We sometimes use the term *family* when we really mean *household.* The term **household** includes all those sharing a dwelling, whether or not they are related by blood, marriage, or adoption. When we talk about our family, however, we could be referring to a number of different social entities. The great variety in living arrangements in present-day North America has led to some confusion about what the word family actually means.

The most common meaning involves the presence of children. When we ask a young couple if they have a family, we mean do they have any children. The term *couple* is used for husband and wife without children, as well as two unmarried people who are sexually involved with each other.

Social scientists and researchers have attempted to be more specific in their definitions of the word family. In 1949, for example, the American anthropologist George Murdock provided a definition of family that has been widely used since then. According to Murdock, a family is "a social group characterized by common residence, economic co-operation, and reproduction. It includes adults of both sexes, at least two of whom maintain a socially-approved sexual relationship, and one or more children, own or adopted, of the sexually cohabiting adults" (Murdock, 1949:1).

Considering recent changes in lifestyle, this definition is now less appropriate than it might have been 40 years ago. Canadian sociologist Emily Nett has revised previous definitions of family to suggest that the word should now refer to "any group of people *considered* to be related to each other by blood or marriage" (Nett, 1980:354). She extended the definition beyond those who share a dwelling place to include a wider network of related persons. She argued that the family is an abstraction involving ideal, expected, and observed behaviour.

When we speak about our families, we might mean the related people who live in the same household with us—our parents and siblings, or our spouse and children. Social scientists have called the living unit consisting of parents and their offspring the **nuclear family**. Anthropologists writing in the early twentieth century, such as Bronislaw Malinowski, noted the universality or near universality of family life, especially the living unit comprised of a husband, wife, and their children. Although marriage and family forms vary widely throughout the world, the nuclear family has been the common living arrangement in most industrialized countries, including Canada. Despite the prevalence of this pattern, however, only 52 percent of Canadian families consist of married couples with children (Vanier Institute of the Family, 1991:5). The remainder consist of one-parent households, married couples without children, and common-law couples with or without children (Ibid, p. 5).

When we use the word family, we could also be referring to the larger kin group that includes grandparents, aunts, uncles, cousins, married brothers and sisters, older parents, or in-laws. In the terminology of social science, an **extended family** involves three or more generations usually sharing the same household. In some countries, such as India, Indonesia, and some countries in southern Europe and the Middle East, married couples live with one set of parents from the beginning of their marriage until the death of their parents. Extended families have also been prevalent among certain cultural groups living

Figure 1.1 **Family Structure in Canada**

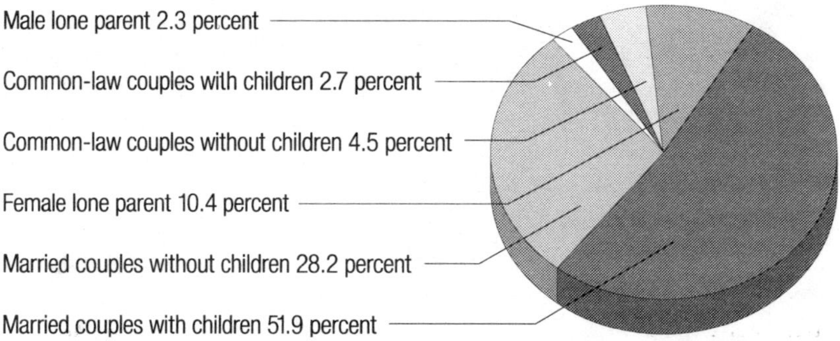

- Five and a half million couples are married.
- Half a million couples are cohabiting.
- Two million families have no children at home.
- Of those, approximately one in three are those whose children have grown up and left home.
- Of the almost 4.5 million families with children, four out of five are two-parent families.
- Nearly 1.5 million of these two-parent families have children under six at home.
- Almost a quarter of a million lone-parent families have children under six at home.

Source: Statistics Canada and Canada Employment and Immigration Advisory Council

in North America. These include southern European and Chinese immigrants and some First Nations' groups.

The most common type of extended family in Canada includes a nuclear family plus a widowed parent unable to live alone. In 1986, 7 percent of women aged 65 and over compared with 3 percent of elderly men lived in extended family situations (Ram, 1990:46). In North America and Europe, at least since the seventeenth century, extended families were more prevalent among lower-income people who needed to share accommodation and couples with parents in need of constant care (Goldthorpe, 1987). There is no evidence from historical research that extended families were considered ideal arrangements in North America or Europe, at least within the past few centuries (Nett, 1981; Goldthorpe, 1987).

An extended family involves three or more generations living within the same household.

Photo: Tessa Macintosh, Government N.W.T.

Statistics Canada collects data on the percentage of "multi-family households," which is as close as we can come to the social science concept of extended family households. Despite the fact that many immigrants come to Canada from countries in which people live in extended families, and that widowed parents sometimes live with their married children, the percentage of such households has declined from 6.7 percent in 1951 to only 1.1 percent in 1986 (Ram, 1990:44). This decline may be explained largely because most Canadians now consider living alone more acceptable and feasible both for single persons and elderly widows or widowers.

In modern-day North America, where separation, divorce, and remarriage are increasingly prevalent, there are many different family forms and several definitions depending on which variation is being researched or which social program is being discussed. When the federal government conducts a census, for example, several specific definitions of family are used depending on how the government wants to use the data. According to Statistics Canada, the **census family** involves a married couple living with or without never-married children (regardless of age) or one parent living with never-married children (regardless of age). Statistics Canada also use the term

economic family to refer to a group of two or more people related by blood, marriage, or adoption sharing the same household.

Instead of referring to *the family* which implies that there is only one acceptable form, social scientists now use the term *families* to connote the variations in family life. When we discuss family life, we should try to be as specific as possible about the type of family we are talking about. It may be useful to simply add an adjective in front of the word family to make its definition clearer. We could then talk about nuclear families, extended families, one-parent families (or households), common-law families, blended families, census families, or economic families.

We may think that it makes no difference how a word is defined. However, accurate information about family life is essential to many different types of organizations and to social scientists. For example, governments collect information on families and households in order to plan schools, hospitals, housing projects, social services, and social security programs (such as Family Allowance and the Canada Pension Plan). Without clear definitions, governments could not obtain

THE FAMILY—VARIATIONS ON A THEME

There are approximately 26 million people in Canada, and more than 6 million families. Essentially, there is no longer one typical family in Canada. Many names are used to describe different kinds of families:

- "Nuclear" families composed of two parents and their one or more children, living together. When the nuclear family was led by a male wage-earner, it was the conventional family of the 1950s, although now it is only one of many types of family.
- "Extended" families composed of parents, children, aunts, uncles, grandparents, and other blood relations living together, or not.
- "Blended" or "recombined" or "reconstituted" families composed of parents who have divorced their first spouses, remarried someone else, and formed a new family that includes children from one or both first marriages, and/or from the remarriage.
- "Childless" families consisting of a couple.
- "Lone-parent" families composed of a parent, most often a mother, with a child or children.
- "Cohabiting couples," and "Common-Law marriages,"—family arrangements that resemble other forms, but without legalized marriage.
- "Traditional" familes—a confusing term that reflects the changing nature of Canadian families in that people tend to use it to refer to their own families, or to the family type that they have encountered most often.

Vanier Institute of the Family. *Canadian Families*, Ottawa 1991:3. Reprinted courtesy of The Vanier Institute of the Family, Ottawa.

accurate statistics relating to age, sex, marriages, births, deaths, divorces, and income levels, and would consequently be unable to plan for the future. Furthermore, researchers could not compare the results of their studies if they did not clearly define their concepts. In the classroom and in student projects, it is just as important to use specific language and to define concepts when describing and analyzing family life.

Before proceeding further, it is important to present some background material to introduce the study of families. The rest of this chapter will outline some cultural variations in family structure and life. The next chapter will provide an overview of various theoretical perspectives and research methods used within the field of family studies.

CULTURAL VARIATIONS IN FAMILIES

Nuclear vs. Extended Families

In a culturally diverse society such as Canada, it is inaccurate as stated earlier to talk about "the family" as though a single type of family exists or ever did exist. In actual fact, various cultural groups tend to organize their family life differently, depending on such factors as their socio-economic backgrounds, their historical experiences in this country, their relations with other cultural groups, their religious beliefs, whether they were indigenous to the country or immigrants, and if they were immigrants, when they arrived.

According to some researchers, however, there has been a convergence throughout the world toward the nuclear or **conjugal family** structure as societies and regions become industrialized (Goode, 1963). In the conjugal family, husband and wife live with their children and place more importance on their marital relationship than on ties with their parents or kin group. Industrialization often forces young people to migrate in order to find work, and they eventually settle in urban areas where housing is expensive, especially for large families. It is more difficult for extended families to remain in the same household when younger members are seeking employment for a wage than when families worked as productive units on a farm, at fishing, or in a family business.

Sociologists in the 1950s lamented the isolation of the modern nuclear family, implying that the extended family was more prevalent prior to industrialization (Parsons and Bales, 1955). In recent years, however, historical researchers have found that nuclear families were always more typical living arrangements than extended families both in Europe or North America (Laslett, 1972; Goldthorpe, 1987), where most Canadians originated. Neither has it been common for married couples to live with their parents at any time in Canadian history, except for short periods in a couple's marriage when their parents were widowed and unable to live alone (Nett, 1981) or among certain cultural groups, such as Asians or Africans. Nuclear families were more prevalent because life expectancy was short and many parents died before their children reached adulthood. Furthermore, many young people established separate households when they moved from their parents' homes to find work. Keep in mind that although many recent immigrants come from countries with extended families, these immigrants form only a small portion of the population. For example, 6.3 percent of Canadian adults are considered "visible minorities" (Moreau, 1991:26), and not all of these people come from countries where extended families are the norm.

The extended family, however, remains important in Canada and in many other countries as a support group. Relatives who do not share a residence, may try to live in the same neighbourhood, visit regularly, telephone daily, assist each other with child care, provide economic and emotional support, and help find one another employment and accommodation (Ishwaran, 1980). This kind of living arrangement has been called the **modified extended family**.

Close physical and emotional ties with the extended family are more apparent for some groups of people than for others. For example, after they marry, people in certain cultural groups maintain close ties with siblings and parents. Working class people tend to live closer to other family members and to maintain closer ties than those in the middle classes (Bott, 1951; Baker, 1983; McPherson, 1990:348). Furthermore, research has indicated that women from all social classes tend to maintain closer family relationships throughout their lives than men do (Rosenthal, 1982, 1985; Connidis, 1989).

High unemployment and prolonged education, however, has led to some young people in their twenties returning to live in their parents' home. In addition, widowed parents sometimes come to live with their children for their remaining years. Certain cultural groups living in Canada are more likely than others to live in extended households. These include recent immigrants from southern Europe, China, and India, as well as people in many First Nations' groups (Elliot, 1983; Ishwaran, 1980). In 1986, however, the proportion of Canadians living in multiple-family households was only about

1 percent. It may be that living in an extended family situation in Canada is still a temporary phenomenon. Such a family situation may exist when members who arrive as immigrants to Canada cannot set up their own households until they find work, when it is too costly for young people to rent an apartment, or when elderly parents are unable to live alone.

Monogamy vs. Polygamy

When George Murdock completed his *World Ethnographic Sample* in 1949, he noted that only about 20 percent of the societies he studied were designated as strictly monogamous. In Canada and most industrialized countries, **monogamy**, or having one legal spouse at a time, is the social custom and the law. Yet, many Canadians marry, divorce, and remarry during their lives. This lifetime pattern of marriage has been called **serial monogamy**.

Having more than one spouse at a time is referred to as plural marriage or **polygamy**. Polygamy is generally viewed as a status symbol in societies where it is practised, but it has also existed in hunting and gathering societies where there were fewer males due to hunting accidents or warfare (Leslie and Korman, 1989:25-32).

According to Murdock's 1949 study of 554 societies, most societies (415) permitted **polygyny**, or having more than one wife at a time, and were characterized by a mixture of polygyny and monogamy. In some African and Moslem countries, for example, polygyny continues to be practised by wealthier men who can afford to support more than one wife.

Polygyny could involve sisters or unrelated women. Wives in polygynous marriages may welcome the addition of a new wife to the family to help with household duties and child care, to share work in the fields, or for companionship (Leslie and Korman, 1989:27). Polygyny is much more prevalent than **polyandry**, or having multiple husbands at a time. This probably relates to the fact that only one male is needed to impregnate several wives and to the question of paternity that would arise with more than one husband. In many societies, obligations and rights flow from lineage or to whom a child is related.

In recent years, polygamy has been prohibited by law in westernized countries. This is due, in part, to the assumed difficulties in providing adequate financial and emotional support for more than one partner and religious ideas of sexual exclusivity.

ARRANGED VS. FREE CHOICE MARRIAGE

In many parts of the world, marriages are **arranged** in order to protect inheritance, increase family resources, enhance family reputation, and because parents feel that they are more qualified to choose partners for their children. Some marriages continue to be arranged in Middle Eastern countries, in parts of Japan, in Moslem African countries, and in parts of Indonesia. The family of either the bride or the groom may make the initial arrangements. **Marriage brokers** or intermediaries are occasionally used to assist the family to find a suitable mate for their offspring. This intermediary may be a family friend or relative, or a friend of a friend with an extensive network of contacts.

Some marriages are arranged among Middle Eastern, Japanese, and east Asian immigrants living in Canada. These arrangements may involve going back to the home country to marry a partner who has been selected by family members still living there. On other occasions, a man and a woman from the same cultural group living in Canada may be introduced to each other by family members and may be encouraged to marry. Among cultural groups in Canada that maintain arranged marriages, young people expect to have veto power if they strongly object to their parents' choice. In their home country, however, there is still considerable pressure to abide by the judgment of the elders (Nanda, 1991:238).

In arranged marriages, more importance is placed on extended family solidarity, financial security, and potential heirs, than on personal gratification and feelings of love between the young people (Nanda, 1991:237-239). Marital partners are urged to respect their family's wishes and each other, and it is hoped that love will develop

ARRANGED MARRIAGES

KWAKIUTL, VANCOUVER ISLAND

"When I was old enough to get a wife—I was about twenty-five—my brother looked for a girl in the same position that I and my brothers had. Without my consent, they picked a wife for me—Lagius' daughter. The one I wanted was prettier than the one they chose for me, but she was in a lower position than me, so they wouldn't let me marry her. I argued about it and was very angry with my brother, but I couldn't do anything... Anyway, my older brother made arrangements for my marriage. He gave Lagius, the head chief of the Nimkis, two hundred blankets to keep Lagius from letting others have his daughter."

Clellan S. Ford. *Smoke From Their Fires.* New Haven: Yale University Press, 1941:149.

after they have married and shared a home. In actual fact, arranged marriages are often more stable than free choice unions because both families have a stake in marriage stability, divorce is often legally restricted, and women cannot always support themselves outside of marriage. The process of urbanization and westernization, however, has encouraged young people to anticipate "falling in love" and to seek a more intensive marital relationship.

In societies practising arranged marriages, a **dowry** is sometimes used to attract a husband and to insure that women have money in case of divorce or premature widowhood. Under the dowry system, families with marriageable daughters must show families with eligible sons that they can provide money or property upon marriage. If a woman has a large dowry, she can find a "better" husband, which usually means one who is wealthier, healthier, highly educated, and from a respected family. The dowry system has been a great financial burden for poorer families, especially if they have several daughters. Because males can more easily find jobs and support themselves, acquire property through marriage, perpetuate the family name, and do not cost the family as much money when they marry, the dowry system tends to encourage families to prefer sons. For this reason, it has been outlawed in some countries such as India, although it continues to operate clandestinely in rural areas.

FINDING HUSBAND EXACTS HIGH PRICE FROM INDIAN WOMEN

Official figures show 11 259 brides died over dowries in past three years

Reuters News Agency

NEW DELHI—More than 11 000 young Indian wives have committed suicide or been killed in the past three years because of illegal but ubiquitous dowry demands, official figures released yesterday indicate.

The government statistics, given in parliament, confirm the fears of women's organizations that more and more Indian families are flouting the law to demand ever-increasing quantities of money and consumer goods from the families of young brides.

"We're so poor, we could not give the dowry to save my child," one mother told reporters this month after her recently and unhappily married 21-year-old daughter was found dead.

Newspaper commentators said she had summed up the plight of millions. Dowry demands have been comprehensively outlawed in India since 1961, but the social stigma falls on the families who fail to pay up, not those who levy the demands.

The official death toll has risen steadily to 4835 in 1990 from 2209 in 1988—

partly because of increasing convictions under a new law that makes it easier to convict families known to have mistreated young wives who die in suspect circumstances.

Women's organizations, social workers and New Delhi residents agree that dowry demands are increasing and spreading from the system's stronghold in the lower middle classes throughout society.

"Our daughter will cost us a fortune," said a New Delhi businesswoman.

"First, the education, with private sports and arts classes to attract the right sort of man. Then, the dowry—we'll have to buy a car, a refrigerator, furniture, jewelry...

"How can I buck the system? It's her happiness that's at stake. Of course, we'd make sure her husband wouldn't beat her, but in every family there's an aunt or cousin who could make her life a misery in more subtle ways."

Indian women traditionally go to live with their husbands' families and become answerable to their mothers-in-law when they marry, making them hostage to new demands or to complaints that dowry promises have not been met.

Given the social climate, many dowry deaths might go unreported.

Newspaper commentators often note that it is always young women whose saris catch fire as they bend over kerosene stoves, while such reported accidents rarely happen to elderly, infirm women who might be thought to be more vulnerable.

Yesterday's statistics, given in response to a question from a woman deputy, show that of the total 11 259 dowry-related deaths registered in 1988, 1989, and 1990, 4038 were suicides.

At the upper end of the social scale, dowry money is believed to account for a significant proportion of India's vast black economy, estimated to total the equivalent of up to $34.5 billion.

Demands among the middle and upper-middle classes include houses or such status symbols as imported video cassette recorders and stereo systems.

At the bottom of the pile, social workers say, even beggars have to find pots, pans and a bit of gold jewelry to marry off their daughters.

Despite the frequent public agonizing over the distortion of the dowry system—originally meant to give brides some financial security—protests against it are rare and attract only women willing to court social ostracism.

In other societies with arranged marriages, such as eastern Indonesia, the groom's family was expected until recently to pay the bride's parents a **bride price** as permission to marry their daughter. If the bride was beautiful or came from a wealthy or well-respected family, the price would rise. When the groom and his family were short of cash or property, the bride price could sometimes be paid through the groom's labour. In the folklore of these cultures, there are tales of men who were expected to labour long and hard for their fathers-in-law in order to marry their daughters.

Although both dowries and bride prices are associated with

arranged marriages, free choice marriages have retained some symbolic remnants of these practices in their wedding traditions. For example, the **trousseau**, or the clothing and household items collected for the wedding, the honeymoon, and the marriage itself are symbolic of dowries. In addition, the engagement ring and gold wedding band given to the bride are remnants of bride prices.

In Canada, most young men and women choose their social and marital partners without formal assistance. It is not uncommon for siblings or friends to introduce two people to each other, however, but there is certainly no expectation of marriage after such a meeting. Mate selection in both types of marriage will be discussed in more detail in chapter three.

Patterns of Authority, Descent, and Residence

In all societies, there are established rules or traditional practices guiding behaviour in families. Most family systems have a family "head" who makes major decisions within the family and represents the group to the outside world. In both western and eastern societies, the oldest male is typically the family head, a system referred to as **patriarchy**. An example of extreme patriarchy could be found in ancient Roman families before the Punic Wars, in which the father had the power of life and death over his children and held all legal and political authority on behalf of his wife (Leslie and Korman, 1989:160).

An authority system in which women are granted more authority than men is called **matriarchy**. Matriarchal systems are rare. However, some Black families in the Caribbean and the United States have been referred to as matriarchal (Queen and Habenstein, 1974:351), as have the Tchambuli people of New Guinea (Mead, 1935). In both of these examples, women hold considerable control over the economy and have decision-making power within their families.

Although Canadian families used to be patriarchal, men and women now have equal rights. When Canadian young people marry, they usually consider that their primary relationship is with each other rather than with either set of parents or siblings. In most cases, however, the newly married couple is still considered to be a part of both the groom's and the bride's extended families or kin groups. This is called a **bilateral descent** pattern. The couple is expected to maintain contact with both sides of the family, participate in family gatherings, and inherit property or money from either or both sides of the family.

Brides and grooms, however, are sometimes considered to be members of only one kin group. Patterns of descent may determine where the couple lives, how they address members of each other's family, what surname their children will receive, and from whom they will inherit if the family has any property to pass on. If they belong to the groom's kin group, we call this **patrilineal descent.**This form of descent is the most prevalent and has a long history in both eastern and western civilizations (Leslie and Korman, 1989:48). The important ties are from father to son to grandson. A wife would marry into her husband's family, and their children would become members of his kin group rather than hers.

With **matrilineal descent**, relationships are traced through females and the female line, disregarding the father's relatives. Matrilineal descent as well as **matrilocality**, or living with the bride's kin group, were typical of the peoples of the Iroquois Confederacy in North America (Brown, 1988).

In Canada, we have bilateral descent for kin membership and inheritance, but traditionally have used patrilineal descent for surnames. Until recently, the name taken by the bride and the couple's subsequent children was the groom's family name. Canadian brides were expected (but not always legally required) to take their husband's name because he was legally considered to be the "head" of the household and because having one family name was a symbol of their legal and social union.

Some cultural groups living in Canada, however, have used the wife's maiden name as a middle name for both the bride and the couple's subsequent children. In Quebec, the law was recently changed to allow a bride to retain her own family name, which she may use along with or hyphenated to her husband's surname. Children use the mother's maiden name as a middle name and the father's name as a surname, or use both their parents' names hyphenated.

In Ontario, women now have the choice of taking their husband's name, retaining their own, or hyphenating theirs to their husband's, and children can take either parent's surname. Because these changes are recent, however, most married women and the couple's children use the husband/father's surname. Changes away from the using the groom's surname have not taken place in all provinces, but advocates of reform have argued that a birth name is important to retain after marriage because it is a part of a person's identity and a form of continuity with the past.

If the newly married couple moves into the wife's kin group or into her family's household, we say that the marriage system is **matrilocal.** If the couple moves into the husband's kin group or family, the marriage system is **patrilocal.** Often, matrilineal family systems are also matrilocal, but this does not mean that women have the authority within the community or the family. More often, it means that the maternal uncle or the wife's brother is the authority figure.

Most North American marriages are **neolocal**, which means that the newly married couple establishes a place of residence separate from either the bride's or the groom's kin. Although the couple may live with either set of in-laws for a temporary period during their marriage, especially if they are in financial difficulty or are waiting to get into a new home, most young couples prefer to establish a separate residence and lifestyle from their family of origin.

CONCLUSION

In this chapter, the importance of family in influencing our values, our aspirations, and future life patterns was considered. The ways in which social scientists have studied families was discussed, and the term *family* was defined and differentiated from the term *household*. Cultural variations in family life were outlined revealing differences in patterns of authority, descent, and residence. Although there has been a trend toward monogamous nuclear families in urbanized and westernized cultures, many societies have retained polygynous marriages and extended families, especially in rural areas.

In addition to cultural variations, social scientists have examined how family life has changed with industrialization and modernization. This includes the impact of wage labour on family formation and the impact that the entrance of married women into the paid labour force had on the division of labour within families and on the upbringing of children. Some researchers have focused on particular stages in the family life cycle, such as adolescence or mid-life, while others have studied a particular topic such as family decision making throughout the entire family life cycle.

Decisions about which aspects of family life to study depend on the researcher's particular personal and professional interests, but also upon available funding for research, what topics are considered to be important by other researchers, and how thoroughly a topic has been studied in the past.

The next chapter will look at the theoretical or conceptual frameworks underlying family studies, as well as some of the different ways in which researchers have carried out their empirical studies. This chapter is important for the critical evaluation of research published in journals or books, as well as in the preparation of projects or papers.

SUGGESTED READINGS

Anderson, Karen L. "Historical Perspectives on the Family." *Family Matters. Sociology and Contemporary Canadian Families.* Edited by K. Anderson et al. Scarborough: Nelson, 1988.

Carter, Elizabeth A. and Monica McGoldrick. *The Changing Family Life Cycle: A Framework for Family Therapy.* 2nd ed. New York: Gardner Press, 1988.

Collier, Jane, Michelle Rosaldo, and Sylvia Yanagisako. "Is There a Family? New Anthropological Views." *Family Bonds and Gender Divisions.* Edited by Bonnie Fox. Toronto: Canadian Scholars' Press, 1988.

Gittens, Diana. "What is the Family? Is it Universal?" *Family Bonds and Gender Divisions.* Edited by Bonnie Fox. Toronto: Canadian Scholars' Press, 1988:19–30.

Goldthorpe, J.E. *Family Life in Western Societies. A Historical Sociology of Family Relationships in Britain and North America.* Cambridge: Cambridge University Press, 1987.

Goode, William J. *World Revolution and Family Patterns.* New York: Free Press, 1963 (revised with new preface 1970).

Ishwaran, K. (ed.). *Canadian Families: Ethnic Variations.* Scarborough: McGraw-Hill Ryerson, 1980.

Leslie, Gerald R. and Sheila K. Korman. *The Family in Social Context.* 7th ed. New York: Oxford University Press, 1989.

Nett, Emily. "Canadian Families in Social-Historical Perspective." *Canadian Journal of Sociology.* 6 (3). 1981:239–260.

Nett, Emily. *Canadian Families Past and Present.* Toronto: Butterworths, 1988.

Ontario Ministry of Education. *Family Studies, 1987.* Toronto.

Queen, S.A., R.W. Habenstein, and J.S. Quadango. *The Family in Various Cultures.* 5th ed. New York: Harper and Row, 1985.

Ram, Bali. *New Trends in the Family. Demographic Facts and Figures.* Statistics Canada. Cat. 91-535E. Ottawa: Minister of Supply and Services, March 1990.

Stephens, William N. *The Family in Cross-Cultural Perspective.* New York: Holt Rinehart, 1963.

Issues for Discussion

1. Why is the government concerned about regulating marriages, births, and divorces?
2. If marriage to two wives is the ideal for wealthy men in one country but is illegal in another, is there any "natural" form of marriage? What is the relationship between culture and marriage?
3. In what ways are expectations concerning marriage in other cultures different from your own experiences?
4. If you do not, would you like to live in a cultural group where your marriage partner will be chosen by your parents or relatives? Why or why not?
5. If dowries are against the law in modern India, why has the practice continued to exist? Are there socio-economic reasons why the practice continues?
6. How could a matriarchal family system evolve among certain cultural groups?
7. Is your family "typical" compared with others you have observed in Canada? Provide details of similarities and differences.
8. Should Canadian women be required to take their husband's name upon marriage? Why or why not?
9. If parents remarry and the bride and groom both keep their previous names, whose name should the children take? What about the next generation?
10. Are there nuclear families in our society whose members do not live together?

Further Activities

1. Is the nuclear family universal? Search the anthropological literature for examples of cultural groups who did not or do not live in nuclear family units.
2. Critically review the literature on family life in preindustrial Canada. How did families in the eighteenth century differ from families today? What socio-economic factors have led to changes in the structure of families and the behaviour of family members?

3. Until the early twentieth century, Mormons living in western United States and Canada justified polygyny with their religious beliefs. Consult your public or school library to find out what reasons they gave for accepting polygyny. How do these reasons differ from those given by certain African societies that continue to accept polygyny?
4. Interview a person from a culture that arranges marriages, or a person whose own marriage was arranged. How do their ideas of marriage compare with the North American model of free choice marriage?
5. Interview a person in a free choice marriage. Ask what influences to marry they experienced from friends and family during courtship. What characteristics did they consider to be important in a spouse before they married compared with after they married?

2

THEORIES AND RESEARCH METHODS

OVERVIEW OF CONCEPTUAL FRAMEWORKS IN FAMILY STUDIES

All studies in social science are based on certain underlying philosophical assumptions about how society is organized, what motivates human beings, which behaviours are biologically based, and the "best" way to discover patterns in human behaviour. These assumptions cannot be proved or disproved but serve as starting points for research.

Some of the more popular perspectives or conceptual frameworks from which to study the family are structural functionalism, the systems approach, the political economy approach, symbolic interactionism, social exchange theory, the feminist perspective, and the family life cycle approach. In the following section, the basic premises of each of these perspectives will be outlined and some of their strengths and weaknesses will be discussed.

STRUCTURAL FUNCTIONALISM

Since the nineteenth century, the **structural-functional** approach to social analysis has been used by anthropologists and sociologists to explain variations in family structure among preliterate cultures, the main responsibilities or functions of the family in that particular society, and adaptive changes to economic or cultural influences. This approach has also provided the framework for studies of modern industrialized societies. Within this perspective, the structures of society, rather than interpersonal relations or unique individual behaviour, are the units of analysis. These include laws, the political system, educational institutions, and the family.

The basic assumption of structural functionalism is that people's behaviour is governed not only by personal choice but by laws, rules, regulations, and expectations of behaviour. Individuals cannot behave any way they want, but must abide by the social expectations and rules of their cultural group, which they are taught early in life. Adherence to these rules and expectations helps maintain a cohesive and stable society, and **deviant behaviour** or behaviour that violates the rules and expectations must be carefully controlled.

Although structural functionalists do not deny the existence of free will, they argue that family and cultural upbringing to a large extent determine a person's future attitudes and behaviour. As the major social institution in society, the family is an important contributor to the maintenance of social order. According to this perspective, the family has many **functions** for society and for individuals. It provides individuals with emotional support and companionship, as well as a setting for sexual expression, reproduction, and the socialization of children. The family, especially the extended family, offers protection from outsiders, while individuals often relate to the outside world through their family head. People, especially children, are controlled and disciplined by families. If a child under a certain age gets into trouble with the law, for example, the police and social workers go to the parents, who are then expected to discipline the child. Families also co-operate economically and help each other through hard times by sharing resources. Finally, people acquire money and property through inheritance from family members, which suggests that the social status of people is largely established by their family of origin.

Discussions of family functions are meant to be theoretical, rather than to imply that all families are supportive or share resources. This is a model of what the family is expected to be in North American society, but it is sometimes presented within the structural-functional perspective as a representation of social reality. We all know that many families do not match this model, yet, it is retained as a conceptualization or what sociologists call an **ideal type.**

One of the key concepts used within the structural-functional perspective is **role,** which is a behavioural guideline or script. This concept suggests that individuals do not create their own ways of behaving but instead adopt cultural patterns of behaviour. For example, the role of father in 1950s North American culture was to earn an income for other family members, act as the major disciplinarian for the children, and represent the family to the outside world. Over the years, however, the role of father has been modified to become less authoritarian, to include more child care activities, and to share earning with his spouse.

The concept of **role strain** implies that any person may have several roles to play at the same time, and the expectations may conflict with one another. For example, a woman who is a mother may be expected to be with her children as much as possible and take care of their emotional and physical needs. As an employee, she may be expected to work long hours in a demanding job or career. As a spouse, she may be expected to be a supportive partner, keep the house in order, and maintain contact with both kin groups. All these different roles may overlap in terms of time requirements and emotional energy.

Bronislaw Malinowski, Talcott Parsons, and Robert Bales wrote within a structural-functionalist perspective. The anthropologist Malinowski (1944) emphasized the functions of the family and argued that despite the prevalence of other family structures, the nuclear family is a universal institution because it fulfils a basic human need in all societies, the nurturing of children. Sociologists Parsons and Bales (1955) theorized that with the development of industrialization and the shift to production outside the home, the small and relatively isolated nuclear family began to specialize in the socialization of children and meeting the personal needs of family members (Thorne, 1982:7). They assumed that the family has two basic structures: a **hierarchy** of generations and a differentiation of adults into **instrumental** and **expressive roles.** Parsons and Bales argued that the wife necessarily takes the expressive role in the family, i.e., she maintains social relations and cares for others. On the other hand, the husband assumes the instrumental role, i.e., he earns the money for the family and deals with the outside world (Ibid).

Although present-day structural functionalists acknowledge role change in families, they have been criticized for being out-of-date and conservative for several reasons. First, structural functionalists often talk about the family as though there is one acceptable family form rather than many variations. Second, to a large extent, behaviour is viewed as being determined by social expectations and family upbringing and, therefore, not easily altered by the individual. Third, structural functionalists have also implied, using a circular argument, that a certain type of family structure (such as husband as breadwinner and wife as homemaker) was maintained throughout history because it was functional for society, when it may have been functional for only one group in society (Thorne, 1982). Fourth, change is seen as disruptive rather than normal, progressive, or beneficial, and individual opposition to social pressure has been viewed as "deviance." Consequently, the structural functionalists have not dealt with conflict and change as well as other approaches, nor have they focused on the dynamic nature of interpersonal relations. For these reasons, many younger researchers who want to examine inequality, conflict, and change find this theoretical perspective less useful than others to explain the social world.

Structural functionalism, however, has shown that the rules and **norms** of society have a compelling influence on our behaviour. Individuals subjected to years of **socialization** to a particular way of behaving and viewing the world are unlikely to be able to change easily. Furthermore, this perspective has taught us that there are patterns in our behaviour based on social and cultural expectations and rules, and that we are not as unique as we would like to think.

SYSTEMS THEORY

Systems theory, like structural functionalism, is a structural approach in which the family as a whole is more than its component parts. General systems theory originated in engineering and cybernetics, but was introduced into family studies by family therapists, human ecologists, home economists, and sociologists during the 1970s (Cheal, 1991:64). According to American sociologist Reuben Hill, the family is considered to be a social system because its members are interdependent and any change in the **behaviour** of one member will affect the behaviour of others. It is also a relatively closed boundary-maintaining unit and an adaptive organization. Furthermore, the family is a task-performing unit, which is expected to meet the requirements of both the larger society and its own internal needs (Hill, 1971:12).

Systems theorists talk of the neighbourhood and larger society within which families operate as the **ecosystem**. Individual families are composed of **subsystems** arranged in hierarchical order. Parents and siblings are examples of separate subsystems. The parents are usually the directors or "architects" of the family system (Satir, 1967), responsible for creating the rules under which the family lives and the socialization of the children, while the siblings have little responsibility to establish family structure.

Some parents encourage rigid boundaries between parental and sibling subsystems, allowing for little information exchange or role flexibility. An example of a rigid **boundary maintenance** would be a family in which parents have difficulty responding to their children's needs or playing with them. These parents may also not listen to their children's opinions because they think that parents should make all the decisions and should maintain control. In the same family, children would not be allowed to be nurturant toward their parents because that would be parentlike behaviour. The opposite to rigid boundary maintenance would be **diffuse**, in which the roles of parent and child might become interchangeable at times. According to systems theory, this could lead to confusion in **role expectations** (Fine, 1986).

Another concept within systems theory is **recurring behaviour**, triggered by similar situations or responses. This concept can be illustrated by using the example of family violence, as the cyclical nature of this behaviour and perpetuation from one generation to the next has been noted by systems theorists. A boy is physically abused by his parents, for example, and when he grows up, he beats up his wife and children. The behaviour may be triggered by low self-esteem, concern that he is losing his authority in his family, and heavy drinking. Although he regrets his actions afterwards and vows that he loves his family and will never again mistreat his wife and children, he does. They lose respect for him and disregard his attempts to become a valued family member, which accentuates his feelings of worthlessness. His children grow up learning that violence is the "normal" way to express anger and hostility. When they marry, they also express their feelings of inadequacy and aggression by abusing their children.

As systems theory is derived from cybernetics and communications, other key concepts include **control** and **feedback**. Family members depend on feedback from each other to tell them how effectively they are relating to each other or how acceptable their behaviour is. In order to keep the system in a state of **homeostasis** or equilibrium, behaviour that oversteps the boundaries or rules is controlled. Feedback can be negative, which may involve a reprimand or withdrawal of privileges. Alternatively, feedback can be positive, which could involve praise, help, or encouragement.

Social work practitioners have used the systems approach in treating clients, to show how the entire family can become involved in and contribute to an apparently personal problem such as being an abusive parent or an alcoholic. Since a person's life is interrelated with the lives of other family members, referred to as **enmeshment** in systems theory, dealing with the individual's problem may involve treating the ways in which the entire family relates and functions.

The family can be viewed as an open or closed system, depending on how much input is received from friends, neighbours, social workers, employers or the outside world in general, including the media, the education system, and the legal system. Although viewing the family as an open system takes into consideration social and economic influences on family interaction, the systems approach does not focus on the social, economic, or political context within which families live. The analysis is generally ahistorical and limited to one culture. Critics of family systems theory point out that focusing on interactions leaves no way of explaining why some clients exhibit certain kinds of problems more than others (Cheal, 1991:82).

FAMILY SYSTEMS THEORY

Perhaps the main achievement of family systems theory, however, has been to provide an intellectual framework for beliefs in family strengths (Olsen et al., 1983). From a systems perspective, families represent potent therapeutic resources. The potential for positive change is therefore thought to be greatly enhanced when family members are involved in plans for intervention. More generally, systems theories reaffirm the strength of family ties in atomistic modern societies, in which the breakdown of family life is always a possibility. As well, they confirm the resilience of families as groups that are able to gain some control over the conditions of their existence, despite the often disruptive effects of economic, political, and military institutions. Pauline Boss has clearly stated the relevance of this point of view for family stress theory:

We emphasize, therefore, that a crisis does not have to permanently disable a family...Human systems, unlike mechanical ones, can learn from their experiences, even painful ones. After a crisis, families can redefine themselves and their resources... or reconstruct their reality by changing the rules by which their system operates... Such shifts in the family's perception and organization constitute a turning point, and the recovery process begins. Crisis does not have to break the family structure. It only temporarily immobilizes it and may, in fact, lead to an even higher level of functioning after recovery than before.

David Cheal. *Family and the State of Theory*. Toronto: University of Toronto Press, 1991:67–68. Reprinted by permission of the publisher. (Quote from Pauline Boss, "Family Stress" in *Handbook of Marriage and the Family*, editors Marvin Sussman and Suzanne Steinmetz, New York: Plenum, 1987:701.)

Despite these criticisms, family systems theory has had a broad appeal and a wide influence on theories of family in several disciplines. It has provided a framework for multidisciplinary study in which various theories and approaches have been combined. It has been particularly useful in psychiatry and family therapy in focusing attention on how the behaviour of individuals is interrelated with that of other family members. This has enabled family therapists to assist their clients to work together to enhance communication and work toward positive change (Cheal, 1991:66,67).

POLITICAL ECONOMY APPROACH

The **political economy** or **conflict perspective** is also a structural approach, but emphasizes the impact of economic and political forces on interpersonal relations and family life, and how these vary by family social class. The basic thesis is that changes in family composition and relations between family members are influenced by the nature and location of the work people do, the lifestyle they can afford, the types of social and economic policies enacted by governments, and the national and international economies. According to this perspective, social change is constant and inevitable, resulting from clashes between groups with conflicting interests, such as employers and employees.

Social class is an important concept within conflict theory. People who earn a living in the same way and who have a similar source and amount of income are classified as members of the same social group. These commonalities are considered to have a significant influence on a person's lifestyle, attitudes, and behaviour.

The conflict perspective originates from the work of two men who wrote in nineteenth-century Europe. The German philosopher Karl Marx (1818–1833) theorized about the effect of different economic systems on people's ideas, their work, and their personal lives. He suggested that political changes would inevitably take place when working people understood that the way capitalist economy is organized disregards the interests of people who work for wages. In the same era, the German researcher Frederick Engels wrote about the ways in which family life has been altered by major transitions in economies from hunting and gathering societies, to horticultural, to preindustrial, and finally to industrial societies.

More recently, conflict theorists such as Eli Zaretsky (1976) and Canadian historian Chad Gaffield (1990) have noted that the industrial revolution in the eighteenth and nineteenth centuries led to major changes in personal and family life. Because the place of work was removed from the home, working class husbands and wives began to work in **manufactories** and later factories, as well as mines. When men worked outside the home, they could no longer maintain the same level of authority over other family members, and there was a gradual decline in patriarchal authority. Furthermore, many of the goods and services that people had provided at home for their own use were eventually made more cheaply in factories. This meant that families eventually became units of consumption and shared incomes rather than producing goods and services as a unit. Once most production of goods and services took place outside the home, the family became private and separate from the public world of business and politics. This **private/public** distinction also came to be associated with women's and men's roles.

Other Canadian researchers, such as Bonnie Fox (1980), Meg Luxton (1980), and Wally Seccombe (1980), have studied the relationship between changes from a preindustrial to an industrial economy and the organization of housework or **domestic labour**. They have noted that industrial economies have depended on women's unpaid labour to keep wages low and to enable companies to make a profit. As more wives and mothers have been drawn into the labour force during this century, however, the value of unpaid work in the home has declined, the distinction between the private and the public realm has become blurred, and the division of labour within families is evolving.

The political economy approach emphasizes the impact of industrialization and workplace activities on family and personal life and the fact that economic changes often preclude changes in ideas. For example, political economists would argue that the entrance of married women into the labour force occurred mainly for economic reasons rather than for reasons of **ideology.** The service sector of the labour market expanded with changes in the domestic economy and foreign markets requiring new workers. While married women had always worked as a **reserve labour force,** the creation of these new job opportunities, as well as inflation, the rising cost of living, and changing ideologies about the role of women in public life encouraged more wives to work full-time for pay. The **dual-income family** has increased marital conflicts over housework, created the need for public child care services, and been a major factor necessitating changes in **gender relations.** Divorce has become more prevalent partly because women now have their own incomes. In addition,

THE EFFECT OF THE INDUSTRIAL ECONOMY ON FAMILIES: POLITICAL ECONOMY APPROACH

In the modern industrial economy, the responsibility of the family for the material welfare of its members declined with the professionalization of health care and the slow emergence of state aid for those in need. The traditional pattern of home births, home remedies, and informal kinship support systems was increasingly replaced by hospitals, clinics, and publicly funded welfare offices. In this sense, the general direction of the twentieth century has been toward the building of public institutions to support individual existence (Strong-Boag, 1979; Struthers, 1983). Nonetheless, these institutions do not fully respond to individual needs, and families have maintained an important support role for family members as well as for kin. The processes of social and economic change may have encouraged some sense of individualism, but family and kin still provide an important framework for personal welfare in the late twentieth century much as they have since the seventeenth century.

The instability of the family during the urban growth and industrial development of the mid-nineteenth century caused considerable concern among politicians and other public leaders, who feared that widespread social disorder would result from the rapid pace of social change. These leaders believed that the family was in peril as a social institution, and so they promoted new ideals for family members, especially for women and children, who were most affected by the new modes of production. The major development for children was the establishment of schooling as a dominant experience in growing up. For women, the result was a definition of their responsibilities that limited them to the home and to the roles of wives and mothers.

Chad Gaffield. "The Social and Economic Origins of Contemporary Families." *Families: Changing Trends in Canada*. Edited by M. Baker. Scarborough: McGraw-Hill Ryerson, 1990:33.

increasing numbers of one-parent households have expanded the need for income-support programs and other social services.

While structural functionalists have discussed the family as though it existed in a political and economic vacuum, political economists have de-emphasized interpersonal relations, stability, and social cohesion. Instead, they have examined historical changes in family life, social class differences in family interaction, conflicts of interest between generations and spouses, family disruption and violence, and the effect of economic and social policies on personal choices. Interpersonal relations and family dynamics are studied only from the viewpoint of how they are influenced by work patterns, the family's economic situation, or historical comparisons.

SYMBOLIC INTERACTIONISM

Social interaction or communication within families has also been studied by sociologists and social psychologists, focusing on the shared meanings that keep families together. Within the **symbolic interaction perspective**, humans interact with one another through symbols such as words, gestures, or facial expressions, and modify their behaviour depending on how others react to them. How people define and interpret reality shapes their behaviour, and this process of interpretation is aided by nonverbal as well as verbal cues that are picked up during social interaction.

The idea that our self-concept is shaped by how we think others see us is called the **looking-glass self** and is an important concept in the socialization of both children and adults. While individuals are influenced by others, they may also influence the behaviour of their family members, friends, and co-workers.

Within symbolic interactionism, it is assumed that we are all "actors" who play a part in the **social construction of reality**. Life does not just happen to us; we make things happen by exerting our free will. While the structural-functionalist approach assumes that people are, at least to some extent, passive recipients of societal rules and regulations, symbolic interactionism emphasizes the active participation of people in creating their own destinies.

Symbolic interactionism originated with the work of Charles H. Cooley (1864–1929) and George Herbert Mead (1863–1931) who studied the processes of **socialization** and the ways individuals actively participate in this process (Wilson, 1991:107). Both these social scientists were interested in how children develop a sense of self and the importance of family interaction in socialization.

Key concepts within this perspective include **primary groups**, which are characterized by face-to-face interaction and co-operation. Families and friendship groups are considered to be primary groups, while larger impersonal groups like schools or corporations would be secondary groups. The concept of **reference group**, through which individuals model, compare, and judge their own behaviour, is also used within this perspective. Children may view older siblings and their friends as a reference group, as well as people not personally known to them, such as rock groups or movie stars. If a child watches how older people behave and attempts to try out this new form of behaviour, symbolic interactionists call this **anticipatory socialization**.

Symbolic interaction studies may take place within a natural setting, but they often occur in a small-groups laboratory, using simulations of family behaviour. Researchers observe the subjects from behind one-way mirrors. Interaction between parents and their children, among children in a play group, and between husbands and wives has been studied in this kind of setting. Sometimes researchers will ask the subjects to comment on their own behaviour and compare these remarks with their own observations. In a Canadian laboratory study of family decision making, for example, Turk and Bell (1972) found that husbands overestimated and wives underestimated their own decision-making power, compared with the observations of the researcher.

Within the symbolic interactionist framework, research is often centred on communication processes during everyday experiences. It is not enough within this perspective to observe what people *do*; it is essential to ascertain how they *feel* about what they do, and why (Scanzoni and Scanzoni, 1988:10). People's actions and feelings are assumed to be influenced by their **definition of the situation**. As American researcher W.I. Thomas said in 1923, if people "define situations as real, they are real in their consequences." For example, elderly people often fear that they will be victims of violent crime, and consequently lock their doors and stay at home in the evenings. In actual fact, elderly people are far less likely to be victims of violent crime than younger people. However, if elderly people think they are going to be victimized, they will act as though the community is a dangerous place.

SOCIAL EXCHANGE THEORY

Researchers have also studied families using **social exchange theory**, which is derived from symbolic interactionism but uses economic analogies from cost-benefit analysis. In the early 1900s, German sociologist Georg Simmel emphasized the importance of reciprocity in everyday life and how human interactions are a form of exchange. His work was translated into English during the 1950s and became very influential in American sociological theory.

In 1961, the American sociologist George Homans argued that although values and norms govern behaviour, people attempt to maximize benefits and minimize costs when interacting with others. Within social exchange theory, social behaviour is seen to be influenced by the anticipation of a reward such as social approval, a better standard of living, or freedom from responsibility. All interpersonal relationships including dating, marriage, and family relationships are assumed to involve a process of negotiation and bargaining (Scanzoni, 1982)

Several studies have used social exchange theory to describe and explain the process of dating and mate selection. For example, in 1978 Robert Staples argued that individuals attempt to maximize their gains while minimizing their efforts, and focused on the "game-playing" in the dating practices of college students in the United States. Others have analyzed the implicit bargaining during dating which is based on traditional gender roles. When men provide the transportation and pay for the evening's activities, they often feel that they are owed something in return, and this is often sexual intimacy (Richman, 1977).

Recently, social exchange theory has been used to explain why some relationships break up and others last. When one partner contributes more time or emotional energy than the other to a relationship, he or she may become resentful and start looking elsewhere for gratification. For example, Huber and Spitze (1980) found that among a variety of subject groups in an American study, married women who worked for pay and whose husbands did not share the housework were most likely to consider divorce.

While symbolic interactionism and social exchange theory do not focus on historical or cultural change, they can explain social interaction within families and provide considerable insight into the dynamics of marriage and marital satisfaction. The interactionist approach has been popular in the United States since the early 1900s and still forms the basis of some research on topics such as childhood and adult socialization, marital adjustment, and the development of self-esteem.

Feminist Perspective

In recent years, an increasing number of researchers in family studies have been using the **feminist perspective**, which focuses on women's experiences, gender roles, and socio-economic inequalities between men and women. Some feminist theorists have used a structural approach to focus on the ways in which inequality is perpetuated through the economic system and prevailing ideologies. Others have concentrated on interpersonal relations between men and women, examining nonverbal communication, attitudes, and values (Mandell and Duffy, 1988:vii).

The feminist perspective developed since the 1970s as an increasing number of students and professional researchers concluded that women's experiences and contributions to society were overlooked, downplayed, or misrepresented in history books and social science research. Since that time, feminist scholars have developed new ways of conceptualizing social organization and introduced new research topics.

Within the feminist perspective, a distinction is made between sex and **gender.** While sex is meant to be a biological distinction, gender connotes the social and cultural meanings attached to being male and female in a particular culture.Researchers have noted that North American females are socialized differently than males and are taught to emphasize different priorities and skills. For example, male gender roles have focused on occupational prestige and earning capacity, while female gender roles tended to encourage women to focus their energy on personal relationships. This includes being the family **kin-keeper**—the person who is expected to keep in touch with other members of both kin groups. While females are socialized to acquire many important characteristics and skills, the female gender role as well as structural barriers to occupational mobility disadvantage women in terms of their socio-economic status. In fact, feminist scholars have argued that whatever is considered "feminine" in our culture is given lower status than masculine achievements or characteristics.

Feminist researchers have reconceptualized child care and household tasks as "work," noting that much of the work women do is unpaid and low status. Housework, for example, is unpaid when done by a wife/mother and has no holidays or benefits attached to it. Researchers have also noted that most adult women now work for pay in the labour force and continue to take the responsibility for housework. This has been referred to as **women's double day**, and the tasks mothers do in the household have been called **motherwork**. Researchers have noted that women's continuing responsibility for child care and household tasks works against their attempts to gain economic equality or employment equity.

Feminist researchers have also exposed the biases of **sexist research**, or research based on false assumptions about women's abilities or experiences and pertaining mainly to men even though the results are generalized to all people. This theoretical perspective has highlighted the consequences, for women and for science or knowledge, of sexist research. Some feminist theoreticians are attempting to create a new type of social science that takes women's experiences and world views into consideration (Smith, 1979; Eichler, 1980, 1987).

Canadian sociologist Margrit Eichler (1983, 1988) has written about family research using a feminist and largely structural perspective. She has criticized earlier research for talking about "the family" as though there were only one form. She has argued that researchers have presented "the family" as a **monolithic** institution and made assumptions about typical family structure and dynamics that were not and are not an accurate representation of reality. She also noted that early family studies often made the assumption that family policies had an equal impact on all individual members. Family research has often been based on samples of women, assuming that their answers adequately represented the views of other family members. Eichler has argued that men and women experience family life differently and have different perceptions of what is happening in the family unit.

While 20 years ago, the feminist perspective tended to be seen as biased or ideological rather than scientific, it is an accepted theoretical perspective today. For example, the perspective is used in much of the present research in family studies, is included in recent textbooks, and forms the basis of numerous courses in universities. Furthermore, several Canadian universities offer degrees in Women's Studies. Greater acceptance of the idea that there is no absolute truth and that one perceives the world differently depending on one's social position has assisted the acceptance of the feminist perspective in academic research. This perspective often glosses over men's experiences and points of view, however, arguing that they are already well-represented by traditional social science.

Family Life Cycle

The **family life cycle** or **developmental approach** began in the 1930s in an attempt to incorporate several perspectives into one. Family life is seen within this approach as ever-changing, influenced by psychosexual development and transitional events such as marriage, divorce, child-launching, or retirement. Several stages of development have been noted in family life, including the period between families when young people are living alone, the early years of marriage, the family with young children, the family with adolescents, child-launching, the empty nest, retirement, and being widowed. With these stages of development, roles shift, the division of labour may change, relationships are modified, and levels of satisfaction fluctuate.

The family life cycle approach shares with structural functionalism the idea that certain prerequisites must be met for continued maintenance of family life. In the family life cycle approach, these are called **developmental tasks**, and they vary with each stage of development. For example, young people who have recently left home and are in a transitional stage need to go through the process of **individuation**

A Bar Mitzvah is a rite of passage marking the formal admission of a boy into the Jewish religious community. This celebration usually takes place when the boy is thirteen years old. Can you think of other rites of passage?

Reuters/Bettmann

and **separation** from parents before they can establish a successful marital relationship. The family life cycle approach also shares with structural functionalism the idea that events such as unemployment will influence other aspects of family relationships. The family life cycle approach does not see the family as a static institution, however, but as a series of relationships that grow and develop over time.

There are several key concepts within this perspective. Developmental tasks are decisions or psychological changes that need to take place before a person can successfully move on to the next stage of development. **Rites of passage** refer to social ceremonies or rituals celebrating the move from one stage of development to another.

One criticism of the family life cycle approach is that it has tended to view the family as a unit that is separate from the political, economic, and social world. While some researchers have used this perspective in cross-cultural and historical studies, most have focused on only one society in modern times. Another criticism is that this approach falsely assumes that both marital partners are passing through the same stages of development at the same time. It often happens today that a divorced man, with children from a previous marriage, remarries a younger woman who is at quite a different stage in her personal and family development. Furthermore, not everyone passes through all stages; some people never marry, others marry and then divorce, others remain childless throughout their lives.

In this book, the family life cycle approach is used to organize the chapters, but research based on the other theoretical frameworks will be introduced as well. Although the focus is on Canadian statistics and published research, theories, research, and cross-cultural and historical examples from other societies will also be examined.

RECENT TRENDS IN FAMILY RESEARCH

Although researchers have been studying family life in North America since the 1890s, most of the research prior to the 1920s was closer to social work than theoretical social science. The gradual separation between academic researchers and practitioners began after World War I (Adams, 1975:5). From the 1920s to the 1940s, anthropologists studied cross-cultural variations in family life in many societies, including Native peoples and other ethnic groups in North America. These researchers relied mainly on the structural-functional framework and tried to apply the scientific method to human behaviour. They searched for universal behavioural patterns and related variations in these patterns to the entire culture. Margaret Mead (1935), for example, investigated the influence of culture and learning on the behavioural patterns of males and females. Although American social scientists of that time thought that gender roles were largely a product of biology, Mead showed that among certain tribes in New Guinea, these roles were reversed and therefore a product of culture.

During the 1930s and 1940s, American researchers began to investigate their own cultural patterns and small group behaviour. Romantic love and personal attraction were analyzed, as well as social patterns in sexual behaviour. The famous Kinsey studies of male sexuality, published in 1948, revealed a widespread disregard for sexual exclusivity, monogamy, and the disapproval of premarital sex, despite giving lip-service to these norms. These findings encouraged

SEX AND GENDER

An important study on the question of whether the characteristics defined as "feminine" in Western culture were universal was carried out by Margaret Mead in New Guinea (1963). Mead studied three different cultures and found that male and female roles and masculine and feminine temperament were patterned differently in each culture. Among the Arapesh, both men and women were expected to act in ways we in the United States consider "naturally" feminine. Both sexes were concerned with taking care of children and with nurturing generally. Neither sex was expected to be aggressive. In the second culture, the Mundugamor, both sexes were what we would call "masculine"—aggressive, violent, and with little interest in children. In the third society, the Tchambuli, the personalities of males and females were different from each other but opposite to our own conceptions of masculine and feminine. Women had the major economic role, showed "common sense" and business shrewdness, and carried out the mundane tasks. Men were interested in esthetics. They spent much time decorating themselves and gossiping. They also had their feelings hurt and sulked a lot.

Mead's study showed that the whole repertoire of behavior, emotions, and interests that go into being masculine and feminine are patterned by culture. In the process of growing up, each child learns hundreds of culturally patterned details of behavior that become incorporated into his or her gender identity. In addition to all the direct instructions about being masculine or feminine that every culture imparts, culture unconsciously affects masculinity and femininity by providing different images, aspirations, and adult role models for girls and boys. In assessing the idea that biology determines gender, anthropologists have pointed to the great variability in human societies regarding the behavior, temperaments, and roles of women and men. As always, the anthropologist attempts to deal with the question of the relation of biology to culture by looking outside our own Western traditions, for it is only in this way that we can grasp the variety of human life. What we see is that whatever biological dispositions may be characteristic of one sex or the other, these are responsive to a tremendously wide range of cultural patterning.

Nanda Serena. *Cultural Anthropology*. 4th ed. Belmont, California: Wadsworth Publishing Company, 1991:100.

other researchers to investigate young people's (and especially students') attitudes and practices concerning dating behaviour and premarital sex.

During the postwar period of rising marriage rates, high fertility, and the suburbanization of North American cities, family researchers began to investigate marital satisfaction and happiness, and continued their interest in patterns of mate selection. When the work of Sigmund Freud was translated into English and became available to the North American reader, research into early childhood development and maternal behaviour became popular. The English child psychologist John Bowlby synthesized earlier studies on the importance of mothering and began his controversial work on **maternal deprivation.** This kind of research continued into the 1950s and explored bonding between mother and infant in nonhumans as well as humans. These research findings appeared to reinforce the expectation that mothers would become homemakers rather than work in the labour force.

Until the postwar period there were few Canadian studies specifically on family life, largely because sociology was not taught as a separate discipline in Canadian universities until the 1950s. Most analysis of Canadian families was found within community studies such as *Crestwood Heights*, a study of a Toronto community by Seeley et al., (1956), rather than on separate projects on family life. In French Canada, family research focused on rural and religious traditions (Garigue, 1962), but studies of **social mobility** and urbanization also made reference to family life as one of the factors influencing patterns of mobility (Elkin, 1964:68).

As the proportion of married women in the labour force increased, many studies of the 1950s and 1960s investigated the relationship between working mothers and juvenile delinquency. Researchers also continued their studies in the social work tradition of "problem families" or those affected by absent fathers or alcohol. In the studies of sociologists such as Parsons and Bales (1955), the ideal family was implicitly portrayed as a two-parent, one-income family, with father as breadwinner and mother as homemaker, and with two or three children. All other family forms were seen as "deviant."

As more women entered the labour force, however, the **dual-career family** emerged as an important concept. Later it was acknowledged that the **two-income family** was a more appropriate concept because many people worked at jobs rather than careers. Research of this era had a white middle-class bias as researchers focused on professional couples rather than on working class ones. The fact that working class wives had always worked for pay was passed over and researchers saw the two-income family as revolutionary and likely to be detrimental to children and marital relationships.

Toward the end of the 1960s, several new themes became important: the concept of **open marriage** in which partners operated as separate individuals and explored their "full potential," possible alternatives to the nuclear family such as communal living or a series of nonlegal intimate relationships, and concern about the death of the family as an institution (Cooper, 1971). The changing role of women and its implications for family life were also the subjects of many studies. The egalitarian family was viewed as the new emerging form, despite the fact that little evidence was available that equality actually existed between husbands and wives.

In the mid-1970s, several studies destroyed the myth of the egalitarian family. Time-budget studies showed that the husbands of working wives did about six minutes more housework per day than the husbands of homemakers (Meissner et al., 1975; Clark and Harvey, 1976). Other research indicated that while women's lives had changed considerably, men's had remained largely unaltered.

Throughout the 1970s, divorce rates soared in Canada and other industrialized countries, leading to more marriage dissolution, one-parent households, child custody disputes, and poverty for divorced mothers and their children. Research began to focus on these issues, as well as domestic labour, family violence, and child care, as they became controversial topics in the media.

By the 1980s, the family was seen less as a haven from commercialism and violence and more as a complex institution that is potentially destructive yet continues to be popular. Governments sponsored studies of child abuse, wife battering, division of matrimonial property after divorce, and child custody, all of which reinforced a negative view of the family. At the same time, feminist scholars revived the sociology and history of the family by adding a female point of view and women's experiences to the study of family life (Parr, 1982; Eichler, 1983; Mandell and Duffy, 1988; Morton, 1988).

In the 1990s, Canadian family research is becoming more historical and focusing on the implications of legal, political, and economic systems for families rather than interpersonal relations. Many younger researchers are using the political economy or feminist perspectives, rather than structural-functional or systems approach, to study families. For example, the consequences of divorce, patterns of child custody, support, and remarriage for individual family members and social policy are being further explored. Social scientists are now presenting a more analytical and critical picture of family life, law, and policy than researchers provided in previous decades (Cheal, 1991).

Researchers are now less likely to see families as units and less likely to expect that one member can represent the experiences and answer surveys on behalf of all others. Social scientists now recognize that husbands, wives, and children often have different perceptions of the same family unit and sometimes have separate goals. In fact, researchers are now showing that legal and social policies on family-related issues have different consequences for men and women (Morton, 1988; Baker, 1990). Family law reform, for example, appears to have hastened the **feminization of poverty**, by eliminating alimony and awarding only temporary support to ex-wives, on the assumption that they can become self-supporting. Researchers are also examining the social and legal implications of the new reproductive technologies (Eichler, 1988).

Rather than analyzing the complexities and variations of family life, early family researchers based their studies on a simplistic or monolithic model of the family (Eichler, 1988). More recently, researchers have acknowledged that family experiences differ by gender, social class, cultural group, and sexual orientation. Family interaction is psychologically complex and difficult to study because many people are not in touch with their innermost feelings or may not be able to articulate them. Furthermore, people may not want to discuss delicate personal matters with social researchers because they value their privacy.

METHODS OF STUDYING FAMILIES

Social scientists have drawn upon many different research methods in their attempt to understand family life. How one studies families, however, depends on many practical concerns, such as the availability of research grant money, collaborators, previous experience, and expertise. The demographic placement (age, gender, race) and personal preferences of the researcher will also affect the choice of methodology. Personal value systems may influence how a topic is researched and what is considered important to study, especially when the researcher does cross-cultural research. Some researchers have more experience or faith in different types of research. Social scientists base their research topics and methods on their own understanding of the way society works and individual people function, as well as their judgment of the best way to gain knowledge about the world or to do research. Five major methods of research will be discussed in the following pages.

HISTORICAL RESEARCH

Both historians and sociologists have drawn upon historical documents to provide information on family life in different eras. Such documents as church registers, municipal records, wills, and letters have formed the basis of many past studies (Aries, 1962; Shorter, 1975; Tilly and Scott, 1978; Gagan, 1981). In oral traditions, stories and legends have yielded important insights into family life.

Although official records can provide information such as age and occupation of marriage partners, number of children born to a marriage, cause of death, and the structure of families and households, they cannot tell us much about the quality of family life, personal experiences, or feelings. Letters, diaries, novels, and personal accounts, however, can supplement the information from official records to shed some light on family life in the past.

In recent years, more researchers have been drawing upon historical accounts to gain a broader understanding of changes in family life (Lee, 1982; Wilson, 1986; Zaretsky, 1982). They have concluded, for

THE CHILDREN OF 18TH CENTURY NEW FRANCE

... Illegitimate births were an increasing problem in eighteenth-century New France and the royal officials were slow to react. Pregnancies out of wedlock were indicative of the breakdown of communal social restraints in the rural parishes where, according to Intendant Michel Bégon, "this disorder is becoming extremely common." From 1701 to 1760 the church registers in what is now the Province of Quebec recorded the baptism of 1112 illegitimate children. At the beginning of this period bastards accounted for two out of every thousand births; in the last decades of the French regime they represented 12.2 out of every thousand. Because the rate fell after the conquest, wartime conditions and the presence of thousands of French regular troops must have contributed to the growing number of illegitimate births in the 1740s and 1750s. These figures are incomplete because, in spite of laws requiring the disclosure of illicit pregnancies, illegitimate children born to *Canadiennes* were frequently given to the Amerindians in preference to letting the infants die of exposure. Infanticide was a capital crime. In the villages of the Christian Amerindians, Louis Franquet observed numerous illegitimate children of the French colonists as well as white children abducted from the English colonies. The youngsters were adopted by the native peoples and they fully accepted the aborigines' way of life.

Peter N. Moogk. "Les Petits Sauvages: The Children of 18th Century New France." *Childhood and Family in Canadian History*. Edited by Joy Parr. Toronto: McClelland and Stewart, 1982:26, 27. Used by permission of the Canadian publishers, McClelland and Stewart, Toronto.

example, that fluctuations in the need for children's labour in the eighteenth and nineteenth centuries influenced the way people viewed childhood (Lee, 1982; Gaffield, 1990). Early twentieth-century laws restricting the immigration of Chinese people to Canada, combined with nineteenth-century patterns of immigration, led to a disproportionate number of unmarried Chinese-Canadian men (Lai, 1980). Canadian research on the historical origins of the Indian Act have shown the impact of this piece of legislation on preventing economic initiatives from developing on reservations and lowering the socio-economic status of status Indians living on reservations, as well as First Nations' people living off reserves (Frideres, 1983). Black slavery, the underground railroad to Canada, and later immigration laws requiring Caribbean women to leave their children behind when they came to Canada as nannies have influenced family structure among Blacks in Canada (Krauter and Morris, 1978; Williams, 1983).

OFFICIAL STATISTICS

Since the nineteenth century, the government of Canada has been collecting information about births, deaths, marriages, employment, family and household income, and family composition. In recent years, Statistics Canada and government departments such as Health and Welfare Canada and Labour Canada have collected, analyzed, and compiled statistical data of interest to scholars and students of family life. These statistics, along with those collected by provincial governments, enable governments to maintain an accurate record of the population and to plan future social and economic policies, such as the building of new schools and changes to social benefits.

When using official statistics, we have to remember that these figures were gathered for specific government purposes and according to certain definitions of "family" which may not have been consistent with social scientific or popular definitions. Furthermore, answers given to government representatives may differ from those offered to nongovernment researchers.

Although reliable data prior to 1851 is not available, statisticians sometimes estimate past figures and project future ones. Projections of population trends are speculative because of the difficulty of anticipating future marriage, birth, immigration, and mortality rates. Nevertheless, governments attempt to predict future trends in order to facilitate social and economic planning.

Insurance companies rely on demographic data such as life expectancies at birth, marriage and divorce rates, and mortality rates at different ages to help calculate the risk of accidents or death. Once they have calculated risk, they can assess the rates they need to charge. Other business organizations also use demographic statistics along with information about family formation and labour force activity to analyze future market trends. Knowledge of how many children are born each year, what percentage of teenagers are living with their parents, or what percentage of mothers are working outside the home may help them estimate the need for certain products or services or to plan their marketing strategies.

Social scientists sometimes rely on official government statistics to study family life, keeping in mind that the figures were gathered by governments for purposes other than social science research. Although official statistics may not fit the exact needs of a researcher, they are often used, even when incomplete, because collecting new information can be very expensive. For example, in studying marriage dissolution, researchers have had to rely on divorce statistics solely because no official statistics are available for marital separation.

With official statistics compiled by governments, social scientists can study the structure of families over a long period of time.

Figure 2.1 **Marriages and Divorces, 1970–1986**

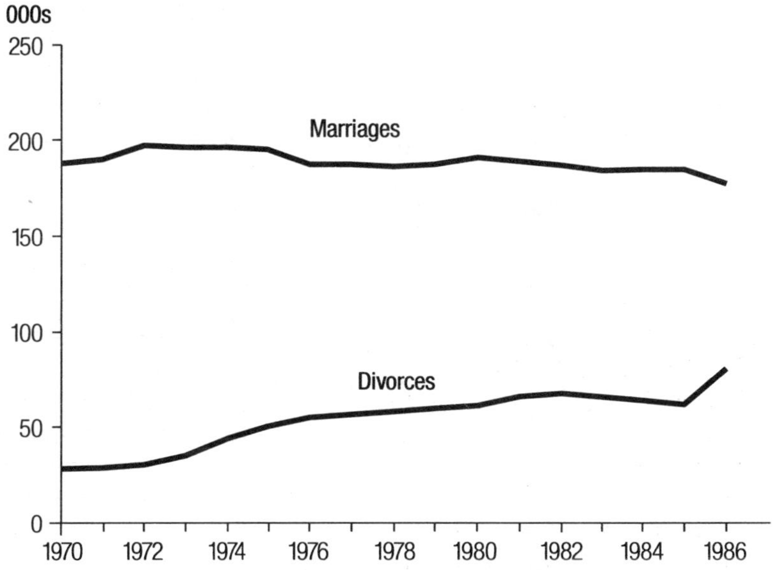

Source: Statistics Canada. Catalogue 84-205. Reproduced with the permission of the Minister of Supply and Services Canada, 1992.

Figure 2.2 **Proportion of Total Life Spent in Different Marital Statuses, by Sex, 1984–1986**

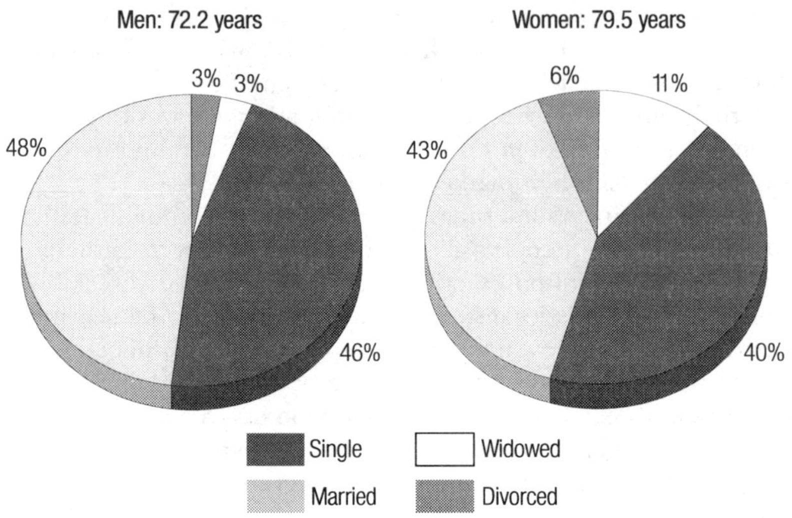

Source: Statistics Canada. Catalogue 84-536. Reproduced with the permission of the Minister of Supply and Services Canada, 1992.

Computer analysis can help them understand past and present family life. Statistical information on the family is often very superficial, however, and only reveals the structure of family life rather than the quality of relationships. If we wanted to probe into the quality of family life, we would have to rely on another method of research, such as interviews or personal observation.

Researchers may also gather their own data and compile statistics about family life. Answers acquired from questionnaires or interviews are **coded**, or transposed into numbers, to create **quantitative** data. Alternatively, researchers can gather **qualitative** data on family life, or details gained from indepth interviews, retaining the interviewees' verbatim comments about their family experiences.

SURVEY RESEARCH

If we wanted to go beyond official statistics but still gather brief answers from many people, we would use **survey research** techniques involving questionnaires. Survey researchers first create a

sample, or a typical subgroup from the entire category of people they want to study (a population). If it is a **representative** sample, an attempt is made to include most of the major variations in the population, such as different cultural groups or age categories. In a random sample, subjects are chosen randomly so that each person has an equal chance of being selected for the sample, and subjects are unlikely to differ from other people in the population. The sample could also be **purposive** and include certain categories of people of interest to the particular study. Whatever the type of sample, it needs to be chosen carefully. If the sample is too small or is not selected carefully, the results could be biased. Factors to consider when choosing a sample might include gender, class, race, and ethnicity.

The subjects are given questionnaires by mail, by telephone, or in person either at home or in a public place, such as a shopping mall. Survey research methods imply that the questions must be simple, unambiguous, and conducive to short answers. Each question must be constructed carefully to eliminate any preconceptions about how the subject might answer, and all questions must be asked in the same way to all subjects. Furthermore, some survey researchers feel that the subjects should not know the exact **hypothesis** of the study or they may try to give the "correct" answers. However, others feel that the ethics of research require that participants have the right to know at least the purpose of any study.

When all the questions are completed, the responses are usually coded, or categorized by numbers that can be analyzed on a computer. If the sample is representative of the population or randomly chosen, and if the response rate is high, researchers feel that they can generalize their results to the larger society with some degree of certainty.

The value of survey research is that large numbers of people can be questioned about their behaviour, attitudes, or opinions in a relatively short time period. It is not possible, however, to obtain in-depth material through this method because people are usually unwilling to provide long and intimate answers on a questionnaire, either in writing, by telephone, or in person. Furthermore, if answers are mailed, the researcher cannot be sure that the designated individual actually answered the questionnaire. In addition, the response rate is often relatively low with a mailed questionnaire (usually less than 50 percent and sometimes much lower). While a large amount of information can be gathered in a short period of time using survey research methods, subtle or in-depth issues are usually studied by personal interviews.

Many government-funded research projects use survey research methods. One example is a study of divorce mediation sponsored by the federal Department of Justice in Winnipeg. It was based on questionnaires to 282 clients entering the Family Conciliation Services, as well as telephone interviews with clients who had completed mediation, telephone interviews with lawyers, and an examination of client files and archival records. A major conclusion of this study was that mediation achieves results that are consistently, though not dramatically, better than those achieved through negotiation between lawyers or fighting things out in court (Richardson, 1988).

IN-DEPTH PERSONAL INTERVIEWS

While conducting large numbers of personal interviews can be costly and time-consuming, researchers can gain a greater knowledge of lifestyles and personal feelings from participants. Through the use of systematic questioning and probes, personal histories or other detailed information can be either recorded on tape or written on an **interview schedule** (a list of questions with appropriate spaces for the answers).

Interviewers do not always ask direct questions in interviews, however, but may encourage subjects to project their feelings and attitudes by providing personal diaries or finishing a sentence to create a hypothetical story. Interviewees may also be allowed to talk at length about some aspect of their life experience, without the researcher using a structured interview schedule.

If rapport develops between the interviewer and the subject, interviewing can uncover valuable information. Yet, it is difficult sometimes to develop rapport, especially for interviewers who cannot empathize with their subjects. The interviewer's personal characteristics may also influence the answers given by the interviewee or subject, especially if approval or disapproval is shown for certain types of responses. Bias can be reduced by using several carefully trained interviewers who are similar in gender and age to the subjects, who ask carefully phrased questions in the same way, and who do not show how they feel about the responses.

Information gathered in interviews can be treated as survey research, and coded and analyzed with a computer (quantitative analysis). Alternatively, the answers can be analyzed to retain the rich personal details and the interviewees' own words and point of view (qualitative analysis). Regardless of whether the information is treated as quantitative or qualitative data, comparisons are usually made between answers given by subjects in different demographic and socio-economic circumstances. In other words, answers of males and females, older and younger subjects, richer and poorer people, or those from different cultural groups might be compared to find trends in interview data.

An example of an interview study is *What Will Tomorrow Bring? A Study of the Aspirations of Adolescent Women*, prepared for the Canadian Advisory Council on the Status of Women (Baker, 1985). After asking a series of questions about the adolescents' backgrounds and present lives, the study focused on what they said they would be doing on a typical day when they were 30 years old. After analyzing these stories, Baker found that many Canadian adolescents have little idea of the expectations and demands of adult society, including marriage and the labour market.

PERSONAL OBSERVATION

Family interaction can also be studied through direct or indirect observation. While the presence of the observer may influence the subject's behaviour, there are ways of minimizing this form of bias. One way is to observe subjects inside a laboratory from behind one-way mirrors. This allows researchers to eliminate extraneous factors that might influence the subjects' behaviour. The setting is unnatural, however, and the subjects may not behave normally because they know that they are being observed. In observation studies in natural settings, the observers usually remain as unobtrusive as possible in the hope that the subjects will barely notice that they are being observed and therefore will behave as they normally do.

In another type of observation study, researchers either disguise themselves as group members or become so familiar with other members that their presence is barely noticed. This method is called **participant observation**. Since it may be considered unethical for researchers to misrepresent their identity, an alternative would be for the researchers to approach the group openly, at the risk of refusal, and request permission to study it as participant observers.

In observation studies, several well-trained observers are sometimes employed to minimize bias. These observers are not usually aware of the hypothesis or main purpose of the study, so they cannot be accused of seeing only what the chief investigator of the study expects to find. Observation studies are usually analyzed by searching for recurring themes or patterns in people's behaviour, interaction, or conversations. Once these patterns are identified, the researcher can note the conditions under which they occur.

Several famous sociological studies have been based on participant observation. One example is William Foote Whyte's American study of a Boston gang, called *Street Corner Society* (1943). Whyte lived in a slum neighbourhood while he was a graduate student at Harvard and participated in gang activities while gathering information about the structure and dynamics of the group. Although this study was done about 50 years ago, it is still considered a prime example of the participant observation method. More recently, films such as *Talk 16* and *Up 21* were also based on participant observation.

COMBINING METHODOLOGIES

Although the various research methodologies have been discussed separately here, it should be emphasized that most researchers use several types of research in the same project. In studying the issue of child care in Ontario, for example, the researcher may first read previous studies on this topic, then consult official statistics about the availability of child care spaces, visit several types of child care centres to gain an understanding of the issues, and then interview parents, child care workers, and operators of child care centres. Few modern studies would rely simply on one research method.

From reading magazines, watching television, or even reading the newspaper, one can get a very distorted picture of family life because unusual cases rather than typical family activities are dramatically portrayed. For example, many people think that young people no longer want to have children because television serials, movies, and magazine features so often show "DINKS" (couples with Double Income and No Kids). Similarly, many television serials show people living in large expensive houses, that most people could never afford, and in families where the traditional gender roles are reversed. Before we assume these cases are typical and that we know about family life, it is necessary to move beyond our personal experience and beyond media features, to look at social science research. Most studies make a real effort to investigate people who are representative of those in the general population, providing a more accurate view of family life than personal experience or media portrayals.

BEGINNING A RESEARCH PROJECT

Independent study projects are designed to encourage you as a student to acquire and apply critical evaluative skills. In planning such a project, it is sometimes difficult to know where to begin. Here are some simple rules that may assist you in selecting your topics, beginning research, organizing and analyzing your material, and preparing your research report.

1. When selecting your research topic, choose one that you find most interesting, but not necessarily one about which you hold strong opinions.
2. Try to break down the topic into its many aspects and focus on one specific issue. For example, if you have chosen divorce in Canada, you should not research the entire issue of divorce but rather one specific question. You might choose from questions such as these:
   a. In what social and economic situations are people most likely to become divorced? Why?
   b. What are the social and emotional consequences for children when their parents divorce?
   c. Does joint custody enforced by the courts work well for children?
3. The topic you choose should be phrased as a specific question or as a hypothesis to be tested. A hypothesis is a statement of relationship between variables, such as "Joint custody arrangements that are court-enforced are less likely to be healthy for children than similar arrangements that are mutually agreed upon by divorcing parents."
4. Before you try to answer your central question, you should read about other similar studies to see what has been found. This **survey of the literature** will help you to define the important issues that require further research, choose a theoretical framework, compare the research methods used by others to study the same issue, and later allow you to compare your findings with those of professional researchers.
5. When you read other studies, make sure they are credible sources, such as academic journal articles or academic books. Popular magazines, newspapers, or trade books should be treated with care. When you read journal articles about empirical studies, try to use a critical approach. For example, notice which method of research was used, how many subjects were included in the sample, and how this sample was obtained. Identify the theoretical framework and its basic assumptions in order to assess the author's conclusions. Make sure the conclusions follow logically from the data or main argument and that

these conclusions are consistent with those in other studies. Just because something is published does not mean that it cannot contain problems or errors!

6. When searching for journal articles, you could look in periodical indexes such as the *Canadian Periodical Index* or the *Social Science Index*. Your library may also contain a computerized index, but it possibly contains only the titles of books and journals, rather than the titles of specific articles in journals.
7. Your topic should be placed within a theoretical framework, such as structural functionalism, systems theory, symbolic interactionism, social exchange, the family life cycle perspective, the feminist perspective, or political economy approach, to help you focus on the **unit of analysis** of your project. By this we mean whether you are studying the structures of society (such as laws or social expectations) or interpersonal relationships. Your theoretical perspective will establish the conceptual framework or the actual concepts you will use to analyze your topic.
8. If you are planning an interview or questionnaire, constructing the questions may be more difficult than you think. The questions must not encourage the subject to give the answers you expect and must be as clear and unambiguous as possible. Questions should not be double-barrelled or contain two questions within one. Be sure to have your teacher and/or principal approve your questions before you begin. (Professional researchers are usually expected to pass their questions through an ethics committee before the project begins.)
9. Make sure you choose your research subjects carefully if you are using an interview or questionnaire. For student projects, you would not need to be as rigorous as in a professional study, and could probably find subjects from your school, club, or a shopping mall. But of course, you could not generalize your results from such a sample to the entire population.
10. When analyzing your interviews or questionnaires, remember that you are looking for patterns in people's behaviour. Keep asking yourself what social, economic, or cultural factors are influencing people's attitudes, behaviour, or personal experiences.
11. When you begin writing your report, you should state clearly your research question at the beginning of the paper so that there can be no misunderstandings. Provide a rationale for your topic choice by indicating why it is a relevant issue for family studies, social science, or social policy analysis.

12. Remember to define your terms and be as specific as possible.
13. Make sure you indicate how you did the study. For example, you should state how you chose your sample, the size of your sample, and whether you used a questionnaire, an interview, observation, official statistics, library research, or a combination of methods.
14. Your paper should make an argument that is substantiated by research findings or statistics. Try to remain objective. Do not put your own opinions into the paper. Do not generalize or exaggerate your points. Provide a balanced argument that presents as many sides to the issue as you can.
15. It is always a good idea to briefly summarize the other studies you read about, so you can later compare your results with theirs. In order to protect yourself from the accusation of plagiarism, be sure you clearly reference other studies and do not present them as though they are your ideas. Any direct quotation from someone else's work or a summary of their main findings must be referenced with either a footnote or the author and date of publication in brackets i.e., (Smith, 1989).
16. In the conclusions of your paper, you should refer back to the theoretical perspective and compare your findings with those of the other studies you read about. Your central question should be answered to the best of your ability in the conclusion of the paper. Your conclusions should be based on the information provided in the paper rather than on implicit assumptions.
17. At the end of your paper, you must include a complete list of all the books and articles you used in your paper, including the author's name, the title of the article or book, the title of journal (if used), the name of the publisher, and the place and date of publication. For style of individual entries in your references or bibliography, refer to a style manual provided by your teacher, board of education, or one of the professional associations, such as the American Psychological Association, which is widely used in Canada.

The point of most independent study projects or research essays is to develop critical thinking, problem solving, and time management skills. This project should help you acquire some of the necessary skills to enable you to continue your studies of families or related social science fields. In the process, you may develop an understanding and awareness of your own attitudes and values concerning specific issues in family studies.

CONCLUSION

Topics of research within family studies have varied with the times, reflecting the concerns and debates of the educated public and the media. Social scientists have reacted to demographic and social trends, funding decisions, legal controversies, media events, and popular ideologies and have chosen their research projects accordingly. While in other decades, researchers were studying instincts, maternal deprivation, romantic love, and attitudes about premarital sex, they are now studying the impact of legal changes in divorce and custody laws on individual family members, the perpetuation of family violence from one generation to the next, government intervention in the family, custody and support issues after divorce, and kin relations in the reconstituted family after remarriage. This suggests that the study of the family now involves more of an understanding of politics, economics, and the law than in previous decades.

SUGGESTED READINGS

Carter, Elizabeth A. and Monica McGoldrick. *The Changing Family Life Cycle: A Framework for Family Therapy*. New York: Gardner Press, 1988.

Cheal, David. *Family and the State of Theory*. Toronto: University of Toronto Press, 1991.

Eichler, Margrit. *Families in Canada Today*. 2nd ed. Toronto: Gage, 1988.

Elkin, Frederick and Gerald Handel. *The Child and Society: The Process of Socialization*. 5th ed. New York: Random House, 1988.

Fine, Marshall. "Basic Characteristics of Family Systems Theory: Some Implications for the OAC in Family Studies." *OFSHEEA Journal*. 5 (1). June 1986:2–6.

Gaffield, Chad. "The Social and Economic Origins of Contemporary Families." *Families: Changing Trends in Canada*. 2nd ed. Edited by Maureen Baker. Scarborough: McGraw-Hill Ryerson, 1990:23–40.

Li, Peter. "Sociological Methods of Research." *An Introduction to The Social World*. Edited by R. Jack Richardson and Lorne Tepperman. Scarborough: McGraw-Hill Ryerson, 1987:35–57.

Mansfield, Nick. "Inquiry and Explanations." *Introductory Sociology: Canadian Perspectives*. Don Mills: Collier MacMillan, 1982.

Meikeljohn, Phyllis, Annette Yeager, and Lenore Kuch (eds.). *Today's Family: A Critical Focus*. Don Mills: Collier Macmillan, 1990.

Parr, Joy (ed.). *Childhood and Family in Canadian History*. Toronto: McClelland and Stewart, 1982.

Scanzoni, John. *Sexual Bargaining: Power Politics in the American Marriage*. 2nd ed. Chicago: University of Chicago Press, 1982.

Tepperman, Lorne and R. Jack Richardson (eds). *The Social World: An Introduction to Sociology*. 2nd ed. Scarborough: McGraw-Hill Ryerson, 1991.

Thorne, Barrie. "Feminist Rethinking of the Family: An Overview." *Rethinking the Family: Some Feminist Questions*. Edited by Barrie Thorne with Marilyn Yalom. New York: Longmans, 1982.

Zaretsky, Eli. *Capitalism, The Family and Personal Life*. New York: Harper and Row, 1976.

Issues for Discussion

1. What do we mean when we say that family life can be studied from different theoretical perspectives? How would structural functionalists, political economists, social exchange theorists, and feminists analyze the changing division of labour in the home?
2. If the acceptance of different theoretical perspectives means that researchers begin with assumptions about what is important to study and how the world works, is the field of family studies unscientific? Explain your position.
3. If we wanted to study the following topics, what research method would we choose? What are your reasons for this choice?
   a. decision-making between husbands and wives;
   b. the division of labour in the family;
   c. the incidence of cohabitation among young people;
   d. the prevalence of child abuse now compared with 30 years ago;
   e. birth rates since Confederation;
   f. parental reaction to the news that their child's illness is AIDS;
   g. the trend for women to have first babies after the age of 35 years.

4. How can a researcher guard against bias in:
   a. a participant observation study;
   b. personal interviews;
   c. mailed questionnaires?
5. Which theoretical perspective best describes family life as you have experienced it?

FURTHER ACTIVITIES

1. How has the percentage of people in each category of marital status changed from 1901 to 1986 in Canada? Is a greater percentage of the Canadian population now married compared with the turn of the century? How could you account for this trend?
2. Most Canadian newspapers contain personal columns in which people advertise for partners. Compare the content of these advertisements using the following criteria: the age and sex of the advertisers, the nature of the relationship people are seeking, how they describe themselves, and how they describe their potential mate.
3. As an exercise in observation, visit a long-term care facility for physically or mentally challenged children or elderly people. What can you observe about the social and psychological characteristics of the residents and the caregivers? What kind of services are provided for the residents?
4. Design a study to find out what categories of people are most likely to want to marry and have children. You might want to consider social class, racial or cultural background, gender, and educational attainment.

3 Between Families: the Single Life

SINGLES: FROM FAMILY TO NONFAMILY HOUSEHOLDS

Throughout the 1980s, the proportion of single people in the Canadian population increased. In 1986, for example, 11 percent of Canadians had never been married by the age of 36. This percentage rose slightly from 1976, when 8 percent had never married by that age (Boyd and Pryor, 1990:188). Furthermore, the percentage of people aged 25 to 34 who reported themselves single (never-married) in the 1986 census was 25 percent compared with 20 percent in 1981 (Devereaux, 1990:139). These figures reflect the current trend toward delayed marriage and **cohabitation** rather than legal marriage.

Over this century, there have been substantial changes in living **arrangements and family composition** among all age groups (Boyd and Pryor, 1990:188). Single adults (never-married as well as separated, divorced, or widowed) have been encouraged to establish separate households from their families by prolonged formal schooling, delayed marriage, high rates of separation and divorce, higher wages, improved social welfare benefits and changes in attitudes toward sexuality, gender roles, and individuality. Independent living has become more valued among all age groups, and more apartment units have been built enabling single people to live alone or with friends.

Table 3.1 **Population Aged 15 and Over, by Marital Status, 1981 and 1986**

MARITAL STATUS	1981	1986	% CHANGE 1981-1986
Total population aged 15 and over	18 862 085	19 917 365	5.6
Single	5 255 110	5 425 290	3.2
Married	11 478 715	12 033 670	4.8
Separated	470 455	517 530	10.0
Divorced	500 135	690 490	38.1
Widowed	1 157 670	1 250 395	8.0

Source: Statistics Canada, 1981 and 1986 Census of Canada. Reproduced with the permission of the Minister of Supply and Services Canada, 1992.

While the percentage of unmarried people aged 15 to 34 who continue to live with their parents declined from 1971 to 1981, recent evidence from the Canadian Census has shown a reversal of this trend from 1981 to 1986 (Ibid). During this period, there was an increase in young people living in their parents' home. This reversal can be attributed to economic factors such as high unemployment rates, relatively lower wages for youth, and the high cost of rental accommodation, as well as the need for more years of schooling. These economic trends have encouraged some single people to stay at home longer and others to return to their parents' home after a period of living on their own.

Whether unmarried people establish a household separate from their families depends on a number of factors, including age, sex, membership in a particular ethnic group, educational attainment, labour force participation, and individual income (Boyd and Pryor, 1990:189). For example, as women tend to marry earlier than men, young men live at home longer. Certain ethnic groups, such as Italians and Greeks, encourage their children to live at home until marriage (Chimbos, 1980; Sturino, 1980). Regardless of gender or ethnicity, young people earning enough money to support themselves can leave home earlier. As educational requirements expand, more students are extending their education and often live at home if they attend a local college or university. However, post-secondary education is also a factor encouraging young people to leave their parents' home before marriage, especially if there is no college or university nearby.

Figure 3.1 **Single and Married People as a Proportion of Young Adults, 1981 and 1986**

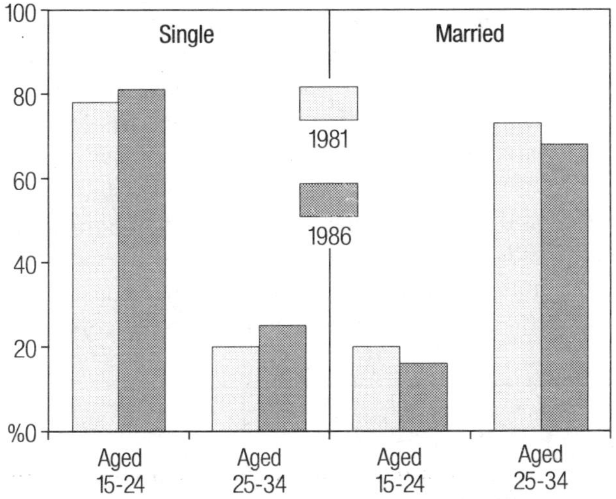

Source: Statistics Canada, 1981 and 1986 Census of Canada. Reproduced with the permission of the Minister of Supply and Services Canada, 1992.

SPECIFIC TASKS

SEPARATION FROM FAMILY AND INDIVIDUATION

Because the population of single people includes all age groups who may be at quite different stages in their personal development, it is difficult to talk about the specific developmental tasks for the entire category. For young people leaving home for the first time, the establishment of their own identities and values separate from those of their parents is very important. They must develop self-confidence, their own political and social attitudes, a gender identity, and social allegiances. They must establish a separate household and learn to budget, shop, cook, clean, and do laundry without their parents' assistance or interference. Since they may also be college or university students, young people living on their own may need to make educational and occupational choices. In addition, some will be establishing intimate relationships for the first time or may be searching for suitable partners.

In *Identity: Youth and Crisis*, American psychologist Erik Erikson

(1968) argued that if young people are not given adequate opportunities to work through these developmental tasks and fail to develop a clear sense of identity, they may be unable to accept adult responsibilities and settle down in an occupation or permanent relationship. The family of orientation is very important in providing role models for young people. If parents have low self-esteem, quit school before graduation, work at jobs that they find unsatisfying, experience marital conflict, and have trouble interacting with their children, their children may have more difficulty staying in school and achieving a satisfying life than children whose parents provided more positive examples. Regardless of what parents say, their actions tend to speak louder than words.

For those making the transition from married to single life, either through separation or bereavement, some of the developmental tasks

Reprinted by permission of Tribune Media Services

may be similar to those of young people who have recently left their parents' home. Like unmarried young people, those recently separated or widowed need to learn to see themselves as individuals rather than as part of a couple. They may need to relearn decision-making skills as well as develop assertiveness and an independent identity. Living alone after being part of a couple may also require learning practical skills in realms that the spouse formerly looked after, such as cooking or driving a car. It may also involve becoming used to one's own company.

Moving out of the family home or a couple relationship may not involve living alone but rather establishing a nonfamily household with friends. This may require making joint decisions about a suitable apartment, furnishings, and lifestyle, or establishing a division of labour or budget for the household.

HISTORICAL PERSPECTIVES

THE WORK AND EDUCATION PATTERNS OF YOUTH

Before industrialization, parents and their children contributed to the family economy, which might have been based on farming, fishing, hunting, crafts, or a family business. Young adults either stayed at home working with their parents until they married, or they worked as domestic servants, apprentices, or labourers in a neighbour's household. Work was segregated on the basis of age, gender, social class, and race, and working hours were typically much longer than they are today.

With large-scale industrialization in Canada in the nineteenth and early twentieth centuries, many young people left the family home and moved to urban areas in search of work. They often found working for wages preferable to personal service or farm work because it offered higher pay, shorter hours, and more personal autonomy (Gaffield, 1984).

Men always had the option to work and remain single, but considering the hardships of early Canadian life and the strict division of labour between men and women, there were few incentives to remain unmarried. Men needed wives to cook, clean, and sew for them; women needed husbands to perform heavy work, to support them, and to represent them legally in the larger society. However, marriages were often delayed for financial reasons. Because men were expected to support their wives and children, and contraception was not widely practised, they could not marry until they had established themselves in an occupation and accumulated sufficient funds to set up a separate household and support a family.

Although there were many ways in which young men could earn a living after they left home, the choices of visible minority men were influenced by prejudice and discrimination. Certain occupations were acceptable for particular racial or cultural groups, but other occupations were closed to them. For example, at the turn of the century, African-Canadian men were typically found in household service and in urban jobs such as railroad porters, but were excluded from labour unions (Krauter and Davis, 1978:51-54). Chinese-Canadian men originally worked as labourers and miners. Many specifically came to Canada to help build the Canadian Pacific Railroad in the 1880s. After the railroad was completed, these men became a large reservoir of cheap labour (Krauter and Davis, 1978:61). Later, they established profitable businesses.

At certain periods of Canadian history, such as after World War I and during the Depression of the 1930s, hostility to "foreigners" was strong (Avery, 1979), as they were seen as taking jobs away from Europeans. But Native men were also discriminated against in urban labour forces. Consequently, they became heavily involved in labour and service jobs, such as logging and guiding (Forcese, 1986:47).

Women's occupational choices were also restricted by ideas of what work was appropriate for them. Prior to the nineteenth century, single women could join a religious order and make a vow of chastity and poverty. They could work as governesses or lady's companions in wealthy homes, or they could live with relatives and help around the house and farm. Many young women from poorer families worked as domestic servants in other people's homes. After industrialization, single women worked in factory or office jobs, but could barely support themselves on their wages. The inability to earn a living outside of marriage and the desire to establish a household separate from parents motivated women to marry.

Industrialization and urbanization soon led to the expansion of formal schooling. When families moved to urban areas, they no longer needed their children for farm labour. Many of the available occupations in cities required literacy and arithmetical skills that could be better taught in schools than through on-the-job training. Moreover, higher unemployment rates from mass production led to concern that idleness among young people would lead to social unrest. Consequently, parents, educators, and policy-makers began to place more emphasis on formal schooling, both to keep young people off the streets and to better prepare them for the changing needs of the labour market (Houston and Prentice, 1988).

Until the twentieth century, only children from wealthy families were able to continue their education beyond a rudimentary level. These young people were taught at private schools or at home by tutors, and when they were older they were sent to prestigious universities, often in Britain or France (Clement, 1975; Forcese, 1986). Priority was always given to the education of boys because they were expected to earn a living. Upper class girls, however, were sometimes educated in the arts, foreign languages, and home management to prepare them to be interesting wives, hostesses, and mothers.

Before Confederation, most communities in Canada required no school taxes, and schools were organized by churches and private educators. Students purchased their own supplies and paid fees to cover the cost of running the school and the teacher's salary. This meant that formal education was more feasible for children from wealthier families.

The first province to provide free education was Prince Edward Island in 1852. Following Confederation, the provinces formed departments of education and tax measures were introduced to pay for provincial educational needs. Compulsory attendance laws were also established (Kalbach and McVey, 1979:242). From 1901 to the present day, the percentage of 5- to 19-year-olds attending school has increased substantially from 51.1 percent to 90.8 percent (Statistics Canada, 1986). Since school attendance until age 16 became compulsory (in Ontario, this was in 1921), children and young people have become increasingly separated from the adult world. This has been especially true for young people from wealthier families, who could afford to stay in school longer delaying employment and adult responsibilities until well into their twenties.

Students in larger schools were divided into classes based on age and performance, while rural classrooms usually contained students of all ages until these schools were phased out in the 1950s. Prior to the Second World War, those from poorer families were sometimes required by their parents to stay home to help around the house or farm, and often left school as soon as they legally could. In many cases, parents obtained special permission from the truant officer (who was responsible for enforcing compulsory education) for their children to leave school at age 14 to help support the family.

When young people left school and worked for wages, they were expected to give a portion to their parents for room and board. Since unmarried people were usually paid lower wages than married people before World War II, a man often had to ask his employer for a raise before he could afford to marry. On the other hand, until the Second World War women were expected to resign from their positions shortly after they announced their engagements. Consequently, marriage was often delayed while young people saved up a "nest egg," but unlike today, they usually lived in a family household until marriage.

Although many families could afford to assist their adult children to marry and establish new households, young couples from poorer families had to accumulate their own funds or temporarily move in with one set of parents until they could afford their own home or until they inherited their parents' house. Although some cultural groups were accustomed to living as an extended family, this arrangement was not considered ideal by most Euro-Canadians at any time during Canadian history (Nett, 1980).

During the Second World War when many Canadian men went overseas, young women entered the labour force in increasing numbers to work in munitions factories and offices. More women worked for pay, more employed women were married, and more women were hired in nontraditional jobs (Wilson, 1991:80,81). When men returned from the war, however, they expected their jobs back. While many married women returned to homemaking, single women and married women whose husbands were unemployed or had low incomes stayed in the labour force and worked in office jobs, retail sales, or factory work. During the 1960s, women were encouraged to work for pay by rising costs, high interest rates, the development of new jobs in the service sector, the creation of part-time work, and a desire to use their education, become self-supporting, or contribute to the family income. Gradually, single women developed work patterns similar to those of men, although they usually performed different jobs with lower pay (Wilson, 1991).

During the 1960s, technological change in the labour force, the expansion of the service sector, rising expectations of **upward mobility**, and expanding world markets led to an expansion of the post-secondary education in North America. Many new colleges and universities were built and enrolments increased. Since the 1950s, for example, the proportion of 18- to 24-year-olds enrolled in post-secondary institutions has risen dramatically. As table 3.2 shows, 6 percent of this age group attended college or university in 1951. By 1989-90, however, this figure had risen to 29.4 percent.

The rise of part-time work throughout the 1960s and 1970s enabled many young people to continue their education beyond secondary school. Prior to this period, those without family financing

Table 3.2 **Full-Time Post-Secondary Enrolment as a Percentage of 18- to 24-Year-Olds in the Population, Canada, 1951–1990.**

1951	6.0
1961	10.6
1971	18.5
1981	20.5
1986–87	26.3
1989–90	29.4

Source: Statistics Canada. *Education in Canada, 1987*. Cat. 81-229. Ottawa: Supply and Services Canada, June 1988:123; *Education in Canada, 1989–90*. Cat. 81-229. August 1991:117. Reproduced with the permission of the Minister of Supply and Services Canada, 1992.

WORKING STUDENTS: LOW WAGES, LOW GRADES

Students make up a huge and ever increasing work force which earns minimum wage, receives few benefits, works odd hours and split shifts, makes no wage demands, and can be fired without severance pay or even any notice. On top of that, most student employees are woefully ignorant of their rights and can potentially be denied many of the safety and health considerations that full-time employees take for granted. Even more important, the use of student labour allows owners to maximize their profits which explains why students will continue to be exploited for cheap labour.

I have seen students unable to participate in field trips or extracurricular events because they cannot get time off for any after-school events. Marion, a grade 11 student, is required to give her employer one-month's notice if she needs time off for any after-school activity. "We make up the scedules one month in advance," she says, "and it's not easy for my boss to replace me if I'm not there." On a recent field trip to the National Arts Centre in Ottawa, another student told me that her job commitment came first and that she could not go if we were not back by 3:15. For the sake of a minimal wage many students deny themselves the very socializing aspects that make school much more than books and tests.

It is, of course, a vicious circle. Students who fail school because of a menial job in the service sector usually end up working these same jobs after they quit school and are unable to look forward to any meaningful advancement in status or pay for many years. To make matters worse, these former students must then compete against current students who will do the same job but for less money.

Ray Saitz. "Moonlighting. How after-school jobs prevent our students from making the grade." *Education Forum*. Vol. 15, no. 2. Summer 1989. Ray Saitz, former Head of English at North Grenville D.H.S. in Kemptville, Ontario, is now teaching in Northumberland and Newcastle.

had to quit school or at least work for a few years in order to save up enough money to continue studying. During the 1960s, the federal government initiated a student loan program that helped poorer students to further their education. Yet, part-time work was still necessary to supplement this loan.

Much of the increase in enrolment in post-secondary education in Canada can be attributed to the substantial rise in the enrolment of young women as well as students from low-income families throughout the 1960s and 1970s. The trend toward post-secondary education kept more young people out of the full-time labour force and prolonged their financial dependence on their families. In smaller communities without a college or university, however, it has forced many young people to leave home and establish their own households.

Changing Attitudes Toward Singleness

While there have always been people who remained single, it was difficult for them to live outside a family household until the twentieth century. Unmarried children (especially daughters) sometimes stayed to care for their aging parents, moved in with relatives, or boarded with other families, but they seldom established their own separate households. Without labour-saving devices and with 10- or 12-hour workdays, single people needed a partner or other family members to help maintain a household.

Until the Second World War, if single people went to the city to find work or attend school, they boarded with other families or lived in supervised residences, but they seldom lived alone or with friends as single people often do today. Adult supervision or chaperones were considered necessary to prevent young people from "ruining their reputations" or engaging in "immoral" activities.

Different connotations have been placed on singleness for men and women because of the different roles they have been expected to play in society (Scanzoni and Scanzoni, 1988). Men have been expected to become educated, acquire occupational skills, and eventually to support their wives and children. Their **social status** has been defined by their education, occupation, and income rather than through their marital status or relationships. According to tradition, the man proposes marriage to the woman, and if a man is not married, it is assumed to be because he chooses not to be. For women, however, being married has been consequential because few expectations have been placed on them to acquire education or occupational skills. Until recently, when women could establish their own paid occupation, their social status was usually assumed to be the same as that of their father or husband. Even now, their occupational pursuits are often viewed as secondary to the pursuit of marriage and childbearing. Furthermore, if women are unmarried, it is sometimes assumed to be because they have not been asked, rather than because of their personal choice.

Women have also been defined more in terms of their sexuality and fertility. For example, historically, beauty, virginity, and childbearing capacity have been considered important characteristics for a bride-to-be, but not for a potential groom. The status of married woman and mother is still elevated in comparison with the single woman. The higher status for mothers is especially noticeable in countries such as Latin America and Africa and within certain cultural groups in Canada, such as southern Europeans (Scanzoni and Scanzoni, 1988; Dinan, 1983). People sometimes ridicule or pity single women, assuming that no man wants them (Shostak, 1987), while men in a similar situation are assumed to be "sowing their wild oats" and "having a good time" as bachelors. Although in traditional societies that value reproduction, remaining single may be devalued and even punished. In Romania, for example, a policy to encourage a higher birth rate introduced higher taxes for unmarried people and gave them lower priority than married people with children when they applied for an apartment (Romaniuc, 1984).

Attitudes toward singleness and independent living became more positive as more young people of both sexes left their home towns for higher education and employment opportunities, and relatives could no longer enforce the same restrictions. With the expansion of the university and college systems during the 1960s, a greater proportion of young people continued their education. Campus life encouraged a less family-oriented lifestyle and even a certain rebellion against "middle-class values," including monogamous marriage with children, working hard to pay the mortgage, the expectation of career mobility, and the accumulation of wealth. In fact, many students participated in a wave of social change during the 1960s and 1970s. They became involved in protest movements relating to student democracy, sexual revolution, feminism, anti-consumerism, and intensive criticisms of the traditional nuclear family. Some experimented with alternatives to monogamous marriage, including communal living and a series of casual sexual relationships. More effective contraception, especially the introduction of the birth control pill in the early 1960s, enabled these alternatives with fewer unwanted pregnancies. The rekindling of the centuries-old feminist movement further encouraged the criticism of traditional gender roles and the expectation that all women would marry, leave their paid jobs, and become homemakers.

Since the 1960s, it has become increasingly possible for both men and women to remain unmarried, support themselves through paid work, and maintain a healthy social and sexual life. Yet ironically, the proportion of women remaining single continued to fall until the 1980s, as table 3.3 shows. This trend toward a greater percentage of the population marrying in the 1960s and 1970s can be explained by the fact that couples had fewer reasons to postpone marriage when they could delay childbearing and continue enjoying two incomes. Furthermore, once divorce laws were liberalized in 1968, marriage was less likely to be seen as a life-long commitment. Although it was never socially acceptable to think of marriage as impermanent, liberalizing the divorce laws could indirectly encourage more people to marry. After all, it is easier to make the decision to marry if it is legally possible to get a divorce. In addition, increased geographic mobility and more women in the work force created more opportunities to meet potential partners.

The feminist and gay liberation movements have contributed to greater social acceptance of single and childless lifestyles. Some gay rights activists talked about the different but valid lifestyles of gay

Table 3.3 **Percentage of Women who are Never-Married by Age 45 to 49, Canada, 1881–1986**

1881	11.3
1891	9.4
1911	12.0
1921	11.1
1931	10.3
1941	11.2
1951	11.7
1961	9.5
1971	7.0
1981	5.8
1986	5.8

Source: Statistics Canada, Ellen M. Gee. "The Life Course of Canadian Women: an Historical and Demographic Analysis." *Social Indicators Research* 18 (1986):266; Statistics Canada. *The Nation. Age, Sex and Marital Status.* Cat. 93-101, Ottawa, September 1987 (calculated from Table 5-3). Reproduced with the permission of the Minister of Supply and Services Canada, 1992.

people and fought against **homophobia** and **heterosexism.** Feminists have encouraged women to educate themselves, develop their talents, participate more in public life, and become more financially independent. They have questioned the traditional idea that women must be wives and mothers in order to be personally fulfilled and "successful." Yet, from interviews with adolescents across Canada, Baker (1985b) noted that adolescents from both sexes expect to enjoy both marriage and children as well as occupational achievement in the future. Furthermore, the young women in this study appeared to be prejudiced against unmarried women, even those who are occupationally successful. They assumed, for example, that unmarried women are unhappy and lack friends and lovers.

In the past two decades, it has become possible for single people to be sexually active with less concern about pregnancy. While birth control has been practised for thousands of years, religious values linking sexuality with marriage and historical efforts to raise the birth rate have led to laws prohibiting the advertisement and dissemination of contraceptive material and devices in both Canada and the United States. Although there were many periods in which these laws were not enforced, an American birth control advocate, Margaret Sanger, was given a prison sentence in the early 1920s for writing a pamphlet on contraception.

The development of the birth control pill and its marketing in the early 1960s helped to challenge existing laws in both the United States and Canada. In 1969, after years of lobbying by the medical profession, lawyers, and women's groups, the federal government legalized the dissemination of birth control devices and made hospital abortions available if a committee concluded that the woman's life or health was in danger. In 1988, however, the abortion law was declared unconstitutional by the Supreme Court of Canada because abortions were not equally available to women in all regions of the country, as some hospitals had no abortion committees and performed no abortions. The federal government has been considering drafting a new law, yet the issue remains very contentious.

In the 1990s, an increasing number of couples are sexually active outside legal marriage and many live together in **common-law relationships** until they marry or break up. Many couples delay marriage and childbearing, especially middle-class young people completing their education or establishing their careers. As more couples live together, remain childless, have smaller families, bear children without a legal spouse, separate, and divorce, additional credence is given to new family forms, singleness, and nonfamily households.

CULTURAL PERSPECTIVES

EDUCATION, WORK, AND ADULTHOOD IN OTHER CULTURES

Children are **socialized** or taught the norms and values of their society by their parents, peers, community, and the education system. Formal schooling is expected to provide them with the knowledge and skills to become informed citizens, to find work, and to become independent from their families. In many countries, laws require compulsory education until a specified age (often 16) and prohibit children and youth from working in jobs considered appropriate only for adults. In many developing countries such as India or Nicaragua, however, the laws cannot always be enforced because children and young adults must assist their families to survive economically by working at home or in the community.

Even in countries with compulsory education and laws prohibiting child labour, children and youth from poorer families are often forced to work to ensure their own and their family's survival. When these young people work during the daytime, they are denied a formal education. Frequently, they are exploited as a source of cheap labour and expected to perform jobs that adults would prefer not to do. Because they are usually working illegally and are too young to join labour unions, employers can subject them to arduous and dangerous conditions. Even in countries with legislation preventing child labour, there is a wide gap between law and practice (Bequele and Boyden, 1988).

The kind of work young people do in developing countries is usually segregated by gender and age. Young women often work with their mothers and other women of the community, while young men learn their occupational skills from their fathers or other men. By the time these young people have reached adulthood, they have developed occupational skills, life skills, and interpersonal contacts to enable them to survive on their own.

Prolonging the period of dependence on family with post-secondary education is more typical of industrialized countries than developing countries. In developing countries, some young people from poorer families can receive bursaries or scholarships to continue their education. However, most young people from poorer families cannot afford to stay in school, and most governments cannot afford to provide free tuition beyond the secondary level or an extensive loan or bursary program. Young men and increasingly young women from wealthy families are expected to graduate from college or university before they establish an occupation and marry. Sometimes they are sent away to get an education at foreign universities in Europe,

Australia, or North America. In these countries, they may live as western young people do, but women and especially women from countries where marriages are arranged may be strictly supervised by kin members so that they do not develop western ideas about **dating** and relations between the sexes. When they have completed their studies, however, they may be expected by their families and by the government of the country in which they are studying to return to their home country. If they have developed personal relationships or have employment opportunities, they may be able to change their immigration status to become landed immigrants.

In impoverished regions of the world, such as Central America or parts of Africa where there is a shortage of work, young people are forced to migrate to a city to find a job. Sometimes they have to leave their countries to work as migrant labourers in foreign lands where they could be faced with difficult jobs, loneliness, and employment discrimination. Although both single and married men and women choose this alternative, single men are most likely to become migrant labourers. These men are often expected to send home money to support their parents as well as save for their future marriage.

Canada has used and continues to use foreign workers to fill gaps in the labour force. Many of these workers are single or come without their spouses and families to work in Canada. For example in the 1880s, immigrant men from China were encouraged to work as labourers on the construction of the Canadian Pacific Railway. Because the idea was to provide a cheap and transitory labour force, Chinese women were excluded and severe social sanctions discouraged relationships with white women (Krauter and Davis, 1978:61). Head taxes on Chinese immigrants and future laws prohibiting Chinese immigration until the 1960s led to an imbalance of the sex ratio and a high percentage of single men in the Chinese immigrant population. The conditions under which Chinese migrant labourers came to Canada and subsequent immigration laws influenced future patterns of family life for many generations of Chinese immigrants, including lowering marriage and birth rates. Now, many Chinese families enter Canada as immigrants each year, especially from Hong Kong.

Changes to Canadian immigration laws may again influence the composition of immigrant families in this country. In an attempt to limit the number of people eligible to enter Canada through the family class category, the Canadian immigration department initially introduced new regulations saying that unmarried children of immigrants could no longer automatically accompany their parents to Canada if they were over the age of 19 and working. These children would no

NEW RULES TO LIMIT FAMILY IMMIGRATION

Non-dependent children over 19 will no longer be eligible

BY ESTANISLAO OZIEWICZ
Immigration Reporter

The Immigration Department expects new rules limiting the sponsorship of children to cut the number of people qualifying as family-class immigrants by 20 000 a year starting in 1993.

Under the new regulations, due to take effect in January, non-dependent children over 19 will no longer be eligible to immigrate under the family class.

All unmarried children under 19 will be determined to be dependent, and adult children will be considered dependent if they are studying full-time and have been continuously supported by their parents.

The current regulations were introduced in 1988 and include children of any age, provided that they have never been married. Before the 1988 changes, only children under 21 qualified.

The explanatory notes to the new rules, published in the Canada Gazette, say the move will help maintain a reasonable balance among the three main immigration categories—family, refugee, and independent.

Immigration Minister Bernard Valcourt said the new definition will more "effectively capture the concept of family as it is generally understood in Canada."

But Lewis Chan, president of the Canadian Ethnocultural Council, a non-partisan coalition of 37 national organizations, sharply criticized the change.

"This represents a retreat by the government from the pro-family and family-reunification policies," he said. "For people who have family members abroad, this represents a partial slam of the door in their faces."

Nancy Pocock, co-ordinator of the Toronto-based Quaker Committee for Refugees, went further in her criticisms, saying the narrower definition of dependency does not embrace Canada's multicultural makeup and eventually will hurt immigrants from the Third World and elsewhere where the concept of family is wider.

"It's all part of the government's effort to get rid of refugees," she said. "I don't know what they expect them to do. Go home and die, I guess."

Refugee advocates argue that refugee claimants are often separated from their families for years while their claims are heard. In cases where they receive refugee status, they must then begin the process of acquiring landed-immigrant status before they can sponsor their families. Now, the new regulations will more narrowly limit whom they can sponsor.

Howard Greenberg, a Toronto immigration lawyer who is chairman of the immigration section of the Canadian Bar Association (Ontario), said the regulation is clearly designed to restrict the entry of children of prospective immigrants to those who can satisfy dependency criteria and those who have job skills Canada wants.

"This approach is consistent with the government's five-year immigration plan in terms of controlling immigrants based on their contribution to Canada," he said.

Mr. Valcourt's report to Parliament released last Friday projects 95 000 family-class members becoming landed immigrants in 1993. The target for 1992 is 100 000. This year the target was 85 000, but 91 000 landings are expected.

The Globe and Mail, 6 November 1991:A4.

longer be considered part of the immediate family. After an outcry from community groups, the age limit was dropped, but the basic idea still applies that only children who are unmarried and financially dependent because they have been previously enrolled as full-time students are considered "immediate family." This definition of family membership is much narrower than many cultural groups accept.

If young people can find work in their own country and in their own community, they usually continue to live with their parents and siblings until they reach a certain age, accumulate enough money or property, or until they marry. If the marriage is to be arranged by family members, the young people are expected to live in their parents' home and wait until the arrangements are made.

In North America, there is often a discontinuity between the expectations of young people and of adults, yet there are few rituals to indicate when young people become adults. Going away to college may serve as a rite of passage to adulthood for some people, but only about 30 percent of Canadian young people pursue post-secondary education (Statistics Canada, 1991:117). Wedding ceremonies are a more universal way of celebrating a change in status to adulthood, but a growing percentage of Canadians are living together without marriage. Those who choose to live together without going through a public wedding ceremony may not necessarily be perceived as fully adult through the eyes of their relatives or older friends.

Often, North American youths are left to initiate themselves into adulthood through peer-group activities or youth gangs (Nanda, 1991:146). For example, young men sometimes become involved in high-risk activities when their friends dare them to prove their strength or bravery, which are considered to be important characteristics of adult males in some segments of society. In other cultures, such as the Cheyenne in south central United States, young people are never marginal to their society, but are gradually given more responsibilities until they become adults and establish their own households. In still other societies, such as parts of Africa, there is a requirement that a youth must change in order to become an adult. This could involve dramatic rituals of initiation to ensure that the change has been made and has been recognized by the community (Nanda, 1991:146).

ATTITUDES TOWARD DATING AND MARRIAGE

Although Canadian parents usually encourage their adult children to get to know a variety of young people and to socialize with members of the opposite sex before choosing their marriage partners, there are many cultural and ethnic variations in the expectations about dating and sexuality. By *dating*, we mean spending leisure time together for the sake of enjoyment, without any intention to marry in the near future. (Even though the word dating sounds old-fashioned, it will be used throughout this book because there does not seem to be a better alternative and because it is still used in sociological texts.) Most parents want their children to date and eventually marry members of their own cultural group. Marrying similar people in terms of their social or cultural characteristics is called **homogamy**. Although this desire to have their children marry within their cultural group may simply be a form of **ethnocentrism**, most parents want their children to maintain their language and culture and to produce children who will appreciate and continue this cultural heritage (Reitz, 1980; Ishwaran, 1980). Parents often see interracial or interethnic dating as an example of loss of control over their children's upbringing, rebellion against their culture, and an indication of future problems with a mixed marriage (Scanzoni and Scanzoni, 1988:82).

From the young person's point of view, dating people from other ethnic or cultural groups may simply indicate lack of prejudice. On the other hand, it may be forced upon them by a shortage of available partners from their own ethnic or cultural group. Interethnic and

Social scientists have used intermarriage as an indicator of cultural or racial assimilation.

Canapress Photo Services

interracial dating is sometimes seen by parents as a subconscious or conscious rebellion against their wishes and by group members as a betrayal of the group (Scanzoni and Scanzoni, 1988:82). Social scientists have used intermarriage as an indicator of cultural or racial assimilation (Ram, 1990:213).

Certain ethnic groups more than others have encouraged dating and marriage within their group. Among Hutterites in Western Canada, for example, dating itself is kept to a minimum because of their religious beliefs and their rural and nonconsumer lifestyle (Peter, 1979). Dating implies spending time and money on pleasure, which is perceived as a waste of time and "sinful." Attending events and activities in nearby towns could lead to forming relationships with non-Hutterites and to premarital sex (Peter, 1979). Hutterites feel that sexuality should only be an expression of marital love. Since religion is an integral part of marriage and community life, **endogamy**, or marriage within the group, is seen to be important for both marital and community cohesion.

Ethnic or racial groups that live in remote areas, in urban "ghettos," or in other closely-knit neighbourhoods tend to promote endogamy. Endogamy is practised more frequently by first generation immigrants because of language barriers and because they have less opportunity to meet people from other cultural groups through their jobs or in their close-knit neighbourhoods. Endogamy is also encouraged by groups who feel their cultural heritage is being threatened (Kalbach and McVey, 1979; Reitz, 1980; Ram, 1990).

As the cultural backgrounds of Canadians becomes more diverse, there are increased opportunities for interracial and intercultural dating and marriage. But some cultural groups are less likely to intermarry than others. From the 1961 and 1971 Canadian census, we know that people with Jewish backgrounds had the highest rates of endogamy, at 91 percent among all family heads and 88 percent to 90 percent for native-born heads of families (Kalbach and McVey, 1979:321). More recent studies (Reitz, 1980:120) showed that southern Europeans and Chinese in Canada also had high rates of endogamy. In a recent Canadian study by Ram (1990), it was noted that 97 percent of men born in South Korea but living in Canada were married to women of the same origin, compared with only 19 percent of Australian men. He concluded in this study based on 1981 census data that intermarriage is most prevalent among persons originating from Australia, United States, and western and northern European countries, and least prevalent among those originating from Asia, the Caribbean, and southern European countries. The duration of residence in Canada and the tendency to work with people from other cultures were both strongly related to intermarriage. This suggests that one reason for lower rates of intermarriage is less opportunity to meet people from other cultural groups (Ram, 1990:225). Groups that are integrated or dispersed among the general population are typically less concerned about **exogamy**, or marriage to partners from other cultural groups. The generation born in Canada has more opportunity to meet, date, and subsequently to marry people from the majority ethnic group. Each future generation is more likely to integrate into the larger society and to marry members of other cultural or racial groups.

Intermarriage among Native women has long been a political and

Table 3.4 **Intermarriage in Canada**

RANK POSITIONS OF 40 NATIONAL ORIGINS (COUNTRIES OF BIRTH) ACCORDING TO THE INCIDENCE OF INTERMARRIAGE, CANADA, 1981

Rank	Wife's Country of Birth	% Married to Husband of the Same Origin	Rank	Wife's Country of Birth	% Married to Husband of the Same Origin
1	Australia	16.8	21	Netherlands	66.9
2	U.S.	21.0	22	Egypt	69.0
3	Sweden	30.7	23	Trinidad & Tobago	69.4
4	Ireland, Rep. of	35.3	24	Former U.S.S.R.	69.8
5	Norway	35.7	25	Hungary	69.9
6	Austria	37.6	26	Malta	70.3
7	Belgium	37.8	27	Jamaica	76.8
8	France	38.7	28	Lebanon	76.9
9	Germany	43.5	29	Guyana	78.6
10	Switzerland	43.5	30	China	78.7
11	Japan	48.8	31	Taiwan	79.2
12	U.K.	49.3	32	Philippines	79.7
13	Romania	50.6	33	Yugoslavia	81.3
14	Denmark	51.3	34	India	86.3
15	Hong Kong	52.1	35	Vietnam	89.7
16	Finland	59.7	36	Haiti	90.2
17	Czechoslovakia	62.0	37	Italy	92.0
18	Poland	62.4	38	Greece	92.1
19	Spain	63.1	39	Korea, S.	92.8
20	Pakistan	63.5	40	Portugal	93.9
			Total		63.5

RANK	HUSBAND'S COUNTRY OF BIRTH	% MARRIED TO WIFE OF THE SAME ORIGIN	RANK	HUSBAND'S COUNTRY OF BIRTH	% MARRIED TO WIFE OF THE SAME ORIGIN
1	Australia	19.4	21	Netherlands	58.4
2	Norway	21.0	22	Hong Kong	59.9
3	Sweden	21.1	23	Finland	60.9
4	U.S.	24.4	24	Japan	62.1
5	Austria	30.8	25	Pakistan	63.5
6	France	33.1	26	Lebanon	65.7
7	Switzerland	33.2	27	Trinidad & Tobago	66.4
8	Belgium	34.4	28	Yugoslavia	67.8
9	Denmark	35.8	29	China	70.5
10	Ireland, Rep. of	36.1	30	Taiwan	73.6
11	Romania	41.8	31	Guyana	76.7
12	Germany	42.6	32	India	77.4
13	U.K.	47.6	33	Italy	77.6
14	Czechoslovakia	49.0	34	Jamaica	77.7
15	Poland	51.0	35	Greece	82.6
16	Hungary	52.5	36	Haiti	84.6
17	Former U.S.S.R.	54.6	37	Portugal	91.1
18	Spain	55.6	38	Vietnam	92.0
19	Malta	57.1	39	Philippines	95.4
20	Egypt	57.6	40	Korea, S.	96.6
			Total		57.7

Source: Bali Ram. "Intermarriage Among Ethnic Groups." *Ethnic Demography*, Edited by S.S. Hali, F. Trovato and L. Driedger. Ottawa: Carleton University Press, 1990:215. Reprinted by permission of Carleton University Press.

legal issue because of the rights and financial benefits awarded to status Indians by the federal government. Until recently, an Indian woman lost her Indian status if she married a man who was not considered to be an "Indian," by the government. However, this loss of status did not take place if an Indian man married a non-Indian. This law, however, did not prevent intermarriage. In the 1986 census, 712 000 people reported themselves or their ancestors as belonging to at least one Native group. Nearly half of these reported multiple origins or combinations of both aboriginal and nonaboriginal origins (Norris, 1990:34). This suggests that there has been considerable intermarriage among Canadian Native peoples.

Various cultural groups also place different emphasis on the importance of virginity before marriage. Although parents do not always have much control over the sexual practices of their adult children, parents' protectiveness of their daughter's "reputation," their reactions to unexpected premarital pregnancy, and acceptance of single parenting indicate that there are cultural differences. Some cultural groups living in Canada, such as Italians and Greeks, might insist on an immediate marriage as soon as a premarital pregnancy becomes evident, and may also be less accepting of living together before marriage or single parenting (Ishwaran, 1980). Other cultural groups such as American Blacks with lower incomes or people from Caribbean Islands may feel that single parenthood with assistance from extended family members is a better alternative than a hasty and premature marriage (Leslie and Korman, 1989; Haskey, 1991).

As will be discussed later in this chapter, people generally date and marry those who come from similar racial, cultural, and socioeconomic backgrounds. Yet, more interethnic and interracial dating and marriage takes place now than several decades ago. During the 1930s, for example, it was socially unacceptable not only for a black person to marry a white person, but for a Protestant to marry a Catholic. In this respect, much has changed.

SELECTED ISSUES

DATING, SEXUALITY, AND COHABITATION

Dating Practices and Trends

In North America, most young people socialize freely with members of the opposite sex and spend several years going out with different people with no immediate intention to marry. The American sociologist Waller (1937) was among the first to study dating. He differentiated between *dating*, or cross-sex interaction with the intention of having a good time, and *courtship*, which was oriented toward looking for a marital partner (Scanzoni and Scanzoni, 1988:67). Focusing on fraternity and sorority members in 1929–30, Waller identified a competitive system of dating that he called the "dating-rating complex." Using a social exchange perspective, Waller argued that part of the reason for dating was the pursuit of social status. Men tried to date young women who were "sought after" by others because of their physical attributes and their popularity, while women looked for men with money and a car, who were considered well-dressed and were recognized for their accomplishments on campus. Waller also emphasized the thrill seeking and exploitiveness of dating (Ibid: 68).

Later researchers, such as Michael Gordon (1981), argued that Waller's research findings might have been typical of American campuses with sororities and fraternities during the 1920s, but that this practice was already in decline by the 1930s. However, other researchers, such as Judith Richman (1977) and Robert Staples (1978), have also used the social exchange framework in talking about dating as a "game" in which people attempt to maximize their gains while minimizing their efforts. At the root of such practices are traditional assumptions about male/female inequality and the differential bargaining resources of men and women. Traditionally, the implicit bargain was that men were expected to provide transportation and financial resources, while women were expected to provide expressive qualities, physical attractiveness, and some sexual contact (Scanzoni and Scanzoni, 1988). In recent years, young people have moved away from rigid gender roles in dating etiquette, especially with respect to who asks and pays for dates. There is some evidence, however, that stereotypes still exist in dating expectations. Studies of "date rape" show that a minority of young men and a smaller percentage of young women think that if a man pays for a date that he is entitled to have sexual relations with the woman (Carlson, 1987; O'Leary et al., 1989; Barnes, Greenwood, and Sommer, 1991).

Makepeace (1981) conducted one of the first studies on violence in dating relationships among American university students and reported that one in five relationships contained physical violence. More recently in Canada, The National Clearinghouse on Family Violence (1990) reported that a fifth of female secondary students in a Toronto survey experienced one or more forms of adolescent girlfriend assault. Furthermore, Barnes, Greenwood, and Sommer (1991) found that 42 percent of Canadian college dating relationships included violence. These studies clearly indicate that violence is not confined to marital relationships, that many of the female victims remain with their boyfriends after an incident of violence, and that some victims perceive abuse as an indication of love.[1]

While the research on wife assault indicates that external factors such as economic dependency and presence of children contribute to the woman's decision not to leave her abusive partner, these factors are rarely present in dating relationships (Hird, 1992:5). Some researchers have explained the female victim's unwillingness to leave an abusive relationship by arguing that violence against women is pervasive in our society and that young people are socialized to view

[1] Thanks to my former student Myra Hird for some of the research in this section.

it as a normal part of gender relations. But this does not explain why some young women stay with abusive partners while others leave. Staying in an abusive dating relationship may relate to low self-esteem, to feelings of obligation to the abuser, or to family experiences that normalize physical, sexual, or verbal abuse.

Traditional ideas may linger about gender roles and social exchanges in dating relationships, but patterns also persist in less consequential expectations such as age and height of dates. Men may

STUDY SHOWS THAT 42 PERCENT OF MALE COLLEGE STUDENTS ABUSE DATES

In January 1991, the University of Manitoba released a study on violence of dating partners. Headed by Gordon E. Barnes, a professor in the department of family studies, the study indicates that more than 42 percent of the male Canadian college students studied had committed courtship violence.

Violence was defined as action in times of conflict, ranging from pushing or restraining a woman, to wrestling or slapping her, to forcing her to have sex.

To try to determine when courtship violence begins, Barnes and his team hope to survey Winnipeg high school students this year.

The federal government is also addressing the issue of violence against women. Justice Minister Kim Campbell is committed to reforming Canada's laws to protect women more fully: last June, a conference on women and the law brought together concerned parties including judges, lawyers, social workers and human rights activists. Campbell was to bring recommendations from his conference to the annual September meeting of Canadian attorneys general for further consideration. Specific recommendations may be made public this fall.

Changing attitudes and legislation takes time. For the short term, the Ontario government is funding projects that use a Women's Campus Safety Audit Kit, which will help assess and improve the safe design and maintenance of college and university campuses. Similar audits have been used throughout Ontario to improve public spaces for women, resulting in better lighting, emergency telephones and better signs giving locations and routes.

While such improvements may go far to prevent "stranger danger," they will not address the problem of the majority of rapes of college women that are committed by acqaintances, men at parties and dates. The Ontario government is developing strategies to counter this problem and may turn to researchers like Barnes who feel that a program that attempts to educate men to act out their emotions in ways that do not violate the rights of others would seem to be the most effective method to improve the safety of women. —*Gloria Hildebrandt* choose women who are substantially younger, the same age, or a few years older, but seldom is the woman more than two or three years older. Even more rigid is the notion that the woman cannot be taller than the man. Men can be advanced in their educational and occupational achievements, but seldom do they date women who have considerably more education or higher occupational status than they do. In addition, dates tend to come from a similar racial, cultural, religious, and socio-economic background (Leslie and Korman, 1989; Baker, 1990d:45-48). When people date or marry "down" in terms of age, height, or socio-economic status, the term **hypogamy** is used. Marrying "up" is referred to as **hypergamy.**

Although we usually rely on our friends and families to introduce us to eligible partners, North Americans are increasingly turning to newspaper "companion ads" and dating services to assist them when they no longer are meeting people who interest them. This may be the case for women who have postponed marriage to further their education or career development, who later find there is a shortage of eligible men. Others who have recently moved to the city or who work in a place with no potential partners may also turn to the personal columns. Advertising for a mate is not a new idea, however, as it has been used for decades by immigrants looking for partners from their own cultures.

In a study of personal advertising in the *Toronto Star* (Baker, 1982), men and women tended to present themselves in stereotyped ways when advertising for a partner. For example, men emphasized their height, age, and occupational characteristics and asked for attractive younger women for a lasting relationship or "recreational sex." Women described themselves as "petite," "slim," and "attractive" and asked for men who were the same age or older, and well-established in their careers as business or professional men. Women asked for lasting relationships or marriage.

People who run dating services usually rely on some of the same characteristics found to be important when people seek their own partners. These include age, education, religion, race, and height. In countries with arranged marriages, marriage brokers and relatives also focus on social standing, family reputation, and income when selecting a mate.

Singleness and Sexuality

Attitudes toward sexual behaviour are definitely changing. In the 1950s, sexual abstinence before marriage was a widely held value. In 1970, a Canadian study found that just over 50 percent of young

FOR SINGLES ONLY

MALE 26. Single, attractive, hardworker with moustache. Honest, warm, kind, loving, physically fit, non-smoker, good sense of humour. Enjoys movies, dancing, dining, walks and quiet times, etc. Seeks healthy, honest, sincere, female 18 and over for friendship, object commitment relationship. All replies answered. FSO835.

SINCERE male 23, attractive, fit, university educated, professional, seeks slim female, 18-24, with intelligence and ambition, must like togetherness and sharing. Phone and photo appreciated. FSO105.

MALE 45, healthy, 6', 170 lbs, young in appearance, considered attractive, would like to meet an attractive, petite female 30-45, who enjoys socializing, dancing, movies, quiet evenings and the outdoors. FSO107.

IF you are a warm, independent, attractive and educated young woman of any race, who appreciates music, nature, travel and new experiences, who never wanted to answer an ad before, but still would like to meet an original, stable, handsome and affectionate 31 year old man, to share emotional, intellectual and spiritual growth in a lasting relationship, please send a photo and letter or telephone number. FSO108.

I am a genuinely attractive woman inside and out, 34, 5'10, willowy, blonde, with diverse tastes. I enjoy beaches, skiing, reading, dining out and much more. I am seeking a tall male companion who is established, settled, compassionate, autonomous and sincere. FSO109.

THIS single full time dad, early fifties, non smoker, wishes to meet that special woman for a serious relationship. I enjoy most outdoor sports, and with snow just around the corner, my downhill skis are ready to go. I am very family oriented, and miss not having the pleasures of that balance in my life. I know the woman for me is out there, so please answer and let's talk. FSO110.

EUROPEAN male, 31, scientist, sociable, active, interested in the arts and wilderness camping, would like to meet a confident, independent, professional female, 25-39. FSO215.

PERSONABLE, sincere, petite lady, mid-forties, varied interests, enjoys simple life style with an extra dash of spice, seeking honest, caring, well-educated gentleman (50-60), for genuine relationship. FSO216.

WOULD you risk reading the following ad, and maybe becoming enchanted in the process? Attractive, positive, articulate, considerate, monogamous, bilingual, professional woman with sense of humour, loving life and liking cultural activities, animals, walking, swimming, antiques, creative cooking, would like to hear from mature, flexible financially secure, university educated unattached man in his fifties, able and willing to risk establishing a fulfilling and joyful relationship. FSO213.

THIS tall, slim, good looking lady, late forties, looking for gentleman who likes the outdoors, dancing and quiet times, couch potatoes need not apply. FSO217.

SEARCHING for enchanting female, 25-35. This dashing young bachelor, 5'11, 39, offers adventure, romance, and undying devotion. FSO218.

Ottawa *Pennysaver*, Division of Netmar Inc.

people approved of premarital sex if the couple loved each other (Hobart, 1970). A more recent national study (Bibby and Posterski, 1985) found that 80 percent of young people favoured sex before marriage if the couple loved each other, and 93 percent felt that contraception ought to be available to unmarried young people. We must remember that these studies examined attitudes rather than behaviour. Actual behaviour is far more conservative than the attitudes they report (Bibby and Posterski, 1985). Yet, some young people have retained traditional and sometimes contradictory values relating to sexuality and relations between the sexes.

Parents, educators, and social service workers have expressed concern about the early sexual activity of young people. Canadian and American studies have indicated that about 50 percent of 15- to 19-year-olds and as many as 67 percent of 19-year-olds have had premarital intercourse (Bibby and Posterski, 1985). Despite these figures, only about half of these young people are using contraception, a fact that is causing anxiety among parents and youth workers.

Interviews with young people indicate several reasons why so many do not use contraceptives. Some naively believe that the probability of conception is so low that it is unlikely to happen unless they have sex regularly and frequently. Others do not want to appear to be prepared for the event, but want sex to be or appear to be spontaneous. Others have difficulty admitting to the family doctor that they are planning to have intercourse and need to be protected, or are embarrassed to purchase contraceptives under the eyes of a pharmacist. On the other hand, some young people actually enjoy the excitement of risking pregnancy and going against adult advice (King et al., 1989:105). Finally, the cost of contraceptives, especially birth control pills, is relatively high for low-income people and some have insufficient money to afford contraception unless they have access to a public health or community clinic (Nolté, 1986).

We cannot assume, however, that unmarried pregnancy is unexpected or unwanted. Many young couples have made a decision to live together without marrying, but still want to have a child. Although birth rates have declined for women of all ages, a greater proportion of babies are now born to unmarried women. This is particularly true for women between the ages of 20 and 24 as shown in table 3.5.

In recent years, international concern about the rise in sexually transmitted diseases, especially AIDS, may have curbed the sexual behaviour of young people. There is some evidence, for example, that more people are practising "safe sex." This could mean using condoms, limiting the number of sexual partners, or abstaining from sexual relations except within a monogamous relationship. However, in a national study of 38 000 Canadians between the ages of 11 and 21, only 14 percent of college/university students and 9 percent of recent dropouts who "often" had sexual intercourse, "always" used con-

Table 3.5 **Live Births to Unmarried Women as a Percentage of Births in Her Age Group, 1974–1987**

	AGE GROUPS			
	UNDER 20	20-24	25 AND OVER[1]	ALL AGES
1974[2]	36.3	8.2	3.2	9.3
1975[3]	39.9	8.8	3.7	10.1
1976[3]	43.0	9.5	3.7	10.5
1977	48.4	11.1	4.6	11.3
1978	51.4	12.2	4.7	11.7
1979	53.3	13.5	5.2	12.2
1980	56.8	15.1	5.9	13.2
1981	60.5	17.0	6.6	14.2
1982	64.2	19.3	7.4	15.5
1983	66.0	21.2	8.4	16.2
1984[4]	68.9	23.0	8.9	16.8
1985[4]	71.6	25.4	10.0	17.8
1986[4]	74.8	27.9	10.6	18.8
1987[4]	76.8	30.6	11.8	20.1

[1] Includes "not stated" ages.
[2] Excludes Quebec and Ontario.
[3] Excludes Quebec.
[4] Excludes Newfoundland.

Source: Statistics Canada, Catalogue 84-204, *Vital Statistics, Volume I, Births and Deaths*, and unpublished data from *Vital Statistics*. Reproduced with the permission of the Minister of Supply and Services, 1992.

Figure 3.2 **Live Births to Unmarried Mothers as a Percentage of Total Live Births, 1931–1987**

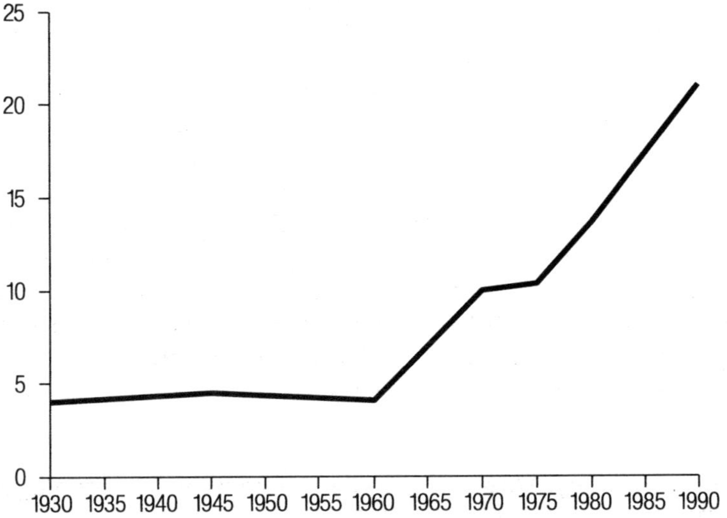

Source: Statistics Canada. Catalogue No. 84-204, *Vital Statistics, Volume 1, Births and Deaths,* and unpublished data from *Vital Statistics.* Reproduced with the permission of the Minister of Supply and Services Canada, 1992.

doms. Among sexually active young people from both groups, more than one quarter never used a condom (King et al., 1989:104).

Cohabitation

In comparison with previous decades, more Canadians are now living together as husband and wife, but without being legally married. In 1990, Statistics Canada reported that 12 percent of all couples were in common-law relationships compared with 6 percent in 1981 (Stout, 1991:18). Provincial variations are apparent in the statistics on common-law relationships. Quebec had the highest percentage of residents aged 15 and over living in common-law relationships (13 percent), while New Brunswick had the lowest (5 percent). Given that most common-law partners are relatively young, it is not surprising that the vast majority have never been legally married. In 1990, 63 percent of common-law partners were never-married, 28 percent were divorced, 7 percent separated and 2 percent were widowed (Stout, 1991:19).

From 1984–90, the proportion of Canadians aged 18 to 64 who had ever lived common-law nearly doubled. Among those aged 40 to 49,

CANADA YOUTH AND AIDS STUDY

Learning about AIDS at home

Parents are not knowledgeable about AIDS—we know as much as they do.
Male, Grade 11.

Parents don't know how sexually active we are and think we don't need information about AIDS.
Female, College.

I would rather learn about AIDS from my mom and dad if they knew enough about it.
Female, secondaire I.

Sexual attitudes and behaviours have changed so much parents can't understand our feelings and activities.
Female, University.

They don't know much about it [AIDS] themselves. They always ask me, they said if they [the school] say anything come and tell us because we want to know, too. They just get it from the television.
Female, Grade 9.

They've talked to me about sex, a lot about sex. They tell me do's and don'ts and stuff like that...They don't believe you should have sex until after you're married.
Male, Grade 7.

Parents use it [AIDS] as a excuse so they don't have to handle it [sex].
Female, Grade 9.

Learning about AIDS at school

The religious views of some adults are keeping AIDS education out of schools.
Male, Grade 11.

We've gotten nothing about AIDS from school, but we should get something.
Female, Grade 9.

Schools usually just give the bare facts, which are not enough. We need to know everything about AIDS.
Female, Grade 11.

Teachers don't know enough about AIDS—they are like the average person. Some of them should become informed and then teach us about it.
Male, College.

Sex education

Today sex education is an established part of the curriculum in most Canadian schools. If the 245 school boards surveyed in this report are representative of English Canada as a whole, it appears that at least 57 percent of the country's school districts offer sex education/family life programs. J. Ajzenstat and I. Gentles, 1988, p.7.

King, Alan J.C. et al. *Canada Youth and AIDS Study*. Kingston: Queen's University, 1988:59–60.

however, the proportion almost tripled, rising to 27 percent in 1990 from 10 percent in 1984 (Stout, 1991:19). In 1986, Statistics Canada found that 8.5 percent of men and 15.1 percent of women between the ages of 20 and 24 were living in a **common-law union**. Among those aged 25 to 29, 20.0 percent of men and 23.4 percent of women were in common-law relationships (Turcotte, 1990:149). By contrast, only 4.3 percent of men and 1.1 percent of women aged 65 and over were living with someone of the opposite sex without being legally married. More than half the women and 43 percent of the men who lived common-law in 1986 were younger than age 30 (Ibid). Since 1984 the median age of common-law partners has continued to rise (Stout, 1991:19).

Statistics Canada's Family History Survey of 1984 found that 63 percent of first common-law unions end in marriage, while 35 percent end in separation, and 2 percent with the death of one of the partners. For this reason, some have referred to the trend of living together before marriage as a new courtship pattern or trial marriage. On the other hand, a few people see cohabitation as an alternative to legal marriage, especially if they are separated but not divorced.

In countries where divorce is impossible, people may leave their legal spouses and live common-law, producing children with the new partners as though they were married. Common-law living may also indicate ideological opposition to marriage. Some people, for example, feel that the government has no right to meddle in people's personal or sexual lives. Others feel that legal marriage involves rigid gender roles and expectations of behaviour that they would like to avoid.

Common-law relationships in Canada used to be considered temporary arrangements that could be seen as trial marriages. Now they are becoming more like legal marriages (Mitchell, 1991:A1). Statistically, common-law relationships still differ from legal marriage in that their duration is shorter and their **fertility rates** are lower. Furthermore, marriages that are preceded by cohabitation have slightly higher rates of dissolution (Burch and Madan, 1986; Beaujot, 1990). However, the 1991 census has shown that these relationships are becoming more prevalent, especially in Quebec. Furthermore, 42 percent of these relationships include children, either born to the common-law partners or brought into the family from other unions (Mitchell, 1992). These family trends are very similar to many European countries, where the distinction between legal marriage and cohabitation is becoming blurred both legally and socially.

MATE SELECTION

Many people do not plan to remain single, but intend to marry when they finish their education, establish themselves in an occupation, earn some money, obtain a divorce, or locate a suitable partner. In cultural groups that practise arranged marriages, selecting a mate may involve consulting kin and a lengthy process of negotiation between the families involved.

Mate Selection With Arranged Marriages

In arranged marriages, parents, elders, or marriage brokers select suitable marital partners for young people based on a number of considerations that they feel will contribute to the well-being of their child and family. These include kin obligations, family wealth and reputation, potential economic productivity, educational background, health, physical appearance, and ability to produce children. Also included in this list are rules of exogamy and endogamy, or rules about whom one may *not* marry and the group within which one *must* marry. In all societies, for example, there are rules of exogamy called **incest taboos** which state that people may not marry certain family members. These rules are intended to prevent inbreeding and congenital disabilities, but are also intended to limit jealousy and conflict within kin groups. Who is defined as a family member varies somewhat from culture to culture, however, but most agree that parents, siblings, and first cousins are not suitable marriage partners because they are too closely related by blood or **ties of consanguinity**. In Canada, there is a long list of those legally ineligible for marriage, including some relations by marriage or adoption (**ties of affinity**).

In some societies, such as India and West Africa, there are also preferential marriage rules. One of the most common, practised in southern India, is that people should marry their cross-cousin, or the child of their mother's brother or father's sister (Nanda, 1991:231), although these relations would be excluded from the list of people eligible to marry in North America. In some polygamous cultures such as the Nuer of Africa, marriage rules specify that a man should marry the widow of his dead brother. This practice, called the **levirate**, provides some means of support for widows in a society where women do not customarily work for pay. In other societies, people practise the **sororate**, which is marriage to a wife's sister. For example, a man may marry his wife's sister if his wife is barren and at least some of the children will be considered those of the first wife. In another situation, when a wife dies, her kin group supplies a sister as a wife for the widower. These rules indicate that marriage is actually an alliance between kin groups rather than between individuals as in our society (Nanda, 1991:231).

As will be discussed in the historical section of the next chapter, romantic love is considered to be a poor basis of marriage in many societies. Some cultures allow a marriage agreement or **child betrothal** before the young people reach physical maturity. This agreement, which could be made when the children are under the age of 10, is seen as a legal contract that cannot be broken without some form of

ARRANGING A MARRIAGE IN INDIA

In India, almost all marriages are arranged. So customary is the practice of arranged marriage that there is a special name for a marriage that is not arranged: It is called a "love match."

As a young woman anthropologist in India for the first time, I found this custom of arranged marriage oppressive. It was contrary to everything I had been taught to believe about the importance of romantic love and individual choice as the only basis of a happy marriage.

At the first opportunity, I questioned young people I met on how they felt about the practice of arranged marriage. One of my first informants was Sita, a college graduate who had been waiting over a year while her parents were arranging a match for her.

"How can you go along with this?" I asked her. "Don't you care who you marry?"

"Of course I care," she answered. "That is why I must have my parents choose a boy for me. My marriage is too important to be arranged by such an inexperienced person as myself."

"But how can you marry the first man you meet? You will miss the fun of meeting a lot of different people and you will not give yourself the chance to know who is the right man for you," I countered.

"Meeting a lot of different men doesn't sound like any fun at all, Sita answered. One hears that in America the girls spend all their time worrying whether they will meet a man and get married. Here we have the chance to enjoy our life and let our parents do this work and worry for us."

"I still can't imagine it," I said. "How can you agree to marry a man you hardly know?"

"But of course he will be known," she replied. "My parents would never arrange a marriage for me without knowing all about the boy and his family background. Naturally we will not rely on what the family tells us. We will check the particulars ourselves and through our friends and relatives. No one will want to marry their daughter into a family that is not good."

"But Sita," I protested, "I don't mean know the family, I mean know the man. How can you think of spending your whole life with someone you don't love or may not even like?"

"If he is a good man, why should I not like him?" she replied. "With you Americans, you know the boy so well before you marry, where is the fun to get married? There is no mystery and no romance. Here we have the whole of our married life to get to know and love our husband. This way is better, is it not?"

From Serena Nanda, "Arranging a Marriage in India," in Philip R. DeVita, ed., *The Naked Anthropologist: Tales from Around the World* (Belmont, Calif.: Wadsworth, 1991).

compensation. Making the agreement so early in the children's lives precludes other marriage agreements and prevents love attachments from developing.

In arranged marriages, personal fulfilment is not necessarily a priority. Young people are taught that marriage represents the union of families, and they must conform to the wishes of older family members. Young people are encouraged to want to marry in order to raise children, to produce heirs for the family, and to continue the family name. Because marriage is the only acceptable adult lifestyle, young people also want to marry to gain more independence from parents and to be treated as adults. In cultures where the continuity of kin lines and family name and the inheritance of wealth are important, arranged marriages or partially arranged marriages are still predominant.

Some immigrants to Canada from Egypt, Lebanon, Japan, India, and Pakistan, for example, prefer to arrange marriages for their children. Parents, aunts or uncles, and family friends will arrange an introduction between two young people which is hoped will lead to marriage. When a suitable partner from the same cultural group is not available in Canada, kin members in the home country will locate a potential partner. The adult children of immigrant parents could be sent back to their home country to participate in an arranged marriage.

In 1963, the American sociologist William Goode noted that industrialization has been accompanied by a trend toward monogamous nuclear families and **free choice marriage**. Where arranged marriages still exist, young people increasingly want the right to veto their parents' decisions about suitable partners. Yet, in many parts of the world, mate selection is considered too important to be left in the inexperienced hands of young people.

Mate Selection With Free Choice Marriages

In free choice marriages, many of the same considerations enter into marital choice as in arranged marriages, yet they are often disguised by the idea that you are supposed to marry for "love." In actual fact, people marry for a variety of reasons, including companionship, sex, children, and additional financial support. Getting away from home is another reason for marriage, as a wedding is still an adult rite of passage or an indication of adult status, even when the couple has been living together. In other words, people marry for more than love, both in North America and other societies.

Most young people in North America choose their own spouses, but they are often introduced to potential partners by friends, siblings, and relatives. Yet, there are sociological patterns involved in these introductions and the final choice of marital partner. The folk music and literature of western cultures are filled with stories of people who fall in love with a person considered inappropriate and marry against their parents' wishes (such as Romeo and Juliet). This folk lore indicates that there are implicit rules governing mate selection.

Parents usually have clear ideas about when and whom their children should marry. They often want their adult children to marry when they have finished their education rather than before. They usually expect that their children have found full-time permanent work with enough income attached to it to enable them to live independently from parents or without social assistance. Parents want their children to marry when they are emotionally mature and when they have found a "suitable" partner.

Suitable often means different things depending on the gender of the partner (Mackie, 1991). A North American man is expected to be educated, to have a "comfortable" income, and a stable job, which is similar in status to that of his own father and his fiancee's. The "suitable" man is expected to be reliable, kind, and emotionally mature. On the other hand, women are expected to have pleasant personalities, "good reputations," to be reasonably attractive, and to want to have children. Increasingly, they may also be expected to be educated and have stable jobs, that will not interfere with marriage and children (Mackie, 1991).

Over the years, psychologists and sociologists have grappled with explanations of love, attraction, and mate selection. In the next section, four theories of mate selection are outlined.

Theories of Mate Selection in Free Choice Marriages

Several theories exist about why people choose particular marriage partners. One of the earliest was called the **social homogamy theory** and suggested that people from similar socio-economic and cultural backgrounds tend to marry because they have more opportunity. People in similar socio-economic circumstances tend to live near each other (**residential propinquity**), go to the same schools, and belong to the same organizations. Large-scale quantitative research has confirmed that North American marital partners are generally of the same race, within three or four years of age, often have similar education, and usually come from families with about the same social status and income level (Leslie and Korman, 1989:365-383). Although the media pay considerable attention to interracial relationships, marriages between older women and younger men, and cases of hypergamy (marrying "up"), such as the employee who marries the boss's daughter, these situations do not happen often.

The **theory of complementary needs**, first formulated by American sociologist Robert Winch in 1955, suggests that psychological variables might be more important than social similarities. This theory states that people marry those whom they think will complement their psychological needs. For example, it suggests that men with dominant mothers may subconsciously look for a mother substitute, people who were abused as children marry someone who continues to abuse them, and people who feel insecure marry someone who flatters them and bolsters their ego. This theory was later generalized to emphasize that similar values were more important than socio-economic characteristics in determining who married whom in North America. Yet, the two theories are not mutually exclusive. From a pool of people who come from a similar socio-economic background, we can still choose someone who we think will complement our psychological needs. We may not really know what our needs are when we marry, or we may later discover that this person no longer fulfils our needs. This could lead to marital conflict or eventual divorce.

Bolton's **developmental theory of mate selection** (1961) emphasizes that the development of courtship is predetermined by neither social nor psychological variables. Instead, it is the end product of a series of interactions characterized by advances and retreats, changing definitions of the situation, and the resolution of tensions. The path to marriage has been portrayed as an escalator — once you get on, it is difficult not to ride to the top. One of the partners may negotiate for more commitment. Friends and family make assumptions about the relationship, put ideas into your head, and apply subtle pressure. In some cases, circumstances change that encourage the couple to live together or break up. A job opportunity in another city, for example, may encourage an already serious couple to decide to marry.

The **ideal mate theory** suggests that based on parental role models and past dating experience we form impressions of an ideal marital partner. We continue to look for a mate having these personality or physical characteristics, and eventually choose the person who best approximates this ideal. The ideal mate theory certainly makes the process of mate selection sound more rational than the developmental theory or the theory of complementary needs. Yet, these theories are not necessarily mutually exclusive.

From a pool of socially similar eligibles, people may choose a partner whom they think will fulfil their needs or will best represent their ideal mate. After the relationship is established, they may move toward commitment tentatively, negotiating new arrangements when they approach road blocks. They may be propelled toward marriage by parents, friends, or circumstances. Although it may be largely a matter of chance that you meet a particular person on a particular day, the social and psychological type of person you are attracted to may follow a pattern.

Although we think we marry for love, most Canadians choose their partners according to certain unspoken rules. It is no coincidence that young people tend to marry at a similar time, generally in their early to mid-twenties. The groom is usually older than the bride by a year or two, has the same or slightly more education, and a higher income (Broderick, 1992:132). Seldom is the groom shorter than the bride (Gillis and Avis, 1980). The daughter of a supreme court judge typically does not marry the son of a garbage collector, nor does the son of a carpenter often marry the daughter of a physician. When we "fall in love," we tend to do so according to these implicit rules about who is attractive and appropriate.

OCCUPATIONAL CHOICE, WORK, AND UNEMPLOYMENT

Occupational Choice

One of the developmental tasks that young people must work through when they leave their family of orientation is the selection of suitable work. Because education systems sometimes require choices that channel students into different educational streams early in adolescence, some decisions might have been made already. Yet, young people who have left home to attend college or university might not have decided what work they want to do when they finish their schooling.

Aspirations or hopes for the future, as well as more realistic expectations, are usually shaped by the models presented to us by our parents, but also by other relatives, friends, neighbours, and what we see in the media or read in books (Martin and Macdonnell, 1982). What our parents explicitly tell us to do with respect to education and occupational choice tends to be far less important than what their own actions imply (Hunter, 1981; Forcese, 1986).

In a national study of the aspirations of Canadian adolescents, Baker (1985) like many other studies found that young people who had parents with little formal education, low wages, and sporadic bouts of unemployment tended to have less confidence in their own abilities to successfully complete university and to find a high-paying job. The role models presented by their parents and their socio-economic circumstances encouraged them to believe that fate or chance plays an important role in their future. Young people from families with high-achieving parents were more likely to say that ability and hard work is more important than chance in their future lives.

Researchers have found that young people generally aspire to occupations much higher in pay and prestige than they can reasonably expect to find. For example, Baker (1985) found that about half of the young women and three-quarters of the young men in her study said that they realistically expected to have professional or managerial jobs by the time they were 30 years old. Yet, according to Statistics Canada, only about 20 percent of Canadian adults of both sexes actually hold these sorts of jobs. Furthermore, only 23 percent of the girls in Baker's study expected that they would have clerical, sales, or service jobs. In fact, about 72 percent of adult women end up doing this kind of work. In light of the realities of the present working environment, the aspirations of this sample of young Canadians seem overly optimistic.

Baker also found that about 20 percent of the girls in her study expected to hold nontraditional jobs that have typically been done by men. Their choices focused on high-level professional positions such as doctor and lawyer, rather than covering the range of technical or nonskilled labour jobs. Furthermore, no boys expected to hold jobs usually performed by women.

The desire that young people have for high-paying and prestigious positions may lead to disappointments as they get older. It is not possible for all people to hold professional or managerial jobs. From present unemployment rates and estimates of underemployment, it is questionable whether many of today's young people will work in their area of choice, reach their aspired level in that occupation, or even receive a permanent position. More than ever, it is important to finish secondary school, complete courses leading to diplomas and degrees, demonstrate initiative, be creative, and develop skills in critical thinking.

Numerous studies have found that North American young people are still making occupational choices based on gender stereotypes (Baker, 1985; Labour Canada, 1986). Children and young people are usually not aware that their occupational choices are influenced by unspoken understandings of what work is appropriate for males and what is more suitable for females. Even when trends in occupational choices are discussed in the classroom, it is difficult for young people to make a connection between their own choices (which they see as independent and uninfluenced by stereotypes) and what studies say about the choices of others.

Patterns in Employment and Unemployment for Young People

When young people initially enter the labour force, they usually find that the jobs they obtain are unskilled and low paying. Young men can sometimes obtain temporary manual labour or factory jobs that pay relatively high wages, but young women can seldom find this type of work. "Pink collar" jobs such as retail sales, clerical positions, and waitressing are more readily available to young women because they have high turnover rates and have been done traditionally by women. While some of the positions that young people initially find while working their way through school might lead to promotional possibilities, many are dead-end jobs with no future. These positions, however, may provide valuable knowledge and skills for future work. The opportunity to develop interpersonal skills and work habits, to acquire knowledge about the expectations of employers, to earn some money and practise money management, and to gain work experience that can be placed on a résumé makes these low-level jobs worthwhile.

Because young people are less likely than older people to have job experience, interpersonal and job-related skills, and employment contacts, they have always had higher unemployment rates than adults. Furthermore, traditionally young women have experienced lower unemployment rates than young men because they had the option of early marriage and childrearing at home, and because clerical and service jobs used to be plentiful. With technological innovations and economic cutbacks, however, many of these clerical and service positions are being eliminated. At the same time, the age of marriage has risen in the past 15 years as more women are continuing their education. Since most families now need two incomes, young women are less likely to use marriage as an alternative to paid work. Consequently, the unemployment rates of females 18 to 24 years old have increased in recent years (Statistics Canada, 1991).

Young people seeking full-time work have always had a more difficult time if they dropped out of school before graduation. For example, unemployment rates are higher for those with lower amounts of education, especially for those 15 to 24 years old as table 3.6 indicates. Furthermore, if these unemployed young people do not live with their parents, they may find themselves virtually excluded from the "safety net" of social security programs, such as unemployment insurance, because so many of these programs are work-related.

A study from the Ontario Ministry of Skills Development (1989:28) of 17- to 28-year-olds confirmed that Ontario high school students who did not graduate had a 50 percent chance of being unemployed since their first job compared with 35 percent for the graduates.

Furthermore, those who did not graduate became unemployed more frequently and stayed unemployed longer than graduates. When those who left school early find work, their job tenure is of relatively short duration. This government report concluded that further education and training are associated with higher incomes and successful long-term participation in the labour force.

Table 3.6 indicates that unemployment rates are highest for those young people with the least schooling. These unemployment rates have been particularly high in recent years as more unskilled entrance level jobs have been taken over by automation or abolished with economic cutbacks. Employees without skills, experience, or union protection have been most vulnerable to "down-sizing," or reducing the number of employees in an organization.

Youth unemployment rates also increased in other western industrialized countries during the 1970s and early 1980s. The influx of the "post-war baby boom" generation into the labour force occurred at the same time as low economic growth. Increased life expectancies and limited job mobility have also led to fewer employment vacancies. At the same time, more women have entered low-level jobs that young men previously used as stepping stones to career positions. Consequently, fewer jobs are now available for unskilled and less educated people. Table 3.7 indicates how youth unemployment rates increased in Canada from the 1960s to the early 1980s, when they began to decline again. In recent years, more full-time unionized jobs in manufacturing and processing as well as white-collar middle-management positions have been eliminated with economic recession and

Table 3.6 **Unemployment Rates by Educational Attainment for 15- to 24-Year-Olds, Canada, 1991**

Educational Attainment	Unemployment Rate
0–8 years	29.5
Some secondary education	20.7
High school graduation	15.7
Some post-secondary	12.6
Post-secondary certificate or diploma	11.7
University degree	8.1
Total	16.2

Source: Statistics Canada. *Labour Force Annual Averages. 1991.* Catalogue 71-220. Ottawa: Ministry of Industry, Science and Technology, February 1992:B11. Reproduced with the permission of the Minister of Supply and Services Canada, 1992.

changes in world markets. In their place, a greater number of part-time, nonunionized, and lower-skilled service jobs have been created providing more opportunities for people entering the labour market for the first time.

Unlike in our parents' or grandparents' time, it is unusual to start with little formal education and work our way up to a management position. Now, employers expect that much of our formal schooling will be complete when we look for our first full-time jobs. **Educational inflation** has increased the qualifications necessary for most positions, in comparison with what was required 20 years ago. This means that staying in school is more important than ever.

While finding full-time work is relatively difficult, the cost of staying in school is also high. Tuition fees and the cost of books, accommodation, food, and clothing is rising, decreasing the likelihood that parents will be able to support their children through college or university. Even with parental financial assistance, it is more difficult than a decade ago for young people to live on their own when they are

Table 3.7 **Unemployment Rates* for 15- to 24-Year-Olds, Canada, 1966–1991**

YEAR	BOTH SEXES	MALE	FEMALE
1966	5.6	6.3	4.8
1971	11.1	12.0	9.8
1981	13.2	14.1	12.3
1982	18.7	21.1	16.1
1983	19.8	22.3	17.0
1984	17.8	19.3	16.1
1985	16.4	18.1	14.5
1986	15.1	16.4	13.6
1987	13.7	14.8	12.4
1988	12.0	12.9	11.0
1989	11.3	12.4	10.1
1990	12.8	14.0	11.4
1991	16.2	18.8	13.4

* unadjusted series, annual averages.

Source: Statistics Canada. *Historical Labour Force Statistics, 1991*. Cat. 71–201. Ottawa: Supply and Services Canada, February 1992:237, 245, 253. Reproduced with the permission of the Minister of Supply and Services Canada, 1992.

completing their education unless they also work part-time. Although staying in school is costly, it is often worth the time and money in terms of future employment possibilities as well as personal enrichment.

AGING AND UNMARRIED PEOPLE

By the age of 36, about 89 percent of the Canadian population is or has been married (Boyd and Pryor, 1990:191). Throughout the life span, unmarried people tend to maintain closer relationships with their parents and siblings than married people who are often preoccupied with their children (Connidis, 1989:40). While unmarried people, especially women, used to live with their parents or other relatives, they are now more likely to rent an apartment or to buy a home on their own (Boyd and Pryor, 1990). While some live with friends of the same or opposite sex, others live alone.

The former stereotype of the maiden lady living alone with her cats or the eccentric bachelor who is unable to care for himself is certainly an image of older single people in the past. Life for single people has changed considerably over the past 20 years. Most never-married men and women maintain active social and sexual lives and hold responsible full-time jobs. However, a few single people continue to live with their elderly parents, especially among the present generation of older women. Some of these people gave up marriage or other opportunities because they felt a responsibility to an aging parent that their married siblings were unable to fulfil.

Unmarried women tend to have similar career patterns to men. They begin working when they have completed their education and continue working full-time throughout most of their adult lives. Yet, single women tend to experience more stable career patterns and higher incomes than married women (Labour Canada, 1990). This may reflect the fact that single women tend to have more formal education than married women and do not need to take time off work for childrearing. In fact, the occupational commitment of single women is similar to that of men (Scanzoni and Scanzoni, 1988:209–210; Labour Canada, 1990:79), although they are less likely than men to have achieved a high-status or well-paid position. This could be attributed to the fact that typically men and women have received their education in different fields and have ended up in different occupations. However, it also suggests that inequalities exist in hiring, promotion, and pay in most segments of the labour force (Armstrong and Armstrong, 1988; Labour Canada, 1990; National Council of Welfare, 1990).

While well-educated men have higher marriage rates than men with lower education, the opposite is true for women (Glick, 1984). In fact, studies have shown that higher levels of intelligence, education, and occupational achievement are associated with singleness among women (Scanzoni and Scanzoni, 1988:208). One theory called the **marriage squeeze** suggests that these women may have postponed marriage while they were developing their careers. Since men tend to marry younger and less educated women than themselves, and since men have lower life expectancies, these highly educated single women may have reduced the probability of later finding a partner. Another explanation is that these women made a conscious or subconscious choice to focus on a career or an independent life rather than marriage.

Although some middle-aged single people of both sexes have always remained **celibate**, we can no longer assume that this is the case. Increasingly, they may maintain permanent but nonmarital heterosexual or homosexual relationships. Some unmarried people have a series of relationships throughout their lives but never settle into a live-in arrangement. Others live like husband and wife, but never legally marry. While 8 percent of all heterosexual couples were living in a common-law union in 1986, this arrangement was more typical of people under 35 rather than older couples (Turcotte, 1988).

In studies of life satisfaction, single people tend to report lower satisfaction than married people (Larson, 1978; Glenn and Weaver, 1988), although this may be changing as the attitude toward singleness is becoming more positive. While single women tend to rate themselves as less happy than married women, unmarried men score the lowest (Bernard, 1982; Glenn and Weaver, 1988). Studies also indicate that unmarried men report more psychiatric symptoms and have higher premature death rates than married men and all women. While Bernard (1982) speculated that men may need wives to keep them happy and healthy, she also noted that men with lower levels of mental or physical health are less likely to marry.

The presence of intimate relationships and the perception of social support are correlated with high levels of satisfaction for both unmarried and married people (Baker, 1988:21). Yet, we cannot assume that unmarried people lack intimate relationships. Many are more gregarious than married people and have a wide network of friends and acquaintances. However, there is still considerable pressure to marry even in later life, and well-meaning friends and relatives sometimes treat unmarried people as less fortunate or in need of match-making. These attitudes could reduce the life satisfaction of unmarried people.

By mid-life, many single people who wanted to marry have probably accepted their present situation and created a satisfying lifestyle outside the nuclear family. Single lifestyles are more visible and socially acceptable now than they used to be as marriage rates have declined, divorce rates remain high, and common-law relationships have become more prevalent. Furthermore, gay and lesbian organizations provide increasing social support for homosexual people living outside family households. These factors contribute to making the single life more visible and probably create more public tolerance toward alternative lifestyles.

In the male gay community, those who have permanent partners may pass through mid-life in a similar way to heterosexual couples (Lee, 1987), except that they seldom have adolescent children and often feel they need to keep their personal situation discreet. Unattached gay men, however, may be disadvantaged in the pursuit of casual sex, as so much emphasis seems to be placed on youth and physical attractiveness in the gay community (but not among lesbians). The spread of AIDS, however, has forced gay men to limit their partners. In a study of aging among gay men, Lee (1987) argues that the theory of accelerated gay aging, or the idea that gay men are considered to be old when they are merely middle-aged, is based on stereotypes and may pertain more to unattached men prior to gay liberation. He claims that the same factors influence life satisfaction for both gay and heterosexual men: perception of health and adequate income, higher educational levels, and meaningful relationships.

Some of the social pressure on homosexual adults may diminish with age, either because they have learned how to cope with it or because they have developed a network of friends with similar values and lifestyle. Furthermore, pressure to marry and bear children would lessen as homosexual people, especially women, pass the customary age of marriage and childbearing. Lesbian mothers who have experienced custody problems may also be better able to live their lives after their children have grown up.

Although most divorced people remarry, about one-third do not. Men are more likely than women both to remarry and to remarry soon after divorce (Kuzel and Krishnan, 1973; Adams and Nagnur, 1990:144). One reason for this is the fact that men are less likely to have custody of their children and are therefore freer to date. They also have higher disposable incomes which might allow them to go out more often and meet people. Furthermore, men have the option of proposing marriage, appear to be more favourable to the idea of remarriage, and typically choose younger women. The probability of remarriage tends to be higher for widowed than divorced women, and for younger rather than older women. But in all cases, the probability of remarriage is higher for men than for women.

In studies of the probability of remarriage, we cannot discount the idea that middle-aged women who are divorced or widowed may prefer to remain unmarried. In *The Future of Marriage* (1982), Jessie Bernard argued that the experience of marriage varies for men and women, and that marriage is more advantageous for men. When women marry, they typically take on more housework and child care, continue their paid jobs, and "look after" the social, emotional, and physical needs of their husbands (Lero, 1990; Eichler, 1988). Men, on the other hand, rarely take full responsibility for housework and child care, and seldom are as supportive to their wives as women are to men. Increasingly, men are no longer totally responsible for earning the family income, as most wives work for pay. Bernard suggests that women are more frequently rejecting traditional marriage because it means taking on two full-time jobs.

By mid-life, many single people have created alternatives to traditional family living that they feel are more satisfying, spontaneous, and sophisticated than the way most others live. Many feel that their present lives more than compensate for the absence of marriage and children, although some may regret that they did not marry and have a family. With more people leaving their marriages in mid-life, there is also an increasing number of opportunities for first marriages later in life. Although the probability of marrying decreases with age for never-married people, about 14 percent of women and 20 percent of men marry at the age of 45 or older (Nagnur and Adams, 1987).

FUTURE TRENDS

Although marriage remains popular in Canada, a larger percentage of people now than in the 1960s and 1970s have never been married. In addition, a growing number of people are separating or divorcing, although many of these are remarrying within a few years. More people are now living in common-law unions rather than legally marrying or choosing to remain unmarried than during the 1970s. These trends are creating a growing percentage of the population living outside traditional family relationships.

Liberal social and sexual attitudes and more effective birth control have encouraged many young people to postpone marriage.

Furthermore, unmarried people of both sexes can increasingly support themselves, although two incomes per household can certainly purchase a better standard of living than one. Efficient apartments, condominiums, and household labour-saving devices have made single living more feasible. People can now work full-time and rely on fast food, same-day dry cleaning and laundry service, dishwashers, vacuum cleaners, microwave ovens, and money machines to save them time.

A growing percentage of people are living between families, and there is no indication that this trend will not continue. To some extent, single people have different lifestyles and concerns than married couples raising children. They often spend little time at home and more time than married people socializing, attending movies, eating in restaurants, or pursuing hobbies outside the home. The search for a suitable partner or mate preoccupies some of them. New forms of dating or finding partners is apparent, especially for those who are older and no longer in school. Personal advertising in newspapers, singles' clubs, bars, and introduction agencies will probably continue to flourish. Living together without legal marriage, with heterosexual or homosexual partners, will continue to become more prevalent.

As the Canadian population becomes more diverse in terms of cultural background, relationships between different racial, ethnic, and religious groups will become more prevalent. Yet, most people will continue to choose partners from similar racial and cultural backgrounds.

Although patterns of sexuality changed dramatically during the 1960s and 1970s, a more conservative approach to sexuality appears to be developing among single people. The fear of sexually transmitted diseases is a major contributing factor to this trend, especially as the AIDS virus is now very apparent in the heterosexual as well as the homosexual population. In addition, there appears to be some concern that the "sexual revolution" of the 1960s and 1970s did not necessarily lead to greater freedom, better relationships, or more happiness.

Since the 1950s, the double standard of sexual behaviour for men and women has been only partially eroded. Men have retained the opportunity to date widely and to enjoy casual sex with fewer negative social consequences than women do. Single women who date a number of men often pay a price in terms of sexual harassment and date rape by friends or colleagues who assume that they are also willing to engage in sexual relations (Baker, 1982; Baker 1983). In other cases, women feel that opportunities to marry may have been reduced by their sexual freedom. These unfortunate experiences have tended to make some women reluctant to believe that there was much of a "revolution" at all. There is no evidence that the double standard of sexual behaviour will disappear in the near future.

Despite common-law relationships, separation, and divorce, the desire for commitment and permanence in relationships appears to be as strong as ever. Perhaps because of uncertainties in their parents' marriages, in the job market, or in the future of the entire world, most young people aspire to fulfilling and lasting relationships even when they do not achieve them. Although they know intellectually that divorce rates have been increasing, they tend to feel personally immune from marriage dissolution when they talk of their future relationships.

Single people increasingly expect to live on their own or with their friends, but not with their parents or other relatives. Whether or not they establish a household separate from their families depends partly on their level of education and income. Without permanent jobs and a stable income, it is difficult to pay the rent and other expenses. Increasingly, post-secondary education is important in finding permanent work, and those who have not completed high school or college will continue to be disadvantaged in the labour market. Although changes are apparent in recent decades and will likely continue in the future, educational and occupational choices are still based largely on stereotypical notions of what work is appropriate for males or females. The same is true for working-class and middle-class young people. They see a segregated labour force in which certain kinds of people typically occupy certain types of jobs. Parental models influence educational and occupational choices, but young people can be motivated to choose from a wider selection of jobs through new role models from teachers, television personalities, visitors brought to the school by guidance counsellors or by friends.

Labour force needs are changing and occupational choices need to consider the fact that much of today's hiring is done on term contracts and an increasing number of workers are becoming consultants and entrepreneurs. If this trend continues, young people may require more interpersonal skills, initiative, and flexibility in their ideas and in the working conditions they are willing to accept in order to make a living. More people in the future will likely work with computers and fax machines at home rather than in offices. These changes in the labour market could have implications for work habits, requiring people to work independently without supervision. They also have implications for housing needs as many of us will require a work space at home, containing more sophisticated and expensive equipment. Many unmarried people living alone depend on their workplace for social contact, and living and working alone may be challenging without increased opportunities for interaction with colleagues and friends. Even those who find full-time employment outside the home may be forced to change jobs or seek alternative careers several times throughout their lives.

Attitudes toward common-law arrangements and childbearing outside legal marriage are becoming more liberal. Singleness and living alone have also become more acceptable at all ages, especially now that being unmarried no longer implies that one lives a celibate life. The social importance of legal marriage will probably continue to subside, as intimacy is seen as a personal choice rather than something regulated by religion or government.

SUGGESTED READINGS

Baker, Maureen. "Finding Partners in the Newspapers: Sex Differences in Personal Advertising." *Atlantis.* 7 (2). 1982:137–146.

_________ . *"What Will Tomorrow Bring?"... A Study of the Aspirations of Adolescent Women.* Canadian Advisory Council on the Status of Women. Ottawa: Minister of Supply and Services Canada, 1985.

Barnes, Gordon E., Leonard Greenwood, and Reena Sommers. "Courtship Violence in a Canadian Sample of Male College Students." *Family Relations.* January 1991:37–44.

Boyd, Monica and Edward T. Pryor. "Young Adults Living in Their Parents' Home." *Canadian Social Trends.* Edited by Craig McKie and Keith Thompson. Toronto: Thompson Educational Publishing, 1990:188–191.

Canada, Special Senate Committee on Youth. *Youth: A Plan of Action.* (Chaired by Senator J. Hébert) Ottawa: Minister of Supply and Services Canada, February 1986.

DeKeseredy, Walter S. *Woman Abuse in Dating Relationships. The Role of Male Peer Support.* Toronto: Canadian Scholars' Press, 1988.

Devereaux, Mary Sue. "Marital Status." *Canadian Social Trends.* Edited by Craig McKie and Keith Thompson. Toronto: Thompson Educational Publishing, 1990:138–141.

King, Alan et al. *Canada Youth and AIDS Study.* Kingston: Queen's University, Social Program Evaluation Group, 1989.

Mackie, Marlene. *Gender Relations in Canada. Further Explorations.* Toronto: Butterworths, 1991.

McKie, Craig. "Common-Law: Living Together as Husband and Wife Without Marriage." *Canadian Social Trends.* 3. Autumn 1986:39–41.

Ontario Ministry of Skills Development. *Pathways. A Study of Labour Market Experiences and Transition Patterns of High School Leavers.* Toronto: Ministry of Skills Development, May 1989.

Ram, Bali. "Intermarriage Among Ethnic Groups." *Ethnic Demography. Canadian Immigrant, Racial and Cultural Variations.* Edited by Shiva S. Halli, Frank Trovato, and Leo Driedger. Ottawa: Carleton University Press, 1990:213–227.

Saitz, Ray. "Moonlighting. How after-school jobs prevent students from making the grade." *Education Forum.* 15 (2). Summer 1989:12–15.

Shostak, Arthur B. "Singlehood." *Handbook of Marriage and the Family.* Edited by M.B. Sussman and S.K. Steinmetz. New York: Plenum Press, 1987:355–367.

Stein, Peter. "Understanding Single Adulthood." *Current Issues in Marriage and the Family.* Edited by J. Gipson Wells. New York: Macmillan, 1988.

Stout, Cam. "Common-Law: A Growing alternative." *Canadian Social Trends.* 23. Winter 1991:18–20.

Turcotte, Pierre. "Common-Law Unions; Nearly Half a Million in 1986." *Canadian Social Trends.* Edited by Craig McKie and Keith Thompson. Toronto: Thompson Educational Publishing, 1990:148–152.

ISSUES FOR DISCUSSION

1. Why do some ethnic groups place more pressure on their children to marry within their own ethnic group?
2. Why are an increasing number of couples living together without legal marriage? What are the advantages and disadvantages of this arrangement?
3. How have stereotypes of unmarried men and women changed in the past 30 years?

4. Imagine that you just turned 40 years old and are still unmarried. How would you feel about your life?
5. What do rising rates of cohabitation tell us about the future of marriage as an institution? Will people dispense with legal marriage in the future?
6. Why do people bother to get their religion or the government to accept their personal living arrangements?
7. Under what conditions would you consider answering an advertisement in the personal columns of a newspaper? Would you consider placing an advertisement? Why or why not?
8. What characteristics do you feel are important to look for in a potential mate? Do you think that a 20-year-old would value the same characteristics as a 45-year-old?
9. If you were asked by a researcher to help develop terminology to be used in a study of contemporary dating practices, how would you deal with the words *dating* and *courtship*? Provide explanations for your terminology.
10. Speculate about the impact of sexually transmitted diseases on the dating and sexual habits of unmarried people in the 1990s.
11. How do you feel about the following statement found on page 92 of this chapter: "From present unemployment rates and estimates of underemployment, it is questionable whether many of today's young people will work in their area of choice, reach their aspired level in that occupation, or even receive a permanent position." Justify your answer.
12. Why is it important for young people to be informed about labour market requirements, job segregation, and potential work/family conflicts?
13. How do you think part-time work affects the grades and extracurricular activities of students?

FURTHER ACTIVITIES

1. Prepare an interview schedule (i.e., a list of questions to ask subjects in an interview) on the aspirations of young people for the future. (Your teacher should approve these questions.) Try to find out what kind of occupation young people really expect to have at a particular point in the future, compared with what

they idealistically would like to do. Interview a few of your acquaintances to see if the questions are clear and to get some indication of what you might find if you actually carried out such a study.

2. Talk to some parents and grandparents (yours or your friends) about dating practices when they were young. Compare what you find to the discussion in your text.
3. In a shopping mall or other public place, observe people who appear to be in couples. Does the theory of social homogamy hold true in terms of age, height, ethnicity, and race? Do you see many interracial relationships? Discuss your findings with your classmates.
4. Talk to a young person who belongs to another culture about dating practices. What are these practices, and how do they differ from your own? What explanations are offered by young people and by their parents for these practices?

4 The Early Stages of Marriage

SPECIFIC TASKS

Marital Adjustment

Many young people in Canada perceive the decision to marry and the wedding ceremony itself as a romantic occasion, even when they live together before marriage. This view is certainly perpetuated by the media, with magazines devoted to brides and weddings and considerable advertising given to wedding attire, rings, receptions, and honeymoons. Furthermore, many families save for years and spend thousands of dollars on wedding clothing and receptions, even though the event lasts only a day or two. Yet, the romance of this "special day" is supposed to last forever. The connection between romantic love and marriage, however, is relatively recent and is seen as unnecessary in some parts of the world where arranged marriages still prevail.

The adjustment to marriage often involves greater co-operation than any other type of human relationship. It includes coming to an agreement about what issues are important, sharing tasks and activities, showing affection to one another, and developing sexual intimacy, effective means of communicating, and a mutually satisfying lifestyle. How difficult this period of adjustment will be depends on differences or similarities in the partners' personalities and upbring-

Bride magazines contain information on all wedding details such as attire, receptions, etiquette, and honeymoons to help plan any type of wedding.

Photo courtesy of *Wedding Bells* magazine

ing, the frequency and quality of communication between them, and the strength of their feelings for each other (Bernard, 1964).

Communication is one of the most important and complex factors in marital adjustment. Communication may be verbal or nonverbal, explicit or tacit, it may clarify or mislead, draw relationships closer together or tear them apart (Eshleman, 1978). In order to understand each other's point of view and needs, marital partners must be able to listen carefully to what the other person says, but also observe the "body language" or other types of nonverbal ways of expressing feelings.

Ideally, engaged couples have already discussed what they want out of marriage and what they expect from their partner. Even if these kinds of discussions have already taken place, the process of identifying and performing role expectations is an ongoing process that inevitably leads to conflict. An important task of the early stages of marriage, therefore, is the management of conflict to the mutual satisfaction of both marital partners (Eshleman, 1978).

Initially, couples may expect that their marital roles be similar rather than complementary. Several generations ago, however, marital

GAMES COUPLES PLAY

BY BARBARA S. SMALLEY

Experts agree that game-playing is not only unhealthy, it can also destroy an intimate relationship. So why do we do it? According to Edward Fish, Ph.D., a Philadelphia psychologist specializing in marriage and family therapy, many strategies we use on our partners were learned from childhood. "If a game works," he says, "we continue to play it. If it doesn't, we try another ploy." Indeed, most of us can recall playing manipulative games as children. We played them with our parents, our siblings, our friends. We used them to win attention, to get our way, and to pump up our egos. And while most of us may *think* we outgrew such tactics, in reality, they are strategies we sometimes use when we are feeling unloved or insecure.

In fact, many experts think that newlyweds are particularly vulnerable to playing games. According to Jeanette C. Lauer, Ph.D., co-author of *'Til Death Do Us Part: How Couples Stay Together*, (Haworth Press, 1986), "Newlyweds are not entirely comfortable with each other yet and haven't developed good communication skills." Fish agrees and adds, "A power struggle exists in every relationship, but it is particularly evident in a new relationship where rules are not yet clear."

Fish believes that by the end of the first or second year of marriage, communication patterns are solidified and that by the end of the third year, patterns are generally set. Furthermore, once communication patterns have been established, they can be extremely difficult to break. "So you have to decide from the beginning whether you want to have a relationship or a contest," Fish says, "and if you opt for a relationship, you can't let games become a substitute for genuine, open communcation."

What steps can newlyweds take to avoid playing games and focus, instead, on developing good communication skills? For starters, it helps to be familiar with some of the games we play and some of the reasons why we play them.

Grudges

The game of holding grudges follows a pattern similar to the following: Partners are confronted with a series of petty annoyances, but instead of expressing, discussing, and handling each one as it arises, they store them all inside and allow them to fester. Fish, for example, compares grudge-holding to a pocket of gas. "If there is no outlet, it will lead to an explosion," he says.

Setting up Tests

There are variations of love exams. For example, how many of us are guilty of muttering this phrase: "If you loved me, you would (or wouldn't) do such and such a thing"? Experts say statements like these are a test of power more than of love, and while this strategy may work, it will also likely result in a lot of resentment. "The game works particularly well with guilt-prone people," Fish believes. "It's a way of using love in a taunting way. It's also asking to prove love, whereas in a good relationship, you don't have to prove love."

A second variation of this game sounds like this: "If you love me, you would change for me." According to William Quinn, Ph.D., director of McPhaul Marriage and Family Therapy Clinic at the University of Georgia, "The romantic notion of love implies that we should possess the highest form of altruism and self-sacrifice despite its poisonous effect on our own integrity. Does this mean that couples who love each other should: Be as much alike as possible? Relinquish their own idiosyncratic dreams or ideas? Fight off their personal history?" Quinn and other experts think not and believe that everyone needs freedom to be his or her own person.

"If you loved me, you would know what I was thinking/feeling" is yet another example of setting up love tests. "Couples who play these games have fallen victim to the illusion of the perfect mate," Quinn suspects. "They get fooled into expecting that love between two people will assure them they will have the same spectacles with which to look at the world. Our culture fools us into believing that our emotions make so much sense to us that they are understood by anyone who would know us."

Transfer Blame

Another "if" game couples play uses displacement—blaming partners for their own problems. "In this game, a spouse becomes a scapegoat when we are reluctant or unable to take responsibility for our own thoughts, feelings, and inadequacies," Quinn explains.

Silent Treatment

Sometimes couples become so angry with each other that they cease communicating altogether. And while not speaking can be advantageous when you are both physically exhausted, when you can't find the privacy to hash out your differences, or when you both need time to cool off and regain your objectivity, in most cases, not communicating can be dangerous to your relationship. "Silence is a way of saying something is really wrong," Lauer believes, "but the other person doesn't know what's wrong, so using the silent treatment can elicit the wrong kind of response."

relationships were thought to be more successful if husbands and wives played different but complementary roles. For example, wives were usually responsible for cooking, housekeeping, child care, and maintaining contact with relatives, while husbands were responsible for earning the family income, performing outdoor chores, maintaining the car, and disciplining the children (Stebbins, 1988). As more married women have entered the labour force and the breadwinning role has become shared, the equality of the division of labour within the home has been questioned. The typical pattern for young, recently married couples is for both to work full-time and for housework to be at least partly shared. Ideas about marital roles tend to evolve throughout the marriage, however, especially with the birth of children, maternity leaves, new jobs, and discrepancies between the earning power of partners.

Although Canadian and international studies have shown that wives accept the responsibility for, and perform, most of the routine household tasks (Maret and Finlay, 1984; Berk, 1985; Kalleberg and Rosenfield, 1990; Marshall, 1990), research also indicates that relationships are likely to be more egalitarian in the early years compared with the middle years of marriage (Albrecht et al., 1979). The sharing of certain household chores is also extended to better communication and the sharing of leisure time, making this stage in the life cycle more companionate than later stages (Rollins and Feldman, 1970; Lupri and Frideres, 1981).

In addition to changes throughout individual marriages, there have also been many changes over time to marriage as an institution. Unlike a few generations ago, the composition, structure, and relationships in Canadian families are highly varied. Despite major social and economic changes since the Second World War, marriage and family life have not become unimportant but rather have adapted to change. We can no longer make the assumptions that spouses have actually been legally married, share their surname, live in the same location, pool their financial resources, or plan to have children.

HISTORICAL PERSPECTIVES

In order to understand family life in previous eras or in other cultures, it is important to distinguish between the ideal and the actual family system. Even before marriages were based on romantic love, there were probably many marital partners who loved each other deeply, and children who persuaded their parents to arrange a marriage with someone they already knew and loved. Similarly, even though fathers traditionally had considerable authority within the family, some men undoubtedly were sensitive to the wishes and needs of their wives and children. Even when **chastity** before marriage was considered to be essential, young men frequented prostitutes or had secret liaisons. Premarital pregnancy was disguised with an immediate marriage or by temporarily sending the woman away until she gave birth and the baby was given up for adoption. In other words, ideal family systems in the past sometimes differed considerably from reality, just as they do today.

ANTECEDENTS OF CANADA'S FAMILY STRUCTURE

The earliest direct antecedent of Canada's family structure, about which we have detailed knowledge, is the family of the ancient Hebrews. If we go back to the earliest Hebrew records of 4000 years ago, we know that their families were patriarchal and their marriages were arranged. According to Talmudic law, the minimum ages of marriage were 13 for boys and 12 for girls. But children were often betrothed by their fathers at much earlier ages, even though the marriage was not consummated until the ceremony later took place. **Betrothal** was a promise to marry, like a formal engagement, that involved the exchange of money or a written contract.

Marriage in many different eras and cultures has been seen as a sacred obligation. Celibacy was a religious crime among the ancient Hebrews and a legal offence among the ancient Greeks (Leslie and Korman, 1989:153, 152). In ancient Greece, marriage was a means to continue the worship of ancestors and to provide for the inheritance of property. The wedding ceremony initially consisted of the groom making gifts to the bride's father—a form of bride price—and the girl being passed over to her husband. Later, betrothal and marriage were separated, and the bride price and dowry were established at the time of betrothal. Marriage was monogamous, but wealthy men could keep concubines, and poorer men could visit prostitutes.

The early Roman family system (prior to 202 B.C.) was the strongest patriarchy of which we have knowledge (Leslie, 1982:169). The father was the only legal person in the family, and even held the right of life and death over his children. Marriage was monogamous, the family was extended to three generations, and emphasis was placed on continuing the family line and worshipping the ancestors. There were three different types of wedding ceremony among the early Romans. In the first, the bride was carried in an elaborate procession to the groom's house, where a sheep was slain, and there was a ritual eating of sacred cake (Leslie, 1982:171). In the second type, the parents of the bride and groom held a mock sale of the bride, passing a coin. Among poorer people, a couple was considered to be married if they lived together for a year without the woman leaving the man's home for more than three consecutive days. After the end of the Punic Wars in 202 B.C., the authority of the father declined, marriage became more a matter of personal satisfaction than a sacred obligation, and divorce became more common.

In the English family from the sixteenth to the eighteenth century, the husband continued to be the official head. Until 1663, in fact, a husband could legally beat his wife. Marriages were arranged by parents, but free choice marriage based on romantic love was beginning. Divorce became legally possible through the bishops' courts, even though the Roman Catholic Church disapproved. Later, divorce was granted to a few influential people through special acts of Parliament.

The origins of **chivalry** and romantic love are thought to date back to feudal times in Europe. During this period, marriages were arranged to suit family alliances, to provide heirs, and to improve or maintain family wealth. Marital partners were not expected to have their emotional needs satisfied in marriage and sought satisfaction elsewhere in extramarital affairs. Among the upper classes especially, these relationships, based on romantic or idealized love, were often between knights and ladies whose husbands were away at war. Affairs were not always overtly sexual but sometimes involved public acts of gallantry, deferential attention to women, and the idealization of love and the partner.

Romantic love and marriage were not considered compatible among the rich because parents did not want to give their children the opportunity to fall in love and to marry the "wrong" person. Instead, they wanted to engineer a marriage that would consolidate or expand the family money and maintain the family reputation. They also wanted a son-in-law who was emotionally and financially stable and a daughter-in-law who was pleasant, healthy, and fertile. Whether or not the couple were romantically involved was considered to be irrelevant, but parents hoped that respect and love would later develop between the couple.

For the vast majority of poor people, the very crowded and difficult living conditions did not allow for much romance or chivalry. In order to maintain a romantic relationship, couples need privacy. Living in the same room with a large number of children, parents would not be able to disguise their bodily functions, their illnesses, or other aspects of life. Even in poorer families, parents wanted their sons and daughters to marry someone wealthier, who would help them out of debt or bring land into the family, and someone strong, healthy, and fertile. Parents in Europe during the Middle Ages felt that marriage was too important to the family to trust children to choose their own marital partners.

Acts of chivalry or deferential treatment of women were much more likely when women were members of the leisure classes. In fact, some authors have argued that treating women with extra respect and deference was a characteristic of an era when wealthy women had no important role in society. They were not allowed to take political office or work in the trades or professions, yet they were too rich to perform their own housework or child care. This chivalry was a form of compensation for a relatively low economic and legal status— a way of keeping women happy despite their low status (Leslie and Korman, 1989:173-74). As societies have changed and developed, some of these customs have remained as rules of etiquette, such as opening doors for women, helping them on with their coats, or protecting them from heavy work.

In the early years of the American colonies and in Canada, parents sometimes arranged their children's marriages, but a young woman could refuse to marry the man her father had selected. The young man was expected to ask the father's permission to **court** his daughter or to develop a relationship leading to marriage. Engagements or betrothal ceremonies sometimes took place, which had the effect of binding contracts. In many locations, it was the practice to have the **banns** read in church. This was the announcement of intention to marry, read for three consecutive Sundays, which requested anyone to declare publicly any reason why the marriage should not take place. Later, when the government became more involved in marriage, a licence was required. Wedding ceremonies were conducted in church in the presence of witnesses, followed by a party. The bride was given a ring by the groom, which was symbolic of the bride price, and she changed her surname to his, which symbolized the fact that he became the legal head of their new household.

From these examples, we can see that engagement and wedding ceremonies involve rituals reflecting the purpose of marriage, transfer of authority, the joining of two families, and fertility symbols. The contractual nature of these customs indicates that getting married is a legal step that may or may not involve romantic love, but it has seldom been considered only a private act between two individuals.

Even after our attitudes and laws about marriage and family have changed, we still tend to retain the traditional symbols of weddings.

WEDDING CEREMONIES

Within the last century, a wedding form that draws heavily on Western European and especially English customs has evolved in North American culture. All its features are not obligatory; in fact, it might be best viewed as a pyramid of customs from which one may choose to incorporate as many levels as taste and recources dictate. A whole industry is supported by these established rules of wedding etiquette. We cannot give or even summarize all the rules here, but they include such familiar elements as the groom's family being seated on the right (facing the altar) and the bride's on the left; the male members of the wedding party being dressed formally; and the bridesmaids, flower girls, and mothers of the bride and groom being dressed in pastel (the pattern chosen by the bride). The wedding march begins with the flower girl and/or ring bearer coming first, then the bridesmaids, and finally the bride on the arm of her father. She is dressed in white and wears a white veil (denoting purity and modesty) and carries a bouquet of flowers. Meanwhile the officiator and the groom have inconspicuously entered from a side door (so as not to distract from the drama of her entrance) and await her at the altar. At the end of the ceremony, rings are exchanged, the groom kisses the bride, and they exit up the main aisle while the organ swells with a triumphal wedding march. As they leave the church they are pelted with rice (an ancient Greek fertility symbol revived during the late nineteenth century).

In contemporary North America nearly all first-time brides are given a wedding reception (88 percent among Whyte's Detroit sample, 1990, p. 57). There, the photographer will take pictures of the bride alone, the bride and groom alone, the bride and groom with the rest of the wedding party, the bride feeding the groom some wedding cake, the bride and groom drinking a cup of punch or champagne. Then, after the tossing of her bouquet to one of the unmarried women in the wedding party (who is thereby assured of an imminent wedding of her own), the bride and her groom leave the reception through a shower of rice to change and depart for the honeymoon. The car they leave in is decorated with streamers and "just married" signs and trails a string of tin cans. In view of the diversity of wedding customs in the subcultures that made up North America, it is remarkable how many of these elements have been incorporated into the weddings of young people from every background.

During the creative 1960s and 1970s, it became a fashion in some circles for the couple to write their own wedding vows. Occasionally, marriage ceremonies were sufficiently innovative to warrant media coverage. Couples were joined in matrimony while the wedding party sped along on motorcycles, hung suspended in free fall after leaping from a plane, or swam over a tropical reef in scuba gear. For better or for worse, it appears that this fashion has passed, and recent surveys show that today it is extremely rare for a couple to forgo the more traditional type of wedding (White 1990, p. 56).

Carlfred B. Broderick. *Marriage and The Family*. 4th ed. Englewood Cliffs, New Jersey: Prentice Hall, 1992:164–166. Adapted by permission of Prentice Hall, Inc., Englewood Cliffs, New Jersey.

When couples have lived together and then decide to marry, for example, many brides wear white wedding dresses, which traditionally symbolized virginity. Although fathers retain no more authority over daughters than sons, they still "give away" their daughter to the groom, which traditionally symbolized the transfer of male authority. While many people no longer accept the traditional patriarchal notion of the family, they may still follow these customs for their cultural value rather than for their true meaning. In many cases, young people do not even know the original meaning of wedding rituals but simply adhere to them because it is the "thing to do."

Legal Changes Affecting Marriage

When the early settlers came to Canada, they brought their marriage customs and their legal traditions with them. In Quebec, the French Napoleonic Code was established as the legal system, while the rest of Canada adopted English Common Law. Under both systems, husbands and fathers had authority over their wives and children. Upon marriage, a woman's property, if she had any, could be taken over and controlled by her husband. After the wedding ceremony, the wife had the status of a minor child; she could not sell or acquire property, and she could not vote. In the rare case that the couple separated and there was any dispute about the custody of the children, the husband was granted custody.

The Married Women's Property Act, which was first passed in England in 1870, was introduced in the Canadian provinces after 1872. This legal change was seen as a milestone because it allowed married women to retain their own wages or property. This was particularly important for middle- or upper-class women, who might have inherited property. At the same time women were also demanding higher education, access to the professions, and the right to participate in politics. It was not until after 1910 that Canadian women obtained the right to retain custody of their children, and after 1918 that women could vote in federal elections. Until 1929, women were not considered to be "legal persons"—the reason to keep them from Senate appointments (Cochrane, 1977). In the province of Quebec, women could not vote in provincial elections until 1940.

In the long fight over women's suffrage, the opposition argued that women did not need to participate in elections because their husband voted on their behalf. Advocates of equal rights for women fought this patriarchal marriage system for many decades before it began to be made more egalitarian after 1870. Yet, some of the battles

YOU MUSTN'T ASK TO VOTE

You may be our close companion
Share our troubles, ease our pain,
You may bear the servant's burden
(But without the servant's gain;)
You may scrub and cook and iron
Sew the buttons on our coat,
But as men we must protect you—
You are far too frail to vote.

You may toil behind our counters,
In our factories you may slave
You are welcome in the sweatshop
From the cradle to the grave.
If you err, altho' a woman
You may dangle by the throat
But our chivalry is outraged
If you soil your hands to vote.

L. Case Russell

The Globe and Mail, 28 September 1912.

are still being fought, such as disputes over the enforcement of child support after divorce and paternity rights for unmarried fathers.

Until the 1960s, marital roles differed by law. A woman promised during the wedding ceremony to love, honour, and obey her husband, while he promised to love, honour, and cherish her. He could establish the place where they lived and she was expected to follow him, to maintain the household, and care for their children. In return, she was entitled to **dower rights**, or the right to one-third of his property, should the marriage dissolve. During the marriage, the husband was supposed to provide her with the necessities of life. What was necessary, however, was decided by him.

Since 1978, most Canadian provinces have changed their laws in an attempt to equalize the relations between husbands and wives. The most publicized changes relate to the division of matrimonial property and the custody of children. Both partners are now expected to financially support each other and their children, and former wives are no longer awarded lifelong alimony. Theoretically, both mothers and fathers have equal rights to the custody of children, but in actual fact, women usually receive custody. In some provinces, including

Ontario, the family home and any property that the family jointly uses (called family assets) are divided equally after divorce. But men have higher earning power than women. Women and children often live on reduced incomes after marriage breakdown, while some men acquire a higher standard of living than when they were married (Weitzman, 1985). This is another example of discrepancies between the ideal and the reality of family life.

In addition to (or instead of) the contract signed during the wedding ceremony, some couples have their own marriage contracts drawn up by their lawyers. Marriage contracts may outline the rights and responsibilities of each partner in marriage, as well as agreements about ownership and division of property, support obligations, and the religious upbringing of the children. Some family counsellors encourage engaged couples to prepare a marriage contract in order to help them identify their expectations of marriage and of each other, and to make sure that they do not have irreconcilable differences (Jarman and Howlett, 1991:162–164). Marriage contracts have always been used in Quebec. Unlike the rest of Canada, Quebec family law originates from the Civil Code of France, which was based on the patriarchal Napoleonic Code. More recently, marriage contracts have also been used in other Canadian provinces as more people disagreed with marital obligations set out in provincial marriage law.

In provinces such as Ontario, the various courts that used to deal with different family matters (divorce, custody of children, child support, and juvenile delinquency) have been consolidated to deal with all family-related issues. The provincial government now provides lawyers to defend children's rights, if the parents are abusive, absent, or in dispute over custody.

To some extent, the family is no longer protected by privacy laws or perceived to be immune from legal intervention. Children are no longer considered to be the property of parents, to be treated any way they want. Wives are no longer required to be obedient or always sexually available to their husbands. While the family used to be viewed as a legal unit represented by the husband/father, individual family members now have their own legal right to protection from each other.

Changing Expectations of Marriage

Until this century, marriage was typically viewed as the normal way to live one's adult life. Although some people entered religious orders or chose to remain single for personal reasons, the vast majority of men and women married and produced children. Marriage was not seen as a vehicle for personal fulfilment and romantic love, but rather as a way to produce children, to be socially acceptable, and to acquire a partner in order to survive economically. Although marriage in previous centuries was particularly crucial for women, who were not permitted to own property or to work alongside men, marriage was also important for men. Since many men worked a twelve-hour day or longer, they needed someone to prepare food, to clean their house, to make and maintain their clothes, and to bear and care for their children. Marriage was therefore seen as a mutually necessary partnership.

Many social and economic changes that affected families took place in the twentieth century. For example, labour unions successfully fought to reduce working hours, which gave working men and women more leisure time to spend with their families. As the church's control over people's lives gradually weakened, more people rejected the religious view that marriages were "made in heaven." Young people demanded more say in whom and when they would marry, how many children they would have, and whether or not they would stay together if they were dissatisfied with their marriage. Gradually, young people placed greater value on the quality of their marital relationships and their own personal development.

Lobby groups pressed for legal change to give married women similar political and legal status to married men. As new jobs in the service sector were created, more married women entered the labour force and their economic independence strengthened their bargaining power in families. As childrearing costs escalated and especially as more mothers entered the labour force, parents opted for fewer children. Divorce became legally available to the middle and lower classes and divorce rates rose. More recently, married women have argued that they have a right to their own lives and should not be expected to focus their lives around their husbands or their husbands' occupations. Gradually, people came to emphasize duty and family obligations less, and to place higher value on personal satisfaction.

CULTURAL PERSPECTIVES

WEDDINGS IN DIFFERENT CULTURES

The variations in engagement and wedding rituals in different historical eras and cultures have fascinated social scientists and students for many years. These ceremonies and rituals indicate that marriage has always been more than a private arrangement between two people and often has been, and still is, an economic and social agreement between extended families or clans. Marriage has been highly valued not only because it inevitably continues the family name and maintains the population, but also because it reinforces alliances between villages, neighbourhoods, and families. It is not surprising, then, that many wedding ceremonies contain symbols of fertility (confetti), the transfer of authority (the bride is "given away" by her father to her husband), and group cohesion (the wedding reception, in which both sets of parents preside).

There are many cultural variations in marriage and family structure. Wedding customs vary greatly throughout the world, but also among cultural groups within a particular country.

WEDDING CUSTOMS

BY LYNNE S. DUMAS

Greek
In a traditional Greek wedding, the bride and groom are crowned with wreaths of orange blossoms to symbolize fruitfulness and happiness; the "Koumbaros," or best man, assists in this crowning. At the close of the ceremony, the couple joins hands and walks three times around the altar while guests pelt them with rice, a symbol of fertility.

Japanese
In Japan, particularly in country-style weddings, the ceremony ends with the couple sipping sake, a rice wine, from ritual cups. In the most traditional of Japanese weddings, the bride and groom each take three sips from a graduated series of three cups.

Italian
For years, brides in Italy carried a bag in which they collected their dowry at the wedding reception. Such bags are available today, although decidedly more upscale, often made of satin and silk and decorated with lace and beads.

In some areas of Italy, guests toss "confetti"—that is, sugared almonds—at the couple in the hopes of bringing sweetness and happiness to the marriage.

Egyptian
At traditional weddings in Egypt, the bride and groom drink "Sharabat," a fruit drink, from individual cups. Then, they exchange cups and take another sip.

Another Egyptian custom still in vogue today is for the guests to toss flowers at the new couple as they enter the reception hall.

Mexican
Charming customs highlight Mexican weddings. During the ceremony, for example, the groom gives his bride 13 gold coins which symbolize his commitment to support her economically.

Another lovely Mexican custom is the "Laso," which is a fancy white string or chain of flowers. One loop is slipped over the bride's head and the other over the groom's, symbolizing their unity.

Thai

Though hundreds of miles from Mexico, the brides of Thailand take part in a similar wedding custom. In the Thai ceremony, the "Mong Kon Faet," a sacred cord blessed by the monks before the ceremony, is draped on the heads of the bride and groom to symbolize their "togetherness always."

Another traditional Thai custom takes place when the parents of the couple take scented powder that has been blessed by monks and lightly place three dots on the foreheads of the bride and groom. This custom calls the good spirits to stay inside the couple.

Chinese

The most striking aspect to the traditional Chinese wedding is the use of the colour red. From the bridal gown to the gift wrappings to the invitations, red is the good luck of the classic Chinese ceremony.

Russian

While modern marriages inside the [former] Soviet Union are exceedingly simple—the bride and groom go to a government deputy and sign a document proclaiming them husband and wife—those who can afford a more expansive celebration often partake in a Russian ritual at the wedding reception. After a champagne toast, everyone throws their champagne glasses on the floor. If the glasses break, the couple will have a future filled with happiness. (If they don't, unhappiness—or even divorce—may be in the cards.)

Another Russian custom is to tie a doll on your wedding car if you want your first child to be a girl, or a bear if you'd prefer a boy.

French

There is one custom that is typically français—the "Coupe de Mariage." In this ceremony, the bride and groom drink from a small, double-handled silver bowl or cup filled with wine or champagne. After the wedding, it is engraved with the name of the couple and the date of the marriage. It is later passed from generation to generation.

Pakistani

Among the most interesting and exotic wedding rituals are those practised by Pakistanis. Even today, most marriages are arranged by the parents; such customs as having the groom ride to the wedding on a white horse bedecked with jewels and other ornaments are still practised.

In the evening, when the Pakistani wedding is over, the bride waits for the groom in a room which is beautifully and elaborately decorated with flourishing flowers.

Excerpted from "Customizing Your Wedding" by Lynne S. Dumas in *Bridal Guide*, Sept./Oct. '88.

The following description is an example of a traditional Jewish wedding taking place in Canada.

Usually the wedding ceremony takes place in a synagogue. The bridal couple exchange the marriage vows under a *chupah* or canopy. The groom places a simple gold ring on the forefinger of the right

A traditional Jewish Orthodox wedding usually takes place in a synagogue. A rabbi reads the *ketubah,* which is the matrimonial contract, under a *chupah,* or canopy. What similarities/differences do you see in this wedding compared with a wedding ceremony in your culture?

Photo courtesy of Mr. and Mrs. Sarfaty

hand of his bride during the ceremony ... twice during the ceremony the couple sip from the same cup of wine to show the unity of their future lives. At the conclusion of the marriage rites, the groom shatters a glass with his foot. This act is symbolic of the destruction of the temple in Jerusalem and the suffering of the Jews throughout their history. It is meant to remind the bride and the groom of their responsibilities to their faith, even at a time of personal joy.

At the dinner after the wedding the children felt a sense of pride when their father was called upon to say the blessing. Then there was music and dancing, both the popular kind and the traditional Yiddish and Hebrew songs that everyone knew. The *Hora*—a lively Israeli circle dance—started the celebration.

(From "The Jews" by Frank Caplan and Norman Sheffe. Excerpt from *Many Cultures, Many Heritages.* Reprinted by permission of McGraw-Hill Ryerson Limited.)

The next section will discuss some examples from the anthropological literature that vary from our family structure in Canada.

Although they are not typical examples of the way people live today in North America, they illustrate how some other cultures actually lived in the recent past.

MARRIAGE IN OTHER CULTURES

Each of the previous chapters has discussed some cross-cultural variations in family composition and customs, but this section will delve into cultural variations of marriage and family in more detail. The first variation is the patriarchal family of the Mennonites and Hutterites, who immigrated into Canada from eastern Europe and Russia from the late nineteenth to early twentieth centuries. The second examples involve families from two First Nation groups in Canada, the Huron and Ojibway, especially before European contact. These examples illustrate the connection between family and personal life and the economic basis of society.

Mennonite and Hutterite Marriage and Families

Large-scale immigration of Mennonites and Hutterites from Germany and Russia began in the late nineteenth century and continued until the 1930s. Although there were differences in religious beliefs between the two ethno-religious groups, both could be considered fundamentalist Christians whose beliefs originated from the Anabaptists in sixteenth century Europe. Both groups settled in the western provinces of Canada, but the Mennonites also established themselves in rural Ontario. The Mennonites and the Hutterites were originally rural agriculturalists who resisted modern urban living longer than other groups (Anderson and Driedger, 1980).

After settling in Canada, Mennonites underwent several divisions. The conservative faction, sometimes referred to as Old Colony, Old Order Mennonites, or Amish, continued to speak German or Russian in an attempt to maintain their culture and religion, and interacted mainly with other Mennonites. The more liberal faction adopted modern dress and urban occupations, and integrated to a greater extent into Canadian society. This section focuses on the more conservative Mennonites who differed most from present-day behavioural patterns.

Until the 1930s, conservative Mennonites restricted opportunities for dating and at least partially arranged marriages for their young people. Marriages between "believers" and "nonbelievers" were not permitted and meant automatic excommunication until 1975 (Hamm,

1987:81). The sanctity of courtship, engagement, and marriage is still upheld, and because marriage is considered to be ordained by God, it cannot be dissolved through divorce. Although people who consider themselves to be religious always have lower divorce rates than those who report no religion, divorce has been rare in Mennonite families. Uniformity of beliefs, customs, and values seems to maintain family solidarity (Anderson and Driedger, 1980).

The conservative Mennonite families living in Canada are patriarchal; the father is considered to be the head of the household and the "priest of the family" (Hamm, 1987:81). The wife and children occupied secondary roles (Anderson and Driedger, 1980). Conservative Mennonites, especially in Ontario, maintained traditional dress, with women wearing long dark-coloured, conservative dresses with bonnets and men wearing dark trousers and jackets, brimmed hats, and beards for married men. Many conservative Mennonites continue to oppose consumerism and high technology, preferring to use horses and buggies instead of cars, and to maintain traditional homes with simple furnishings and few modern conveniences.

When Mennonites were mainly agriculturalists, they had large families, often as many as ten children. Now that many have moved to urban areas and wives are working outside the home, family structure is becoming more democratic (Anderson and Driedger, 1980:171). Birth rates have fallen, but at least in the 1970s Mennonites continued to have more children than the Canadian average (Kalbach and McVey, 1979:107). Since the Canadian census no longer asks questions about religious background, it is difficult to find more recent figures. Redekop (1989) indicated that recent birth rates are also difficult to find for American Mennonites, but a 1982 study indicated that their birth rate had fallen below the U.S. average. Yet, conservative Mennonites continue to oppose abortion and birth control and view children as gifts from God (Hamm, 1987:81).

The extended family plays an important role in perpetuating cultural and religious traditions. Conservative Mennonites have been opposed to ethnic intermarriage, but with each generation, opposition has declined. Opposition to religious intermarriage, however, is still prevalent. Yet, Hutterites are much more likely to be opposed to both ethnic and religious intermarriage than Mennonites (Anderson and Driedger, 1980).

Conservative Mennonites were able to preserve their traditional family structure by living in isolated rural areas. With urbanization, two-income families, and less social isolation, even the more conservative Mennonites are moving to a more democratic and smaller family. Yet, they have retained their family solidarity and opposition to divorce.

Since the last century, Hutterites have lived in colonies, which are largely self-sufficient and very successful in agriculture. They have maintained their rural lifestyle and isolation from other groups in Alberta and Saskatchewan, yet accepted technological advances in farming. Through social isolation and the rejection of "worldliness," they have retained their system of communal property ownership, co-operative values, and patriarchal family structure.

Separation by gender and segregation on the basis of age are apparent both in the socialization of children and in adult work experiences. Baptism and marriage are the final stages of the socialization process for Hutterites (Peter, 1979). Baptism takes place between the ages of 19 and 21, and is usually followed by marriage within a year or two. The baptized man grows a beard to signify his adult status. Since social mobility or powerful positions cannot be held by unmarried people, all young people are encouraged to marry. Dating is restricted and marriages tend to be at least partially arranged by parents and community members (Peter, 1979). Sex outside marriage is forbidden.

Hutterites have tended to prefer sibling exchange marriages between colonies (Hostetler, 1974:238), meaning that two brothers or a brother and sister might marry two sisters or a sister and brother from a different colony. Although marriages used to be arranged by elders, since the 1960s and 1970s the potential groom and his father or other relatives drive (in a horse and buggy) to the colony where the prospective bride lives and formally ask her consent and the consent of the colony for permission to marry. If everyone agrees, the engagement announcement is followed by an engagement service in church and a two-day party. The next week, the bride and her family travel to the groom's colony for the marriage ceremony. Multiple weddings are preferred by Hutterites because of the expense and travel time required for weddings. As the bride continues to live in the groom's colony, the marriage system of Hutterites is patrilocal.

A married couple lives in an apartment in one of the longhouses built on sixteenth century floor plans. Meals are prepared and eaten communally with other families, and laundry and bathing are also performed in communal facilities. Hutterites live much like extended families, with little personal privacy. The man is considered to be family head, while the woman's secondary position is justified by Biblical references to "Adam's fall." Gender roles are very distinct; the women's role tends to be mainly domestic, while men occupy important economic and political positions. The purpose of marriage is procreation and birth control during marriage is restricted (Hostetler, 1974:203). After marriage, women are expected to become pregnant within the year and the childless woman is pitied by her community. Childrearing and socialization is shared by the Hutterite family and the community (Peter, 1979).

Hutterites have not relied on outside institutions to resolve their conflicts, and although their preachers have the legal power to marry people, they cannot divorce them. This may be one reason why marriages appear to be unusually stable because problems are resolved within the colony rather than in the courts (Peter, 1980). However, religious values help to keep families stable as they emphasize self-control, self-denial, and self-sacrifice (Peter, 1983).

Huron and Ojibway Marriage and Families

In the seventeenth and eighteenth centuries, the Huron people lived in villages organized on the basis of clan membership in what is now Ontario. Descent was matrilineal or traced through the female line. The Hurons lived in longhouses divided into four or more pairs of compartments separated by a central passageway that served as a common fire for heating and cooking. The occupants of the longhouse were the descendants of the senior woman, her unmarried sons and daughters, and her married daughters with their husbands and children. Property belonged to the extended family, rather than to individuals or nuclear families (Castellano, 1991).

Because of the matrilocal and matrilineal living arrangements, relationships between mothers and daughters were often strong, and women held considerable power over their daughters after marriage. Men were often away from home for hunting, trading, political reasons, or war, and this absence enabled mother/daughter relationships to be reinforced. The women, who remained at home, were responsible for the stability of the food supply, and the agricultural crops that women grew were important as staples as well as for trade. As men were highly mobile and engaged in hazardous activities such as warfare and hunting, the matrilocal pattern of residence and matrilineal family structure provided both economic security and family stability (Castellano, 1991).

Young men and women were accorded similar sexual freedom and little distinction was made between being married and unmarried. A personal commitment between a man and woman was noted by the clan, but particularly when the couple produced a child.

Although each partner had the right to terminate the relationship, separation and divorce seldom occurred after a child was born. As with any group that live in extended family arrangements, marital problems were dealt with by relatives who intervened to help heal the rift. It was to the advantage of the community to see that couples got along.

Although Huron women and men shared many activities, they retained complementary roles. By this we mean that men more often hunted and engaged in warfare, while women grew and gathered food, cared for the young children (especially female children), and maintained the home. Yet, women enjoyed respect and autonomy "not yet dreamed of by their white female contemporaries" (Castellano, 1991:9).

The Ojibway people were migratory hunters and gatherers who lived in single nuclear families for most of the year, and in groups of families for certain seasonal economic and ceremonial exchanges. They lived in tents or wigwams suitable for highly mobile nuclear families.

Marriage was considered essential for both men and women, because neither could survive economically without the other. Marriages were sometimes arranged by parents, but after marriage the young couple established an independent household with little interference. The Ojibway maintained a clear division of labour based on gender. Yet, like Huron and Iroquois women (Brown, 1988), Ojibway women had important economic roles in addition to cooking, sewing, and child care. These included weaving fish nets, constructing parts of their dwellings, tanning hides, and harvesting rice and maple sap. However, men's activities of hunter, warrior, and shaman were given greater public recognition (Castellano, 1991). For this reason, few men took on "female" tasks but some women, especially only children, were taught "male" skills such as hunting, shamanism, and warfare.

Iroquois society can be contrasted to Huron and Ojibway in women's relative power not only in families but in the economy, politics, and religious ceremonies. Iroquois society has been described as one of the few matriarchies, and relative to European culture at the time of contact and some other Native tribes such as the Huron, women held an unusual amount of power. Judith Brown (1988) argued that the role of women in politics, religion, and domestic life cannot be explained by Iroquois kinship structure or women's contribution to the economy. Instead, she argues that women's powerful position was a result of their control of the economic organization of their tribe. Iroquois women controlled agricultural activities and production, including land, implements, seeds, and stored food. Through this economic control, they could influence Council meetings, war parties, religious festivals, and household activities.

When Upper Canada was settled by Europeans, many changes took place within Native families, because their livelihood and culture were systematically destroyed. The culture and legal system that was forced upon Native people was foreign and in many ways contradictory. For example, family law brought from Europe by both the French and the English was patriarchal. Despite the matrilineal descent patterns of the Huron, Canadian law stated that Native women lost their Indian status when they married a non-Indian, as did their children. Only recently was this law changed (Nett, 1988:95).

Treaties signed between Native people and the English often established reserves on infertile land that could not support the traditional lifestyles of Native people. However, it was mainly men's roles that changed as the result of colonization (Castellano, 1991). Especially for those Native people who were migratory hunters and gatherers, such as the Ojibway, the transition to sedentary life was difficult. Men whose education from infancy was directed to preparing them to assume the roles of hunter, warrior, and visionary saw their opportunities to use these skills shrink with urbanization, industrial development, and eventually environmental pollution. However, women as farmers, gatherers, and homemakers have retained much of their traditional role despite cultural change (Castellano, 1991).

SELECTED ISSUES

MARITAL ADJUSTMENT: SATISFACTION, CONFLICT RESOLUTION, AND MARITAL VIOLENCE

Marital Adjustment and Satisfaction

As early as the 1930s, studies have been done on marital adjustment and marital satisfaction finding that marital adjustment is easier for couples with certain social backgrounds (Terman, 1938; Burgess and Cottrell, 1939). For example, they found that couples who marry slightly above the average age are less likely to experience adjustment problems than couples who marry in their teens. (According to Statistics Canada, the average age for first marriages in 1990 was 26 for women and 28 for men (Wadhera and Strachan, 1992:5, 52).) In addition, those who are not pregnant when they marry, but rather have a few years of childfree marriage tend to make an easier adjustment. Burgess and Cottrell also concluded that partners who come from similar backgrounds in terms of family income and educational level of parents, religion, race, **ethnicity**, and culture experience fewer adjustment problems and report more satisfaction with their marriage. Even if both partners come from similar backgrounds, however, relationships always require a certain amount of compromise and accommodation.

Levels of marital satisfaction and happiness tend to vary according to the family life cycle, however. Satisfaction with a relationship can depend on whether your partner meets your expectations in terms of sharing your values and ideas about lifestyle, providing you with companionship, respect, and a satisfying sexual relationship, earning an adequate income, and eventually becoming a good parent. Marital satisfaction can also be influenced by satisfaction about other aspects of your life, such as job, friendships, in-laws, and children.

Studies that have examined how marital satisfaction changes over the family life cycle have found that satisfaction tends to be at the high point for both men and women in the early years of marriage (Waller and Hill, 1951; Lupri and Frideres, 1981). Some studies have referred to these early weeks and months as the "honeymoon stage," because everything seems new and exciting and considerable satisfaction is gained from spending time together as a couple, developing a sexual relationship, and sharing a home. Very soon after the wedding, however, researchers have noted a generalized disillusionment, often leading to conflict, but also to separation and divorce. This disillusionment has been found to be more prevalent among men than women and is associated with those who see their partner in highly romantic and idealistic terms prior to marriage (Landis, 1948; Hobart, 1958; Pineo, 1969; Rubin, Peplau, and Hill, 1981). When disillusionment sets in, conflict may develop, initially from apparently trivial issues that could permeate the relationship if not resolved.

Conflict Resolution

Living with another person inevitably involves differences of opinion, unresolvable dilemmas, and external pressures, as well as joys and pleasures. Throughout the years of marriage, the most important factor stressed by marriage counsellors for a viable and satisfying relationship is good communication skills. If marital partners understand how the other thinks and feels about a variety of issues, it is easier to weather differences of opinion, conflict over finances or sex, changes in interests, or marital transgressions.

In marriage, conflict is not always detrimental. Open conflict may lead to negotiated order (Scanzoni, 1982), if those involved openly state their positions and attempt to show some respect for the view of the other. If rules are established about the boundaries of conflict, and these rules are always respected, then open disagreement can be resolved. On the other hand, if one partner is forced reluctantly to give in to the other's wishes, this may be worse than open conflict. Although it may appear that the couple is co-operating, this pattern may actually deepen hostility.

People learn ways of interacting and resolving conflict from their family experiences, and often have difficulty relearning "healthier" behavioural patterns. In an argument, for example, before one partner has finished his or her statement, the other may retaliate on the basis

CREATIVE CONFLICT RESOLUTION

By Donald P. Cushman

Conflict. You find it everywhere—in schools, in businesses, in government agencies, in churches, in social clubs, in professional organizations and in families. Conflict occurs whenever people disagree sharply on issues, when they hear but do not listen, look but only see one perspective in a dispute. As a normal part of human interaction, conflict cannot be avoided, but it can be overcome.

Whether between family members, professionals in a work setting or neighbours, disputes are universal. The way in which such conflicts are resolved, however, is not.

Two behaviours influence the methods used to resolve conflicts—assertiveness and co-operation. Assertiveness means the degree to which one person tries to satisfy *personal* interests and needs. Co-operation refers to how much that same individual tries to help others satisfy *their* interests and needs. In any particular conflict, a person might score high on the assertiveness scale and low on the co-operation scale, while someone else scores just the opposite. An individual's "score," or combination of assertiveness and co-operation, determines which of the five strategies will be used to resolve conflicts. (See Figure 4.1.) The five strategies are:

- Withdrawal—When little attempt is made to satisfy either personal needs or the needs of others, a person withdraws from conflict.
- Enforcement—The individual who has a deep personal interest in the outcome of the conflict but does not care much about the needs of others will often use the strategy of enforcement to resolve a dispute. The power to enforce comes from age, control of resources, a person's role in the group, etc.
- Acquiescence—The person who does not have a personal interest or stake in the conflict but who does care about the needs of others will usually give in, or acquiesce.
- Compromise—When an attempt is made to find an answer in which the gains and losses of both parties are equal, compromise is tried. However, compromises leave the interests and needs of each person only *partially* satisfied.
- Collaboration—The collaborative

resolution integrates the interests and needs of each person so that everyone wins in the end. It requires the full understanding of all viewpoints.

In the special case of families, a conflict seldom arises in which those involved do not care about the outcome for themselves or about the needs of the others involved. Because of this interest in self and other family members, compromise and collaboration seem to be the appropriate strategies for the resolution of most family conflicts.

Although compromise can be useful, it can also breed frustration and mistrust. Those involved may become frustrated when their personal needs are only partially met, and they tend to "keep tabs" on others to make sure that the terms of the compromise have not been violated. The strategy of compromise may create a battleground in the struggle to equalize and influence.

Collaborative resolutions, on the other hand, encourage openness and honesty. Because collaborative strategies seek to meet everyone's needs, information is shared freely and without suspicion. Power is shared equally, and consensus is required before any action is taken. Thus, collaboration:

- promotes an understanding of everyone's perspective
- increases communication, co-operation and interdependence
- instills a feeling of integrity, trust and mutual support

A number of steps are required to formulate an effective resolution through collaboration.

1. Identify the issue from which the conflict arose.
2. Understand the interests and needs of each person involved.
3. Construct a resolution that integrates all interests and needs.

Although collaboration seems like a simple method of analyzing and resolving conflicts, it is not. Time, patience, and a belief in the integrity of others are essential. But once this method and its underlying values are adopted, conflict resolution, in whatever setting, has the potential for becoming an effective learning experience for all.

Figure 4.1 **The Degree to Which a Person Tries to Satisfy Personal Needs and the Needs of Others Determines the Choice of Conflict Resolution Strategy**

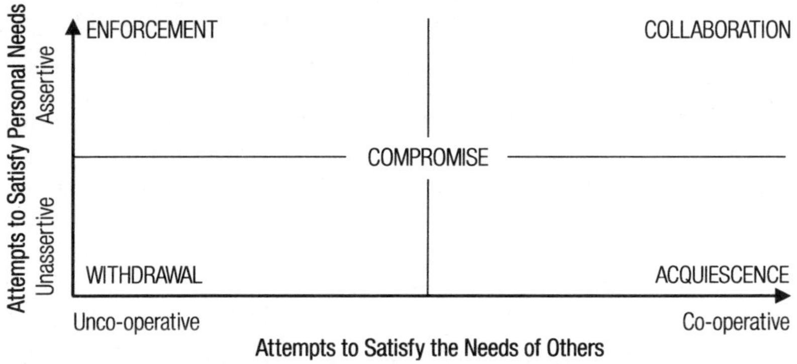

Source: "Creative Conflict Resolution" (article and diagram) by Donald Cushman which appeared in J.C. Penney Forum.

of what they think the other is thinking or is about to say. These misinterpretations may result from feelings of low self-esteem and inadequacy developed in childhood. As part of family therapy, couples are often encouraged to listen carefully to each other without confronting the other or misinterpreting the message. To reinforce that they are communicating effectively, the therapist may ask each to repeat what they think their partner just said, but rephrasing it in their own words.

Covert conflict involving emotional withholding or underlying hostility can be potentially more dangerous to the relationship than open conflict. Some couples attempt to avoid potential conflict by not discussing a troublesome issue or pretending it does not exist. When one partner feels strongly that he or she is right, it is difficult to fight according to the rules and not overstep the invisible boundaries. This could lead to serious fights, including marital violence.

Marital Violence

Every day, we witness violence in sports, movies, comics, and on the televised news. We see it so often that we have almost normalized the idea that power is abused and physical force is used when we are angry or cannot have what we want. More powerful people often try to exert their will on the less powerful by arguing in a louder voice, hurling verbal insults, or threatening them with physical or emotional punishment. This happens all the time, both within families and in other aspects of life.

Physical violence is only one form of abuse within marital relationships, but it has recently come to the attention of the police, social workers, and researchers. Most of the reports of marital violence are from female victims, perhaps because men are less likely to admit being abused by women, but also because men have not been discouraged from taking out their frustration in physical violence in our society. Due to men's greater average size and strength, the potential for physical harm is much greater when men abuse women. Consequently, the public has become very concerned about preventing this kind of conflict and assisting women and children to protect themselves from further abuse.

In recent years, the incidence of marital violence reported to the authorities has grown dramatically throughout North America. Canadian research in the early 1980s estimated that one in ten women in Canada is psychologically, physically, or sexually battered by her husband or live-in partner (McLeod, 1980), even though many of these incidents are not reported to the police. Depending on how "wife battering" or "wife abuse" is defined, estimates have varied, but the one in ten figure is thought to be conservative by people who work with battered women (McLeod, 1989).

Some researchers have tried to relate this apparent increase in family violence to changes in bargaining power within marriage, as well as to increased levels of unemployment, financial stress, and substance abuse. A large part of the apparent increase, however, has been caused by new laws making it illegal to force a spouse to have sex and laws requiring professionals and ordinary citizens to report abusive behaviour. Previously victims were expected to tolerate abuse and keep it behind closed doors. Social attitudes have now changed. Social service workers are becoming more sympathetic and helpful to victims. Partners charged with family violence are now more likely to be arrested and convicted than in the past, when police and the courts saw such violence as a private family matter. In turn, increased enforcement of the law encourages reporting. These factors have increased the visibility of family violence but whether there is actually more abuse than before remains under dispute.

The vast majority of reported abuse cases involve a male perpetrator and a female victim. Some studies, however, claim that women are also heavily involved in abusing their partner, although they acknowledge that this behaviour is less likely to be reported to police or social workers, is less consequential in terms of physical harm, and more often occurs as acts of self-defence (Strauss and Gelles, 1990; Brinkerhoff and Lupri, 1988). Because women are usually the victims and men the perpetrators, some researchers object to the term "family violence" as misleading and even ideological; they prefer to use the phrase "violence against women."

The Canadian Urban **Victimization Study** found that separated women have higher rates of assault than divorced or married women and that fewer than half of cases are reported to the police. In most cases of "spousal violence," physical abuse is not an isolated event (Johnson, 1990). Some abused women are assaulted on numerous occasions by their male partners or former partners and have sought help many times from neighbours, friends, social workers, and police. Several factors, however, work together to maintain women's vulnerability. Men's aggression against women is maintained by patriarchal ideas that men should be in control of a relationship and by the prevalence of violence in the media and other aspects of society.

Until recently, police did not seriously respond to calls about domestic violence because they perceived that women did not want charges laid or would later withdraw them (McLeod, 1989:ii; Johnson, 1990). There is now a nation-wide policy for police to charge men who batter. Shortage of temporary and low-income housing, inability to support themselves and their children, and lack of knowledge about where to turn for assistance prevents many wives from leaving an abusive home with their children. Some women continue to tolerate abuse because of a feeling that it may somehow be their own fault. Especially those abused as children may suffer from low self-esteem and feel that they are not worthy of better treatment. Many more women, however, fear reprisal from their spouses or former spouses who have threatened to kill them if they go to the police. The enormous publicity recently given to women killed by their partners indicates that in many cases, fear of reprisal is entirely justified.

Policy-makers, social service agencies, women's groups, police,

LAYING CHARGES SAVES WIVES

Mandatory counts for wife-beating help reduce violence

BY SEAN FINE
Social Policy Reporter

Laying criminal charges against wife-beaters without giving the assaulted women a say in the matter helps to reduce violence in families, a study by London's Family Court Clinic has found.

The study of the Ontario city's requirement that a charge be laid when a wife is assaulted suggests that it may take years to persuade police departments to carry out such a policy as a matter of course, but that eventually it begins to work.

In May 1981, London became the first jurisdiction in Canada in which police were instructed to ignore the wishes of the assaulted woman and lay charges in all cases where reasonable and probable grounds for charges exist, Dr. Peter Jaffe said. A similar policy has since been instituted for the RCMP, and by provincial solicitors-general for local police forces all across the country.

Based on interviews with 90 assaulted women and 133 police officers, it found that violence was "significantly reduced" in a majority of cases in the year after charges were laid by police.

"There are women who reported literally dozens of beatings where they would be kicked, slapped and punched. After the police investigation it did not happen again, period," Dr. Jaffe, director of the clinic and the report's main researcher, said in an interview.

No such reduction was found among families where the police were not involved, or where police investigated but did not lay charges.

Mandatory laying of charges "makes the violence a public issue," Dr. Jaffe said. "The only reason violence is allowed to continue is people get away with it."

Jim Wilson, 53, said he beat his wife for 15 years and was never charged. He wished he had been.

"If I'd been charged by police I might have gone for help," he said in an interview after being contacted through a London counselling agency. "It used to be the woman laid the charge, but by the time it got to court they're into the honeymoon stage, [the man] crying, 'Oh, I'm so sorry,' then she drops the charges and the next thing you know, he's doing it again.

"When the police lay it, it doesn't get dropped, and the man has to face what he did."

London police laid charges in 89 percent of the wife-assault cases last year, compared with 67 percent in 1983 and 3 percent in 1979, Dr. Jaffe said. And 52 percent of officers interviewed said the policy is effective, up from 33 percent five years earlier.

Other police departments vary widely in their enforcement of mandatory-charging policies, Dr. Jaffe said. "There are still police forces that...unless the victim vigorously demands that charges be laid, the police won't do it."

Among the study's key findings:

- Women are more likely to follow through as witnesses when police lay charges than when they lay charges themselves.
- Courts tend to be tougher on offenders when police, rather than victims, lay charges.
- More experienced police officers tended to express more support for mandatory charging than did junior officers.

The policy does not seem to deter wives from calling the police, Dr. Jaffe said, noting that the women in the study tended to call the police again if another situation arose (25 percent of the women were threatened, and 9 percent were physically abused, while the charges were before the courts). As well, 87 percent said they would call the police again.

Only 11 percent of charges were dismissed or withdrawn in 1988 and 1989, compared with 16 percent in 1983 and 38 percent in 1979.

The Globe and Mail, 5 July 1991.

---

and researchers have developed new ways of dealing with marital violence against women. Many of the programs deal with crisis-intervention with the women involved. When social workers intervene in an incidence of domestic violence, the woman is usually assisted in developing a protection plan that could involve laying charges against her spouse or ex-spouse, finding transitional housing, engaging a lawyer, and if necessary, acquiring welfare payments to cover her living costs. Either through individual counselling or group therapy, battered wives are helped to restructure their thinking about violence and view it as unacceptable regardless of their own behaviour.

Increasingly the male batterer is charged with an offence, but also provided with opportunities for counselling. This often involves explicitly accepting responsibility for his acts of violence rather than blaming his partner, learning to control his emotions, developing better communication skills, and learning nonviolent behaviour from male role models.

Action against family violence has also included public education for most services and governments. For example, sensitization workshops are being provided for judges to increase their knowledge of program options and the implication of this form of violence for women, their families, men who batter, and the wider society (McLeod, 1989:ii). In addition, support services have been provided for families who are perceived to be "at risk" of violence because of their stressful circumstances.

Although governments at all levels have voiced their concern about family violence, and specifically violence against women and children, money is a major impediment to establishing new programs and transitional housing. Many transition houses for battered women are funded by private donations, staffed by volunteers, and operate on the verge of closing due to lack of funds. Follow-up therapy and counselling may also be necessary for the entire family, but these services also cost money to establish and maintain. Despite the serious nature of marital violence, new program funding for the rising number

HELPING ABUSIVE MEN

Studies show counselling reduces violence against women

BY ANDREW DRESCHEL
Hamilton Spectator

HAMILTON, Ont.—Counselling programs for abusive men are effective in stopping violence against women, a host of studies have found.

Research consistently indicates the majority of men stop physically abusive behavior following group treatment.

According to a comprehensive review of research literature published last year, the percentage of men who stop battering after treatment ranges from 53 to 85 percent.

The review, based on more than 120 American and Canadian studies dealing with batterers and treatment programs, is by University of Illinois researchers Richard Tolman and Larry Bennett. It appeared in the *Journal of Interpersonal Violence.*

The authors acknowledge that evaluating program effectiveness is difficult due to different treatment techniques and methods of measuring success.

Some studies use reduction of violent behavior as a criteria; others use complete cessation of violence; others factor in threats and psychological mistreatment.

Lower success rates tended to occur in programs with lengthier follow-ups and when success was based on women's reports.

At least one study found women reported less fear of their partners, decreased conflict, increased comfort in expressing anger, and increased closeness to their partners following men's treatment.

The review also points out police arrests are a more effective deterrent against domestic violence than separation or mediation, and that men who have a shorter history of abuse and who attend treatment programs on the instruction of the courts are more likely to be successful in stopping abuse.

The authors conclude that programs for victims should be the highest priority, but services for men who batter do play a role in ending wife abuse.

Donna Gannon, co-ordinator of the domestic violence treatment program with COHR Family Services in Burlington, says attempts to measure the success of programs for wife abusers is unfair.

Gannon points out men's programming for wife assault is only 11 years old in Ontario and for the first six or so years programs tended to be short-term—10 to 20 weeks.

"We know now that that is crazy. That's far too little, that nothing is going to change in that short of time. It's a much bigger, more complex problem than that."

All research shows counselling is effective to a degree, said Gannon. But true results won't be known until the long-term can be evaluated.

The first programs to stop batterers were developed in the United States about 15 years ago at the urging of women's organizations. There are more than 100 programs in Canada. Many are influenced or shaped by feminist perspectives.

"Men's treatment came out of listening to abused women and what they wanted," said Gannon. "What many abused women want is not to end a relationship but for the abuse to stop.

"The solution is not always kicking him out of the picture. For one thing, he's going to have an ongoing involvement in that family if there are children."

Courtesy of *The Hamilton Spectator*, 27 June 1991.

---

of reported victims and their abusers is difficult to find.

Recent research has noted the prevalence of physical and sexual violence in dating and courtship, and a relationship between courtship violence and marital violence. For example, in a Canadian sample of 202 male college students by Barnes, Greenwood, and Sommer (1991), 42 percent of the sample reported that they engaged in some form of courtship violence. An American study by O'Leary et al., (1989) found that the chance of spouse abuse was over three times greater if violence had also occurred during courtship. Research has also found that adults who batter their spouses or children have often come from families where their parents engaged in similar behaviour.

These studies have led to two theories about marital violence. The intergenerational theory suggests that solving conflicts through physical or verbal violence is learned from previous family or interpersonal experiences. The patriarchal theory adds that the prevalence of violence against wives is symptomatic of the low status of women, the social acceptability of violence toward those considered most vulnerable, and the way in which family life has previously been protected from intrusion by the law. Now that women have objected to abuse by their partners, and social services are available to assist them, this kind of behaviour, which always existed, appears to be more prevalent (Hird, 1992).

A third theory of marital violence sees it as a misguided way of resolving conflicts, which is used by husbands who feel that their authority within the family is being threatened. The solution to the problem within this systems framework is to offer men or couples therapy sessions to improve their communication skills, learn to control emotions, and to become more assertive about their feelings and needs without resorting to violence. This theory is not necessarily incompatible with the intergenerational and patriarchal theories; not everyone who has witnessed spousal abuse or who lives in a society that condones violence against women becomes abusive. Each theory contributes to the explanation of the perpetuation of violence against women and children.

While some battered women remain in abusive relationships for many years, an increasing number are leaving and obtaining divorces. As we will see in the next section, divorce rates are only crude indicators of marital conflict; many couples remain in conflict-ridden marriages; others separate without legal agreements.

Separation and Divorce

Marital Instability, Unhappiness, and Divorce

Despite the wedding vows that are exchanged and people's high expectations of marriage, marital instability is increasingly prevalent in North America. Discussions of the extent of marriage instability are usually based on divorce rates. Statistics Canada compiles and measures the number of divorces per 100 000 population each year or the number of divorces per marriages in the same year. Because there are no official statistics on marital separation, researchers tend to focus on legal divorce. It has been estimated, however, that the rate of marital separation may be as high as the divorce rate (McVey and Robinson, 1981). Therefore, marriage dissolution in any year could be twice as high as government divorce figures imply.

Divorce rates have been rising throughout the twentieth century, but increased sharply in Canada after 1968 when the grounds for divorce were liberalized. Before 1925, legal divorce was very restricted, expensive, and easier for men than for women to obtain. A new ground was created for divorce in 1968 called "marriage breakdown," which was strictly defined but made divorce more accessible.

With the 1986 legal changes, "marriage breakdown" has been more liberally defined by a one-year separation.

Numerous factors have pushed up divorce rates in developed societies. With industrialization, many young people moved away from family restrictions and raised their expectations of personal fulfilment. Growing individualism discouraged the view of marriage as sacred or related primarily to family lineage, obligation, or procreation. People began to feel that they had the right to personal happiness, fair treatment, and love in marriage. The entrance of married women into the labour force allowed women to support themselves outside marriage and gave them increased opportunities to meet new people and to compare their personal situations. Improved birth control made it possible to separate sex and marriage, permitting more discreet extramarital relations for both men and women, but placing a strain on existing marital relationships.

As well as societal changes leading to divorce, marriages under certain social and psychological conditions tend to lead to unresolved conflict and separation. Researchers have found that those who marry well below the average age, especially if the bride is pregnant, have above-average chances of being unhappy in their marriages and divorcing (Lee, 1977; Ambert, 1980:75; Albrecht et al., 1983:29ff). This suggests that emotional and social immaturity, an incomplete education, inability to be self-supporting, and lack of opportunity to adjust to marriage before the strains of pregnancy jeopardize the stability of many marriages.

Studies have also found that those who have been previously divorced and people with divorced parents are also more likely to end their marriages (Beaujot, 1990). This may simply suggest that people with previous experience of marriage dissolution in their family see divorce as a viable alternative to an unhappy marriage. With a divorced person as role model, they know from experience that there is life after marriage, that it is possible to make a transition from being married to being single. They also may be aware of the legal procedures involved. On the other hand, it may indicate that people learn unhealthy ways of resolving marital conflict from their parents. Since more young people now come from families in which their parents' marriages have dissolved, this will likely contribute to high divorce rates in the future.

Large age discrepancies, differences in cultural, religious or socio-economic background, as well as the absence of religious affiliation are also related to high divorce rates. This does not mean that anyone who enters a "mixed" marriage or who does not attend religious services regularly will get a divorce. It simply means that these people have a greater chance, presumably because they are less traditional people.

As will be discussed in the section on the Childfree Alternative, couples without children have higher probabilities of divorce. This should not imply that childless couples are not as satisfied or happy with their marriages as parents, but that it is easier to obtain a legal divorce and survive economically afterwards if a couple does not have to agree on the custody and financial support of the children.

Researchers have also found that employed married women consider divorce as an option more often than homemakers (Huber and Spitze, 1980; Albrecht and Kunz, 1980). Women who can support themselves financially initiate the decision to separate more often than women who are financially dependent on their husbands. Ambert (1983) further concluded that high-income divorced women felt less social and financial pressure to remarry.

These and other studies suggest that although all marriages experience conflict, some may experience more conflict than others. Furthermore, the way in which this conflict is resolved may relate to

Table 4.1 **Divorce Rates in Canada, 1921–1989**

Year	Rate per 100 000 Population
1921	6.4
1931	6.8
1941	21.4
1951	37.6
1961	36.0
1971	137.6
1981	278.0
1982	285.9
1983	275.5
1984	259.5
1985	244.4
1986	308.3
1987	355.1
1988	308.1
1989	307.8

Source: Statistics Canada, *Marriages and Divorces. Vital Statistics,* Vol. II. Ottawa: Supply and Services Canada, annual publication; Wayne J. Millar. "Divorces, Canada and the Provinces, 1989." *Health Reports* 3 (1) 1991:83. Reproduced with the permission of the Minister of Supply and Services Canada, 1992.

Table 4.2 **Divorces per 1000 Population in Selected Countries, 1988**

COUNTRY	DIVORCES PER 1000 POPULATION
Canada	3.10
Australia (1987)	2.44
Denmark	2.88
England and Wales	2.89
France (1987)	1.91
Greece (1986)	0.87
Hungary	2.25
Iran (1987)	0.65
Italy	0.44
Japan	1.25
Poland	1.27
Sri Lanka	0.16
Spain (1982)	0.60
Sweden	2.26
Turkey	0.41
United States	4.80
Former USSR	3.35

Source: United Nations. *Demographic Yearbook 1989.* New York, 1991:513–515.

parental role models but also to opportunities to leave the marriage. Many unhappy couples stay together because they see no alternative to their present relationship or means of support, or they are pressured by friends and relatives to either resolve their differences or learn to live with them. At the same time, other individuals who claim they were happy in their marriages obtain a divorce because their partner appeared to "fall out of love" or became involved with someone else. In other cases, conflict escalated to the point of divorce because neither partner knew how to stop it.

Divorce and Matrimonial Property

Changing gender roles, the liberalization of divorce laws, increasing number of dual-earner families, and greater expectations of marriage as a vehicle of personal fulfilment have both heightened the stresses on modern marriage and increased the opportunities to leave an unhappy marriage. As table 4.1 indicates, the divorce rate in Canada rose almost consistently from 1921 to 1982. Since 1983, however, the rate declined slightly until 1986, when it sharply increased. The 1986 and 1987 increases in the divorce rate were influenced by the legal change that redefined marriage breakdown as one year of separation. There was probably a backlog of petitioners who waited for the law to change before they applied for divorce.

After the 1971 Murdoch case in Alberta, many groups lobbied for changes in the division of matrimonial property after divorce because they felt that women were receiving a smaller share and that their unpaid contributions to households were not being considered. In the Murdoch case, the wife ran the family farm for several months of each year while her husband worked out of town. The 25-year marriage broke up after he physically assaulted her, but the court gave the farm to the husband because his name was on the deed and most of the money used to purchase it came from him. The wife was given $200 per month alimony, but was also allowed to continue to live in the farmhouse (Dranoff, 1977:52). This court case, and others that followed, precipitated legal change in Canada.

Dividing matrimonial property equally after divorce has now become the guiding rule in many Canadian provinces. Yet, because women do not earn equal incomes to men, women often end up living in poverty after marriage dissolution. For these reasons, issues of child support, custody, and the division of matrimonial property remain contentious. The next chapter looks more closely at the situation of one-parent families and why so many live in poverty.

High divorce rates and problems resolving support and custody issues also exist in many other industrialized countries. However, Canada's divorce rate is moderate compared with that of other industrialized countries. While Canada had a rate of 3.10 divorces per 1000 population in 1988, other countries such as England, the United States, and the former Soviet Union had much higher rates. On the other hand, divorce has been legally restricted in countries such as Spain, Italy, Greece, and many Asian nations. This does not mean that marriages do not dissolve in these countries, for couples can sometimes legally separate and live with someone else, or they can obtain a divorce in a neighbouring country. Table 4.2 shows the divorce rate per 1000 population in selected countries.

The next section will examine decision making and the division of labour changes among families in which both partners work outside the home.

DUAL-EARNER FAMILIES: DECISION MAKING AND THE DIVISION OF LABOUR

In the past 20 years, the proportion of married women in the Canadian labour force has risen dramatically. Among married people aged 25 to 44, for example, about 75 percent of women and 96 percent of men were working for pay in 1989. By contrast, only 48 percent of married women and 97 percent of married men between those ages were in the labour force in 1975 (Labour Canada, 1990:21).

According to Statistics Canada, 62 percent of all husband-wife families were dual-earner families in 1986 compared with 34 percent in 1967 (Moore, 1990:162). Since two incomes are increasingly needed to counteract the rising cost of living, it is not surprising that dual-earner families are more likely than traditional-earner families to have higher incomes.

When both partners are working for pay, decisions about major purchases are often made jointly because part of the money comes from each pay cheque. Although many couples have joint bank accounts for household purchases, they might also have separate

Figure 4.2 **Dual- and Traditional-Earner Families as a Percentage of All Husband-Wife Families, 1967 and 1986**

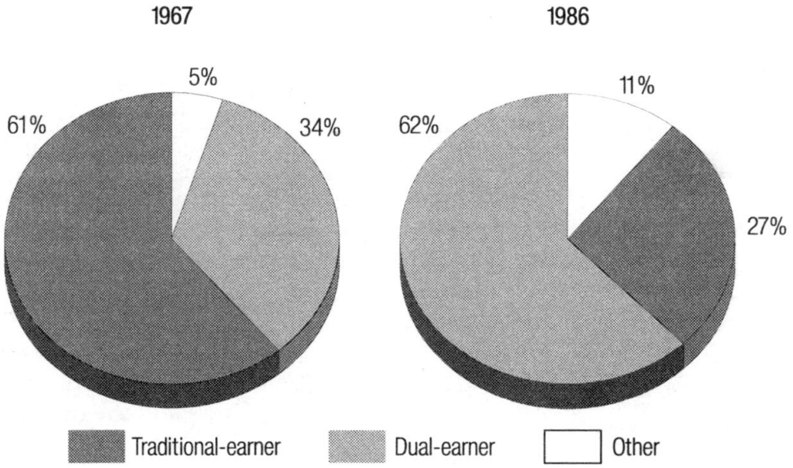

Source: Statistics Canada, Labour and Household Surveys Analysis Division. Reproduced with the permission of the Minister of Supply and Services Canada, 1992.

Figure 4.3 **Dual Earners as a Proportion of Husband-Wife Families, by Income Quintile, 1986**

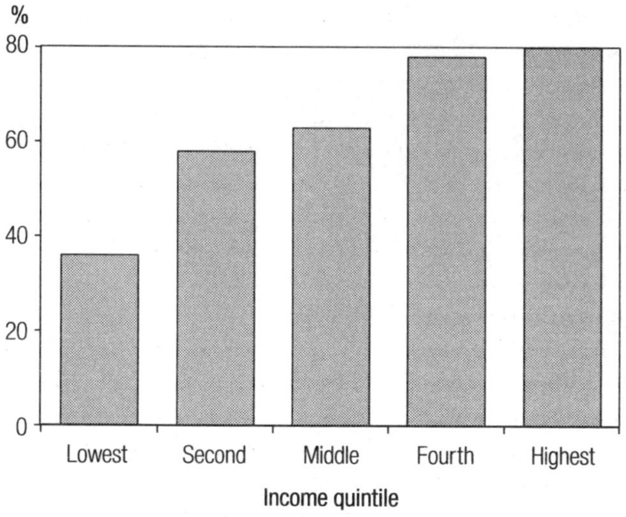

Source: Statistics Canada, Labour and Household Surveys Analysis Division. Reproduced by permission of the Minister of Supply and Services Canada, 1992.

accounts and make purchases without consulting each other. Some couples do not have joint bank accounts; instead each pays for separate items in the household budget or makes contributions as expenses arise. For married women, these latter situations could differ substantially from their grandparents' generation, when many wives had to ask permission to buy something with money earned by their husbands. While we know that some wives controlled the family finances even when their husbands earned most of the money, many husbands in one-income families would have retained the **power of the purse**, or the power to make spending decisions.

Research on family decision making indicates that wives who work for pay increase their bargaining power in the relationship. For one thing their husbands are slightly more likely to be involved in routine housework (Seccombe, 1989; Asner and Livingstone, 1990). Wives' money is often essential in determining whether or not couples can ever afford to buy a house, take a vacation, or clothe themselves and their children. Therefore, wives feel they have a right to be involved in financial decisions. The relationship between family power and wives' earnings is not clear, however, partly because most husbands earn considerably more money than their wives (Labour Canada, 1990).

Studies of family power and decision-making indicate that other factors besides earnings influence who has the final say when husbands and wives cannot agree. Several decades ago, American sociologists Blood and Wolfe (1960) found that bargaining power in a relationship is affected by access to resources, including higher education, social skills, youth and physical beauty, high income, inherited money, or a combination of all of these. Depending on the circumstances, they concluded that decision-making power may shift from one spouse to the other. This theory of family power has been referred to as the **personal resource theory**.

Other authors (Gillespie, 1971; Kandel and Lesser, 1972) have argued that, although personal resources may give individuals more influence in specific interpersonal situations, these resources are not randomly distributed in the population. We live in a society in which men have more opportunity to acquire these resources simply because they are male. This has been called the **patriarchal society theory** of family decision making and power. In addition to the fact that most of the positions of power and influence in public life are held by men, patriarchy is further perpetuated through a marriage system in which women tend to marry older men who are physically taller than themselves, and who have more education, more job experience, and higher incomes (Baker, 1990). In order to counteract some of the effects of the patriarchal structure of our society, women could marry younger men with less job experience and similar or less education (Gillespie, 1971). Yet, two Canadian studies by Baker, one about personal advertisements in a Toronto newspaper (1982) and the other based on interviews with Canadian adolescents (1985), indicated that many young women still want to marry a man they can "look up to," both in terms of height and experience or expertise.

Regardless of which factors influence family power and decision making, there has been a long-term trend in Canada toward social, legal, and economic equality between husband and wife. Over the past century, there have been numerous legal changes leading in this direction. As women gained more education throughout the twentieth century and entered the labour force in increasing numbers, they fought for these legal changes. With higher education, greater earning power, fewer children, and legal equality, women are achieving more autonomy and moving closer to social and economic equality with men. At the same time, however, women may have lost some of their

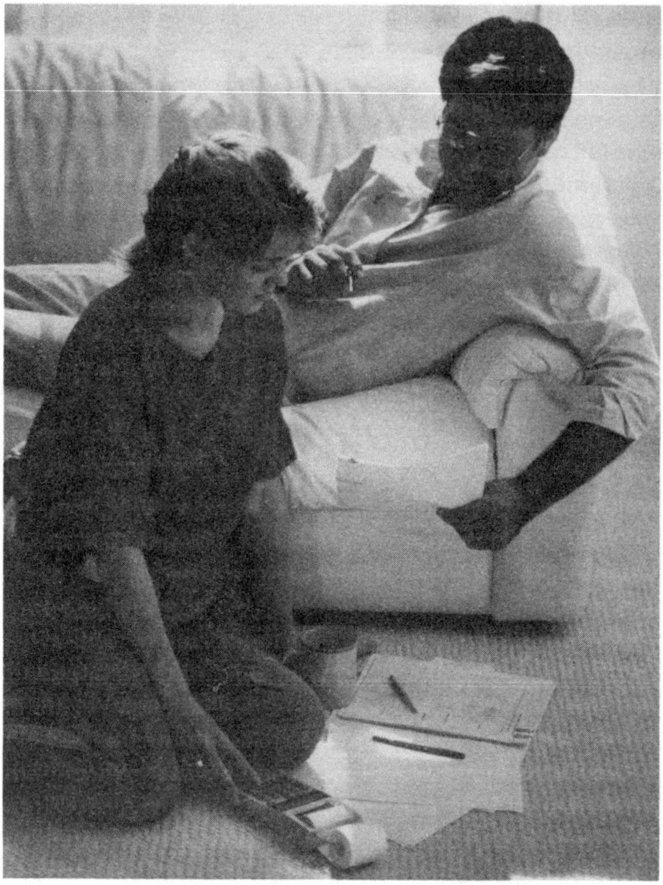

Most couples find it necessary to plan a budget together.

Arthur Tilley/Focus/Tony Stone Worldwide

former control over home and children, now that so many women are absent from the home during the day, and children are cared for by nonfamily members (Armstrong and Armstrong, 1988). Changes in female educational attainment and earning potential have required both men and women to develop new ways of relating.

While changes in role expectations have led to higher educational attainment and paid employment for women, the advantages for men have sometimes been less apparent. Some men have experienced difficulty in adapting to the new reality in which men are no longer heads of households and sole breadwinners. This is especially true when their wives have expected them to do more household chores or have been unwilling to move with their jobs. Other men have been confused about how to address and treat their female colleagues at work, including such minor issues as whether or not to hold open doors, help them with their coats, or allow them to enter the elevator first. More important are some men's concerns that women's employment equality will reduce men's promotional opportunities. If changing gender roles are perceived as a "zero-sum game," men will get less if women gain more.

In the past 50 years, women's family roles have changed considerably while men's have changed more gradually. We could almost say that men have been expected to react and adapt to the changes in women's lives. Because some of the pressure has been taken off men to be the sole or major breadwinner in their families, they may be freer to remain in school longer, to change jobs to find one more conducive to their interests, or develop their leisure interests. Similarly, as gender roles change, men now have the opportunity to express their emotions more honestly and overtly and to develop closer relationships with their children and other adults. They may also be expected

Figure 4.4 **Time Spent on Household Chores, by Main Activity, November 1986**

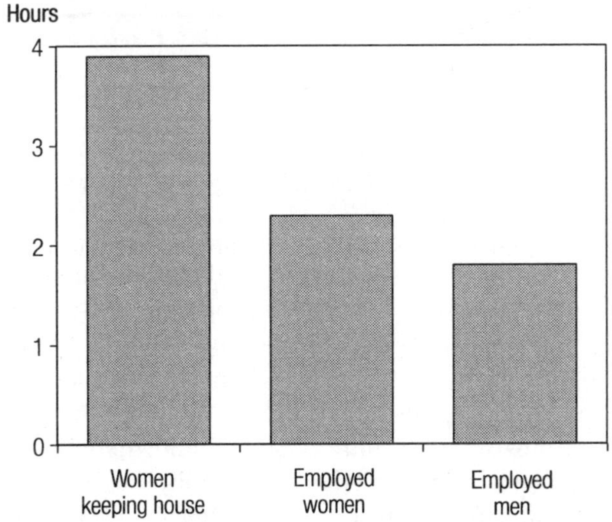

Source: Statistics Canada, *General Social Survey, 1986*. Reproduced with the permission of the Minister of Supply and Services Canada, 1992.

Table 4.3 **Daily Participation in and Time Spent on Household Chores, November 1986**

	PARTICIPATION RATE		AVERAGE TIME SPENT BY PARTICIPANTS	
	WOMEN	MEN	WOMEN	MEN
	%		HOURS/MINUTES	
Age				
15–24	65	40	1:50	1:12
25–44	89	53	3:02	1:50
45–64	93	55	3:24	2:17
65 and over	90	61	3:00	2:11
Total 15 and over	85	52	2:57	1:53
Main activity				
Paid work	83	51	2:16	1:44
Looking for work	84	65	2:43	2:27
Student	57	36	1:28	1:04
Keeping house	97	91	3:52	3:35
Retired	88	62	2:51	2:21
Presence of children under age 19				
Children at home	94	53	3:22	2:01
No children at home	80	51	2:39	1:49

Source: Statistics Canada, General Social Survey, 1986. Reproduced with the permission of the Minister of Supply and Services Canada, 1992.

to do more housework and child care and to consider their wives' interests and employment when making their own personal or family-related decisions.

When women work full-time in the home, the potential for some conflict is reduced as the division of labour is often firmly established (Armstrong and Armstrong, 1988). It is when women work outside the home that the division of labour most often needs to be negotiated. This negotiation process may be most difficult for families in which the wife is re-entering the labour force after many years as a homemaker. This move could require all other family members to adapt to her working hours and the fact that she is unlikely to be able or willing to continue doing most of the housework. In fact, one Canadian study found that wives employed outside the home are less willing than homemakers to move with their husbands' jobs and more likely to make demands on their husband to share the housework (Harrell, 1985).

Despite the legal and labour force changes that have taken place over the past 40 years, studies still conclude that women are responsible for the bulk of household chores. For example, the 1986 Social Survey sponsored by Statistics Canada included questions on household chores, which included meal preparation and clean-up, indoor and outdoor cleaning, laundry, home repairs and maintenance, gardening, pet care, bill paying, and travel to and from these household chores. The survey concluded that while full-time homemakers devoted about four hours a day to housework (excluding child care), women with jobs outside the home are also largely responsible for housework. On a given day, 83 percent of working women did housework and the time they spent averaged about two and a quarter hours. In contrast, half of working men did household chores and they devoted an average of about one and three-quarter hours. Housework patterns for married people were even more divergent: 89 percent of the women compared with 51 percent of the men did housework each day (Marshall, 1990:19).

THE CHILDFREE ALTERNATIVE

Unmarried people have always had opportunities to remain celibate and childfree and to live purposeful and socially accepted lives as members of religious orders. However, traditionally, married couples were expected to bear children, and to some extent this expectation still holds.

Historically, childlessness among married people was a stigma viewed as an indication of ill health, sexual inadequacy, immaturity, a gender identity problem, or selfishness (Veevers, 1980). Sex without procreation also violated the religious belief that the purpose of marriage was procreation. The presence of children in a marriage not only confirmed adult status but also indicated social responsibility, mental and physical health, and selflessness.

As birth control technology has advanced, more married couples have postponed childbearing or have decided to have a childfree marriage. The percentage of couples without children has not increased dramatically, however, because medical technology has also enabled low-fertility couples to reproduce. If some women who previously could not become pregnant are now having children and others are deciding not to have children, the two groups almost cancel each other out in the statistics (Baker, 1990). However, there has been a slight rise in childlessness in Canada in the past decades. About 15-

20 percent of ever-married women are now childless (Eichler, 1988:228) compared with about 14 percent in 1961 (Rao and Balakrishnan, 1986:26). But there are no accurate figures on what percentage of these women are voluntarily childless.

A childfree marriage was not really a viable option for many Canadians until the development and legalization of more effective contraception and abortion in the 1960s. Furthermore, couples lacked positive role models of childfree marriages. About 85 percent of Canadians marry at some point in their lives (Adams and Nagnur, 1990:143) and most of these will produce at least one child. Although motherhood has been portrayed as the major role for women throughout Canada's history, there have always been women who have rebelled against this role.

Many countries, such as Canada, have promoted pronatalist values, encouraging people to reproduce to increase or maintain the population by offering Family Allowances and tax deductions or credits for parents with dependent children. This is presently a major concern in the province of Quebec, where the birth rate is the lowest in Canada and among the lowest in industrialized countries. Consequently, the Quebec government has recently introduced financial incentives in the form of cash grants to parents with newborns to

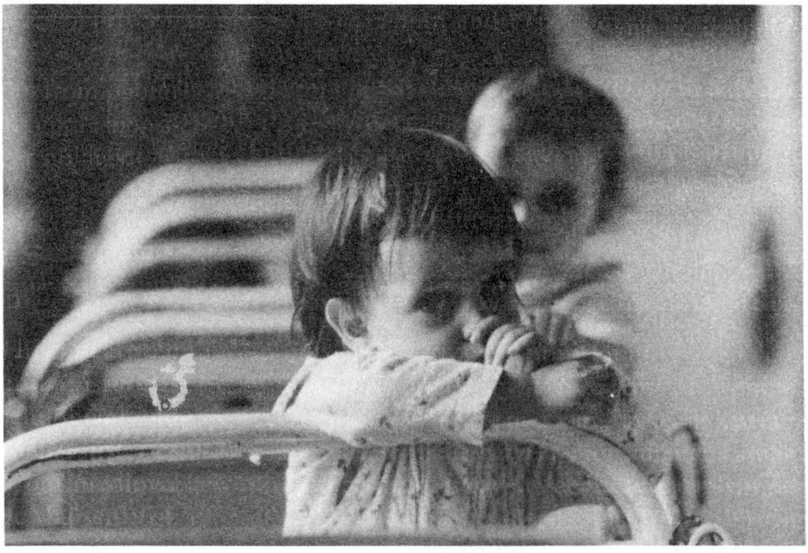

This child is one of many children placed in Romanian orphanages as a result of attempting to raise the birth rate in that country.

Reuters/Bettmann

encourage larger families. Countries such as Romania that prohibited contraception and abortions in an attempt to raise the birth rate later found that many unwanted babies were placed in orphanages.

Despite pronatalist values, contraception and birth control have been practised for thousands of years. Married and unmarried couples practised celibacy to control the population, regulate the sex ratio, or curb their family size. In the best-selling novel by Jean Auel called *Clan of the Cave Bear* (1980), which was based on considerable anthropological research, the prehistoric medicine woman used herbal concoctions to prevent conception and to induce spontaneous abortions. Auel implied that few women knew these "secrets," but those who did kept them to themselves.

In Jean Veevers' Canadian study of childlessness (1980), she found that childless couples tended to perceive that their parents, especially their mothers, had lived unsatisfying lives because they had to sacrifice other activities for childrearing. These childless couples also tended to perceive pregnancy as a form of illness and a condition leading to loss of erotic appeal. They also associated motherhood with dependency and incompetence, and felt that having children would interfere with their career plans, travelling, or the stability of their marriage. According to Veevers' study, voluntarily childless people often lacked child care skills because they were only children, or alternatively, were first-born and experienced too much child care responsibility as children.

The popular myth that couples need children in order to be happy has certainly not been verified in research. Instead, studies have found that childfree couples, and especially men in these marriages, report greater satisfaction with their marriages than parents do (Veroff and Feld, 1970; Ramu, 1984; Burman and de Anda, 1985–86). Childfree couples report various satisfactions with their lifestyle, including spontaneity and avoidance of routine, time to seek out new experiences and develop their skills, and opportunities to travel. While childfree women reported strong commitment to their careers, men tended to emphasize the freedom from having to work to support children, low career involvement, or a varied career history.

Childfree couples tend to have a more egalitarian division of labour according to several studies (Veevers, 1980; Burman and de Anda, 1985-86). The incomes of husbands and wives were more similar than among couples with children, presumably because these wives are not taking time off for childrearing and are more likely than mothers to work full-time. Furthermore, husbands tended to encourage their wives' outside interests and career development.

In industrialized countries, low marriage rates and childlessness have been correlated with high education, continuous employment, and high career involvement for women (but not for men). In a study of women listed in *Who's Who* (Veevers, 1980:81), 24 percent of the ever-married women in the 1970 edition were childless compared with 8 percent of the men. In the 1928 edition, the percentage of childless women was as high as 54 percent. Even though these figures are somewhat outdated, we can see the correlation between high levels of achievement and women's childlessness. If we wanted to update this study, it would be necessary to read the biographies of all women listed in the most recent edition of *Who's Who*, which would be a major study in itself. But since it is now easier to combine career and family, we would expect that the percentage of childless women represented in *Who's Who* has probably fallen below the 1970 level. Yet, the positive correlation between women's childlessness and occupational achievement continues because of the difficulty mothers have in balancing children and career (Lero and Kyle, 1991). This will be discussed in more detail in the Future Trends section of this chapter.

Despite the fact that childless couples tend to report higher levels of satisfaction and happiness in their marriage, they tend to experience higher rates of divorce than couples with children. Although only about 20 percent of couples remain childless throughout their lives, about 50–70 percent of divorces in Canada are obtained by couples with no children (Adams, 1990:147). This can be explained partially by the practical difficulties of divorcing when children are involved and the relative ease in a childfree marriage.

Now that couples have more lifestyle options, more may choose a childless marriage. Yet, there remains considerable social pressure, especially from older friends and relatives, to reproduce to perpetuate the family line or to acquire companionship later in life. In addition, some governments are trying to encourage couples to reproduce in order to maintain the population.

FUTURE TRENDS

THE FUTURE OF MARRIAGE

From the social trends of the past few decades, we can assume that marriage rates will continue to fall as the difference between living together and legal marriage becomes socially and legally blurred.

Increasingly, couples are living together without going through a wedding ceremony although most of these will eventually marry, especially those who intend to have children. Young people who come from divorced families and older divorced adults are often reluctant to enter into legal marriage without some previous knowledge of what it is like to live with their partner. Living together may become more socially acceptable in the future as a "courtship pattern" or preliminary stage to marriage. In addition, those who are ideologically opposed to traditional marital roles will continue to see common-law relationships as an alternative to legal marriage.

People who live together before marriage are often those who question social customs and traditions and who are willing to go against societal norms. Those who for religious or other reasons do not believe that living together without legal marriage is morally right are also less likely to think of divorce as a viable option. While cohabitation may give potential marital partners a more realistic notion of what they are getting into, it is not a way of ensuring a more stable marriage.

Because couples who live together before legal marriage experience higher divorce rates than those who have never lived common-law, we may see more marriage instability in the future. As more people question traditions in gender relations, role expectations, and marriage, we will probably see more variety in living arrangements, marriage contracts, wedding ceremonies, and marriage lifestyle.

An increasing number of couples are living apart for temporary periods or even as permanent arrangements in order to pursue post-secondary education or take on more challenging jobs. Commuting couples may not share one home, but rather have two. Each may maintain their own set of friends, bank account, car, and their own household responsibilities. Working men, such as sales representatives, sailors, members of the armed forces, or migrant workers, have often had to spend weeks and months apart from their wives and families in order to make a living. But now, middle-class women are requiring their partners to accommodate their career plans by moving to another city or by commuting. Commuter marriages are most typical among dual-career couples in which both have high-level jobs and incomes, because this arrangement is expensive and requires high career commitment from both partners. As well-paid professional and managerial positions become harder to find, commuter marriages may become more prevalent. However, because of the expense and difficulties involved, it is not expected that many couples will opt for this kind of lifestyle.

COMMON-LAW RELATIONSHIPS NOT LIKE MARRIAGE, GROUP SAYS

BY ANDRÉ PICARD
Quebec Bureau

MONTREAL—Despite the phenomenal increase in common-law relationships, they should not be considered the legal equivalent of marriage, the Quebec Council on the Status of Women says in a new report.

"It is important to maintain the distinction between marriage and common-law relationships, essentially because they are two different types of commitments and all individuals should maintain freedom of choice when it comes to their personal relationships," council president Marie Lavigne said yesterday at a news conference.

She said marriage is an official, public act that entails legal consequences if there is a breakup, notably division of assets, alimony and child support.

While marriage is a "commitment to the present and the future," Ms. Lavigne said, common-law relationships are a "commitment uniquely to the present" with few legal ramifications.

According to the 1986 census, one in eight Quebec women lived in a common-law relationship—one in four under the age of 35—and the number is estimated to have at least doubled. One clue to the growth of the phenomenon is provided by Statistics Quebec, which found that 38 percent of children were born "outside marriage" in 1990, up from 27 percent in 1986.

Ms. Lavigne said that there is a common misconception that couples "become automatically married" after a certain period of time living together, as is the case in many provinces. Under Quebec's Civil Code, she said, there is no such provision, and none should be added.

Another stereotype is that poor, uneducated people "shack up." In fact, the study found that common-law relationships are most popular with professional women; the majority of women living common-law earn more money and are better educated than both married women and their own male partners.

Ms. Lavigne stressed that the council, an advisory body to the provincial government, is not advocating common-law relationships over marriage or vice versa.

"I can only say that marriage no longer implies a relationship of inequity, as it did in the past," she said. "We respect whatever choice a woman makes."

Ms. Lavigne also noted that various social welfare laws that have provisions for marital equivalency are inconsistent. For example, unemployment insurance programs consider common-law couples married after three years of co-habitation (one year if they have a child). Welfare programs, on the other hand, consider people married if they have a child or if they have lived together for a year.

"The council would like the state, in all its social welfare legislation, to remain neutral, to treat equally all people regardless of their personal choice of marriage or common-law relationship," Ms. Lavigne said.

The Globe and Mail, 20 November 1991.

Delayed marriage and delayed childbearing are definitely on the increase in Canada. This suggests that more couples will live for longer periods of time in nonfamily households, in a lifestyle that focuses on work, career development, leisure pursuits, and travel. Undoubtedly, many will become accustomed to this lifestyle and decide to adopt a childfree marriage permanently. If many people make this choice, policy-makers will certainly become concerned about the future of the nation's population. But in addition to population decline, more childfree marriages could lead to higher divorce rates. Without concerns about child custody and support, the procedures of separation and divorce are much simpler legally, if not emotionally.

Future Gender Roles

As more married women enter the labour force and take on full-time jobs, the division of labour both within the family and in the labour force will gradually change. Initially, however, as working hours shrink for paid workers, men rather than women may have more leisure time. While more men may choose to spend this time with their friends and families, the pressures of women's "double workload" may persuade more men to share child care and housework.

The transition to shared housework may be more difficult than people realize. Few people of either sex want to do housework after working for pay all day. Furthermore, some adults have never taken the time to learn certain skills and may be reluctant to learn. In order to attain equality in the division of labour, parents and educators will have to teach children to perform all household tasks and encourage them to expect equality in their future homes. Yet, children tend to learn by role models rather than explicitly being told something and without egalitarian models, many children will receive a different message.

In the future more households will hire cleaners for a few hours each week, increasing service jobs, but this is likely to remain an option for families with higher incomes, and the occupation is likely to remain female-dominated because of low wages and benefits. New labour-saving devices will undoubtedly be invented as well, although these will also be costly and require higher family incomes. Increasingly, children and husbands in dual-earner families will be expected to do more housework. It is unlikely, however, that many men will want to become homemakers in the future for the same reasons that women are rejecting this job—it is unpaid and retains low status. Yet, many policy-makers and researchers have pointed out that equality in the labour force cannot be achieved without equality in the home (Armstrong, 1990, Lero and Kyle, 1991).

Many people have argued that there has been more change in attitudes than behaviour relating to gender roles. Young couples *say* that they are in favour of equality in marriage, yet studies of the division of labour indicate that traditional roles and expectations are being perpetuated in most households. Women have acquired greater access to paid employment, are now better able to support themselves, have gained bargaining power in marriage, and are better able to leave relationships if they are not working out. Yet, women are still more likely to be offered and to accept jobs which replicate the homemaker/mother role, such as nurse, teacher, cleaning woman, baby-sitter, or secretary. Only recently have women made inroads into nontraditional jobs, including professions such as medicine and law. Although a few women have entered skilled labour jobs, technical and scientific jobs have remained dominated by men (Labour Canada, 1990:16). Furthermore, men have not entered female-dominated jobs, such as day-care worker, nurse, elementary school teacher, or secretary, in any significant numbers for the same reasons they have not voluntarily accepted full responsibility for household chores.

With high rates of unemployment, more opportunities for self-employment and increased rates of separation, divorce, and joint physical custody of children, men may find themselves spending more time in the household with more responsibility for housework. As more women work full-time in the labour force, men may devote time and attention to cooking, shopping, and developing closer ties with their children. In addition, as family roles and obligations affect people's performance on the job, changes in men's family relationships and the increased presence of women in higher-level jobs may force employers to be more cognizant of the family responsibilities of their employees. At the same time, the increased numbers of women in the labour force might encourage employers to be more accepting of women working in nontraditional fields.

Change in gender roles within the workplace will come about slowly, however, as concerns about productivity, efficiency, profit making, and tradition will remain more important than equity. Relations will change as the result of new legal requirements, the enforcement of old laws, union/management negotiations, and conflicts between employees and between employees and employers.

Within families, gender relations will also take time and will require difficult negotiations between spouses (Luxton, Rosenberg and Arat-Koc, 1990). While some couples will adapt with a minimum of conflict, others may separate and seek new relationships that place fewer demands on them. We may find, however, that each generation of younger people is more willing to work toward a marriage where both are equal partners.

Despite the trend toward more common-law living and increased marital instability, marriage remains popular for the vast majority of the Canadian population and will continue to be so in the future. About 70 percent of couples remain married until one partner dies (Adams and Nagnur, 1990:144), and many who eventually divorce have derived considerable satisfaction from their marital relationship. Young people usually expect to marry and to remain with the same partner throughout their lives. Canadian marriages are changing, becoming somewhat less permanent and more voluntary, but there is no indication that either marriage or family life will decline in value. We may actually be raising our expectations.

SUGGESTED READINGS

Adams, Owen B. "Divorce Rates in Canada." *Canadian Social Trends*. Edited by Craig McKie and Keith Thompson. Toronto: Thompson Educational Publishing, 1990:146–147.

Adams, Owen B. and Dhruva Nagnur. "Marrying and Divorcing: A Status Report for Canada." *Canadian Social Trends*. Edited by Craig McKie and Keith Thompson. Toronto: Thompson Educational Publishing, 1990:142–145.

Ambert, Anne-Marie. "Marriage Dissolution: Structural and Ideological Changes." *Families: Changing Trends in Canada*. 2nd ed. Edited by Maureen Baker. Scarborough: McGraw-Hill Ryerson, 1990:192–210.

Armstrong, Pat and Hugh Armstrong. "The Conflicting Demands of 'Work' and 'Home'." *Family Matters. Sociology and Contemporary Families*. Karen L. Anderson et al. Scarborough: Nelson, 1988:113–140.

Beaujot, Roderic. "Dwindling Families." *Policy Options*. 7. September 1986:3–7.

Blumstein, Philip and Pepper Schwartz. *American Couples*. New York: William Morrow and Company, 1983.

Bram, Susan. "Childlessness Revisited: a Longitudinal Study of Voluntarily Childless Couples, Delayed Parents, and Parents." *Lifestyles: A Journal of Changing Patterns*. 8 (2). 1985:46–66.

Fox, Bonnie (ed.). *Hidden in the Household: Women's Domestic Labour Under Capitalism.* Toronto: Women's Educational Press, 1980.

Johnson, Holly. "Wife Abuse." *Canadian Social Trends.* Edited by Craig McKie and Keith Thompson. Toronto: Thompson Educational Publishing, 1990:173–176.

Larson, J. "The Marriage Quiz: College Students' Beliefs in Selected Myths About Marriage." *Family Relations.* January 1988.

Leslie, Gerald R. and Sheila K. Korman. *The Family in Social Context.* 7th ed. New York: Oxford University Press, 1989.

Lupri, Eugen and James Frideres. "The Quality of Marriage and the Passage of Time: Marital Satisfaction Over the Family Life Cycle." *Canadian Journal of Sociology.* 6 (3). Summer 1981:283–306.

Marshall, Katherine. "Household Chores." *Canadian Social Trends.* 16. Spring 1990:18–19.

Moore, Maureen. "Dual-Earner Families: The New Norm." *Canadian Social Trends.* Edited by Craig McKie and Keith Thompson. Toronto: Thompson Educational Publishing, 1990:161–163.

Nagnur, D. and O. Adams. "Tying the Knot: an Overview of Marriage Rates in Canada." *Canadian Social Trends.* 7. Autumn 1987:2–6.

Nave-Herz, Rosemarie. "Childless Marriages." *Marriage and Family Review.* 14 (1-2). 1989:239–250.

Noller, Patricia and Mary Anne Fitzpatrick. "Marital Communication in the Eighties." *Journal of Marriage and the Family.* 52. November 1990:832–839.

Pogrebin, L.C. *Family Politics, Love and Power on an Intimate Frontier.* New York: McGraw-Hill, 1983.

Queen, Stuart, Robert W. Habenstein, and J.S. Quadragno. *The Family in Various Cultures.* 5th ed. New York: Harper and Row, 1985.

Ramu, G.N. "Voluntarily Childless and Parental Couples: A Comparison of Their Lifestyle Characteristics." *Lifestyles: a Journal of Changing Patterns.* 7 (3). 1985:130–145.

Scanzoni, John. *Sexual Bargaining: Power Politics in American Marriage.* 2nd ed. Chicago: University of Chicago Press, 1982.

Schlesinger, Benjamin and Shirley Tenhouse Giblon. *Lasting Marriages.* Toronto: Guidance Centre, Faculty of Education, University of Toronto, 1984.

Schlesinger, Benjamin and Rachel Schlesinger. "Postponed Parenthood: Trends and Issues." *Journal of Comparative Family Studies.* XX (3). Autumn 1989:355–363.

Stebbins, Robert A. "Men, Husbands and Fathers: Beyond Patriarchal Relations." *Reconstructing the Canadian Family: Feminist Perspectives.* Edited by Nancy Mandell and Ann Duffy. Toronto: Butterworths, 1988:27–47.

Veevers, Jean E. *Childless By Choice.* Toronto: Butterworths, 1980.

ISSUES FOR DISCUSSION

1. Why is our system of marriage not necessarily appropriate in other parts of the world?
2. If you and your spouse were both working full-time and you had no children, how would you decide:
   a. where to live;
   b. whether to have separate or joint bank accounts;
   c. whether to relocate if one of you receives a job promotion in another city?
3. Why would participation in the labour force increase a woman's decision-making power in the family? Would it have the same effect for a husband's decision making?
4. If provincial governments offered financial incentives similar to those offered in Quebec , would people have larger families?
5. Why are career-oriented men much more likely than career-oriented women to marry and have children?
6. What personal and social characteristics do you have that might make you a candidate for a stable marriage?
7. Analyze the difficulties for men who have been raised in a traditional family when they are faced with a more egalitarian role for women.
8. What is the relationship between power and violence?
9. What are the future implications for marriage and for our society if more couples choose a childfree marriage?
10. How would you explain the decline in the birth rate using the political economy approach?

FURTHER ACTIVITIES

1. Interview five married couples to determine which customs they retained for their wedding. Find out if they are aware of the historical significance and cultural background of these customs.
2. Although many couples say that they believe in equality between marital partners, are their relationships really equal? Design a research project that differentiates between attitudes about marital equality and actual behaviour.
3. Visit a shelter for battered women in your neighbourhood. Talk to the some of the women (both residents and staff) about the ways in which the criminal justice system, social workers, and women's groups have changed their ways of dealing with family violence in recent years. Prepare a report for your class.
4. Develop a questionnaire about the division of and time spent doing household chores. Give it to a group of men whose wives work full-time for pay outside the home and to a group whose wives are homemakers. Is there a difference in the kind of tasks they do and the amount of time spent on these tasks?
5. Interview three individuals of varying ages or circumstances who are living in common-law relationships. For example, one could be a young student, another could be a parent, and the third could be a middle-aged person who is divorced. Compare their reasons for living together without legal marriage and their perceptions of how others view their relationship.

5 The Family With Young Children

SPECIFIC TASKS

Deciding to Become a Parent

Becoming a parent is a lifetime commitment that involves major changes in the daily lives of couples or single parents. Whether or not to have children, the timing of each pregnancy, and eventual family size can be difficult decisions. Although some women are now making these decisions alone, most people make them as couples. If both partners agree about whether to have children and the timing of pregnancy, their relationship may flourish. However, there could be major conflict if one wants a child while the other does not.

Delayed childbirth is becoming more typical in Canada. For example, the number of first births to women in their thirties more than tripled from 1971 until 1988 (Wadhera and Millar, 1991:154). Reasons for delayed childbirth include the fact that the average age of marriage has risen since the 1970s. Improvements in contraception have allowed many couples to experience more childfree years of marriage, in which both tend to be working for pay and have time for leisure, self-development activities, or travel. Many couples wait until they feel they are psychologically ready for childbearing, until they can establish a financially secure environment for a child, or until they have saved enough money to buy a house. Sometimes, one or both of the people are still in college or university. The timing of a pregnancy involves decisions about whether a woman should take the standard maternity leave from a full-time job, attempt to obtain a longer leave without pay, or quit her job or postpone her education in order to care for a child. Many dual-income couples feel that they cannot afford to lose one income; wages have not kept up with inflation over the years and two incomes are necessary to maintain the same living standard of a generation ago (Maynard, 1988). Some couples delay making a decision for so long that, by the time they attempt to conceive, becoming pregnant is more difficult. At the same time, adopting a baby is increasingly difficult in Canada.

CHILDBIRTH AND LIFESTYLE CHANGES

For many couples, the months of pregnancy involve anticipation, excitement, and emotional closeness. At the same time there is a growing concern about financial security, future child care, and the adjustments required in becoming parents. The expectant mother or the couple sometimes attends prenatal classes and makes regular visits to clinics or doctors to have the progress of the fetus monitored. Unlike a generation ago, men are now encouraged to participate in prenatal classes and to be present at the delivery. Some people have suggested that the father's participation throughout the pregnancy creates a stronger bond between him and the baby—a bond which could last a lifetime (Lamb, 1976; Ricks, 1985). Despite the new parental leave benefits for either parent at childbirth (10 weeks under Unemployment Insurance in addition to 15 weeks of maternity benefits for the mother), both parents cannot take parental leave at the same time. If the couple must decide which one gets the parental leave, it is more likely that they will decide that the mother should add it to her maternity leave (Widerberg, 1987). Many men feel that they are unable to take as much time off work as their wives, either at the time of the birth or in the weeks following.

The experience of childbirth may vary with the woman's physical and emotional health, the presence or absence of the father, and the social conditions surrounding the birthing process. In the past few decades, health care reformers have argued that childbirth has been unnecessarily "medicalized." While prior to the 1920s, most births took place at home with the assistance of midwives or experienced married women, most North American births now occur in hospitals. Numerous medical interventions are typically used, including anesthetics, episiotomies, and Caesarian sections. Some doctors and nurses argue that sterile conditions and medical interventions are necessary for the safety of birth, while other people argue that Canadian **infant mortality rates** are still higher than other industrialized countries that allow home births and midwives, and where doctors perform fewer Caesarians. These controversies have led to several provincial investigations about the licensing of midwives, the safety of home births, the development of more pleasant birthing rooms in local hospitals, and the importance of increased personal or couple choice in the birthing process.

The birth of the first child increases the role complexity for the couple; some of the time they once spent together must now be spent on child care activities. The first few months after childbirth are typified by sheer fatigue brought on by 24-hour care, reduced sexual intimacy, and major lifestyle readjustments (Broderick, 1992:291). Parents who have to get up and go to work after feeding and changing a baby or dealing with a sick child during the night, undoubtedly experience mixed emotions about the "joys" of childrearing. But the amount of work often subsides when the baby no longer requires night feedings, and after toilet-training. Yet, the couple's sleep patterns, sex life, leisure time, housing situation, and their work activities will be affected by the arrival of the new baby (Ambert, 1992).

COMBINING PAID WORK AND PARENTING

Some mothers find it difficult to return to work after the birth of their child, because they are reluctant to leave the baby with anyone else. The shortage and cost of quality child care for infants complicates this situation. Other mothers are anxious to return to work to escape the routine of diapers and feedings, to enjoy more time with adults, or to raise the family income.

According to Statistics Canada (1992:B19), 61.6 percent of women with children under three years old worked in the labour force in 1991. In 1976, only 32 percent were in the labour force. If the mother leaves a paid job to become a full-time homemaker when the baby is born, the couple's previous division of labour may change dramatically. While some household tasks might have been shared when the couple was childless, the woman is now likely to take over the cooking and cleaning, as well as child care. The longer she stays home, the more traditional the division of labour tends to become (Entwisle and Doering, 1981; Cowan et al., 1985), although neither partner may notice this role shift at the time. Sometimes the woman may feel isolated, overworked with routine tasks, and out of touch with adult activities and labour force requirements. Many homemakers are able to overcome these feelings of isolation with community activities, volunteer work, play groups, baby-sitting co-operatives, part-time jobs, mother's support groups, or continuing education courses.

Fathers who stay at home to care for their children while the mothers work may actually experience more problems than women, because they do not fit into mother's support groups or children's play groups. Not having a paying job also seems to lower their decision-making power in the family (Brinkerhoff and Lupri, 1983). Neighbours and relatives may be critical of male homemakers because they are not playing the traditional masculine role of breadwinner and family head. Few men have remained homemakers for more than short time periods because of social pressure from friends and family, as well as financial pressures (Nett, 1988:226).

Considering the structure of the labour force, continuing high unemployment, and rapid technological change, it is increasingly difficult to leave the labour force for childrearing and easily return several years later. For those with higher level or skilled jobs, their training, education, or experience is soon considered outdated. Parents who have remained at home to care for their children might be expected to retrain and start at the bottom of the occupational hierarchy.

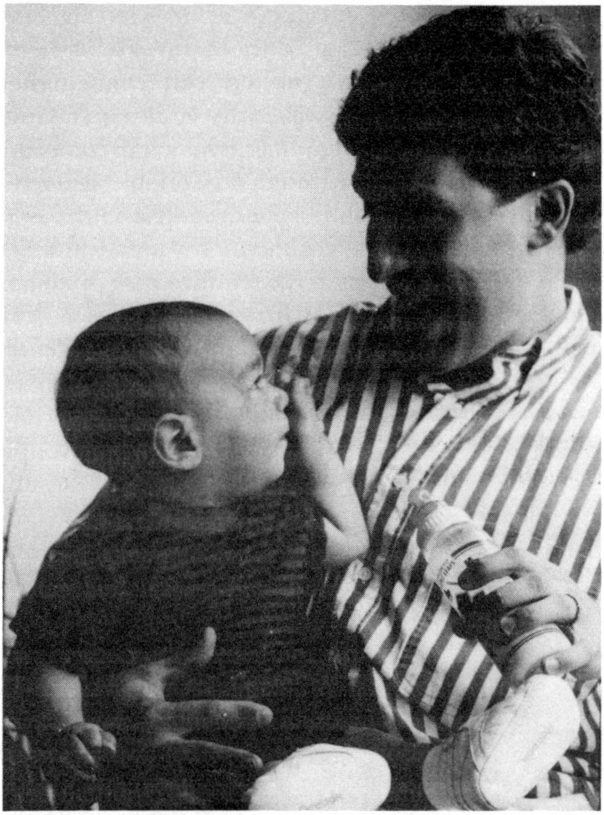

An increasing number of fathers are becoming involved in child care.

Canada Wide/Veronica Milne

Women who care for their own children at home have historically provided a vast amount of volunteer work which has benefitted their communities. Many homemakers have canvassed for charitable organizations, served as fundraisers for religious and cultural organizations, and performed considerable behind-the-scenes work for their communities. In addition, some women have taken in sewing, cared for other people's children, or taught music at home for extra money. Other women have cared for foster children, even when remuneration was low and barely covered their expenses. Increasingly, however, families need a second income and women are less often available for unpaid or underpaid positions.

Despite the fact that so many mothers have entered the labour force either full-time or part-time, most have remained responsible for housework and child care. Some parents feel that mothers can best care for and socialize their own children, and do not want to trust their children to hired baby-sitters or child care workers. But remaining at home reduces the family's income and may deny children certain opportunities that cost money. These dilemmas involved in combining paid work and parenting cause some parents considerable anxiety.

As mentioned in chapter three, childhood and adolescence have been seen as unique stages in the life cycle only in the past hundred years. When children's labour was necessary to families, and children were not legally required to attend school, parents were less likely to protect them from reality or to allow them a carefree existence marked

CHILD-REARING CAN BE TOUGH BUT REWARDING

"My husband and I are in our early 30s and we have just recently started our family. Though we are both university graduates, and consider we've paid our dues to society in that regard, we had to make a choice between buying a home or having a family.

"We don't regret in the least our decision to have the family, but it is a little tough to realize that we won't be able to afford a home, if at all, until our children are in school and we don't have daycare expenses.

"We feel that a society that doesn't even allow us to write off what we actually pay in child care is being unfair in the tax burden it levies on parents."

"People say their families are their most important thing in their lives, but their actions show otherwise: divorce, separation, neglect and abuse of children. I think people only say this because society tells them they should think so. Their actual values are much more self-centred and material."

"If you don't have children, what do you have? Children inspire you, and children just make your day."

"I'm a single mother. I'm 42 and I have a 10-year-old child. I think things are going to work out. We've been through a traumatic divorce and just moved back to Quebec from Ontario. I'm making a good income, over $40,000 a year. That has enabled us to buy a house, which we would not have been able to do had we stayed in Ontario.

"I think my son is growing up knowing the importance of family—not necessarily that a family is a unit composed of a father, mother and child, but an extended family. We are close to my brother and his children. My son, having come back to Quebec, is getting a chance to get close to his grandparents."

"My parents are divorced and I've been living with the same man for five years now, and neither of us really wants to get married. I know I never wanted to get married and have children like all my other schoolmates wanted. It's not my parent's divorce that soured me on marriage; it was their marriage that soured me on marriage."

"I've got two children now, and I hope to have three. I'm extremely happy and wouldn't trade them for anything. But about the people who are childless by choice—it might be fine when they're young, but when they get older what's going to happen to them? Then all they are going to have is hopefully some nieces and nephews somewhere, and hopefully some close friends. But nothing can replace the relationship you have with your children and grandchildren when you're older. And these people are going to miss all this."

"I don't see a bright future for my family because I am a lesbian. Your laws don't allow me to get married and don't recognize my family or my right to have a family although I fully intend to have one and have many lesbian friends who do have families."

"Because families stayed together before didn't mean they were very happy. Women who decide to have children and work full-time like myself didn't know what they were getting into. We didn't have any role models; most of our mothers stayed at home.

"We ended up with 15-hour days—up at 6 and by the time we can relax it's 9 at night, and no weekends off. By the time we are 40 a lot of us are burned out.

"Society is structured as if the majority of women were still at home. For example, appointments for children, for plumbers, orthodontists, etcetera are from 9 to 4."

The Gazette, Montreal, 26 January 1992, p.A5.

by play and personal development. Children, especially from poorer families, were forced to grow up at a young age and to accept responsibility for farm chores, housework, and the care of younger siblings.

HISTORICAL PERSPECTIVES

CHANGING IMAGES OF CHILDREN AND CHILDHOOD

Ways of viewing children and childhood have varied by historical time period, culture, social class, religion, and gender. Family historians and sociologists have begun only recently to study childhood and aspects of everyday family life, and some excellent social histories have been written about childhood and family life from medieval society to the present (Ariès, 1962; Sutherland, 1976; DeMause, 1974; Parr, 1982; Synnott, 1983).

Historians disagree about the treatment of European and North American children in previous centuries (Mackie, 1990:120) because the only available evidence comes from art, the history of costume, literature, and religious writings. They agree, however, that distinctions between adulthood and childhood were not as well defined as they are today (Mandell, 1988:52). Legal documents and historical records indicate that children had no legal rights, which could be protected by churches or governments, but rather were often considered the property of their parents. According to today's standards, children were mistreated in a variety of ways, including infanticide, abandonment, neglect, and physical and sexual abuse.

The treatment of children, however, changed over time with the evolution of religious ideas, demographic trends, and the change in importance of children's labour to the economy. For example, Philippe Ariès (1962), a French cultural historian, argued that from the thirteenth century on, the value placed on children's lives by adults increased dramatically as a result of the growing impact of Christianity and the idea that a child's soul is immortal (Mackie, 1990:120). Whereas previously children had been treated as miniature adults, the appearance of schools at the end of the seventeenth century signaled the view that children needed a period of religious training and preparation for the adult world.

In the nineteenth century, perceptions of childhood varied by the social class of the parents and the economic value of children. While infant and child mortality rates were high, working-class children were more at risk because of their living conditions and diet, and because they were expected to work to help support the family, sometimes in dangerous mines and factories (Synnott, 1983). For the poor, childhood was not much different from adult life. For the rich, however, children were idealized as symbols of innocence (Coveney, 1982:45) and were protected from work and other dangers.

Throughout the past century, attitudes toward childbearing and childrearing have continued to evolve with economic, demographic, and social changes. When more people lived in rural areas, for example, children were less costly to house and feed, and provided additional labour and income for the family. Under urban conditions, children tend to become more expensive especially when both parents are in the labour force and need to purchase child care services. Demographic changes have also influenced attitudes toward children. As shown in figure 5.1, infant mortality rates have fallen and very few children now die in infancy. This demographic change could influence desired family size, the level of attachment parents feel toward individual children, and the timing of pregnancy.

Attitudes toward children are also influenced by family planning, which is now both technically possible and socially acceptable. Women can experience fewer pregnancies to achieve the couple's desired family size and parents can space children according to family and personal needs. With these economic, social, and demographic changes, parents are now more likely to view childhood as a time of innocence, play, learning, and freedom from responsibility.

Despite greater attention by historians to the contribution of children to families, and the continuing attention by psychologists to early childhood development, sociologists have tended to study families from the viewpoint of parents (Eichler, 1988:58; Baker, 1991). Only recently have children been perceived as influencing their parents' behaviour to any great extent (Ambert, 1990, 1992), except in the study of the transition to parenthood and the effect on family life of children with special needs or behavioural problems. In earlier studies in most disciplines, researchers have not emphasized the fact that children often have divergent views about family life from their parents, and different social-psychological needs and legal interests.

Figure 5.1 **Infant[1] Mortality Rates, by Sex, 1926–1986**

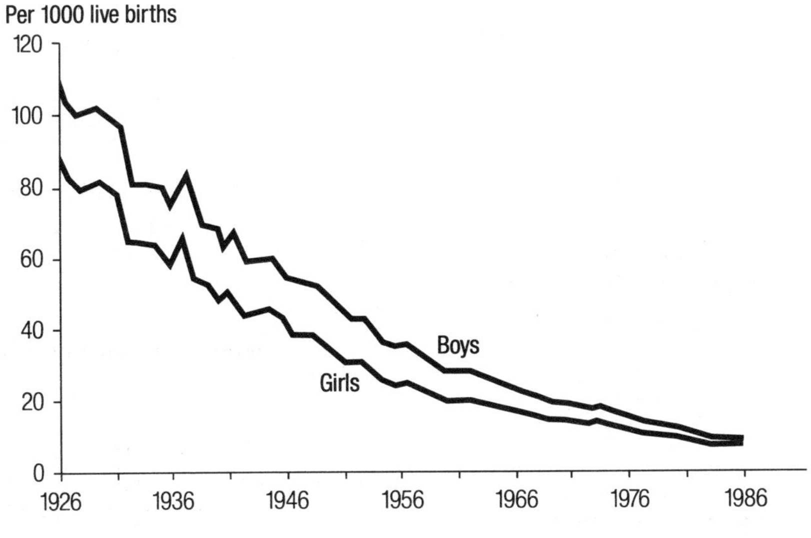

[1] Children under 1 year

Source: Statistics Canada, Vital Statistics and Causes of Death as published from 1926–1986. Reproduced with the permission of the Minister of Supply and Services Canada, 1992.

THE RISE OF CHILDREN'S RIGHTS

The power that parents have over their children has been gradually restricted over the past century. Children were once considered the property of parents. The Romans went further than any other legal system in placing the liberty and lives of children within the power of the father. Early Roman law included the right of fathers to give their children away or to have them put to death.

Under English medieval law, parents had an obligation to exercise guardianship over minors, or those below the legal age defining adulthood. By the eighteenth century, children were regarded as chattels, or property, under English Common Law. Parents had three duties toward their children at that time: maintenance, protection, and education. Because of these obligations, parents could claim authority over children (Bala and Clarke, 1981:2–4).

Prompted by the work of social critics such as Charles Dickens, who described the fate of children in institutions in *Oliver Twist*, the nineteenth century was a period of social reform in Great Britain, the United States, and Canada (Bala, Hornick and Vogl, 1991:2). The first legal challenge of the century to the absolute rights of parents occurred in New York in 1870. A social worker, horrified at the neglect of a child, sought legal assistance and, in desperation, turned to the American Association for the Prevention of Cruelty to Animals as a means of obtaining legal sanction. Soon after this, the American Society for the Prevention of Cruelty to Children was established. Twenty years later, in 1891, the Children's Aid Society was founded in Canada.

From this early beginning in North America legislation flowed to protect children who were neglected and abused. In 1893, reformers persuaded the Ontario legislature to enact the Children's Protection Act, which gave the Children's Aid Society the right to remove neglected or abused children from their homes and become their legal guardians (Bala, Hornick, and Vogl, 1991:3). Such actions demonstrated a concern by the state for the well-being of children and an acknowledgement that parents did not have sole authority over their offspring. From this evolved the idea that children are citizens in their own right, and the state has an obligation to assist them, as minors, in exercising these rights.

According to the Canadian Council on Children and Youth, four main concepts underlie and shape the socio-legal status of children in Canada. The first is *patria potestas*, paternal power, or the integrity and power of the family. The second is *parens patria*, the state as parent, or the authority of the courts to make decisions on behalf of those who cannot act for themselves. The third is the best interests of the child, a concept used to justify state intervention in child neglect and delinquency cases. The fourth is the child as person before the law, which is a relatively recent concept in Canadian law (Ayim, 1987:4).

During the 1970s and 1980s, when Canadian and American family law underwent extensive reform, children's rights became an issue of public concern. At the present time, children's rights are protected by both federal and provincial laws in Canada. For example, the Criminal Code contains sections requiring parents to provide children with the necessities of life and protecting children from physical and sexual abuse. The federal government also shares with the provinces the cost of health and welfare services and provides direct grants for research and education on child abuse. The provinces, however, create and amend their own child welfare legislation and have jurisdiction over child protection agencies.

EARLY CHILD CARE IN CANADA

The daytime care of children became a social issue in the nineteenth century when the number of neglected and delinquent children began to noticeably increase in the industrialized cities. Poor, deserted, and widowed women were often unable to care for their young children because they needed to work for pay or because their incomes were too low. Children from these families would be placed temporarily in institutions or children's homes, cared for by relatives or friends, or left to fend for themselves, while their mothers worked as domestics or in factories.

Since middle-class women seldom worked outside the home, the care of children of working mothers was generally seen as a welfare issue. Orphanages, **foundling homes**, and other children's homes were run by churches or charitable organizations and provided care for infants and children not looked after by their families. These institutions were financed through donations and volunteer labour, and the children, when possible, worked for their board. Children were also placed with families by means of **indenture** and were expected to work for those families in return for their care. Many poor or homeless children were brought from Britain to Canada in the nineteenth and early decades of the twentieth century in order to find them homes and provide labour for Canadian families. For example, the British philanthropist Thomas Barnardo organized the emigration of over 25 000 British children between 1882 and 1915 (Corbett, 1981).

The institutionalization of neglected and delinquent children declined considerably in Toronto in the early decades of the 1900s after a conference, held in Washington D.C., made it clear that these children benefitted from a family environment. The Children's Aid Society in Toronto began to place children in foster homes whenever possible, and after 1920 children's institutions became less prevalent in Ontario, although many still operated across the country. Settlement houses or community welfare centres provided some daytime care for welfare children, as well as programs to improve the health, morals, and the education of the poor.

In the welfare tradition, one controversy had always been whether to provide child care to enable poor women to work for a living or whether to pay a mother welfare benefits to enable her to stay home with her children. Before federal or provincial support for social services, few municipalities or charitable organizations could pay a mother to look after her own children. When mothers were forced to take work to support themselves and their children, they usually made private arrangements with neighbours or relatives for child care. It was not until 1916 that a Canadian province (Manitoba) initiated mothers' allowances, and these were only for "morally upright women" with dependent children (Armitage, 1988:271). Federal universal mothers' allowances were introduced in 1945, as the Family Allowance Program.

While child care services originated from a welfare tradition, public kindergartens and nursery schools arose from educational philosophy. Child psychologists from Europe encouraged conscientious parents to provide their preschool children with disciplined but creative play in a group setting. The first public kindergarten opened in Ontario in 1883 (Sutherland, 1976:174), but it was not until the 1920s that kindergartens were widely accepted in Canada.

After World War I, birth rates were declining but rates of infant mortality and maternal death were still high in Canada compared with some European countries. Concern was expressed by doctors, journalists, members of the clergy, and social workers that mothers themselves were promoting child health problems by their lack of knowledge of child care. During the 1920s and 1930s, strong criticism of the knowledge and expertise of mothers was expressed in magazines such as the *Canadian Home Journal* and *Maclean's*. Concern was voiced that worldly ambitions of the "new woman" (i.e., the desire for education and paid work) would lead to the deterioration of family life (Strong-Boag, 1982:161).

In 1922, the federal government's new Division of Child Welfare produced a series of booklets providing practical childrearing and domestic advice and set up clinics for expectant mothers and babies as part of a campaign to reduce infant mortality. Popular magazines published a barrage of articles celebrating maternalism and recommending strict scheduling in infant and child care.

Within this social environment, nursery schools developed and expanded. In 1925, nursery schools were started for children two to five years old as part of the child study program at McGill University and the University of Toronto (Strong-Boag, 1982:161). All of the children were from middle-class families and had educated parents. They attended an enriched program of creative play and "scientific child care," grounded in behaviourist and Freudian psychology. Unpaid mothers occasionally assisted trained teachers.

Although the McGill nursery experiment lasted only until 1930, the program at the University of Toronto continued and became the model for settlement house and church nurseries. However, there was always a certain amount of opposition to the nursery school idea. From the 1930s to the 1950s, research on early child development emphasized the importance of the bond between mother and child. Some feared that nursery school or day nursery children would be deprived of that bond and consequently would develop abnormally.

Studies done in European orphanages showed that infants and children often became intellectually disadvantaged and emotionally disturbed over time. The results were interpreted as resulting from "maternal deprivation." However, these researchers (including John Bowlby and René Spitz) mistakenly confused the presence of the mother with nurturance, stability, and intellectual stimulation, and suggested that mothers who "neglected" their children all day (i.e., had them cared for by someone else) were voluntarily causing emotional and intellectual problems for them. No one studied the absence of the father during early childhood development; it was assumed that only the mother could provide the nurturance a child needed. And no one seemed to realize that a sample of emotionally disturbed children in an orphanage for 24 hours a day was different from 8 to 9 hours in a professionally run nursery.

The other reason why nursery schools did not become more popular was the traditional idea that the married woman's "career" was motherhood. If she was not caring for her children, some people felt that she was not fulfilling her duty. This was partly perpetuated by Freudian psychology, which was quite popular in North American in the 1930s and 1940s. Some thought that nursery schools would encourage married women to work outside the home and compete with the male breadwinner. They feared that this might lead to the dissolution of the family (Pierson, 1977).

In the 1930s and the 1940s, some people thought that nursery schools might deprive chidren of an emotional bond with their mothers, encourage married women to participate in the labour force, and lead to the dissolution of the family.

National Archives of Canada/PA111359

Despite this attitude against married women working, women's labour was needed during World War II in war industries and in the many positions left vacant by men who had joined the armed forces. As part of a plan to draw women into the work force, Prime Minister Mackenzie King revised the Income Tax Act to allow husbands to claim their wives as dependants regardless of how much money the wives earned. He also offered federal cost-sharing with those provinces providing day-care centres for mothers working in the war industries. This was later extended to all working women. Only Quebec and Ontario, however, made use of the Dominion-Provincial Wartime Day Nurseries Act. Furthermore, these day nurseries were closed when the war was over (Pierson, 1977).

After the Second World War, kindergarten programs were expanded into the elementary school system in some provinces, including Ontario. These programs continued the nursery school philosophy, providing half-day enrichment programs for five-year-olds. Gradually during the 1950s, some schools accepted four-year-olds. During the 1960s in Canada when educational theories emphasized creative play, private preschools developed, including Montessori schools. Parents also co-operatively developed play schools, to provide intellectual and social stimulation for their preschoolers. When mothers' participation in the labour force continued to rise in the 1970s, child care centres were established both by private owners and by nonprofit organizations. While many private centres offered mainly custodial care, some provided educational services comparable to nursery schools and kindergartens (Canada, Task Force on Child Care, 1986).

Federal funding was used again for day-care in 1966. In this year the Canada Assistance Plan (CAP) extended cost-sharing to welfare programs that enabled the provision of day-care for children of families in financial need. As more middle-class mothers entered the labour force and required child care services, lobby groups pressured the federal government to take child care funding out of CAP. In 1988, the government proposed a new cost-sharing arrangement with the provinces but this was never legislated.

In 1992, the federal government announced that there would not be a new child care program because limited resources would be spent instead on child benefits for low-income families and child abuse programs. Some provinces such as Ontario and Quebec, however, are attempting to provide new child spaces and expand their commitment to child care services for all families who need it.

Working parents often experience difficulty finding affordable yet high-quality care for their children. Later in this chapter, the present system of child care and some of these problems will be discussed.

CULTURAL PERSPECTIVES

CULTURAL DIFFERENCES IN FERTILITY

Throughout this century, **birth rates** have been falling in industrialized countries, including Canada. As figure 5.2 illustrates, this is especially the case since the 1960s, with new birth control technology, the two-income family, and a more expansive role for women. While over 100 years ago there were 45 births per 1000 population, this figure had fallen to 14.5 in 1988 before rising to 15.2 in 1991 (Statistics Canada, 1992c). Maintaining high birth rates has been important historically to Canada because our country has always had a relatively low population density and depended on new settlers and their descendants for agricultural and industrial development.

From Canadian census data, we know that different ethnic and language groups have varying fertility rates. Contrary to popular myth, immigrants to Canada traditionally have had lower birth rates than Canadian-born women. This may relate to the fact that many immigrants come to Canada to improve their standard of living and need two incomes to accomplish this. Historically, the participation of women in the labour force has been related to lower birth rates and smaller family size.

Religious variations are also evident in fertility rates. Traditionally, Roman Catholics have produced larger families than Protestants, but there are substantial differences among Protestant denominations. Mennonites, Hutterites, and Mormons, for example, have also opposed birth control and encouraged large families. On the other hand, Jewish people (except Hasidic Jews) have generally produced smaller families than other religious groups (Kalbach and McVey, 1979:107).

Figure 5.2 **Birth Rates in Canada, 1851–1990***

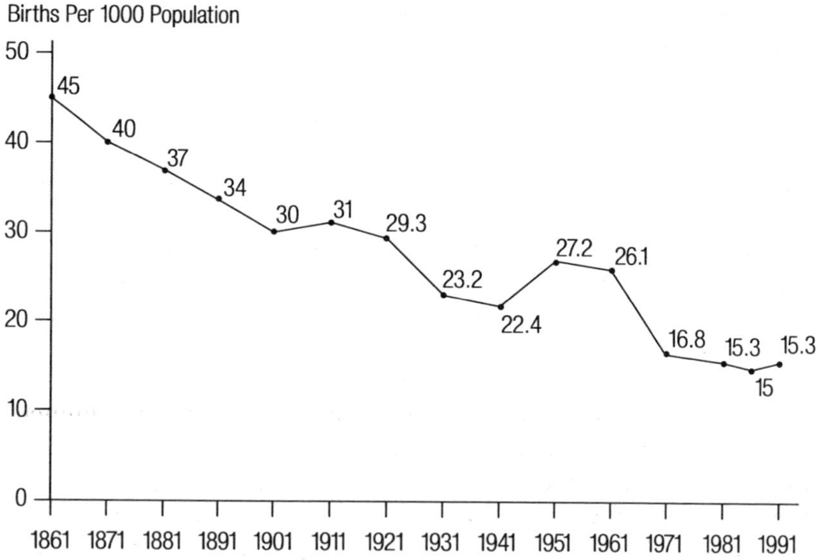

*Rates for 1851 to 1921 are estimates.

Source: Baker, Maureen. *The Family. Changing Trends in Canada.* Scarborough: McGraw-Hill Ryerson, 1984:5; Statistics Canada. "Births 1987–1988." *Health Reports* 2 (1) 1990:2. (Cat. 82-003S), Ottawa: Supply and Services Canada; Jean Dumas (for Statistics Canada). *Report on the Demographic Situation in Canada.* Catalogue 91-209E, Ottawa: Minister of Supply and Services, Nov. 1990:5. Stephen Strauss. "Baby boomlet continues, Statistics Canada reports," *The Globe and Mail,* 31 March 1992:A1, A5. Reproduced with the permission of the Minister of Supply and Services Canada, 1992.

French Canadian birth rates have changed considerably throughout this century. Only a generation ago, Quebec women were still having large families in comparison with all Canadians. In 1954, for example, the birth rate in Quebec was 31.0 per 1000 population (Caldwell and Fournier, 1987), while the Canadian rate was 28.5 in the same year (Statistics Canada, 1983). In 1988, when birth rates reached their lowest point, this pattern was reversed with a lower birth rate in Quebec (13.6) than in Canada (14.5). In 1991, the Quebec rate rose to 14.4 while Canada's rose to 15.2. If we look at the total fertility rate, or the number of children per woman, Quebec women gave birth to an average of 1.72 children in 1990 compared with 1.86 in Canada (Strauss, 1992). Although both Quebec and Canadian total fertility rates have increased since 1988, they are still below the population replacement level, which is 2.1 children per woman (Dumas, 1990:4-5).

The low Quebec birth rates since the 1960s have been attributed to the sweeping cultural changes of the "Quiet Revolution," when the Catholic Church lost much of its control over Quebec society, the education system became more secularized, young people placed more emphasis on occupational success, and young women played down their traditional role as mothers (Lachapelle and Henripin, 1982:116–117). Another reason for the lower birth rates probably relates to the high participation of women in the labour force, and their personal reaction to their mothers' experiences of childbearing and childrearing, perceived by many to be emotionally and physically draining.

Falling birth rates have been considered by some policy-makers, especially those in the province of Quebec, as socially, culturally, and economically dangerous. Concern has been expressed about declining birth rates in that province because of a fear that francophones will become even a smaller minority in the Canadian population. Historically, immigrants residing in Quebec have not adopted the French language as often as expected, and have sometimes moved on to English Canada or the United States rather than integrating into French-speaking Quebec. Because maintaining the birth rate is culturally and politically important, the Quebec government has recently announced cash grants for parents at childbirth, with a larger amount for the second and third child. In 1992, $7500 was paid to parents for third or subsequent children.

Other countries have attempted to induce families to procreate through special family allowances, generous maternity leaves and benefits, and taxation benefits for families with dependent children. These attempts have not been successful in raising the birth rate, but

BABY BOOMLET CONTINUES, STATISTICS CANADA REPORTS

Women 30 and over bear more than a third of babies

BY STEPHEN STRAUSS
The Globe and Mail

The baby boomers' baby boom and Quebec's quiet fertility revolution continued apace in 1990.

Statistics Canada reported yesterday that the number of live babies born per thousand people increased from 15 in 1989 to 15.3 in 1990. This translated into 405 486 babies born in 1990, as opposed to 392 661 in 1989.

On average, Canadian women could expect to have 1.86 children over their lifetimes, up from 1.77 in 1989.

Surinder Wadhera, a senior analyst with Statistics Canada, said the decisions by many women to postpone having children, as well as the relatively large number of baby-boom women now in their 30s and 40s, continued to skew birth statistics. For example, more than one-third of the babies born in 1990 were born to women 30 and over. By comparison, in 1971 only a bit over 21 percent of babies were born to mothers in these age categories. The percentage of women under 20 having children fell to 5.9 percent last year from 11.6 percent in 1971.

The most significant increase took place in Quebec, where the number of babies born increased to 98 048 in 1990 from 92 373 in 1989.

In 1988, the Quebec government announced a bonus of $500 for each of the first two children and $3,000 for each subsequent child to counteract a decline in fertility which was seeing Quebec couples producing on average only 1.3 children. Demographers generally believe that 2.1 children is a society's replacement rate—the number of children who have to be born to keep a population stable.

With the increase, the average number of children born to Quebec women over their reproductive lifetime is now 1.72.

The number of babies in Ontario also increased substantially in 1990, to 150 923 from 145 338 in 1989. This translates into a 2 percent increase, versus 5.1 percent growth in Quebec.

Four provinces, Manitoba, Newfoundland, Saskatchewan, and Alberta, had decreases in the number of children born per thousand inhabitants. Newfoundland had the lowest rate of 13.3 live births per thousand. The highest birth rates were in Yukon and the Northwest Territories—some 21.3 children born to every 1000 people in the Yukon and 29.4 in the NWT. The magnitude of the baby boom in the NWT resembles the high rates which existed in Canada during the late forties and fifties, and is roughly the same as Mexico today.

The Globe and Mail, Toronto, 31 March 1992:A1, A5.

may have prevented it from falling further. Decisions to reproduce depend on many factors, including the economic climate, availability of jobs, educational plans, opportunities to combine family and work, accommodation costs, and prevailing attitudes about women's role and the desirability of family life. In other words, the inducements have been insufficient to counter reasons not to have children.

Unlike Quebec, the Northwest Territories has an extremely high birth rate. In 1990, there were 29.4 births per 1000 population in the Northwest Territories (Strauss, 1992), compared with the Canadian average of 15.3. This has concerned social workers and politicians because of the large percentage of single parents and poor families requiring government assistance in the North.

Although the fertility rates of First Nations' people have been declining since the late 1960s and are becoming closer to non-Native rates, status Indians and Inuit still have larger families than Canadians in general (Siggner, 1986). The birth rate of registered or status Indians was 29.8 per 1000 population in 1985 when Canada's average was 14.8 (Muir, 1988:2). This birth rate is similar to that of developing countries in the Caribbean (United Nations, 1991:143). Historically, high birth rates have been associated with poverty, economic underdevelopment, and high infant mortality rates.

Governments around the world have also had limited success in encouraging their citizens to curb family size, especially in countries with high infant mortality rates and widespread poverty. China has been moderately successful with its enforced one-child policy, but the greatest resistance to it has been in the less developed rural areas. Policies advocating birth control and smaller families are most successful among more prosperous urban families because children are not needed as a source of labour and are more costly to accommodate in urban conditions.

Low fertility rates are certainly not confined to southern Canada, but are also typical of other industrialized countries. As table 5.1 indicates, many countries, including Denmark, Hungary, and Switzerland, have lower birth rates than Canada. Declining birth rates in industrialized countries, as well as rising life expectancies, have generally led to the aging of the population. Older populations require new policies and services, which will be discussed further in chapter eight. In addition, longer lifespan means more time for couples to live together after the childrearing years. As life expectancy rises, so do divorce rates. There are now many years after the children have left home either to remain with one's partner or to begin a new life. In the past, however, many marriages lasted no longer than they do today because life expectancies were shorter.

Table 5.1 **Comparative Birth Rates**

COUNTRY	YEAR	BIRTHS PER 1000 POPULATION
Canada	1988	14.5
Australia	1987	15.0
Czechoslovakia	1987	13.9
Denmark	1987	11.0
England and Wales	1987	13.6
Former West Germany	1987	10.5
France	1987	13.8
Greece	1986	11.3
Hungary	1987	11.8
Ireland	1986	17.3
Israel	1986	23.1
Italy	1985	10.1
Japan	1986	11.4
Mexico	1985–90	29.0
Poland	1987	16.1
Spain	1985	11.7
Sweden	1987	12.5
Switzerland	1987	11.6
United States	1986	15.4
Former USSR	1987	19.8

Source: Statistics Canada, *Health Reports, Births 1987–88*. Vol. 2, no. 1, catalogue 82-003S, 1990, p. 80. Reproduced with the permission of the Minister of Supply and Services Canada, 1992.

CULTURAL VARIATIONS IN CHILDREARING AND CHILD CARE

Childrearing attitudes and practices have changed over the centuries and decades, but many variations remain. A child's upbringing still varies considerably by the family's social class background, cultural or ethnic origin, and religious affiliation. Yet, ethnic and cultural differences in childrearing and child care used to be more pronounced than they are today. Before urbanization, transportation improvements, radio, and television, cultural groups could more easily live in isolation from the mainstream culture and were more likely to maintain distinct family systems. With urbanization and modernization, there has been more integration of cultural groups, especially among teenagers and younger adults. Nevertheless, some groups have managed to resist outside influences and maintain their distinctiveness.

Many parents from cultural minorities make a special point of teaching their children the language, customs, and traditional values of their own cultural group. Some children attend special language classes, often outside school hours. While urban schools in areas with large ethnic communities sometimes offer heritage language classes as part of the regular curriculum, these are usually offered only after parental pressure and if sufficient numbers of children require training in the same language.

Whether or not children should be permitted to be taught in their first language at public expense has been controversial in Canada for over 100 years. Many groups, such as Hutterites and Doukhobors, were induced to immigrate with the promise of language and cultural rights, but more often than not these promises were rescinded within a few years of their arrival. Francophones living outside the province of Quebec are still fighting for the right to educate their children in their first language. Native people are increasingly insisting that their languages be taught as part of school curricula.

Childrearing and child care differences among cultural groups are so extensive that it is difficult to deal with all of the diversity. Instead, the focus here will be on two issues: child care and child welfare among First Nations' or Native populations, and some common trends relating to immigrants and child care.

Isolated Native groups continue to encourage all members of the extended family to share in childrearing, and they have maintained a more relaxed attitude toward child discipline than many European-Canadians. Yet, child care and child welfare among Native people continue to be contentious issues. This is partly because the majority culture attempted to assimilate Native people and obliterate their culture through the system of residential schools and non-Native foster homes. Historically, the lack of concern about cultural differences in the socialization of Native children and the transmission of culture continues to haunt Canadian governments. The roots of these issues are explored in more detail in the next section.

Child Care for First Nations' People

Prior to the 1960s, most Native people lived within extended families in isolated regions, and children in need of care were looked after by other members of the extended family. Among many aboriginal groups, child care was traditionally seen as the responsibility of the extended rather than nuclear family, and looking after a sister's, daughter's, or cousin's children was not unusual. Elders were also

CHILDREARING

Childrearing refers to a method of bringing up children, or practices which are believed to be effective in achieving socialization. Childrearing techniques are socially approved ways of dealing with and teaching children. They are the means by which it is believed that the goals of socialization can best be achieved. Indeed, various kinds of childrearing techniques are effective under different social conditions.

Nowhere in the quintessential features of families, which render them apt socializers, is there any indication that one type of family arrangement is better than another for this purpose. Nor can evidence be found of the superiority of any particular method of childrearing in general. All kinds of domestic and kin units have been considered "best" for children, just as many kinds of childrearing practices have been advocated in different places and at various times.

In regard to variations in childrearing, the debates in North America have centred on authoritarian techniques versus permissive ones. The matter has usually been put in terms of "either/or." On the one hand, it is believed that parents should be strict disciplinarians, impose rules on their children with punishment or negative reinforcement, and expect unquestioning obedience. On the other hand, it is believed that parents should treat their children in a more indulgent manner, permitting them freedom and relying upon reason and the inherent desire of humans for approval, while giving them positive reinforcements for good behaviour. Thus, it can be seen that childrearing practices have a *philosophy* behind them, underlying which are *assumptions* about human nature. Authoritarian techniques are generally based on a belief in the inherent evil in human nature, while permissive ones are based on a belief in goodness. Books which claim to have found the proper techniques for turning children into adults number in the hundreds each year. Larson (1976) has summarized the scientific research on the topic. He concludes that "Children reared with ... guidance, discipline, punishment, and encouragement of autonomy...tend to have more positive self views, attitudes, and behaviours." In this way, Larson seems to be declaring for a balanced technique, midway between too much indulgence and too much strictness. As he points out, excessive permissiveness leads to irresponsibility and impulsiveness; extreme authoritarianism results in aggressiveness and rebelliousness; and extreme neglect fosters anxiety. The balance between authoritarian and permissive techniques applies to our culture at the present time, because our society values responsibility, conformity, and happiness. Other societies may aim for different ideal personal characteristics.

The fact is that the parent/child relationship is a dynamic one in which children influence parents at the same time as parents are shaping their offspring. That this relationship operates in the context of various kinds of family arrangements within even wider social structures accounts for much of the difficulty in arriving at a recipe for turning out perfect children.

Nett, Emily. *Canadian Families Past and Present,* Toronto: Butterworths, 1988:153–155.

involved in child care and instructed young children in language and traditions. In some cases, the Indian agent (the representative of the federal government on the reserve) would place a child with another family on the reserve. Often, however, children were sent away to Indian residential schools (Johnston, 1983).

In 1947, the Canadian Council of Welfare and the Canadian Association of Social Workers presented a brief to a parliamentary committee considering changes to the Indian Act. They argued that Native peoples were not being provided with comparable services to non-Natives, that Indian agents were generally not qualified to make child welfare decisions, and that no legal or social protection was being provided for Native children or their families. They condemned placing neglected children in residential schools and recommended an extension of the provincial services of health, welfare, and education to residents of reserves. In 1951, the federal government made major changes to the Indian Act including extending provincial welfare services, but no additional funding accompanied these legal changes. Consequently, only some provinces actually extended child welfare programs and jurisdictional disputes continued.

When the profession of social work developed and expanded after World War II, attention was focused on the absence of welfare services among Native children, but no major changes were made. During the 1960s, a high proportion of Native children were taken away from their families and placed in substitute care by social service workers. This pattern has been called the "Sixties Scoop" (Johnston, 1983:23) and emerged for several reasons. Colonial policies required English-speaking education for Native children, and population was so low in remote areas that children were sent to centralized residential schools. If these children experienced problems at school, the authorities found them non-Native foster families whom they believed would provide a stable family environment. Alcohol abuse and widespread poverty among Native peoples, cultural misunderstandings, jurisdictional disputes, and paternalistic policies also encouraged the removal of Native children from their cultural environment to be cared for by non-Native families. In recent years, First Nations' people have protested against policies such as residential schools and non-Native foster care for Native children, and have attempted to take control of their own child welfare services (Johnston, 1983; Warry, 1991.

The demand for child care services has generally increased with women's rising participation in the labour force as well as with rising rates of poverty and family disintegration. First Nations women, especially those living on reserves, have had extremely high unemployment rates and lower labour force participation rates than non-Native women. In addition, Native families have experienced severe social and economic problems requiring a variety of social services, including child care and family support programs.

The Native population is growing at a rapid rate (Muir, 1988), which means that demand for child care and child welfare services may increase faster among Native people than the rest of the Canadian population. Furthermore, a large percentage of Native women head one-parent families (Siggner, 1986; Warry, 1991) and require child care services while they work, study, or look for employment. But a major issue concerning First Nations' child care has centred on

Many First Nations' peoples have developed their own schools providing culturally sensitive education.

N.W.T. Government/Tessa MacIntosh

past practices that allowed so many Native people to become alienated from their culture through placement in non-Native foster homes. In addition, finding ways to provide and pay for day-care services that are culturally sensitive remains a concern in aboriginal communities.

First Nations' people now expect child care services in their own language, controlled by their own people, and based on traditional values such as the importance of the extended family and elders (Native Women's Association, 1986; McEvoy, 1991). Some Native groups, such as those in Manitoba, have negotiated tripartite agreements with the provincial and federal governments that allow them to control their own child welfare and child care services with money from both levels of government.

Immigrants and Child Care

Immigrant women as a group are more likely to be in the labour force than Canadian-born women, although there are variations by ethnic origin and length of time in Canada. Although immigrant women from the United States, Great Britain, and northern Europe are more likely than Canadian-born women to have well-paid managerial and administrative jobs, those from southern Europe, Africa, and Asia are often concentrated at the bottom of the occupational scale (Seward and McDade, 1988; Basavarajappa and Verma, 1990). Many work in factories, especially in the clothing industries (Seward, 1990), where they do not need to know English or French, but where their chances of mobility are very slim. Others are forced to accept piecework at home because they cannot make suitable child care arrangements.

In some immigrant families, the grandmother is able and willing to provide child care while the parents are at work. This situation can save money, provide culturally sensitive care, and create a more solid bond between the children and their grandmother. However, it can also lead to disagreements about childrearing techniques between the grandparent, who is likely to have retained more traditional cultural values, and the parents or children, who may see the ideas of the grandmother as "old-fashioned."

If the parents are working on different shifts, they may be able to share childrearing. Again, this solves the problem of hiring a babysitter or sending the child(ren) to an expensive but not necessarily culturally-sensitive centre. Yet, it is difficult for parents working on separate shifts to maintain their own marital relationship, or for the family to share activities as a unit.

Some grandparents care for their grandchildren while the parents are in the labour force.

The Chu family

Although public child care is important to all workers, it is particularly critical for recent immigrants who have little control over their working hours or who are required to work shifts (Seward and McDade, 1988). Most child care centres operate during regular office hours and do not offer culturally sensitive services. Many parents need child care in the evening and care that respects and reinforces their cultural heritage. These parents (especially the women) also need child care to enable them to take language training that could improve their chances of moving to a more lucrative job or assist them to become more independent from their families.

SELECTED ISSUES

In the following section, several issues concerning childbirth and the early years of childrearing have been selected for discussion. The first deals with delayed childbirth and **infertility**. With the rising age of marriage and first birth, there is an apparent increase in infertility. Some of the new technologies created to help couples bear children have led to considerable controversy. The second discussion focuses on theories of socialization, or the ways in which children learn to develop their personalities and acquire the knowledge, skills, and motivation required for participation in social life. Academics have often disagreed about which theories best explain how children are socialized, yet some of these theories have formed the basis of educational policies. The third issue involves the problems parents encounter with child care when they attempt to combine work and family life. Finally, why is the incidence of child abuse increasingly reported in schools, churches, and homes?

DELAYED PARENTING, INFERTILITY, AND REPRODUCTIVE TECHNOLOGIES

In the past two decades, many couples in industrialized countries have been postponing pregnancy in order to finish their education, establish their careers, travel, save money, or buy a house. Life without children allows couples to create a more spontaneous lifestyle with greater emphasis on career development for women, less emphasis on steady work and career development for men, increased pursuit of leisure activities and travel, and a higher standard of living. After five or ten years of a childfree life, however, most couples feel that they are now ready to start a family.

An increasing number of Canadian women, especially middle-class career-oriented women, are having their first babies later in their childbearing lives than women did in previous generations. For example, only 7 percent of women had their first child after the age of 30 in 1971, compared with 18 percent in 1988 (Wadhera and Millar, 1991). Furthermore, delayed childbirth is especially increasing among single women. The total number of births to single women aged 30 to 39 increased thirteenfold from 1974 to 1988, and the number of first births increased 19 times (Wadhera and Millar, 1991).

The reasons for an increasing number and rate of first births at older ages relates to demographic factors such as the large number of postwar baby boomers who have now reached the later stages of their childbearing years. Many have lived a childfree life and are now reaching the end of their fertility. They either reproduce now or not at all. Although many of these women have remained single or have become divorced, as they come to the end of their fertile years they do not want to forego motherhood. They know that there is not much time left according to their "biological clocks."

For the present generation of women who are likely to be in the labour force, it is increasingly possible to support a child without a partner. Consequently, more women are choosing single parenthood when their jobs are reasonably secure or their careers established. Others are living in relationships without legal marriage, but feel that the legal disadvantages of having a child outside marriage are no longer restrictive.

In developed or industrialized countries such as Canada, where childless women are usually involved in a career, there is less social pressure to bear children and less of a stigma attached to childlessness than in developing countries. Yet, most people feel that having and raising a child is an integral part of married life that should not be missed. Increasingly, however, infertility appears to be a problem for a growing percentage of couples. About 15 percent of married couples in industrialized countries are infertile (Leslie and Korman, 1989:462) although this statistic depends on the definition of infertility. Infertility is usually defined as the inability to conceive a viable pregnancy within one year of unprotected intercourse (Bryant, 1990:2). For many couples, the inability to conceive contributes to feelings of guilt, anger, depression, and marital disputes (Matthews and Matthews, 1986).

Although the percentage of married couples who remain childless has never been very large, there were always some couples who could not bear children. In preindustrial or developing societies, fertility is usually considered to be very important for both sexes, and childless couples are often pitied by their neighbours and relatives. Without the available technology to test fertility, it is often assumed that the woman rather than the man is infertile. In the past, having an infertile wife was an acceptable reason for a man to take a mistress or concubine or to obtain a divorce in countries such as traditional China, ancient Greece, and early United States (Leslie and Korman, 1989:97, 159, 462). In some developing countries today, a childless woman is not considered to be fully adult and may be expected to care for her relatives' children or to take on community work rather than pursue her own interests.

The causes of infertility are numerous, including exposure to sexually transmitted diseases, long-term use of certain contraceptives, workplace hazards, environmental pollutants, hormonal imbalances, and lifestyle factors such as tobacco smoking, excessive exercise, a large consumption of caffeine or other drugs, and prolonged stress (Leslie and Korman, 1989:463; Bryant, 1990:17–18). Women who wait until their mid- to late thirties to have their first child sometimes find that although they are more emotionally and financially prepared for childbirth than they were in their twenties, conception is more difficult than they anticipated.

Some couples spend years trying to get pregnant, while others place their names on waiting lists for adoption. However, the number of infants available for adoption has dramatically decreased in the past two decades with lower birth rates among all age groups and fewer single mothers placing their children for adoption. Some couples eventually find an infant or young child in Canada but others turn to countries such as Korea, Romania, Colombia, or Brazil in order to adopt. This process could cost thousands of dollars in travel expenses and adoption, medical, and legal fees.

Those who feel that it is important to experience pregnancy and childbirth themselves can now turn to medical interventions, which have been developed to assist low-fertility couples. ***In vitro***

NEW REPRODUCTIVE TECHNOLOGIES (NRTS)

Infertility negatively affects the quality of life of many individuals in Canada. Indeed, it would appear that the number of individuals affected may actually be increasing. As the prevalence of this condition increases, and the public belief that technology can respond to these problems becomes more widespread, the demand for services will also increase.

However, the success rates of the newest therapies remain low, and the techniques quite experimental. Thus, the short- and long-term results of therapy must be collected and analysed, and this information must be clearly communicated to prospective consumers and the media. In addition, while the biological challenges of infertility are best met by those trained in the medical specialities related to their study, these groups are not the best (and certainly not the only) qualified to address the ethical and cultural issues which relate to these technologies. An atmosphere of open and genuine discussion of controls and concerns of these therapies needs to be created to facilitate discussion between the technologists and multidisciplinary groups which include consumers.

While the debate on NRTs has, to date, focused on the technologies themselves, it should be recalled that infertility's antecedents and effects are largely outside the technical sphere. Although many gaps in knowledge and opportunity exist which undermine chances for immediate success in preventive policies, it is realistic to state that cost-effective programs for infertility prevention are entirely possible. If progress is to be made in combatting infertility, then, the major battleground of the future may well be in the community itself, and not merely in the "test tubes" of research laboratories. Thus, focusing solely on new reproductive technology research runs the risk of overlooking opportunities for diminishing the impact of infertility which affects and disturbs so many women and couples in Canada.

This section is taken from *The Infertility Dilemma: Reproductive Technologies and Prevention* by Heather Bryant, published by the Canadian Advisory Council on the Status of Women, 1990.

fertilization, in which the woman's egg is fertilized outside the uterus, has become more prevalent in the past decade with the development of hospital-based fertility clinics. Success rates of this technique (referred to as "test-tube babies") are often based on pregnancies rather than live births, even though there tends to be an above-average rate of miscarriages with **artificial insemination**. Many couples undergo several cycles of treatment; a cycle includes one attempt at ovulation, recovery, fertilization, and implementation. In a number of studies of artificial (intrauterine) insemination quoted by Bryant in a study for the Canadian Advisory Council on the Status of Women (1990:9,10), the pregnancy rates varied from 3 percent to 14 percent per treatment. If couples underwent multiple treatments, however, the pregnancy rate rose from 40 percent to 50 percent for insemination by donor sperm. For *in vitro* fertilization, the pregnancy rates vary from 10 to 31 percent, but the percent of live births was about 15. Powerful drugs often accompany fertility treatment, producing side effects such as depression, weight gain, and multiple births. Furthermore, the technique is extremely expensive for hospitals to perform and, if the patient has to pay directly, it can cost several thousands of dollars. Because of these concerns, the Canadian government established a Royal Commission on New Reproductive Technologies in 1990 to explore the medical, legal, and social implications of a variety of reproductive technologies.

A very small but increasing number of childless couples have contracted fertile women to bear children for them. These **surrogate mothers** are usually low-income women who see childbearing as a relatively easy way to earn a living, while the childless couple is often financially well-off (McDaniel, 1988c; Bryant, 1990). In addition to any moral concerns there may be, legal complications are ever present. For example, the "Baby M" case, which was widely publicized in North American newspapers in 1988, illustrates the potential legal complications. After the birth, the surrogate mother decided that she wanted to keep the child rather than give her to the biological father and his wife. In this particular case in the United States, William and Elizabeth Stern won custody of the child born by Mary Beth Whitehead, who was artificially inseminated with the sperm of William Stern. But this long and well-publicized court case has underlined the need for public policy on the legality of surrogate motherhood, the role of women in reproductive technology, the acceptability of profit-making or the use of public funds for infertility clinics, and the changing definition of paternity.

THEORIES OF SOCIALIZATION

Theories of socialization are being discussed within this section on Special Issues because, although academics disagree on which theory best explains the socialization process, educational policies and childrearing and social work practices have been developed around certain theories. The socialization of children, refers to "the complex learning process through which individuals develop selfhood and acquire the knowledge, skills, and motivations required for participation in social life" (Mackie, 1990:117). Social scientific views on socialization have evolved with research developments and the popularization of new theories.

Psychoanalytic theorists, such as the Austrian physician Sigmund Freud (1856–1939), believed that socialization takes place in the first few years of life and is influenced by psychosexual development. Children pass through stages marked by sexual preoccupation with different parts of the body, but are also influenced by early family experiences. Children tend to identify with their same-sex parent, and much of personality development is influenced by unconscious emotions (Mackie, 1990). The process of socialization involves taming children's selfish urges.

Psychoanalytic theory has been criticized for being untestable and biased, as the research was based almost exclusively on a sample of middle-class female patients in nineteenth-century Vienna. Furthermore, parts of Freud's earlier theories portrayed women as defective men. Freud also assumed that socialization takes place only in early childhood, but later social scientists found that it continues throughout life. For these reasons, Freud's theories have been criticized, yet we cannot overlook the contribution he made to the study of personality development and the further research he stimulated. Freud's ideas about socialization have been influential both in social science and popular thought. For example, Erik Erikson (1963, 1968) argued that children pass through stages of development or preoccupation in which they must resolve certain crucial life issues in order to reach maturity. These include developing a capacity for trust, autonomy, initiative, industry, identity, and intimacy. Erikson has been very influential in the fields of family studies and child development.

Another theory of socialization, **learning theory**, emphasizes the importance of nurture in the historic **nature/nurture debate**. This debate over whether inherited characteristics or social environment and learning play a more important role in personality development continues. Learning theory became predominant in the 1920s with experiments on **conditioning** and imitation. According to this theory, children are socialized by being rewarded or punished for certain behaviour and from observing and imitating adults, especially their parents.

The developmental approach to socialization arose from the work of the Swiss psychologist Jean Piaget during the 1920s and 1930s. Piaget was interested in the systematic changes that occur over time in children's thought processes. Like psychoanalytic theory, Piaget's approach suggests that all children pass through similar stages of cognitive development. Piaget also concluded that children could not learn particular tasks or concepts until they had reached a certain stage in their development. He further theorized that these stages were influenced by children's experiences and interpretations of the physical and social world. Unlike learning theory, this approach suggests that children actively participate in their own socialization.

Research by David Elkind (1981) on **hurried children** uses the developmental approach to socialization and suggests that children cannot be rushed through certain stages in their development. Middle- and upper-class children are often pushed by their parents to excel in language, reasoning, and mathematical skills, and encouraged to progress through the school system faster than other children. Working-class children, on the other hand, are often forced to earn a living in order to help support the family or to leave home before they can adequately cope. Pushing children beyond their capacities can lead to later emotional and behavioural problems, according to this theory.

Symbolic interactionists argue that children are socialized through their interpretations of other people's reactions to them, especially family members and friends. There is a strong association between what we believe others think of us and our self-concept (Cooley, 1902, Mead, 1934). At the same time, what people actually think of us can also be affected by the image we project. Social interactionism also theorizes that part of socialization is looking at the world through the eyes of other people and anticipating a particular role before taking it. According to this theory, however, socialization takes place throughout the life cycle.

More recently, social scientists have argued that socialization is influenced not only by environmental factors but also by the genetic make-up of an individual. **Sociobiology** emphasizes the nature part of the nature/nurture debate, just as scientists did prior to the 1920s. This approach has stimulated considerable controversy within sociology (Mackie, 1990) because it is reminiscent of earlier theories that suggested behaviour was determined by instincts and drives. Furthermore, sociobiologists sometimes assume that research results which are valid for animals also pertain to humans.

The systems approach to socialization combines all of these theories, but also deals with the child's special circumstances in the family and how the family relationships influence the child's personality and social development (Tesson, 1988:101). Parental authority, however, is increasingly shared with baby-sitters, television, school teachers, and the peer group (Mackie, 1990:130), and it cannot be assumed that the influence of parents is the only important one in the lives of young children. As more children are cared for by nonfamily members during working hours, parents may lose more of their influence in the socialization process in the future.

Feminists have used elements of psychoanalytic theory, developmental theory, and symbolic interactionism to explain socialization, but usually focus on development and maintenance of gender differences. Most feminists argue that girls and boys develop differences in personality, priorities, interests, and achievements because of their unique psychological and sexual experiences as well as different treatment by parents, teachers, and employers, rather than from any inherent physiological differences. For example, Nancy Chodorow (1989) combines psychoanalysis and feminist theory, showing how unconscious awareness of self and gender, developed from earliest infancy, shapes the experiences of males and females as well as the patterns of inequality that permeate our culture. Carol Gilligan argued in *In a Different Voice* (1982) that moral development of men and women is quite different. While men tend to focus on human rights, justice, and freedom, the principles of human responsibility, caring, and commitment form the basis of women's sense of morality. Feminists now refer to all aspects of society differentiating between masculine and feminine, such as different toys for girls and boys, a segregated labour force, and advertisements that accentuate cultural ideas of masculinity and femininity, as elements of a **gendered society**.

Child Care Concerns

A generation ago, most children were raised at home by their mothers during their preschool years. In the last two decades, an increasing number of mothers with young children have entered the labour force partly because a single income can no longer maintain the same standard of living it did in the 1950s.

Raising children is very expensive in modern society. Over the life cycle, two-child families in Ontario spend at least 18 percent of their gross income to meet childrearing costs (Douthitt and Fedyk, 1990:29). Couples meet these costs by raising their incomes, increasing the amount of time spent on household work rather than hiring help or using labour-saving products, reallocating income from other expenditures to child-related goods, or decreasing their savings. Families with children tend to spend less on restaurant meals, recreation, tobacco, alcohol, adult clothing, and gifts in order to meet childrearing costs. In addition, families with children save less money than childfree couples. For example, two-child families in Ontario save about 17 percent of their gross income during childrearing years, compared with an average savings rate of 29 percent by childfree couples over the same period (Ibid, 1990:29).

The Social Planning Council of Metropolitan Toronto estimated that the cost of raising a child from birth to age 18 in the Toronto area was $94 500 in 1987 dollars. If they had added the cost of 10 years of nonsubsidized child care, the cost would have increased to about $140 100. This conservative estimate assumes that the family rents an apartment and does not own a car. Day-care can more than double the annual cost of raising younger children, and is usually the greatest single child-related expense a family incurs (Mitchell, 1987).

The two-income family is one of the most important social changes of this century. The additional income raises the standard of living but further increases income inequality between one-income and two-income families. In addition, two-income families create the need for new services such as convenience foods, home cleaning companies, and public child care facilities.

Since 1966, child care for low-income or one-parent families has been cost-shared between the provinces and the federal government under the Canada Assistance Plan. For these families, subsidized spaces are set aside, generally in nonprofit government-regulated day-care centres or licensed homes. Two-parent families that are not low-income families, however, must pay the full cost if they require nonfamily child care. In Ontario, infant care costs about $10 000, while

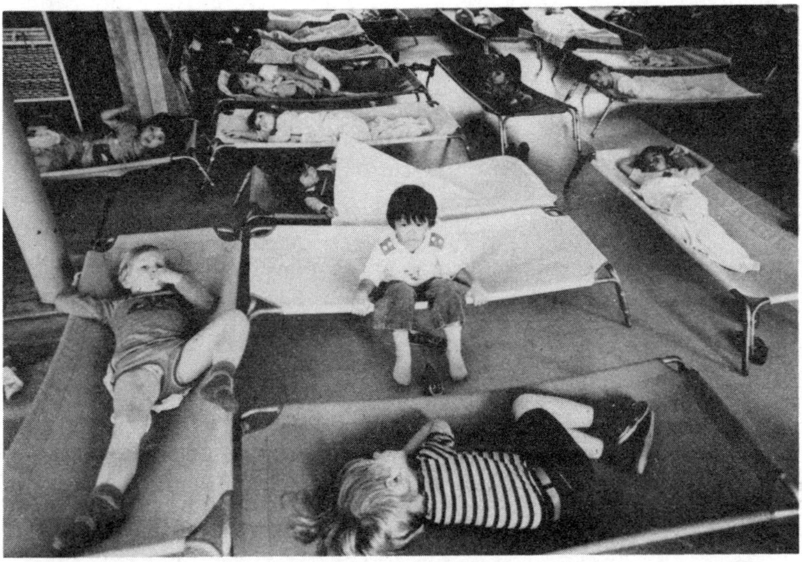

Because of the shortage of child care spaces, most parents do not use licensed child care, but rely on unregulated baby-sitters to care for their preschool children.

Canapress Photo Service/Ian Barrett

a high-quality preschool program costs about $6000 to $7000 per child each year (Canada, House of Commons, December 1991). Because of the shortage of child care spaces, most parents do not use licensed child care centres or licensed family home care, however, but rely on unregulated baby-sitters to care for their preschool children.

Although the federal government provides an income tax deduction for child care expenses, it is not used by a substantial minority of parents who pay for child care services because they are unable to obtain receipts from caretakers working informally within the **underground economy**. The federal government further provides child care allowances for trainees in Canada Employment and Immigration programs.

Although the federal government contributes to child care funding, the provision of services and the regulation of care falls under provincial jurisdiction. As a result the system lacks national unity and varies in consistency and quality. Many nonprofit day-care centres have long waiting lists; the number of families that need child care far outstrips the availability of spaces. In 1990, for example, there were more than 1.3 million preschoolers (under age 6) and 1.7 million school-age children (6–12) whose mothers were in the labour force. Therefore, as many as 3 million children may have been in need of alternative care arrangements, yet in 1990 there were only 321 000 licensed spaces for children of those ages in Canada. Only 18 percent of preschool children with mothers in the labour force were in licensed family or day-care centre full-time, up from 4 percent in 1981 (Burke, Crompton, Jones and Nessner, 1991).

The quality of child care both in licensed centres and in private homes by baby-sitters concerns many parents. Child care centre employees in some provinces and baby-sitters in all provinces are not required to have any special training. These jobs generally pay the minimum wage or below, and have difficulty attracting trained people. The quality of care received by most children of working parents can be monitored only by parents, who seldom have the opportunity or time to investigate conditions fully. Because parents often cannot find alternative care within their neighbourhood, they must accept whatever is available.

A number of consumer groups have formed around this issue, including the Canadian Day Care Advocacy Association and day-care committees within large unions. Some have asked for the federal government to take a role in funding child care similar to its role in funding post-secondary education or Medicare. Other groups have demanded better training, fringe benefits, and pay for nannies and child care workers, who they say are paid less than zoo keepers. The difference between the qualifications and salaries of child care workers and kindergarten teachers, for example, has been widely discrepant. Kindergarten teachers are unionized and are paid through funds from the Ministry of Education. On the other hand, day-care employees are seldom unionized and are paid through funds from the Ministry of Community and Social Services.

Parents with children who have special needs have not had an easy time finding suitable day care for them. Before institutions and hospitals were built in the 1960s, mothers were the main caretakers of these children. This traditional source of unpaid labour is once again being examined as a way to reduce health and chronic care costs with policies of de-institutionalization. But adequate attention is not always given to the fact that many mothers are now in the labour force. Without some remuneration and community assistance, these women will be unable to provide the close supervision some of these children require because of their own work responsibilities. Furthermore, many parents now expect their children, despite their special needs, to be integrated into the local day-care centre or public school in order to receive the same education as other children. In fact, court cases using the equality clause of the Charter of Rights and Freedoms have been fought over this issue.

Whether or not governments should be more involved in child care remains a contentious issue. Lobby groups have argued for more income tax relief for one-income families, wages for homemakers to enable parents to look after their own children, and pensions for homemakers. But the amount of these benefits would have to be much less than the income from working in the labour force, or taxes would rise considerably.

Although most young parents are now in the labour force, problems with nonparental child care have encouraged some parents (usually mothers) to remain at home to care for their children. Many day-care centres do not take children under the age of two unless they are toilet-trained. Even if space is available, parents want to ensure that the centre employs an adequate number of staff members to keep the infants clean, fed, and stimulated. In addition, parents are often concerned about the spread of infectious diseases with infants in centre care.

Finding a qualified baby-sitter who will come to the child's home or will welcome an extra child in her or his home is also difficult. Although there are licensed family homes in some provinces, most sitters operate outside provincial regulations. Sitter care is unregulated by any level of government, yet remains the typical solution to the problems with centre care.

Increasingly, employers are allowing parents extended unpaid leave of up to five years to care for their children at home. However, not all employers offer such leave programs, and usually only mothers accept extended leave. Furthermore, few families can survive on one income and the parent who stays at home may experience difficulty re-entering the labour force.

CHILD ABUSE

In recent years, considerable concern has been expressed about the rising number of reported child abuse cases in North America. Although children were probably always mistreated by some parents and guardians, definitions of "abuse" and "mistreatment" have changed. People have only recently started talking about these instances publicly and demanding increased protection for children. We no longer feel that children are the property of parents nor that parents or teachers have the right to beat or even physically punish children under their care.

Child abuse is a general term used to describe a variety of injuries inflicted by a parent or guardian. There are four main types of abuse: physical abuse or battering; neglect, usually involving food or water deprivation; sexual abuse, which includes pornographic exploitation, incest, violent molestation, rape, or pedophile contact; and emotional abuse, which could involve withholding affection or praise and belittling the child and reducing his or her self-esteem (Wachtel, 1989).

The vast amount of unreported child abuse makes estimating the extent of this problem very difficult. Most Canadian provinces have child abuse registries, but child protection workers and victimization studies indicate that these registries record only a fraction of cases. However, the number of reported cases has been rising dramatically every year across the country. Whether this indicates a rise in the actual number of abuse cases or simply is a result of new regulations requiring that such behaviour be reported is not known.

Research has documented the cyclical nature of child abuse (Van Stolk, 1978). Abused children generally develop low self-esteem and are likely to experience future emotional problems. Many young people who become involved in prostitution have been abused throughout their childhood. Abused children also tend to become abusive parents because they learn violent ways of dealing with frustration within their families. Over the past decade, the rise in reported cases of child abuse has led to a public demand for better child protection laws and new ways of dealing with abusers.

Parents and guardians who abuse children often feel that they are simply disciplining them. In some cases, the child is labelled "difficult" because of a health or behavioural problem. But an abused child may be victimized simply because he or she is vulnerable. Some abusers realize that they cannot control themselves and join self-help groups to try to change their violent behaviour. But many continue the abuse until the child becomes too big to beat up, leaves home, or notifies the authorities.

Although physical abuse remains an issue, recent attention has focused on the sexual abuse of children. The Badgley Report in 1984 concluded through a variety of research techniques that the proportion of Canadian adults who had been the victims of "unwanted sexual acts" as children was much higher than previously acknowledged. The report noted that sexual abuse generally occurs during the daytime, in the victim's or a friend's home, and is likely to be carried out by a male relative or family friend. While girls are more vulnerable to abuse than boys, a sizable minority of young boys are sexually abused. Recently, school and church leaders have become concerned

CHILD SEX ABUSE CONSTANT, STUDY SAYS

BY DEBORAH JONES
Special to The Globe and Mail

HALIFAX—A study of sexual abuse of children conducted by researchers in Ottawa suggests that contrary to other recent studies, the phenomenon is not increasing but merely being reported more.

"Although many child protection programs are reporting more clinical cases of childhood sexual abuse, it is likely that (it) is not increasing but, in a new social climate, more children and their families are coming forward," said the study by a team at the Children's Hospital of Eastern Ontario in Ottawa.

The study, presented at the annual meeting of the Canadian Pediatric Society in Halifax yesterday, analysed data from 17 North American studies on the prevalence of such abuse in the 1940s, the 1970s and the 1980s.

Co-author William Feldman said the criteria used in the studies differed and that some studies were seriously flawed by the small number of responses or by the selection of people surveyed. Some of these studies would suggest childhood sexual abuse was dramatically increasing if these flaws were not taken into account, he said.

Dr. Feldman and his wife, anthropologist Eva Feldman, compared the prevalence of abuse by concentrating on girls under age 14 who were sexually abused by a male over 14 who was at least five years older than the victim.

Using those criteria, the Feldmans found a consistent rate of about 12 percent of females were victims of childhood sexual abuse from the 1940s to the present.

Dr. Feldman said reports of such abuse are soaring because society is changing. "Women and children are no longer considered objects," he said.

Dr. Feldman started the study after becoming concerned by reports that such abuse had increased by 600 percent and was becoming epidemic.

By Deborah Jones. This article was originally printed in *The Globe and Mail.*

about sexual abuse by teachers, youth workers, and priests and are looking for ways to detect potential abusers before an incident occurs and to deal with those accused of abuse.

Because provincial legislation covers many family and child protection issues, ways of responding to family violence, regulations, and procedures for reporting vary across the country. Grants for social services, including transition houses, counselling, and family courts, fluctuate by province. Increasingly, there is a lack of intervention in known child abuse cases because of insufficient staff and the sheer number of cases reported.

The federal government has not established a central child abuse registry, as recommended by several reports including Badgley's, but rather appointed a co-ordinator to work through the National

Clearinghouse on Family Violence at the Department of Health and Welfare in Ottawa. Federal legislation was passed in 1987 introducing tough penalties to those sexually abusing children and giving children's evidence in child abuse cases more credence (Baker, 1988b).

FUTURE TRENDS

The Future of Parenting

Throughout this century, family size has continued to decline as women bear fewer children, and more parents separate and divorce. Most demographers project that declining birth rates will continue in the near future because children are increasingly costly in modern urban environments, and combining work and family life is difficult when both parents are in the labour force.

Although government reports have reiterated that "children are our greatest future resource," little has been done in North America to assist couples in combining work and family life. Yet, governments, especially in Quebec and Europe, are increasingly concerned about the economic and political implications of below-replacement fertility rates. There have been many policy discussions about possible changes to enhance family and work life. Although it would be costly, employers and governments could make it easier by allowing more generous maternity and parental leaves and benefits. Parents also need to be allowed to take time off work to care for sick children or for other family responsibilities. Both of these changes, however, would cost employers and governments more money. More flexible work hours or shared work without loss of benefits would also assist working parents.

Governments cannot realistically expect that one-time cash grants or even moderate increases in tax credits will encourage many couples to have larger families when some employers will not accommodate employees with family responsibilities (Baker, 1992). Governments and employers could assist working parents by providing more child care spaces in neighbourhoods or in the workplace. Parents would then be relieved from the burden of transporting their children to and from a day-cares that are close to neither home nor work. In addition, they could provide extended retail shopping and business hours to allow parents working weekdays to complete their errands on more than one day a week. However, in times of economic recession, many of these reforms are unlikely to happen because they would increase either taxes or employer costs. Many employers are more concerned with staying in business than assisting employees to combine work and family life.

One-parent families, small families, and childfree couples will continue to be more prevalent in the future. While more low-fertility couples will be able to reproduce with the assistance of new reproductive technologies, a larger number of couples may opt for a childfree lifestyle. Already, some couples have postponed childbearing to the point where conception becomes more difficult, and the risks of fetal deformities are higher. Increasingly, more couples will postpone childbearing until they can no longer conceive.

During the 1950s, **pronatal values**, or values that encouraged childbearing, were dominant in both the popular media and academic research. On the other hand, we have been inundated with negative portrayals of family in the 1980s and 1990s, by emphasizing child abuse, the high cost of raising children, the probabilities of birth defects after a certain age, and the problems of juggling family life and job. After romanticizing family life, we are now focusing on the negative aspects, instead of simply presenting a more realistic picture.

Yet, some governments are again trying to encourage childbearing because they are concerned that declining birth rates will eventually lead to an older population requiring higher government expenditures. At the present time, a disproportionate amount of government money is being spent on health care and pensions for seniors in comparison with services for children. Some researchers argue that more retired people in the population will lead to a lower tax base and a drain on social programs. However, if governments want to encourage people to have more children, they will have to create a more conducive social environment.

In addition to the suggestions previously mentioned, governments could also increase tax incentives for families with dependent children or adults with special needs. They could provide more generous family allowances and seriously consider some payment to those parents who choose to care for their own children at home. These reforms are unlikely to be introduced, however, because they would entail such politically unfeasible alternatives as tax increases or a shift in government priorities.

SUGGESTED READINGS

Ambert, Anne-Marie. *The Effect of Children on Parents*. New York: The Haworth Press, 1992.

Bala, Nicholas, Joseph P. Hornick, and Robin Vogl (eds.). *Canadian Child Welfare Law. Children, Families and the State*. Toronto: Thompson Educational Publishing, 1991.

Bryant, Heather. *The Infertility Dilemma: Reproductive Technologies and Prevention*. Canadian Advisory Council on the Status of Women. Ottawa: Minister of Supply and Services Canada, February 1990.

Burke, Mary Anne, Susan Crompton, Alison Jones, and Katherine Nessner. "Caring for Children." *Canadian Social Trends*. 22. Autumn 1991:12–15.

DeMause, L. (ed.) *The History of Childhood*. New York: The Psychohistory Press, 1974.

Drakich, Janice and Connie Guberman. "Violence in the Family." *Family Matters. Sociology and Contemporary Canadian Families*. Edited by Karen Anderson et al. Scarborough: Nelson, 1988.

Elkind, David. *The Hurried Child*. Don Mills: Addison-Wesley, 1981.

Ishwaran, K. (ed.). *Canadian Families: Ethnic Variations*. Scarborough: McGraw-Hill Ryerson, 1980.

Ishwaran, K. (ed.). *Childhood and Adolescence in Canada*. Scarborough: McGraw-Hill Ryerson, 1979.

Johnston, Patrick. *Native Children and the Child Welfare System*. Toronto: James Lorimer and Company, 1983.

Mackie, Marlene. "Socialization: Changing Views of Child Rearing and Adolescence." *Families: Changing Trends in Canada*. 2nd ed. Edited by Maureen Baker. Scarborough: McGraw-Hill Ryerson, 1990:115–148.

Mandell, Nancy. "The Child Question: Links Between Women and Children in the Family." *Reconstructing the Canadian Family: Feminist Perspectives*. Edited by Nancy Mandell and Ann Duffy. Toronto: Butterworths, 1988:49–81.

Martin Matthews, Anne, and Ralph Matthews. "Beyond the Mechanics of Infertility: Perspectives on the Social Psychology of Infertility and Involuntary Childlessness." *Family Relations*. 35. October 1986:479–487.

McEvoy, Maureen. "Native Communities Revise and Redesign the Child Welfare System." *Transition*. 21(4). December 1991:11–14.

Statistics Canada. *A Portrait of Children in Canada*. Cat. 89-520. Ottawa: Supply and Services Canada, 1990a.

___ . *Women in Canada. A Statistical Report*. 2nd ed. Cat. 89-503E. Ottawa: Minister of Supply and Services, February 1990c.

Strong-Boag, Veronica. "Intruders in the Nursery: Childcare Professionals Reshape the Years One to Five, 1920–1940." *Childhood and Family in Canadian History*. Edited by Joy Parr. Toronto: McClelland and Stewart, 1982:160–178.

Tesson, Geoffrey. "Socialization and Parenting." *Family Matters. Sociology and Contemporary Canadian Families*. Edited by Karen Anderson et al. Scarborough: Nelson, 1988:87–112.

Wadhera, Surinder and Wayne J. Millar. "Patterns and Change in Canadian Fertility 1971–1988: First Births After Age 30." *Health Reports*. 3 (2). 1991:149–161.

Warry, Wayne. "Ontario's First People: Native Children." *Children, Families and Public Policies in the 90s*. Edited by Laura C. Johnson and Dick Barnhorst. Toronto: Thompson Educational Publishing, 1991:207–230.

ISSUES FOR DISCUSSION

1. Which factors do you think have made the greatest impact on historical changes to childhood?
2. Develop a case study to illustrate the socialization process according to symbolic interactionism (or another theory of your choice).
3. How much of the personality and behaviour considered to be appropriate for males and females is learned and how much is innate?
4. Can parents effectively counteract other socialization influences, such as peers or television, if they think they are bad for their children?
5. What is meant by the "underground economy?" Why do so many baby-sitters neglect to give parents receipts when they are paid for child care? What are the implications of not obtaining a receipt from the parents' point of view?
6. If you need to find day-care for your child, what kind of care would you want? How would you decide on the quality of care provided at a day-care centre or by a baby-sitter?

7. Imagine that you are a married mother with two children. You have been out of the labour force for five years, and your husband has been supporting the family. Before your children were born, you worked as a typist in a secretarial pool. Now you are planning to separate, and your husband says that he cannot afford to pay more than $200 a month for child support. What would you do?
8. Should government benefits be provided to enable women to stay at home and care for their children, or should governments be providing child care services to enable women to go out to work? Would it make a difference if these women were on social assistance?
9. At what stage in a child's life is childrearing most difficult for parents? Justify your answer.
10. What are the major differences among couples who have children soon after marriage, those who choose to remain childfree, and those delaying childbirth until later in life?
11. Identify strengths in your family that will help you to become a better parent in the future.

FURTHER ACTIVITIES

1. What services are available in your community for each of the following groups:
   a. the care of children of working parents;
   b. children abused by their parents;
   c. the education and stimulation of preschool children with mothers at home?

   Which organizations offer these services, where do their funds come from, and how much do parents pay?
2. Construct a questionnaire that could be used to evaluate the above services.
3. Observe at least two types of child care arrangements. List advantages and disadvantages of each.
4. Interview a number of fathers and ask them about their experiences with their partner's pregnancy, with childbirth, and with their newborn baby.

6

MID-LIFE AND THE FAMILY WITH ADOLESCENTS

SPECIFIC TASKS

THE REFORMULATION OF PARENT-CHILD ROLES

In modern-day Canadian families, we distinguish between childhood and **adolescence** by granting adolescents more autonomy and privacy, allowing them certain privileges and rights, giving them more choice in their daily lives, and encouraging them to develop adult skills and to plan for their independence. Young people are usually encouraged to establish their own beliefs and ideas, and to look forward to setting up their own households separate from their **family of orientation**. It is generally assumed that young people will want to leave home, marry, and have children or create their own **family of procreation**. Yet, the family environment is very important in providing role models for young people, including examples of the importance of staying in school, the kinds of jobs that are desirable, what it is like to develop an intimate relationship, how to raise children, and what is important in life.

Older people tend to think of adolescence as a time of hope, anticipation, and preparation for the future. Some young people, however, find it difficult to plan for the future considering the threat of nuclear war, the uncertainty of the labour market, and the apparent impermanence of marriage. Other adolescents demand more autonomy than their parents are willing to give them, or attempt to show in socially unacceptable ways that they are individuals .

Families with adolescents often experience considerable conflict. Many studies indicate that at this stage, life and marital satisfaction for parents tends to be at the lowest level of the life cycle (Rollins and Feldman, 1970; Lupri and Frideres, 1981). Lupri and Frideres (1981) found that having teenage children tends to have a negative impact on marital satisfaction. Their research of Calgary couples found a U-shaped pattern of marital satisfaction, with the lowest levels reported between the years when the children are teenagers until they leave home. However, they also found that fathers were more positive about teenage children than mothers.

Reasons for the low levels of satisfaction reported by the parents of teenagers are several. Nett (1990) argues that with parenting, interactions between couples become less person-oriented and more structured in terms of roles and obligations. As the children grow older, financial demands increase. Parents may be caught between responsibilities for their adolescents and their aging parents. Both husband and wife are likely to be in the labour force, and to have jobs that require greater commitment and responsibility than in previous

FOR BETTER OR FOR WORSE © 1989 Lynn Johnston Prod., Inc. Reprinted with permission of Universal Press Syndicate. All rights reserved.

years. It is not surprising that many parents feel that there are too many demands being placed on them.

Parents may also find family life difficult at this stage because they are reaching the point in their lives when they are increasingly aware of what they have yet to accomplish, and question what lies ahead of them. At a time when parents' self-worth might be fragile, teenage children are often highly critical of their parents' appearance, values, accomplishments, and lifestyle (Lamanna and Reid, 1988). Furthermore, there may be friction between the parents over how to deal with disagreements and misunderstanding in the household.

Parents with teenage children may find that rearing them is a complex task involving patience and understanding. As their teenagers wrestle with what kind of people they want to be, what kind of life they want to live, and what they believe in, their moods often swing rapidly with little prior warning. Parents are often excluded from sharing their thoughts, perhaps because the teens fear being ridiculed or because they do not respect their parents' opinions. Some adolescents become very confused and emotionally distressed, turning to alcohol and illegal drugs. Rates of suicide and attempted suicide are relatively high during adolescence. However, suicide rates are highest for men aged 20 to 24 (Beneteau, 1990).

Adolescents have to cope with physiological and emotional changes, new social expectations, dating, educational choices, and imminent occupational decisions. They tend to be caught between adulthood and childhood, and often feel that parental and social expectations are inappropriate for them. While many young people are physically mature, they are not educationally and socially prepared to live independently and earn a living. As dependants of their parents, adolescents tend to resent restrictions on their personal freedom, feel that their parents are unreasonable and old-fashioned, and demand more rights and independence than parents are prepared to give. Both parents and adolescents sometimes feel that the gap between generations is insurmountable.

Reprinted with special permission of King Features Syndicate.

If adolescents are financially dependent on their parents, as most North Americans are, they may make economic demands that parents cannot or will not meet. Adolescents often feel that they require certain types of clothing, material goods such as stereos and cars, and specific forms of entertainment to conform to peer standards. These expenses frequently violate parental standards of what young people need. Furthermore, young people often want to be different from their parents, both in their lifestyle and in their ideas, while parents usually expect them to adopt parental values. Disputes about physical appearance, clothing, musical taste, leisure activities, and choice of friends sometimes cause considerable friction between parents and their adolescent children.

In their desire to fit in with the crowd, adolescents may be more influenced by their peer group than by their parents. Many become caught up in the **adolescent subculture**, with values emphasizing conformity, spontaneity, sexuality, and fashion, that often violate parents' ideas of propriety and maturity. In some extreme cases, teens become involved in youth gangs that may provide a sense of belonging and acceptance, but can overemphasize conformity and sometimes become violent and destructive. The ideals and activities of these gangs may be difficult for parents to understand.

Resolving the conflicts between parents and their adolescent children may require parents to read the hidden messages behind their adolescent's hostility and apparent rejection, noting that these emotions and outbursts often accompany the process of individuation and separation from family. At the same time, adolescents need to remember that parents are concerned about their children's safety and well-being, that they need to maintain some remnant of control over their children's behaviour, and need to maintain their self-respect.

Adolescence is usually a time of questioning, and young people often crave information about their family history. While those born into a family can ask their biological parents specific questions about the past, young people who are adopted may have a more difficult time finding these answers. While many adoptive parents readily tell their children what they know of their past, others are concerned that the desire to find out about their origins and the birth parents means rejection of all the years of adoptive parenting. Young people may register at age 18 for disclosure with adoption agencies or self-help groups, but adopted young people may not be pleased with what they discover about their birth parents. Through this process, they may come to appreciate more the parents who raised them.

Although life with adolescents may be trying for some parents or at certain times, others enjoy their children more when they grow up. Many parents can feel proud of the children they have raised, and derive considerable satisfaction from watching them develop new interests, talents, and unique personalities. Occasionally, parents become remotivated and adopt some of their adolescent's interests or hobbies. They may also enjoy a kind of companionship not possible in earlier stages of the family life cycle when their children were less mature.

Although adolescence is often a time of psychological and parental conflict, many young people later find that they have more in common with their parents and siblings than they initially thought. Early family experiences create a solid bond and lasting impression about desirable lifestyles and acceptable values. In fact, children often unknowingly pattern their behaviour and their relationships after their parents'. This may include duplicating the same patterns of interaction and types of conflict with their own children that they experienced with their parents.

Over the years, typical relations between parents and their adolescent children have varied with changes in education and the labour market, living arrangements, and relations between the sexes. For example, adolescents are more likely now than in the 1950s to work part-time while they study. They are also more likely to plan to attend college or university. Many engage in sexual relations and expect to leave home before marriage. At the same time, they are less likely than adolescents in the 1950s to pay "room and board" to their parents while they are working. They are also less likely than young people in the 1950s to legally marry or to remain married for life.

The creation of adolescence as a distinct stage in the family life cycle is relatively recent. This stage between childhood and adulthood was only possible after the abolition of child labour, the insistence on compulsory education, and the necessity for young people to receive higher education in order to find work.

HISTORICAL PERSPECTIVES

TYPICAL EDUCATION AND WORK PATTERNS OF ADOLESCENTS

Until this century, most Canadian adolescents left school when their families needed their incomes. Young people from the working and middle classes would find jobs such as domestic servants, apprentices, labourers, and office clerks, or would work at home for their families in return for room and board. A large percentage of adolescents' wages, if they received any, went to their parents. Without insurance for medical care, accidents, unemployment, or permanent disability, many parents needed their adolescent children's income to pay the bills and to set aside money for future uncertainties.

Before World War II, children of low-income parents often left school before graduation in order to help support the family. With parental consent, the Ontario law requiring compulsory education until age 16 could be waived at the age of 14. Although these school leavers had to accept unskilled jobs, they often expected to work their way into more responsible positions with experience.

In the 1930s, only about one-third of Canadian adolescents aged 15 to 19 were in school. The proportion rose, however, after the 1960s, as table 6.1 indicates. School attendance increased with the need for a more literate labour force, the expansion of the service sector, and the development of office technology, which created more white collar jobs. In addition, the professions expanded and professional qualifications were upgraded during this period. Colleges and universities also expanded to accommodate the large population of young people in the postwar baby boom.

During the early 1980s, the proportion of 15- to 19-year-olds attending school temporarily declined. Part of this decline could be attributed to lower birth rates, which led to a higher proportion of 18- and 19-year-olds in this age group, who are more likely to leave school. But in addition, high unemployment rates, increasing competition to enter post-secondary institutions, and the economic recession encouraged students to accept any job they could find rather than stay in school in the anticipation of a better job later.

When parents are unemployed or are experiencing financial difficulty, families may need the income of their adolescents and cannot afford to keep them in school. Those adolescents from the neediest families, however, usually have the most difficulty finding work, and their lack of formal education usually signals sporadic employment. Consequently, many who are forced to quit school for financial reasons may be permanently disadvantaged in the work

Table 6.1 **Percentage of 15- to 19-Year-Olds Attending School Full-Time, by Sex, Canada, 1931–1990**

	MALES	FEMALES
1931	32.2	35.1
1941	33.8	37.0
1951	40.8	40.1
1961	61.2	55.7
1971	73.8	71.1
1981	65.5	66.2
1986	72.9	72.9
1989–90	73.3	74.8

Source: Minister of State for Youth. *Youth: A New Statistical Perspective on Youth in Canada.* Ottawa: Supply and Services Canada, 1984:94; Statistics Canada. Education, Culture and Tourism Division, telephone conversation to obtain 1986 and 1989–90 figures, August 1988 and February 1992. Reproduced with the permission of the Minister of Supply and Services Canada, 1992.

force. According to a study from the Ontario Institute for Studies in Education, the Ontario school drop-out rate remained high from 1983 until 1987. In other provinces, however, school attendance has apparently risen for 15- to 19-year-olds since the early 1980s.

Over the past 20 years, **educational inflation** has elevated the required qualifications of many jobs, and the education and occupational aspirations of adolescents have risen as they realize they need more schooling to find work. At one time, students were required to attend college for one or two years after high school to qualify for elementary school teaching; now they need a university degree. As job opportunities decline, young people must become more competitive by increasing their educational attainment, searching harder for work, becoming more entrepreneurial and flexible about the kind of work they will do, and improving their interpersonal skills.

As new colleges and universities were established and old ones expanded during the 1960s and 1970s, more young people have furthered their education. Since educational expenses and the cost of living have increased, many families would not be able to afford to educate their children without some financial contribution from the children themselves. Part-time work has enabled many young people to stay in school, but at the same time it has led to greater financial independence from parents. This may be one more factor contributing to parents' loss of control over their adolescent children. Young people are now supervised by employers as well as teachers, and spend a larger proportion of their time with other adolescents or at their part-time jobs than they did in previous decades. These nonfamily influences may not coincide with parental values and could lead to antagonisms between parents and children.

From the 1960s until very recently, part-time work grew at a rapid pace. These workers are valued by employers because they work for low wages and are not legally entitled to receive the same fringe benefits or severance pay as full-time workers. Part-timers are still less likely to be protected by union contracts and consequently can be laid off more easily than full-time employees. Yet, many young people value part-time work because it allows them to earn money and gain work experience while pursuing their studies. By 1986, however, the trend of hiring more part-time than full-time workers slowed down as part-time workers began to unionize and to gain more rights (Coates, 1988). With the recession of the early 1990s, the preference for nonunionized part-timers continued.

When adolescents seek part-time work, they usually find only low-level service, clerical, or manual labour jobs because of their lack of experience and skills. Baker (1985) found that nearly half the adolescent students in her Canadian study worked part-time during evenings and weekends in low-level jobs, especially retail sales. These students were typically enthusiastic about their work and their pay cheques, and did not define their jobs as monotonous. Their part-time work enabled them to continue their education, yet cut into their time for homework, extra-curricular activities organized by the school, and social and family activities. School administrators and teachers have lamented that part-time work is having a negative effect on grades, willingness to do homework, and participation in extra-curricular activities.

Ironically, research has found that students from higher socio-economic families are able to find part-time jobs more easily than students from lower socio-economic families, even though the latter need the money more (Baker, 1985). This probably relates to the fact that adolescents from higher socio-economic backgrounds often present a middle-class image which is more in line with employer expectations. But it may also be explained by the fact that higher socio-economic parents are in a better position to assist their children to find work, either through personal advice or through friends who are also employers.

In Baker's 1985 study of the aspirations of Canadian adolescents, over three-quarters of the adolescents interviewed planned to continue their education beyond high school. Yet, only about one-quarter to one-third will actually continue, if provincial and federal government statistics are any indication. For example, figure 6.1 shows that while 100 percent of 15-year-olds attend school full-time, only about 22 percent of 20- to 22-year-olds do. Although many will be unable to study at the post-secondary level for financial or intellectual reasons, the fact remains that the desire for formal schooling and the levels of post-secondary school attendance are higher than ever before. In the past few years, education costs have escalated for both governments and students, college and university class sizes have increased, and the quality of Canadian education has been debated. Table 6.2 shows some typical costs of enroling in an Ontario university in 1991–1992. Raising entrance qualifications and increasing tuition fees will undoubtedly restrict enrolment in the future, pushing some young people back into the job market. The youth unemployment rates have been

Figure 6.1 **Full-Time School Enrolment* Related to Population, by Age, Canada, 1989–1990**

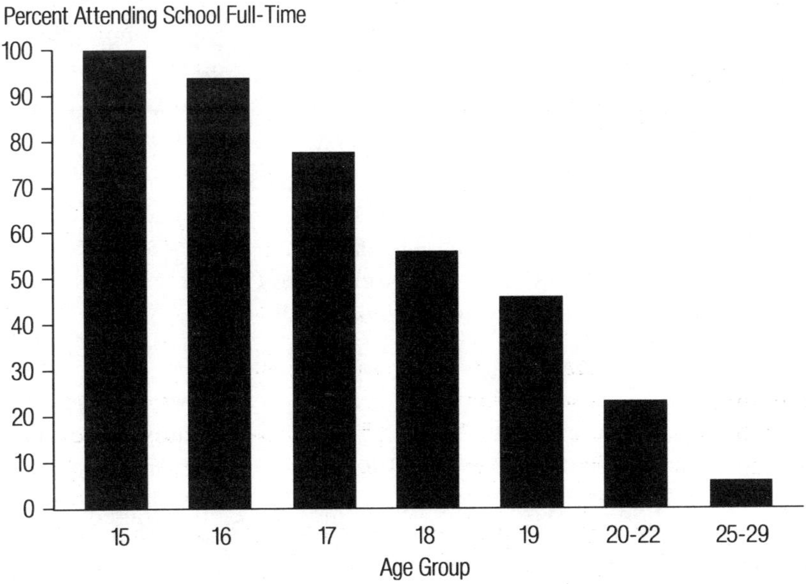

*Includes elementary, secondary, and post-secondary enrolment.

Source: Statistics Canada. *Education in Canada. A Statistical Review for 1989–90.* Cat. 81-229. Ottawa: Supply and Services Canada, August 1991:130. Reproduced with the permission of the Minister of Supply and Services Canada, 1992.

Table 6.2 **Typical Costs to Attend an Ontario University*, 1991–1992**

Tuition fees for full-time students	$1770
Tuition fees for foreign students	$6673
Living accommodation in residence (room and board for a single student)	$4844

*General Arts Program, University of Western Ontario.

Source: Statistics Canada. *Tuition and Living Accommodation Costs at Canadian Universities, 1990–91 and 1991–92.* Cat. 81-219. Ottawa: Supply and Services Canada, October 1991:16, 20, and 25. Reproduced with the permission of the Minister of Supply and Services Canada, 1992.

very high in recent years, however, and many young people have been forced to stay in school despite financial hardships or a lack of interest.

During the 1960s and early 1970s, when part-time or full-time jobs were plentiful and post-secondary institutions were expanding, many young people left their family homes to live on their own. They usually shared accommodation with other young people, and did not worry too much about completing their education in the required time because there was always a job waiting. Sometimes young people worked for a while, travelled, or studied. But the 1980s brought higher unemployment rates, rising educational expenses, and high living costs.

Urbanization and the development of regional schools have encouraged greater **age segregation**, or the separation of people on the basis of chronological age. Since most schools are now age-graded and leisure activities are often school-related, age segregation extends from the classroom to sports, games, clubs, and less organized leisure pursuits. This trend has encouraged the development of a youth culture, with behavioural standards and attitudes distinct from the adult world.

PAID AND UNPAID WORK IN MID-LIFE

Prior to the Second World War, young men were encouraged to find jobs when they left school, to remain with one employer throughout their working lives, and to provide reliable service in return for job security. By mid-life, some men had worked their way into supervisory or managerial positions, while others were less successful. After so many years of working in the same job, some middle-aged men were bored and sought satisfaction in family activities or leisure pursuits. However, prior to the 1920s, most men worked a 10-hour day, usually six days a week, and did not have much leisure time.

Working-class men who were marginally employed in temporary or seasonal work often had to work long hours at several jobs in order to feed their families. From the 1920s to the 1940s, the work week was reduced to 48 hours or five-and-a-half days. Paid vacation leave, however, had to be negotiated with the employer until the 1940s and 1950s, when legislation in most provinces required employers to provide one week paid vacation (Malles, 1976:11, 12).

These facts from labour history indicate that most working men had little leisure time to spend with their families, and that earning a living consumed most of their time. Leisure was for wealthier people who did not have to earn a living and who could afford to hire others to work for them. Because men were responsible for supporting their wives and children at that time, they could not quit their jobs to try something more rewarding. Instead, they were expected to be thankful for steady work.

Prior to the Second World War and especially during the 1930s Depression, women were expected to leave paid work when they married. Job priority was given to men, and if men and women worked in the same job, men were paid higher wages (Wilson, 1991). The concept of the **family wage**, in which men were supposed to be paid enough to support themselves and their families, gradually lost favour after World War II. As the cost of living rose, more women entered the work force demanding equal pay. Gradually, employees tended to be paid for the work they did rather than on the basis of their marital or family status.

Despite the fact that few Canadian wives worked in the labour force prior to the Second World War, many earned money and contributed to the family income. Homemakers sometimes took in boarders, did dressmaking for wealthier neighbours, gave piano lessons to local children, washed and ironed other people's laundry, or looked after neighbours' children. Rural wives often worked hard in the fields or barnyard, sold eggs or vegetables, and cared for the house and children.

Some married women did work for pay outside the home, however, especially in family businesses. Women were also employed as factory workers, domestics, hairdressers, nurses, school teachers (especially in elementary schools), rural post mistresses, bookkeepers, stenographers, and retail sales clerks. In fact, married women were often considered by governments and employers to be a reserve labour force. When extra employees were needed, such as in retail stores in December or in farm areas at harvest time, married women were expected to work hard alongside men. Working-class wives especially needed to supplement the family income if their husbands were sporadically unemployed or earned low wages.

Until about 20 years ago, homemaking and childrearing were considered the most acceptable occupation for married women. Most marriages in North America were marked by a distinct division of labour with complementary roles, which were said to be equal. Typically, wives were expected to be homemakers, even when there were no children at home. Husbands were usually the sole breadwinners, and they did not learn how to cook or do the laundry because they could rely on their wives to perform these tasks.

Contrary to popular thought, Canadian families in the early twentieth century were not necessarily more stable than families are now. Although divorce was nearly unheard of, desertion and separation were not uncommon. In poorer families, a husband often simply left home, while wealthier people who did not want the expense or scandal of legal divorce could maintain separate lives by sleeping in different rooms. Some openly maintained other relationships, despite the fact that they were still legally married. Furthermore, many marriages, regardless of their happiness, were curtailed by the premature death of a spouse.

Without income security programs, one-parent families could not stay together as easily as they can now. Younger children were often informally adopted by other families, spent time in children's homes or orphanages, or were temporarily cared for by friends while the surviving parent tried to reestablish the family income or household. If the children were old enough to work, they were urged to contribute to the family income or to leave home. Older daughters who were not in the work force were expected to care for younger siblings and do the housework.

Women's workload gradually lessened in mid-life, when all the children attended school for a full day. During the 1950s, some mothers used this opportunity to return to school, upgrade their skills, and move back into the permanent work force. In fact, the typical work pattern for married women during the 1950s and 1960s was the two-phase work cycle. This meant that young women first entered the labour force when they finished school, then left work when they were pregnant with the first child. For 10 or 20 years, they stayed home to raise children, and then re-entered the labour force when the last child was in school. By the 1970s, this pattern was changing as inflation and higher unemployment rates made it more difficult for women to leave the work force to raise children. Yet, many mothers chose part-time rather than full-time work as a strategy for managing work/family conflicts, as employed mothers retained responsibility for child care and housework.

Prior to the expansion of part-time work in the 1960s, parents assisted their children with educational expenses or young people worked full-time for several years before enroling in college or university. In the 1960s, however, the federal government introduced student loans and grants to assist those from poorer families to obtain post-secondary education. Around the same time, employers began to hire part-time workers to increase their flexibility and reduce labour costs. The availability of part-time work has been important for students working their way through college, as well as for married women who need to earn money while caring for their children.

In previous decades as well as now, people's work lives and family relationships varied by culture. The next section examines the ways in which the lives of parents with adolescents and the expectations they hold for their children differ in various ethnic and cultural groups.

CULTURAL PERSPECTIVES

The Division of Labour and Parental Expectations

Immigrant families are more likely to have both parents working for pay than Canadian-born families (Seward and McDade, 1988; Moore, 1989:21), perhaps because many have come to this country to improve their standard of living and provide a better life for their children. In lower-income families, parents may work in shifts, or women may do piecework at home when the children are young in order to avoid extra child care costs. When the children are teenagers, the mother can work outside the home with less concern about child care.

Teenage girls, especially those from southern European backgrounds, are usually expected to baby-sit their younger siblings after school and to start preparing the evening meal for the rest of the family. Yet, regardless of cultural background, teenagers of both sexes are likely to have part-time jobs after school and on weekends if they are still students, or full-time jobs if they have left school. This means that meals may become less formal because some family member will almost always be absent, and that housework has to be done in the evenings and on the weekend.

Many ethnic groups, especially southern Europeans, Latin Americans, and most Asians, still view housework as women's work, even when female family members are also working full-time (Sturino, 1980; Baker, 1985). This could contribute to conflicts between adolescent girls and their parents, as the girls may see their parents as old-fashioned and unreasonable. In addition, it could contribute to rivalry between male and female siblings, if females perceive the division of labour and expectations for themselves and their brothers or male cousins to be unfair.

Attitudes toward how much independence teenage children should have vary by cultural group. Some groups, such as southern Europeans, not only make a distinction between the responsibilities of male and female children in the household but also protect and control female children more (Ambert, 1992). Females tend to be encouraged to stay near the family, performing household chores and child care for younger siblings. Their potential to find a suitable husband is considered important (Sturino, 1980). While girls are encouraged to do well in school, occupational preparation often takes second place to marriage prospects. Parental pressure focuses on maintaining a good reputation, the development of traditional female skills and an acquiescent personality, and physical attractiveness. Young women from working-class immigrant families are often encouraged by their relatives to marry at a relatively young age and to begin raising a family within a few years (Sturino, 1980; Grindstaff, 1990).

In many immigrant groups, adolescent males are given more independence and personal freedom, but are expected to assist their fathers with household repairs and the disciplining of younger children. Furthermore, sons are seen as future breadwinners and household heads, and considerable pressure is placed on them to develop physical and emotional strength, bravado, good judgment, and occupational skills. Although young men are often expected to leave school early to help support the family, as are daughters, greater importance is given to the sons' education. In families with a patriarchal tradition, the son is granted additional importance because he will continue the family name into the next generation (Sturino, 1980).

In Chinese-Canadian and -American families, adolescents are expected to show respect for their elders, to listen carefully to their advice, to protect the family's reputation, and to reduce family conflicts (Jim and Suen, 1990; Lin and Fu, 1990; Lee, 1992). Relations between adolescents and their parents are sometimes more formal than in families from other cultures, and are often less overtly conflictual (Sung, 1985). Yet, Canadian-born Chinese teenagers sometimes complain that their parents do not allow them to make their own

INTERVIEWS WITH CHINESE ADOLESCENTS ABOUT THEIR RELATIONSHIPS WITH PARENTS

"I dare not share opinions that are different from my parents' since they see it as talking back. I don't want to anger them, so I keep silent."
15-year-old immigrant girl

"There's no point to object to my parents' words. All is final and it is what I must follow."
16-year-old Canadian-born boy

"Dad is afraid of losing respect from us in this Western society. Thus he sets a clear parent-child boundary."
16-year-old girl

"Dad, please open to me personally. I want to understand you as a person, to know who you are, your thoughts and feelings, and not just your role as a father."
17-year-old boy

"My dad tries to avoid embarrassment and he never talks directly with me about dating. He's too scared."
14-year-old Canadian-born girl

"Dad just gets mad at my phone calls with male friends. Yet, he never discusses directly with me about the dating issue."
17-year-old Canadian-born girl

"There is something more important than study, such as happiness. High marks do not always reflect what you learn. Yet, I want to get a PhD degree."
16-year-old girl

"My parents expect me to ever improve in my study. They give me no praise nor encouragement. They don't know much about the school system. Do they really care for me?"
17-year-old girl

"I feel good being a Chinese, but still need a balance between the two cultures. I need help from my parents. If they are more open and Westernized, it is easier for me."
16-year-old girl

"I need to improve my Chinese language so as to increase communication with my parents."
14-year-old girl

"After immigration, we've got more time together as a family. We can understand each other more than in Hong Kong."
15-year-old immigrant girl

Leanna Lai Chu Lee. "Parent-Adolescent Relationships From Adolescent Eyes: A Comparison Between Recent Immigrants and Canadian-Born Chinese Adolescents." MSW Research Report, McGill University, June 1992. (Reprinted with permission.)

decisions about friendships, dating, leisure activities, or educational choices, and that they demand too much respect (Yeung, 1982; Lee, 1992). Furthermore, Chinese immigrant parents often pressure both female and male adolescents to work hard at their studies, to continue on to university, and find a responsible and well-paying job. Sometimes, young people find this pressure excessive and difficult to handle (Lin and Fu, 1990; Lee, 1992).

The educational and occupational aspirations of young people are influenced by the achievements of their parents, although some immigrant parents have been downwardly mobile since coming to Canada. Despite the verbal encouragement given to their children to stay in school, young people often leave before graduation and accept unskilled jobs. Although many young people from cultural minorities do surpass their parents' education level and occupational achievements, their aspirations are partly shaped by the role models they see around them—their parents, their other relatives, their parents' friends, and the parents of their own friends. Canadian-born children often achieve higher levels of education than their immigrant parents, and sometimes make a dramatic leap up the status hierarchy in comparison with their older relatives. Yet, even when they continue their education, some young people from **visible minorities** experience difficulty finding work because of racial or cultural discrimination. Furthermore, young people from all family backgrounds are receiving more education these days and are competing for jobs and status.

Canada's ethnic make-up is becoming increasingly diverse. For example, just under 10 percent of adolescents living in Ontario come from a visible minority families, as calculations from table 6.3 would indicate. A recent report by Stephen Lewis, commissioned by the Ontario government, on the May 1992 race riots in Toronto highlighted visible minorities, especially black people, as the targets of **systemic discrimination** permeating all our institutions, including the police, the school system, and the labour force.

The next section will examine three selective issues: Teen Pregnancy, One-Parent Families, and Remarriage and Blended Families. While the first clearly fits into The Family With Adolescents, a discussion of One-Parent Families and Remarriage could have been placed in several other stages. They are dealt with here for the sake of unity.

Table 6.3 **Ontario Children Aged 0–24 Years in Census Families, by Designated Group Status, 1986[a]**

	Total Children 0–24	Total Children Percent	4 Years and Less	5–9 Years	10–14 Years	15–19 Years	20–24 Years	Percent
Total	2 871 775	100.0	615 375	598 130	617 530	623 720	417 025	100.0
Aboriginals[b]	71 700	2.5	18 335	17 600	16 755	13 255	5 755	2.5
Black visible minorities	83 310	2.9	16 745	17 010	18 310	19 345	11 900	2.9
Indo-Pakistan[c]	60 995	2.1	15 320	15 275	12 975	10 295	7 130	2.1
Chinese	60 290	2.1	13 650	13 120	12 010	11 640	9 870	2.1
All other visible minorities[c]	91 255	3.2	21 035	21 825	19 885	17 430	11 040	3.2
Total visible minorities[c]	295 815	10.3	66 755	67 225	63 180	58 715	39 940	10.3
Multiple Aboriginal and visible minorities	2 570	0.1	700	580	600	475	215	0.1
All Aboriginal[d]	74 265	2.6	19 030	18 180	17 355	13 730	5 970	2.6
All visible minorities[e]	298 390	10.4	67 450	67 810	63 785	59 185	40 150	10.4
Non-Aboriginal and non-visible minorities	2 501 690	87.1	529 585	512 720	536 990	551 280	371 115	87.1

[a] Visible minority variable created by the Federal Employment Equity Group from Census ethnicity data, combined with language and place of birth data.
[b] Excluding multiple responses with visible minorities.
[c] Excluding multiple responses with Aboriginal people.
[d] Including multiple responses with visible minorities.
[e] Including multiple responses with Aboriginal people.

Source: Statistics Canada, Census of Canada, 1986, Special Tabulations, February 1990. Reproduced with the permission of the Minister of Supply and Services Canada, 1992.

SELECTED ISSUES

TEENAGE PREGNANCY

Teenage pregnancy and early marriage resulting from pregnancy concern parents, teachers, social workers, and policy-makers because the personal and societal costs could be considerable. Now that more adolescents are becoming sexually active at earlier ages, pregnancy may occur well before one can legally work, vote, drive a car, or marry. Increasingly, young people must have at least a secondary school diploma in order to find work, yet early pregnancy frequently disrupts a young woman's education and could lead to years of poverty. For both sexes, early marriage and childrearing tend to be associated with low educational attainment, low income and continuing financial problems, separation and divorce, and social assistance (Broderick, 1992:156).

Despite the earlier age at which adolescents are becoming sexually active, the actual birth rate of teenagers has decreased considerably since the 1960s. In fact, the birth rate for women of all age categories has decreased from 1921 to 1989 (Wadhera and Strachan, 1991). The availability of more effective contraceptives and legalized abortions has undoubtedly contributed to the reduction of the birth rate of Canadian women. Yet, there is some indication that teenage girls from low-income families are more likely than those from middle- or higher-income families to become pregnant and more likely to give birth rather than obtaining abortions (Stark, 1986). Girls from middle-class families are more likely to see an early premarital pregnancy as interfering with their education and career plans (Stark, 1986).

Although the teenage birth rate fell between the years 1961 and 1989, about 25 in every 1000 women aged 15 to 19 produced a child in 1989, as table 6.4 indicates. The more important development, however, is the trend since the 1970s for unmarried mothers to keep their babies rather than allow them to be adopted. Although 40 years ago psychologists and social workers encouraged unwed mothers to give their newborns up for adoption without even seeing them, professionals now think that this could be detrimental for both mothers and children. Teenage mothers can now receive social assistance and support from programs such as "Teen Moms" at the YWCA. Some schools are providing special classes to enable teen mothers to continue their education until graduation by supplying on-site child care services.

The trend for unmarried mothers to keep their babies and to raise them with family and social support has been strengthened by changing social ideas about pregnancy outside of marriage. More couples are living together without legally marrying, and new opportunities exist for single mothers to support their babies through employment or social assistance. Generally, attitudes toward sexuality and marriage are more relaxed, and unmarried mothers are less likely to be ostracized by their families and communities than they were 30 years ago. Despite these changes, the adolescent mother who drops out of school is still likely to be unemployed and on welfare (Dornbusch and Strober, 1988:282).

While only 30 percent of unwed mothers in Ontario kept their babies in 1968, 88 percent did so in 1977 (Eichler, 1983:281). This trend has continued into the 1980s, although reliable data to support

Table 6.4 **Fertility Rates, by Age*, Canada, 1921–1989.**

	AGE OF WOMAN					
	15–19	20–24	25–29	30–34	35–39	40–44
1921	38.0	165.4	186.0	154.6	110.0	46.7
1931	29.9	137.1	175.1	145.3	103.1	44.0
1941	30.7	138.4	159.8	122.3	80.0	31.6
1951	48.1	188.7	198.8	144.5	86.5	30.9
1961	58.2	233.6	219.2	144.9	81.1	28.5
1971	40.1	134.4	142.0	77.3	33.6	9.4
1981	26.4	96.7	126.9	68.0	19.4	3.2
1989	25.4	84.7	128.8	83.7	27.0	3.8

*Births per 1000 women of each category.

Source: Surinder Wadhera and Jill Strachan. "Births and Birth Rates, 1989." *Health Reports*. 3 (1). 1991:80. Reproduced with the permission of the Minister of Supply and Services Canada, 1992.

this conclusion are unavailable. The trend for single mothers to raise their own children has been viewed with alarm by some teachers, social workers, and parents. Many teenage mothers drop out of school and have no job skills with which to support themselves. These mothers are most likely to depend on social assistance to survive and may be unable to give their children the economic and social resources they need to successfully live in a competitive society. Not all teen mothers who initially keep their babies find that they can cope two years later (Wood and Nuttall, 1984).

Despite the availability of birth control, some adolescent women become pregnant when their contraceptives fail, yet they decide to keep their baby out of real feelings of personal and social responsibility. Others become pregnant when they fail to use contraceptives, which they are too embarrassed to buy. Others do not use contraceptives at all because they feel that pregnancy cannot happen to them. Some young women appear to become pregnant consciously or subconsciously in order to keep their boyfriend, to have someone to love them, or to give their lives increased meaning and purpose (Stark, 1986). Teenage mothers sometimes discover later, however, that caring for another human being is not only emotionally and physically exhausting, but is not always best for them or for the child (Wood and Nuttall, 1984; Baker, 1985; Dornbusch and Strober, 1988:284).

Teenage parents usually delay or postpone their education, which makes it difficult to find jobs. Money is often in short supply, child care is costly, and friends and family are not always supportive. Once teenage mothers are on social assistance, it is difficult to become financially independent with employment and child care worries. While school boards and social agencies provide assistance to teenage mothers, their problems are often difficult to solve.

Research on socio-economic factors relating to divorce consistently show that teenage marriages precipitated by premarital pregnancy have above average divorce rates (Ambert, 1980:75; Broderick, 1992:156). The reasons behind this are quite simple: adolescents usually have not completed their education and consequently cannot find permanent and well-paid work. Without a reliable pay cheque, they are constantly in need of money, which adds stress to their relationship. Typically, neither partner is emotionally mature and both may experience difficulty coping with the responsibilities of marriage and parenting. They may not even be suited to each other in terms of interests or personality, but may have married only to prevent a family scandal with the premarital pregnancy.

At a time when social service workers are trying to hold families together and keep children out of foster homes, encouragement is given to teen mothers to raise their own children. Some find this encouragement disturbing because of the high rate of poverty among young parents. More than half of single-parent families led by women and over 30 percent of two-parent families under the age of 25 had incomes below the poverty line in 1986 (National Council of Welfare, 1988b:32, 37).

In Canada, custody of the children of unmarried parents has usually been granted to the mother. Yet, some unmarried fathers have

A TYPICAL DAY OF ONE TEEN MOTHER

"I get up at 8:00 or 9:00 and make breakfast for my boyfriend and myself. He leaves for work at 10:30 (he works in a factory). I watch T.V.: "Wheel of Fortune," "Game Go," and the soaps. I also look after the baby. From 12:00 to 1:00 I have lunch and do some housework. In the afternoon, I watch T.V. and look after the baby. At 9:00 my boyfriend comes home. I make supper, we eat, and then I clean up. I watch some more T.V., or go out for a walk. I go to bed around 11:00. The baby wakes up all night and cries, so I'm always tired."

"I go shopping (which she saw as "leisure"). I listen to the stereo. I watch T. V. ...about 10 hours a day. I go to the teen mothers' group (at the local YWCA). I don't go out with my boyfriend because he gets home from work at 9:00 p.m."

Monica: 17 years old, Toronto

This section is taken from "*What Will Tomorrow Bring?...*" *A Study of the Aspirations of Adolescent Women,* prepared by Maureen Baker and published by the Canadian Advisory Council on the Status of Women: Ottawa, 1985.

recently used the courts, and especially the equality rights clause in the Canadian Charter of Rights and Freedoms, to obtain more say in decisions relating to abortion, custody, adoption, family benefits, and child support (Gotell, 1990:36).

Ironically, at the same time that unwed teen mothers are struggling to raise their children, childless couples are unable to find babies or even young children to adopt. This trend has forced couples to accept older children for adoption or to attempt overseas arrangements.

ONE-PARENT FAMILIES

Two factors have led to an increase in one-parent families since the 1960s: separation and divorce rates have risen dramatically, and a small but increasing number of women are raising their children without living with or marrying the father. Although the official rate of one-parent families has not yet reached the 1930s level, the increase since the 1960s has been considerable, as table 6.5 indicates. While one-parent families used to be caused by desertion and widowhood, they can now be attributed mainly to separation and divorce.

Single parenting, even when it is a personal choice, can be very challenging. The difficulties include financial problems, social isolation and loneliness, and role conflict and strain. As most unmarried single parents are mothers, and as custody is granted to the mother in about three-quarters of Canadian divorce cases, some of the problems of single parents are closely related to women's issues. For example, numerous studies have indicated that divorced women and female family heads are more likely to be poor than their male counterparts (Baker, 1983; Ambert, 1990; National Council on Welfare, 1990). Not only do women tend to earn lower wages when they are in the full-time labour force, but female family heads are less likely to be working full-time than male heads of one-parent families. Increasingly, two incomes are necessary to maintain the same standard of living that one wage could maintain in the 1950s. Furthermore, many divorced or noncustodial fathers do not continue to pay child support even when the court has ordered them to do so (Richardson, 1988b, Galarneau, 1992).

The sheer numbers of one-parent families and the tendency for these families to be living in poverty must be considered in making policy decisions about family benefits, social assistance, and child care facilities. Allowing children to live in low-income families may have unanticipated consequences more costly than the various schemes to improve the economic status of one-parent families (Baker, 1991).

Although living with children can be rewarding, having no other

Table 6.5 **Percentage of One-Parent Families of Total Families in Canada, 1931–1986**

1931	13.6
1941	12.2
1951	9.9
1961	8.4
1971	9.4
1981	11.3
1986	12.7

Source: Statistics Canada. *Canada's Lone-Parent Families*. Cat. 99-933, Ottawa, 1984; Statistics Canada. Families: Part 1. Cat. 93-106, Ottawa, November 1987. Reproduced with the permission of the Minister of Supply and Services Canada, 1992.

adults to talk to, especially about childrearing issues, can be isolating. Loneliness can be aggravated if you cannot afford to hire a baby-sitter in order to go out with friends. Many single mothers cannot afford to go out very often without their children because they have low incomes and cannot pay baby-sitters. Single mothers tend to be poorer than single fathers and are more likely to be unemployed and at home during the daytime. Therefore they experience more problems than single fathers in meeting potential mates and making the transition from married to unmarried life (Baker, 1983).

Single parents of either sex often experience work overload and strains. In many cases, they are attempting to fulfil the role of both mother and father to their children, earn a living, and perform household chores and childcaring tasks often done by two people. The demands of paid work, parenting, and care of a home can be exhausting (Hanson and Sporakowski, 1986; Lowe, 1989). In addition, many of these parents are involved in custody or child support disputes, even years after the separation or divorce occurred. In some cases, the children are caught up in the dispute and forced to take sides.

Receiving custody of children may soften the initial blow of marital separation because of the constant source of affection and companionship from the children. However, custody may also make readjustment to single life more difficult for parents. The presence of children constantly reminds the parent of their family status and their former life. In addition, the children require supervision and money, and usually experience some behavioural problems around the time of the separation. Attempting to provide the children with a stable environment on a low income may occupy much of the time and energy of separated and divorced parents.

Many researchers agree that the way children adjust to divorce is influenced by how their parents deal with it.

Tom Shields, Creative and Editorial Services

Effects of Divorce on Children

Numerous studies concerning the effects of divorce on children have indicated that the meaning of divorce differs greatly depending on the family context and the children's ages. Research has yielded contradictory results that imply that studying the impact of divorce on children is very complex and numerous factors need to be considered. First of all, studies indicate that children's social and emotional adjustment is often better in harmonious separated homes than it is in intact conflictual homes (Raschke, 1987; Ambert, 1990a). In hostile intact homes, children imitate their parents' behaviour and gradually adopt unhealthy ways of interacting with the opposite sex. Having no constant role model appears to be better than having a negative one. That is why staying in a violent or openly unhappy marriage "for the sake of the children" is not a wise decision, and may in fact be more harmful than separating.

The most obvious behavioural problems tend to occur around the time of the parents' separation, when tension in the household is usually the greatest. Children sometimes blame themselves for their parents' separation and feel rejected by the absent parent. Very young children and older teenage children may be less affected by the separation than school-aged children, because they are either unaware of the situation or are able to absent themselves from the home. Boys appear to be stressed more than girls by the absence of their fathers (Santrock and Warshak, 1986; Ambert, 1990a). By the time of the legal divorce, many of these problems have subsided or disappeared. Emotional difficulties, however, may surface later in life, even years after the separation (Wallerstein, 1985; Southworth and Schwarz, 1987).

Some studies show that children from divorced families tend to have lower educational and socio-economic attainment (Ambert and Saucier, 1984; Keith and Finlay, 1988). But this finding may partially reflect the fact that they are usually living in reduced economic circumstances, as a result of the separation. Low incomes and poverty are associated with poor educational and occupational attainment regardless of the parents' marital status (Clement, 1975; Porter, Porter and Blishen, 1982; Guppy, 1984).

Researchers have also found that divorced mothers tend to be punitive but inconsistent disciplinarians, which may also influence their children's behaviour. Hetherington, Cox, and Cox (1978) explain this as resulting from divorced mothers' low incomes, their social isolation, and high levels of frustration.

Divorced women often experience conflict over their children's reaction to the men they see, although some of this conflict is caused by assumptions about what their children's reactions might be. While women often feel that they need to be circumspect about their sexual liaisons because of their children's presence, divorced men often experience a period of heightened sexual activity with a variety of partners. In a sense, this activity is often a futile attempt to regain intimacy and to improve self-esteem.

Children of divorced parents tend to have higher divorce rates when they later marry than those from intact marriages (Beaujot, 1990). This may be a result of the "unhealthy" interaction patterns learned from their parents or negative attitudes toward marriage and the opposite sex. Alternatively, the higher divorce rates of children from divorced parents may simply indicate that they feel that divorce is a possible way to end an unhappy marriage. Children from intact marriages may be less likely to see divorce as feasible or less likely to feel that it is possible to make a better life after marriage dissolution.

The research indicates that some of the effects of separation and divorce on children and teenagers can be modified by changes in parents' behaviour and circumstances. If children and adolescents understand that their parents are unhappy and are adequately prepared for the break-up, the children tend to experience fewer emotional problems associated with their parents' separation. If the father continues to play an important role in the socialization of the children, and they do not feel abandoned by him, this seems to be a mediating factor. More importantly, if the father continues to financially support the family, the consequences of parental divorce appear to be weakened (Furstenberg, 1987). Problems are most intense when the child is taken by surprise or forced to take sides in parental disputes, especially those over custody (Schlesinger, 1983). Because many of the studies of the effect of divorce on children are done with clinical samples or use theoretical models of pathology or social disorganization, the negative consequences may be overestimated compared with positive effects (Sev'er, 1992:240).

Custody Issues

In recent years, there has been considerable controversy over how custody decisions are and should be made, as well as the effects of various custody arrangements on children. Until recently, one parent was given sole custody, while the other was given visiting rights or access. Some parents have been voluntarily arranging joint custody, however, which could involve **joint physical custody** in which both parents share the physical care of the child or **joint legal custody** in which both parents share decision making about the child, even though the child may live with only one parent.

Joint custody is now being promoted by fathers' rights groups who want more involvement in decisions relating to their children's lives, and may want to share their physical care. Some women's groups have also seen joint custody as a more egalitarian division of parental roles, and a number of professionals view it as beneficial to the children that they continue to be cared for by both parents after divorce, as long as the care is loving and consistent. On the other hand, involuntary or court-ordered joint custody has been opposed by some feminist groups who argue that it often works against the interests of divorced women. Joint custody, they say, tends to reduce the amount of child support which judges award to mothers because they assume that fathers are also sharing the cost. Yet, because a child spends some of the time in his father's home does not mean that the mother's costs are reduced. Joint custody also gives the children's father veto power over decisions made by the children's mother, even when the children live with her most of the time (Drakich, 1988).

Some therapists and child psychologists argue that children cannot relate positively to parents who are in continual conflict. Unfortunately, divorced parents rarely co-operate in their parental roles (Furstenberg and Nord, 1985). Furthermore, therapists and researchers have noted that joint custody only works for children when it is voluntary rather than court-ordered.

Although joint custody was seldom awarded by Canadian courts prior to 1986, the 1989 Canadian statistics indicate that there has been a rise in joint custody and a slight decline in sole custody for mothers. For divorce cases in which custody was awarded by the court, 74.2 percent of children were awarded to their mothers, 12.6 percent were given to their fathers, and 12.9 percent were involved in a joint custody arrangement. Less than 1 percent of children were awarded to a person other than the mother or father (Millar, 1991). However, some couples make private joint custody agreements, occasionally with the

WHY DON'T FATHERS SEEK PRIMARY CUSTODY?

Some authors argue that more fathers could have primary custody. This argument is based on the fact that when fathers do seek custody, they obtain custody in about 50 percent of the cases. Some of the reasons put forth to account for fathers not seeking primary custody include the following:

1. Fathers fear a bitter court battle and the subsequent possibility of having a poor relationship with their children and former spouses.
2. Fathers see it as unchivalrous, if not unmanly, to attack the character of their wives and to seek to carry out what society has defined largely as a female role, i.e., childrearing.
3. Many fathers merely do not want what they perceive as the burdensome responsibility of having primary responsibility for childrearing.
4. Many mothers fervently seek primary custody to enhance their general financial settlement and/or to avoid social stigma when, in fact, they might be very satisfied with their former husband's having primary custody.
5. The Equal Rights for Fathers Organization contends there is a "quiet conspiracy" among judges, probation departments, conciliation courts, and even fathers' attorneys to dissuade divorced men from seeking custody.
6. Courts still base custody decisions to some extent on fault, and it is easier to prove the father at fault and thus a less-able parent than the mother.

assistance of divorce mediators, and courts are not always involved in these decisions. Because joint custody arrangements require considerable post-divorce co-operation, they are less prevalent. Yet, an increasing number of children from divorced parents seem to spend portions of each week in both parents' homes.

In most states of the United States, joint custody is presumed to be the normal arrangement unless it is demonstrated that it would be harmful for the child (Pearson and Theoness, 1990). Yet, despite this presumption, joint physical custody comprised less than 2 percent of custody arrangements in the United States in 1988. In 95 percent of joint legal custody arrangements in California in that year, the children lived with the mother most of the time (Coller, 1988).

Studies of the impact of joint custody on children note the importance of cordial relations between the divorced parents and frequent positive contact with the child. **Shared parenting** after divorce tends to be a middle-class voluntary arrangement which requires two places for the child to live, and therefore more resources. There is some evidence that parents and children involved in court-ordered joint custody are less satisfied with the arrangement than those who arranged it themselves (Irving, Benjamin and Troeme, 1984). Especially when parents are involved in custody and visitation disputes, joint legal custody can lead to emotional and behavioural problems in the children (Johnston, Kline and Tschann, 1989). The child's life is least disrupted if divorced parents live in the same neighbourhood, if they can provide their children with a room in each of their homes, and if they are both concerned about their child's welfare and can co-operate over childrearing issues. Because these conditions are so difficult (Ambert, 1988), however, this form of custody is an option considered by a minority of educated middle-class couples.

In summary, research indicates that in situations of voluntary joint physical and legal custody, children are happier and better adjusted than children in sole custody arrangements. There is also evidence that imposed shared parenting may not work. This implies that couples who have voluntarily chosen joint custody may be different from most divorcing couples. They may have had less conflictual marriages and may now be better able to co-operate after their marriages are over.[1]

---

[1] Thanks to my former student Barbara Mitchell for some of the research on custody arrangements.

Low Incomes of Custodial Mothers

Custodial mothers often experience low income from employment or social assistance and lack of child support from the children's father. Lenore Weitzman (1985) of Stanford University, whose research became very influential for future studies and child support policies in both Canada and the United States, found that divorced mothers experienced an average drop in household income of 73 percent after marriage dissolution, while divorced fathers' income increased by 42 percent on average. From an analysis of American divorce settlements over a number of years, Weitzman concluded that "no fault" divorce laws have led to greater inequality than before family law reform. Prior to these changes, women could have been awarded alimony and could have delayed the divorce hearing until they negotiated a higher settlement. Weitzman argued that new American divorce laws are based on the false assumption of economic equality between the sexes.

Canadians have made a similar argument, pointing out that traditional procedures for enforcing support payments are inadequate because they leave the onus on the financially-dependent spouse to take the other to court. This has usually meant that the woman has to hire a lawyer to take her ex-husband to court. Although he might pay for a while, the woman has to repeat this exhausting and expensive procedure the next time he fails to pay (Canada, Federal/Provincial/Territorial Family Law Committee, 1991). Most provinces, including Ontario, have begun to devise new enforcement systems in which the government pays child support directly to the custodial parent and automatically retrieves the money from the other parent. This system has raised the likelihood of the custodial parent receiving money for the child .

ONTARIO TO START NEW FAMILY SUPPORT PLAN

BY JOHN BEAUFOY
Ontario Correspondent

TORONTO—Ontario is about to launch a new Family Support Plan in an effort to cut the massive default rate in payment of support orders to women and children.

Currently, about 75 percent of all support orders filed with the existing government program are in arrears to some extent.

According to Attorney General Howard Hampton, that translates into about $465 million in money owed about 110 000 children and their mothers. Without their support payments, such families have to rely on social assistance—at a cost to Ontario of $140 million since 1987. "These figures are intolerable. There is no good reason for not paying family support, and that is the message we want to get out," Hampton said.

The government has launched an advertising campaign to emphasize the social and economic costs of defaulters. Starting March 1, [1991] the new Family Support Plan will allow for automatic deduction of support payments from income—much as income tax and similar deductions are made at source.

Under the program, employers will be required to automatically deduct support payments from an employee's pay cheque and forward these payments to the Family Support office for distribution.

The support deductions will follow an employee when he changes jobs, placing the onus on the employer and the support payer to advise the program of a change or termination of employment.

Sanctions could be applied if the program is not notified of changes, but employees' rights have been safeguarded through an amendment to the Employment Standards Act which protects employees from being fired because of the support deduction process.

The new program will apply to all new court orders, cases already filed and, where applicable, to domestic contracts. Courts making a support order will also make a "support deduction order" and send that to the Family Support Plan program for implementation through the payor's employer.

The program will not generally apply to self-employed individuals. If they are in default of a support order, they will be subject to default hearings, "intensive use of federal diversion (i.e., income tax refunds)," writs of seizure, sales and liens.

The government will allocate an additional $3 million to the program in addition to the current $24 million budget. The deduction plan was to have started in 1991, but was delayed as part of the government's budget-cutting last fall.

Similar programs operate in at least 35 U.S. states and the U.S. Congress has enacted its Family Support Act requiring every state to have an automatic support deduction system in place by 1994.

Nancy Mossip, Chair of the CBAO's [Canadian Bar Association of Ontario] Family Law Section, welcomed the implementation of the new program. "I think it is a step in the right direction." She added that once the program is launched, the government can pay more attention to self-employed defaulters and other difficult cases.

Hampton cautioned that this alone won't solve the problem of unpaid family support. The message his government has for defaulters, most of them men, he said, is that "it is simply unacceptable not to live up to your responsibilities to your children."

National. Canadian Bar Association. Vol. 19, no. 1. February 1992.

As table 6.6 and figure 6.2 indicate, mother-led one-parent families are much more likely than father-led one-parent families to be living in poverty. Since most one-parent families now originate from separation and divorce, policy-makers have tried to improve enforcement procedures for child support payments. Yet, the typical amount of these payments is relatively small, less than $200 per month in the United States (Seltzer, 1991) and a median payment of about $250 in Canada

Table 6.6 **Percentage of Canadian Families Living in Poverty, 1981–1990**

	Female Single Parents	Male Single Parents	Couples With Children
1981	52.8	15.5	9.5
1982	57.1	22.2	11.2
1983	59.3	27.1	12.0
1984	59.6	27.1	12.4
1985	60.3	26.8	11.1
1986	56.0	22.9	10.4
1990	60.6	—	9.6

Source: Adapted from Statistics Canada. *Low Income Persons*. Ottawa, January 1992.

(Galarneau, 1992). This suggests that most one-parent families would still be poor even if court-awarded payments were regularly made.

A more radical solution to the poverty of one-parent families would be to systematically attempt to improve women's status in the labour force, since women head most one-parent families. Women could be assisted to find better-paying positions through continuing education and retraining programs. At the same time, pay equity laws would need to be enforced so that pink collar jobs were not paid less than jobs normally held by men. Continuing education programs could provide on-site child care to enable women to attend classes without concern about their children. More subsidized child care spaces could be provided throughout the community and at the workplace to encourage single-parent mothers to enter the labour force or continue working when they have children. Expanding child care services would cost additional money, yet living on welfare is also costly to governments. Accepting welfare is certainly detrimental to the self-esteem and opportunities of divorced mothers, but the consequences might be even greater for their children.

Although divorce rates have been rising in Canada, many divorced people remarry and move back into two-parent families. About three-quarters of divorced men and two-thirds of divorced women remarry (Adams and Nagnur, 1990:144), although these figures are declining with more common-law relationships. Yet, most divorced parents move into a new live-in relationship within a few years of their divorce. According to Adams and Nagnur (1990:144), women were divorced an average of five years and men an average of three years before remarriage in the mid-1980s, up from two years for women and one for

Figure 6.2 **Poverty Rates of Single-Parent Mothers With Children Under 18, 1987**

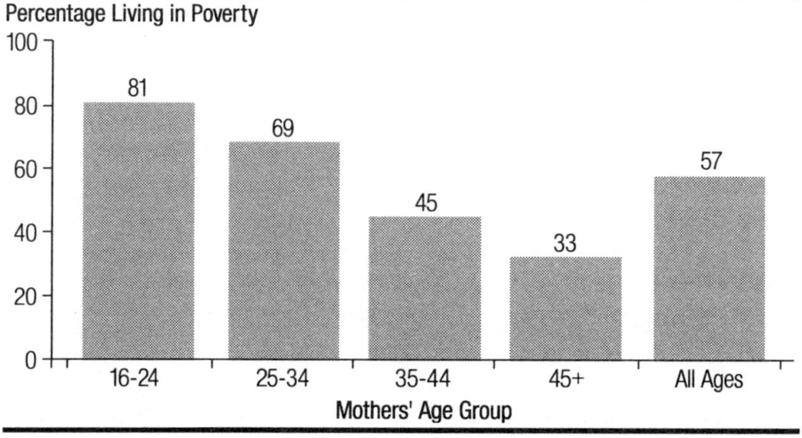

Source: National Council of Welfare. *Women and Poverty Revisited.* Ottawa. Summer 1990:58.

men in 1971. This means that many children from divorced parents are living in one-parent family settings for only a few years of their lives, although relative to their age that might be a large portion of their lives. In addition, the period of time spent with divorced parents is increasing, although many parents might be living with a partner.

Although the focus of this section has been on one-parent families, most children are still raised in intact families and most marriages, regardless of how happy they are, are lasting ones. However, in order to complete the discussion of divorce and its consequences, the next section will focus on remarriage and blended families, which are rapidly increasing in North America.

REMARRIAGE AND BLENDED FAMILIES

Although divorced people who remarry tend to do so in their late thirties, widowed people who remarry are more likely to do so in their late fifties. Because it is not possible to find a specific stage of the life cycle that fits both types of remarriage, remarriage and blended families are discussed along with one-parent families.

According to Owens and Nagnur (1990:144), about 84 percent of the Canadian population marry at some point in their lives, and in the mid-1980s about 28 percent of marriages ended in divorce. In Canada, about three-quarters of divorced men and two-thirds of divorced women remarry as figure 6.3 and table 6.7 indicate. These figures are

Figure 6.3 **Percentage of Marriages Ending in Divorce, by Region, 1984–1986**

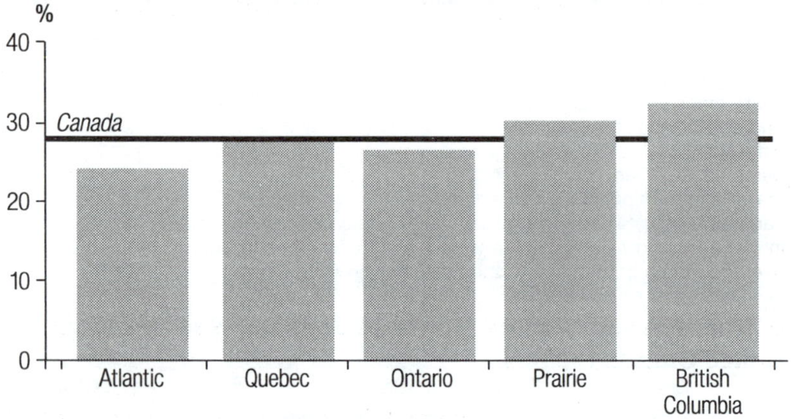

Source: Statistics Canada, Cat. 84-536. Reproduced with the permission of the Minister of Supply and Services Canada, 1992.

much lower than the American statistics. In Canada, remarriage after divorce has declined since the 1970s with the trend toward common-law relationships (Adams and Nagnur, 1990:144). Until 1992, two single parents with children living in Canada could receive more taxation benefits or transfer payments if they lived common-law than if they legally married (Morrison and Oderkirk, 1991).

In the United States, about 44 percent of marriages ended in divorce in the mid-1980s, and about 85 percent of men and 76 percent of women remarried after divorce (Adams and Nagnur, 1990:144). In 1987, stepfamilies constituted over 17 percent of all married-couple families with young children, but it has been projected that 40 percent of married-couple families will become stepfamilies before the youngest child is 18 (Orleans, Palisi, and Caddell, 1989:371).

For widowed compared with divorced persons, the Canadian and American remarriage rates are much lower—about 14 percent of Canadian men and 5 percent of women remarry after their spouses die (Adams and Nagnur, 1990). Widowed people have a lower probability of remarriage than divorced people mainly because of the age at which their marriages end. In 1990, almost 20 percent of marriages involved divorced people (*The Globe and Mail*, 26 February 1992:A4). The average age of remarriage for divorced persons is about 36 for women and 40 for men, while the average age of remarriage for widowed persons is 54 for women and 60 for men (Statistics Canada, 1986b:9).

Older widowed people are less likely to want to begin a new

Table 6.7

a. Marriage and Divorce in Canada and the United States

Although Canada and the United States share many cultural influences, marriage and divorce statistics in the two countries differ significantly. While roughly the same percentage of Canadians and Americans marry, a much higher proportion of American marriages, 44% compared with 28% in Canada, end in divorce. As well, the average length of marriage in the United States is 24 years, compared with 31 years in Canada.

Nevertheless, Americans can expect to live in a marriage almost as long as Canadians, although they will marry more often to do so. Remarriage rates for both men and women are higher in the United States than in Canada.

b. Marriage and Divorce Trends in Canada (1984–1986) and the United States (1983)

	Men		Women	
	Canada	United States	Canada	United States
		%		
Population ever marrying	83	84	86	88
Marriages ending in divorce	28	44	28	44
Widowed persons remarrying	14	19	5	7
Divorced persons remarrying	76	85	64	76

Source: Statistics Canada. Cat. 84-536. Reproduced with the permission of the Minister of Supply and Services Canada, 1992.

marriage because they sometimes feel that no one can measure up to their former spouse. They are more likely than divorced persons to own their own home and to see no need to change their lifestyle. In addition, some widows feel that if they remarry, they will have to look after another man, which will increase their housework and caregiving (Connidis, 1989a:37). In reality, few widows have an opportunity to remarry because the sex ratio (ratio of males to females) becomes increasingly imbalanced with age and because men tend to marry younger women, especially when they remarry .

Stepfamilies are different from biological nuclear families because they involve a greater complexity of relationships and may include people living in different households. Adjustment may be complicated by the presence of the ex-spouse, by lingering hostility between formerly married people, and unresolved conflicts surrounding child custody and support. However, social scientists have often focused on the negative aspects of these families because they have been trained to research "problems." In addition, many samples have come from people seeking couple counselling, marriage therapy, or assistance with children's behavioural problems. Divorce and remarriage continue to be portrayed in somewhat negative ways in social science research, especially when studying the effects on children (Sev'er, 1992:243–245).

Systems theorists argue that with remarriage, the boundaries of the family are often ambiguous. For example, members included in one child's family may not be the same as those in their stepsibling's, since noncustodial parents may be included in this definition (Hobart, 1988a). Furthermore, a child may have more sets of grandparents and other relatives than children from intact marriages. This occurs through the remarriage of the noncustodial parent and further complicates the definition of who is a family member. This is yet another example of the changing structure of family life and the complexities created through the remarriage of two parents. But systems theorists have further argued that lack of clarity about family membership, and the resulting difficulty in determining the roles and the rules of the system, is related to increased stress and family dysfunction (Boss, 1987).

When parents remarry, they often bring two sets of children into the same household. This **blended family** can often be the source of

"Which parent do you want to sign it: my natural father, my stepfather, my mother's third husband, my real mother or my natural father's fourth wife who lives with us?"

conflict as well as renewed prosperity and security. Since the involvement of noncustodial fathers tends to decline with the passage of time (Amato, 1987), stepfathers frequently function as paternal figures for their stepchildren (Orleans, Palisi, and Caddell, 1989:372). Yet, noncustodial fathers sometimes retain decision-making power over their children even when they do not live with them. If the mother remarries and the children continue to live with her, their biological father and their stepfather may occupy similar roles in the children's minds. They may not be able to perceive their stepfather as a "real father" because of the continuing presence of their biological father or their lingering loyalty to him.

In popular mythology, the stepmother has been portrayed as unloving and punitive, while the stepfather is seen as somewhat more benign. Not surprisingly, some studies indicate that relations between children and their stepmothers are more often contentious than with natural parents of the same sex or with stepfathers (Hobart, 1988a). This is probably because mothers spend more time in the home with responsibility for child supervision, but may also be affected by the negative stereotypes of stepmothers.

Another indication of possible conflict in blended families is the finding that children leave home at earlier ages than children in first marriages (White and Booth, 1985). However, this may indicate that these children have become more independent at an earlier age, especially if they have lived in a one-parent family situation before the custodial parent remarried. On the other hand, it may indicate that children in blended families are attempting to escape a home situation that they find uncomfortable for some reason. One source of contention may be that parents associate a certain child with the discredited spouse, and treat this child as though he or she were "tainted" (Hobart, 1988a), or parents may make disparaging comments about the absent biological parent. In addition, children and adolescents may be jealous of or dislike the parent's new partner and his or her children.

Remarried people sometimes take on parenting roles of their partner's children reluctantly. They may not feel close to these children, yet have a responsibility to look after them, discipline, and help to raise them. Because they have grown up in different families, there may be substantial differences in the values and interests of step-parents and stepchildren. Given the lack of common history, it may be improbable that a step-parent could achieve a full parental role with a teenager (Mills, 1986: 262). Problems often arise when a step-parent inappropriately tries to act like a parent, instead of supporting the same-sex parent in the child's other household.

If custodial parents remarry, young children tend to adapt better than teenagers (Ambert, 1990:206). Teenagers are more likely to remember the absent parent, make negative comparisons between the step-parent and the biological parent, and see the step-parent as an intruder. Research has also shown that the mere presence of stepchildren in remarriage is related to lower levels of marital satisfaction for parents and increased marital instability (Ambert, 1986; Booth and White, 1980). A few studies, however, have noted that remarriage often provides a stabilizing influence for children and their parents, and is much better for children than remaining in an intact family with conflicting parents or living in a low-income one-parent household (Sev'er, 1992:244–245).

STEPFAMILIES

When Susan Borkin married Jerry Hurwitz almost nine years ago, she became an "instant mother" to Jerry's three children, Dan, Noah, and Ramee. Susan had never planned on having a family; her career as a psychotherapist always came first, she says. Jerry's ex-wife, who lived in Oregon, had custody so Susan and Jerry expected the kids to visit them in San Francisco only on holidays and vacations. But as the children became teenagers, the living arrangements changed. Both Noah and Ramee spent long and sometimes difficult periods with Susan and Jerry; the family sought outside therapy several times. Now, with the older boys in college and Ramee, 16, finishing high school, Susan and Jerry believe they have overcome most of the hurdles—although they haven't forgotten them. "You have to have a commitment that you're going to stay married." says Jerry. "That has to be your bottom line."...

For couples who each bring children to the marriage, childrearing styles are often a problem. Terry and Leanne Hochstein of Norfolk, Nebraska, each had two children when they got married five years ago. Terry had custody of his two daughters, Niki, now 14, and Angie, 13. Leanne and her two sons, Phillip, now 11, and Joey, 9, moved into Terry's house. Each was critical of the other's methods of discipline. Says Terry: "I was more strict and would punish more. I felt that Leanne would just talk to them and they would keep it up." At first they tried just disciplining their own kids, but now, as the situation has settled down, they have been acting more as a couple. Their rule is to try to present a unified front; otherwise, they say, the kids play one parent off against the other.

In this phase of stepfamily life, many couples just decide to give up. "Remarriages are very fragile," says Johns Hopkins University sociologist Andrew Cherlin. "There's a high rate of divorce for the first several years, almost as though these couples have gone through one bad marriage and they're determined not to go through another. Their antennae are up and they're prepared to leave if necessary."

Grandparents sometimes lose contact with their grandchildren through the dissolution of the parents' marriage. Lack of involvement by the noncustodial spouse, unresolved conflicts, and geographic distance lead to decreased visiting with the noncustodial parent's parents (Gladstone, 1987). The parents of the custodial parent tend to see the child more frequently, but both sets of grandparents could be a valuable resource to children in stepfamilies.

One problem with the life cycle approach is that it assumes that "the family" goes through a particular stage at the same time. In actual fact, individual members may experience quite different stages simultaneously. Especially remarried couples may find that their aspirations differ because of their varying ages and life experiences. In this case, future plans affecting the family unit may have to be negotiated with each other to prevent family conflict.

With rising rates of remarriage, there is evidence that the age gap in second and subsequent marriages is larger than in first marriages. While the age gap averages two years in the first marriage, it is about four years in the remarriage of divorced people and seven years with widowed people (Statistics Canada, 1990a:28, 29). In many second marriages, the husband is more than four years older than his wife, although in a few cases, she may be older than he is. Furthermore, many men divorce and remarry younger women, with whom they begin a new family. Although a remarried husband may be old enough to consider early retirement, he may still have young children from his second wife and adult children from his first. This merely illustrates that husbands and wives are not always at the same stage in the life cycle. In addition, a very young wife may find herself in a stepmother relationship to children not much older than she is.

We cannot assume that both members of a couple reach mid-life at the same time. Men who marry younger women may be considering early retirement just as their younger wives are reestablishing themselves in the labour force. This could cause friction in their relationship. Traditionally, women have retired when their husbands retired, but younger wives may have no desire to leave work when they are still under 50, especially if they are not yet entitled to a full pension.

FUTURE TRENDS

Although mid-life has been associated with crises and menopausal women in the minds of some people, these in fact are myths for most Canadians. Increasingly, both men and women are in the labour force during middle age and their occupational lives may be just starting to solidify during their forties. In addition, many men are now making major job or career changes at this time of life, either because of layoffs or a desire to develop other interests or become self-employed.

Although Canadians are bearing fewer children, and finishing childbearing at younger ages (Wadhera, 1989:216), their children are dependent on them for more years than in previous decades. While this prolonged dependency could lead to more companionate relationships between parents and their adult children, it could also encourage adolescent rebellion. As educational requirements for employment continue to be inflated, more young adults will continue to live with their parents, and their parents will be expected to help these students pay for their education. Part-time jobs seldom provide sufficient income for educational and living expenses. In addition, continuing education and job retraining may become more necessary not only for youth but also for adults in the future.

Studies on the children of divorced parents indicate that these young people tend to leave home at an earlier age. As the percentage of children from divorced families rises in the population, we may see more young people leaving home earlier and forfeiting higher education in their effort to establish their own households away from the complications of blended families. Yet, high accommodation costs and inability to support themselves may prevent some from leaving home even when they want to do so.

Although divorce rates continue to rise, there is some indication that remarriage is becoming less prevalent (Adams and Nagnur, 1990). More couples will live together without legally marrying in the future, but remarriage will probably remain popular for divorced parents. With increasing rates of joint custody, the boundaries of blended families may become even more blurred as greater numbers of children live in the households of both biological parents.

SUGGESTED READINGS

Ambert, Anne-Marie. *Divorce in Canada.* Don Mills: Academic Press, 1980.

___. "Marriage Dissolution: Structural and Ideological Change." *Families: Changing Trends in Canada.* 2nd ed. Edited by Maureen Baker. Scarborough: McGraw-Hill Ryerson, 1990:192–210.

___. "The Other Perspective: Children's Effect on Parents." *Families: Changing Trends in Canada.* 2nd ed. Edited by Maureen Baker. Scarborough: McGraw-Hill Ryerson, 1990:149–165.

Baker, Maureen. "*What Will Tomorrow Bring?...*" *The Aspirations of Adolescent Women.* Canadian Advisory Council on the Status of Women. Ottawa: Minister of Supply and Services Canada, 1985.

Bibby, Reginald W. and Donald C. Posterski. *The Emerging Generation. An Inside Look at Canada's Teenagers.* Toronto: Irwin, 1985.

Canada, Special Senate Committee on Youth. *Youth. A Plan of Action.* (Chaired by Senator J. Hébert). Ottawa: Minister of Supply and Services, February 1986.

Clingempeel, W.G. and S.Segal. "Stepparent-Stepchild Relationships and the Psychological Adjustment of Children in Stepmother and Stepfather Families." *Child Development.* 57 (1). 1986:474–484.

Drakich, Janice. "In Whose Best Interest? The Politics of Joint Custody." *Family Bonds and Gender Divisions.* Edited by Bonnie Fox. Toronto: Canadian Scholars' Press, 1988:477–496.

Elkind, David. *All Grown Up and No Place to Go. Teenagers in Crisis.* Reading, MA: Addison-Wesley, 1984.

Galarneau, Diane. "Alimony and Child Support." *Perspectives on Labour and Income.* 4 (2). Summer 1992:8–21.

Gecas, Viktor and Monica A. Seff. "Families and Adolescents: A Review of the 1980s." *Journal of Marriage and the Family.* 52. November 1990:941–958.

Gehring, Thomas M. et al. "Conflict in Families of Adolescents: The Impact of Cohesion and Power Structures." *Journal of Family Psychology.* 3 (3). March 1990:290–309.

Gladstone, James W. "Factors Associated With Changes in Visiting Between Grandmothers and Grandchildren Following an Adult Child's Marriage Breakdown." *Canadian Journal on Aging.* 6 (2). 1987:117–127.

Hobart, Charles. "Relationships in Remarried Families." *Canadian Journal of Sociology.* 13 (3). 1988:261–282.

Lin, C.C. and Fu, V.R. "A Comparison of Child-Rearing Practices Among Chinese, Immigrant Chinese, and Caucasian-American Parents." *Child Development.* 61. 1990:429–433.

Mackie, Marlene. "Socialization: Changing Views of Child Rearing and Adolescence." *Families: Changing Trends in Canada.* 2nd. ed. Edited by Maureen Baker. Scarborough: McGraw-Hill Ryerson, 1990:115–148.

Meiklejohn, Phyllis et al. "Separation, Divorce and Remarriage" (189–195), "Blended Families" (207–214), and "The Sandwich Generation" (227–231). *Today's Family: A Critical Focus.* Toronto: Collier Macmillan, 1990.

Mills, David M. "A Model for Stepfamily Development." *Family Relations.* 33. July 1986:261–273.

Moore, Maureen. "Women Parenting Alone." *Canadian Social Trends.* 8. Winter 1987:31–36.

National Council of Welfare. *Women and Poverty Revisited.* Ottawa: National Council of Welfare, Summer 1990.

Nett, Emily. *Canadian Families Past and Present* (Chapters 6 and 8). Toronto: Butterworths, 1988.

Orleans, Myron, B.J. Palisi, and D. Caddell. "Marriage Adjustment and Satisfaction of Stepfathers: Their Feelings and Perceptions of Decision Making and Stepchildren Relations." *Family Relations.* 38. October 1989:371–377.

Pasley, B. Kay and Marilyn Ihinger-Tallman. "Boundary Ambiguity in Remarriage: Does Ambiguity Differentiate Degree of Marital Adjustment and Integration?" *Family Relations.* 38. January 1989:46–52.

Richardson, C. James. "Children of Divorce." *Family Matters. Sociology and Contemporary Canadian Families.* Edited by Karen L. Anderson et al. Scarborough: Nelson, 1988a:163–200.

Seltzer, J.A. "Relationships Between Fathers and Children Who Live Apart: The Father's Role After Separation." *Journal of Marriage and the Family.* 53 (1). 1991:79–110.

Sev'er, Aysan. *Women and Divorce in Canada.* Toronto: Canadian Scholars' Press, 1992.

Stark, Elizabeth. "Young, Innocent and Pregnant." *Psychology Today.* October 1986:28–35.

Wakil, Parvez S., C.M. Siddique, and F.A. Wakil. "Between Two Cultures: A Study in Socialization of Children of Immigrants." *Journal of Marriage and the Family.* 43. November 1981:929–940.

ISSUES FOR DISCUSSION

1. Explain how the political economy perspective might be used to explain the prolonging of adolescence.
2. Analyze the implications of the following statement: "Allowing children to live in low-income families may have unanticipated consequences more costly than the various schemes to improve the economic status of one-parent families."
3. Write a brief case study of a co-parenting or a joint custody arrangement that is successful.
4. Why do you think that men remarry faster than women after divorce?
5. What do we mean by educational inflation? Provide some examples of where this has occurred with specific jobs.
6. The clothing and hair styles of many young people imply a rebellion against accepted adult norms; similarly, the words of the music preferred by many young people emphasize sex, violence, or hedonism. Is this a new phenomenon? What causes young people to embrace these aspects of youth "counter-culture?"
7. Explain how the family with adolescents is similar to and different from other stages in the family life cycle.
8. Analyze the impact of dual-earner families or teen employment on the division of labour, power, conflict resolution, and relationships in families.
9. How would an unplanned pregnancy at this time in your life affect your education, occupational plans, and present relationships?
10. Debate the following: "Teenage mothers sometimes discover later, however, that caring for another human being is not only emotionally and physically exhausting, but is not always best for them or for the child."
11. Imagine that you are 45 years old, and your children have left home. Your spouse of 25 years has just informed you that he/she is leaving you for another relationship. What plans would you need for the future?
12. Why do remarriage rates decline with age, especially for women? Why would divorced people have higher remarriage rates than widowed people?

FURTHER ACTIVITIES

1. Interview adolescents from different cultural groups to discover similarities and differences in their relationships with their parents, the amount of independence granted to them, and when they plan to leave home.
2. Interview several stepchildren, including some whose mothers have remarried and some whose fathers have remarried. Have them share their feelings about adjusting to these remarriages.
3. Visit a teen mothers' group at your community centre. Listen to them discuss their lives and their future plans, and prepare a report for your class on what it is like to be a teen mother.
4. Invite to your classroom a father who has sole custody, a custodial mother, and a divorced person with joint physical custody to discuss their ideas on what arrangements are best for children as well as divorced parents.
5. What kind of assistance would be available in your community for each of the following people :
   a. an adolescent using cocaine;
   b. a pregnant 16-year-old;
   c. a single mother living below the poverty line, with two adolescents;
   d. an adolescent with AIDS;
   e. a gay youth;
   f. a date-raped teen?

7 The Post-Parental Stage

SPECIFIC TASKS

From Child-launching to Retirement

The **post-parental stage** begins when the last child leaves home or is "launched" and ends when one or both parents retire from work. With longer life expectancies, fewer children per family and improved family planning, parents no longer spend their entire adult lives raising children. When the last child leaves home, parents could have 10 or 15 years left in their working lives before retirement. However, the recent trend toward delayed marriage and childbirth among women and couples (Wadhera and Millar, 1991), as well as the trend for early retirement may reduce the time between launching and retirement in the future.

Mid-life may involve a reassessment of the meaning of aging, of the importance of sexuality and fertility, and the comparative value of work and family relationships. For many people, mid-life involves renewed interest in work or career development, in friendships and family relationships, or in hobbies. Others anticipate their children's weddings and eventually the birth of grandchildren.

Because the post-parental stage often corresponds with menopause for women, it may be a time when some think more about aging and growing old. Some women maintain the appearance of youthfulness with the assistance of hair colouring, cosmetic surgery, or more tailored and expensive clothing. However, others vow to age more naturally and merely adjust their definition of "old" so that it continues to be higher than their own chronological age.

Chronological age has become a poor predictor of life events with rising rates of divorce and remarriage, teenage childbearing and mothering in some segments of the population, and delayed marriage and childbearing in others (Neugarten and Neugarten, 1987:30). Women may be having their first children or becoming grandparents at the age of 40. Men may be divorcing, embarking on new marriages, or starting new families with a much younger wives at age 50 or 60. Chronological age may also be a poor predictor of health, work status, interests, preoccupations, and needs (Neugarten and Neugarten, 1987:30). However, it is possible to portray typical life patterns of Canadian men and women, as figures 7.1 and 7.2 illustrate.

What is considered an appropriate lifestyle for people of different chronological ages varies with each **birth cohort**, as well as by gender,

Figure 7.1 **Life Patterns of Canadian Women**

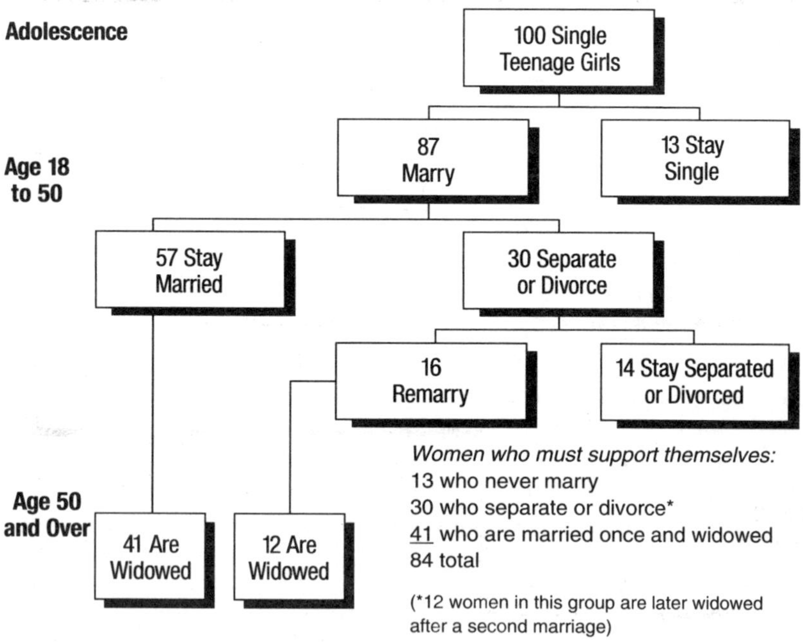

Source: National Council of Welfare. *Women and Poverty Revisited*, Ottawa: Summer 1990:16.

social class, and culture. We may compare ourselves at 45 or 50 with our parents' or grandparents' generation, and feel more active, independent, and youthful. Especially the lives of women have changed over the years, where today's middle-aged woman is likely to be working for pay and to have important activities in her life in addition to her children and home. For this reason, the **empty nest syndrome** involving depression and anxiety about loss of reproductive capacity and parenting tends to be less relevant today than it used to be. What are more likely to precipitate crises are unexpected life events, such as the death of a parent during a child's adolescence, a teenage pregnancy, a child who does not leave home at the appropriate time, or an unanticipated divorce (Neugarten and Neugarten, 1987:33).

When children leave home, parents with intact marriages could be alone for the first time in years. At the same time, they may become increasingly concerned about the health and well-being of their own parents, who are growing older and now may need some assistance.

Figure 7.2 **Life Patterns of Canadian Men**

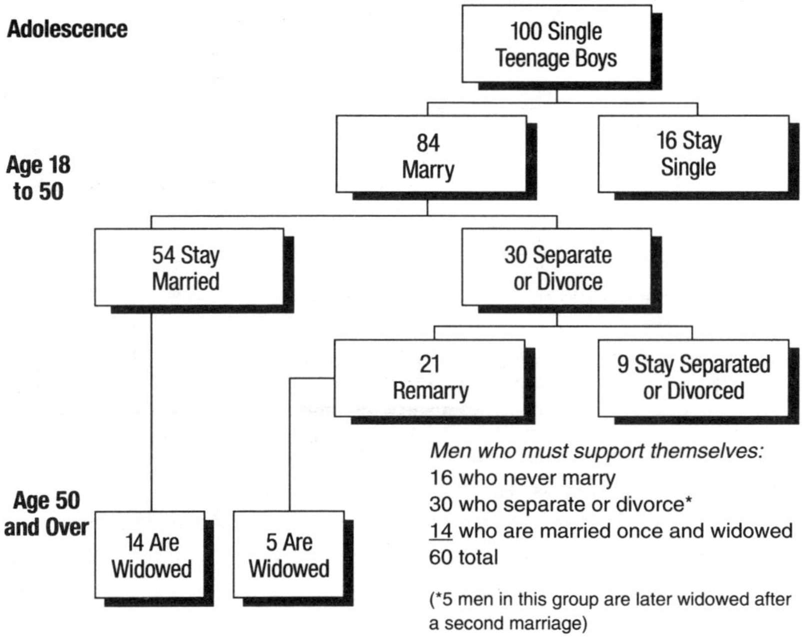

Source: National Council of Welfare. *Women and Poverty Revisited.* Ottawa: Summer 1990:134.

Adjusting to Changing Roles and Relationships

Since their wedding, married people may have experienced childbirth and childrearing together, and undoubtedly enjoyed good times as well as suffering through some tribulations. Their years of childraising may have brought them closer together, but could also have pushed them apart into rigid complementary roles in which they shared few activities. By **complementary roles** we mean marital roles in which each specializes in a different area, such as husband as the breadwinner and wife as the homemaker. When all the children leave home and the parents are alone, they may need to reestablish themselves as a couple rather than seeing each other mainly as parents. Those who have always emphasized the importance of their marital relationship compared with their parental roles may make this transition easily, while those who gave parenting priority may continue to interact with each other as parents. For example, some couples in the post-parental stage continue to call each other "father" or "mother" rather than by their actual names.

Interacting with the adult "children" who have left home requires a shift in power relations and new ways of interacting. When the children arrive as visitors and chat about their new activities and relationships, parents may realize that they now have little control over their children's lives. Unless they still support them financially, parents are often made to feel they have no right to continue to talk to and discipline these adults as though they were still children. Although they can set house rules which must be followed while their children are in the parental home, parents may find that their adult children do not share all their ideas about appropriate behaviour and lifestyle. Similarly, young people can no longer assume that their parents will provide services for them, such as cooking or laundry. This readjustment of parent-child roles may require some practice and a period of negotiating new forms of interaction.

As Nett (1988) mentions in her book, children may be assisted or "sponsored" to become more independent or they may leave home suddenly, with little advance warning to allow parents and children to readjust. When parents are reluctant to let their children begin a new life, future interaction with them may be difficult. Adult children may see their parents infrequently and remain alienated from them for some time.

It is now more acceptable than it was before the 1960s for young people to leave home to set up their own apartments or to live with friends without parental supervision. Furthermore, these friends are

SPONSORED AND UNSPONSORED INDEPENDENCE

"Sponsored independence" (Adams, 1980) involves gradually relinquishing control over the adolescent's behaviour in an atmosphere of emotional support, thereby permitting the youngster to assume more and more responsibility for decisions and actions related to her or himself. There is variation, however, in the degree to which the strategy is applied to teenaged boys and girls, even in the middle class. The developmental tasks assigned to girls are different from those given to boys at adolescence in North American culture. As Mackie (1987, 147) observes, "For both sexes, the peak of gender role differentiation occurs in adolescence and early adulthood." The moves of adolescent boys toward autonomy are much more likely to be encouraged, and at earlier ages, than those of girls. More passivity is expected of girls, who do indeed as a rule stay closer to home and accept more parental restrictions than males during these years. The differences between strategies practised on adolescents by sex are accentuated in certain ethnic groups, where the culture dictates *machismo* (masculine sexual experimentation and aggression) for males, and modesty and virginity for young women. Girls are subject to curfews; boys have no hours imposed on them by parents. (This is true in fact of most families in North America.)

Another strategy less widely subscribed to today is unsponsored independence. It occurs where parents view the move from childhood to adulthood as happening abruptly. This strategy was more commonly used in an earlier era by working-class parents (skilled and unskilled labourers) who required income from paid work into which children could enter more easily than adults could....

Other adolescents in rural areas, because the family had too many children for the farm to support, would be given a small amount of cash and sent out to make their own way in the adult world. In other cases, strict discipline or other unpleasantness at home led adolescents themselves to strike out on their own. Today, the abrupt move toward independence frequently takes place in a context of parent/adolescent conflict, although this is not necessarily the case. Because adolescents have such limited opportunities for supporting themselves by legal means in modern society, those who do not receive familial support (and are not yet of a legal age to be eligible for welfare) are at risk of exploitation on the streets. In their destitution they resort to delinquent acts and prostitution....

The results of unsponsored independence are highly unpredictable. Some persons who are thrust into adult behaviours and responsibilities in their early teen years, whether voluntarily or involuntarily, are alienated in every way from their parents and siblings. They never go back home, or they continue to "act out" against family values, and in some cases they refuse to understand or forgive parents even while staying in contact. The same situation can occur when a parent insists that a teenager must go into the same occupation as the parent, or live out some other parental dream.

Nett, Emily. *Canadian Families Past and Present.* Toronto: Butterworths, 1988:173–175.

increasingly of the opposite sex. While many parents oppose their children's common-law relationships, some accept this arrangement as a form of trial marriage. Others feel that they have little control over their children when they leave home, and sometimes prefer to remain ignorant of their children's activities for fear of what they might uncover. Today's parents are particularly concerned about the use of illegal drugs, but also worry about immoderate alcohol consumption, drinking and driving, and sexual activities. Most parents, however, would like to feel that they can trust their adolescent or adult children to behave sensibly when they live independently.

Some children, especially those with special needs, never leave home or leave later in life when community services are accessible and subsidized accommodation available. The absence or delay of the launching stage may make it very difficult for parents to perceive these children as adults. If they require daily assistance, the parent providing the care (usually the mother) may find her continuing situation stressful unless she has access to respite care programs or some outside assistance from community services.

Increasingly, adult children leave home and then return temporarily to live with their parents. Some go away to college or university, and when they graduate or leave school, they cannot always find a job that pays well enough to move into a place of their own. Other young people move out, lose their jobs, cannot afford to continue paying rent, and return home to their parents for a temporary stay. After being accustomed to living on their own and having few behavioural restrictions, young people and their parents may need to negotiate new arrangements about parental discipline, curfews, and division of household chores.

Occasionally, when the marriages of young people dissolve through separation and divorce, they temporarily return home for assistance with finances or child care. Increasingly, this is becoming an uncom-

FRANK & ERNEST® by Bob Thaves

Reprinted by permission of Newspaper Enterprise Association.

mon solution, which is considered undesirable by both divorced children and their parents (Baker, 1983). If the divorced "children" are parents themselves, and they return to live with their parents, both parties need to negotiate new roles, behavioural standards for the young children, house rules, new forms of interaction, and a new division of responsibilities in order for this living arrangement to be successful.

Although many young people now live with partners before marriage, most eventually marry and bear children, which means that the majority of parents become grandparents. During the post-parental stage, parents may be getting to know their children's spouses and may be anticipating becoming grandparents. In time, they hope that their children will reproduce, that the family will grow larger, and that they will soon be developing a relationship with their grandchildren.

Since each generation is having fewer children and some young people are opting for a childfree life, however, parents can no longer assume that their children will provide grandchildren. Nor can they assume that when there are grandchildren they will live near enough for regular visits. In addition, divorce and remarriage sometimes means that grandparents lose contact with their grandchildren, especially if their adult child is not awarded custody or does not maintain contact with the children.

Social trends toward fewer children or no children and later first births (Wadhera and Millar, 1991) suggest that the number of grandchildren will decline in the future, and the years between generations may once again increase. In addition, the post-parental stage may not involve grandparenting for a substantial minority of the population. Instead, it might involve increased commitment to work, friendships, leisure activities, or caring for aging parents.

At the stage when many people are free from daily parenting responsibilities, their own parents may require personal assistance. Longer life expectancy means that the parents of more middle-aged people will still be alive, and some of them will require assistance. One of the developmental tasks of middle age may be to accept responsibility toward an aging parent (Troll, 1971).

Because middle-aged people could have children and even grandchildren who require attention, as well as parents who require personal assistance, they have been called the **sandwich generation** (Miller, 1981). Some adult children invite elderly parents to live with them, but more often help them to maintain their own homes. Children may shop for aging parents, cut lawns or shovel snow, visit, and provide companionship and emotional support. They also may help elderly parents to identify and access available social services, purchase home care, or move into new accommodation more convenient to their needs.

The middle-aged couple's parents need not be very elderly or need assistance, however. Many people live well into their eighties or nineties without major illness and without requiring much assistance. In fact, older parents often continue to provide support to their adult children as well as receiving it from them. Relationships between adult children and their parents are often reciprocal and mutually supporting, and only become asymmetrical when parents become very elderly, ill, or need assistance.

WORK IN MID-LIFE

For those able to maintain full-time steady employment since they left school, work in mid-life could involve increased responsibility and commitment leading to higher wages or salaries. Even those who have not prospered financially might find that they now have an easier time at work because they know their jobs and co-workers well. Due to the reduction in family responsibilities, working parents now have more leisure time after work and fewer financial responsibilities when children leave home. If parents own a home, the mortgage could be paid off by this time. If both husband and wife are in the labour force full-time, the couple may have accumulated enough money for frequent entertainment and travel. For the first time in years, they may have money to spend on themselves.

For women who have not remained in the labour force or reentered at a younger age, child-launching may require some reevaluation of life goals. This often involves making educational or employment plans. In most Canadian homes, however, mothers have already reentered the labour force by the time their children have left home or have never left paid work. In fact, younger women now tend to remain in the labour force throughout their life cycle (Statistics Canada, 1992a) and take only short maternity leaves. When children leave home and family responsibilities subside, however, commitment to work may increase.

If both husband and wife have careers that involve progression through the ranks, mid-life might be one of their most productive times and much of their energy could be devoted to furthering their careers. Some employees even accept positions in other cities, and maintain a commuter marriage in order to take advantage of promo-

Mid-life could be one of the most productive and enjoyable times in terms of career as couples in this stage tend to have fewer financial and childrearing responsibilities.

Courtesy of Carolyn and Gord Leaver.

tional opportunities. At this point in their lives, their income might be higher than they ever anticipated. Income statistics indicate, for example, that personal income usually peaks at age 35 to 45 (Statistics Canada, 1990b).

For those whose work is merely a way of earning money with few promotional possibilities, mid-life may be a time when work is becoming monotonous and unsatisfying. There are several ways of dealing with this lack of satisfaction, including telling yourself that you are fortunate to have a job while others are unemployed, spending more time and energy with co-workers at breaks, or becoming more involved with leisure activities after work.

In times of recession such as the early 1990s, many middle-aged employees are concerned about job security. With rapid changes in technology and a globalized economy, an increasing number of older workers are being laid off well before retirement age. Severance pay to full-time permanent employees may not amount to very much money, while those in part-time or temporary work may not receive any at all. Consequently many older workers are forced into long-term unemployment or early retirement. The unemployed worker over the age of 45 or 50 often has considerable difficulty finding a new job, especially those with low educational attainment or experience with only one type of work (McDonald and Wanner, 1990:107).

Depending on personal or family finances, job status and the level of job satisfaction, mid-life may be the time to consider a job or career change, to branch out into self-employment, or take early retirement. With improvements in employer pensions, registered retirement savings plans, and government pensions, more people are now able to retire before the age of 65. Despite the 1985 Supreme Court decision prohibiting the fixing of a compulsory retirement age, a greater percentage of the Canadian population is now choosing to retire before 65 than a few decades ago (McDonald and Wanner, 1990:34). Only a very small minority of self-employed business people or high-status professionals tend to choose to remain in the labour force after that age.

HISTORICAL PERSPECTIVES

When Children Left Home

Until the 1960s, young people generally left their parental home and established their own households only when they married. For parents whose children took over the family farm or business, the post-parental stage involved reduced control over their children's behaviour and the family business, but they remained in close contact with them and may have even worked with them. Adult children who could not take over the family farm might have moved to another farm or into town to find work before marriage, but they would have boarded with another family rather than living on their own. Married children settled on nearby farms or moved to the nearest town, visiting their parents and other siblings as often as they could.

Wealthier young people, usually men, sometimes left home before marriage to attend university, but often lived in supervised residences. After they finished their studies, they usually came home to live with their parents until they could establish their profession and marry.

Unmarried young people, especially men, sometimes migrated to Canada or other places, but usually they were expected to seek out relatives or neighbours who had emigrated earlier and to live with or near them. Many parents in Europe, and later other parts of the world, "launched" their children and never saw them again because the

Many parents never saw their adult children again after they emigrated.

National Archives of Canada, Negative no. C68842

children emigrated from Europe to North America or Australia. In previous centuries and even up to the 1960s, many young emigrants could not afford to return home, nor could their parents afford the time or money to visit them. Of course, some young people emigrated to escape parents and relatives whom they saw as meddling and intrusive, and they made little or no attempt to maintain contact with their families.

Prior to airplanes and automobiles, adult children who left home and moved farther away than walking distance or a carriage ride could not see their parents very often, although literate people often wrote letters. These letters have provided social historians with valuable information about family life and specifically about parent-child relations in the past.

Until a few decades ago, the post-parental stage began when all the children were successfully launched or married and had left home. Because most parents could not afford to support them indefinitely, they were anxious to see their children married. In addition, a stigma was attached to remaining unmarried, and the person might be considered immature or unfortunate. Parents hoped that their children's marriages would be advantageous in terms of finances, because their own well-being might be at stake. They also wanted their children's marriages to be fruitful in terms of childbearing in order to continue the family line, provide a future labour force for the family and community, and to raise their status as grandparents.

Trends in the Timing of Launching and First Marriage

Economic and labour force factors have always influenced the timing of launching, although personal choice was also involved. For example, during the recession at the turn of this century, during the 1930s Depression, and throughout the 1980s and early 1990s, the age of first marriage was older than in more prosperous times such as the 1960s.

Before the Second World War, men departed from their parents' home when they could afford to marry, as well as when they were permitted by their parents, their fiancée's parents, and their employers to do so. Men needed to be able to support themselves, as well as their wives and children, and had to wait until they acquired the skills, education, and opportunity to work and save money. After all, marriage for men meant immediate financial responsibility. Men also delayed marriage because fewer restrictions were placed on their sexual behaviour compared with women's, and there was less pressure to marry early to prevent sexual indiscretions.

For many centuries, daughters left their parental home only when they married or joined a religious institution, and they married at younger ages than sons. The major reason for this was that women looked to men for financial support, and it took time before men were capable of supporting a family. In addition, men wanted wives who were young and healthy, sexually inexperienced, and with many years of childbearing ahead of them.

Even when unmarried women began working outside the home, leaving home and marrying were delayed while the couple saved money for their new household. Until about 1940, women were expected to quit work upon marriage because it was assumed that they could get pregnant at any time after the wedding. Without reliable contraception or maternity leave/benefits, women were not considered dependable employees. Credit cards, medical insurance, and unemployment insurance benefits were not available to help young people establish a household, pay their living expenses, or deal with emergency expenses.

Before the Second World War, adult children living with their parents usually were expected to give their parents a substantial portion of their earnings for room and board. Consequently, leaving home and marrying could be delayed until their parents allowed them to save their earnings. Young people also had to wait for parental consent to marry if they were below the minimum age, if their parents were supporting them, or if their parents objected to their marriage and refused to assist them. Sometimes a man was expected to ask the father for permission to marry his daughter, and to wait until this permission was granted.

The timing of marriage and launching was also influenced by wages and employment practices. A male employee often had to persuade his boss to give him a raise before he could afford to set up his own household. Prior to World War II, wages were based partially on an employee's gender, marital status, and financial need. A man was paid more than a woman for the same work, and a married man was often paid more than a single man with the assumption that he had greater expenses. Since women were expected to quit work after the wedding, the couple would also have to wait until they saved up enough money so that they could afford to live on one income.

As table 7.1 indicates, the median age of first marriage (and leaving home) was relatively high at the beginning of this century. In addition, the age gap between husbands and wives was larger than it is now, reflecting women's lower levels of education and lack of investment in the labour force. Furthermore, at the turn of this century, many young people did not marry at all for various reasons: they did not meet a suitable partner; they remained at home to care for their elderly parents; they chose to remain single for personal reasons; or, if they were men, they could not afford to support another person. Gradually, the median age of marriage in Canada declined until the early 1970s, when it began to rise again with higher unemployment rates, prolonged education, and common-law relationships.

Variations in the timing of marriage and launching have also been studied through birth cohorts, or people born within the same time period. Ellen Gee (1986) analyzed birth cohorts and noted that the median age of first marriage for women was 26.0 years, if they were born between 1841 and 1850, and 21.1, if they were born between 1931 and 1940. Interestingly, the age of first marriage has now risen again as more people delay marriage to complete their education. Furthermore, the age of launching and marriage no longer coincides as more young people now live together before legally marrying.

People married and left home at younger ages when it was easy to find work, when wages were high relative to the cost of living, and in urban settings where men and women mixed freely and there were

Table 7.1 **Median Age at First Marriage, Canada, 1901–1989**

	Brides	Grooms
1901	24.7	29.1
1911	23.2	27.2
1921	22.8	26.2
1931	23.8	26.8
1941	23.5	26.5
1951	21.7	24.8
1961	21.1	24.0
1971	21.3	23.5
1981	22.5	24.6
1986	23.9	25.8
1989	24.9	25.8

Source: Figures from 1901–1951: *Journal of Marriage and the Family,* "The Family Cycle in Twentieth-Century Canada," Roy H. Rodgers and Gail Witney; 43:3 pp. 727–740 using figure p. 729. Copyrighted 1981 by the National Council on Family Relations, 3989 Central Ave. N.E. Suite 550, Minneapolis, MN 55421. Reprinted by permission.

Figures from 1961–1989 from Statistics Canada. *Health Reports. Marriages 1989.* Supplement 16, vol. 2, no. 4, 1990, cat. 82-003S, Ottawa: Statistics Canada, 1991:26, 27. Reproduced with the permission of the Minister of Supply and Services Canada, 1992.

more opportunities to meet potential marriage partners. Decisions to leave the parental home have also been influenced by the availability of student loans and grants. If governments provide financial assistance to students, young people may not have to wait until graduation to leave home. Furthermore, now that women typically enter the labour force after leaving school and continue working throughout their lives (Statistics Canada, 1992b), it is possible for men and women to establish separate households from their parents, to live together, or to marry when one of them has work. If colleges and universities have subsidized apartments for married students, it may be more advantageous financially for young people to marry while they are still students than to wait until after graduation. Yet, early marriages are more susceptible to divorce because of financial problems, undeveloped career plans, and emotional immaturity.

Women with high educational attainment tend to have lower marriage rates and higher divorce rates than those with less formal education, while the opposite is true for men (Glick, 1984). Because women tend to look for partners with the same or higher educational qualifications, and because educated professional women are less likely to have to marry for financial reasons, they sometimes delay marriage, thereby raising the probability of remaining single. Yet, unmarried people are now more likely to leave home than before the Second World War when many continued to live in the parental home until the death of their parents.

In addition to gender differences, the average age of marriage and launching has also varied by socio-economic status. Wealthier people tend to stay in school longer (Porter, 1965; Clement, 1975; Forcese, 1986). The occupations they choose usually require more education and take longer to establish. In addition, young people from wealthier families may delay launching because they have more spacious and attractive living quarters with their families than they could afford on their own. In their parents' house, they may have their own room, the use of their parents' possessions, and their financial support, so there may be little pressure to establish their own households. On the other hand, young people from poorer families may look forward to acquiring more privacy, and their parents may find it difficult to continue supporting them beyond a certain age.

In 1986, more unmarried young people were remaining in their parents' home than in 1981 (Boyd and Pryor, 1990), owing to rising rates of unemployment, more immigrants from cultures valuing extended families, and the need for more schooling. This trend is delaying the onset of parents' post-parental stage. As table 7.2 shows, more unmarried men than women live with their parents, but for both sexes, the percentage rose from 1981 to 1986.

Establishing a separate household is becoming more difficult with rising rents and education costs, increased pressure to stay in school

Table 7.2 **Unmarried* Adults Living With Their Parents, by Age and Sex, Canada, 1971–1986**

AGE		1971	1981	1986
20–24	Male	72.4	68.1	71.2
	Female	62.1	59.3	63.3
25–29	Male	46.8	40.0	44.6
	Female	34.5	27.2	31.6
30–34	Male	35.1	27.8	28.8
	Female	24.7	17.1	17.7

* Includes never-married, separated, divorced, and widowed.

Source: From *Canadian Social Trends*, Summer 1989, cat. 17-20, no. 3. Reproduced with the permission of the Minister of Supply and Services Canada, 1992.

longer, the loss of full-time permanent jobs, and fewer opportunities to accumulate savings. Consequently, the median age of leaving home and first marriage in the 1980s is higher than the 1960s, and more similar to the pattern of the turn of the century. However, the major difference between the present and the early 1900s is that more unmarried couples now have sexual relations and live together before marriage.

CULTURAL PERSPECTIVES

CULTURAL VARIATIONS IN LAUNCHING

Although the timing of child-launching varies for different ethnic groups, we cannot overlook generational differences. The generation born in Canada may be similar in attitudes and behaviour, but is not always the same as those born in the homeland (Ujimoto, 1987:115). As mentioned in chapter three, some ethnic groups, especially those who are less prosperous, encourage their children to marry early. The timing may vary for daughters and sons, however. Italians and Greeks, for example, usually encourage their daughters to remain at home until marriage, but marriage is expected to take place around the age of 20. Girls are also given little opportunity to date and are expected to be virgins at the time of marriage. Boys are given more social and sexual independence before marriage, but are expected to marry later (Sturino, 1980).

There is little information about when young people from different cultural groups leave their parents' homes apart from the age of marriage. There has been some analysis of Canadian census data that examines the age of first marriage by ethnicity, but only a few ethnic groups were included, and the 1981 census is the most recent that includes clear-cut questions about ethnicity.[1] For example, Shiva Halli (1990:67), using 1981 Canadian census data, found that the average age of ever-married women at first marriage was 20.9 for British, 20.2 for French, 20.6 for Italians, and 21.8 for Jewish people. Although she found that most cultural groups marry at about the same time, there were some small differences among them. Jewish young people have tended to marry later than most other groups, while French and Italians have married slightly younger.

[1] In the 1986 census, questions about ethnicity more clearly reflected the multiple backgrounds of many new Canadians, but these data were more difficult to analyze.

Many adult immigrants bring their elderly parents with them to Canada, or later sponsor them as landed immigrants. After the parents arrive, the older generation may experience difficulty adapting to the new culture, especially if they cannot speak the language and are retired from work (Driedger and Chappell, 1987). If there is a cohesive ethnic community, such as among the Chinese in Toronto, the older parents may be able to function well, to continue to speak their native language, and to associate with others in similar situations.

Immigrant groups, such as Italians and Chinese, tend to invite their parents to live with them in extended family households (Driedger and Chappell, 1987:71; Novak, 1988:281). Even when accommodation is crowded, this is considered to be a preferable arrangement to having their parents live alone. Although this pattern relates to traditional customs and living arrangements in their country of origin, living as three generations makes particular sense when the elderly parent cannot speak English or French and when income is low.

Child care, meal preparation, and house cleaning is often done by older women in three-generation households. For example, grandmothers in Asian and southern European households provide valuable household assistance when their daughters or daughters-in-law work outside the home. In particularly crowded living conditions, however, the potential for conflict is high between grandparents and adolescent or young adult children.

While children are expected to care for their elderly parents in the homeland, once they are in Canada it is easy for immigrants to adopt the North American pattern of encouraging their parents to live alone or in seniors' residences (Ujimoto, 1987:116). This may lead to conflict between the generations, however. Elderly parents are especially likely to feel rejected if they were encouraged to leave their homeland and friends in order to join their children, only to find that they are expected to live alone when they arrive.

If aging parents are placed in institutions designed for the **majority group**, where everyone is expected to speak the official language and eat the same food, there may be cultural misunderstandings. If they do not speak the language or are not as assertive as some other cultural groups, they cannot make their needs known and may therefore feel neglected by staff (MacLean and Bonar, 1983:52). In addition, some ethnic groups such as Japanese, Chinese, Koreans, and Filipinos strongly value the emotional and symbolic support provided by family members when they are in institutions. Yet, when adult children assist their aging parent to eat or bathe, or obtain medical information on their behalf, this is sometimes seen as interference by hospital staff

(Ujimoto, 1987:118). Cultural groups that have been established in Canada for many years have created their own seniors' clubs and residences in order to overcome these cultural misunderstandings.

We cannot assume that immigrants to Canada bring all of the cultural values of the homeland with them, to be passed on to their children (Ujimoto, 1987:116). For example, the traditional Japanese model of old age places primary emphasis on the concept of **filial piety**. Children have an obligation to look after their parents in old age to repay their parents for caring for them as children. Yet, research on Japanese immigrants in Canada has noted that neither immigrants nor their Canadian-born children want to rely solely on their children for support in old age (Sugiman and Nishio, 1983). Childhood patterns of socialization and cultural values are often modified by immigrants when they come to North America.

Many immigrants come to Canada without other family members. For example, numerous young women arrive in Canada from Europe, the Philippines, and various countries in the Caribbean to work as nannies or caregivers to children in Canada. Other young people come as refugees from war-torn countries in Central America, Africa, Asia, eastern Europe, and the Middle East. These refugees are not able to return to visit their family and friends, nor in some cases can they write letters without endangering the lives of their relatives or friends. Launching for these young people may mean making a long-term break from parents and other family members until the war is over, until they can get landed immigrant status and sponsor their relatives to come to Canada as immigrants, or until they can save enough money to visit.

GENERATION GAPS

Among some ethnic and cultural groups, parents become concerned that their adolescent and adult children are losing their cultural traditions and becoming assimilated by the dominant culture. In some cases, the young people cannot speak their parents' language properly even though they can understand it and translate for them. Children may have acted as interpreters for parents for many years, especially for their mothers, who are less likely than fathers to learn English or French (Seward and McDage, 1988). Parents often expect their children to speak their own language at home, but most second-generation immigrants (or the children born to immigrant parents) would rather learn English or French to fit in with others at school.

When Canadian-born children grow up, they may be embarrassed by their parents' traditional appearance and behaviour (Ambert, 1992:139). In some cases, they may have little in common with their parents, and find communication difficult. As long as they live at home, they can talk about daily routines and events. But when these young people leave home and then return as visitors, the culture gap may widen. First-generation parents and the Canadian-born children may have little to talk about.

This culture gap is sometimes partially bridged when grandchildren are born. Grandparents can then focus on the care and activities of the grandchild, but disputes can still arise over childrearing techniques. Canadian-born parents may have quite different ideas about childrearing than immigrant grandparents. Yet, the grandchild can serve as a focus for interaction between the generations and between the first- and second-generation immigrants (Connidis, 1989a:64).

SELECTED ISSUES

THE EMPTY NEST AND THE NOT-SO-EMPTY NEST

The Empty Nest

Life satisfaction tends to rise for both men and women after their children have left home. The empty-nest, which in the 1950s was assumed to be the cause of depression in middle-aged women, now appears to increase well-being among women (Palmore et al., 1979; Barnett and Baruch, 1978–79; George et al., 1980). The rate of labour force participation among women 45 to 64 has increased considerably in the last decade, as table 7.3 shows. Furthermore, a qualitative shift appears to have taken place in the meaning of work for women (Connidis, 1982). In the 1950s, married women in financial need composed a large portion of the female labour force, but now, with rising levels of educational attainment for women, more married women work for personal satisfaction as well as financial reasons.

Several studies have found that employed women compared with homemakers generally report higher levels of life satisfaction and adjustment throughout the life cycle to old age (Lehr, 1978; George et al., 1980). Having their own money, enjoying daily contact with adults, and making a contribution to society are reasons given for the higher reported satisfaction of working women. Although homemakers also make an important contribution to their families and to society by rearing children, they receive no formal recognition such as a pay cheque or fringe benefits. Over the years, the lives of homemakers and their husbands could become increasingly separate because their

Table 7.3 **Labour Force Participation, by Age and Sex, Canada, 1951–1991.**

	MALES				
	1951	**1961**	**1971**	**1981**	**1991**
25–34	98.2	98.4	92.6	95.8	92.6
35–44	—	—	92.8	95.6	93.8
45–54	95.0	95.3	90.3	92.7	90.6
55–64	—	—	80.1	77.8	62.6
65+	39.5	30.6	23.6	17.1	11.3
	FEMALES				
	1951	**1961**	**1971**	**1981**	**1991**
25–34	25.5	29.2	44.5	66.2	77.2
35–44	22.4	31.2	43.9	64.6	78.4
45–54	21.1	32.9	44.4	55.9	69.9
55–64	13.5	23.1	34.4	35.4	35.7
65+	4.5	6.2	8.3	5.3	3.5

Source: Statistics Canada. *Labour Force Annual Averages. 1991*. Ottawa: Ministry of Industry, Science and Technology, February 1992. Statistics Canada. *The Labour Force*. June 1988. Cat. 71-0001. Supply and Services Canada, July 1988:26; Statistics Canada. *Historical Statistics of Canada*. 2nd ed. Supply and Services Canada: Ottawa, 1983:D107-123; Labour Canada, Women's Bureau. *Changing Patterns in Women's Employment*, Ottawa: Supply and Services Canada, 1966:7; Jac-Andre Boulet and Laval Lavallee. *The Changing Economic Status of Women*. For the Economic Council of Canada. Supply and Services Canada: Ottawa, 1984:7. Reproduced with permission of the Minister of Supply and Services Canada, 1992.

daily routines are so different. Furthermore, the prestige of the occupation of homemaker seems to have declined in status over the past 20 years as more women have entered the labour force, although the prestige of a homemaker is still based on her husband's occupation (Eichler, 1977). Homemakers sometimes feel that they must justify their decision to stay home, whereas a generation ago, working women had to defend their decision to work outside the home.

For parents who are separated, divorced, or remarried, the timing of launching and the empty nest tends to be earlier than for those in intact marriages. Recent studies have found that children from single-parent, step-parent, or adoptive parent families, as well as those living in nonparental situations, are more likely to leave home prior to the age of 19 than those from intact families (White and Booth, 1985;

Aquilino, 1991). Girls from these families especially tend to leave home early to establish their own residences. In most cases, these young people are entering the labour force or marrying early, rather than continuing their education. The reasons given in the research for early home-leaving in single-parent families and remarried households are often related to problematic parent-child relations and financial reasons for children of single-parent families.

A growing percentage of women between the ages of 55 and 64 are now living on their own, and the increase is mainly due to the rising divorce rates and low remarriage rates for older divorced women. At the same time, however, there has also been a long-term trend for older never-married women to live alone rather than with relatives. By 1986, 29 percent of women between the ages of 55 to 64 were living on their own. About half of these were widowed, 29 percent divorced, 22 percent never-married, and 11 percent were separated (Burke and Spector, 1991:15). Many of these women are economically disadvantaged and have difficulty finding appropriate and affordable housing. Those who have been lone parents especially may be entering a vulnerable stage of their life as they approach 55. When their children leave home, they no longer receive certain benefits such as child tax credits, Family Allowances cheques, child support payments, and in some provinces subsidized housing. Because of low incomes, these parents are often not able to lend money to their children for their education or to help them establish their homes. At the same time, their children are not able to help their mothers because of their own low incomes (Burke and Spector, 1991:17). In addition, these lone parents may also be emotionally vulnerable as they anticipate poverty in their old age.

When all the children have left home, older parents often reorganize the household to make better use of available space. They may choose to leave the children's bedrooms intact for future visits. On the other hand, many couples want to use their housing space more efficiently and convert children's bedrooms into offices, sitting rooms, sewing rooms, or guest rooms. Other couples or single parents may choose to move to a smaller home or apartment for financial reasons or to reduce their workload.

Once they are alone, the division of labour of middle-aged couples may gradually return to the prechildren stage, especially if both are in the labour force. Meal times may become less formal, and they might eat out in restaurants more frequently. Furthermore, leisure activities can now be more spontaneous. While some couples may feel lonely without the children, marital satisfaction tends to rise after the

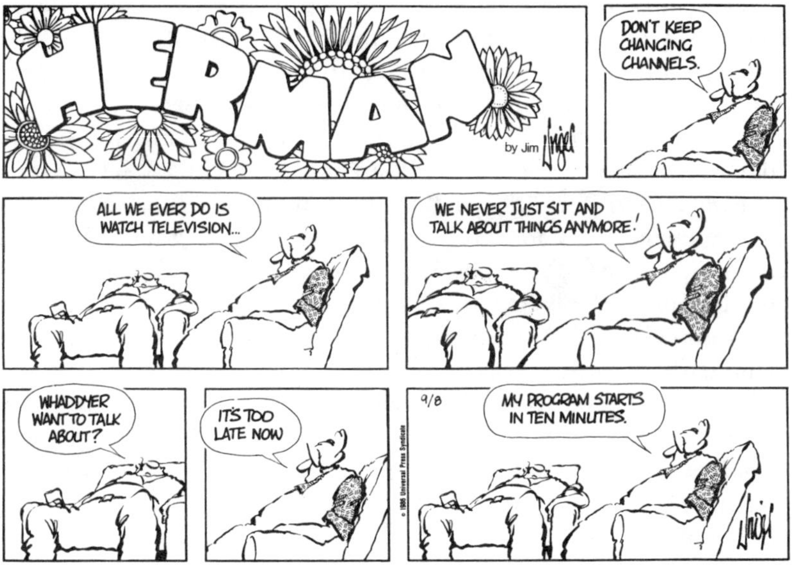

HERMAN copyright 1986 and 1988 Jim Unger. Reprinted with permission of Universal Press Sydicate.

children have left, because everyday tensions have diminished. There is more space in the home, less noise, and fewer people with whom to argue.

Children Who Remain at Home or Return

As the educational requirements for employment rise, young people need to stay in school longer in order to be able to compete for the shrinking number of jobs. Since the 1960s and 1970s, a greater percentage of the population has been attending post-secondary education on a full-time basis. As mentioned in chapter three, almost 30 percent of young people between the ages of 18 and 24 are still in school full-time (Statistics Canada, August 1991:117). Since the early 1980s, educational and accommodation costs have risen, making it difficult for young people to attend a college or university in another location from their parents' home. Increasingly, young people are living at home while they attend college or university or returning home on vacations and after graduation, until they can save up enough money to establish their own residence.

Perhaps because young people are now given more autonomy when living in their parents' homes than in previous generations, and because marriage is no longer a necessity for sexual relations, there is less pressure on young people to leave home. In the 1960s, when jobs were plentiful, young people could leave home and expect to find full-time work more easily than in the economic climate of the 1990s.

In addition, high rates of unemployment and marriage breakdown tend to jeopardize the independence of young people who have already left home. Those who have lost jobs or whose marriages have dissolved may temporarily return to the "nest," for emotional or financial reasons. Although their stay may be short, it may be enough to give middle-aged parents the impression that their children will continue to need their assistance and will remain a responsibility. Under these circumstances, parents may continue to worry about their adult children, and consider them as dependents who may at any time need parental help.

Young people with special needs may feel compelled to depend on their parents far beyond the usual launching period. Although independent living is encouraged through sheltered workshops and specialized accommodation, there is often a long waiting list to get into these programs or apartments. Middle-aged parents, therefore, may be required to provide some care for these children at home or to hire someone to assist them during the daytime while parents are working.

Although medical technology has enabled more persons with special needs to live longer, policies of de-institutionalization and shortage of funds for community care have led to increased care by family members. Mothers especially are expected to care for adult children because other services are not available.

If young people are given opportunities to make decisions and manage responsibilities, they are more likely to have the coping skills to establish their own households. On the other hand, if parents make living at home too easy, with many perks and few responsibilities, children may have no incentive to leave. Parents who prolong their children's living at home may not be doing the children or themselves a favour.

Coping With Elderly Parents

At a time when many couples are still responsible for their children and are beginning to feel old themselves, their parents are often widowed, are becoming less able to care for themselves, or are in need of some assistance. Because home care services, retirement homes, and seniors apartments are only in the initial stages of development in this country, much of the organizational work and actual care of disabled elderly parents falls on the shoulders of their children. According to Canadian figures, about 80 percent of caregiving to elderly people is provided by family members and friends rather than institutions (Connidis, 1989a:49). Traditionally, much of this care was given by middle-aged women, who were free from labour force participation. Now, most of these women are working in the labour force and carry the stress of a double workload of paid work and housework. Some couples are able to hire caregivers for their elderly parents or may help older family members to seek home-care services from governments.

Many of today's seniors are not used to relying on government services because they grew up in an era without Medicare, Unemployment Insurance, or visiting homemakers. Even when they are in need and are eligible for assistance, they sometimes hesitate to ask (McPherson, 1990:355). They may feel that other people are more deserving, or that they should be able to cope without formal assistance. Knowing that formal services are available for their parents, adult children may try to bring someone into their parents' homes to assist them. There is a thin line, however, between helping elderly parents and meddling in their affairs. Many seniors who have been self-reliant, have their own ways of doing things and resent someone else in their household arranging their affairs (McPherson, 1990:355).

A traditional solution to the problem of caring for elderly widowed parents is to bring them into the children's home when they can no longer care for themselves. While this could be the best living arrangement for some families, it could strain the marital relationship of the adult child and cause friction with the grandchildren. Yet, for many lower- or middle-income families, there are few alternatives. Institutional care is not always desirable or available. Furthermore, many middle-aged parents feel that institutionalizing their parents is abandoning them to an inflexible, cold, and impersonal living arrangement (Connidis, 1989a:52).

Increasing life expectancy has broadened the responsibilities of some adults, and these responsibilities are expected to grow in the future as the percentage of seniors rises and birth rates fall. While some young people are delaying their independence to continue their education, many senior people are living until their eighties or nineties. This means that more middle-aged parents will retain the responsibility for two generations — their children and their parents. Adult children may begin to help out gradually, such as tending their parents' garden or helping with financial decision making, and gradually take over more task such as shopping and housework (Underwood with DeMont, 1991:32).

Although provincial governments and private agencies are developing home and community care services, such as visiting homemakers and meals-on-wheels, these initiatives are only in the early stages in some parts of Canada. In addition, they continue to be underfunded because government money for health care is disproportionately going into acute-care hospitals and medical services rather than community care. Although more seniors' residences are being built, some with meals and personal care services, there are usually long waiting lists to get into them. Also, many seniors prefer to remain in their own homes without moving to age-homogeneous apartments, especially if they feel that they are relatively healthy and can cope with personal care. Yet, their children may not agree that they are able to care for themselves adequately and may feel obligated to help out.

Easing the family's burden for the care of elderly parents may be a matter of reallocation of government funding into chronic care and

Although provincial governments and private agencies are developing home and community care services, these initiatives are only in the early stages in some parts of Canada.

Canapress Photo Service

community services rather than hospital-based medical services. In addition, respite care programs allow adult children to leave their parent with an alternate caregiver for the day, while they attend to other matters. But programs to assist family caregivers should focus on caregivers' and elderly persons' perceptions of need, as perceptions are more important than actual need (Walker et al., 1991). Some government programs also encourage elderly people to remain independent longer by financing alterations to their homes, such as hand grips in washrooms, main floor bathrooms, wheel chair ramps, and lower kitchen cupboards for those in wheel chairs. Also, some government programs offer home repair services, snow removal, lawn cutting, transportation, and home security checks for low-income seniors. The cost of these programs to the user is often based on ability to pay, which means that taxpayers subsidize them.

MID-LIFE SATISFACTION AND ASPIRATIONS

Since couples are now having fewer children, many women have completed their childbearing and childrearing years earlier than a generation ago. With a life expectancy of about 80 years, this leaves considerable time to pursue other activities. Contrary to popular belief, mid-life often means renewed energy for women (Gee and Kimball, 1987:49). With freedom from time-consuming childrearing tasks, women can return to school or reenter the labour force, although an increasing number of married women are not leaving the labour market except for maternity leaves.

Women's lives used to be characterized by childrearing and housework, and they were publicly portrayed mainly as wives and mothers. When they reached middle age and passed through menopause, the end of fertility sometimes caused a **mid-life crisis** because so much of their social value was related to childbearing, sexuality, and physical attractiveness. Yet, many middle-aged women welcomed menopause because the relentless fear of pregnancy was over and their childrearing tasks were reduced when their children became more self-sufficient.

For men, the experience of mid-life may be different. They could be tiring of the occupation that they have been pursuing for 20 years or more, or they may feel frustrated that they have not achieved their occupational goals. At the same time, many men find that they have devoted so much time to their jobs that their children have grown up to be strangers. Middle-class fathers are more likely than working-class fathers to be involved in child care and housework, and fathers tend to be more involved in rearing their sons than their daughters (Morgan, Lye and Condran, 1988). Despite these trends, most men are at work much of the day and interact far less than their wives with their children. Furthermore, men are not taught as women are to listen and pay attention to nonverbal cues, which may lead to a different quality of relationship between men and children (Baker, 1983; Aronson, 1991).

In mid-life, some men also realize that they have devoted so much time to their jobs that they have also neglected friendships with other men. Others may have male companions, but tend not to confide in them or to really know much about their feelings or concerns. Frequently, middle-class men see each other as business associates and competitors and do not create close personal relationships with each other as women do. Middle-aged and older men consequently spend more of their leisure time alone or in the company of work buddies who are merely acquaintances rather than intimate friends (Connidis, 1989a).

Marital Dissatisfaction in Mid-Life

Early studies of marital satisfaction and happiness have found that for many couples there is a drop in satisfaction over time (Pineo, 1961). Later research indicates a **curvilinear relationship** between marital satisfaction and length of marriage, as figure 7.3 indicates. By this we mean that satisfaction tends to decline in the middle years and then rise again in the post-parental years (Rollins and Feldman, 1970; Lupri and Frideres, 1981).

In some cases, the expectations of marriage may be too high. Young people often view marriage in highly romantic terms and expect their partner to fulfil all their emotional, social, physical, and intellectual needs. This is obviously an impossibility for any one person. Individuals require time to themselves, to develop outside interests, and cultivate other friendships. When marital satisfaction is low, individuals may develop new sexual liaisons and may attempt to recapture the passion of sex and the excitement of a new relationship. Sometimes this provides renewed vigour to an otherwise boring lifestyle, but, in many cases, the new relationship itself becomes mundane. People often discover this too late, occasionally after a divorce and remarriage.

On the other hand, marital dissatisfaction after 20 years is not necessarily related to making the wrong choice of partners or to the idealization of marriage. It is often related to changing circumstances

Figure 7.3 **Percentages of Husbands and Wives in Each of Seven Stages and Four Phases of the Family Life Cycle Reporting "Very Satisfying" Marriages**

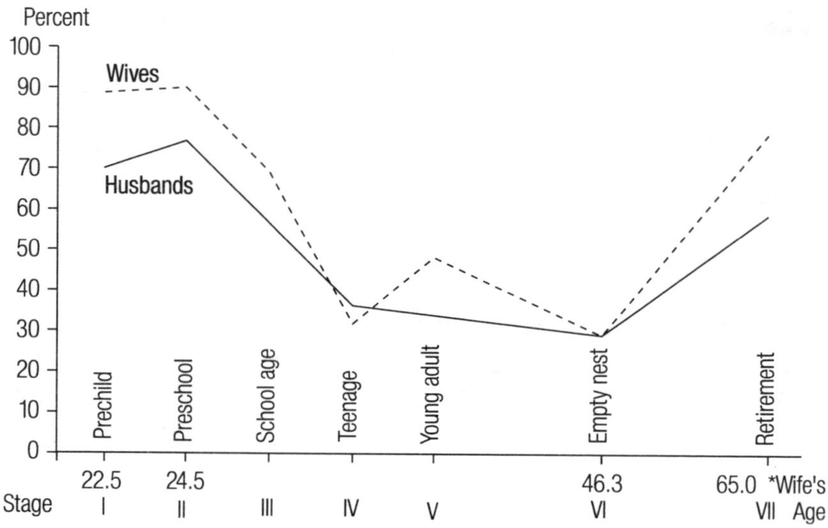

*Except for the age at retirement, the figures are median ages for women in the birth cohort 1951–1960.

Source: Eugen Lupri and James Frideres. "The Quality of Marriage and the Passage of Time: Marital Satisfaction Over the Family Life Cycle." *Canadian Journal of Sociology. (3).* 6, 1981:289.

and personal growth. While the couple may have been suited to each other when they married, 20 years later they could have grown apart. They may have developed new personal interests that are not shared by their spouses. For example, she may have developed a passion for hiking and camping, while he became increasingly interested in theatre and other urban activities.

Marital satisfaction is also influenced by factors outside the marriage. Unemployment, sporadic employment, or insufficient income can put strains on relationships and heighten dissatisfaction. The family with adolescents is likely to have higher expenses than when the children are younger, and this appears to lower the satisfaction of fathers. If their wives are also in the labour force, middle-aged men are less likely to express dissatisfaction than husbands of homemakers (Lupri and Frideres, 1981).

Mid-life marital dissatisfaction can also be influenced by other

HERMAN copyright 1986 and 1988 Jim Unger. Reprinted with permission of Universal Press Syndicate. All rights reserved.

factors. For example, lack of fulfilment in a job or career that can be generalized to feelings about marriage or personal relationships. Alcohol or drug addiction can also affect relationships negatively, and attempts to seek renewed excitement through extramarital relationships can be disastrous to some marriages.

Couples who divorce are most likely to do so between the ages of 25 and 35, as figure 7.4 indicates. Yet, the divorce rate for men aged 45 to 49 is nearly as high as the rate for men 20 to 24 years old. These figures imply that while adjustment is most difficult in the early years, a sizable minority of couples do break up after lengthy marriages.

Rollins and Galligan (1978) have argued that the level of dissatisfaction in the middle years is not particularly high, but has been overplayed in earlier studies. Despite high divorce rates among young people, most middle-aged and older people remain in lasting marriages.

Lasting Marriages

Studies of lasting marriages are difficult because some people who were very dissatisfied with their marriages would have already separated or divorced, while others remain married. Marriages that survive 20 years are not exactly a representative sample of all marriages. With

Figure 7.4 Age-Specific Divorce Rates, by Sex, Canada, 1989

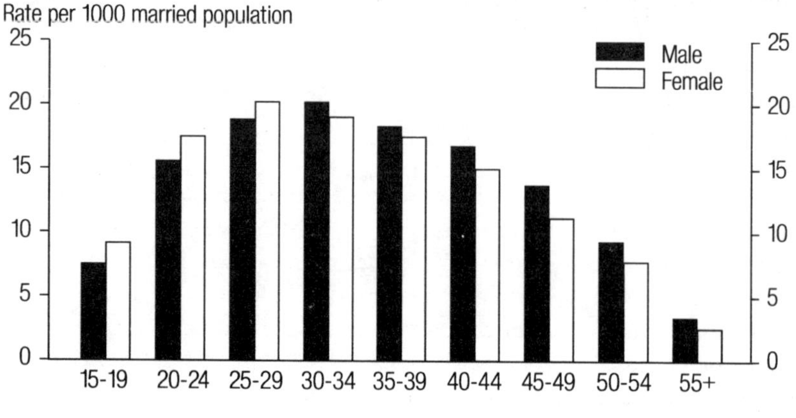

Based on married persons

Source: Wayne J. Millar. "Divorces, Canada and the Provinces, 1989." *Health Reports.* 3 (1) 1991:85. Reproduced with the permission of the Minister of Supply and Services Canada, 1992.

the difficulties of conducting longitudinal studies, however, little research is available to tell us why most marriages stay together. Yet, most couples do stay together, especially those who have already remained married for 10 to 15 years.

Perhaps the more interesting question then is why do so many marriages last despite all the pressures on modern relationships. There are many answers. Some people have satisfying marriages that actually improve over time. Others are unhappy, but cannot bring themselves to the point of divorce. After a certain length of time, the emotional investment in marriage may be too great to give up. Some people who have been married for many years might jokingly say: "I have spent so many years training him/her, that I would hate to have to start all over again with someone else!"

In 1981, Benjamin Schlesinger did a study of 129 couples in Toronto who had been married for 15 years or more and had at least one child. He found that couples in lasting marriages said that they respected and trusted each other, were loyal, and willing to make sacrifices. They said they were comfortable with each other, loved and counted on each other, they valued honesty in their communication, and were committed to making the marriage last. They also valued give-and-take in the relationship, recognized their partner's needs and were able to solve problems together (Schlesinger and Giblon, 1984).

After the age of 35 or 40, the probability of finding a new partner diminishes, especially for women (Gee, 1986). Awareness of this fact may prevent some people from admitting dissatisfaction or actively seeking divorce. Spouses also get used to each other's ways. They have children together whom they could not bear to lose. They buy houses together and know that they could not afford to live as well alone (Ambert, 1990:198).

Married couples share activities and memories. Even if some of the emotion is gone from marriage, many spouses choose not to part. Contentment, companionship, friendship, and shared children keep many marriages together. For other couples, however, their marriages grow more satisfying over time because of these shared activities. It does not necessarily follow, therefore, that marital satisfaction declines over time, even though social scientists have spent more time studying marriage dissolution than lasting marriages.

BECOMING A GRANDPARENT

Because the post-parental phase begins when the last child leaves home, parents could already be grandparents from their first-born child when their youngest is just being launched. Depending on the age of pregnancy in each generation, parents could become grandparents in their forties or much later in their lives. According to Statistics Canada, a woman is likely to be about 50 years old when her last child is married (Ram, 1990b:12).

Most parents look forward to becoming grandparents because they can have the pleasure of playing with infants and young children, and watching them grow, without the concerns of daily care. Most grandparents report that they enjoy their grandchildren, especially watching them gain skills and develop their own personalities. They enjoy spending time with them and developing a relationship (Connidis, 1989a:67).

Women often report enjoying being grandmothers more than being mothers (Robertson, 1977), perhaps because grandmothers are not as involved in the hard work of daily care and discipline. Yet, some grandmothers provide child care services for their employed daughters and daughters-in-law. In addition, women tend to find their relationships with grandchildren more satisfying than grandfathers do (Thomas, 1986). Regardless of the children's genders, women tend to be more involved than men with their grandchildren (Connidis, 1989a:68). Enjoyment of grandparenting tends to be the highest when children are young, rather than when they are teenagers (Cherlin and Furstenberg Jr., 1986).

The relationships between grandparents and grandchildren are often mediated by parents (Leslie and Korman, 1989:572). When parents separate or divorce, the grandparents are less likely to maintain contact with the children if their adult child does not have custody. In these situations, an adult child's divorce may mean loss of contact with young grandchildren unless the custodial parent (usually the daughter-in-law) encourages easy access to the children.

Relationships between adults and their parents usually involve exchange. Parents rely on grandparents for instrumental assistance such as child care but also for emotional assistance, especially in times

QUALITATIVE ASPECTS OF THE GRANDPARENT–GRANDCHILD RELATIONSHIP

If you can keep in touch with young people it will rub off on you. I get a big kick. My grandchildren will come down tonight—three of them. Now, I will change and I will be laughing. And they are so natural and they are cheerful. And natural rubs off on you and I think it keeps you young. But some people don't have grandchildren and I say there is a certain amount of luck in life.

66-year-old grandfather

I have three grandchildren and my goodness me there is no generation gap there at all. ...I say they either make me feel old or they make me feel young. But, I will say this, they certainly do keep the wheels lubricated—mentally and physically.

76-year-old grandmother

My two older granddaughters who live near here are 16 and 18. They have their own little worlds now. You don't expect to see as much of them. I miss them and I would love it if they would just drop in, you know. They do occasionally but I know what it is to be young. I know that ... they have their own schedules and they are working and going to school ... and their social lives. But I do enjoy particularly the ones that are too young to be out on their own like that. And I think that they enjoy us. They love to come to Grandma's and I like to keep it that way.

67-year-old grandmother

The babe (grandson) was crying the second night he was home and I got out of bed and tottled in and my son is up looking after the babe. I said, "Here give him to me." So I took him to a rocking chair, and I said, "This makes me think of my Grandma." Whenever we were upset or there was something that we didn't like, or we were unhappy, Grandma used to take us and she would sit one on here, one on one arm and one on the other arm or knee and just rock. And she would sing.

65-year-old grandmother

Connidis, Ingrid. *Family Ties and Aging.* Toronto: Butterworths, 1989:61, 63, 67.

of crisis such as unemployment, the death of a child, or divorce. The balance becomes less than equal, however, as the older parents age. Older widows are especially likely to live with their children and grandchildren, and depend on them for advice, companionship, and financial assistance.

Adult children and their parents do not always agree over childrearing practices. Grandparents sometimes interfere with child-rearing, expressing unwanted opinions about how the children should be raised. Furthermore, some grandparents are considered by parents to be too indulgent with money or sweets for the grandchildren.

The grandparent role, however, may be important to the family unit because it brings the adults closer together (Bengtson, 1985). Grandchildren tend to provide a common focus, enhancing communication between their parents and grandparents. Emotional closeness between grandparents and grandchildren depends on a number of variables, however, such as geographic proximity and contact frequency.

Despite the rewards of grandparenting, older parents are no closer to children who produce grandchildren than those who do not (Connidis, 1989a:70). Instead, older parents tend to maintain closer ties with never-married children and divorced children (especially daughters) who have children. Aldous (1985:131) has argued that the critical variable in intergenerational contact is not the role of grandparents, but the demonstrated need for instrumental and emotional aid (Connidis, 1989a:70).

FUTURE TRENDS

The process of launching children is becoming more gradual for parents and the transition to the post-parental stage is being prolonged and becoming increasingly complicated. More young people over 18 are now living with their parents while attending college or university than in the early 1980s (Boyd and Pryor, 1990). With educational inflation, high unemployment rates, and a high cost of living, this trend will probably continue.

The trend to delay parenting until women are in their thirties, which is apparent among a growing minority of Canadians, will also delay the post-parental stage. These parents could easily be in their sixties when they begin the launching stage. The trend toward delayed first births, which is most noticeable among middle-class educated single women and couples, will not only postpone child-launching but also delay the age of retirement in the future. With continuing childrearing expenses, these parents will not be able to afford early retirement.

As more married women enter the full-time labour force and remain employed throughout the life cycle, the meaning of mid-life will undoubtedly change. When most middle-aged women were homemakers and their lives were focused around childbearing and childrearing, menopause and child-launching often were perceived to be synonymous with the end of their usefulness. In the future, child-launching will mean a reduction of responsibilities for adolescent discipline, food shopping, meal preparation, and laundry for an increasing number of women, yet a retention of their employment and income.

As more women become self-supporting, their personal and marital satisfaction may rise. Those in unhappy relationships will be better able to separate and divorce because each partner will have an income. However, there are indications in the research that women are now less likely than men to remarry after divorce, and this trend will probably continue in the future. Because neither custody arrangements nor women's relative incomes have changed much in recent years, custodial mothers will continue to live on lower incomes than their male counterparts, and their financial conditions, as well as the unfavourable sex ratio, will prevent them from remarrying. In addition, women appear to be less eager to remarry than men because of their unreciprocal experiences with caregiving in marriage.

Yet, more middle-aged people in the coming decades will leave unhappy marriages and establish more satisfying lives in new relationships, either within or outside legal marriage. On the other hand, growing financial pressures and the need for two incomes may keep some couples together, regardless of the quality of their relationship.

With rising life expectancies, however, mid-life could also mean an increase in responsibilities for aging parents and parents-in-law. Furthermore, there is no indication that the tendency for women to be the primary caregivers for both children and elderly relatives will not continue in the future. As more middle-aged women are in the labour force and are unable to provide day-to-day care for their elderly relatives themselves, they will become managers of care rather than caregivers. In other words, they will be the ones to hire service providers and negotiate with governments and private agencies on behalf of their elderly parents. But as birth rates decline, there will be fewer adult children in the future to care for elderly parents, and we may need more community services.

The greater prosperity of the two-income family and early retirement incentives will continue to allow mid-life couples to travel, to spend more money on entertainment, or to choose early retirement. At the same time, the development of computer technology and competition from younger workers may encourage an increasing number of employees to leave their positions in mid-life, either through choice or lay-off, and to set up their own businesses. This kind of occupational gamble is most feasible when there are no longer children to support or the spouse has a steady income. Higher disposable incomes and more generous early retirement programs may encourage others to retire in their fifties and spend more time on leisure activities.

Most people have children, and their children eventually produce grandchildren. Relationships between grandparents and their grandchildren may become more salient in the future as life expectancies rise and the relationship has longer to develop. On the other hand, the trend toward delayed childbirth will mean that some children will be quite young when their grandparents die, as the years between generations lengthen.

SUGGESTED READINGS

Aquilino, William S. "Family Structure and Home Leaving: A Further Specification of the Relationship." *Journal of Marriage and the Family*. 53. November 1991:999–1010.

Armstrong, Pat and Hugh Armstrong. *The Double Ghetto. Canadian Women and Their Segregated Work*. 2nd ed. Toronto: McClelland and Stewart, 1984.

Beaujot, Roderic. "Dwindling Families." *Policy Options*. 7. September 1986:3–7.

Boyd, Monica and Edward Pryor. "Young Adults Living in Their Parents' Homes." *Canadian Social Trends*. Edited by Craig McKie and Keith Thompson. Toronto: Thompson Educational Publishing, 1990:188–191.

Burke, Mary Anne and Aron Spector. "Falling Through the Cracks: Women Aged 55–64 Living on Their Own." *Canadian Social Trends*. 23. Winter 1991:14–17.

Gee, Ellen M. "The Life Course of Canadian Women: An Historical and Demographic Analysis." *Social Indicators Research*. 18. 1986:263–283.

Lupri, Eugen and James Frideres. "The Quality of Marriage and the Passage of Time: Marital Satisfaction Over the Family Life Cycle." *Canadian Journal of Sociology*. 6 (3). Summer 1981:283–306.

Miller, D.A. "The 'Sandwich' Generation. The Adult Children of the Aging." *Social Work*. 1981:419–423.

Moore, Maureen. *The Characteristics of Dual-Earner Families*. Cat. 13-588, no. 3. Ottawa: Minister of Supply and Services Canada, July 1989.

Neugarten, Bernice L. and Dail A. Neugarten. "The Changing Meanings of Age." *Psychology Today*. May 1987:29–33.

Rosenfeld, Anne and Elizabeth Stark. "The Prime of Our Lives." *Psychology Today*. May 1987:62–72.

Schlesinger, Benjamin and Shirley Tenhouse Giblon. *Lasting Marriages*. Toronto: Guidance Centre, Faculty of Education, University of Toronto, 1984. (Reprinted in part in *Today's Family: A Critical Focus*. Edited by Meiklejohn et al. Don Mills: Collier Macmillan, 1990:253–258).

Sheehy, Gail. *Passages: Predictable Crises in Adult Life*. New York: Dutton, 1974.

Underwood, Nora with John DeMont. "Mid-Life Panic." *Maclean's* 19 August 1991:30–33.

Wise, George and Velma McBride Murray. "The Empty Nest: The Silent Invasion on Two Fronts." *Journal of Home Economics*. Spring 1987:49–53.

ISSUES FOR DISCUSSION

1. You have always wanted to be a grandparent, but your only child has just informed you that she doesn't want to have any children. You try to convince her of the social importance of childbearing, and tell her how much it means to you personally to be a grandparent. She gets very angry and says that it is her life. How could conflict resolution techniques be used to resolve this conflict and what might be the consequence?
2. Imagine that your widowed mother has Alzheimer's disease and cannot care for herself. You have a good job and cannot

look after your mother during the day. No institutional care is available to her at the present time. You want her to live with you, but your spouse and children (who still live at home) do not think it is a good idea. What would you do?

3. What do we mean by sponsored and unsponsored independence?
4. What "developmental tasks" are most important for parents during the time when their children are leaving home? What are some potential consequences of encouraging children to stay at home longer?
6. Why is there so little research on the child-launching stage of the family life cycle? What research could be done on this stage?
7. What is the difference between launching for a young person who emigrates from his or her country and your plans for leaving home?
8. What coping strategies are necessary for three-generation families? Suggest as many as possible.
9. What kind of care and support do adult children provide for their elderly parents? What kind of services and support do seniors provide for their adult children?
10. Has too much emphasis been placed on "the empty nest syndrome?" Do men experience this syndrome? Provide reasons for your answers.
11. Many parents "feel that they have little control over their children when they leave home, and sometimes prefer to remain ignorant of their children's activities for fear of what they might uncover." Would you want to know the details of your children's lives after they leave home? Why or why not?
12. Consider the advantages and disadvantages of a commuter marriage. Under what conditions would it be worth living in a different town or city from your spouse? Would it be easier at the launching stage or at one of the stages with children at home? Explain your choice.
13. What are the advantages and disadvantages of marrying before graduation from college or university?
14. Why do more unmarried men than women between the ages 20 to 35 live with their parents?

FURTHER ACTIVITIES

1. Choose an ethnic or racial group different from your own living in Canada, and interview several young adults (males and females) from this group in order to discover their experiences of leaving home. Compare these experiences with those of your older siblings, cousins, or friends.
2. Interview two immigrants to Canada, one who came alone as a young adult and one who came with his or her parents and siblings. Ask them both about the adjustment period and their relationships with their parents.
3. Interview a family in which an unmarried or married child has returned to live with parents. What are the advantages and disadvantages of this living arrangement from the perspectives of both the adult children and the parents?
4. Interview couples who have been married 20 years to discover how their relationships have changed over time.
5. Interview your grandparents (or a friend's) to learn how their relationships with their children have changed since the birth of their first grandchild, and how their relationships with their grandchildren have changed as everyone grows older.

8 The Family in Later Life

SPECIFIC TASKS

From Retirement to Bereavement

The last stage in the family life cycle begins with the retirement of one or both spouses from work outside the home and ends with the death of one spouse. With a trend toward early retirement and the abolition of mandatory retirement in some jurisdictions, 65 is no longer necessarily the age at which retirement begins. Based on the findings of the 1989 General Social Survey, most Canadians are opposed to the idea of mandatory retirement, and only a small minority plan to retire at 65 or later (Lowe, 1991:16). Yet, the federal government currently begins Old Age Security benefits at 65, and this age still retains symbolic meaning as the beginning of "old age."

Successful retirement usually involves financial and psychological planning, and increasingly, employees try to retire when they have obtained enough years of service to qualify for an adequate pension as well as when they are psychologically prepared to leave their paid work and take up other pursuits. Men are more likely than women to make concrete retirement plans, and retiring early is a definite preference expressed by baby boomers (Lowe, 1991:12).

Some employees find retirement psychologically difficult because they lose daily contact with their colleagues or co-workers.

Furthermore, many are living on a reduced and fixed income, and have so much discretionary time that they feel at "loose ends." However, retirement appears to be less disruptive for older couples and involves fewer adjustment problems than people sometimes assume (Ekerdt and Vinick, 1991). Those who always maintained outside interests are better able to find meaningful activities to fill their days. People who feel that they have an adequate income, good health, and strong social support tend to adapt well to retirement and old age (McDonald and Wanner, 1990:94, 95).

Men often establish the time of retirement for both themselves and their wives. Many married couples plan to retire at the same time so that they can travel or share other leisure activities. Since wives tend to be younger than their husbands, they are less likely to be financially and psychologically ready to retire when their husbands are ready. Due to sporadic or part-time positions without pension plan membership in their younger years, women are less likely than men to receive work pensions. While three in five retired men receive pension benefits from former employers, less than three in ten women

---

WOMEN HAVE DIFFICULTY ACCEPTING RETIREMENT

BY SHARON KIRKEY
Citizen Staff Writer

Women are finding it more difficult than men to adjust to retirement, and are less likely to be happy in their retirement years, says an expert on aging.

The widely held image that women don't invest as much of themselves into their job as men isn't true, says Anne Martin Matthews, director of the University of Guelph's gerontology centre.

Matthew's 1982 study of 475 retired men and women in Kitchener-Waterloo found both scored equally on the "job deprivation index," a measure she used to determine how important their jobs were to them.

"There was absolutely no difference between men and women on how much of themselves they invested in their jobs, how much their jobs meant to them and how much they missed their jobs," says Matthews, who led a workshop on the issues of aging at the Canadian Home Economics Association conference in Guelph earlier this month...

Matthew's study found that women reported much lower levels of satisfaction with their retirement than men. That finding can be attributed to the reasons why women retire, she says.

The study showed that most men reported they retired because they had reached company retirement age, or for health reasons. However, women typically indicated they retired because their husbands had, or because of the health of their husband or another family member.

"The women were much more likely to say they retired earlier than they expected to, and that they hadn't wanted to retire when they did," says Matthews.

"When people retire when they want to, it seems to make a tremendous difference in terms of how well they adjust."

In 1983, one-third of all women between 54 and 64 were in the labour force. The same year, 60 percent of all women aged 45 to 54 were working outside the home.

"We're looking to a time where it will increasingly become the pattern that both members of the couple retire," says Matthews.

"We're undergoing a tremendous historical change."

More people are retiring at an earlier age, adds Matthews. "Mandatory retirement is a non-issue for most people because the average age of retirement is just over 62. But we still have a lot of pressure over the whole controversial issue of mandatory retirement"...

Courtesy of *The Ottawa Citizen*, 18 July 1988.

do (Lowe, 1991:16). Furthermore, because pensions are based on previous earnings, women tend to have smaller pensions than men because of their lower incomes. Although many wives are not ready for retirement at the same time as their husbands, they are often persuaded to retire at the same time.

At the time of retirement, a new division of labour may need to be established within the household. If the wife works as a homemaker, she now has companionship from her husband during the daytime. Yet, she may continue to be responsible for shopping, cooking, and cleaning even though her husband is retired and has more discretionary time. While retired husbands sometimes share the household tasks with their wives, women often feel that their husbands' very presence disrupts their household routine (Connidis, 1989a). Furthermore, wives of retired men sometimes feel that, while their husbands are enjoying leisure time and new activities, they are doing the same housework with no hope of retirement or pension. If both were in the labour force before retirement, their household division of labour may have been more egalitarian than a couple with traditional complementary roles. Yet, a new division of labour still needs to be negotiated when one or both retire.

Not all couples are still married in their senior years and not all are well-matched or enjoy their marital relationship. Yet, a number of studies have indicated that married seniors tend to be as happy or happier than they ever were (Abu-Laban, 1978; Lupri and Frideres, 1981; Yarrow, Marcus, and MacLean, 1981). For example, Sharon Abu-Laban (1978) has compared the post-retirement family with recently married couples experiencing the honeymoon period. She noted that both are times of relative leisure, a more egalitarian division of labour, and emotional intensity. In the honeymoon period, the relationship is new and exciting: in senior years, the imminence of death means that each moment becomes important. Furthermore, communication problems have probably been worked out after many years of marriage and the couple has developed some form of conflict-resolution.

With declining birth rates and rising life expectancies, the average age of the Canadian population is rising. About 12 percent of the population is now aged 65 or older (Gauthier, 1991:16), but this percentage is expected to increase considerably in future years. If birth rates remain low, 25 percent of our population could comprise people 65 and older by the year 2036 (Gauthier 1991:16). Population aging has led to considerable concern among policy-makers because of the implications for pension funds, health services, the labour force, and economic growth.

Although the lifespan has not increased since the 1930s (Simmons-Tropea and Osborn, 1987), more people are reaching old age. Since women now live an average of seven years longer than men and because men tend to marry younger women, more elderly women outlive their husbands. Because of the imbalance of the sex ratio among older people, especially over the age of 80, much of the research on elderly families deals with widows and their relationships.

In 1986, women made up 58 percent of Canadians 65 and over and 62 percent of those 75 and over. The number of people aged 75 and over, or the **older elderly** as they are sometimes called, increased 56 percent from 1971 to 1986, and is the fastest growing age category. In 1986, the Canadian population comprised about 4.1 percent of the older elderly, but this is expected to increase to 6 percent by 2001 (Priest, 1990:184). About two-thirds of older elderly women are widows compared with one-quarter of men that age.

Differences are noticeable in the living arrangements of older elderly people due to gender differences in marital status. As shown in figure 8.1, older elderly women are more likely than men to live alone, with others, or in institutions because most men are still living with their wives (Priest, 1990:184–5). Unfortunately, the Canadian government does not gather statistics on elderly people living with their children, only "with others." This means that this information can only estimated.

Most elderly people are in good health and maintain their own households even after being widowed. Most also choose to live independently rather than burden their children (Connidis, 1989a). Seniors' apartments have assisted elderly people to maintain their

Figure 8.1 **Living Arrangements of Population Aged 75 and Over, by Sex, 1971, 1986, and 2001**

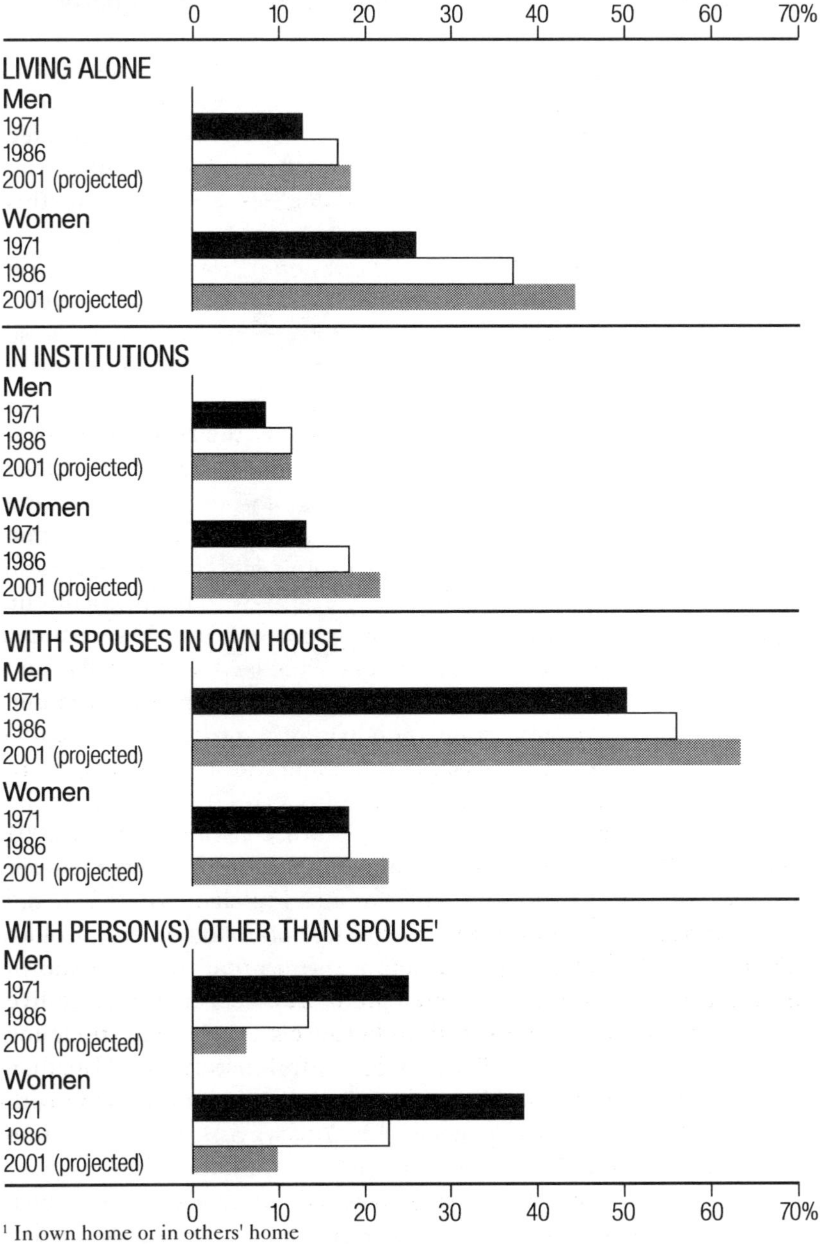

[1] In own home or in others' home

Source: Statistics Canada, Census of Canada, and Housing, Family and Social Statistics Division. Reproduced with the permission of the Minister of Supply and Services Canada, 1992.

independence and have provided a ready-made support group. The development of more home care programs, which many see as less expensive and preferable to institutionalization, may further enable more seniors to stay as long as they choose in their own homes.

More women than men are widowed because women tend to live longer than men and usually marry older men. Although many people try to prepare themselves psychologically for bereavement, most feel inadequately prepared for the loneliness and sense of loss. In addition to the emotional difficulty of dealing with bereavement, the death of a husband (but not a wife) often means living on a reduced income and moving from the family home to a smaller apartment or house. In addition, it may involve gradually changing friendships to include more widows and increasing the level of dependence on children and grandchildren for companionship and advice.

Most seniors remain relatively healthy until the last few years of their lives and require little physical care. With increasing age, however, physical health tends to decline and chronic diseases, such as arthritis, become more prevalent. Although most seniors report that their health is good, many eventually require some assistance in their daily lives. They may require help with finances, housework, home maintenance, or personal care. Coming to grips with failing health and dependence is difficult for most people, especially if one is also suffering the loss of a spouse and some friends.

Despite the fact that many children have left their home communities and moved away from their parents, most keep in regular contact with elderly parents and assist them when necessary. In fact, about 80 percent of the caretaking is done by family members or friends, rather than in nursing homes or other institutions (Connidis, 1989a). Several social and economic trends have affected family relations, however. For one thing, many middle-aged women are now in the labour force and, therefore, are less often available to care for their elderly parents. At the same time, health care policy-makers are calling for more home care, because it is assumed to be less expensive and more humane. Traditionally, mothers, sisters, and daughters have done much of the personal care for elderly relatives, and women tend to perform the bulk of volunteer work (and paid employment) with seniors and people with special needs. Yet, we can no longer assume that women can afford to continue doing volunteer work, since two incomes are increasingly needed to keep up with the cost of living.

Secondly, smaller families mean that more responsibility will be placed on each adult child to care for aging parents. In the last century, when families were larger, the responsibility for elderly parents might have been shared by several siblings as well as other relatives. Now that the average number of children per family is less than two, family responsibilities become more intense as these children reach middle age.

Today more seniors are able to maintain financial independence due to improvements in public pensions during the 1970s. Furthermore, increased numbers of the senior population have given new credence to their concerns (Gifford, 1990) and new meaning to "old age." The next section examines the history of retirement and pensions, mainly from a political economy perspective.

HISTORICAL PERSPECTIVES

WORK, RETIREMENT, AND THE INTRODUCTION OF PENSIONS

Before the introduction of retirement benefits, people were expected to be thrifty throughout their entire lifespan and save for their old age. Retirement from work before disability was a privilege for the rich. Poorer people worked until they were unable to continue, and then relied on their children's assistance, on their community's good will, or on their savings. Yet, most people were unable to save much money because of low wages, sporadic unemployment, illness, and unexpected expenses. Without insurance for unemployment, disability, or medical care, families sometimes went heavily into debt when the breadwinner became ill (Baker, 1988).

North Americans hesitated to accept the idea of old age insurance, annuities, and health insurance because they felt that people should be able to save for their own future. Furthermore, these programs tended to be associated with socialism, which has had negative connotations in Canada and still does in the United States. Yet, some European governments, such as Germany, had introduced compulsory old age insurance as early as the 1880s. Similar programs were not implemented in Canada until 1927, when the Old Age Pension first provided benefits for poor people aged 70 and over.

Some researchers have suggested that retirement benefits were not offered by governments or employers until there was a surplus of older workers in the labour force. At the end of the nineteenth century and the beginning of the twentieth century, life expectancies increased at the same time that industrial growth and technological advancement placed new emphasis on speed, efficiency, and fitness, which disadvantaged older workers (Achenbaum, 1978; Graebner, 1980). With the rise of the assembly line, skilled craftsmen became less important (Myles, 1989). Younger workers who could more readily adapt to technological changes were often preferred for factory jobs. Out of these economic and social changes, the idea of mandatory retirement as a solution to the older worker "problem" arose from industrialists and reformers, rather than the workers (Haber, 1978:78). But only a few large companies offered pensions to retiring workers, and these were usually reserved for employees who had given a lifetime of good service to the company.

The demand for universal retirement, government insurance, and public pensions in Canada was given impetus by widespread unemployment during the Depression of the 1930s. Many people lost their life savings, which undermined confidence in the traditions of thrift and self-reliance. It became apparent to many politicians and reformers that unemployment and poverty were partially affected by

Until the 1920s when the Canadian Government created Old Age Security, only a few large companies offered pensions to retiring workers.

Reuben R. Sallows/National Archives of Canada/C42636

international market forces, bad weather, and the shortage of work, rather than lack of individual initiative. This meant that governments could justifiably become involved with insurance and pension programs.

After World War II, economic prosperity allowed many countries to develop social security programs, including old age pensions. Gradually, attitudes changed from viewing government benefits as assistance to the poor, to seeing them as rights for all citizens. More older workers were able to retire as benefits improved and replaced a larger portion of their preretirement wages. Furthermore, the development of contributory pension plans (such as the Canada Pension Plan) allowed benefits to increase with the rising cost of living.

A government old age pension was discussed for many years in Canada before it was actually introduced. Private insurance companies lobbied against any attempt from the federal government to take over their business. In 1927, the federal government finally passed legislation to cost-share with the provinces a "means-tested" benefit (for low-income people without much property) to be paid monthly to residents aged 70 or over. Since the life expectancy was only about 60 at the time, many Canadians never benefitted from this pension. In 1952, legislation was amended to remove the income restrictions and in 1966 the age was lowered to 65 (Baker, 1988).

After 1966, several other government pensions were introduced, including the Canada/Quebec Pension Plans for those in the work force, the Guaranteed Income Supplement for low-income pensioners, and the Spouse's Allowance for the younger spouses of pensioners. Federal and provincial governments also encouraged employers to introduce work-related retirement benefits and individuals to initiate their own Registered Retirement Savings Plans (RRSPs).

Until the last few decades, poverty in old age was widespread. In fact, families with heads aged 65 and over used to be the poorest category of Canadian families. With the introduction of government and private pensions and with high interest rates for investments in the late 1970s and 1980s, the economic status of seniors has risen relative to younger families as figure 8.2 indicates.

While the economic status of elderly families has improved over the last few years, many elderly individuals live in poverty, especially unattached women—those who are widowed, never-married, separated, or divorced. Nearly one half of unattached elderly women in Canada live below the poverty line (Gauthier, 1991:18). The reasons why elderly women are so often poor relate to financial dependency throughout their lives, the lack of social recognition for housework and child care, the nature of women's jobs (part-time, temporary, and

Figure 8.2 **Incidence of Low Income Among Families and Unattached Individuals, 1983 and 1988**

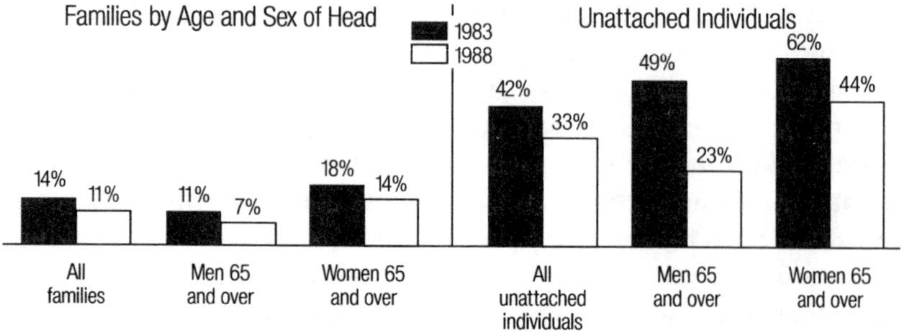

Source: Statistics Canada, Catalogue 89-519. Reproduced with the permission of the Minister of Supply and Services Canada, 1992.

within the "pink collar ghetto"), and low wages. Women are less likely than men to belong to pension plans at work because the kinds of jobs they perform tend not to offer these fringe benefits. Even when they belong to pension plans, their benefits are calculated as a percentage of annual income, which tends to be lower for women (Wilson, 1991).

As women's labour force participation rises, as more employers offer pension benefits, and as governments legislate pay equity, the poverty of elderly women in the future may diminish. Yet, high rates of female-led one-parent families and unequal labour force practices will continue to disadvantage women in comparison with men and contribute to the poverty of senior women. Furthermore, many older people from cultural minorities are in jobs without pension plan coverage, and they will have to continue to rely on savings or their families in old age.

CULTURAL PERSPECTIVES

Living Arrangements

When discussing elderly families, it is important to keep in mind that lifestyle varies by cultural and income differences, as well as by gender and family status. Some ethnic groups, such as Italians and Chinese, encourage older family members to live with their children. Even when they may have little privacy, widowed parents may prefer this arrangement to remaining in their homes alone or living in a self-contained seniors' apartment. Other ethnic groups, such as Jewish,

Polish, or British people, more often live independently from their children. Variations by ethnicity tend to relate to cultural values, but also to the timing of immigration, the relative economic prosperity of the cultural group, and to the financial resources of individual families.

Immigrant groups that came to Canada in large numbers prior to the Second World War now have larger proportions of elderly people in Canada. As they grew in numbers and prosperity, these groups have tended to create seniors' clubs and retirement homes for group members. Among eastern European Jewish people living in Canada, for example, 16 percent are 65 and older. At the same time, average incomes within this cultural group are relatively high in comparison with other cultural groups (Grindstaff, 1990:315).

More recent immigrants, such as Chinese, Italians, and people from the Caribbean, as well as First Nations' peoples have a lower proportion of elderly people and have not yet developed such an extensive network of organizations for seniors. For example, among the Indo-Chinese in Canada (including Chinese, Vietnamese, and Southeast Asians), only 2 percent were 65 and older in 1986 (White, 1990). About 3.5 percent of Native people in Canada are 65 or older (Driedger and Chappell (1990:230). As the proportion of seniors within these groups rises, they will probably develop more retirement

One study found about 19 percent of Chinese Canadians were living in extended families.

Courtesy of Winnie Chu.

homes, although the tradition of extended family living is still relatively strong in these culture. For example, one study found that about 19 percent of Chinese Canadians were living in extended families (Verma et al., 1980).

Cultural values and the size of the elderly population in the ethnic group are not the only factors influencing living arrangements among seniors. Income is also a major factor. Wealthier people tend to prefer to remain independent from their children, and to either stay in their own homes or move to luxury retirement homes. Furthermore, men tend to remain independent longer than women, perhaps because they are more likely to have access to employment savings or pension plans. In addition, ethnic groups with lower fertility rates are less likely to live in multigenerational households. In fact, living with their children tends to be a typical pattern for women from poorer immigrant groups with low percentages of elderly people and with large extended families (Baker, 1988).

Some immigrants from cultures which traditionally revere the elderly may find that, when they migrate to Canada, it is no longer considered necessary or practical to have their elderly parents live with them (Ujimoto, 1987). In Canada, there is little social pressure to accept three-generation households, and immigrants may be encouraged by their friends and colleagues to find a room, apartment, or seniors' residence for their widowed parent. Without Canadian language skills and with different expectations, older immigrants may feel isolated and estranged by these arrangements.

ATTITUDES TOWARD AGING: CULTURAL DIFFERENCES

Canadian ethnic groups also differ in their attitudes toward aging and the respect which they are willing to grant to elderly family members. Those from Southeast Asian and East Asian cultures, for example, have continued their tradition of respect even though the older person may be financially dependent on adult children. Other cultural groups, such as Italians, Hutterites, Greeks, Portuguese, and some Native groups, place a strong emphasis on the authority of the eldest male. Other Native groups are deferential to elders in general, regardless of gender. But the generation and cultural gap between immigrants and their Canadian-born children, or between older and younger Native people, often becomes a source of contention among family members, especially over issues such as this.

Many older people, especially first-generation immigrants, have lived frugal lives in crowded living quarters, and through hard work and entrepreneurial activities have accumulated considerable money for their old age. The reason for this frugal lifestyle was sometimes to enable their children to live a better life, rather than to live comfortably themselves in old age. Many older ethnic members, however, occupied low status positions in the labour force because of discrimination, language problems, and low or unacknowledged educational qualifications. Without pensions or significant accumulations of property or money, some members of cultural groups must share accommodation with their children after retirement.

Other immigrant groups prospered from their family connections, education, or ethnic networks, or were relatively well-off when they came to Canada. Many migrants from Britain, United States, India, Hong Kong, and eastern Europe, for example, came to Canada as professionals, and were able to obtain high-level positions and gradually to improve their wealth and social status. As seniors, they continue to live in prosperity, travelling south in the winter or back to their homelands for periodic visits, and hiring people to assist them with home maintenance tasks.

The generation born in Canada and Native people who have

NATIVE ELDERS: THE ANICINABE OF GEORGIAN BAY

In prereserve times, and prior to the influence of missionaries and schools, Anicinabe elder status was understood partly in terms of the individual's progress through the life-cycle statuses. Those who were grandparents, or who belonged to the grandparental generation, tended to be perceived (and to perceive themselves) as elders. However, the nature of the individual's contribution to the survival of the kin group was another important aspect of the meaning of elderhood.

The younger adult members of the group were busy with the daily subsistence round, based partly on hunting and gathering and partly on horticulture. Members of the parental generation had little time for childrearing. Those perceived as elders, on the other hand, played a major role in the socialization of new members of the group; this socialization role was their major contribution to group survival. Thus, any individual who was no longer actively involved in the subsistence round tended to be viewed, whatever his or her age, as an elder. Frequently the socializing elder was a grandparent, but the Anicinabe child referred to anyone in the grandparental generation, or who fulfilled an elder's role, as "grandparent."

"Grandparents" expected, and received, deference and respect from "grandchildren." Within these broad guidelines the relationship between elder and child was warm and almost fraternal. In contrast, the relationship between parent and child was patterned along authoritarian lines.

It is difficult to ascertain whether *any* person in the appropriate generation, and in a socializing role, was invariably perceived as an elder. Aged informants today mention the additional criteria of acquired wisdom and successful experience in surviving life's vicissitudes. At any rate, Anicinabe "grandparents" were repositories of knowledge, of essential cultural information and they were responsible for transmitting that information to the "grandchildren."

Anicinabe elders in the Georgian Bay area were (and still are) experts on both mythic and local history, on Native language usage, on healing and (to a lesser extent today because of the depth of missionizing) on ritual. In sum, they controlled the core values of their culture as these were embodied in myths/legends and in the forms of their language. Anicinabe core values have always been concerned with what are perceived as the most basic aspects of survival: the control of social interaction and of the "supernatural," both essential for survival and success at the group and individual levels.

Social interaction involved not only human persons, but also the interaction of humans with "other-than-human" persons, i.e., animal and supernatural "persons" (Hallowell, 1960). In addition, the incremental building up of individual power during the life course through proper social relations with the supernatural was the major road to success and renown. Survival to elder status underlined and validated the existence of this personal power, and elders could transmit some of their power to children through the naming ceremony, as well as through the passing on of specific skills in dealing with the supernatural.

By Rosamond M. Vanderburgh. From *Aging in Canada, Social Perspectives.* 2nd ed. Edited by V. Marshall. Richmond Hill, Ontario: Fitzhenry & Whiteside, 1987: 102–103.

---

become educated and moved to southern Canadian cities, tend to have higher educational levels, better command of the English or French language, and more opportunities for integration and upward mobility than their parents (Siggner, 1986:76; Ram, 1990; Kalbach and Richard, 1990). They also have the security of health insurance, unemployment insurance, and government pensions. As they grow older, their values and their attitudes about aging will undoubtedly differ from those of their parents. Their socio-economic status may be higher than their parents, and they will probably not continue all of their ethnic customs, such as respect for male elders or multigenerational living. Within ethnic groups, however, there are class, gender, and generational differences that make generalizations difficult.

There may be more research about this stage of the family life cycle than any other. Consequently, six specific issues relating to aging are examined in this chapter: myths and attitudes about aging, relationships and the elderly, elder abuse, several policy issues, coping with bereavement, and theoretical approaches to aging.

SELECTED ISSUES

AGING: MYTHS AND ATTITUDES

For both sexes in North America, growing old has held negative connotations. This is especially true for women with so much emphasis on youth, beauty, and fertility. Traditionally, women have been encouraged to lie about their age, to dye their grey hair, to brighten their appearance with cosmetics, and to support their aging bodies with uncomfortable foundation garments. Both sexes have been forced to retire from work and accept a drop in income, usually at the age of 65, on the assumption that they can no longer make useful contributions or must create vacancies for younger people.

Negative and misleading attitudes or portrayals of elderly people have been referred to as **agism**. Older people are sometimes assumed to be out of touch with modern life, forgetful, doddery, conservative, and uninterested in politics or sex. These stereotypes may damage older people's self-esteem, isolate them socially from other age groups, and prevent them from continuing to work or remaining independent. Agism may be particularly difficult for retired people who previously held important positions in the work force.

Negative stereotypes have been prevalent in the media, and most of the research on mass media portrayals of old age have focused on American television, due to its potent impact as a medium. The most obvious form of media misrepresentation lies in the underestimation of the numbers of seniors in the population, implying their lack of importance to social and economic life. For example, several American studies have found that only about 2 percent of the characters in television commercials and prime time programs appeared to be over 65, despite the fact that 11 percent of the United States' population was in that age category (Powell and Williamson, 1985). The age distribution tended to represent instead the "prime demographic market" used by commercial advertisers in targeting consumers. The more recent study by Dail (1988) implies that American television has become more responsive to the aging population by showing more older adults.

When elderly characters do appear in mass media, their roles are often negative. Numerous American studies have indicated that older males are more likely than younger ones to be portrayed as "bad guys," and are presented as less powerful and less competent than younger men. Older women were often portrayed as victims, eccentric, and foolish. Appearing younger is clearly seen as socially acceptable and necessary for women, especially in television commercials.

Older women are also less likely to be shown in romantic situations, and tend to be portrayed as sexless. Furthermore, elderly characters are often treated with disrespect by other characters in television programs (Elliott, 1984; Powell and Williamson, 1985; Dail 1988).

The portrayal of older men as stronger and more dominant than older women is, of course, contrary to the facts. Women live longer and older women manage to live alone more successfully than men do, that is with fewer psychological problems and more friends (Connidis, 1989a). Yet, the myth of the weak and passive older woman still permeates North American culture.

Dail (1988) found that seniors are portrayed more positively than middle-aged people, which suggests that middle age is now viewed as more difficult and problematic than the older years. One explanation for the more positive portrayal of old age is an explicit effort to eliminate agism from the mass media for reasons of fairness and because seniors are viewed as an important marketing target. Most of the studies on this topic conclude that television plays an important role in shaping attitudes, beliefs, and self-images. Therefore, it is important to attempt to eliminate negative stereotypes of aging, gender, and culture in order to create a more just society.

Many of the popular myths about aging and the elderly have been challenged in gerontology textbooks and by governments attempting to improve the image of seniors. One myth is that most elderly people live with their children or in nursing homes. Although there are no accurate figures on the percentage of seniors living with their children, census data reveal that 23 percent of women 75 and over and 13 percent of men lived with a person other than their spouse. Although this could be their children, it could also be a friend, a sibling, or another relative. Despite popular ideas that the nuclear family is a relatively new institution, the three-generation household, where elderly parents are supported by their children, has always been an exception in North America (Laslett, 1971; Synge, 1980). Furthermore, only about 8 percent of Canadians 65 and older live in institutions (Forbes, Jackson and Kraus, 1987:43).

The myth that families are now abandoning their elderly also needs to be emphatically refuted, for elderly parents and children still rely on each other for companionship and assistance, especially in times of crises (Rosenthal, 1987). Moreover, many older people find it difficult to talk to strangers about personal matters or to hire professionals to perform personal care or household tasks, preferring to rely on family members. In fact, the elderly are more likely to turn to their families and friends for both emotional and concrete forms of support than to community services or professionals (Kaye, 1985; Chappell et al., 1986). While family members express a willingness to care for older members, however, they are not always able to do so because of employment commitments, distance, their own ailments, or obligations to their children or spouses.

Contrary to what many people think, most seniors report high levels of satisfaction with their lives. In the 1990 General Social Survey, 95 percent reported themselves as "very happy" or "somewhat happy" (Gauthier, 1991:19). Although this study did not find substantial differences between seniors and younger people, other research has found that a higher percentage of older people than younger people report that they are "very satisfied" with various aspects of their lives. From teenage years to age 70, life satisfaction has been found to consistently increase by Atkinson (1979) and Northcott (1982). Even the low-income elderly report high levels of satisfaction.

There are several possible explanations for reports of higher levels of satisfaction among seniors than younger people. First, aspirations are more often in line with the current situation of advancing age. Secondly, retired people have more opportunities to pursue their own interests as they have fewer obligations than younger people. Thirdly, elderly people may be reluctant to complain because they do not want to appear ungrateful, or because they feel that circumstances are beyond their control. Probably all these factors contribute to the finding that life satisfaction increases with age.

Various studies have tried to identify other correlates with life satisfaction besides chronological age. Perceived good health in comparison with the health of others the same age seems to be a major factor influencing a positive outlook among seniors (Chappell et al. 1986). Poor health, or the perception of poor health, may curtail visiting and social relationships and necessitate institutionalization, which would involve losing control over one's daily schedule.

Life satisfaction, however, does not necessarily coincide with external circumstances, but rather is a reflection of the perception of circumstances (McPherson, 1990). Since old age has such negative associations in our society, many older people may expect to be somewhat disabled. They may also look around at others with severe arthritis or Alzheimer's disease and feel relatively well-off.

Other factors relating to life satisfaction among older people are perceptions of adequate financial resources and perception of supportive relationships. These perceptions, however, vary by gender. Women appear to be satisfied with lower levels of income, but place a high value on relationships with both kin and friends (Connidis, 1989a).

Despite the negative stereotypes about old age, major differences in attitudes and outlook are apparent between age groups. Studies have found that the current cohort of older people tend to be more conservative, cautious, egocentric, introverted, passive, and less emotional than younger groups (McPherson, 1990). Researchers have theorized about whether people develop these attitudes as they physically and socially mature or whether different age cohorts have their personality patterns set for life by similar social and political experiences in the past (continuity theory). Much of the research suggests that certain characteristics of seniors are not the inevitable result of aging, but are caused either by life events (Nicholson, 1980) or at least the interaction between personality and the social situation (Epstein, 1979).

Being raised in a low-income household during the 1930s Depression, for example, can help to establish a lifetime of frugal habits and cautious behaviour. On the other hand, being raised in a middle-class family during the 1960s, student revolts and experiments in communal living can create liberal social and political attitudes until old age. As indicated in previous chapters socialization continues throughout

"Sure, you were good at it.
You were *there* for most of it."

the life span, and numerous life events such as divorce, retirement, or bereavement can modify attitudes and behaviour developed earlier in life (developmental theory). Although these theories will be discussed in more detail later in this chapter, it is sufficient to say at this time that the characteristics noted in elderly people are not necessarily caused by physiological aging, but rather by political, social, and economic circumstances of their lives.

RELATIONSHIPS AND THE ELDERLY

As mentioned previously, marital relationships tend to vary in strength throughout the life cycle and appear to be stronger in old age than in early middle age. Reports of marital satisfaction tend to peak at the beginning of marriage, decline in the middle years, and rise again in the post-parental phase until after retirement (Rollins and Feldman, 1970; Lupri and Frideres, 1981).

Studies of marital satisfaction, however, are usually **cross-sectional** rather than **longitudinal**. This means that instead of studying the same couples over 50 years of marriage (obviously a very difficult research task), individuals married for varying lengths of time are compared. This may be an unfair comparison because older couples whose marriages were unsatisfying may have divorced in mid-life or earlier and these divorced individuals would not be interviewed as part of any study (Connidis, 1989b:17). Furthermore, after 40 or more years of marriage, people have shared many experiences and are expected to say they are happy. Otherwise, how could they justify staying together for so many years?

In actual fact, there may be many strains on marriage in later life. For example, not all retirees make a smooth adjustment to loss of status, income, and work companions. Wives often complain that their husbands are difficult to deal with when they are adjusting to retirement, and the burden often falls on wives to provide emotional support and companionship (Jorgensen, 1986:427).

Poor health often places a heavy burden on one spouse who cares for the other. Because of different life expectancies and the age gap between marital partners, it is often the wife who cares for her failing husband. In some cases, she may be worse off emotionally and socially than a widow because she cannot go out with friends and leave her husband alone (Connidis, 1989a; Aronson, 1991). Yet, if his condition is serious, he may not be much of a companion. Without adequate respite care or home care services, the strain of caregiving may create serious problems for their relationship as well as reduce the personal satisfaction of the caregiver.

Although sexual activity tends to decline in later life, many researchers argue that activity level is influenced more by situational factors, such as loss of spouse or illness of spouse, than by physiological ones (Gee and Kimball, 1987). Those who have maintained a high level of sexual activity throughout their marriage may continue their sex lives well into old age. In addition, interest in sex often continues beyond actual activity level. Even when sexual intercourse ceases because of illness or disability, it may be important for the couple to maintain other forms of physical contact to reinforce closeness.

Poor physical health, overuse of prescription drugs, institutionali-

Marital relationships tend to vary in strength throughout the life cycle and appear to be stronger in later years than in early middle age.

Canada Wide/Fred Thornhill

zation, and being widowed can reduce or eliminate sexual activity for both men and women (Gee and Kimball, 1987:103). Older people living in institutions are seldom provided with adequate privacy to remain sexually active. Furthermore, there is a tendency to equate sexuality with youth and not see older people as sexual beings.

In later life, relationships with siblings tend to be weaker than with children, even though people often renew contact with their siblings as they approach the end of their lives. While female family linkages have often been strong throughout life, especially between sisters, men who have spent little time with their siblings in the middle years tend to renew relationships as they age. The never-married, divorced, and widowed generally have more contact with siblings than married people, since couples are often preoccupied with each other to the exclusion of friends and relatives (Connidis, 1989a).

Contact with children and grandchildren varies by sex and social class. Working-class parents, especially women, are more likely to live with children, to exchange services such as baby-sitting, and to visit their children. Middle-class parents speak to their children on the telephone or write letters, but are less likely than working-class parents to visit in person. Instead of exchanging services, middle-class elderly parents typically send money or gifts to their children and grandchildren (Lopata, 1979; Synge et al., 1981). Mothers perceive their children as providing more emotional support than fathers do, and older women compared with older men more often use their children as confidants (Babchuk, 1978–79).

Various studies have found that the grandparent role is more salient for women, for the working class, and for retired people. By their very presence, grandparents may provide a sense of family continuity, acting as mediators of and deterrents to family disruption (Bengtson, 1985). Moreover, the grandparent role may become more important in the future with rising life expectancies, when more people will live to see their grandchildren become adults.

Adult children typically dominate the support networks of the elderly, but not all research has distinguished the quality from the quantity of support. Furthermore, not all studies separate instrumental aid such as home repairs from emotional assistance such as acting as confidant. If family members are available to assist elderly relatives, does this mean that seniors are less likely to use formal support such as housekeeping services, senior citizen homes, or visiting nurses (Connidis, 1985)? While this is unclear, studies have found that seniors are more satisfied with life if they perceive that relatives and friends are available to help them if needed. Whether or not they

Grandparents may provide a sense of family continuity, acting as mediators of and deterrents to family disruption.

Photo: Tessa MacIntosh, Government N.W.T.

actually draw on these people for support is less important than the belief that they are available.

Regular contact with friends and neighbours seems to be important to the well-being of seniors. As people grow older, however, more of their friends die and making new friends is difficult as life becomes more sedentary and income drops (Dulude, 1978). Church groups and senior citizens' clubs help provide new friendships and activities. Membership in seniors' clubs, however, tends to be dominated by women because of the lower life expectancies of men. This makes cross-sex friendships difficult for older people.

While family relationships are particularly important for most seniors, strains develop especially if the older person becomes less independent and more demanding. As the next section indicates, elder abuse often involves family caregivers who feel trapped by the burden of looking after a spouse or parent.

ELDER ABUSE

Although there is no standard definition of elder abuse, most studies and discussions deal with physical and psychological abuse, while others include financial abuse and neglect. Numerous studies have concluded that most elder abuse victims are women, and that there is often a history of family violence or spousal abuse in earlier years (Gnaedinger, 1989). North American estimates of the incidence of elder abuse range from 2 percent to 3 percent of all elderly persons, but like other forms of family violence, this kind of behaviour is likely to be under-reported.

Elderly people are most often abused by relatives who care for them, but are also abused by paid caretakers. In cases of family abuse, victims are frequently disabled elderly women, often over 75 years old, who are physically dependent on their husband or adult child for daily care. Family caregivers sometimes neglect or abuse their spouse or parent out of frustration, fatigue, and lack of supportive services, but are more likely to do so if they came from an abusive home. Caregivers are sometimes old themselves, with insufficient energy to deal with a disabled person, or they may be a younger person who feels overwhelmed by the responsibility for children as well as elderly parents (Gnaedinger, 1989; McDonald et al., 1991).

Elder abuse is not always physical or verbal. Children who expect to inherit money have sometimes deprived their parents of suitable care, accommodation, and food in the hopes of promoting a larger and earlier inheritance. In other cases, children or other relatives have tricked their elderly parents into signing over their money to them.

Elder abuse is similar to other forms of family violence in that both involve socially isolated people and families. Victims are in a powerless and dependent relationship with the abuser, and abusers often have a history of alcohol abuse, low self-esteem, unemployment, and family violence (Bolton and Bolton, 1987).

Elder abuse, however, does not always involve family members or male perpetrators. Caregivers in residential institutions, who are usually women, sometimes abuse elderly patients when they appear to be too demanding or increase their workload. Although some commit physically abusive acts, more often the abuse is psychological. Nursing homes with high staff/patient ratios, low salaries, and poor working conditions foster such abuse (Bélanger, 1981; Pillemer and Finkelhor, 1987).

Awareness of elder abuse is not as great as awareness of child abuse or violence against women. Debates continue over mandatory reporting laws, reporting protocols, and guidelines for detection. Increasingly, however, governments are recognizing that elder abuse is often a form of family violence and should be part of prevention and treatment programs. Some provinces (including Ontario, Nova Scotia, Prince Edward Island, Alberta, and New Brunswick) have enacted special legislation that recognizes elder abuse and the vulnerability of older adults.

As seniors become a larger percentage of the population, issues such as elder abuse will receive greater attention, leading to support services that may help to reduce this form of abuse. In addition, elder abuse may diminish if, in the future, seniors become more financially and physically independent. However, other policy issues, such as providing adequate pensions, affordable health care services, and housing for a growing percentage of seniors also need to be dealt with for an aging population.

POLICY ISSUES: PENSIONS, HEALTH CARE, AND HOUSING

The percentage of seniors in the population varies considerably by province. Some provinces, such as British Columbia, Manitoba, Saskatchewan, and Prince Edward Island, have above-average percentages of seniors, while other such as the Northwest Territories have a percentage of seniors as low as 3 percent (Baker, 1988). From policy documents, it appears that not all provinces are equally concerned about providing and financing services for seniors or about the aging population. This may be explained by provincial and territorial variations in the percentage of elderly.

In the past few years, however, all levels of government have been discussing the needs of seniors. Are the programs and services presently available still relevant to today's seniors, or were they designed in previous years for a group with different needs? How can appropriate services be provided to the growing percentage of elderly people at a reasonable cost to seniors and taxpayers? Answering these questions has led to controversy about future population projections, the need to reform present programs, who should pay for expanding services, whether or not people should be asked to retire at a certain age, and when they should be eligible for pensions.

Retirement and Pension Plans

It is important to differentiate between public plans (such as Old Age Security and the Canada/Quebec Pension Plan) and private pensions (those from former employers, RRSPs, and annuities). Public pensions are sponsored and funded mainly by the federal government, while private pensions, although regulated by government legislation, are sponsored by employers, unions, and individuals.

Although labour force participation rates have increased for women in the past decade, less than 30 percent of retired women compared with less than 60 percent of retired men presently receive pension benefits from their former employers (Lowe, 1991:16), as figure 8.3 indicates. This percentage, however, has increased considerably over the past 15 years. Not everyone is equally likely to belong to work-related pension plans, however. Those who do belong tend to be in the highly paid and organized work forces where women are under represented, or in government employment. Because employer pensions are relatively recent, older retirees are less likely than recent retirees to receive benefits from their former employers. In addition, only 58 percent of present Canadian retirees are receiving pensions that are at least partially indexed for inflation (Lowe, 1991:16). Without full indexation, the real value of a pension falls each year.

Until recently, membership in work pension plans was seldom transferable from job to job, and most plans required an employee to work at the same place for at least 10 years and to be 45 years old before they could transfer the employers' contributions. If employees left within this period, their own contributions were returned with low interest but the employers' contributions were usually forfeited. In recent years, most provinces have shortened the **vesting period**, or the

Figure 8.3 **Percentage of Seniors With Private Retirement Pensions, Canada, 1977 and 1988**

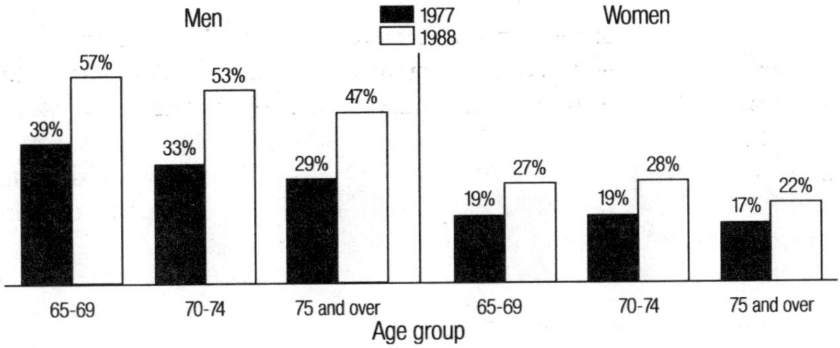

Source: Statistics Canada, Catalogue 89-519. Reproduced with the permission of the Minister of Supply and Services Canada, 1992.

length of service required before the employer's contributions legally belong to employees, from ten years to between two and five years and removed the age limit. New legislation also requires employers to contribute 50 percent to the pension plan. These reforms will undoubtedly improve the economic position of future retired people.

In the late 1960s, the federal government created the Canada/Quebec Pension Plan, which was funded by employer and employee contributions. Only those working for pay, however, could belong to this plan, which excluded full-time homemakers with no personal earnings. At the same time, the federal government introduced the Guaranteed Income Supplement, designed to assist low-income pensioners to improve their standard of living. Later, the Spouse's Allowance was created for the younger spouse (usually the wife) of a pensioner, so that an older couple would have more to live on than one pension for two people. Figure 8.4 shows the percentage of men and women receiving benefits from CPP/QPP in 1977 and 1988.

Despite the introduction of these public pensions, improvements in employer-sponsored pensions, and the expansion of Registered Retirement Savings Plan (RRSPs), a significant percentage of seniors continue to live in poverty. In 1988, for example, 44 percent of elderly unattached women and 23 percent of elderly unattached men had incomes below the Statistics Canada poverty lines (Gauthier, 1991:18). Although poverty among the elderly declined substantially throughout the 1980s, elderly people remain poor because they have no employment savings from low-income jobs, sporadic unemployment,

Figure 8.4 **Percentage of Seniors Receiving CPP/QPP, 1977 and 1988**

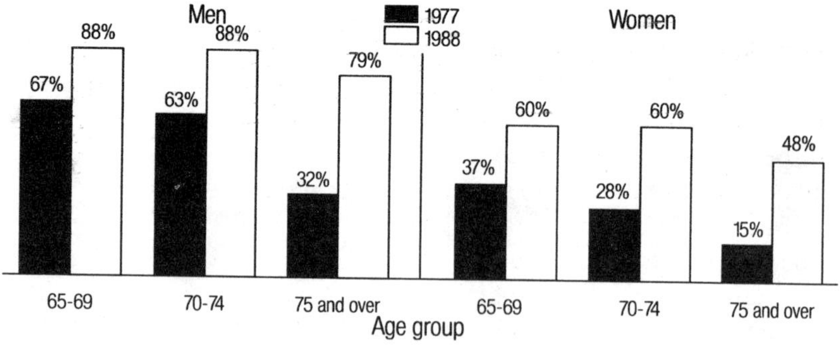

Source: Statistics Canada, Catalogue 89-519. Reproduced with the permission of the Minister of Supply and Services Canada, 1992.

or unpaid positions, and many have no work pensions. Poverty has been aggravated by pensions that have no survivor benefits, which means that when a spouse dies, the pension is terminated and the surviving spouse gets nothing.

Pension reform is important for all employees, but particularly for women. For one thing, work pension plans usually exclude part-time workers and many more women than men work part-time. Furthermore, the service, clerical, and retail sales positions that women typically occupy tend not to offer pension plans. Since women change jobs more often than men, usually for family-related reasons, retired women could easily have worked most of their adult life, yet receive no pension from their former employers. Furthermore, pensions are based on previous income, often the best five years. Since elderly women are less likely than their male counterparts to be in the labour force and when they are, they earn about 60 percent of the income earned by elderly men (Galarneau, 1991:28), they tend to receive lower monthly pension benefits.

Women who have worked exclusively as homemakers have neither a work pension nor Canada Pension Plan benefits. The issue of pensions for homemakers has been controversial because of the difficulty of agreeing on the economic value of housework and deciding who would make the contributions to the benefits women would receive. At the present time, only those who drop out of the labour force for a temporary period are covered by the Canada Pension Plan. Long-term homemakers must rely on their husband's pension when he retires, or government benefits for the poor such as the Guaranteed Income Supplement. All these reasons contribute to higher poverty rates for older women, especially if they are widowed, never-married, or divorced.

Health Status and Health Care

Numerous studies have indicated that perceptions of health status are more influential than actual health in affecting people's feelings of well-being and their levels of activity. Although perception of health tends to decline somewhat after middle age, most older people continue to feel that they are in good health. The 1985 Health and Social Support Study by the Canadian government found that while 39 percent of 25- to 44-year-olds rated their health as "excellent," this declined to 32 percent for 45- to 54-years-olds, 29 percent for 55- to 64-year-olds, 22 percent for 65- to 74-year-olds, and 15 percent for those 75 or older.

Aging, however, is not synonymous with illness and disability. Few seniors require assistance with their daily activities, although this percentage increases with age. For example, the same government study looked at the percentage of the population aged 55 and over that require some help or are unable to carry out selected activities. Table 8.1 compares people 55 and over and the sub-group of people aged 75 and over, showing that a relatively large percentage of even the "old elderly" can manage daily tasks without assistance.

Despite poorer objective conditions in both health and income, older people tend to report high levels of well-being, frequently exceeding those of younger people. This may simply indicate that they do not want to complain to researchers. Alternatively, they may compare themselves to other seniors who are in poor health. However, like the rest of the population, seniors may hold negative stereotypes of aging that include poor health. When they reach old age, they may be pleasantly surprised that they feel so good.

Some people continue to exercise, remain socially active, and maintain their positive outlook and good health well into old age. Researchers have argued that declines in physical function have more to do with decreased activity than true aging. Lack of activity can lead

"That's what it says: 'one tablespoonful, 300 times a day.'"

Table 8.1 **Percentage of the Population Requiring Some Help or Unable to Carry Out Selected Activities, Canada, 1985**

	Aged 55 and Over (percent)	Aged 75 and Over (percent)
Yard work	33	64
Heavy housework	21	46
Grocery shopping	12	33
Meal preparation	7	17
Managing money	4	12
Light housework	3	9
Personal care	2	7

Source: Statistics Canada. *Health and Social Support, 1985.* Cat. 11-612, no. 1. Ottawa, 1987:177. Reproduced with the permission of the Minister of Supply and Services Canada, 1992.

to mental and physical problems, while increases in activity can reverse or prevent these problems. Attitudes toward fitness and aging are definitely changing in Canada, with Seniors Games, wheel chair facilities in National Parks, and exercise classes for seniors.

Studies of happiness, satisfaction, depression, mental and physical health, and loneliness among the elderly indicate that the married fare better than the widowed and never-married (Connidis, 1989a). There is also some evidence that those with children have higher levels of subjective well-being, perhaps because children are perceived as a source of future assistance (Connidis, 1989a).

Despite high levels of reported satisfaction, seniors tend to report more health problems than younger age groups, and hospitalization and disability rates also increase with age. The most prevalent health problem reported by seniors in a federal government study was arthritis, with 63 percent of women and 46 percent of men reporting this problem, as figure 8.5 indicates. However, the majority of seniors in private households report that their health is "good" or "excellent" (Gauthier, 1991:19).

According to much of the literature, institutionalization of the elderly is more prevalent in Canada than in many European countries with higher proportions of seniors. Even so, only about 8 percent of elderly Canadians live in nursing homes or other institutions (Forbes, Jackson and Kraus, 1987:43), compared with about 5 percent in Britain where 15 percent of the population are seniors. The trend toward home care rather than institutionalization is well developed in Swe-

Figure 8.5 **Selected Health Problems Among Seniors, by Sex, 1985**

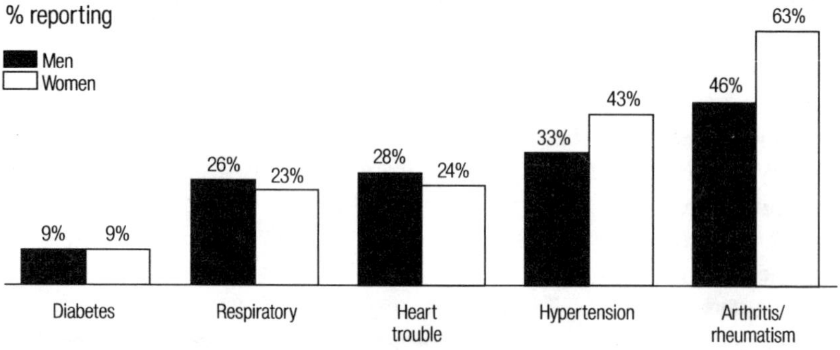

Source: Statistics Canada, Catalogue 89-519. Reproduced with the permission of the Minister of Supply and Services Canada, 1992.

den and Great Britain, but is only in the early stages in Canada (Forbes, Jackson and Kraus, 1987:43).

A number of studies indicate that most seniors prefer to remain in their own homes as long as possible, even when they are ill or disabled (Chappell, Strain, and Blandford, 1986:119; Connidis, 1989a:5). In addition, home care services appear to be less expensive than hospitalization or chronic care facilities, partly because services are provided by lower-paid nonprofessional workers rather than by registered nurses and doctors, but mainly because unpaid family members are doing most of the caregiving (Chappell et al., 1986:119).

Increasingly, however, female family members are not available to care for elderly relatives because they are in the labour force. Some European countries, such as Sweden and Britain, have attempted to encourage home care services and family caregiving by paying the expenses of caregivers or paying them a small wage (Forbes et al., 1987:104). This payment also provides a clear message that caring for elderly relatives at home is important work which is valued by governments.

Especially in the last few years of life, older people are more likely to be hospitalized than younger people. One government report has noted that health care spending on people 65 and over was 4.5 times greater than for those under 65. Health care for those 75 and over was even more costly—6.7 times greater than for those under 65 (Chappell et al., 1986). Policy-makers and health administrators are expressing concern about the cost of Medicare at the present and the projected cost for the future.

The current Medicare system in Canada, however, focuses on institutional care rather than community care, on acute care rather than chronic care, and on medical care rather than health care broadly defined. Many critics argue that we need to change the health care system to deal more with prevention, chronic care, and home care services. Doctors have also been criticized for viewing elders as sick people in need of medication and surgery (Chappell et al., 1986). Many health care analysts have argued that at present, acute care hospitals are being used to accommodate chronic care patients at a high cost to the taxpayer, because of the shortage of home care services and chronic care facilities. They say that greater use could be made of visiting nurses, homemakers, and day hospitals, which would provide care to the elderly at a much lower cost than is presently done by physicians in general hospitals. If these changes were made, they argue, health care costs for seniors would not be so high. However, there is competition among the various segments of the health care system for government funding (Chappell et al., 1986; Sutherland and Fulton, 1988; Clarke, 1990).

Housing

The housing needs of seniors are varied, depending on age, physical health, financial status, and interests. While some elders may choose to live in their son's or daughter's homes, others may prefer a subsidized apartment with communal dining facilities and nursing assistance. Wealthier people may select a luxury condominium in an urban or rural setting, while others may prefer to stay in the house where they have always lived. A variety of housing is necessary to meet these different requirements.

Over the past two decades, developers have built mainly large family homes in the suburbs or high-rise units targeted to young professionals. But seniors often have different housing needs and preferences than younger people. While new seniors' apartments are built to accommodate people with physical disabilities, there are long waiting lists to get in. Furthermore, these apartments tend to be small and seem to be more suited to unattached and frugal individuals rather than couples, individuals who like to entertain, or those who simply want more space. Few small one-storey homes with gardens, similar to those in Britain, have been built in Canada. Consequently, there are few housing choices between larger luxury retirement complexes and small subsidized apartments.

The proportion of seniors living alone has increased in the past two decades, especially widows. In 1986, 38 percent of women aged 75 and over lived alone compared with 17 percent of men of that age group (Priest, 1990:183–184). Connidis (1989a:5) notes that living alone is often a preferred arrangement for seniors who value their independence. The trend for more seniors living alone relates to rising life expectancies for women, new attitudes about the importance of

CONTINUUM OF HOUSING BY DEGREE OF INDEPENDENCE

Housing Type	Criteria
Independent Household	
Fully Independent (approx. 87 percent of Canadians aged 65 and over)	Self-contained and self-sufficient; resident does 90 percent of housework. Includes house, apartment, townhouse, duplex, condominium.
Supported Independent Living (4 percent of Canadians aged 65 and over)	Self-contained but some help with chores (e.g., Meals on Wheels, Homemaker Services, etc.). Sheltered or enriched housing. Cooking and household chores may be part of community life (e.g., communal dining room).
Collective Dwellings	
Collective Dwellings (9 percent of Canadians aged 65 percent and over)	Dependent Living
Hotels and Rooming Houses (2 percent of Canadians aged 65 and over)	Serviced dwellings may provide meals and housekeeping services.
Personal care home, Home for the Aged, or Nursing home (7 percent of Canadians aged 65 and over)	Not self-contained, not self-sufficient. Personal care help in health care, grooming, bathing, and household work.

This chart shows that the need for support increases as people's ability to care for themselves decreases. A good system gives people the support they need, while allowing them to do as much for themselves as they can.

independence, greater prosperity for elderly people, and the building of more rental apartment units.

Several studies have concluded that while elderly people usually enjoy living near their children, they value their independence and their tranquillity (Connidis, 1989a; Nett, 1990:261). Living in seniors' apartments allows them independence without the usual noise level of general rental accommodation. They are also more likely to have interests and concerns in common with people of their own age group, and therefore to make friends more easily and join in group activities. The organizers of some seniors' residences hire visiting nurses, recreation directors, or other staff members to provide the necessary services. But waiting lists are often long to get into such accommodation.

Some low-income seniors are forced to sell their houses because they have insufficient income to pay for property taxes and maintenance. Others move to senior citizen housing or nursing homes because they need home care services, yet none are available. Visiting homemakers and home care nurses are needed, but also assistance with home repairs, lawn maintenance, and snow removal. While some municipalities have organized such services, they are in the initial stages of development in many areas. If these services were available, seniors who want to would have the satisfaction of remaining in their own homes rather than moving in with relatives or institutional living.

Increasingly, a larger proportion of seniors live alone, especially after the death of their spouse. Although the transition from married to single status often involves a change in housing arrangements, it may also involve changes in friendships, a drop in income, and the formal end of marriage.

Coping With Bereavement

According to the family life cycle approach, the nuclear family ends with the death of one spouse. We cannot always assume, however, this occurs only in old age, as many people die from disease, suicide, or accident before the end of their natural lives. The unexpected death of a child, parent, or spouse may be far more difficult to handle than an expected death in old age, and may require more inner strength and social support than any other life experience.

Although everyone knows that people do not live forever, not everyone plans how they will spend their remaining years. Those who plan their future tend to have more positive attitudes toward death. The process of mentally reviewing and legitimizing one's life activities and decisions is a normal and typical one, and most people use this process to come to accept their inevitable death (Lamanna and Reidmann, 1988:494). For the terminally ill, caregivers working in hospices and palliative care units may assist them to accept their death with dignity.

Formalized preparation for death is as absent from our society as specific preparation for marriage and childrearing. We tend to discourage people from talking about the potential death of their spouse, even though doing so is a form of preparation or "anticipatory socialization." Certain categories of people, such as those whose spouses have undergone prolonged illness, may be better prepared to handle the practical aspects of living alone. But seldom do people anticipate the emotional problems of bereavement, such as the loneliness, the perceived lack of purpose, and the social isolation from former married friends.

In the past two decades, there have been many studies on bereavement in North America, some focusing on women and others highlighting gender differences. Helena Lopata's American research was one of the first studies on women, highlighting the lack of preparation women have for living without husbands (1973). Anne Martin Matthews' recent Canadian book (1991) indicates that women who have centred their lives around husbands and families often experience a serious loss of identity when their husbands die. Many women also perceive that their status drops when they are no longer married (Martin Matthews, 1987a), and they view the company of other women as second best. Widows are also more likely than the married elderly to think of themselves as "old," and are more inclined to be unhappy, to worry, and to anticipate death in the near future (Riley and Foner, 1968:353; Martin Matthews, 1991).

Although most of the research on bereavement focuses on women, men appear to experience more emotional difficulties both with marriage breakdown and bereavement. Reasons for this may relate to the fact that men seldom develop close same-sex relationships as women do. Nor do men retain meaningful relationships with their children and grandchildren throughout life. Furthermore, more women than men are left without spouses, and by old age, women usually have a ready-made support group of widows. Women are also more experienced in looking after themselves and in cooking and cleaning. Men who have devoted significant amounts of time to their jobs may also have few hobbies and may find themselves with little to do when their wives die (Martin Matthews, 1987a:349).

Researchers have investigated the various stages of bereavement, beginning with the work of American sociologist Elisabeth Kubler-

More women than men are left without spouses, and by old age, women usually have a ready-made support group of widows.

Canapress Photo Service/Jim Cochrane

Ross (1969), as well as the patterns of adjustment and the changing self-concept of the widow. The initial mourning period appears to be the most stressful and may last for over a year. Widows and widowers often experience contradictory emotions throughout this stage of bereavement, including disbelief, numbness, yearning, anger, and guilt. The mourning stage may also involve insomnia, weight loss, and deteriorating health (Vachon, 1979; McPherson, 1990).

In some cultures, such as those in southern Europe, bereavement is followed by elaborate rituals and dress regulations. People openly mourn the loss of a loved one. Widows must wear black clothing and are discouraged from socializing with men or remarrying. Many North Americans have dispensed with these rituals and bereavement is often internalized. Whether or not this assists or interferes with overcoming grief has not been adequately researched.

The transition from married to single status is usually made with the assistance of religion, family, friends, or support groups. Psychological preparation for the spouse's death can assist long-term adjustment and is more possible if friends have also been widowed or with involvement in a formal support group. But adjustment to being widowed is more difficult if there are also financial problems, poor health, and few opportunities to meet new people (McPherson, 1990:326).

While widows are more likely to experience financial problems and to divert themselves by spending more time with family and friends, widowers are more likely to remarry soon after bereavement—often within two years. Because of the imbalance of the sex ratio in later life, women have much more difficulty finding partners. Remarriage often revitalizes the lives of older people, and provides a source of companionship, love, sex, physical and emotional care, and financial support. Yet, some widows report little desire to remarry because they feel they might lose their independence and would be expected to be housekeeper and eventually nurse to a new husband

REMARRIAGE IN LATER LIFE

Comments from numerous widows in the London study make it clear that taking care of a man is precisely the role many older women shun. A widow of 66 says she would not remarry because "I am enjoying my freedom too much now. I brought up my children and I looked after my husband to the best of my ability. I cared for my parents until they died and it was a joy and I liked it but I am enjoying the freedom now of not having to account to anybody for what I do." An 81-year-old widow is even more direct:

"I wouldn't get married again for all the tea in China. ... Oh no. ... I am set in my ways and I wouldn't want a young fellow running around all the time and I wouldn't want an old man with one foot in the grave either. Then stop and think that you would have to wash for them, you would have to iron, you would have to have meals to suit them. Now, if I feel like eating, I eat, and if I feel like going out, I go out."

Marital success is more likely among those whose first marriage was successful, who have adjusted well to changes associated with aging, who are better off financially, and who begin their marriage in their own home rather than one previously shared with a former spouse (McKain, 1972). One reason for the greater stability of later-life remarriages is the long time that most remarried older persons have known their new spouse, a factor associated with greater marital success.

In sum, a very small percentage of all older individuals remarry but it appears that most of those who do so are happy with their marriage. There is still much that is unknown about remarriage in later life and its impact on other family relationships. ...

Connidis, Ingrid Arnet. *Family Ties and Aging.* Toronto: Butterworths, 1989:37.

(Lopata, 1970, Connidis, 1989a). Remarriages later in life also have the potential to disrupt relationships with children and patterns of inheritance, as well as reduce individual pension benefits. Yet, these possible negative aspects are usually outweighed by the benefits of beginning a new life.

THEORETICAL APPROACHES TO AGING

Within the field of **gerontology**, social scientists have attempted to explain patterns in aging and differences in personality, attitudes, living arrangements, and relationships between older and younger people. Theories that focus on behaviour, interpersonal relationships, and inner feelings have been called **micro-theories**. The unit of analysis in these studies is behaviour and relationships, and is narrower in scope than theories that look at social institutions. Despite the fact that individuals are always different in some ways, researchers search for patterns in the behaviour of people of the same age, gender, cultural group, or social class. Gerontologists have also attempted to explain relations between different age groups and how the status of the elderly has changed over time, especially since industrialization. These theories have been referred to as **macro-theories** because they look beyond behaviour and relationships to focus on social institutions, such as the economy and politics.

Several micro-theories are examined in this discussion of theoretical approaches to aging. The theoretical framework that sets the structure of this book is the family life cycle approach. In gerontology, this is similar to the **life-span approach**, which examines the role of social interaction and family responsibilities in developing social skills and a sense of identity. The assumption is that certain characteristics and attitudes are likely to develop after particular life experiences, such as going through an unhappy marriage and divorce, having a child with special needs, retiring from work, or losing a spouse from cancer. This theory finds patterns in personal and social development among people at the same stage of the family life cycle and attempts to explain changes or lack of change in individuals over the years.

The **disengagement theory** (Cumming et al., 1960) attempted to explain the tendency for elderly people to be fatalistic, nonassertive, and to gradually withdraw from social activity. Advocates of this theory have argued that it is normal for aging people to lose interest in activities and relationships and to drop out of active participation in society. Critics, however, have argued that much of this "disengagement" may in fact be involuntary. Seniors are forced out of the workplace through mandatory retirement policies and expected to "take it easy" on a reduced income. Lack of transportation and other services prevent some seniors from going out and fully participating in community activities. Other critics have noted that social participation tends to depend on former lifestyles, and those who have been active throughout their lives tend to remain active well into old age.

Activity theory contradicts disengagement theory, making the opposite claim that successful aging depends on older people remaining active. This theory suggests that as people lose a social role, such as worker or spouse, they need to replace it with another to promote "successful" aging (Havighurst et al., 1968; Novak, 1985). The retired man, for example, may need to find new hobbies or volunteer work to replace the loss of self-esteem and social contact caused by retirement. Similarly, the recent widow needs to become more actively involved with her grandchildren or female friends in order to make up for the emotional and physical absence of her late husband. But the research on the relationship between activity level and life satisfac-

Activity theory argues that successful aging depends on older people remaining active.

The Toronto Star/B. Spremo

tion is contradictory and complicated by gender and class differences. In addition, relationships and activities in old age tend to be related to former occupation and lifestyles. While some people will be content to relax in old age, those who were always active will need to find substitute activities for those no longer available to them.

Continuity theory examines how personality and attitudes change throughout the life cycle. It suggests that rather than people becoming more cautious and conservative with age, personality and attitudes are established early in life and tend to persist as a person grows older, despite life events (Neugarten et al., 1968). Critics argue that this apparent continuity may be promoted by a stable lifestyle. The death of a spouse or retirement from work may necessitate both lifestyle and personality changes.

Phenomenological theories of aging emphasize the meaning attached to growing old in a particular culture. In some societies, people consider themselves and are considered by others as "old" and useless or unattractive when they are 40. Old people adopt certain attitudes and lifestyles and expect to be treated in certain ways. Phenomenological approaches emphasize that how people see themselves is more important in terms of behaviour and relationships than the way others see them. For example, people who think they are too frail and elderly to participate in community activities will not do so even if a researcher evaluates their health as being better than the health of others who are active participants in all community functions.

These micro-level theories have been only partially successful in explaining aspects of the aging process because they do not seriously consider variables external to individuals, such as cultural norms, environmental influences, changes in the structure of the labour force, or social policies. However, many theorists focusing on social interaction have been successful in showing that the elderly are not passive recipients of the behaviour and expectations of others. Instead, they have found that elderly people, like other age groups, create their own relationships and negotiate their status with other people. They initiate social arrangements that are beneficial to themselves and attempt to maintain their self-esteem and dignity as long as possible.

Macro-level theories of aging, which use entire societies or segments of society as units of analysis, have generally compared seniors to other groups, or traced historical trends in the status of the elderly. In the 1950s and 1960s, parallels were drawn between elderly people and disadvantaged ethnic or racial groups in an attempt to explain low status and self-deprecation of both groups. However, since then, the political and economic status of seniors in Canada has improved considerably with population aging and the expansion of public pensions. Furthermore, researchers have noted that elderly people are not a homogeneous group, but rather vary in their attitudes and lifestyles by ethnicity, gender, and social class. Many differences exist among seniors, and some researchers have argued that the characteristics of elderly people do not set them apart from younger people (Abu-Laban and Abu-Laban, 1977).

Exchange theory of aging compares the bargaining power of seniors to other age groups, and examines how social status is negotiated. This theory argues that changes in technology, the education system, and labour market needs have encouraged younger people to obtain higher education, better-paid jobs, and higher status than many seniors (Dowd, 1975). Many retired elderly people have only their former accomplishments or a claim to reciprocity from their children to use as bargaining power for greater respect (McPherson, 1990:132).

Political economy theories of aging, like social exchange theories, focus on how changes in the labour force, the economy, and governments influence the position of seniors in a society. Unlike social exchange theory, the focus is not on interpersonal negotiations, but rather on the development of public policies and the social and economic implications of an aging population. Political economy theories may try to explain disputes over public resources that could be used for facilities and services either for children or for seniors. They emphasize that conflicts over public resources do not take place between people of different generations, but rather between organizations whose interests are connected with particular age groups. For example, the education system, which generally caters to children and youth, may be competing with chronic care hospitals for future resources as the proportion of elderly people in the population becomes larger and the proportion of children dwindles.

Feminist theories of aging tend to focus on gender differences in attitudes and behaviour, and the experiences of older women. They note that throughout the life span, differences in socialization, expectations, and life experiences have created substantial variations in the lifestyles of older men and women. Despite cultural and class differences, older women are more likely to be dependent on family members, to derive satisfaction from relationships, and to live alone or with their children in comparison with older men. Furthermore, because of labour force practices and women's domestic responsibilities throughout the life cycle, older women are more likely than older men to be living in poverty. In addition, older women tend to view the world in their own way and to have a different set of priorities than men.

Environmental theories of aging have examined how various aspects of the physical or social environment affect attitudes, behaviour, or the physical aging process. For example, researchers have studied how diet, housing conditions, income, and exercise can promote physical and social aging. Demographers have also studied probabilities of disability or death depending on gender, social class, and date of birth, and noted that poor people live shorter lives with more chronic illness than wealthier people.

Many theoretical approaches to the study of aging and the elderly exist. As mentioned in chapter two, all theoretical perspectives are based on untestable philosophical assumptions about the way the world works and what is important in life. Some theories address certain issues better than others, as they focus on different aspects of the aging process or the status of the elderly. For example, some theories focus on interpersonal relations, while others focus on societal changes affecting elderly people. Which approach is used in research depends on the purpose of the study, the preference of the researcher, and the availability of money, time, and personnel. Throughout this chapter, a political economy approach was used to emphasize historical trends in pensions, but various other theories (such as phenomenological, activity, and continuity) were used to discuss attitudes and interpersonal relationships.

FUTURE TRENDS

CHANGING LIFESTYLES AND ATTITUDES TOWARD AGING

Since most studies of aging compare different generations living at the same time rather than several generations throughout their entire lifespan, we cannot say that variations between age groups are the result of the aging process. Differences could have been caused by growing up under varying political, economic, and social conditions. Certainly the generation of Canadians now aged 65 and over have grown old in a different social and economic world than will the elderly of the future.

Many of today's seniors were greatly affected by the 1930s Depression and the Second World War. The Depression may have curtailed their education, delayed their marriage, or forced them to accept work that was secure rather than challenging. Trying to make ends meet during those years encouraged both thrift and financial anxiety. Travelling overseas to fight in the war may have been their first opportunity to see the world, leave their hometowns, and make some money, as well as serve their country. Yet, many surviving veterans and their families were changed by the destruction of war, the death of their friends, food rationing, loneliness, and physical and mental disabilities. Both the Depression and the Second World War made lasting impressions on today's elderly, affecting their attitudes, expectations, and behaviour (Baker, 1988).

Past generations needed to be prepared for the unexpected in life in a way that today's young people find difficult to understand. Without social security programs, Medicare, credit, or reliable birth control, today's seniors had to prepare themselves for the future by saving their money, maintaining a support network of friends and family, or by cultivating an attitude of resignation. Many of today's elderly relied on their family for assistance, especially their children, whom they hoped would feel a reciprocal responsibility and would assist them in their old age.

Those born after World War II have been raised to take income security programs, private insurance, government medical insurance, inflation, and credit for granted. They feel that it is not necessary to save for the future, to defer gratification, or to stay in an unsatisfying job or even an unhappy marriage out of duty or obligation. They are more likely to move in and out of jobs and relationships, and live for the present rather than the future. The acceptance of government and employment fringe benefits, such as pensions, is well entrenched in the psyche of this generation, and affects their present lifestyle as well as their outlook on the future.

The generation raised during the 1960s and 1970s is likely to view old age differently from their parents. They may feel that they have more control over their lives and more right to speak up and demand to be heard. Younger women are more likely to have their own jobs, interests, and money, and to see their families as a part of their lives but not their entire lives. More older people will be divorced in the future, and have grandchildren and other relationships from previous marriages and remarriages, further blurring the boundaries of families. But the high divorce rates and the increasing percentages of one-parent households could mean that poverty among older women will continue despite women's labour force participation.

Because of rising life expectancies, however, young people often anticipate a more active old age than their parents' generation. With the aging of the baby boom generation, there will certainly be a larger proportion of elderly in the future who could acquire the political power to demand improved services and facilities. Some of these seniors will be financially secure with their RRSPs, work pensions, and public pensions. These seniors will create the need for particular services and facilities, and in doing so, will probably challenge present notions about the capabilities and interests of seniors. Our stereotypes about old age tend to be based on our perceptions of relatives, friends, and acquaintances, as well as images in the media. However, there are many reasons to believe that future seniors will be different from past generations and even from today's seniors.

Tomorrow's elderly may not follow the same trends or experience all the problems of today's elderly, and policy-makers should be wary of relying on predictions based solely on demographic projections without considering economic and social variables. Stages in the life cycle are less distinct than even 30 years ago. Rather than keeping to the pattern of finishing school, working, marrying, raising children, seeing the children leave home, and retiring, more people will marry and remarry and perhaps start a second family. They may return to school at an older age, and change careers or jobs several times. Planning for the future must take into consideration changing trends in education, family formation, labour force participation, and ideology, as well as demography.

Those born after the Second World War are better educated than previous generations. While about 5 percent of people aged 65 and older have university degrees (McPherson, 1990:86), about 16 percent of 25- to 34-year-olds have graduated from university (Statistics Canada, Feb. 1990:67). Their college and university degrees have enabled them to find higher-paying jobs, and with the assistance of credit cards and two incomes, they have come to expect a high standard of living. With higher education, they are more likely than their parents to read, travel internationally, exercise, take adult education courses, remain politically active well into old age, question authority, and be more articulate about their needs.

The postwar generation has grown up with a variety of social security programs. Unlike their parents, these people have not had to worry about saving in case of unemployment, ill health, or disability in old age. They are likely to continue to consume at a higher rate than their parents' generation, with the expectation that social security benefits will continue and that credit will always be available.

The postwar generation may live longer and healthier lives than their parents' generation since they were fortunate to grow up with better nutrition, sanitation and health services, and with an increased knowledge of the relationship between fitness, nutrition, smoking, and health.

If the trend for early retirement continues, many men will want to retire early and live off their private savings and investments, their employer-sponsored pension benefits, and public pensions. On the other hand, more women will remain in the labour force until retirement and will be more likely to have adequate pension incomes in the future.

The postwar generation will probably place less emphasis on individualism in their old age than previous generations, because they could always rely on collective or government assistance rather than their own individual initiative. With fewer children, they may need to purchase more assistance in their old age. With higher levels of education and more experience with hiring help, they may become more demanding about the availability and quality of services than the present elderly.

POLICY ISSUES FOR AN AGING POPULATION

If aging is examined from the political economy perspective, it becomes apparent that an aging population implies major changes in social security benefits, health services, and housing to accommodate this population growth. The rising percentage of seniors will place heavy demands especially on federal government pension funds and perhaps on health services, which are financed by both federal and provincial governments.

In studying the consequences of demographic trends, **dependency ratios** are sometimes used as rough measures of societal needs for social security benefits and medical, educational, or other facilities. These ratios compare the proportion presumed to be dependent (by nature of their age) with the proportion of the population presumed to be in the labour force (those between the ages of 18 and 64). In actual fact, we know that not all 18- to 64-year-olds are working for pay (especially women), and not all adolescents and seniors are financially dependent. Dependency ratios are usually used with other social and economic data, however, when setting priorities for social programs (Baker, 1988).

While the dependency ratio for children has been declining, the ratio for seniors has been rising. Although this suggests that the working-age or "productive" population will remain stable, it will eventually decline. Yet, if we use the more precise measure of the actual percentage of the population in the labour force, the rising numbers of women could increase the size of the productive population. In addition, they will increase the amount of money in contributory pensions plans such as the Canada Pension Plan.

In an attempt to improve the economic position of elderly people, the federal government has raised Canada Pension Plan contribution rates and both levels of government are encouraging employers to expand their work-related pension coverage. The federal government, however, still faces difficult political decisions when dealing with the rising costs of Old Age Security and the Guaranteed Income Supplement (GIS). Money to cover these benefits comes from income taxes, yet raising taxes is politically unpopular.

Pension plans are based on the idea that each generation will be supported by the one that follows. This means that when the baby boom generation retires in the 2020s or 2030s, their pensions will come from the pockets of the smaller "baby bust" generation born in the 1970s and 1980s. It has been suggested that by the year 2021, the cost of public pensions could increase at least three and a half times (McDaniel, 1986:69). But in the meantime, the working-age population is increasing slightly (mainly through more women entering the workforce) and decision makers should have time to bolster pension funds for the increase expected after 2020.

Major reforms in health services appear to be essential because of rising Medicare costs. Although Canada's public health care system is less expensive than the United States' private system, both to the individual and as a proportion of the Gross Domestic Product, expenditures will rise with the aging population unless changes are made (Heller et al., 1986). Some of these costs could be reduced with greater emphasis on preventive health care. In addition, community clinics could employ a variety of (lower paid) professionals to share health care with physicians. And palliative care units or hospices could accommodate dying patients and help them accept death without trying to prolong their life with sophisticated and expensive technology. Furthermore, home care services could postpone institutionalization for some people with chronic ailments or special needs.

The future elderly have had the benefits of public health insurance and preventive health care, but are they going to be healthier as they age? Canadians are now paying more attention to diet and the need for exercise than previous generations. Yet, at the same time, most people get less exercise in their daily lives with labour-saving devices, elevators, cars, and public transport. Rates of cigarette smoking rose to high levels in the 1970s, especially among young people, and have only recently declined. In fact, more teenage women smoke now than previously. Cancer rates and automobile accident rates remain high, and unknown problems could arise from environmental pollutants. Furthermore, medical technology is prolonging the life of people who formerly would have died, creating a larger population of people with special needs. Researchers have tried to evaluate the future impact of all these factors, but cannot agree whether the younger generation will be freer from disabling illnesses when they reach old age than the present generation of elderly.

Researchers are still arguing about whether the rise in life expectancies will be accompanied by improved health or whether we will also see an increase in disability among the growing numbers of seniors. While medical technology can prolong life, some have argued that there has been no comparable improvement in health in the later years. In fact, new diseases related to pollution or lifestyle now disable more people. Other researchers, however, point to the recent "revolution" in diet, increased emphasis on exercise, and improvements in living standards as indicators that the future elderly will probably be healthier and require less medical care and hospitalization. In the gerontological literature, this has been called the **compression of morbidity thesis** because it predicts that illness and disability in the future will be compressed into a shorter period of time at the end of people's lives. This thesis cannot really be tested, however, until the postwar generation begins to reach old age.

Recently, federal and provincial governments have begun to plan for the housing needs of a growing elderly population. They have created different housing options, including subsidies for home improvements for those with disabilities and the provision of home care services for those who need assistance but want to stay in their present homes. They have also provided subsidies for the construction of seniors' apartments, retirement condominiums, garden suites, home sharing, group homes, and adult foster care.

Some authors have suggested that the presence of an aging population in Canada will encourage intergenerational conflict between the young, who are competing for jobs and resources, and the older citizens, who are holding on to their jobs. Ultimately, however, the young and the middle-aged have a self-interest in improving pensions and benefits for the elderly. The real conflict will more likely break out between groups that have catered to the needs of or benefited from a youthful population and those whose interests lie with the elderly. Many of our social organizations, such as schools, which based their funding policies on large numbers of students, will fight to change the funding formulae when these are no longer to their advantage. Improved conditions for the elderly will eventually benefit all individuals in the community, but not necessarily all organizations.

SUGGESTED READINGS

Baker, Maureen. *Aging in Canadian Society: A Survey*. Scarborough: McGraw-Hill Ryerson, 1988.

Bonar, Rita and Michael J. MacLean. "Multicultural Issues in Old Age." *Multiculturalism*. VIII (2). 1985.

Burke, Mary Anne. "Implications of an Aging Society." *Canadian Social Trends*. 20. Spring 1991:6–8.

Chappell, Neena. "Aging and the Family." *Marriage and the Family in Canada Today*. Edited by G.N. Ramu. Scarborough: Prentice-Hall, 1989:185–206.

Chappell, Neena, Laurel A. Strain, and Audrey A. Blandford. *Aging and Health Care. A Social Perspective*. Toronto: Holt, Rinehart and Winston, 1986.

Chawla, Raj K. "Dependency Ratios." *Canadian Social Trends*. 20. Spring 1991:3–5.

Comfort, Alex. "Sexuality in Later Life." *Handbook of Mental Health and Aging*. Edited by J. Birren and R. Sloane. Englewood Cliffs, NJ: Prentice-Hall, 1980.

Connidis, Ingrid Arnet. *Family Ties and Aging*. Toronto: Butterworths, 1989.

Dail, Paula. "Prime-Time Television Portrayals of Older Adults in the Context of Family Life." *The Gerontologist*. 28 (5). October 1988:700–706.

Driedger, Leo and Neena Chappell. *Aging and Ethnicity*. Toronto: Butterworths, 1987.

Gauthier, Pierre. "Canada's Seniors." *Canadian Social Trends*. 22. Autumn 1991:16–20.

Gee, Ellen. M. and Meredith M. Kimball. *Women and Aging*. Toronto: Butterworths, 1987.

Gifford, C.G. *Canada's Fighting Seniors*. Toronto: James Lorimer and Company, 1990.

Gnaedinger, Nancy. *Elder Abuse: A Discussion Paper*. Ottawa: Health and Welfare Canada (For the National Clearinghouse on Family Violence), May 1989.

Lowe, Graham S. "Retirement Attitudes, Plans and Behaviour." *Perspectives on Labour and Income*. 3 (3). Autumn 1991:8–17.

Marshall, Victor W. (ed.). *Aging in Canada, Social Perspectives.* 2nd ed. Markham: Fitzhenry and Whiteside, 1987.

Martin Matthews, Anne. *Widowhood in Later Life.* Toronto: Butterworths, 1991.

McDonald, P. Lynn and Richard A. Wanner. *Retirement in Canada.* Toronto: Butterworths, 1990.

McDonald, P. Lynn, J.P. Hornick, G.B. Robertson, and J.E. Wallace. *Elder Abuse and Neglect in Canada.* Toronto: Butterworths, 1991.

McPherson, Barry D. *Aging as a Social Process.* 2nd ed. Toronto: Butterworths, 1990.

Meikeljohn, Phyllis et al. (eds.). "Being Old" (by Leah Cohen, 141–145) and "Intergenerational Connections" (by Joyce Maynard, 148–151), *Today's Family: A Critical Focus.* Don Mills: Collier Macmillan, 1991.

Methot, Suzanne. "Employment Patterns of Elderly Canadians." *Canadian Social Trends.* 7. Autumn 1987:7–11.

Naidoo, J.C. "The South Asian Experience of Aging." *Multiculturalism.* VIII (3). 1985:3–6.

Nett, Emily. "The Family and Aging." *Families: Changing Trends in Canada.* 2nd ed. Edited by Maureen Baker. Scarborough: McGraw-Hill Ryerson, 1990:241–271.

Novak, Mark. *Aging and Society. A Canadian Perspective.* Scarborough: Nelson, 1988.

Priest, Gordon E. "Living Arrangements of Canada's "Older Elderly" Population." *Canadian Social Trends.* Edited by Craig McKie and Keith Thompson. Toronto: Thompson Educational Publishing, 1990:183–187.

Schlesinger, Benjamin and Rachel A. Schlesinger. *Abuse of the Elderly: Issues and Annotated Bibliography.* Toronto: University of Toronto Press, 1988.

"Seniors With Disabilities." *Canadian Social Trends.* 20. Spring 1991.

Ujimoto, K. Victor. "The Ethnic Dimension of Aging in Canada." *Aging in Canada. Social Perspectives.* 2nd ed. Edited by Victor W. Marshall. Markham: Fitzhenry and Whiteside, 1987: 111–137.

ISSUES FOR DISCUSSION

1. Analyze the implications of the following: "Past generations needed to be prepared for the unexpected in life in a way that today's young people find difficult to understand."
2. Imagine that you are an older immigrant from Hong Kong, who came to Canada with your son and daughter-in-law. Although you expected to live with them, they have now told you that they have found a nice seniors' apartment for you. You cannot speak English very well. How would you live? How might you spend your time?
3. Develop a case study that demonstrates how the historical and cultural context shapes an individual's perception of old age and grandparenting.
4. Imagine that you are elderly and widowed. You are too disabled with arthritis to care for yourself. Your daughter has suggested that you come to live with her, her husband, and two children. However, you would have to share a room with one of your grandchildren. Another alternative is to go into the local nursing home, which has a reputation for low-quality care. What would you do? What reasons could you give for your choice?
5. Why are widowers more likely than widows to remarry?
6. If women continue to aspire to professional and managerial jobs, smoke and drink, and live a high-pressured life, will their life expectancies continue to surpass those of men? Explain the impact of this in the future.
7. Give examples of the portrayal of old age in television serials and advertising. Are these images accurate? Are they changing?
8. Compare and contrast the honeymoon stage of marriage and the retired couple, with respect to division of labour, communication, financial planning, and leisure time.
9. Describe what steps you would need to take at each stage of the family life cycle in order to ensure a satisfying retirement.
10. Compare and contrast the different theories of aging. Which theories do you think best explain the aging process and the differences between age groups?
11. How do you feel about discussing the sexuality of elderly people? Why do you think you feel this way?
12. Suppose that both your grandmothers are living. One suddenly decides to have a facelift, lose weight, and dye her grey hair in

order to look younger. The other grandmother says that this behaviour is silly and she should act her age. She is proud of her grey hair and feels that she has earned every wrinkle. Who do you think has the best argument? How would you respond?

13. Why do you think our society discourages "anticipatory socialization" for bereavement, even though doing so might alleviate some of the difficulties when a spouse dies?
14. How might the political power of seniors change in the future? What kind of social and legal changes might they demand?
15. What is the possible impact of current housing trends on family life and feelings of well-being for seniors?
16. Upon your death, how will you want to be remembered in your family's history?

FURTHER ACTIVITIES

1. Investigate how much money an unattached person and a married couple over 65 would receive in pension income. What other sources of income might they have? Is it possible to live on such a fixed income? What would you be able to afford and what would you have to do without?
2. Volunteer for a day in a seniors' recreation centre, a nursing home, an adult day care, or visit a hospice program. Through your observations and conversations with staff and residents, are the current needs of seniors being met by these organizations and services?
3. Watch in your local newspaper for announcements of 50th wedding anniversary celebrations. See if you can contact several couples and interview them about how their relationship has changed over the past 50 years and what they feel contributes to a successful marriage.
4. Interview two or three elderly widows and widowers about the transition to being widowed. What coping mechanisms proved effective for them? What advice would they give to others?
5. Interview a gerontologist or someone working with the elderly about policy issues relating to an aging society. Relate this to the political economy conceptual framework.

9 Trends in Canadian Families

INTRODUCTION

This final chapter will summarize some of the economic, legal, and social changes that have altered each stage of family life over the past century and draw some general conclusions about social trends and the future of family life in Canada.

Since the focus is on broad societal change, macro-level analysis will be used to identify and explain trends. Political economy and feminist theory have been especially prevalent in recent Canadian family research and are useful in describing and explaining how people's lives and interpersonal relations are influenced by factors outside family life.

So often in families studies courses, emphasis is placed on psychological variables, including feelings, attitudes, and interpersonal relationships. Although these processes are important, they take place within a social, cultural, political, and economic context. It is important to understand how our world has been shaped and how our personal decisions and interpersonal relations have been modified by economic, legal, and social changes in the larger society.

ECONOMIC CHANGES

This section will review the ways in which changes in the structure of the labour force or the nature of work have influenced family life. Changes in family size, the interdependence of members, authority structure, gender roles, and the division of labour within families will be discussed.

With the transformation from an agrarian to an industrial society in Europe and North America, families had to accommodate the work patterns of their earners. Farm families often lived at a subsistence level, growing their own food, making their clothing, and trading their surplus crops or animals for basic necessities or cash to purchase those products they could not grow or make. With industrialization, men and later poorer women and children began to work away from home, first in manufactories and later in factories (Gaffield, 1990). This separation of work and home weakened the father's authority in families because he was no longer present to supervise the children or become involved in household activities. Working away from the home also required new child care arrangements and a different daily schedule of meal preparation and domestic work. Increasingly, men became excluded from childrearing and concerns about household production, because most men were absent from the home for 10 to

Farm families often lived at a subsistence level, growing their own food, making their clothing, and trading their surplus crops or animals for basic necessities or cash.

National Archives of Canada/C30165

12 hours a day in order to earn a living.

The expansion of industry required more people to work in unskilled jobs. Employers preferred younger workers, who were perceived as quicker, more flexible and compliant, and more efficient on the new assembly lines. With widespread industrialization, the demand for skilled craftsmen gradually decreased, as goods could be mass produced at lower cost. Employers began to recruit more employees as their enterprises expanded, and people in need of work flocked to towns and cities searching for wage labour. Many domestic servants left their positions for factory jobs because they were paid higher wages, offered more time off, and enjoyed more personal autonomy. Children and young women were hired in the factories as well as younger men, but many older workers found themselves out of work.

When working-class wives and children went out to work, fewer goods and services were produced at home, and families were less able to get together for shared activities. While agrarian families were often units of production, the new urban families tended to become units of consumption. Yet, family members still pooled their wages and remained an economic unit. Furthermore, wives continued to produce many goods and services for family members within the home, while older children and the husband earned most of the income.

The problem of child care for working parents was temporarily addressed by taking children to the factories, where they worked alongside their parents. In agrarian communities, children had always worked as soon as they were able, as their labour was essential to the family enterprise. In the new industrial towns and cities, however, the employment of children soon became controversial, largely because of the dangers associated with factory work. In some cases, children of working parents were left in the care of other relatives or neighbours, or expected to fend for themselves while their parents worked. Increasingly, children and young people left on their own became involved in delinquency and petty crime.

In the early years of industrialization, employees worked long hours under difficult working conditions with no fringe benefits, such as paid vacations. Improvements to working conditions came with unionization, but also from the outcry about the potential impact of poor working conditions on the health and safety of children, youth, and women. Reformers were particularly concerned that heavy physical work in factories and mines, high levels of noise and dirt, and lack of sunlight would harm children's growth and development, as well as the health and potential fertility of women.

The potential decline of the birth rate and the destruction of family life became the focus of the movement to reform working conditions, but the emphasis was on women and children employees. Reformers successfully organized against employers hiring very young children and encouraged protective legislation for both women and older children to limit hours of work, restrict the amount of weight they could be asked to lift, provide proper washroom facilities, and improve safety and working conditions. Eventually, most of these laws were generalized to all workers regardless of their age or gender.

In the late nineteenth century, employers saw men as family "heads" or potential heads and paid them a "family wage" to enable them to support their present or future dependents. When women and children entered the paid labour force, their wages were lower because their incomes were perceived to be secondary. Prior to the 1920s, wives entered the labour force only if their husbands were

In the early years of industrialization, reformers were concerned about the impact of heavy physical work, high levels of noise and dirt, and lack of sunlight on working children's growth and development.

National Archives

unemployed or marginally employed because family wages were supposed to be enough to cover a man's dependants. However, many wives contributed to the family income by working at home for their neighbours, such as baby-sitting, taking in laundry, or dressmaking.

Until the 1920s, middle-class wives whose husbands could adequately support the entire family tended to remain at home to supervise servants and engage in hobbies or charitable activities rather than working for pay. Increasingly, husbands became the major breadwinner in most families and middle-class wives became financially dependent. For middle- and upper-class wives, work outside the home was seen as demeaning and taking jobs away from men (Wilson, 1991).

As richer women became more removed from the world of work, an ideology supporting the "natural" domesticity of women was perpetuated. Wives of wealthier men were encouraged to stay at home and engage in homemaking, conspicuous consumption, and leisure activities. Husbands tried to protect their wives from the "cold" world of economics and politics, for at that time, having a homemaker wife indicated that the husband was a good breadwinner (Zaretsky, 1976). After World War I, men's breadwinning role and women's role as wife, mother, and homemaker were strongly emphasized as separate but equal.

As the demands of the labour force began to change and become more technical, and as concern grew about delinquent youth, literacy and school attendance became more important to employers and policy-makers. Children and youth were encouraged to acquire more formal education and stay in school longer. Females as well as males were now expected to acquire an education, but women were still not expected to be self-supporting after marriage. Instead, adolescent women were expected to prepare themselves for a profession or occupation. Most young women worked briefly before marriage, but needed some education and training in case they did not marry and needed to be self-supporting. In addition, they might need to work for pay if their husbands became disabled or died young and left them to support themselves and their children.

During the 1920s and 1930s, great improvements were made in health, nutrition, and sanitation. Infant and maternal death rates began to fall, and health care professionals started to advise mothers on how to care for and raise their infants and children. In addition, some people started to advocate the use of birth control, especially those concerned about the high birth rates in poor urban ghettos, and those involved in the **eugenics movement**. Urbanized lifestyles and higher education tended to encourage families to produce fewer children. As the cost of labour rose, fewer middle-class families could afford live-in servants and large houses, and households gradually became smaller units.

During the 1930s Depression, it became apparent that many people could no longer rely on their own initiative, hard work, and savings to support their families. It became increasingly evident to policy-makers and the general public that unemployment and poverty were not necessarily the result of lack of individual initiative, but were related to national or world-wide economic conditions, employer's practices, unfortunate weather, or even bad luck. Reformers pressed for government insurance for unemployment, illness, retirement, disability, and for a family allowance to help parents with

During the 1930s Depression, it became evident that poverty and unemployment were not necessarily the result of lack of individual initiative.

National Archives of Canada, Negative no. PA 108300

childrearing expenses. Several new federal government programs were introduced in Canada in the 1940s, such as Unemployment Insurance in 1941 and Family Allowances in 1945.

After the Second World War, the government rewarded returning war veterans for their service by assisting some with tuition fees, land grants, money to pay off mortgages, and priority for jobs. Although women's contribution to the war effort during both wars showed that women were capable of more than domesticity, many couples wanted to focus on making a home, having children, and raising a family after the lonely and dangerous war years. Contrary to popular opinion, there were relatively few married women in the labour force during World War II. For example, the proportion of married women in the official labour force was only about 4 percent in 1941 (Baker, 1990d:8), although many more wives contributed to the household finances in informal ways.

Throughout the prosperous 1950s, many North American families sought less expensive and new homes in the suburbs, often far away from the workplace and cultural or entertainment activities. As immigration and birth rates increased, conditions in inner cities became more crowded and expensive. The suburbs offered inexpensive land and homes, and were seen as good places to raise children, with clean air, less traffic, lower crime rates, larger "ranch-style" houses, and yards in which children could play. Many North American developers converted thousands of hectares of productive farmland near cities into new subdivisions to meet housing demands (Clark, 1966).

The one-income family with complementary roles was most prevalent during the 1950s, although not all families lived this way. Many couples had a strict division of labour in which the wife cared for the home and children, and the husband earned the money, disciplined the children, drove and cared for the car, and performed outdoor work around the house. But this division of labour left men excluded from the daily lives of their children and unknowledgeable about household management. Similarly, wives sometimes remained uninformed about money matters, car repairs, and the labour force and were often left alone all day without transportation or adult company.

As the service sector of the labour force began to expand in the 1960s, new jobs were created. Education systems throughout North America expanded to include more colleges and universities, drawing on students from a wider variety of economic and cultural backgrounds. As the economy grew, people's expectations about how they wanted to live increased. Inflation rates rose, and more couples looked for ways to raise their income.

The "family wage" was no longer acceptable to human rights advocates, who argued that employees should be paid for their work, rather than on the basis of their marital status, ethnicity, race, or gender. Women whose children were in school began to enter the labour force, initially as a reserve labour force during busy times or as part-time workers. Without child care facilities, however, and with a strong public sentiment that women should care for their own children at home, mothers with young children were discouraged from working outside the home.

During the 1970s and 1980s wages declined relative to the cost of living and inflation continued to soar. More middle-class women, including married women with young children, entered the labour force. Numerous factors encouraged women out of the home and into the workforce, including the rising cost of living, expectations of higher living standards, the expansion of the service sector, the need for new employees, the development of part-time work, and the relative decline in wages. But women were also influenced by the need to make a contribution to society, new ideas about women's role, and the desire to use their education.

The employment of married women has been viewed as a major impetus to social change, because it has encouraged nonfamily child care services, the development of household cleaning companies and fast food outlets, and advancements in household technology. Working outside the home and contributing to the family income has changed power relations within marriage and contributed to an egalitarian family. It may have also contributed to rising divorce rates and a less permanent family unit because it is more feasible to consider divorce if both partners can be self-supporting (Huber and Spitze, 1980).

The development of part-time work and educational upgrading has also influenced teenagers and youth and their relative position in families. Educational requirements for many occupations have been inflated recently and many entry-level positions have been eliminated. Consequently, it is now more difficult to find a permanent job before graduation and to work one's way up in an organization as people did before World War II. This means that today's young people need to complete secondary school, college, or university to find the same kind of job that their parents or grandparents could get with some high school education. Consequently, young people remain dependent longer on their families than a generation ago, although they are eventually likely to receive more formal education than their parents. While living at home, however, most young people work part-time and have a higher disposable income than their parents' generation.

Although adolescents may be physically mature and have more formal schooling than their parents, they generally have not acquired the employment and social skills to survive on their own without parental financial assistance. This prolonged dependency places additional stresses on students' parents, who may also be providing some assistance to their elderly parents. These stresses could lead to considerable conflict about values, lifestyle, choice of friends, and house rules.

With further advances in industrialization and more seniors in the population, mandatory retirement was initiated to create more jobs for young people by removing older workers considered to be less efficient and less educated. Governments and a few employers offered pension plans, but until public and private pension plans became well developed and widespread in the 1980s, seniors often found themselves living on diminishing savings, small public pensions, or employer pensions, which were not indexed to the rising cost of living.

As the retirement incomes of elderly Canadians rose through the 1980s, life expectancies and geographic mobility increased, and as more apartment units were constructed, more older people began to live independently from family members. Although cultural values still encourage multigenerational families within some segments of the population, most older couples and individuals prefer to live independently from their children if their finances allow it.

The recession of the early 1990s once again led to high rates of unemployment and business and personal bankruptcy, placing financial stress on families and individuals. Lack of jobs and the competitive labour market have kept young people in school and dependent on their parents longer. The recession may also have discouraged unhappy couples from separating, because of the financial difficulties of dividing wages and property and trying to live on one income. Financial hard times have also pushed more wives and adolescents into the labour force. Increasingly, families have two or more incomes and it is not possible for most to live on the earnings of only one member without reducing their standard of living or going into debt. This severely disadvantages one-parent households, and enlarges the poverty gap between families with two earners and those with only one.

Further changes in the labour force, such as working at home with computers, modems, and fax machines, will continue to alter personal relationships and family life. This may modify the design of our homes, requiring home offices, change child care needs, and lead to new ways of maintaining social contact. Furthermore, if more people become self-employed, financial security in old age may be reduced by the elimination of some employment-related fringe benefits, such as pension plan membership.

Although all these changes may derive from labour force restructuring, they affect our personal decisions, our relationships, and our family lives.

LEGAL CHANGES IN FAMILIES

Economic change accompanying industrialization was the major impetus for legal changes in European and North American families, as will be shown in this section. The family in Europe and North America was legally patriarchal, although some Native societies in North America, such as Huron and Ojibwa, had families based on matrilineal descent and were governed by a different legal system (Castellano, 1991). Patriarchal means that the father and husband was legally responsible for his wife and children and spoke on their behalf to the community and government. Furthermore, husbands voted on behalf of their wives and became guardians of their wives' property and earnings. Fathers were legal guardians of children in families; they had the right to discipline them with corporal punishment and to make decisions about their education and training.

Because most families in Europe and North America were patriarchal until the twentieth century, many of the legal changes relate to women and children gaining rights that men already had. As children's rights are in the very initial stages, much of this discussion will focus on changes in the status of married women from the 1880s to the present.

Although improvements in children's rights are still being advocated, many legal changes in the status of women and some for children arose when large numbers of women and children entered the labour force to perform jobs formerly done by men. When women and children worked alongside men in the factories, reformers became concerned about family health and pressed for legislation improving working conditions. Protective legislation and the abolition of child labour resulted from these initiatives, and as mentioned earlier, some of these laws about working conditions and the length of the working day were eventually generalized to all workers. In order to compete in the job market with men, women needed and demanded formal schooling, including the right to study in professional colleges and universities. Furthermore, as wage earners, they felt that they should have equal pay, the right to vote, and the opportunity to participate in policy-making.

From the late 1800s to well into the twentieth century, women gradually gained more political rights, but only after many years of speeches, protests, and legal battles. In Britain, the Married Women's Property Act of 1870 was seen as a milestone for women's rights because it enabled married women to control their earnings, their bank accounts, and their property. Of course, only wealthier women had any property to control. Similar laws were introduced into most Canadian provinces within the next few years.

From 1910 to 1923, provincial legislation changed laws relating to child custody. These laws allowed mothers as well as fathers to have legal custody of their children both during marriage and after separation. This meant that mothers had the right to make decisions about their children's welfare, education, and medical treatment. In 1918, women gained the right to vote in federal elections although they could not vote in Quebec provincial elections until as late as 1940. These legal changes were precipitated by the participation of women in the labour force, from the determined efforts of the Women's Rights Movement, and by ideologies of equality emanating from other political movements.

While family celebrations and disputes were formerly the realm of religion, the state or governments and their agencies gradually gained more control. Marriage was traditionally a religious contract, but gradually it became a legal contract that could be broken through divorce proceedings. Laws were created that prevented people from marrying until they reach the chronological age, which the government decided represented maturity. In 1925, the grounds for divorce became the same for both men and women, and in 1968 and again in 1985, the grounds for divorce were liberalized. Property had to be divided according to certain rules, and one parent was usually granted custody of the children. New laws stipulated that marital partners could neither physically nor sexually abuse each other.

Compulsory education laws were also developed from the late nineteenth century until about 1920, which stated that children had to be sent to school until a certain age, usually 16. The lobby for compulsory education came from reformers interested in the education of children, but also those concerned about the potential effects of "idle youth" on social unrest. Employers also wanted to ensure that they had a literate labour force, whose members were disciplined, punctual, and eager to learn new skills.

In the early years of this century, child protection agencies were established throughout Canada, and legislation was introduced in each province. Most of the legal changes for children, however, have been made since 1960 (Bala, 1991:3). Since then child abuse registers have been established and mandatory reporting laws enacted. Laws have been changed to give children born to unmarried parents, formerly called illegitimate, equal rights to children born within marriage.

The Family Law Reform Commission initiated major changes in family law from the late 1970s throughout the 1980s. One change was to make men and women equally responsible for the support and care of their children, both within marriage and after separation. Although the custody of most children is still awarded to mothers upon divorce, an increasing number of joint custody awards are being made. In addition, a small but increasing percentage of fathers receive sole custody. Legislation has also been changed in most provinces, notably Manitoba and Ontario, to enforce child support awards by the court when the noncustodial parent defaults on payments.

Since the 1960s, the development of human rights legislation has made it possible to challenge employers and landlords who are allegedly discriminating on the basis of race, ethnicity, cultural background, religious belief, or marital status, but these laws have not eliminated prejudice and discrimination. However, laws in some jurisdictions still do not protect people from discrimination based on sexual preference. The federal employment equity law has identified four target groups—women, Native persons, visible minorities, and disabled persons—as vulnerable to employment discrimination. Yet, the law was written in such a way that reporting on the representation of these target groups in the labour force is mandatory, but enforcement is difficult.

The separation of marriage and reproduction has presented a number of legal problems that have not been fully resolved in Canada. The rights of biological and legal fathers, for example, have been complicated by increasing rates of common-law marriages, artificial insemination, surrogate motherhood, and motherhood outside an established relationship.

Increasing numbers of single mothers have encouraged social assistance departments to define carefully their eligibility rules for benefits. Assumptions about men's role in supporting women with whom they live have led to controversies and new rules about

SURROGATE MOTHERHOOD

A branch that has grown out of adoption law in the absence of any statutory law to address the issue is surrogate motherhood, although one can trace its roots to Old Testament times. The arrangement basically involves a woman agreeing to be artificially inseminated by a man who is not her husband and then, at the child's birth, relinquishing all parental rights and responsibilities to him and his wife through adoption. The problem is that most surrogate parenting arrangements involve financial compensation of the woman who has agreed to bear the child, and agreements that involve payment of a fee in exchange for a consent to an adoption or a placement for adoption are illegal under provincial adoption legislation. This strict control of payments made in connection with an adoption creates a legal barrier for surrogate parenting contracts in Canada, since such arrangements involve an application for adoption by the wife of the biological father with the consent of the biological mother.

Surrogate motherhood is morally and politically controversial. In 1985 the Ontario Law Reform Commission issued a report proposing that the government legalize the practice, but closely regulate it, with the courts required to scrutinize any agreements before they are given legal effect to ensure that they are not unconscionable[1]. The Ontario government has failed to act on this report, and in the fall of 1989 the federal government established a Royal Commission to study a range of issues related to developments in reproductive technology, including surrogate motherhood.

American states have had a variety of responses to surrogate motherhood. Some have declared the practice illegal, either as a result of legislation or judicial decision. In a few states, however, the practice is legal, and it is apparent that some Canadians are going to the United States to execute and perform surrogate motherhood contracts under the supervision of American lawyers.

[1] There is a growing body of literature on surrogate motherhood. See, e.g., Ontario Law Reform Commission, *Report on Human Artificial Reproduction and Related Matters* (Toronto: 1985); and E. Faulkner, "The Case of Baby M." (1989) 3 C.J.W.L. 239.

Katarynych, Heather L. "Adoption." *Canadian Child Welfare Law*. Edited by Nicholas Bala, Joseph Hornick, and Robin Vogl. Toronto: Thompson Educational Publishing, Inc. 1991:168–169.

provincial social assistance. The "man in the house" rule, or the assumption that all men who live with women are household breadwinners for these women and their children, has led to a court challenge based on the 1982 Canadian Charter of Rights and Freedoms. This challenge prompted the Ontario government to change its social assistance regulations in September 1986.

The Charter has been used to challenge a number of issues relating to family law (Bala et al., 1991:5). One example includes parents' right to choose the location and person assisting the birth of their child, including whether this person is a midwife or a physician. Parents of children with special needs have used the Charter to argue that these children have the right to be integrated into the public school system, rather than being forced to attend special schools. The Charter has also been used successfully to argue that a person has the right to decide not to continue medical treatment if there is no hope of recovery.

Whether or not an unmarried father has the right to prevent his girlfriend from having an abortion or from allowing his child to be placed for adoption has also been argued under the Charter of Rights and Freedoms. In addition, the Charter has been successfully used to argue that a biological father has a right to parental leave when his child is born because this leave was already granted to adoptive fathers. Gay couples are using the equality rights clause of the Charter of Rights to argue that the law should recognize same-sex marriages.

Gotell (1990) has argued that contrary to expectations, the Charter has not really assisted women, cultural minorities, or persons with special needs to expand their rights; it has been used more successfully by groups with strong financial backing to argue that the provision of special services is not required. In 1992, the federal government announced that The Court Challenges Program, which offered financial assistance to groups wishing to challenge laws under The Charter of Rights and Freedoms, would no longer be funded by the federal government. This would mean that challenges to The Charter would be less possible for individuals and groups without considerable money.

SOCIAL CHANGES IN FAMILIES

Demographic changes, such as declining birth rates, can also be attributed to economic factors such as the declining value of children's labour and the high cost of rearing children in an urban environment. But declining birth rates also have social causes. The decline in infant mortality from improved sanitation, nutrition, living standards, health care, and inoculations encouraged people to have smaller families because they knew that more babies would live to adulthood. The increased social acceptability of contraception and legalized abortion also led to lower birth rates, even though some religious organizations continue to object to any mechanical method of preventing conception.

Widespread use of birth control has encouraged more liberal

attitudes toward sexuality, allowed women to pursue advanced education and careers without interruptions for childbirth, and made possible cohabitation without children. Whether or not more people will choose to have childless marriages in the future is difficult to say, but voluntary childlessness, or desire for a childfree lifestyle, appears to be increasing.

Combining work and family life is becoming more difficult because although more mothers work in the labour force, governments and employers have not responded by creating leave for family responsibilities, extending parental leave, or providing affordable child care services. Although some husbands and older children share child care and other domestic responsibilities, employed mothers tend to take responsibility for and perform most of the household tasks formerly done by full-time homemakers (MacBride-King, 1990). One way in which couples, especially women, have responded to the difficulties of combining work and family life is by having fewer children.

Couples have also produced fewer children because they believe that children need quality care which they themselves cannot provide.

One way in which couples have responded to the difficulties of combining work and family life is by having fewer children.

The Chu family

Theoretically, fewer children enable more family resources (such as time, energy, and money) to be spent on each child, thereby improving the quality of the child's life as well as the parents'. Yet, most parents are in the labour force either part-time or full-time. The children are often at the sitter's, at school, out with their peers, or at work. Some conservative critics such as R.E.A.L. Women of Canada have argued that families are not spending enough time together in order to promote healthy child development and family cohesion. Most social scientists, however, have argued that it is the quality of time spent with children rather than the quantity that is important. Furthermore, low family income appears to be more detrimental to the welfare of children than nonfamily care (Weitzman, 1985; Ambert, 1990; Armstrong, 1990). In addition, there is no evidence that parents are more neglectful of their children now than in earlier decades.

Most parents always worked even though it was not always in the formal labour force. When mothers stayed home, they were often busy with housework or the care of younger children and did not spend all their time playing with or even watching all their children. When families were larger, each individual child seldom received much time and attention from mothers or fathers, but older children were often available for child care. However, nonfamily child care, as well as the influence of television, peer groups, schools, and adolescents' employers, may decrease parental influence over the values and behaviour of their children and adolescents.

With so much publicity given to family violence, custody disputes, and contested property settlements, we may be less likely to think of marriage as romantic, as we did in the 1950s. If we are considering getting married or divorced, and use the cost-benefit analysis of social exchange theory, we might ask what can marriage provide that is not available to me as a single person? Or why should I stay in a marriage that is not personally satisfying if I can support myself and find intimate relationships outside marriage?

With more emphasis on individualism and independence, most people feel less bound by duty to tolerate social pressure to marry a particular person or to be content with an unhappy marriage. With more opportunities for sexual gratification outside of marriage or to cohabit than in the 1950s, people are now more likely to get married because they really want to rather than through social pressure. For the same reasons, they can separate from their spouse or obtain a divorce much more easily than in the 1950s. This implies that marriage is becoming more of a voluntary institution.

Yet, in recent years with high unemployment and rising costs of accommodation, some people are entering marriage for openly pragmatic reasons. This is nothing new, however, as widows and widowers sometimes looked to remarriage as providing a new parent for their children and an additional income. In addition, many ethnic groups formerly resorted to mail-order brides or advertising in the ethnic press for marriage partners when their numbers were small in North America. This pragmatic approach to marriage may be more typical of divorced or widowed people, especially young single parents, who cannot adequately support their children on their own incomes or care for them alone, as well as cultural groups which have always preferred arranged marriages.

At the same time, a small but growing minority of women are bearing and raising children outside of marriage. The separation of marriage and childbearing has been enhanced by new reproductive technologies, anti-family ideologies, and more liberal social and sexual attitudes. While women have always produced illegitimate children, single women from wealthier families were better able to conceal their pregnancies by travelling abroad for costly abortions or by quickly marrying. Prior to the 1970s, children from middle-class single mothers were usually given up for adoption and raised by legally married couples rather than by the biological mother. Middle-class women could not raise their illegitimate children alone and still be considered "respectable."

Now, a small number of women are choosing to get pregnant outside of marriage and raise the children alone. Although being a single parent is still financially and emotionally difficult, women's ability to be self-supporting in the labour force and improved social assistance programs have made this option possible. The separation of marriage and childbearing will probably continue because social attitudes have become more liberal and legitimacy laws have changed.

Although the 1960s to the 1970s was labelled "the sexual revolution," some sexual attitudes and practices appear to be more conservative since the 1980s. One reason for this conservative approach is the rise in sexually transmitted diseases such as herpes and AIDS. Sexual and lifestyle experimentation of the 1960s and 1970s appears to have diminished as many people restrict the number of sexual partners and insist on monogamous relationships for fear of contracting sexually transmitted diseases. In addition, with fewer jobs and temporary positions, employees may be forced to present a more conservative personal demeanour in order to find or keep their jobs. Appearing too radical in one's personal life may now interfere with one's occupational life or economic survival.

Despite some restrictions in sexual behaviour, many couples now engage in sex before marriage, and an increasing percentage live together before or outside legal marriage (Turcotte, 1990). This trend is most prevalent among people in their twenties or thirties, but is spreading to older couples as well. Increasingly, the social and legal distinction between being legally married and cohabiting is becoming blurred.

With cutbacks in social programs in some provinces and fears of rising costs in others, expectations are being placed on families and the community to care for their unemployed, disabled, and elderly. The aging population and policies of de-institutionalization have led to the development of home care programs, which assume that someone is at home to provide care. This someone is usually the wife or daughter (Connidis, 1989a; Baines, Evans, and Neysmith, 1991). Furthermore, policies of de-institutionalization imply that community facilities and services will take the place of professionals in acute care or chronic care hospitals or nursing homes. In many cases, family members are expected to take over, yet increasingly, they cannot because of work commitments. Community care programs are not always available to replace institutional care because of financial constraints, yet policies of de-institutionalization continue.

Although the rationale for recent changes in family law has been to make the family a more egalitarian institution, critics have argued that the end results have sometimes impoverished wives and children (Morton, 1988). Part of the problem is that many family policies are based on erroneous models of family life that either assume that husbands are the only breadwinners, or suggest that women should be capable of supporting themselves and their children (Baker, 1990c). In actual fact, labour market practices and domestic responsibilities prevent women from earning equal wages to men, despite employment equity laws. Especially as single parents, women often cannot support themselves and their children without assistance from former husbands or governments.

From the social exchange or political economy perspective, the traditional division of labour, with father as breadwinner and mother as homemaker or even secondary worker, has allowed men to devote more time to their occupations and to accrue more assets than their wives. Since many judges have not yet recognized that much of the unpaid labour traditionally done by wives and mothers contributes to men's financial assets, they have not always placed a monetary value on homemaker's contributions to family assets (Morton, 1988).

At the same time, judges have not always seen men as potential fathers and caregivers. Although few men apply for custody after divorce, an increasing number are applying for and receiving custody. At the same time, there has been a trend toward shared parenting, especially among more educated couples, as well as legal decisions about joint custody. Both divorced husbands and single fathers are demanding that the courts give them more say in legal decisions about their children when couples cannot agree. The Fathers' Rights Movement has encouraged fathers to be more assertive about exercising their rights as legal custodians and caregivers, and this will probably increase in the future.

Marriage is no longer viewed as permanent by many young people, especially those whose parents have divorced (Baker, 1985). Legal divorce and single parenting are becoming more prevalent and more socially acceptable. Yet, because of the financial difficulties of single parenting, the continued popularity of marriage, and rising life expectancies, remarriage or at least recoupling will continue to rise. Serial monogamy, or one marriage partner at a time but several over a lifetime, is becoming more prevalent in Canada, as it has been in the United States for over a decade. Figures 9.1 and 9.2 show the changes in the number of common-law unions, lone-parent families, one-person households, and husband-wife families from 1981 to 1986.

While most people still maintain close contact with their kin, families have a weaker influence over the daily actions of their

Figure 9.1 **Percentage Increases in the Number of Families and One-Person Households, 1981–1986**

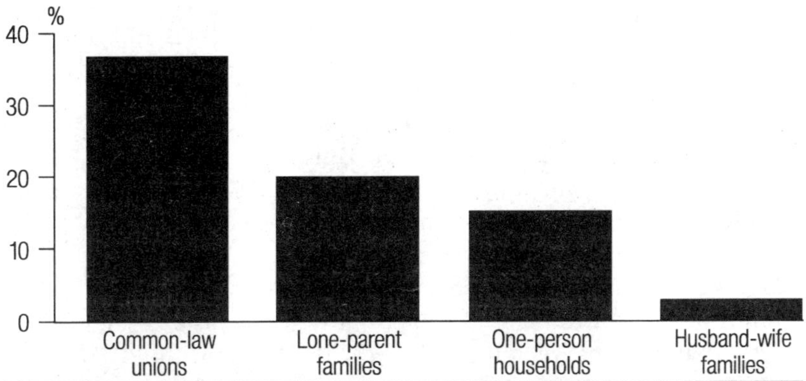

Source: Statistics Canada, Census of Canada. Reproduced with the permission of the Minister of Supply and Services Canada, 1992.

Figure 9.2 **Average Family Size and Average Number of Children at Home, 1961 and 1986**

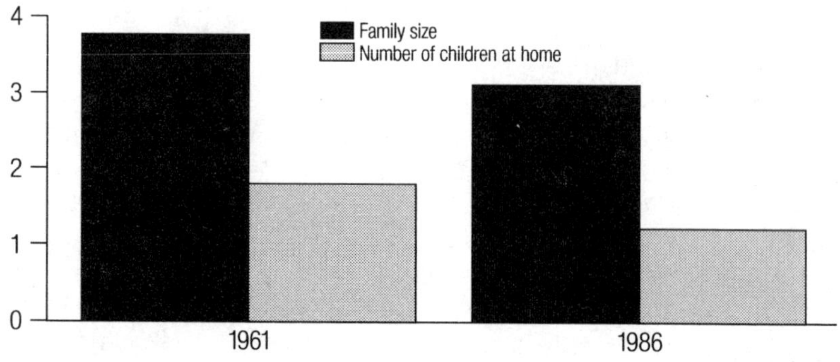

Source: Statistics Canada, Census of Canada. Reproduced with the permission of the Minister of Supply and Services Canada, 1992.

members than a few generations ago. This has been furthered by children spending hours in front of the television set, teenagers working outside the home, and young people staying in school longer and obtaining more formal education than their parents. In addition, people are mobile geographically and more likely to move far away from family and former friends. From a structural-functional perspective, we could argue that through travel, higher education, the media, and our jobs, we are all presented with norms and values that are likely to differ from those of our parents.

Despite all the influences and changes noted above, marriage and childbearing remain popular, and families are now united more through affection than through necessity and duty. More couples live together without marriage, and a slightly higher percentage of couples plan to remain permanently childfree. But most common-law couples eventually marry, and the majority of married couples eventually decide to reproduce, although more are now delaying childbearing. After divorce, over two-thirds of divorced people remarry, which implies that family living remains the major choice of Canadians. It cannot be argued though, as structural functionalists argued in the 1970s, that families are dying. While the myth of "the family" may be dying, there are now more acceptable variations in lifestyle and family living.

CONCLUSIONS

In this book, the family life cycle approach has been used to present historical and cross-cultural material about each stage and examine some of the well-researched and controversial social issues affecting each stage. At the same time, however, it is important to remember that not all individuals pass through each of these stages. Neither do marital partners necessarily experience these stages at the same time.

The life-cycle approach implies that all people share similar experiences in marrying, raising children, having the children leave home, retiring, and growing old. Even among those who pass through all the stages noted, there are differences in their experiences. The importance of gender differences, socio-economic variations, and cultural differences in how individuals experience the various stages of family life are also emphasized.

Husbands and wives do not always form a unit in terms of family experiences, attitudes, and goals. Men and women often experience both the single life and marriage differently (Eichler, 1988). These variations can be attributed in part to gender role socialization leading to different ways of thinking, feeling, and seeing the world. Some of these differences might also be attributed to physiological differences in hormone levels or reproductive capacities, but what appears to be more important is how these physiological differences are culturally defined and magnified.

Men and women experience different interpersonal relations, acquire different types and levels of education, job opportunities, earning power, parental and caregiving roles, retirement benefits, and poverty rates. Their experience outside the family has a strong impact upon the way they see themselves, the kinds of relationships they are willing to engage in, and their levels of marital satisfaction.

The early experiences of children are very much influenced by the way their parents interact with each other as well as with them. Furthermore, the education, occupation, and economic status of parents—or their social class—certainly influences children's opportunities, their likelihood of illness or accident, their experiences of parenting, and the entire family's lifestyle. In addition, social class background influences the amount of privacy as well as the possessions that family members are able to buy, their experiences in the workforce, sometimes their life satisfaction, their retirement experiences, and even their life expectancies.

It has also been emphasized throughout this book that all ethnic and cultural groups do not necessarily share the same life or family experiences. Different cultural values are placed on the desirability and nature of independence from parents, the timing of marriage and pregnancy, living arrangements, preferred family size, child care arrangements, marital roles, and respect for elders. In addition to values, the lives of some cultural groups may differ because of racism, discrimination, and poverty. They may be forced to accept jobs not wanted by others, to work in places of employment requiring shift work, or to experience periodic unemployment. Although some immigrants and cultural groups may integrate enough to find employment and be accepted by their fellow workers, they may continue their traditional family values and practices within the privacy of their own homes. Others do not integrate well, either through choice or lack of opportunity. Those most likely to maintain different cultural patterns in their families are recent immigrants from countries with a very different cultural background, those who do not speak or understand either of the dominant languages, those who live in remote areas, and those who prefer to live according to traditional customs.

Because of these variations by gender, social class, and cultural background, it is difficult to accurately generalize about the family. Although all ethnic and cultural minorities share some form of courtship, marriage ceremonies, economic co-operation, childrearing practices, child-launching, and norms about aging, there are many variations in family behaviour. While there are patterns in family behaviour, there are also differences. For this reason, the term families rather than the family has been used throughout this book to express the variety of family forms and practices in Canada today.

SUGGESTED READINGS

Armstrong, Pat and Hugh Armstrong. "The Conflicting Demands of 'Work' and 'Home'." *Family Matters. Sociology and Contemporary Canadian Families.* Edited by K. Anderson et al. Scarborough: Nelson, 1988:113–140.

Baker, Maureen. "The Future of Family Life." *Families: Changing Trends in Canada.* 2nd ed. Edited by Maureen Baker. Scarborough: McGraw-Hill Ryerson, 1990:330–345.

Burke, Mary Anne. "Families: Diversity the New Norm." *Canadian Social Trends.* 2. Summer 1986:6–10.

Devereaux, Mary Sue. "Changes in Living Arrangements." *Canadian Social Trends*. Edited by Craig McKie and Keith Thompson. Toronto: Thompson Educational Publishing, 1990:135–137.

Eichler, Margrit. "Family Change and Social Policy." *Family Matters. Sociology and Contemporary Canadian Families*. Edited by K. Anderson et al. Scarborough: Nelson, 1988:63–86.

Gaffield, Chad. "The Social and Economic Origins of Contemporary Families." *Families: Changing Trends in Canada*. 2nd ed. Edited by Maureen Baker. Scarborough: McGraw-Hill Ryerson, 1990:23–40.

Luxton, Meg. "Thinking About the Future." *Family Matters. Sociology and Contemporary Canadian Families*. Edited by K. Anderson et al. Scarborough: Nelson, 1988:237–257.

McKie, Craig and Keith Thompson (eds.). *Canadian Social Trends*. Toronto: Thompson Educational Publishing, 1990.

Nett, Emily M. *Canadian Families: Past and Present*. Toronto: Butterworths, 1988.

Whitehurst, Robert. "Alternative Life Styles: Two Decades of Change." *Marriage and the Family in Canada Today*. Edited by G.N. Ramu. Scarborough: Prentice-Hall, 1989:253–270.

ISSUES FOR DISCUSSION

1. Is a complementary division of labour more efficient and effective than shared roles in dual-income families? Discuss the pros and cons of each type of family structure.
2. From your readings, do family members still maintain contact with their kin? Has there been a change in such contact over the past 50 years? Will this trend continue?
3. Should couples planning to marry prepare a legal contract with each other? What are the advantages and disadvantages of such contracts?
4. Is marriage as an institution likely to survive in the future? Justify your answer.
5. What recurring patterns of behaviour can you see in your own family that were present in either set of your grandparents' families? If you cannot remember your grandparents, ask your parents for information.

6. Which theoretical framework best explains:
   a. the rise of children's rights;
   b. the rise of father's rights;
   c. the rise of women's rights?

   State your reasons.
7. If you could redesign family life, what kind of arrangement do you think would be more satisfying to most men, women, and children, as well as to governments?
8. Use one or more of the conceptual frameworks in the text to predict what family life will be like in the year 2051.

FURTHER ACTIVITIES

1. With their permission, interview an elderly woman and an elderly man and prepare written biographies for each of them. Include their explanations of why they made crucial decisions in their lives and their assessment of their life experiences. Without identifying these people, read the biographies in class and see if you can find any patterns in the explanations.
2. Interview someone who is living in one of the following arrangements: common-law, divorced and remarried, or a sole parent with dependent children. Using one of the conceptual frameworks in the text, discuss trends in the living arrangement you chose and make projections for the future.
3. Select a number of family photographs either from your own or a friend's family. What do they tell you about the family's values? Prepare a short essay on this, and discuss what values you would like to pass on to your children, if you have any in the future.

APPENDIX

Careers Related to Family Issues

It is difficult to find a career in any subject area without a specialized college or university degree. Family studies at the secondary school level provides students with a valuable background for many post-secondary courses in the social sciences, such as sociology, social work, home economics, family studies, and social psychology. In Canadian colleges and universities, there are many courses that deal with the issues discussed in this book. Students at the secondary level can research careers related to family studies through the guidance departments in their schools.

To work directly with families, it is usually necessary to obtain a professional diploma or degree in an area such as early childhood development, family life education, family studies, home economics, or social work. To work as a social work supervisor, a historian, sociologist, or psychologist, further education is needed after a bachelor's degree.

Most policy-related positions dealing with family issues would require a master's degree in sociology, social work, social administration, or social welfare. Government departments, parliamentary research services, and research departments of large voluntary organizations hire people with degrees in these areas to work on issues related to child benefits, child welfare policies, marriage and divorce, child support, and policies for an aging society.

In order to teach family studies at the high school level, it is necessary to acquire a bachelor's degree in family studies, sociology, home economics, history, or early childhood education, in addition to an education degree. To teach at the college or university level, a doctorate is now required to obtain a full-time permanent position.

Family studies can provide the understanding of human relationships necessary to develop any career that involves working with people, whether it be teaching, retail sales, law, medicine, human relations, nursing, psychology, or child care. A knowledge of changing family structures and relations is a valuable part of a general education.

GLOSSARY

Activity Theory A theory that suggests that as people lose or give up social roles or activities, they need to replace them with others to promote "successful" aging.
Adolescence The period between childhood and adulthood.
Adolescent Subculture Values and behavioural patterns shared by teenagers but not necessarily by other age groups.
Age Segregation The separation of people on the basis of chronological age.
Agism Discrimination based on chronological age; negative or misleading attitudes about elderly people.
Anticipatory Socialization Preparing for a future role by watching someone in the role and anticipating expected behaviour in advance.
Arranged Marriage A marriage in which the bride or groom is chosen by relatives.
Artificial Insemination Starting a new life through artificial means. Sperm is obtained from the husband or donor and placed in the vagina with a syringe.

Banns A spoken or published announcement in a church of an intended marriage.
Behaviour All the responses made by an organism in any situation.
Best Interests of the Child The idea that all legal decisions made on behalf of the child, such as removal from the parental home or custody decisions, must be carried out only if they are considered best for the child (rather than for the parents).
Betrothal A promise to marry that involves the exchange of money or a verbal or written contract.
Bilateral Descent Descent or lineage is traced through both the families of the bride and groom.
Birth Cohort All people born in the same year or between the same years, within a given jurisdiction.
Birth Rate (crude) The number of live births per 1000 population in a given year.
Blended Family A remarriage that brings two sets of children into the same household. Also called reconstituted family.
Boundary Maintenance Ensurance that the limits to roles or membership of the group are clear. If maintenance is rigid, there may be little flexibility in role performance or in defining the group as larger or smaller. If maintenance is diffuse, role performance may be flexible

or others may be included in the group, depending on the circumstances.

Bride Price An amount paid in currency or labour by the groom's family as permission for the marriage in an arranged marriage system.

Celibacy The condition of abstaining from sexual intercourse, especially by reason of religious vows of chastity.

Census Family A term used by Statistics Canada to refer to husband and wife living with or without never-married children, or a lone-parent living with never-married children.

Chastity The state of being pure, chaste, or virginal.

Child Betrothal A formal agreement between the children's parents to have them marry when they reach the legal age of marriage.

Chivalry The qualities idealized by knighthood in medieval Europe, such as bravery and courtesy; courtesy toward women.

Coding Categorizing answers in a questionnaire and transforming them into numbers so that they can be analyzed by computer.

Cohabitation Living together without legal marriage.

Common-Law Relationship or Union A relationship in which a couple lives together without being legally married.

Complementary Needs A theory of mate selection that states that people marry those whom they think will complement their psychological needs.

Complementary Roles Marital roles in which the husband and wife specialize in different areas in the family.

Compression of Morbidity Thesis A theory that predicts that, in the future, illness and disability will be compressed into a shorter period of time at the end of people's lives.

Conditioning Systematically rewarding or punishing a behaviour in order to increase or decrease its occurrence.

Conflict Perspective A theoretical perspective within social science that emphasizes power differentials and conflicts of interest between groups or organizations. (See Political Economy Perspective.)

Conjugal Family A husband and wife living together with their children and placing greater importance on their relationship with each other than on their relationship with either set of relatives. Similar to a nuclear family, but with emphasis on the relationship rather than on the structure.

Consanguinity See Ties of Consanguinity.

Continuity Theory A theory suggesting that personality tends to persist as people age, despite life events.

Control A term from systems theory emphasizing social pressure to keep people behaving in such a way that the family system is maintained.
Couple Two people of either sex who are sexually or intimately involved.
Court To attempt to gain the love of someone and develop a relationship leading to marriage.
Cross-sectional Study A study in which the same characteristics or attributes of different groups are compared at one time.
Curvilinear Relationship A statistical term referring to a relationship between variables which is characterized by a bell curve.

Dating The leisure time two people of the opposite sex spend together for the same of enjoyment, without any intention to marry in the near future.
Definition of the Situation The way in which people personally interpret a social situation that affects their behaviour.
Dependency Ratio The population assumed to be financially dependent (children and retired people) as a ratio of the working age population used to predict the need for future services and facilities.
Developmental Approach A theoretical perspective based on the work of Jean Piaget who suggested that children pass through stages of cognitive, motor, and psychological development. Particular tasks or concepts must be learned adequately before a child passes through the next stage of development. (See Family Life Cycle.)
Developmental Task A skill or psychological lesson to be learned before a person can move on to the next level of development.
Developmental Theory of Mate Selection A theory suggesting that once people begin a relationship, there is no way to predict who will marry whom except by analyzing the couple's emotional advances and retreats, changing definitions of the situation, resolution of tensions, and external circumstances pressuring them to marry.
Deviant Behaviour Behaviour that violates society's norms or laws.
Diffuse See Boundary Maintenance.
Disengagement Theory A theory of aging that suggests that it is normal for seniors to lose interest in activities and relationships and to drop out of active participation in society.
Domestic Labour Housework, yard work, and child care usually provided for no pay by family members.
Dower Rights A wife's right to a portion of her husband's property should the marriage dissolve, because of the domestic and sexual services she provided throughout the marriage.

Dowry Money or property provided by a woman's family in order to find her a husband. This money becomes her "insurance" in case her husband dies or leaves her.
Dual-Career Family A family in which both adults have careers or occupations that consume large amounts of their time and in which they expect to advance over time.
Dual-Income Family A family in which both adults work for pay.

Economic Family A term used by Statistics Canada to refer to related people sharing a household.
Ecosystem A term from systems theory referring to the socio-economic environment, neighbourhood, or community within which a family lives.
Educational Inflation The elevation of educational requirements for jobs.
Empty Nest Syndrome The assumption that parents, especially mothers, will feel depressed and unfulfilled when all the children have left home.
Endogamy Marriage to a partner within the same social or cultural group.
Enmeshment Emotional attachment and dependence in a family or other close group.
Environmental Theories of Aging Theories that examine how various aspects of the physical or social environment affect attitudes, behaviour, and the physical aging process.
Ethnic Origin National or cultural identity or affiliation.
Ethnicity See Ethnic Origin.
Ethnocentrism Viewing and judging the world from the vantage point of one's own ethnic or cultural group.
Eugenics Movement A social movement to improve the quality of the human race, especially through selective breeding.
Exchange Theory of Aging A theory that suggests that people from different age groups interact and bargain with each other on the basis of what resources they control, either interpersonally or societally.
Exogamy Marriage to a partner from outside one's social or cultural group.
Expressive Role A pattern of behaviour that is nurturant or concerned with the feelings of others.
Extended Family A multigenerational household that could comprise grandparents, parents, children and their aunts, uncles, and cousins.

Family There are many acceptable definitions of family including a couple and their children sharing a dwelling and co-operating

economically; a parent and dependant children sharing a dwelling; all persons considered to be related.
Family Life Cycle The family is seen as an ever-changing unit in which relationships and interaction vary with psycho-sexual development and social events such a marriage, birth, divorce, or retirement.
Family of Orientation The family into which a person is born.
Family of Procreation The family that a person creates through marriage and childbearing.
Family Wage A wage that was supposed to cover the cost of supporting a man and his family.
Feedback A term from systems theory that refers to spoken or unspoken information from others in reaction to a person's behaviour.
Feminist Perspective A theoretical perspective that focuses on women's point of view and experiences, as well as on how social systems impact on women.
Feminist Theories of Aging Theories that focus on differences in the socio-economic status, relationships, and attitudes of older men and women.
Feminization of Poverty The trend for more poor people to be female or more poor families to be female-led.
Fertility Rate (total) The average number of children a woman is likely to have in her childbearing years.
Filial Piety Respect and deference given to parents by their children as repayment for raising them.
Foundling Homes Institutions, often run by religious organizations, that provided care for infants and children who had been orphaned or abandoned by their parents.
Free Choice Marriage A marriage in which people choose their own partners.
Function The intended or unintended purpose or goal.
Functionalism See Structural-Functional Perspective.

Gender The social or cultural connotations attached to being male or female in a particular society.
Gender Relations The ways in which males and females interact in a given society, considering the differential socialization of males and females and their different life experiences.
Gendered Society A society in which males and females are encouraged to develop different skills and interests, in which the labour market is segregated by gender, and in which males and females do not relate to each other equally.
Gerontology The study of aging and the elderly.

Heterosexism A bias that assumes everyone is heterosexual or that homosexuality is abnormal or insignificant.
Hierarchy An arrangement of a group or organization into strata so that each one is considered superior to those below.
Homeostasis The maintenance of equilibrium in a social group.
Homogamy The tendency for people from a similar social background to interact and marry.
Homophobia Fear or disapproval of homosexuals or homosexuality.
Household People who live in the same dwelling, regardless of whether they are related.
Hurried Children Children who are rushed through certain stages of development and pushed to excel by their parents in language, reasoning, and mathematical skills earlier than other children.
Hypergamy Marriage with a partner of higher social status, age, or height.
Hypogamy Marriage with a partner of lower social status, age, or height.
Hypothesis A statement of a possible relationship between variables that can be tested through research.

Ideal Mate Theory A theory suggesting that, based on past parental role models and dating experience, people form impressions of an ideal marital partner and search for someone who approximates this ideal.
Ideal Type A conceptualization or mental construct based on many observations but not representing any actual case.
Ideology A body of ideas that reflects the interests and beliefs of a social group or society and forms the basis of political action.
Incest Taboo A rule that forbids sexual activity between family members.
Indenture A contract binding a party into the service of another for a specific period of time.
Individuation The process by which a person becomes an individual and develops his or her own ideas, personality, and lifestyle separate from those of the parents.
Infant Mortality Rate The number of deaths of children under the age of one per 1000 live births.
Infertility The inability to bear children; the inability to conceive a viable pregnancy within one year of unprotected intercourse.
Instrumental Role A pattern of behaviour that focuses on task orientation, or getting the job done, rather than on concern about people's feelings or interpersonal relations.

Interactionist Theory See Symbolic Interactionist Perspective.
Interview Schedule A written list of questions to be asked orally in a research project.
***In Vitro* Fertilization** The process of removing an egg from the ovary and placing it in a petri dish with semen for fertilization. The fertilized egg is then placed in the uterus of the birth mother.

Joint Legal Custody Both parents have the legal right to make decisions about the child's education, religious upbringing, and general welfare, regardless of which parent physically cares for the child after divorce.
Joint Physical Custody The physical care of the child is the legal responsibility of both parents after divorce, and the child may live in each parent's household for a portion of the year.

Kin-Keeper The person who socially maintains the family as a group and organizes family celebrations and rituals.

Learning Theory A theory of socialization that emphasizes the importance of social environment and learning rather than inherited qualities in personality development.
Levirate The practice of a man marrying his brother's widow.
Life-Span Approach A theory that studies behaviour from childhood to old age and assumes that certain characteristics and attitudes are likely to develop after particular life experiences.
Longitudinal Study A study in which the same individuals or groups are observed or monitored over a number of years.
Looking-Glass Self A self-image that is developed as the result of the way others see that person.

Macro-Level Theory A theory that explains human behaviour by focusing on how societal structures, such as the law or education systems, influence people's lives.
Majority Group A group that is dominant in power rather than in numbers. In anglophone Canada, white people of British ancestry would be considered the majority group. In modern Quebec, white francophones with ancestral roots in France would be considered the majority group.
Manufactories Places outside the home where craftspeople worked together in the same room, and each person created an entire product for sale.

Marriage Broker A person who specializes in finding suitable marriage partners for arranged marriages.
Marriage Squeeze A theory that suggests that, since men tend to marry younger and less educated women, older women who postponed marriage for education and careers tend to get squeezed out of the marriage market.
Maternal Deprivation The condition of being deprived of a mother's warmth and attention, formerly assumed to result from mothers working outside the home as well as children being confined to an institution.
Matriarchy A society or family system in which women have more authority than men.
Matrilineal Descent Lineage or family relationship is traced through the bride's kin group.
Matrilocal Residence The bride and groom live with the bride's family or in her community after marriage.
Means-Tested Benefit Entitlement to social benefits is based on financial assets, property, and income.
Micro-Level Theory A theory that explains human behaviour by focusing on interpersonal relations and individuals rather than on the structures of society.
Mid-Life Crisis Overwhelming feelings of depression or futility related to a perceived decline in physical attractiveness or a feeling of lack of accomplishment in life.
Minority Group A cultural or ethnic group that has its own values and practices.
Modified Extended Family Grandparents, parents, children, and other relatives who maintain frequent and close contact with each other, but live in separate households.
Monogamy A system of marriage in which each adult is allowed only one spouse at a time.
Monolithic Family One family type that remains unchanged.
Motherwork The housework and child care that most mothers must perform for no wage; formerly not considered "work" by social scientists.

Nature/Nurture Debate The debate that centres around the question of whether inheritance or social environment plays the more important role in personality development and behaviour.
Neolocal A marriage in which the bride and groom live in a residence separate from both sides of the family.
Norms Unwritten rules or expectations of social behaviour.

Nuclear Family Husband, wife, and their children sharing the same household and co-operating economically.

Older Elderly People aged 75 and older.
Open Marriage A relationship in which marriage partners operate as separate individuals in order to explore their full potential.

Participant Observation The method whereby researchers participate in group activities to obtain first-hand information about the group.
Patriarchal Society Theory The theory that suggests men tend to have more bargaining power than women in relationships because they have greater access to resources such as education, income, and prestige.
Patriarchy A society or family system in which men have more authority than women.
Patrilineal Descent Lineage or family relationships are traced through the male side of the family.
Patrilocal Residence The family structure in which the bride moves into or near her husband's family home.
Personal Resource Theory The theory of family power that suggests that the person who has more resources, such as higher education or income, good looks, or youth, has more bargaining power in a relationship.
Phenomenological Theory of Aging A theory that emphasizes the meaning individuals in a particular society attach to growing old.
Political Economy Perspective A perspective that emphasizes the link between changes in the economy, the work people do, political decisions, and people's personal lives. Also called the conflict approach because conflicts between vested interests and power relations are emphasized.
Polyandry A system of marriage in which women are allowed more than one husband at a time.
Polygamy A system of marriage in which adults are allowed more than one spouse at a time.
Polygyny A system of marriage in which men are allowed more than one wife at a time.
Power of the Purse The theory that the person who earns most of the money controls the relationship or has greater decision-making power.
Primary Group A small group involving face-to-face contact and strong feelings of attachment.

Private/Public Dichotomy The distinction made between family matters and work or public life. These areas of life used to be viewed as distinct and synonymous with the roles of women and men.
Pronatal Values Values that encourage childbearing.
Psychoanalytic Theories of Socialization Theories that stress the importance of subconscious emotions in shaping personality.
Purposive Sample An attempt to include certain types of people in a study who might not appear in a random sample, such as single mothers who have never been married or men who have custody of their children.

Qualitative Research Research that focuses on the quality of people's lives, their perceptions, and ways of viewing the world and that does not use statistics to analyze the information obtained.
Quantitative Research Research that gathers information with the intention of analyzing it numerically and statistically.

Random Sample People selected for a study from a list of random numbers.
Recurring Behaviour Behaviour that happens over and over again according to a pattern.
Reference Group The group people look to for their ideas of acceptable behaviour and their self-image.
Representative Sample A sample that contains the same categories of people and in the same proportion as in the actual population.
Reserve Labour Force A pool of workers that employers draw upon when they need additional employees.
Residential Propinquity The theory that people of the same socio-economic circumstances tend to live close together or in the same neighbourhood, which encourages social interaction and eventual marriage.
Rite of Passage A ritualized acknowledgement that a person has changed his or her status, such as from adolescent to adult or from employee to retiree.
Role A pattern of behaviour governed by social expectations, rights, and duties and associated with a specific position in a social situation, such as a husband in a family.
Role Expectations Assumptions about appropriate behaviour for a specific position in a social situation.
Role Differentiation The assignment of different duties and rights, as well as expected ways of behaving, to people in a social situation, such as husband and wife in a family.

Role Strain Feelings of pressure caused by too many different and incompatible obligations and expectations.
Romantic Love Idealized or sentimental love.

Sample A typical subgroup from an entire category of people to be studied.
Sandwich Generation Middle-aged adults who retain responsibility for two generations—their children and their aging parents.
Separation A term from the family life cycle approach to indicate psychological distancing of a child from his or her parents or young people leaving home.
Serial Monogamy A pattern of marriage, divorce, and remarriage; one partner at a time, but several over a lifetime.
Sexist Research Research that focuses on only one gender and generalizes to both; usually considered male-biased research.
Shared Parenting Both parents share in the decision making and physical care of the child during marriage or after divorce regardless of which parent legally has custody.
Social Class A division of people grouped by similar social and economic position.
Social Construction of Reality The theory that our social reality, i.e., our relationships and experiences in life, is created by our own view of the world, our family and cultural experiences, and personal decisions. Therefore, this "reality" differs for each person.
Social Exchange Theory A theory that uses economic analogies from cost-benefit analysis to show that marriage and family relationships involve a process of negotiation and bargaining.
Social Homogamy Theory A theory of marriage that suggests people with similar socio-economic backgrounds have more opportunities to meet and are more likely to marry than people from different backgrounds.
Social Institution An established set of roles, norms, and relationships organized around some central activity or social need.
Social Mobility Movement between social classes or socio-economic levels of society.
Social Norms Traditional patterns and/or expectations of social behaviour.
Social Status A hierarchical position in society equated with rank or prestige.
Socialization The complex learning process through which individuals develop their personalities and acquire the knowledge, skills, and motivation necessary for participation in social life.

Sociobiology The study of the biological or genetic component of social behaviour.
Sororate The custom for a widower to marry the sister of his deceased wife.
Structural-Functional Perspective A theoretical approach that focuses on how social structure influences individual behaviour and assumes that behaviour is governed by rules, laws, and expectations that function or serve to maintain the structure of society.
Subsystem A term from systems theory referring to a group within a group.
Surrogate Mother A woman who bears a child for a childless couple, possibly for financial gain.
Survey of the Literature A careful reading of relevant research, which is done before an empirical study, in order to guide the research design and compare results.
Survey Research Gathering quantitative information from a large sample of people through questionnaires.
Symbolic Interactionist Perspective The perspective that assumes that people create their own social reality through social interactions by defining and interpreting the symbolic meanings of others' reactions and responding to them.
Systemic Discrimination Differential and unfair treatment, targeted toward visible minorities, disabled persons, or women, that permeates the values and understandings of a society or a social organization.
Systems Theory A theory that suggests the family is a system of interactions and relationships in which the behaviour of one member influences all others. The focus is on patterns of recurring behaviour triggered by similar situations.

Ties of Affinity Related by marriage or adoption.
Ties of Consanguinity Related through "blood" or birth, such as siblings or parents and children.
Trial Marriage Living together before making the decision to marry.
Trousseau Clothes and household items that a bride assembles for her marriage.
Two-Income Family A family with two earners, usually husband and wife.
Underground Economy Working or earning money unofficially without receipts, without the government's knowledge, and without paying income tax.

Unit of Analysis The segment of society under study, such as the individual, a specific organization, or the legal system.
Upward Mobility Movement to a higher socio-economic level of society.

Vesting Period The number of years of service and/or age requirements before pension contributions paid by an employer become the legal property of an employee.
Victimization Studies Studies that ask the subjects if they have ever been victims of violence or certain illegal acts, such as break and enter.
Visible Minorities People who can be identified as members of a minority racial or cultural group by their skin colour, facial features, or manner of speaking.

Women's Double Day Working for pay during the day and doing unpaid housework and child care in the evenings.

BIBLIOGRAPHY

Abu-Laban, Sharon McIrvin. "The Family Life of Older Canadians." *Canadian Home Economics Journal.* January 1978:16–25.

Abu-Laban, Sharon and Baha Abu-Laban. "Women and the Aged as Minority Groups. A Critique." *Canadian Review of Sociology and Anthropology.* 14 (1). 1977:103–116.

Achenbaum, W. Andrew. *Old Age in the New Land: The American Experience Since 1790.* Baltimore: Johns Hopkins University Press, 1978.

Adams, Bert N. "Isolation, Function and Beyond: American Kinship in the 1960s." *A Decade of Family Research and Action.* Edited by Carlfred B. Broderick. Minneapolis: National Council of Family Relations, 1975.

___. *The Family.* 3rd ed. Chicago: Rand McNally College Publishing, 1980.

Adams, Owen B. "Divorce Rates in Canada." *Canadian Social Trends.* Edited by Craig McKie and Keith Thompson. Toronto: Thompson Educational Publishing, 1990:146–147.

Adams, Owen B. and Dhruva Nagnur. "Marrying and Divorcing: A Status Report for Canada." *Canadian Social Trends.* Edited by Craig McKie and Keith Thompson. Toronto: Thompson Educational Publishing, 1990:142–145.

Akyeampong, Ernest. "Absences From Work Revisited." *Perspectives on Labour and Income.* 4 (1). Spring 1992:44–51.

Albrecht, Stan L., Howard M. Bahr, and Bruce A. Chadwick. "Changing Family and Sex Roles: An Assessment of Age Differences." *Journal of Marriage and the Family.* 41. 1979:41–50.

Albrecht, Stan L., Howard M. Bahr, and Kristen L. Goodman. *Divorce and Remarriage: Problems, Adaptations and Adjustments.* Westport, CT: Greenwood, 1983.

Albrecht, Stan L. and P.R. Kunz. "The Decision to Divorce: A Social Exchange Perspective." *Journal of Divorce.* 3. 1980:319–337.

Aldous, Joan. "Parent-Adult Child Relations as Affected by the Grandparent Status." *Grandparenthood.* Edited by Vern L. Bengtson and Joan F. Robertson. Beverly Hills: Sage, 1985:117–132.

Amato, Paul R. "Family Processes in One-Parent, Stepparent, and Intact Families: The Child's Point of View." *Journal of Marriage and the Family*. 49. 1987:327–337.

Ambert, Anne-Marie. "Being a Step-Parent: Live-In and Visiting Step-Children." *Journal of Marriage and the Family*. 48. 1986:795–804.

___. *Divorce in Canada*. Don Mills: Academic Press, 1980.

___. *Ex-Spouses and New Spouses*. London: J.A.I. Press, 1990.

___. "Longitudinal Changes in Children's Behavior Toward Custodial Parents." *Journal of Marriage and the Family*. 46. 1984:463–468.

___. "Marriage Dissolution: Structural and Ideological Changes." *Families: Changing Trends in Canada*. 2nd ed. Edited by Maureen Baker. Scarborough: McGraw-Hill Ryerson, 1990a:192–210.

___. "Relationships Between Ex-Spouses: Individual and Dyadic Perspectives." *Journal of Social and Personal Relationships*. 5. 1988:327–346.

___. "Relationships With Former In-Laws After Divorce: A Research Note." *Journal of Marriage and the Family*. 50. 1988:679–686.

___. "Separated Women and Remarriage Behaviour: A Comparison of Financially Secure Women and Financially Insecure Women." *Journal of Divorce*. 6. 1983:43–54.

___. *The Effect of Children on Parents*. New York: The Haworth Press, 1992.

___. "The Effect of Divorce on Women's Attitude Toward Feminism." *Sociological Focus*. 18. 1985:265–272.

___. "The Other Perspective: Children's Effect on Parents." *Families: Changing Trends in Canada*. 2nd ed. Edited by Maureen Baker. Scarborough: McGraw-Hill Ryerson, 1990b:149–165.

Ambert Anne-Marie and J.F. Saucier. "Adolescents' Academic Success and Aspirations by Parental Marital Status." *Canadian Review of Sociology and Anthropology*. 21 (1). February 1984:62–74.

Anderson, Alan and Leo Driedger. "The Mennonite Family: Culture and Kin in Rural Saskatchewan." *Canadian Families: Ethnic Variations*. Edited by K. Ishwaran. Scarborough: McGraw-Hill Ryerson, 1980:161–180.

Anderson, Karen L. et al. *Family Matters. Sociology and Contemporary Canadian Families*. Scarborough: Nelson, 1988.

Anderson, Karen L. "Historical Perspectives on the Family." *Family Matters. Sociology and Contemporary Canadian Families*. Edited by K. Anderson et al. Scarborough: Nelson, 1988.

Angenent, Huub and Anton DeMan. *Childrearing. Personality Development and Deviant Behavior*. Toronto: Thompson Educational Publishing, 1992.

Aquilino, William S. "Family Structure and Home Leaving: A Further Specification of the Relationship." *Journal of Marriage and the Family*. 53. November 1991:999–1010.

Ariès, Philippe. *Centuries of Childhood: A Social History of Family Life*. New York: Vintage Books, 1962.

___. "Two Successive Motivations for the Declining Birth Rate in the West." *Population and Development Review*. 6 (4). 1980:645–650.

Armitage, Andrew. *Social Welfare in Canada*. 2nd ed. Toronto: McClelland and Stewart, 1988.

Armstrong, Pat. "Economic Conditions and Family Structures." *Families: Changing Trends in Canada*. 2nd ed. Edited by M. Baker. Scarborough: McGraw-Hill Ryerson, 1990:67–92.

Armstrong, Pat and Hugh Armstrong. *A Working Majority: What Women Must Do for Pay*. Canadian Advisory Council on the Status of Women. Ottawa: Minister of Supply and Services Canada, 1983.

___. "The Conflicting Demands of 'Work' and 'Home'." *Family Matters. Sociology and Contemporary Canadian Families*. Karen L. Anderson et al. Scarborough: Nelson, 1988:113–140.

___. *The Double Ghetto. Canadian Women and Their Segregated Work*. 2nd ed. Toronto: McClelland and Stewart, 1984.

___. *Theorizing Women's Work*. Toronto: Garamond, 1990.

Aronson, Jane. "Dutiful Daughters and Undemanding Mothers: Contrasting Images of Giving and Receiving Care in Middle and Later Life." *Women's Caring. Feminist Perspectives on Social Welfare*. Edited by C. Baines et al. Toronto: McClelland and Stewart, 1991:138–168.

Asner, Elizabeth and David Livingstone. "Household Class, Divisions of Labour and Political Attitudes in Steeltown." Paper Presented at Canadian Socialist Association Meetings, Victoria, BC, 1990.

Auel, Jean M. *Clan of the Cave Bear*. New York: Crown Publishers, 1980.

Avery, Donald. *'Dangerous Foreigners'. European Immigrant Workers and Labour Radicalism in Canada, 1896–1932*. Toronto: McClelland and Stewart, 1979.

Ayim, Maryann. "Children's Rights in Canada." Paper presented to the Canadian Society for Women in Philosophy, Montreal. November 1987.

Babchuk, Nicolas. "Aging and Primary Relations." *International Journal of Aging and Human Development*. 9 (2). 1978–79:137–151.

Badgley, Robin (Chairperson). *Sexual Offences Against Children*. Report of the Committee on Sexual Offences Against Children and Youth. Ottawa: Minister of Supply and Services Canada, 1984.

Bagley, Christopher R. and Kathleen King. *Child Sexual Abuse. The Search for Healing*. London: Tavistock/Routledge, 1990.

Bagley, Christopher R. and Ray J. Thomlinson (eds.). *Child Sexual Abuse: Critical Perspectives on Prevention, Intervention and Treatment*. Toronto: Wall and Amerson, 1991.

Baines, Carol, Patricia Evans, and Sheila Neysmith (eds.). *Women's Caring. Feminist Perspectives on Social Welfare*. Toronto: McClelland and Stewart, 1991.

Baker, Maureen. "A New Status for Midwifery: Women and Public Policy." *Canadian Review of Social Policy*. 26. 1990a:54–63.

___. *Aging in Canadian Society: A Survey*. Scarborough: McGraw-Hill Ryerson, 1988a.

___. "Child Abuse." Ottawa: Library of Parliament, Research Branch (Current Issue Review 82–17). August 1988b.

___. "Divorce: Its Consequences and Meanings." *The Canadian Family*. Edited by K. Ishwaran. Toronto: Gage, 1983:289–300.

___. (ed.). *Families: Changing Trends in Canada*. 2nd ed. Scarborough: McGraw-Hill Ryerson, 1990b.

___. "Family and Population Policy in Quebec: Implications for Women." *Canadian Journal of Women and the Law*. 6 (2). 1993.

___. "Finding Partners in the Newspaper: Sex Differences in Personal Advertising." *Atlantis*. 7 (2). 1982:137–146.

___. "His and Her Divorce Research: New Theoretical Directions in Canadian and American Research." *Continuity and Change in Marriage and Family*. Toronto: Holt, Rinehart and Winston, 1991. (Reprint of article in *Journal of Comparative Family Studies*, 1984).

___. "Introduction: Theories, Methods, and Concerns of Family Sociology." *Families: Changing Trends in Canada.* 2nd ed. Edited by Maureen Baker. Scarborough: McGraw-Hill Ryerson, 1990c:1–22.

___. "Mate Selection and Marital Dynamics." *Families: Changing Trends in Canada.* 2nd ed. Edited by Maureen Baker. Scarborough: McGraw-Hill Ryerson, 1990d:41–66.

___. "The Future of Family Life." *Families: Changing Trends in Canada.* 2nd ed. Edited by Maureen Baker. Scarborough: McGraw-Hill Ryerson, 1990e:330–345.

___. "The Perpetuation of Misleading Family Models in Social Policy: Implications for Women." *Canadian Review of Social Work* Summer 1990f.

___. *"What Will Tomorrow Bring?..." A Study of the Aspirations of Adolescent Women.* Canadian Advisory Council on the Status of Women. Ottawa: Minister of Supply and Services Canada, 1985.

___. "Women Helping Women: The Transition From Separation to Divorce." *Conciliation Courts Review.* 22. 1984:53–63.

Baker, Maureen and Hans J.I. Bakker. "The Double Bind of the Middle Class Male: Men's Liberation and the Male Sex Role." *Journal of Comparative Family Studies.* XI (4). Autumn 1980:547–561.

Bala, Nicholas. "Child and Family Policies for the 1990s." *Children, Families and Public Policy in the 90s.* Edited by Laura C. Johnson and Dick Barnhorst. Toronto: Thompson Educational Publishing, 1991:105–132.

Bala, Nicholas and Kenneth L. Clarke. *The Child and the Law.* Scarborough: McGraw-Hill Ryerson, 1981.

Bala, Nicholas, Joseph P. Hornick, and Robin Vogl (eds.). *Canadian Child Welfare Law. Children Families and the State.* Toronto: Thompson Educational Publishing, 1991.

Barnes, Gordon E., Leonard Greenwood, and Reena Sommers. "Courtship Violence in a Canadian Sample of Male College Students." *Family Relations.* 40. January 1991:37–44.

Barnhorst, Richard and Laura C. Johnson (eds.). *The State of the Child in Ontario.* Toronto: Oxford University Press, 1991.

Basavarajappa, K.G. and Ravi B.P. Verma. "Occupational Composition of Immigrant Women." *Ethnic Demography.* Edited by Shiva Halli, Frank Trovato, and Leo Driedger. Ottawa: Carleton University Press, 1990:297–314.

Battle, Ken. "Child Benefits in Decline." *Policy Options.* January 1988:3–6.

Beaujot, Roderic. "Dwindling Families." *Policy Options.* 7. September 1986:3–7.

___. *Population Change in Canada: The Challenges of Policy Adaptation.* Toronto: McClelland and Stewart, 1991.

___. "The Family and Demographic Change in Canada: Economic and Cultural Interpretations and Solutions." *Journal of Comparative Family Studies.* XXI (1). Spring 1990:25–38.

Belanger, Lise. "The Types of Violence the Elderly are Victims of: Results of a Survey Done with Personnel Working with the Elderly." Paper presented at the 34th Annual Scientific Meeting of the Gerontological Association of America, November 1981.

Beneteau, Renée. "Trends in Suicide." *Canadian Social Trends.* Edited by Craig McKie and Keith Thompson. Toronto: Thompson Educational Publishing 1990:93–95.

Bengtson, Vern L. "Diversity and Symbolism in Grandparental Roles." *Grandparenthood.* Edited by Vern L. Bengtson and Joan F. Robertson. Beverly Hills: Sage, 1985:11–25.

Bequele, Assefa and Jo Boyden (eds.). *Combatting Child Labour.* Geneva: International Labour Organization, 1988.

Berk, Sarah Fenstermaker. *The Gender Factory: The Apportionment of Work in American Households.* New York: Plenum, 1985.

Bernard, Jessie. "The Adjustment of Married Mates." *Handbook of Marriage and the Family.* Edited by Harold T. Christensen. Chicago: Rand McNally, 1964.

___. *The Future of Marriage.* 2nd ed. New Haven, CT: Yale University Press, 1982.

Berthelette, Jerome (interview with). "Aboriginal Communities. Familial Societies, Familiar Pressures." *Transition.* 21 (4). December 1991:4–6.

Besharov, Douglas J. *Recognizing Child Abuse. A Guide For the Concerned.* New York: The Free Press, 1990.

Bibby, Reginald W. and Donald C. Posterski. *The Emerging Generation: An Inside Look at Canada's Teenagers.* Toronto: Irwin, 1985.

Blood, Robert O. and D.M. Wolfe. *Husbands and Wives.* New York: The Free Press, 1960.

Blumstein, Philip and Pepper Schwartz. *American Couples*. New York: William Morrow and Company, 1983.

Bolton, Charles D. "Mate Selection as the Development of a Relationship." *Marriage and Family Living*. 23. August 1961:234–240.

Bolton, Frank and Susan Bolton. *Working With Violent Families: A Guide for Clinical and Legal Practice*. Newbury Park, CA: Sage Publications, 1987.

Bonar, Rita and Michael J. MacLean. "Multicultural Issues in Old Age." *Multiculturalism*. VIII (2). 1985:13–15.

Booth, A. and L. White. "Thinking About Divorce." *Journal of Marriage and the Family*. 42. 1980:605–616.

Boss, P. "Family Stress." *Handbook of Marriage and the Family*. Edited by M. Sussman and S. Steimetz. New York: Plenum, 1987.

Bott, Elizabeth. *Family and Social Network: Roles, Norms and External Relationships in Ordinary Urban Families*. London: Tavistock Publications, 1951.

Bowlby, John. *Maternal Care and Mental Health*. Geneva: World Health Organization, 1951.

Boyd, Monica, John Goyder, Frank Jones, Hugh McRoberts, Peter Pineo, and John Porter. *Ascription and Achievement: Studies in Mobility and Status Attainment in Canada*. Ottawa: Carleton University Press, 1985.

Boyd, Monica and Edward T. Pryor. "Young Adults Living in Their Parents' Home." *Canadian Social Trends*. Edited by Craig McKie and Keith Thompson. Toronto: Thompson Educational Publishing, 1990:188–191.

Boyle, Michael. "Child Health in Ontario." *The State of the Child in Ontario*. Edited by Richard Barnhorst and Laura C. Johnson. Toronto: Oxford University Press, 1991:92–116.

Bram, Susan. "Childlessness Revisited: A Longitudinal Study of Voluntarily Childless Couples, Delayed Parents, and Parents." *Lifestyles: A Journal of Changing Patterns*. 8 (2). 1985:46–66.

Brillon, Yves. *Victimization and Fear of Crime Among the Elderly*. Toronto: Butterworths, 1987.

Brinkerhoff, Merlin B. and Eugen Lupri. "Conjugal Power and Family Relationships: Some Theoretical and Methodological Issues." *The Canadian Family*. Edited by K. Ishwaran. Toronto: Gage, 1983.

___. "Interspousal Violence." *The Canadian Journal of Sociology*. 13 (4). Fall 1988:407–434.

Broderick, Carlfred B. (ed.). *A Decade of Family Research and Action*. Minneapolis: National Council of Family Relations, 1971.

___. *Marriage and the Family* 4th ed. Englewood Cliffs, NJ: Prentice-Hall, 1992.

Bronstein, P. and C. Cowan (eds.). *Fatherhood Today: Men's Changing Role in Society*. New York: Wiley and Sons, 1988.

Brown, Judith. "Iroquois Women: an Ethnohistoric Note." *Family Bonds and Gender Divisions*. Edited by Bonnie Fox. Toronto: Scholars' Press, 1988:83–98.

Bryant, Heather. *The Infertility Dilemma: Reproductive Technologies and Prevention*. Canadian Advisory Council on the Status of Women. Ottawa: Minister of Supply and Services Canada, February 1990.

Burch, Thomas K. *Families in Canada*. Statistics Canada. 1986 Census of Canada, Cat. 98-127. Ottawa: Minister of Supply and Services Canada, March 1990.

___. "Remarriage of Older Canadians. Description and Interpretation." *Research on Aging*. 12 (4). 1990:546–559.

Burch, Thomas K. and Ashok Madan. *Union Formation and Dissolution: Results from the 1984 Family History Survey*. Statistics Canada. Cat. 99-963. Ottawa: Minister of Supply and Services Canada, 1986.

Burgess, Ernest W. and Leonard S. Cottrell Jr. *Predicting Success or Failure in Marriage*. New York: Prentice-Hall, 1939.

Burke, Mary Anne. "Canada's Immigrant Children." *Canadian Social Trends*. 24. Spring 1992:15–20.

___. "Families: Diversity the New Norm." *Canadian Social Trends*. 2. Summer 1986:6–10.

___. "Implications of An Aging Society." *Canadian Social Trends*. 20. Spring 1991:6–8.

Burke, Mary Anne, Susan Crompton, Alison Jones, and Katherine Nessner. "Caring for Children." *Canadian Social Trends*. 22. Autumn 1991:12–15.

Burke, Mary Anne and Aron Spector. "Falling Through the Cracks: Women Aged 55-64 Living On Their Own." *Canadian Social Trends*. 23. Winter 1991:14–17.

Burman, Bonnie and Diane de Anda. "Parenthood or Nonparenthood: A Comparison of Intentional Families." *Lifestyles: A Journal of Changing Patterns.* 8 (2). 1985–86:69–84.

Caldwell, Gary and Daniel Fournier. "The Quebec Question: A Matter of Population." *Canadian Journal of Sociology.* 12 (1-2). Spring 1987:16–41.

Canada, Federal/Provincial/Territorial Family Law Committee. *Child Support: Public Discussion Paper.* Ottawa: Family Law Committee, June 1991.

Canada, Health and Welfare. *Dating Violence.* Ottawa: The National Clearinghouse on Family Violence, 1990.

Canada, House of Commons. *Canada's Children: Investing in Our Future.* Report of the Standing Committee on Health and Welfare, Social Affairs, Seniors and the Status of Women. SubCommittee on Poverty (Chaired by Barbara Greene, M.P.) Ottawa: Minister of Supply and Services Canada, December 1991.

___. *Sharing Our Responsibility.* Report of the Special Committee on Child Care, (Chaired by Shirley Martin, M.P.) Ottawa: Minister of Supply and Services Canada, March 1987.

___. *The War Against Women.* Report of the Standing Committee on Health and Welfare, Social Affairs, Seniors and the Status of Women. (Chaired by Barbara Greene, M.P.) Ottawa: Minister of Supply and Services Canada, June 1991.

Canada. Standing Senate Committee on Social Affairs, Science and Technology. *Children in Poverty: Toward a Better Future.* (Chaired by Senators Lorna Marsden and Brenda Robertson.) Ottawa: Minister of Supply and Services, January 1991.

Canada, Special Senate Committee on Youth. *Youth: A Plan of Action.* (Chaired by Senator Jacques Hébert.) Ottawa: Minister of Supply and Services, February 1986.

Canada, Task Force on Child Care. *Report of the Task Force on Child Care.* (Chaired by Katie Cooke.) Ottawa: Minister of Supply and Services Canada, 1986.

Carlson, B.E. "Dating Violence: a Research Review and Comparison with Spousal Abuse." *Social Casework.* 68 (1). 1987:16–23.

Carter, Elizabeth A. and Monica McGoldrick. *Family Life Cycle: A Framework for Family Therapy.* New York: Gardner Press, 1980.

___. *The Changing Family Life Cycle: A Framework for Family Therapy.*

2nd ed. New York: Gardner Press, 1988.

Castellano, Marlene Brant. "Women In Huron and Ojibwa Societies." *Transition*. 21 (4). December 1991:6–10.

Cath, S.H., A. Gurwitt, and L. Gunsberg (eds.). *Fathers and Their Families*. Hillsdale, NJ: Analytic Press, 1989.

Chappell, Neena. "Aging and the Family." *Marriage and the Family in Canada Today*. Edited by G.N. Ramu. Scarborough: Prentice-Hall, 1989:185–206.

Chappell, Neena L., Laurel A. Strain, and Audrey A. Blandford. *Aging and Health Care. A Social Perspective*. Toronto: Holt, Rinehart and Winston, 1986.

Chawla, Raj K. "Dependency Ratios." *Canadian Social Trends*. 20. Spring 1991:3–5.

___. "The Changing Profile of Dual-Earner Families." *Perspectives of Labour and Income*. 4 (2). Summer 1992:22–29.

Cheal, David. *Family and the State of Theory*. Toronto: University of Toronto Press, 1991.

___. "Theoretical Frameworks." *Marriage and Family in Canada Today*. Edited by G.N. Ramu. Scarborough: Prentice-Hall, 1989:19–34.

Cherlin, Andrew J. and Frank F. Furstenberg Jr. *The New American Grandparent. A Place in the Family, A Life Apart*. New York: Basic Books, 1986.

Chimbos, Peter D. "The Greek-Canadian Family: Tradition and Change." *Canadian Families: Ethnic Variations*. Edited by K. Ishwaran. Scarborough: McGraw-Hill Ryerson, 1980:27–40.

Chipperfield, Judith G. and Betty Havens. "A Longitudinal Analysis of Perceived Respect Among Elders: Changing Perceptions for Some Ethnic Groups." *Canadian Journal on Aging*. 11 (1). 1992:15–30.

Chodorow, Nancy. *Feminism and Psychoanalytic Theory*. New Haven, CT: Yale University Press, 1989.

Clark, S.D. *The Suburban Society*. Toronto: University of Toronto Press, 1966.

Clark, Susan and Andrew Harvey. "The Sexual Division of Labour: The Use of Time." *Atlantis*. 2 (1). 1976:46–66.

Clarke, Juanne Nancarrow. *Health, Illness and Medicine in Canada*. Toronto: McClelland and Stewart, 1990.

Clement, Wallace. *The Canadian Corporate Elite*. Toronto: McClelland and Stewart, 1975.

Clingempeel, W.G. and S. Segal. "Stepparent-Stepchild Relationships and the Psychological Adjustment of Children in Stepmother and Stepfather Families." *Child Development*. 57 (1). 1986:474–484.

Coates, Mary Lou. *Part-Time Employment: Labour Market Flexibility and Equity Issues*. Kingston: Queen's University, Industrial Relations Centre, 1988.

Cochrane, Jean. *Women in Canadian Life. Politics*. Scarborough: Fitzhenry and Whiteside, 1977.

Coller, D. "Joint Custody: Research, Theory and Policy." *Family Process*. 27 (4). December 1988:459–469.

Collier, Jane, Michelle Rosaldo, and Sylvia Yanagisako. "Is There a Family? New Anthropological Views." *Family Bonds and Gender Divisions*. Edited by Bonnie Fox. Toronto: Scholars' Press, 1988:31–46.

Coltrane, Scott. "Father-Child Relationships and the Status of Women: A Cross-Cultural Study." *American Journal of Sociology*. 93 (5). March 1988:1060–1095.

Comfort, Alex. "Sexuality in Later Life." *Handbook of Mental Health and Aging*. Edited by J. Birren and R. Sloane. Englewood Cliffs, NJ: Prentice-Hall, 1980.

Connidis, Ingrid Arnet. *Family Ties and Aging*. Toronto: Butterworths, 1989a.

___. "The Service Needs of Older People: Implications for Public Policy." *Canadian Journal on Aging*. 4 (1). 1985:3–10.

___. "The Subjective Experience of Aging: Correlates of Divergent Views." *Canadian Journal on Aging*. 8 (1). 1989b:7–18.

___. "Women and Retirement: The Effect of Multiple Careers on Retirement Adjustment." *Canadian Journal on Aging*. 1. (1982):17–27.

Cooley, Charles H. *Human Nature and the Social Order*. New York: Charles Scribner's Sons, 1902.

Cooper, David. *The Death of the Family*. London: Penguin Books, 1971.

Corbett, Gail H. *Barnardo Children in Canada*. Peterborough: Woodland Publishing, 1981.

Coveney, Peter. "The Image of the Child." *The Sociology of Childhood*. Edited by Chris Jenks. London: Batsford, 1982:42–47.

Cowan, Carolyn P. et al. "Transition to Parenthood: His, Hers and Theirs." *Journal of Family Issues*. 6. 1985:451–481.

Cregheur, Alain and Mary Sue Devereaux. "Canada's Children." *Canadian Social Trends*. 21. Summer 1991:2–5.

Crompton, Susan. "Who's Looking After the Kids? Child Care Arrangements of Working Mothers." *Perspectives on Labour and Income*. 3 (2). Summer 1991:68–76.

Crysdale, Stewart. *Families Under Stress. Community, Work, and Economic Change in Eastside, A Workers' Area*. Toronto: Thompson Educational Publishing, 1991.

Cumming, E. et al. "Disengagement: a Tentative Theory of Aging." *Sociometry*. 23 (1). 1960:23–25.

Cushman, Donald P. "Creative Conflict Resolution." *J.C. Penney Forum*. September 1983:8.

Dail, Paula. "Prime-Time Television Portrayals of Older Adults in the Context of Family Life." *The Gerontologist*. 28 (5). October 1988:700–706.

Danziger, Kurt. "Attitudes to Parental Control and Adolescents' Aspirations–A Comparison of Immigrants and Non-Immigrants." *Childhood and Adolescence in Canada*. Edited by K. Ishwaran. Scarborough: McGraw-Hill Ryerson, 1979:179–194.

DeKeseredy, Walter S. *Woman Abuse in Dating Relationships: The Role of Male Peer Support*. Toronto: Canadian Scholars' Press, 1988.

DeKeseredy, Walter S. and Ronald Hinch. *Woman Abuse: Sociological Perspectives*. Toronto: Thompson Educational Publishing, 1991.

DeMause, Lloyd. (ed.) *The History of Childhood*. New York: The Psychohistory Press, 1974.

Devereaux, Mary Sue. "Changes in Living Arrangements." *Canadian Social Trends*. Edited by Craig McKie and Keith Thompson. Toronto: Thompson Educational Publishing, 1990:135–137.

___. "Decline in the Number of Children." *Canadian Social Trends*. 18. Autumn 1990:32–34.

___. "Marital Status." *Canadian Social Trends.* Edited by Craig McKie and Keith Thompson. Toronto: Thompson Educational Publishing, 1990:138–141.

Dickenson, James and Bob Russell (eds.). *Family, Economy and State.* Toronto: Garamond, 1986.

Dinan, Carmel. "Sugar Daddies and Gold-Diggers: the White-Collar Single Women in Accra." *Male and Female in West Africa*, Edited by Christine Oppong. London: George Allen and Unwin, 1983.

Dornbusch, Sanford M. and Myra H. Strober (eds.). *Feminism, Children and the New Families.* New York: The Guildford Press, 1988.

Douthitt, Robin A. and Joanne Fedyk. *The Cost of Raising Children in Canada.* Toronto: Butterworths, 1990.

Dowd, James J. "Aging as Exchange: a Preface to Theory." *Journal of Gerontology.* 30. 1975:584–594.

Drakich, Janice. "In Whose Best Interest? The Politics of Joint Custody." *Family Bonds and Gender Divisions.* Edited by Bonnie Fox. Toronto: Canadian Scholars' Press, 1988:477–496.

Drakich, Janice and Connie Guberman. "Violence in the Family." *Family Matters. Sociology and Contemporary Canadian Families.* By Karen L. Anderson et al. Scarborough: Nelson, 1988:201–236.

Dranoff, Linda Silver. *Women in Canadian Life.* Scarborough: Fitzhenry and Whiteside, 1977.

Driedger, Leo and Neena Chappell. *Aging and Ethnicity.* Toronto: Butterworths, 1987.

Duchesne, Doreen. "The Decline in Unpaid Family Work." *Canadian Social Trends.* 11. Winter 1988:20–21.

Duffy, Ann. "Struggling With Power: Feminist Critiques of Family Inequality." *Reconstructing the Canadian Family.* Edited by Nancy Mandell and Ann Duffy. Toronto: Butterworths, 1988:111–139.

Dulude, Louise. *Women and Aging: a Report on the Rest of Our Lives.* Canadian Advisory Council on the Status of Women. Ottawa: Minister of Supply and Services Canada, 1978.

Dumas, Jean. *Report on the Demographic Situation in Canada 1990.* Statistics Canada. Cat. 91-209E. Ottawa: Minister of Supply and Services Canada, November 1990.

Eichler, Margrit. *Families in Canada Today.* 2nd ed. Toronto: Gage, 1988.

___. "Family Change and Social Policy." *Family Matters. Sociology and Contemporary Canadian Families.* Edited by K. Anderson et al. Scarborough: Nelson, 1988:63–86.

___. "Fifty Questions: Problems and Issues in Developing Policies for Canadian Families." Ottawa: Canadian Centre for Policy Alternatives, 1988.

___. "The Prestige of the Occupation Housewife." *The Working Sexes.* Edited by Patricia Marchak. Vancouver: University of British Columbia Press, 1977.

Eichler, Margrit and M. Bullen. *Families in Canada: An Introduction.* Toronto: OISE Press, 1986.

Ekerdt, David J. and Barbara H. Vinick. "Marital Complaints in Husband-Working and Husband-Retired Couples." *Research on Aging.* 13 (3). September 1991:364–382.

Elkin, Frederick. *The Family in Canada.* Ottawa: The Vanier Institute of the Family, 1964.

Elkin, Frederick and Gerald Handel. *The Child and Society: The Process of Socialization.* 5th ed. New York: Random House, 1988.

Elkind, David. *All Grown Up and No Place to Go. Teenagers in Crisis.* Reading, MA: Addison-Wesley, 1984.

___. *Miseducation–Preschoolers at Risk.* Toronto: Random House, 1987.

___. *The Hurried Child.* Don Mills: Addison-Wesley, 1981.

Elliott, Jean Leonard. *Two Nations, Many Cultures. Ethnic Groups in Canada.* 2nd ed. Toronto: Prentice-Hall, 1983.

Elliott, Joyce. "The Daytime Television Drama Portrayal of Older Adults." *The Gerontologist.* 24 (6). November 1984:628–633.

Engels, Frederick. *The Origins of the Family, Private Property and the State.* Moscow: Foreign Languages Publishing House, 1954. (Originally published in 1884.)

Entwisle, D. and S. Doering. *The First Birth: A Family Turning Point.* Baltimore: Johns Hopkins University Press, 1981.

Epstein, S. "The Stability of Behaviour: On Predicting Most of the People Much of the Time." *Journal of Personality and Social Psychology.* 37 (7). 1979:1097–1126.

Erikson, Erik. *Childhood and Society.* 2nd ed. New York: Norton, 1963.

___. *Identity: Youth and Crisis.* New York: Norton, 1968.

Eshleman, J. Ross. *The Family: An Introduction*. Needham Heights, MA: Allyn and Bacon, 1978.

Fine, Marshall. "Basic Characteristics of Family Systems Theory: Some Implications for the OAC in Family Studies." *OFSHEEA Journal*. 5 (1). June 1986:2–6.

Forbes, William F., Jennifer A. Jackson, and Arthur S. Kraus. *Institutionalization of the Elderly in Canada*. Toronto: Butterworths, 1987.

Forcese, Dennis. *The Canadian Class Structure*. 3rd ed. Scarborough: McGraw-Hill Ryerson, 1986.

Ford, Clellan S. *Smoke From Their Fires*. New Haven, CT: Yale University Press, 1941.

Fox, Bonnie (ed.). *Family Bonds and Gender Relations. Readings in the Sociology of the Family*. Toronto: Canadian Scholars' Press, 1988.

___. (ed.). *Hidden in the Household: Women's Domestic Labour Under Capitalism*. Toronto: Women's Educational Press, 1980.

___. "Women's Double Work Day: Twentieth Century Changes in the Reproduction of Daily Life." *Hidden in the Household*. Edited by Bonnie Fox. Toronto: Women's Educational Press, 1980:173–216.

Frenken, Hubert. "Marriage, Money and Retirement." *Perspectives on Labour and Income*. 3 (4). Winter 1991:31–34.

Furstenberg, Frank Jr. "The New Standard Family: The Experience of Parents and Children After Remarriage." *Remarriage and Step-Parenting*. Edited by K. Pasley and M. Ihinger-Tallman. New York: Guilford Press, 1987:42–61.

Furstenberg, Frank Jr. and C. Nord. "Parenting Apart: Patterns of Childrearing After Divorce." *Journal of Marriage and the Family*. 47. 1985:893–904.

Furstenberg, Frank Jr. and G.B. Spanier. *Recycling the Family: Remarriage After Divorce*. Beverly Hills: Sage, 1984.

Gaffield, Chad. "The Social and Economic Origins of Contemporary Families." *Families: Changing Trends in Canada*. 2nd ed. Edited by Maureen Baker. Scarborough: McGraw-Hill Ryerson, 1990:23–40.

___. "Wage Labour, Industrialization, and the Origins of the Modern Family." *The Family: Changing Trends in Canada*. Edited by Maureen Baker. Scarborough: McGraw-Hill Ryerson, 1984:21–34.

Gagan, David. *Hopeful Travellers: Families, Land and Social Change in Mid-Victorian Peel County, Canada West*. Toronto: University of

Toronto Press, 1981.

Galarneau, Diane. "Alimony and Child Support." *Perspectives on Labour and Income*. 4 (2). Summer 1992:8–21.

___. "Women Approaching Retirement." *Perspectives on Labour and Income*. 3 (3). Autumn 1991:28–39.

Garigue, Philippe. *La Vie familiale des Canadiens Français*. Montréal: Presses de l'Université de Montréal, 1962.

Gauthier, Anne H. "Nouvelles estimations du coût de l'enfant au Canada." *Cahiers québecois de demographie*. 16 (2). octobre 1987:187–208.

Gauthier, Pierre. "Canada's Seniors." *Canadian Social Trends*. 22. Autumn 1991:16–20.

Gecas, Viktor and Monica A. Seff. "Families and Adolescents: A Review of the 1980s." *Journal of Marriage and the Family*. 52. November 1990: 941-958.

Gee, Ellen M. "The Life Course of Canadian Women: An Historical and Demographic Analysis." *Social Indicators Research*. 18. 1986:263–283.

___. "The Transition to Grandmotherhood: A Quantitative Study." *Canadian Journal on Aging*. 10 (3). 1991:254–270.

Gee, Ellen M. and Meredith M. Kimball. *Women and Aging*. Toronto: Butterworths, 1987.

Gehring, Thomas M. et al. "Conflict in Families of Adolescents: The Impact of Cohesion and Power Structures." *Journal of Family Psychology*. 3 (3). March 1990:290–309.

George, Linda K., Elizabeth J. Mutran and Margaret R. Pennybacker. "The Meaning and Measurement of Age Identity." *Experimental Aging Research*. 6 (3). 1980:283–298.

Gifford, C.G. *Canada's Fighting Seniors*. Toronto: James Lorimer and Company, 1990.

Gillespie, Dair. "Who Has the Power? The Marital Struggle." *Journal of Marriage and the Family*. 33. 1971:445–458.

Gilligan, Carol. *In a Different Voice: Psychoanalytic Theory and Women's Development*. Cambridge, MA: Harvard University Press, 1982.

Gillis, J.S. and W.E. Avis. "The Male-taller Norm in Mate Selection." *Personality and Social Psychology Bulletin*. 6. 1980:396–401.

Gilmore, David D. *Manhood in the Making. Cultural Concepts of Masculinity*. New Haven, CT: Yale University Press, 1990.

Gittens, Diana. "What is the Family? Is it Universal?" *Family Bonds and Gender Divisions*. Edited by Bonnie Fox. Toronto: Canadian Scholars' Press, 1988:19–30.

Gladstone, James W. "An Analysis of Changes in Grandparent-Grandchild Visitation Following An Adult Child's Remarriage." *Canadian Journal on Aging*. 10 (2). 1991:113–126.

___. "Factors Associated With Changes in Visiting Between Grandmothers and Grandchildren Following an Adult Child's Marriage Breakdown." *Canadian Journal on Aging*. 6 (2). 1987: 117–127.

Glenn, Norval D. and Charles N. Weaver. "The Changing Relationship of Marital Status to Reported Happiness." *Journal of Marriage and the Family*. 50. 1988:317–324.

Glick, Paul. "Marriage, Divorce, and Living Arrangements: Prospective Changes." *Journal of Family Issues*. 5. March 1984:7–26.

Gnaedinger, Nancy. *Elder Abuse: A Discussion Paper*. Ottawa: Health and Welfare Canada (For the National Clearinghouse on Family Violence), May 1989.

Goldthorpe, J.E. *Family Life in Western Societies. A Historical Sociology of Family Relationships in Britain and North America*. Cambridge: Cambridge University Press, 1987.

Goode, William J. *Women In Divorce*. New York: The Free Press, 1956.

___. *World Revolution and Family Patterns*. New York: The Free Press, 1963 (revised with new preface 1970).

Gordon, Michael. "Was Waller Ever Right? The Rating and Dating Complex Reconsidered." *Journal of Marriage and the Family*. 43. February 1981:67–76.

Gorlick, Carolyn A. "Economic Stress, Social Support and Health/Well-Being of Low-Income Female Single Parents." *Today's Family. A Critical Focus*. Edited by Phyllis Meikeljohn, Annette Yeager, and Lenore Kuch. Don Mills: Collier Macmillan, 1990:200–202.

Gotell, Lise. *The Canadian Women's Movement, Equality Rights and the Charter*. Ottawa: Canadian Research Institute for the Advancement of Women, January 1990.

Graebner, William. *A History of Retirement*. New Haven, CT: Yale University Press, 1980.

Grindstaff, Carl F. "Ethnic, Marital and Economic Status of Women." *Ethnic Demography. Canadian Immigrant, Racial and Cultural Variations*. Edited by Shiva D. Halli, Frank Trovato, and Leo Driedger. Ottawa: Carleton University Press, 1990:315–342.

___. "The High Cost of Childbearing: The Fertility of Women Age 30–44." Ottawa: Review of Demography and its Implications for Economic and Social Policy, 1986.

Gross, Penny. *Kinship Structures in Remarriage Families*. Toronto: Ph.D Thesis, University of Toronto, 1985.

Gunderson, Morley and Leon Muszynski (with Jennifer Keck). *Women and Labour Market Poverty*. Canadian Advisory Council on the Status of Women. Ottawa: Minister of Supply and Services Canada, June 1990.

Guppy, Neil. "Access to Higher Education in Canada." *Canadian Journal of Higher Education*. 14 (3). 1984:79–93.

Haber, Carole. "Mandatory Retirement In Nineteenth-Century America: The Conceptual Basis for a New Work Cycle." *Journal of Social History*. 12. 1978:77–96.

Hamm, Peter Martin. *Continuity and Change Among Canadian Mennonite Brethren*. Waterloo: Wilfrid Laurier Press, 1987.

Hanson, S.H. and M.J. Sporakowski. "Single-Parent Families." *Family Relations*. 35. 1986:3–8.

Harrell, Andrew. "Husband's Involvement in Housework: The Effects of Relative Earning Power and Masculine Orientation." Edmonton AB: Edmonton Studies Area Series #39, 1985.

Haskey, John. "Lone Parenthood and Demographic Change." *Lone Parenthood. Coping With Constraints and Making Opportunities in Single-Parent Families*. Edited by Michael Hardey and Graham Crow. Toronto: University of Toronto Press, 1991:19–46.

Havighurst, Robert J. et al. "Disengagement and Patterns of Aging." *Middle Age and Aging*. Edited by B. Neugarten. Chicago: University of Chicago Press, 1968.

Heller, Peter S., Richard Hemming, and Peter W. Kohnert. *Aging and Social Expenditure in the Major Industrial Countries, 1980–2025*. Washington, DC: International Monetary Fund, September 1986.

Hetherington, E.M., M. Cox, and R. Cox. "The Aftermath of Divorce." *Mother/Child, Father/Child Relationships*. Edited by J.H. Stevens, Jr. and M. Mathews. Washington, DC: The National Association for the Education of Young Children, 1978.

Hill, Reuben. "Modern Systems Theory and the Family." *Social Science Information*. 10. 1971:7–26.

Himelfarb, Alexander and C. James Richardson (eds.) *Sociology for Canadians. A Reader*. 2nd ed. Toronto: McGraw-Hill Ryerson, 1992.

Hird, Myra Jean. *Adolescent Attitudes Towards Adolescent Girlfriend Assault*. Montreal: McGill University, School of Social Work (MSW Research Report), March 1992.

Hobart, Charles. "Changing Orientations to Courtship: a Study of Young Canadians." *Canada: a Sociological Profile*. Vol. 2. Edited by W.E. Mann. Toronto: Copp Clark, 1970.

___. "Disillusionment in Marriage, and Romanticism", *Marriage and Family Living*. 20. May 1958:156–162.

---. "Premarital Sexuality." *Marriage and the Family in Canada Today*. Edited by G.N. Ramu. Scarborough: Prentice-Hall, 1989:53–76.

___. "Relationships in Remarried Families." *Canadian Journal of Sociology*. 13 (3). 1988A:261–282.

___. "Relationships Between the Formerly Married." *Journal of Comparative Family Studies*. 21. 1990:81–97.

___. "The Family System in Remarriage: An Exploratory Study." *Journal of Marriage and the Family*. 50. 1988b:649–662.

Hobart, Charles and D. Brown. "Effects of Prior Marriage Children On Adjustment in Remarriage: A Canadian Study." *Journal of Comparative Family Studies*. 13. 1988:37–47.

Holmes, Janelle and Eliane Leslau Silverman. *We're Here, Listen to Us! A Survey of Young Women in Canada*. Canadian Advisory Council on the Status of Women. Ottawa: Minister of Supply and Services Canada, March 1992.

Hostetler, John A. *Hutterite Society*. Baltimore: Johns Hopkins University Press, 1974.

Houston, Susan E. and Allison Prentice. *Schooling and Scholars in Nineteenth-Century Ontario*. Toronto: University of Toronto Press, 1988.

Huber, Joan and Glenna Spitze. "Considering Divorce: An Expansion of Becker's Theory of Marital Instability." *American Journal of Sociology*. 86 (1). 1980:75–89.

Hunter, Alfred A. *Class Tells. On Social Inequality in Canada*. Toronto: Butterworths, 1981.

Irving, Howard H., Michael Benjamin, and Nicolas Troeme. "Shared Parenting: An Empirical Analysis Utilizing a Large Data Base." *Family Process*. 23. December 1984:561–569.

Ishwaran, K. (ed.). *Canadian Families: Ethnic Variations*. Scarborough: McGraw-Hill Ryerson, 1980.

___. (ed.). *Childhood and Adolescence in Canada*. Scarborough: McGraw-Hill Ryerson, 1979.

___. (ed.). *Family and Marriage. Cross-Cultural Perspectives*. Toronto: Thompson Educational Publishing, 1992.

___. (ed.). *The Canadian Family*. Toronto: Gage, 1983.

Jarman, Frederick E., Susan Howlett, et al. *The Living Family. A Canadian Perspective*. Toronto: John Wiley and Sons, 1991.

Jim, Eva and Peggy Suen. "Chinese Parents and Teenagers in Canada: Cultural Conflicts." Burnaby, B.C.: Burnaby Multicultural Society and the Canadian Mental Health Association, December 1990.

Johnson, Holly. "Wife Abuse." *Canadian Social Trends*. Edited by Craig McKie and Keith Thompson. Toronto: Thompson Educational Publishing, 1990:173–176.

Johnson, Laura S. and Dick Barnhorst (eds.). *Children, Families and Public Policy in the 90s*. Toronto: Thompson Educational Publishing, 1991.

Johnson, Laura with Robert E. Johnson. *The Seam Allowance. Industrial Sewing in Canada*. Toronto: Women's Educational Press, 1982.

Johnston, Patrick. *Native Children and the Child Welfare System*. Toronto: James Lorimer and Company, 1983.

Johnston, Janet R., Marsha Kline, and Jeanne M. Tschann. "Ongoing Postdivorce Conflict: Effects on Children of Joint Custody and Frequent Access." *American Journal of Orthopsychiatry*. 59. October 1989:576–592.

Jones, Charles, Lorna Marsden, and Lorne Tepperman. *Lives of Their Own*. Toronto: Oxford University Press, 1990.

Jorgenson, S.R. *Marriage and the Family: Development and Change.* Toronto: Collier Macmillan, 1986.

Kahn, Joan R. and Kathryn A. London. "Premarital Sex and the Risk of Divorce." *Journal of Marriage and the Family*. 53 (4). November 1991.

Kalbach, Warren E. and Wayne W. McVey. *The Demographic Basis of Canadian Society*. 2nd ed. Scarborough: McGraw-Hill Ryerson, 1979.

Kalbach, Warren E. and Madeleine A. Richard. "Ethno-Religious Identity and Acculturation." *Ethnic Demography. Canadian Immigrant, Racial and Cultural Variations*. Edited by Shiva S. Halli, Frank Trovato, and Leo Driedger. Ottawa: Carleton University Press, 1990:179–198.

Kalleberg, Arne L. and Rachel A. Rosenfield. "Work in the Family and in the Labor Market: A Cross-National Reciprocal Analysis." *Journal of Marriage and the Family*. 52. 1990:331–346.

Kandel, Denise and Gerald S. Lesser. "Marital Decision-Making in America and Danish Urban Families." *Journal of Marriage and the Family*. 34. February 1972:134–138.

Katarynych, Heather L. "Adoption." *Canadian Child Welfare Law*. Edited by N. Bala, J. Hornick, and R. Vogl. Toronto: Thompson Educational Publishing, 1991:133–169.

Kaye, Lenard W. "Home Care for the Aged: A Fragile Partnership." *Social Work*. 30 (4). 1985:312–317.

Keith, Verna and Barbara Finlay. "The Impact of Parental Divorce on Children's Educational Attainment, Marital Timing, and Likelihood of Divorce." *Journal of Marriage and the Family*. 50. 1988:797–809.

Kierans, Sheila. *The Family Matters: Two Centuries of Family Law and Life in Ontario*. Toronto: Key Porter Books, 1986.

King, Alan et al. *Canada Youth and AIDS Study*. Kingston: Queen's University, Social Program Evaluation Group, 1989.

King, Margaret, John Gartrell, and Frank Trovato. "Early Childhood Mortality, 1926–1986." *Canadian Social Trends*. 21. Summer 1991:6–10.

Kinsey, Alfred C., C.W. Pomeroy, and C.E. Martin. *Sexual Behaviour in the Human Male*. Philadelphia: Saunders, 1958.

Kitchen, Brigitte. "Family Policy." *Families: Changing Trends in Canada*. 2nd ed. Edited by Maureen Baker. Scarborough: McGraw-Hill Ryerson, 1990:306–329.

Knoppers, Bartha Maria (ed.). *Canadian Child Health Law. Health Rights and Risks of Children*. Toronto: Thompson Educational Publishing, 1992.

Krahn, Harvey. "Youth Employment." *The State of the Child in Ontario*. Edited by Richard Barnhorst and Laura C. Johnson. Toronto: Oxford University Press, 1991:139–159.

Kraus, Arthur S. "The Increase in the Usual Life Span in North America." *Canadian Journal on Aging*. 6 (1). 1987:19–31.

Krauter, Joseph F. and Morris Davis. *Minority Canadians: Ethnic Groups*. Toronto: Methuen, 1978.

Kubler-Ross, Elisabeth. *On Death and Dying*. New York: Macmillan, 1969.

Kuzel, Paul and P.Krishnan. "Changing Patterns of Remarriage in Canada." *Journal of Comparative Family Studies*. 4 (2). 1973:215–224.

Labour Canada, Women's Bureau. *When I Grow Up... Career Expectations and Aspirations of Canadian Schoolchildren*. Ottawa: Minister of Supply and Services Canada, 1986.

___. *Women in the Labour Force. 1990–91 Edition*. Ottawa: Minister of Supply and Services, 1990a.

___. *Work-Related Child Care in Canada*. (Prepared by Margie I. Mayfield). Ottawa: Labour Canada, 1990b.

Lachapelle, R. and J. Henripin. *The Demolinguistic Situation in Canada: Past Trends and Future Prospects*. Montreal: The Institute for Research on Public Policy, 1982.

Lai, Chuen-yan David. "The Population Structure of North American Chinatowns In the Mid-Twentieth Century: A Case Study." *Visible Minorities and Multiculturalism: Asians in Canada*. Edited by K. Victor Ujimoto and Gordon Hirabayashi. Toronto: Butterworths, 1980:13–21.

Lam, Lawrence and Tony Haddad. *Reconstructing Canadian Men and Masculinities*. Toronto: Canadian Scholars' Press, 1993.

Lamanna, Mary Ann and Agnes Riedmann. *Marriage and Families: Making Choices and Facing Change*. 3rd ed. Belmont, CA: Wadsworth, 1988.

Lamb, Michael E.(ed.). *The Role of the Father in Child Development.* New York: Wiley 1976.

Lamb, Michael E. and D. Oppenheim. "Fatherhood and Father-child Relationships: Five Years of Research." *Fathers and Their Families.* Edited by S.H. Cath et al. Hillsdale, NJ: Analytic Press, 1989.

Landis, Judson T. "On the Campus." *Survey Midmonthly.* 84. January 1948:17–19.

Larson, Lyle. *The Canadian Family in Comparative Perspective.* Scarborough: Prentice-Hall, 1976.

Larson, J. "The Marriage Quiz: College Students' Beliefs in Selected Myths About Marriage." *Family Relations.* January 1988.

Larson, Reed. "Thirty Years of Research on the Subjective Well-Being of Older Americans." *Journal of Gerontology.* 33 (1). 1978:109–125.

Laslett, Peter. *The World We Have Lost.* London: University Paperbacks, 1971.

Le Bourdais, Celine, Pierre J. Hamel, et Paul Bernard. "Le travail et l'ouvrage. Charge et partage des tâches domestiques chez les couples québecois", *Sociologie et Societés.* XIX (1). avril 1987:37–55.

Lee, G.R. "Age at Marriage and Marital Satisfaction: A Multivariate Analysis for Implications for Marital Stability." *Journal of Marriage and the Family.* 39. 1977:493–504.

Lee, John Alan. "The Invisible Lives of Canada's Gray Gays." *Aging in Canada. Social Perspectives.* 2nd ed. Edited by Victor W. Marshall. Markham: Fitzhenry and Whiteside, 1987: 138–155.

___. "Three Paradigms of Childhood." *Canadian Review of Sociology and Anthropology.* 19 (4). 1982:591–608.

Lee, Leanna L.C. "Parent-Child Relationships From Adolescent Eyes: A Comparison Between Recent Immigrants and Canadian-Born Chinese Adolescents." Montreal: McGill University, MSW Research Report. June 1992.

Lehr, Ursula. "The Situation of Elderly Women: Psychological and Social Aspects." *Zeitschrift für Gerontologie.* 11 (1). 1978:6–26. (Abstracted in *Psychology Abstracts* 61:1356).

Lero, Donna. "Child Care as an Element in Family Policy." Paper Presented at the Annual Meetings of the Canadian Sociology and Anthropology Association, University of Victoria, 1990.

Lero, Donna and Irene Kyle. "Families and Children in Ontario." *Children, Families and Public Policy in the 90s*. Edited by Laura C. Johnson and Dick Barnhorst. Toronto: Thompson Educational Publishing, 1991:25–72.

Lero, Donna, A. Pence, M. Shields, L. Brockman, and H. Goelman. *Canadian National Child Care Study. Introductory Report*. Ottawa: Supply and Services Canada, February 1992.

Leslie, Gerald R. *The Family in Social Context*. 5th ed. New York: Oxford University Press, 1982.

Leslie, Gerald R. and Sheila K. Korman. *The Family in Social Context*. 7th ed. New York: Oxford University Press, 1989.

Li, Peter S. *Ethnic Inequality in a Class Society*. Toronto: Thompson Educational Publishing, 1988.

___. "Sociological Methods of Research." *An Introduction to the Social World*. Edited by R. Jack Richardson and Lorne Tepperman. Scarborough: McGraw-Hill Ryerson, 1987:35–57.

___. *The Chinese in Canada*. Toronto: Oxford University Press, 1988.

Lin, C.C. and Fu, V.R. "A Comparison of Child-Rearing Practices Among Chinese, Immigrant Chinese, and Caucasian-American Parents." *Child Development*. 61. 1990:429–433.

Linton, Ralph. *The Study of Man: An Introduction*. Englewood Cliffs, NJ: Prentice-Hall, 1936.

Lopata, Helena Z. "Social Involvement of American Widows." *American Behavioural Scientist*. 14 (1). 1970:40–56.

___. *Widowhood in an American City*. Cambridge, MA: Schenkman Publishing Company, 1973.

___. *Women as Widows: Support Systems*. New York: Elseviers, 1979.

Love, Roger and Suan Poulin. "Family Income Inequality in the 1980s." *Perspectives on Labour and Income*. 3 (3). Autumn 1991:51–57.

Lowe, Graham S. "Retirement Attitudes, Plans and Behaviour." *Perspectives on Labour and Income*. 3 (3). Autumn 1991:8–17.

___. *Women, Paid/Unpaid Work, and Stress. New Directions for Research*. Canadian Advisory Council on the Status of Women. Ottawa: Minister of Supply and Services Canada, 1989.

Lupri, Eugen and James Frideres. "The Quality of Marriage and the Passage of Time: Marital Satisfaction Over the Family Life

Cycle." *Canadian Journal of Sociology*. 6 (3). Summer 1981:283–306.

Luxton, Meg. *More Than a Labour of Love*. Toronto: Women's Educational Press, 1980.

___. "Thinking About the Future." *Family Matters. Sociology and Contemporary Canadian Families*. Edited by K. Anderson et al. Scarborough: Nelson, 1988:237–257.

Luxton, Meg, Harriet Rosenberg, and Sedef Arat-Koc. *Through the Kitchen Window: The Politics of Home and Family*. 2nd ed. Toronto: Garamond Press, 1990.

MacBride-King, Judith L. *Work and Family: Employment Challenge of the 90s*. Ottawa: Conference Board of Canada, November 1990.

Mackie, Marlene. *Constructing Women and Men: Gender Socialization*. Toronto: Holt, Rinehart and Winston, 1987.

___. *Gender Relations in Canada. Further Explorations*. Toronto: Butterworths, 1991.

___. "Socialization: Changing Views of Child Rearing and Adolescence." *Families: Changing Trends in Canada*. 2nd ed. Edited by Maureen Baker. Scarborough: McGraw-Hill Ryerson, 1990:115–148.

MacLean, Michael and Rita Bonar. "The Ethnic Elderly in a Dominant Culture Long-Term Care Facility." *Canadian Ethnic Studies*. 15 (3). 1983:51–59.

MacLeod, Linda. *Battered But Not Beaten: Preventing Wife Abuse in Canada*. Canadian Advisory Council on the Status of Women. Ottawa: Minister of Supply and Services Canada, 1987.

MacLeod, Linda. *Wife Battering and the Web of Hope: Progress, Dilemmas and the Visions of Prevention*. Prepared for the Family Violence Prevention Division. Ottawa: Health and Welfare Canada, May 1989.

MacLeod, Linda. *Wife Battering in Canada: The Vicious Circle*. Canadian Advisory Council on the Status of Women. Ottawa: Minister of Supply and Services Canada, 1980.

Makepeace, J. "Courtship Violence Among College Students." *Family Relations* 30 1981:97–102.

Malinowski, Bronislaw. *A Scientific Theory of Culture*. Chapel Hill: University of North Carolina Press, 1944.

Malles, Paul. *Canadian Labour Standards in Law, Agreement, and Practice*. Economic Council of Canada. Ottawa: Minister of Supply and Services, 1976.

Mandell, Nancy. "The Child Question: Links Between Women and Children in the Family." *Reconstructing the Canadian Family: Feminist Perspectives.* Edited by Nancy Mandell and Ann Duffy. Toronto: Butterworths, 1988:49–81.

Mandell, Nancy and Ann Duffy. *Reconstructing the Canadian Family: Feminist Perspectives.* Toronto: Butterworths, 1988.

Mansfield, Nick. "Inquiry and Explanations." *Introductory Sociology: Canadian Perspectives.* Don Mills: Collier Macmillan, 1982.

Marcil-Gratton, Nicole and Jacques Légaré. "Will Reduced Fertility Lead to Greater Isolation in Old Age for Tomorrow's Elderly?" *Canadian Journal on Aging.* 11 (1). 1992:54–71.

Maret, Elizabeth and Barbara Finlay. "The Distribution of Household Labor Among Women in Dual-earner Families." *Journal of Marriage and the Family.* 46 (2). May 1984:357–364.

Marshall, Katherine. "Household Chores." *Canadian Social Trends.* 16. Spring 1990:18–19.

Marshall, Victor W. (ed.) *Aging in Canada. Social Perspectives.* 2nd ed. Markham: Fitzhenry and Whiteside, 1987.

Martin, Wilfred B.W. and Allan J. Macdonnell. *Canadian Education. A Sociological Analysis.* Scarborough: Prentice-Hall, 1982.

Martin Matthews, Anne. *Widowhood in Later Life.* Toronto: Butterworths, 1991.

___. "Widowhood as an Expectable Life Event." *Aging in Canada. Social Perspectives.* 2nd ed. Edited by Victor W. Marshall. Markham: Fitzhenry and Whiteside, 1987a:343–366.

Martin Matthews, Anne and Kathleen Brown. "Retirement as a Critical Life Event." *Research on Aging.* 9 (4). 1987b:548–571.

Martin Matthews, Anne and Ralph Matthews. "Beyond the Mechanics of Infertility: Perspectives on the Social Psychology of Infertility and Involuntary Childlessness." *Family Relations.* 35. October 1986:479–487.

Maynard, Rona. "Were They Better Off Than We Are?" *Report on Business Magazine.* May 1988:39–47.

McDaniel, Susan A. *Canada's Aging Population.* Toronto: Butterworths, 1986.

___. "Women's Roles and Reproduction: The Changing Picture in Canada in the 1980s." *Atlantis.* 14 (1). 1988a:1–12.

___. "Women's Roles, Reproduction and the New Reproductive Technologies: A New Stork Rising." *Reconstructing the Canadian Family*. Edited by Nancy Mandell and Ann Duffy. Toronto: Butterworths, 1988b:175–206.

McDonald, P. Lynn and Richard A. Wanner. *Retirement in Canada*. Toronto: Butterworths, 1990.

McDonald, P. Lynn, J.P. Hornick, G.B. Robertson, and J.E.Wallace. *Elder Abuse and Neglect in Canada*. Toronto: Butterworths, 1991.

McDonald, Ryan J. "Missing Children." *Canadian Social Trends*. 24. Spring 1992:2–5.

McEvoy, Maureen. "Native Communities Revise and Redesign the Child Welfare System." *Transition*. 21 (4). December 1991:11–14.

McKie, Craig. "Common-Law: Living Together as Husband and Wife Without Marriage." *Canadian Social Trends*. 3. Autumn 1986:39–41.

McKie, Craig and Keith Thompson (eds.). *Canadian Social Trends*. Toronto: Thompson Educational Publishing, 1990.

McLaren, Angus and Arlene Tigar McLaren. *The Bedroom and the State: The Changing Practices and Politics of Contraception and Abortion in Canada, 1880–1980*. Toronto: McClelland and Stewart, 1986.

McLaren, Arlene Tigar. *Gender and Society*. Toronto: Copp Clark Pitman, 1988.

McPherson, Barry D. *Aging as a Social Process*. 2nd ed. Toronto: Butterworths, 1990.

McVey, Wayne W. and Barrie W. Robinson. "Separation in Canada: New Insights Concerning Marriage Dissolution." *The Canadian Journal of Sociology*. 6 (3). 1981:353–366.

Mead, George Herbert. *Mind, Self and Society*. Chicago: University of Chicago Press, 1934.

Mead, Margaret. *Sex and Temperament in Three Primitive Societies*. New York: Dell, 1935.

Meiklejohn, Phyllis, Annette Yeager, and Lenore Kuch (eds.). *Today's Family: A Critical Focus*. Don Mills: Collier Macmillan, 1990.

Meissner, Martin, Elizabeth W. Humphreys, Scott M. Meis, and William J.Scheu. "No Exit for Wives: Sexual Division of Labour and the Cumulation of Household Demands." *Canadian Review of Sociology and Anthropology*. 12 (Part 1). 1975:424–439.

Mercer, S. "Not a Pretty Picture: An Exploratory Study of Violence Against Women in High School Dating Relationships." *Resources for Feminist Research.* 17 (2). 1986:15–23.

Methot, Suzanne. "Employment Patterns of Elderly Canadians." *Canadian Social Trends.* 7. Autumn 1987:7–11.

Michelson, William. *From Sun To Sun. Daily Obligations and Community Structure in the Lives of Employed Women and Their Families.* New Jersey: Rowman and Allanheld, 1985.

Millar, Wayne. "Divorces, Canada and the Provinces 1989." *Health Reports.* 3 (2). June 1991:83–86.

Miller, D.A. "The 'Sandwich' Generation. The Adult Children of the Aging." *Social Work.* 1981:419–423.

Mills, David M. "A Model for Stepfamily Development." *Family Relations.* 33. July 1986:261–273.

Mitchell, Andrew. "The Cost of Raising a Child in the Toronto Area in 1986." Social Planning Council of Metropolitan Toronto. *Social Infopac.* 6 (5). November 1987:1–5.

___. "The Economic Circumstances of Ontario's Families and Children." *The State of the Child in Ontario.* Edited by Richard Barnhorst and Laura C. Johnson. Toronto: Oxford University Press, 1991:22–47.

Moogk, Peter N. "Les Petits Sauvages: The Children of Eighteenth Century New France." *Childhood and Family in Canadian History.* Edited by Joy Parr. Toronto: McClelland and Stewart, 1982:17–43.

Moore, Maureen. "Dual-Earner Families: The New Norm." *Canadian Social Trends.* Edited by Craig McKie and Keith Thompson. Toronto: Thompson Educational Publishing, 1990:161–163.

___. *The Characteristics of Dual-Earner Families.* Statistics Canada. Cat. 13-588, no. 3. Ottawa: Minister of Supply and Services Canada, July 1989.

___. "Women Parenting Alone." *Canadian Social Trends.* 8. Winter 1987:31–36.

Moreau, Joanne. "Employment Equity." *Canadian Social Trends.* 22. Autumn 1991:26–28.

Morgan, S. Philip, Diane N. Lye, and Gretchen A. Condran. "Sons, Daughters, and the Risk of Marital Disruption." *American Journal of Sociology.* 94 (1). July 1988:110–129.

Morris, Cerise. *The Politics and Experience of Co-Parenting: An Exploratory Study of Shared Custody in Canada*. Ottawa: Canadian Research Institute for the Advancement of Women, 1988.

Morris, Monica. *Last Chance Children. Growing Up With Older Parents.* New York: Columbia University Press, 1988.

Morrison, Richard J. and Jillian Oderkirk. "Married and Unmarried Couples: The Tax Question." *Canadian Social Trends*. 21. Summer 1991:15–21.

Morton, Mary E. "Dividing the Wealth, Sharing the Poverty: the (Re)formation of 'Family' in Law." *The Canadian Review of Sociology and Anthropology*. 25 (2). 1988:254–275.

Morton, Mildred. "Controversies Within Family Law." *Families: Changing Trends in Canada*. 2nd ed. Edited by Maureen Baker. Scarborough: McGraw-Hill Ryerson, 1990:211–240.

Muir, Bernice L. *Health Status of Canadian Indians and Inuit*. Indian and Northern Health Services. Ottawa: Health and Welfare Canada, 1988.

Murdock, George. *Social Structure*. New York: Macmillan, 1949.

Myles, John. *Old Age in the Welfare State: Political Economy of Public Pensions*. 2nd ed. Lawrence, KS: University Press of Kansas, 1989.

Nagnur, Dhruva and Owen Adams. "Tying the Knot: An Overview of Marriage Rates in Canada." *Canadian Social Trends*. 7. Autumn 1987:2–6.

Naidoo, J.C. "The South Asian Experience of Aging." *Multiculturalism*. VIII (3). 1985:3–6.

Nanda, Serena. "Arranging a Marriage in India." *The Humbled Anthropologist: Tales From Around the World*. Edited by Philip R. DeVita. Belmont, CA: Wadsworth, 1991.

___. *Cultural Anthropology*. Belmont, CA: Wadsworth, 1991.

National Council of Welfare. *Child Care. A Better Alternative*. Ottawa: National Council of Welfare, December 1988a.

___. *Poverty Profile 1988*. Ottawa: Minister of Supply and Services Canada, April 1988b.

___. *Women and Poverty Revisited*. Ottawa: National Council of Welfare, Summer 1990.

Native Women's Association of Canada. *Presentation to the Special House of Commons Committee on Child Care*. Ottawa, 10 June 1986.

Nave-Herz, Rosemarie. "Childless Marriages." *Marriage and Family Review*. 14 (1–2). 1989:239–250.

Nessner, Katherine. "Children With Disabilities." *Canadian Social Trends*. 18. Winter 1990:18–21.

Nett, Emily. "Canadian Families in Social-Historical Perspective." *Canadian Journal of Sociology*. 6 (3). 1981:239–260.

___. *Canadian Families Past and Present*. Toronto: Butterworths, 1988.

___. "The Family." *Sociology*. Edited by Robert Hagedorn et al. Toronto: Holt, Rinehart and Winston, 1980.

___. "The Family and Aging." *Families: Changing Trends in Canada*. 2nd ed. Edited by Maureen Baker. Scarborough: McGraw-Hill Ryerson, 1990:241–271.

Neugarten, Bernice L., Robert Havighurst, and Sheldon S. Tobin. "Personality and Patterns of Aging." *Middle Age and Aging*. Edited by B. Neugarten. Chicago: Chicago University Press, 1968:173–177.

Neugarten, Bernice L. and Dail A. Neugarten. "The Changing Meanings of Age." *Psychology Today*. May 1987:29–33.

Nicholson, John. *Seven Ages*. Glasgow: Fontana Paperbacks, 1980.

Ng, Edward. "Children and Elderly People: Sharing Public Income Resources." *Canadian Social Trends*. 25. Summer 1992:12–15.

Noller, Patricia and Fitzpatrick, Mary Anne. "Marital Communication in the Eighties." *Journal of Marriage and the Family*. 52. November 1990:832–839.

Nolté, Judith. "Teenage Sexuality: Myths and Reality." *Le Temps d'y Voir*. Summary of Papers presented at the International Conference on the Status of Girls, Montreal October 1985. Montreal: Guérin 1986.

Norris, Mary Jane. "The Demography of Aboriginal People in Canada." *Ethnic Demography. Canadian Immigrant, Racial and Cultural Variations*. Edited by Shiva Halli, Frank Tovato and Leo Driedger. Ottawa: Carleton University Press, 1990:15–59.

Novak, Mark. *Aging and Society. A Canadian Perspective*. Scarborough: Nelson, 1988.

___. *Successful Aging. The Myths, Realities and Future of Aging in Canada*. Markham: Penguin, 1985.

Okin, Susan Moller. *Justice, Gender, and the Family*. New York: Basic Books, 1989.

O'Leary, K.D., et al. "Prevalence and Stability of Physical Aggression Between Spouses: A Longitudinal Analysis." *Journal of Consulting and Clinical Psychology*. 57. 1989:263–268.

Ontario Law Reform Commission. *Report on Human Artificial Reproduction and Related Matters*. Toronto, Ontario Ministry of Education, 1985.

Ontario Ministry of Skills Development. *Out of School Youth in Ontario: Their Labour Market Experience*. Toronto: Ministry of Skills Development, 1987.

___. *Pathways. A Study of Labour Market Experiences and Transition Patterns of High School Leavers*. Toronto: Ministry of Skills Development, May 1989.

Orleans, Myron, Bartolomeo J. Palisi, and David Caddell. "Marriage Adjustment and Satisfaction of Stepfathers: Their Feelings and Perceptions of Decision Making and Stepchildren Relations." *Family Relations*. 38. October 1989:371–377.

Ornstein, Michael. *AIDS in Canada. Knowledge, Behaviour, and Attitudes of Adults*. Toronto: York University Institute for Social Research, 1989.

Paris, Hélène. *The Corporate Response to Workers With Family Responsibilities*. Report 43–89. Ottawa: The Conference Board of Canada, August 1989.

Parr, Joy (ed.). *Childhood and Family in Canadian History*. Toronto: McClelland and Stewart, 1982.

Parsons, Talcott and Robert F. Bales. *Family Socialization and Interaction Process*. New York: The Free Press, 1955.

Pasley, Kay and Marilyn Ihinger-Tallman. "Boundary Ambiguity in Remarriage: Does Ambiguity Differentiate Degree of Marital Adjustment and Integration?" *Family Relations*. 38. January 1989:46–52.

Pearson, Jessica and Nancy Theoness. "Custody After Divorce: Demographic and Attitudinal Patterns." *American Journal of Orthopsychiatry*. 60. April 1990:233–249.

Peter, Karl A. "Childhood and Adolescent Socialization Among Hutterites." *Childhood and Adolescence in Canada*. Edited by K. Ishwaran. Toronto: Gage, 1979.

___. "Problems in the Family, Community, and Culture of Hutterites." *Canadian Families: Ethnic Variations.* Edited by K. Ishwaran. Scarborough: McGraw-Hill, 1980.

___. "Religion, Community Relations, and Self-Identity Among Hutterites." *The Canadian Family.* Edited by K. Ishwaran. Toronto: Gage, 1983.

Peters, John F. "Cultural Variations: Past and Present. *Families: Changing Trends in Canada.* 2nd ed. Scarborough: McGraw-Hill Ryerson, 1990:166–191.

___. "Divorce and Remarriage." *Marriage and the Family in Canada Today.* Edited by G.N. Ramu. Scarborough: Prentice-Hall, 1989.

Piaget, Jean. *The Moral Judgment of the Child.* New York: The Free Press, 1965.

Piaget, Jean and Barbel Inhelder. *The Psychology of the Child.* New York: Basic Books, 1969.

Pierson, Ruth. "Women's Emancipation and the Recruitment of Women into the Labour Force in World War II." *The Neglected Majority: Essays in Canadian Women's History.* Edited by Susan Mann Trofimenkoff and Alison Prentice. Toronto: McClelland and Stewart, 1977.

Pillemer, Karl and David Finkelhor. "The Prevalence of Elder Abuse: A Random Sample Survey." Paper distributed at the National Conference For Family Violence Researchers, Durham, New Hampshire, July 1987.

Pineo, Peter C. "Disenchantment in the Later Years of Marriage." *Marriage and Family Living.* 23. 1961:3–11.

Pineo, Peter C. "Development Patterns in Marriage." *Family Coordinator.* 18. April 1969:135–140.

Pogrebin, L.C. *Family Politics, Love and Power on an Intimate Frontier.* New York: McGraw-Hill, 1983.

Porter, John. *The Vertical Mosaic.* Toronto: University of Toronto Press, 1965.

Porter, John, Marion Porter, and Bernard Blishen. *Stations and Callings.* Toronto: Methuen, 1982.

Powell, Lawrence A. and John B. Williamson. "The Mass Media and the Aged." *Social Policy.* Summer 1985:38–49.

Priest, Gordon E. "Living Arrangements of Canada's "Older Elderly" Population." *Canadian Social Trends*. Edited by Craig McKie and Keith Thompson. Toronto: Thompson Educational Publishing, 1990:183–187.

Propper, Alice. "Patterns of Family Violence." *Families: Changing Trends in Canada*. 2nd ed. Edited by Maureen Baker. Scarborough: McGraw-Hill Ryerson, 1990:272–305.

Pupo, Norene. "Preserving Patriarchy: Women, The Family and The State." *Reconstructing the Canadian Family: Feminist Perspectives*. Edited by Nancy Mandell and Ann Duffy. Toronto: Butterworths, 1988:207–237.

Queen, Stuart and Robert W. Habenstein. *The Family in Various Cultures*. 4th ed. New York: J.B. Lippincott Company, 1974.

Queen, Stuart A., Robert W. Habenstein, and J.S. Quadagno. *The Family in Various Cultures*. 5th ed. New York: Harper and Row, 1985.

Ram, Bali. "Intermarriage Among Ethnic Groups." *Ethnic Demography. Canadian Immigrant, Racial and Cultural Variations*. Edited by Shiva S. Halli, Frank Trovato, and Leo Driedger. Ottawa: Carleton University Press, 1990a:213–227.

___. *New Trends in the Family. Demographic Facts and Figures*. Statistics Canada. Cat. 91-535E. Ottawa: Minister of Supply and Services Canada, March 1990b.

Ramu. G.N. "Family Background and Perceived Marital Happiness: A Comparison on Voluntarily Childless Couples and Parents." *The Canadian Journal of Sociology*. 9 (1). 1984:47–67.

___. (ed.). *Marriage and the Family in Canada Today*. Scarborough: Prentice-Hall, 1989.

___. "Voluntarily Childless and Parental Couples: A Comparison of Their Lifestyle Characteristics." *Lifestyles: a Journal of Changing Patterns*. 7 (3). 1985:130–145.

Rao, K. Vaninadha and T.R. Balakrishnan. "Childlessness as a Factor of Fertility Decline in Canada." Prepared for the Review of Demography and its Implications for Economic and Social Policy. Ottawa: Health and Welfare Canada, October 1986.

Raschke, Helen J. "Divorce." *Handbook of Marriage and the Family*. Edited by M.B. Sussman and S.K. Steinmetz. New York: Plenum, 1987:597–624.

Redekop, Calvin. *Mennonite Society*. Baltimore: Johns Hopkins University Press, 1989.

Reitz, Jeffrey G. *The Survival of Ethnic Groups*. Toronto: McGraw-Hill Ryerson, 1980.

Richardson, C. James. "Children of Divorce." *Family Matters. Sociology and Contemporary Canadian Families*. Edited by Karen L. Anderson et al. Scarborough: Nelson, 1988a:163–200.

___. *Court-based Divorce Mediation in Four Canadian Cities: An Overview of Research Results*. Prepared for the Department of Justice Canada. Ottawa: Minister of Supply and Services Canada, February 1988b.

___. "Family Law Research in a Decade of Change." *Sociology for Canadians*. 2nd ed. Edited by Alexander Himmelfarb and C. James Richardson. Toronto: McGraw-Hill Ryerson, 1992:231–239.

Richman, Judith. "Bargaining for Sex and Status: The Dating Service and Sex Role Change." *The Family: Functions, Conflicts, and Symbols*. Edited by Peter J. Stein, Judith Richman, and Natalie Hannon. Reading, MA: Addison-Wesley, 1977:158–165.

Ricks, Shirley. "Father-Infant Interactions: A Review of Empirical Research." *Family Relations*. 34. October 1985:505–511.

Robertson, Joan F. "Grandparenthood: A Study of Role Conceptions." *Journal of Marriage and the Family*. 39 (1). 1977:165–174.

Rollins, Boyd and Harold Feldman. "Marital Satisfaction Over the Family Life Cycle." *Journal of Marriage and the Family*. 26. 1970:20–28.

Romaniuc, A. *Fertility in Canada: From Baby-Boom to Baby-Bust*. Statistics Canada. Ottawa: Minister of Supply and Services Canada, 1984.

Rosenfeld, Anne and Elizabeth Stark. "The Prime of Our Lives." *Psychology Today*. May 1987:62–72.

Rosenthal, Carolyn J. "Aging and Intergenerational Relations in Canada." *Aging in Canada. Social Perspectives*. 2nd ed. Edited by Victor W. Marshall. Markham: Fitzhenry and Whiteside, 1987:311–342.

___. "Family Responsibilities and Concerns: A Perspective on the Lives of Middle-aged Women." *Resources for Feminist Research*. 11 (2). 1982:211–212.

___. "Kinkeeping in the Familial Division of Labour." *Journal of Marriage and the Family*. 47 (4). 1985:965–974.

Rossi, Alice S. and Peter H. Rossi. *Parent-Child Relations Across the Life Course*. New York: Aldine de Gruyter, 1990.

Rubin, Zick, Letitia Anne Peplau, and Charles T. Hill. "Loving and Leaving: Sex Differences in Romantic Attachments." *Sex Roles*. 7. August 1981:821–825.

Russell, Diana E.H. *Rape in Marriage*. Bloomington, IN: Indiana University Press, 1990.

Russel, Susan. "The Hidden Curriculum in School: Reproducing Gender and Class Hierarchies." *Sociology for Canadians. A Reader*. 2nd ed. Edited by Alexander Himelfarb and C. James Richardson. Toronto: McGraw-Hill Ryerson, 1992:444–456.

Saitz, Ray. "Moonlighting. How after-school jobs prevent our students from making the grade." *Education Forum*. 15 (2). Summer 1989:12–15.

Santrock, John and R.A. Warshak. "Developmental Relationships and Legal/Clinical Considerations in Father-Custody Families." *The Father's Role: Applied Perspectives*. Edited by M.E. Lamb. New York: Wiley, 1986.

Satir, V. *Conjoint Family Theory*. Palo Alto, CA: Science and Behavior Books, 1967.

Scanzoni, John. *Sexual Bargaining: Power Politics in the American Marriage*. 2nd ed. Chicago: University of Chicago Press, 1982.

Scanzoni, Letha Dawson and John Scanzoni. *Men, Women and Change*. 3rd ed. New York: McGraw-Hill Ryerson, 1988.

Schlesinger, Benjamin. "Living in One-Parent Families: The Children's Viewpoint." *The Canadian Family*. Edited by K. Ishwaran. Toronto: Gage, 1983.

Schlesinger, Benjamin and Rachel Schlesinger. "Postponed Parenthood: Trends and Issues." *Journal of Comparative Family Studies*. XX (3). Autumn 1989:355–363.

___. *Canadian Families: A Resource Guide*. Toronto: OISE Press Guidance Centre, 1988.

___. *Abuse of the Elderly: Issues and Annotated Bibliography*. Toronto: University of Toronto Press, 1988.

Schlesinger, Benjamin and Shirley Tenhouse Giblon. *Lasting Marriages*. Toronto: Guidance Centre, Faculty of Education, University of Toronto, 1984. (Reprinted in part in *Today's Family. A Critical Focus*. Edited by Phyllis Meikeljohn, Annette Yeager, and Lenore Kuch. Don Mills: Collier Macmillan, 1990:253–258.)

Schlesinger, Rachel Aber. "Granny-Bashing: An Introduction to the Problem." *Canadian Woman Studies*. 5 (3). 1984:55–59.

Seccombe, Wally. "Domestic Labour and the Working-Class Household." *Hidden in the Household*. Edited by Bonnie Fox. Toronto: Women's Educational Press, 1980:25–100.

___. " 'Helping Her Out': The Participation of Husbands in Domestic Labour When Wives Go Out to Work." Unpublished paper. Toronto: OISE.

Seeley, J., A. Sim and E. Loosely. *Crestwood Heights*. Toronto: University of Toronto Press, 1956.

Seltzer, J.A. "Relationships Between Fathers and Children Who Live Apart: The Father's Role After Separation." *Journal of Marriage and the Family*. 53 (1). 1991:79–110.

Sev'er, Aysan. *Women and Divorce in Canada*. Toronto: Canadian Scholars' Press, 1992.

Seward, Shirley B. "Immigrant Women in the Clothing Industry." *Ethnic Demography*. Edited by Shiva Halli, Frank Trovato, and Leo Driedger. Ottawa: Carleton University Press, 1990:343–362.

Seward, Shirley B. and Kathryn McDade. "A New Deal for Immigrant Women." *Policy Options*. June 1988:15–18.

Sheehy, Gail. *Passages: Predictable Crises in Adult Life*. New York: Dutton, 1974.

Shorter, Edward. *The Making of the Modern Family*. New York: Basic Books, 1975.

Shostak, Arthur B. "Singlehood." *Handbook of Marriage and the Family*. Edited by M.B. Sussman and S.K. Steinmetz. New York: Plenum Press, 1987:355–367.

Siggner, Andrew J. "The Socio-Demographic Conditions of Registered Indians." *Arduous Journey*. Edited by J. Rick Ponting. Toronto: McClelland and Stewart, 1986.

Simmons-Troppea, Daryl and Richard Osborn. "Disease, Survival and Death: the Health Status of Canada's Elderly." *Aging in Canada. Social Perspectives*. 2nd ed. Edited by Victor W. Marshall. Markham: Fitzhenry and Whiteside, 1987:399–423.

Sloan, Pamela. "From School to Work." *Children, Families and Public Policy in the 90s*. Edited by L.C. Johnson and D. Barnhorst. Toronto: Thompson Educational Publishing, 1991:175–206.

Sloss, Elizabeth (ed.). *Family Law in Canada: New Directions.* Ottawa: Canadian Advisory Council on the Status of Women, 1985.

Smart, Carol and Selma Sevenhuijsen. *Child Custody and the Politics of Gender.* New York: Routledge, 1989.

Smith, Dorothy. "A Sociology For Women." *The Prism of Sex: Essays in the Sociology of Knowledge.* Edited by J. Sherman and T. Beck. Madison: University of Wisconsin Press, 1979.

Southworth, Suzanne and J.C. Schwarz. "Post-Divorce Contact, Relationship With Father, and Heterosexual Trust in Female College Students." *American Journal of Orthopsychiatry.* 57. 1987:371–382.

Staples, Robert (ed.). *The Black Family: Essays and Studies.* 2nd ed. Belmont, CA: Wadsworth, 1978.

Stark, Elizabeth. "Young, Innocent and Pregnant." *Psychology Today.* October 1986:28–35.

Statistics Canada. *A Portrait of Children in Canada.* Cat. 89-520. Ottawa: Minister of Supply and Services Canada, 1990a.

___. *Births and Deaths 1985. Vital Statistics Volume 1.* Cat. 84-204. Ottawa: Minister of Supply and Services Canada, November 1986a.

___. *Education in Canada. A Statistical Review for 1989–90.* Cat. 81-229. Ottawa: Minister of Supply and Services Canada, August 1991.

___. *Health Reports. Marriages 1989.* Cat. 82-003S. Supplement 16, Vol 2 (4). 1990. Ottawa: Minister of Supply and Services Canada, 1991.

___. *Historical Labour Force Statistics, 1991.* Cat. 71-201. Ottawa: Minister of Supply and Services Canada, February 1992a.

___. *Historical Statistics of Canada.* 2nd ed. Ottawa: Minister of Supply and Services Canada, 1983.

___. *Income Distribution by Size in Canada.* Cat. 13-206. Ottawa: Minister of Supply and Services Canada, 1990b.

___. *Labour Force Annual Averages. 1991.* Cat. 71-220. Ottawa: Ministry of Industry, Science and Technology, 1992b.

___. *Marriages and Divorces 1985. Vital Statistics. Volume 2.* Cat. 84-205. Ottawa: Minister of Supply and Services Canada, September 1986b.

___. *Quarterly Demographic Statistics. July–September 1991.* Cat. 91-002, Vol. 5 (3). Ottawa: Minister of Supply and Services Canada, January 1992c.

___. *The Family in Canada. Selected Highlights.* Ottawa: Minister of Supply and Services, January 1989.

___. *The Labour Force.* Cat. 71-001. Ottawa: Minister of Supply and Services Canada, monthly.

___. *Tuition and Living Accommodation Costs at Canadian Universities, 1990–91 and 1991–92.* Cat. 81-219. Ottawa: Minister of Supply and Services Canada, October 1991.

___. *Women in Canada. A Statistical Report.* 2nd ed. Cat. 89-503E. Ottawa: Minister of Supply and Services Canada, February 1990c.

Stebbins, Robert A. "Men, Husbands and Fathers: Beyond Patriarchal Relations." *Restructuring the Canadian Family: Feminist Perspectives.* Edited by Nancy Mandell and Ann Duffy. Toronto: Butterworths, 1988:27–47.

Stein, Peter. "Understanding Single Adulthood." *Current Issues in Marriage and the Family.* Edited by J. Gipson Wells. New York: Macmillan, 1988.

Stephens, William N. *The Family in Cross-Cultural Perspective.* New York: Holt Rinehart, 1963.

Stets, J. and D. Henderson. "Contextual Factors Surrounding Conflict Resolution While Dating: Results From a National Study." *Family Relations.* 40. 1991:29–36.

Stout, Cam. "Common-Law: A Growing Alternative." *Canadian Social Trends.* 23. Winter 1991:18–20.

Strain, Laurel A. and Barbara J. Payne. "Social Networks and Patterns of Social Interaction among Ever-Single and Separated/Divorced Elderly Canadians." *Canadian Journal on Aging.* 11 (1). 1992:31–53.

Strauss, Murray A. and Richard J. Gelles. *Physical Violence in American Families. Risk Factors and Adaptations to Violence in 8,145 Families.* New Brunswick, NJ: Transaction Press, 1990.

Strauss, Stephen. "Baby boomlet continues, Statistics Canada reports." *The Globe and Mail,* 31 March 1992:A1, A5.

Strike, Carol. "AIDS Into the 1990s." *Canadian Social Trends.* 21. Winter 1991:22–24.

Strong-Boag, Veronica. "Intruders in the Nursery: Childcare Professionals Reshape the Years One to Five, 1920–1940." *Childhood and Family in Canadian History.* Edited by Joy Parr. Toronto: McClelland and Stewart, 1982:160–178.

Sturino, Franc. "Family and Kin Cohesion Among Southern Italian Immigrants in Toronto." *Canadian Families: Ethnic Variations.* Edited by K. Ishwaran. Scarborough: McGraw-Hill Ryerson, 1980:84–104.

Sugiman, Pamela and Harry K. Nishio. "Socialization and Cultural Duality Among Aging Japanese Canadians." *Canadian Ethnic Studies.* 15 (3). 1983:17–35.

Sullivan, Terrence. *Sexual Abuse and the Rights of Children. Reforming Canadian Law.* Toronto: University of Toronto Press, 1992.

Sung, B.L. "Bicultural Conflicts in Chinese Immigrants." *Journal of Comparative Family Studies.* 16 (2). 1985:255–269.

Sutherland, Neil. *Children in English-Canadian Society: Framing the Twentieth Century Consensus.* Toronto: University of Toronto Press, 1976.

Sutherland, Ralph W. and M. Jane Fulton. *Health Care in Canada.* Ottawa: The Health Group, 1988.

Swift, Karen. "Contradictions in Child Welfare: Neglect and Responsibility." *Women's Caring. Feminist Perspectives on Social Welfare.* Edited by C. Baines et al. Toronto: McClelland and Stewart, 1991:234–271.

Sydie, Rosalind. *Natural Women, Cultured Men: A Feminist Perspective on Sociological Theory.* Toronto: Methuen, 1987.

Synge, Jane. "Work and Family Support Patterns of the Aged in the Early Twentieth Century." *Aging in Canada. Social Perspectives.* Edited by Victor W. Marshall. Markham: Fitzhenry and Whiteside, 1980:135–144.

Synge, Jane et al. "Phoning and Writing as Means of Keeping in Touch in the Family in Later Life." Paper presented to the Annual Meetings of the Canadian Association on Gerontology, Toronto, November 1981.

Synnott, Anthony. "Little Angels, Little Devils: A Sociology of Children." *The Canadian Review of Sociology and Anthropology.* 20 (1). February 1983:79–95.

Tavuchis, Nicholas. "Ethnicity and the Family." *Marriage and the Family in Canada Today.* Edited by G.N. Ramu. Scarborough: Prentice-Hall, 1989:167–184.

Tepperman, Lorne and R. Jack Richardson (eds.). *The Social World.* 2nd ed. Scarborough: McGraw-Hill Ryerson, 1991.

Terman, Lewis M. *Psychological Factors in Marital Happiness.* New York: McGraw-Hill, 1938.

Tesson, Geoffrey. "Socialization and Parenting." *Family Matters. Sociology and Contemporary Canadian Families.* Edited by Karen Anderson et al. Scarborough: Nelson, 1988:87–112.

Thomas, Jeanne L. *Adulthood and Aging.* Needham Heights, MA: Allyn and Bacon, 1992.

___. "Age and Sex Differences in the Perception of Grandparenting." *Journal of Gerontology.* 41 (3). 1986:417–423.

Thorne, Barrie. "Feminist Rethinking of the Family: An Overview." *Rethinking the Family: Some Feminist Questions.* Edited by Barrie Thorne with Marilyn Yalom. New York: Longmans, 1982.

Thorne-Finch, Ron. *Ending the Silence. The Origins and Treatment of Male Violence Against Women.* Toronto: University of Toronto Press, 1992.

Tilly, Louise and Joan Scott. *Women, Work and the Family.* New York: Holt, Rinehart and Winston, 1978.

Townson, Monica. *Leave for Employees With Family Responsibilities.* Ottawa: Labour Canada, 1988.

Troll, L.E. "The Family in Later Life: A Decade Review." *Journal of Marriage and the Family.* 33. 1971:263–290.

Turcotte, Pierre. "Common-Law Unions: Nearly Half a Million in 1986." *Canadian Social Trends.* Edited by Craig McKie and Keith Thompson. Toronto: Thompson Educational Publishing, 1990:148–152.

Turk, James and Norman Bell. "Measuring Power in Families." *Journal of Marriage and the Family.* 34. 1972:215–222.

Ujimoto, K. Victor. "The Ethnic Dimension of Aging in Canada." *Aging in Canada. Social Perspectives.* 2nd ed. Edited by Victor. W. Marshall. Markham: Fitzhenry and Whiteside, 1987:111–137.

Underwood, Nora with John DeMont. "Mid-Life Panic." *Maclean's* 19 August 1991:30–33.

United Nations. *Demographic Yearbook 1989.* New York, 1991.

Vachon, Mary L.S. *Identity Change over the First Two Years of Bereavement: Social Relationships and Social Support.* Toronto: York University (Ph.D Dissertation) 1979.

Vanier Institute of the Family. *Canadian Families.* Ottawa: Vanier

Institute of the Family, 1991.

___. "Of Birds, Bees and Petri Dishes." *Transition*. March 1988:4–5.

___. "Workers With Family Responsibilities in a Changing Society: Who Cares?" *Transition*. 17 (3). September 1987:10–11.

Van Stolk, Mary. *The Battered Child in Canada*. Toronto: McClelland and Stewart, 1978.

Veevers, Jean E. *Childless By Choice*. Toronto: Butterworths, 1980.

___. (ed.). *Continuity and Change in Marriage and Family*. Toronto: Holt, Rinehart and Winston, 1991.

___. "Traumas versus Strens: A Paradigm of Positive versus Negative Divorce Outcomes." *Marital Instability and Divorce Outcomes*. Edited by C.A. Everett. Binghamton, NY: The Haworth Press, 1991:99–126.

Verma, Ravi, Chan B. Kwok and Larry Lam. "The Chinese-Canadian Family: A Socio-Economic Profile." *Canadian Families: Ethnic Variations*. Edited by K. Ishwaran. Scarborough: McGraw-Hill Ryerson, 1980:138–156.

Veroff, Joseph and Sheila Feld. *Marriage and Work in America*. New York: Van Nostrand-Reinhold, 1970.

Volgy, Sandra S. (ed.). *Women and Divorce Men and Divorce. Gender Differences in Separation, Divorce and Remarriage*. Binghamton, NY: The Haworth Press, 1991.

Wachtel, Andy. *Child Abuse: Discussion Paper*. Ottawa: Health and Welfare Canada (National Clearinghouse on Family Violence), May 1989.

Wadhera, Surinder. "Trends in Birth and Fertility Rates, Canada, 1921–1987." *Health Reports*. 1 (2). 1989:211–223.

Wadhera, Surinder and Wayne J. Millar. "Patterns and Change in Canadian Fertility 1971–1988: First Births After Age 30." *Health Reports*. 3 (2). 1991:149–161.

Wadhera, Surinder and Jill Strachan. "Births and Birth Rates, Canada, 1989." *Health Reports*. 3 (2). 1991:79–82.

___. *Selected Marriage Statistics, 1921–1990*. Statistics Canada. Cat. 82-552. Ottawa: Minister of Supply and Services Canada, July 1992.

Wakil, Parvez S., C.M. Siddique, and F.A. Wakil. "Between Two Cultures: A Study in Socialization of Children of Immigrants." *Journal of Marriage and the Family*. 43. November 1981:929–940.

Walker, Alexis J. et al. "Perceptions of Aid and Actual Aid in Intergenerational Caregiving." *Family Relations*. 40. 1991:318–323.

Walker, Gillian A. *Family Violence and the Women's Movement. The Conceptual Politics of Struggle*. Toronto: University of Toronto Press, 1990.

Waller, Willard. "The Rating-Dating Complex." *American Sociological Review*. 2. October 1937:727–735.

Waller, Willard and Reuben Hill. *The Family: A Dynamic Interpretation*. New York: Cordon, 1951.

Wallerstein, Judith S. "Children of Divorce: Preliminary Report of a Ten-Year Follow-Up of Older Children and Adolescents." *Journal of the American Academy of Child Psychiatry*. 24. 1985:545–554.

Warry, Wayne. "Ontario's First People: Native Children." *Children, Families and Public Policy in the 90s*. Edited by Laura C. Johnson and Dick Barnhorst. Toronto: Thompson Educational Publishing, 1991:207–230.

Weitzman, Lenore J. *The Divorce Revolution: The Unexpected Social and Economic Consequences for Women and Children in America*. New York: The Free Press, 1985.

White, Lynn. "Determinants of Divorce: A Review of Research in the Eighties." *Journal of Marriage and the Family*. 52. 1990:904–912.

White, L.K. and A. Booth. "The Quality and Stability of Remarriages: the Role of Stepchildren." *American Sociological Review*. 50. 1985:689–698.

White, Pamela M. "The Indo-Chinese in Canada." *Canadian Social Trends*. 18. Autumn 1990:7–10.

Whitehurst, Robert. "Alternative Life Styles: Two Decades of Change." *Marriage and the Family in Canada Today*. Edited by G.N. Ramu. Scarborough: Prentice-Hall, 1989:253–270.

Whyte, William Foote. *Street Corner Society*. Chicago: University of Chicago Press, 1961. (Originally published in 1943.)

Widerberg, Karen. "Reforms for Women—on Male Terms—The Example of the Swedish Legislation on Parental Leave." Paper presented to the 22nd International Congress of Applied Psychology. Kyoto, Japan, July 22–27, 1987.

Williams, Savanah E. "Two Hundred Years in the Development of the Afro-Canadians in Nova Scotia, 1782–1982." *Two Nations,*

Many Cultures. Ethnic Groups in Canada. 2nd ed. Edited by Jean Leonard Elliott. Scarborough: Prentice-Hall, 1983:444–461.

Wilson, S.J. *Women, the Family and the Economy.* 3rd ed. Scarborough: McGraw-Hill Ryerson, 1991.

Winch, Robert F. "The Theory of Complementary Needs in Mate Selection: A Test of One Kind of Complementariness." *American Sociological Review.* 20. October 1955:552–555.

Wineberg, H. "Delayed Childbearing, Childlessness, and Marital Disruption." *Journal of Comparative Family Studies.* 21. 1989: 99–112.

Wise, George W. and Velma McBride Murray. "The Empty Nest: The Silent Invasion on Two Fronts." *Journal of Home Economics.* Spring 1987:49–53.

Wood, D.W. and S. Nuttall. "Single Adolescent Mothers: Dimensions of Unscheduled Parenting." Paper Presented to the Annual Meetings of the Canadian Sociology and Anthropology Association, 1984.

Yarrow, Andrew L. *Latecomers. Children of Parents Over 35.* New York: The Free Press, 1991.

Yarrow, Pamela, Lotte Marcus, and Michael J. MacLean. "Marriage and the Elderly: A Literature Review." *Canadian Journal of Social Work Education.* 7 (2). 1981:65–79.

Yeung, H. *Adaptation and Assimilation of Young Chinese in a Bicultural Setting.* Montreal: McGill University (MSW Research Report), 1982.

Zaretsky, Eli. *Captialism, The Family and Personal Life.* New York: Harper and Row, 1976.

___. "The Place of the Family in the Origins of the Welfare State." *Rethinking the Family: Some Feminist Questions.* Edited by Barrie Thorne with Marilyn Yalom. New York: Longmans, 1982:188–223.

Ziegler, Suzanne. "A Multicultural Perspective on Inter-Generational Conflicts in Immigrant Families." *Multiculturalism.* 3. 1982:12–13.

INDEX

MW01686356

Bahá'u'lláh

A Brief Survey of His Life and His Works

Shahrokh Monjazeb

The Furútan Academy

Furútan Academy Publications

Library and Archives Canada Cataloguing in Publication

Monjazeb, Shahrokh, 1966 -
Bahá'u'lláh: a brief history of his life and works / Shahrokh Monjazeb.

Includes bibliographical references.
ISBN 978-0-9783571-0-8

1. Bahá'u'lláh, 1817-1892. 2. Bahá'í Faith 3. Bahá'í Faith -- Biography.
I. Title

BP362.2.M66 2007 297.9'3 C2007-904125-6

FIRST EDITION

Cover design by Rose Bertolo

Bahá'u'lláh: A Brief Survey of His Life and Works.

 For information address Furútan Academy Publications, 2272 Courtice Avenue, Ottawa, ON, Canada, K1H 7G8 or publications@furutanacademy.org.

This book is dedicated to my teacher and mentor, Dr. Riaz K. Ghadimi (1927-2006), through whose inspirational lectures and writings I discovered a new way of studying Bahá'u'lláh and His Creative Words.

Contents

Appendices

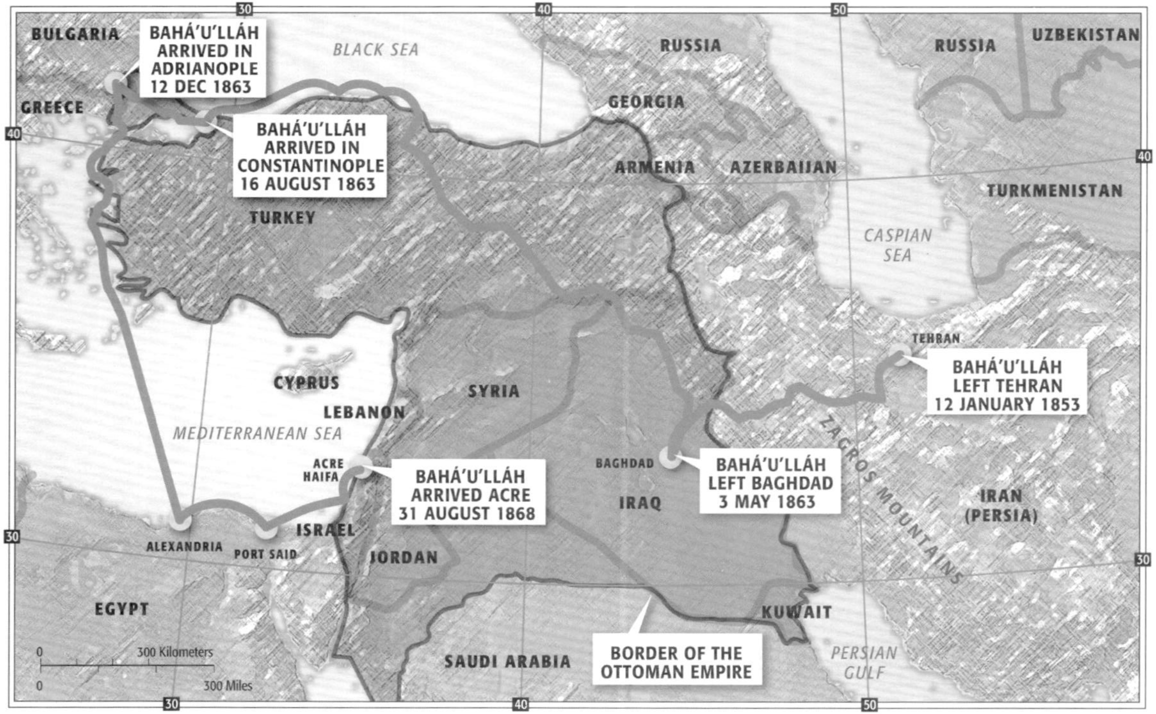

The route of Bahá'u'lláh's exiles

Reproduced with permission of the Bahá'í International Community.

Foreword

In November of 1981 the Research Department at the Bahá'í World Centre prepared a compilation called "Excellence in All Things." As its title suggested, and as the Universal House of Justice, the world governing body of the Bahá'í Faith, wrote to all National Spiritual Assemblies, the purpose of the compilation "...aimed at presenting texts and extracts which encourage the friends to attain distinction and excellence in all their undertakings" (3 November 1981). The author of the following brief survey of the life and works of Bahá'u'lláh, Mr. Shahrokh Monjazeb has, in this writer's opinion, achieved this excellence as a dynamic teacher, translator and lecturer on the sacred writings of the Bahá'í Faith.

Shahrokh Monjazeb is a man with a mission who pursues his goals with single-minded determination and purpose. That mission is to bring the knowledge of Bahá'í history and the sacred writings to the community of his fellow-believers, and interested seekers, and to remind them of the supreme importance of this goal that has been repeatedly stressed by Bahá'u'lláh, and His successors, 'Abdu'l-Bahá and Shoghi Effendi. In 2004, Mr. Monjazeb took concrete steps to further Bahá'í learning by founding the Furutan Academy (www.furutanacademy.org), with branches in Vancouver and Ottawa, an organization that is devoted to the post-secondary study of the sacred writings and history of the Bahá'í Faith.

Since 1989, Mr. Monjazeb has written a number of scholarly articles, too numerous to mention here, some of them regrettably unpublished, that have enhanced the understanding of the Bahá'í community of its corpus of superlative sacred writings. While he has written articles bearing on the life and work of the renowned Bábí-Bahá'í chronicler, Nabíl-i-A'ẓam, and 'Abdu'l-Bahá, his first love remains translation and commentary of the writings of

Bahá'u'lláh. His competence in both Persian and Arabic, the two source languages of the Bahá'í Faith, and his academic and independent study, have served him well in his chosen vocation. Mr. Monjazeb's presentations at the Annual Conferences of the Association for Bahá'í Studies (North America) have generated much interest and are well-attended.

The present survey might best be described as a research tool or study adjunct for the aspiring student of Bahá'í history and the sacred writings. The target-audience of this brief survey is not the deepened scholar, nor the polished, professional academic, but rather the intellectual and spiritual seeker, or new believer who aspires to achieve more systematic learning by delving further into the sacred writings and secondary literature of the Bahá'í Faith. The following brief survey consists of four parts, of which numbers three and four are appendices: (1) A concise linear history of Bahá'u'lláh's life that focuses on the most important events of His ministry primarily in Bahá'u'lláh's own words. (2) An anthology of thirteen selected writings. While these selections have been previously published in standard Bahá'í texts, each is preceded by a short introduction that gives the context of the scripture in question. (3) A title-list of 150 of Bahá'u'lláh's best-known works arranged alphabetically and chronologically, spanning the pre-exilic Tehran days, followed by the Baghdad, Istanbul, Edirne and Akká periods. (4) A chronology of some important dates of Bahá'u'lláh's life.

Mr. Monjazeb's contribution to the field is deserving of commendation, especially since his stated purpose is to direct the thoughtful student to the sacred writings themselves, and to more detailed historical accounts of the life and work of Bahá'u'lláh.

Jack McLean (Ottawa, Canada)

Preface

As the official web site of the Bahá'í World Community (http://www.bahai.org) states: "the Bahá'í Faith is today among the fastest-growing of the world's religions. . . . The Faith's Founder was Bahá'u'lláh, a Persian nobleman from Tehran who, in mid-nineteenth century, left a life of princely comfort and security and, in the face of intense persecution and deprivation, brought to humanity a stirring new message of peace and unity.

"Bahá'u'lláh claimed to be nothing less than a new and independent Messenger from God. His life, work, and influence parallel that of Abraham, Krishna, Moses, Zoroaster, Buddha, Christ, and Muhammad. Bahá'ís view Bahá'u'lláh as the most recent in this succession of divine Messengers.

"The essential message of Bahá'u'lláh is that of unity. He taught that there is only one God, that there is only one human race, and that all the world's religions represent stages in the revelation of God's will and purpose for humanity. In this day, Bahá'u'lláh said, humanity has collectively come of age. As foretold in all the world's scriptures, the time has arrived for the uniting of all peoples into a peaceful and integrated global society."

This book is a short introduction to the life and works of this great spiritual teacher of our time.

The mightiest proof of a Prophet has ever been found in Himself and in the efficacy of His word. Bahá'u'lláh rekindled the fires of faith and of happiness in the hearts of men. His knowledge was innate and spontaneous, not acquired in any school. None could gainsay or resist His wisdom and even His worst enemies admitted His greatness. All human perfections were embodied in Him. His strength was infinite. Trials and sufferings increased His firmness and power. As a divine physician He diagnosed the malady of the Age and prescribed the remedy. His teachings were universal and conferred illumination on all mankind. His power has been poured forth more abundantly since His death. In His prescience He stood alone and events have proved and are still proving its accuracy.

George Townshend (1876-1957)
Former Archdeacon of Clonfert and Canon of St. Patrick's Cathedral, Dublin, Ireland

His Days Amongst Humanity

Bahá'u'lláh was born in the city of Tehran as Mírzá Ḥusayn-'Alí Núrí on November 12, 1817. The place of His birth, in the great capital city of Iran, where He also spent His childhood, was in a house in the district known as Darvázih-Shimrán (Shimran Gate)[1]. According to His family genealogy[2], Bahá'u'lláh derived His lineage, on one side, from the prophet Abraham through his third wife Katurah, and on the other from the Persian prophet Zoroaster and the king Yazdigird III (r. 632-641 C.E.), the last Sásáníyan monarch of pre-Islamic Iran. He was also a descendant of Jesse[3] (father of the Hebrew King David) and was connected, through His father, Mírzá 'Abbás Núrí, to one of the oldest and most distinguished families in the northern Iranian province of Mázindarán.

Mírzá 'Abbás, the father of Bahá'u'lláh, was an eminent administrator in the court of the Qájar king Fatḥ-'Alí Sháh (r. 1797-1834 C.E.). He was also known as Mírzá Buzurg (the Great Mírzá) a title conferred on him by the Sháh himself in commendation of his exceptional talent in calligraphy. During the years of his service in the government, Mírzá Buzurg had come to hold many important and sensitive posts in the ministerial circle. At one time he was a vazír (minister) to the chief of the imperial guard, Imám Virdí Mírzá, Fatḥ-'Alí Sháh's twelfth son and the head of the Qájar tribe, and at another he was the provincial governor of Burújird and Luristán. Paying a special tribute to the memory of His illustrious father, Bahá'u'lláh has spoken these words:

> The late Vazír, My father, enjoyed a most enviable position among his countrymen. His vast wealth, his noble ancestry, his artistic attainments, his unrivalled prestige and exalted rank made him the object of the admiration of all who knew him. For a period of over twenty years, no one among the wide circle of his family and kindred, which extended over

Núr and Ṭihrán, suffered distress, injury, or illness. They enjoyed, during a long and uninterrupted period, rich and manifold blessings.[4]

Childhood and Early Youth

From His early days Bahá'u'lláh showed signs of extraordinary powers and remarkable qualities. His personal warmth and gentle character prompted great admiration and respect in those who came in contact with Him. Speaking of Bahá'u'lláh's early life, His eldest son 'Abdu'l-Bahá has related the following:

> From His childhood He was extremely kind and generous. He was a great lover of outdoor life, most of His time being spent in the garden or the fields. He had an extraordinary power of attraction, which was felt by all. People always crowded around Him, and the children also were devoted to Him.[5]

Unlike the other members of nobility who were taught the contemporary arts and sciences, Bahá'u'lláh's education was limited to what little instruction He received at home. Bahá'u'lláh Himself states in the *Epistle* to Shaykh Najafí: "This Wronged One hath frequented no school, neither hath He attended the controversies of the learned."[6] And similarly in the *Lawḥ-i-Sulṭán*, His monumental proclamation to the Persian king Náṣiri'd-Dín Sháh, Bahá'u'lláh avers: "The learning current amongst men I studied not, their schools I entered not. Ask of the city wherein I dwelt, that thou mayest be well assured that I am not of them who speak falsely."[7]

Although formally untutored, Bahá'u'lláh became renowned for His knowledge as early as age fourteen. As a member of the nobility He was occasionally invited to gatherings where famous religious doctors and scholars were in attendance. The learned present at these congregations would often be astounded by Bahá'u'lláh's mastery of argument and His cogent explanations of intricate matters with which even they themselves had difficulty. Yet, Bahá'u'lláh was never presumptuous nor derisive in His assertions. He always spoke in a courteous language with utmost humility and forbearance.

In 1835, when Bahá'u'lláh was eighteen years of age, He married Ásíyih Khánum, the daughter of another prominent court official. Seven children were born of this wedlock, although only a daughter and two sons survived. The eldest son was named 'Abbás (he later became known as 'Abdu'l-Bahá), the daughter Bahá'íyyih and the youngest son Mihdí. These three children were to remain faithful and dedicated to the Cause of their beloved father all throughout their lives.

Ásíyih Khánum, addressed as Navváb (the revered one) by Bahá'u'lláh, and designated by Him in His writings as "the Most Exalted Leaf", was a true and faithful helpmate of Bahá'u'lláh who stood by her beloved Husband with great love and acquiescence through the trials and afflictions of His four successive exiles. After her death in 1886 Bahá'u'lláh in a prayer, composed in her memory, extols her love and devotion and states that she will be His "perpetual consort in all the worlds of God".

Bahá'u'lláh passed his childhood and youth as a highly revered and distinguished nobleman amid a comfortable and opulent environment. He was only twenty-two years old when His father passed away, leaving Him responsible for managing the household and the extensive family estates. The government offered Bahá'u'lláh His father's ministerial post, but to everyone's surprise He declined this lucrative position, only to continue attending to the interests of the poor and the needy.

Early Adulthood as a Bábí in Tehran

In 1844, following His declaration as the inaugurator of a new religion, the Báb[8] sent a letter, through His first disciple Mullá Ḥusayn-i-Bushrú'í, to Bahá'u'lláh. Upon reading a portion of the Báb's epistle, Bahá'u'lláh is known to have said the following: "Verily I say, whoso believes in the Qur'án and recognises its Divine origin, and yet hesitates, though it be for a moment, to admit that these soul-stirring words are endowed with the same regenerating power, has most assuredly erred in his judgment and has strayed far from the path of justice."[9]

From that day Bahá'u'lláh cast aside all thought of personal interest and arose with great enthusiasm to promote the cause of the new religion and espouse its teachings. His first journey to promulgate the Báb's message was to His native province of Mázindarán. In Núr, His ancestral district, Bahá'u'lláh's teaching efforts resulted in the conversion of a large number of its prominent citizens to the Faith including many of His own relatives.

For the first few years after He gave His allegiance to the cause of the Báb, the social position of Bahá'u'lláh and His highly acclaimed reputation for personal integrity protected Him from the dire persecutions which the other members of the Bábí community were experiencing. But before long, He too became the target of enmity of the country's ruling stratum. Bahá'u'lláh's first imprisonment (in 1847) was in connection with the murder of a well-known mujtahid (shí'a jurist) of Qazvín. The story goes that four men, one of whom the actual murderer, were taken to Tehran to be tried and sentenced for their conspiracy in the killing of the clergyman. Bahá'u'lláh, who knew of the innocence of the three detainees, went to visit them and gave them some money for food and clothing. In the meantime, the man who had assassinated the mujtahid and openly confessed his act, seeing the authorities' disbelief in his confession, escaped from jail. Since Bahá'u'lláh had been to see the prisoners and had given them financial assistance, He was accused of having helped the murderer escape. For this, Bahá'u'lláh was arrested and imprisoned. He remained in captivity for one day until the accusation was proved false and then He was released.

A year after this incident, the Conference of Badasht took place. In a remote hamlet situated on the eastern boundaries of Mázindarán, the harassed and persecuted followers of the Báb gathered to formally examine the spiritual verities of the new religion and deliberate on its future. During the twenty-two days of the Conference all eighty-one believers that had come from various provinces were Bahá'u'lláh's guests. It was at this historic occasion that Bahá'u'lláh became known in the

Bábí community as Jináb-i-Bahá (His honour Bahá).

From Badasht Bahá'u'lláh set out for Núr. On His way to that district He stayed at Bandar-Jaz on the shores of the Caspian Sea where He was entertained by some of the notables of the town. Meanwhile back in the capital, Bahá'u'lláh's adversaries in the royal court had induced such hostility in the mind of Muḥammad Sháh (r. 1834-1848) against Bahá'u'lláh that the Sháh eventually issued Bahá'u'lláh's death sentence. The royal edict ordering His arrest came while Bahá'u'lláh was at Bandar-Jaz. The imperial summons was received by Bahá'u'lláh's host who was very devoted to Him. Though greatly perturbed by the news, he did not disclose it to anyone. Perceiving the distressful mood of His host, Bahá'u'lláh advised him to submit to the will of God. The next day a messenger from Tehran brought the news of Muḥammad Sháh's death, and thus Bahá'u'lláh's arrest was nullified.

While at Núr, hearing of some three hundred Bábís who had been forced to take refuge in the forests of Mázindarán, Bahá'u'lláh decided to visit the site. He reached Shaykh Tabarsí, sometime in November of 1848, where the faithful defenders had built a fortress. Bahá'u'lláh met with Mullá Husayn and gave him some valuable instructions. He then left for Tehran promising to return at a later date. A month later, to fulfil His promise, Bahá'u'lláh set out with eleven other Bábís for a second visit to the Fort of Shaykh Tabarsí. But on the way He and His retinue were apprehended by government soldiers and were taken to the nearby town of Ámul. In Ámul, some enemies of the new Faith who had heard of the detention of a number of Bábís demanded their immediate death. The acting governor, who had great respect for Bahá'u'lláh, in order to appease the unfriendly crowd, decided to have Bahá'u'lláh's companions bastinadoed[10]. At this point, Bahá'u'lláh intervened by saying: "None of these men are guilty of any crime. If you insist on inflicting your punishment, I offer Myself as a willing Victim of your chastisement."[11] Upon hearing Bahá'u'lláh's offer, the acting governor reluctantly complied. Bahá'u'lláh was then bastinadoed so severely that His feet bled. In the *Epistle*

to Shaykh Najafí, written decades later, Bahá'u'lláh refers to this incident in the following words: "While confined in the prison of the Land of Mím (Mázindarán) We were one day delivered into the hands of the divines. Thou canst well imagine what befell Us."[12]

The martyrdom of the Báb on July 9th, 1850, inflicted a crushing blow to the foundation of the already beleaguered and tyrannized Bábí community. Now with the sudden and tragic removal of its Founder, the only channel of sustenance which the infant Faith could hope for was Bahá'u'lláh's unceasing comfort and guidance. In accordance with Bahá'u'lláh's instructions, the remains of the Báb and the companion martyred with him were rescued from the hands of their enemies and safely transferred from Tabríz to Tehran where they were carefully and secretly concealed in a safe location. Eulogizing the Martyred-Prophet for his constancy and resolve in proclaiming his religion to the world, Bahá'u'lláh, in His highly acclaimed work *The Book of Certitude*, writes:

> Though young and tender of age, and though the Cause He revealed was contrary to the desire of all the peoples of earth, both high and low, rich and poor, exalted and abased, king and subject, yet He arose and steadfastly proclaimed it. All have known and heard this. He was afraid of no one; He was regardless of consequences. . . . The whole world rose to hinder Him, yet it utterly failed. The more severe the persecution they inflicted on that Sadrih [Tree] of Blessedness, the more His fervour increased, and the brighter burned the flame of His love. All this is evident, and none disputeth its truth. Finally, He surrendered His soul, and winged His flight unto the realms above.[13]

In June, 1851, Bahá'u'lláh left Tehran to visit the holy cities of Iraq. There the Bábís, bewildered and dispirited from the shock of the Báb's martyrdom, had been deceived by a clergyman who had gone so far as to declare that he was the incarnation of the Holy Spirit. Bahá'u'lláh approached the priest and the power of His argument and presence was such that the priest was persuaded to withdraw his claim and openly confess his real intentions. Bahá'u'lláh then reinvigorated that

community with a new spirit of faith and exhorted its members to remain steadfast in the cause of the Báb. No sooner had Bahá'u'lláh returned to the capital than a highly consequential event occurred.

On August 15, 1852, obsessed by the tragic and unjust martyrdom of the Báb, three obscure Bábís who held the Sháh directly responsible of that crime ventured to kill the young Náṣiri'd-Dín Sháh and failed. Immediately after this episode, the blame for its design was directly placed on the entire body of the Bábí community. The result was a bloody and horrific campaign of mass persecution by the Persian government who, with the help of the Shí'a clergy, set out to exterminate all the followers of the Báb.

At the time of the attempt on the sovereign's life, Bahá'u'lláh was the guest of the prime minister at the village of Afchih, in the outskirts of Tehran. As soon as the appalling news reached Him, He decided to immediately present Himself to the authorities. Bahá'u'lláh knew that, because of His reputation as a Bábí leader, He would inevitably fall under suspicion. Hence, refusing the advice of His host to remain for a time hidden in that vicinity, He mounted His horse the following morning and rode intrepidly to the headquarters of the imperial army at Níyávarán.

Upon His arrival at Níyávarán, Bahá'u'lláh was immediately arrested by the royal troops and held for questioning at the army encampment for three days. On the fourth day He was forced to walk barefoot and in chains, a distance of some twenty-four kilometres to Tehran under the blazing sun of a midsummer day. On the way Bahá'u'lláh was scorned, ridiculed and pelted with stones by the hostile crowd who thronged the roadsides. It is reported that among the abusive populace was an old woman who wished to fling a stone at Bahá'u'lláh, but was unable to keep up with the procession. Seeing her condition, Bahá'u'lláh requested the escorting guards to slow down so that the elderly woman could achieve her desire. In Tehran Bahá'u'lláh was taken at once to the Síyáh-Chál (the Black Pit), the most foul, unsanitary and disease-ridden

underground dungeon in the capital. In the pages of His celebrated *Epistle* to Shaykh Najafí, Bahá'u'lláh recounts the circumstance of His arrest and imprisonment in connection with the attempt on the life of the Sháh. He writes:

> By the righteousness of God! We were in no wise connected with that evil deed, and Our innocence was indisputably established by the tribunals. Nevertheless, they apprehended Us, and from Níyávarán, which was then the residence of His Majesty, conducted Us, on foot and in chains, with bared head and bare feet, to the dungeon of Tihrán. A brutal man, accompanying Us on horseback, snatched off Our hat, whilst We were being hurried along by a troop of executioners and officials. We were consigned for four months to a place foul beyond comparison.[14]

The subterranean dungeon into which Bahá'u'lláh was thrown had originally served as a water reservoir for one of the city's public baths. Having been abandoned for some years, the government had turned it into a torturous prison where it would consign only the worst prisoners. Bahá'u'lláh Himself describes the condition of that horrendous place in graphic detail:

> As to the dungeon in which this Wronged One and others similarly wronged were confined, a dark and narrow pit were preferable. Upon Our arrival We were first conducted along a pitch-black corridor, from whence We descended three steep flights of stairs to the place of confinement assigned to Us. The dungeon was wrapped in thick darkness, and Our fellow-prisoners numbered nearly a hundred and fifty souls: thieves, assassins and highwaymen. Though crowded, it had no other outlet than the passage by which We entered. No pen can depict that place, nor any tongue describe its loathsome smell. Most of these men had neither clothes nor bedding to lie on. God alone knoweth what befell Us in that most foul-smelling and gloomy place![15]

In the Síyáh Chál Bahá'u'lláh's feet were put in stocks and around His neck were placed chains of such heavy weight that their mark remained imprinted upon His body until the end of His life. For the first three days and three nights Bahá'u'lláh was not allowed any food or drink. Even when He was permitted a small ration of food it was poisoned by the guards.

This attempt, though ineffective, left grave traces on His health for years to come. In such cruel and afflictive conditions Bahá'u'lláh was kept for four months. Years later, Bahá'u'lláh provided to Nabíl-i-Zarandí, who was then writing a chronicle of the early years of the Bábí-Bahá'í religions, a detailed account of His incarceration in the infamous Síyáh Chál. What follows is an excerpt from Bahá'u'lláh's words as recorded by Nabíl:

> We were all huddled together in one cell, our feet in stocks, and around our necks fastened the most galling of chains. The air we breathed was laden with the foulest impurities, while the floor on which we sat was covered with filth and infested with vermin. No ray of light was allowed to penetrate that pestilential dungeon or to warm its icy-coldness. We were placed in two rows, each facing the other. We had taught them to repeat certain verses which, every night, they chanted with extreme fervour. "God is sufficient unto me; He verily is the All-sufficing!" one row would intone, while the other would reply: "In Him let the trusting trust." The chorus of these gladsome voices would continue to peal out until the early hours of the morning. Their reverberation would fill the dungeon, and, piercing its massive walls, would reach the ears of Náṣiri'd-Dín Sháh, whose palace was not far distant from the place where we were imprisoned. "What means this sound?" he was reported to have exclaimed. "It is the anthem the Bábís are intoning in their prison," they replied. The Sháh made no further remarks, nor did he attempt to restrain the enthusiasm his prisoners, despite the horrors of their confinement, continued to display. . . .
>
> Every day Our gaolers, entering Our cell, would call the name of one of Our companions, bidding him arise and follow them to the foot of the gallows. With what eagerness would the owner of that name respond to that solemn call! Relieved of his chains, he would spring to his feet and, in a state of uncontrollable delight, would approach and embrace Us. We would seek to comfort him with the assurance of an everlasting life in the world beyond, and, filling his heart with hope and joy, would send him forth to win the crown of glory. He would embrace, in turn, the rest of his fellow-prisoners and then proceed to die as dauntlessly as he had

> lived. Soon after the martyrdom of each of these companions, We would be informed by the executioner, who had grown to be friendly to Us, of the circumstances of the death of his victim, and of the joy with which he had endured his sufferings to the very end.[16]

While Bahá'u'lláh remained immured in the Síyáh Chál the government soldiers stormed the district of Núr and confiscated all His properties. In the village of Tákur, Bahá'u'lláh's expensively furnished home, which He had inherited from His father, was completely robbed of its material wealth and the building itself was demolished. His luxurious house in Tehran was also ransacked and its valuables carried away. In fact so grave was the plundering that Bahá'u'lláh's family were forced to flee their home and seek refuge in a destitute part of town.

According to Bahá'u'lláh Himself, it was in the midpoint of these torturous months in "the Great Prison" that the mandate of His divine Mission was made known to Him by God. In the *Epistle* to Shaykh Najafí Bahá'u'lláh vividly describes His experience of this momentous event:

> During the days I lay in the prison of Ṭihrán, though the galling weight of the chains and the stench-filled air allowed Me but little sleep, still in those infrequent moments of slumber I felt as if something flowed from the crown of My head over My breast, even as a mighty torrent that precipitateth itself upon the earth from the summit of a lofty mountain. Every limb of my body would, as a result, be set afire. At such moments My tongue recited what no man could bear to hear.
>
> One night, in a dream, these exalted words were heard on every side: "Verily, We shall render Thee victorious by Thyself and by Thy Pen. Grieve Thou not for that which hath befallen Thee, neither be Thou afraid, for Thou art in safety. Erelong will God raise up the treasures of the earth–men who will aid Thee through Thyself and through Thy Name, wherewith God hath revived the hearts of such as have recognized Him."[17]

Similarly, in His *Súratu'l-Haykal (The Epistle of the Temple)*, written some two decades later, Bahá'u'lláh recounts in symbolic terms how the "Most Great Spirit", personified as a

maiden, appeared before Him and announced His station to the rest of the world:

> While engulfed in tribulation I heard a most wondrous, a most sweet voice, calling above My head. Turning My face, I beheld a Maiden–the embodiment of the remembrance of the name of My Lord–suspended in the air before Me. So rejoiced was she in her very soul that her countenance shone with the ornament of the good-pleasure of God, and her cheeks glowed with the brightness of the All-Merciful. Betwixt earth and heaven she was raising a call which captivated the hearts and minds of men. She was imparting to both My inward and outer beings tidings which rejoiced My soul, and the souls of God's honoured servants. Pointing with her finger unto My head, she addressed all who are in heaven and all who are on earth, saying: "By God! This is the Best-Beloved of the worlds, and yet ye comprehend not. This is the Beauty of God amongst you, and the power of His sovereignty within you, could ye but understand. This is the Mystery of God and His Treasure, the Cause of God and His glory unto all who are in the kingdom of Revelations and of creation, if ye be of them that perceive."[18]

Bahá'u'lláh was released from the Síyáh Chál in December of the same year after overwhelming testimonies had established beyond the shadow of a doubt His non-complicity in the plot against the Sháh. When He was discharged from the prison, Bahá'u'lláh did not divulge to anyone His experience of divine revelation; His Mission was destined to remain concealed from the eyes of humanity for another decade. Nevertheless those who were in close contact with Him could not help but realize a spiritual transformation in His person.

Bahá'u'lláh had hardly come out of confinement when He received a decree from Náṣiri'd-Dín Sháh ordering His expulsion from the Persian territory. The royal edict had given Bahá'u'lláh one month to leave the country permitting Him to choose the land of His exile. The Russian minister[19] in Tehran, who had been instrumental in securing Bahá'u'lláh's release from the Black Pit Prison, hearing of the imperial decision, offered Bahá'u'lláh his country as a place of refuge. In one of His Tablets written some years after, Bahá'u'lláh acknowledges

the assistance extended to Him by the Russian ambassador in these words:

> In the days when this Wronged One was sore-afflicted in prison, the minister of the highly esteemed government (of Russia)–may God, glorified and exalted be He, assist him!–exerted his utmost endeavour to compass My deliverance. Several times permission for My release was granted. Some of the 'ulamás of the city [Tehran], however, would prevent it. Finally, My freedom was gained through the solicitude and the endeavour of His Excellency the Minister.[20]

Bahá'u'lláh declined, however, the invitation of the Russian government and chose instead Iraq, then a province of the neighbouring Ottoman empire, as His place of exile.

At the time when the Sháh's summons was communicated to Him, Bahá'u'lláh was very ill and could not set out on a long journey. His house and properties having been confiscated, He had no place of His own. So for the next month preceding His departure to Iraq, Bahá'u'lláh stayed at the house of His half-brother Mírzá Riḍá-Qulí[21]. Here Mírzá Riḍá Qulí's wife, Maryam, together with His own wife, Ásíyih Khánum, nursed Bahá'u'lláh with great love and care until His health improved. This short recuperation period allowed Bahá'u'lláh to regain the strength He required for embarking on His exile.

Bahá'u'lláh left Tehran for Baghdad on January 12, 1853 accompanied by some members of His family, and "two mounted escorts"[22] consisting of an officer of the Persian government and an official of the Russian legation. The journey lasted three months and was fraught with hardship. The small band of exiles traveled through cold and perilous environments across the Zágrus mountain ranges of western Iran. The arduous route coupled with lack of proper facilities made the suffering all the more intense for the outcast travellers. Bahá'u'lláh refers to the adverse conditions of that "terrible journey" in a prayer written at that time:

> My God, My Master, My Desire! . . .Thou hast created this atom of dust through the consummate power of Thy might, and nurtured Him with Thine hands which none can chain up. . . . Thou hast destined for Him trials and tribulations

> which no tongue can describe, nor any of Thy Tablets adequately recount. The throat Thou didst accustom to the touch of silk Thou hast, in the end, clasped with strong chains, and the body Thou didst ease with brocades and velvets Thou hast at last subjected to the abasement of a dungeon. . . . finally, Thy decree was irrevocably fixed, and Thy behest summoned this servant to depart out of Persia, accompanied by a number of frail-bodied men and children of tender age, at this time when the cold is so intense that one cannot even speak, and ice and snow so abundant that it is impossible to move.[23]

Baghdad

Bahá'u'lláh and His family reached Baghdad on April 8, 1853. After spending a few days there, Bahá'u'lláh moved to the nearby town of Káẓimayn[24]. Soon after His arrival in that city the Persian council general in Baghdad suggested to Bahá'u'lláh that in view of the masses of visitors frequenting Káẓimayn for pilgrimage, it would be appropriate for Him to return to Baghdad and establish His residence there. Bahá'u'lláh agreed and about a month later, He and His family came back to Baghdad and settled in the rented house of Ḥájí 'Alí Madad situated in the old quarter of the city.

Upon His arrival in Baghdad, Bahá'u'lláh found the Bábís residing there in a pathetic state of waywardness. The events of the past three years had been truly staggering. The Faith had lost most of its leaders, leaving the community tragically divided and utterly demoralized. It was now up to Bahá'u'lláh to rescue the religion of the Báb from impending extinction. At once and without hesitation, Bahá'u'lláh rose with complete vigour to regenerate the spirit of the Bábís and to revitalize their teachings. Initially, Bahá'u'lláh's efforts met with great success and people began turning to Him as a source of guidance. But soon, the fortune of Bahá'u'lláh's endeavours dramatically changed when His enemies, alarmed by His sudden popularity and the growing number of His admirers, began a secret campaign to discredit Bahá'u'lláh's efforts and undermine His reputation. At the centre of this conspiracy

was Bahá'u'lláh's own half brother, Mírzá Yaḥyá[25], whose personal insecurity had made him jealous of his older Brother's fame and prestige. It was this same kindred of Bahá'u'lláh who was destined to become, in later years, His most inveterate and hostile opponent.

Bahá'u'lláh, whose intention was nothing more than rehabilitation of the Bábí community, was greatly saddened by the betrayals. In a Tablet written years later in honour of His faithful cousin Maryam, He states:

> The wrongs which I suffer have blotted out the wrongs suffered by My First Name (the Báb) from the Tablet of creation . . . O Maryam! From the land of Ṭá (Ṭihrán), after countless afflictions, We reached 'Iráq, at the bidding of the Tyrant of Persia [Náṣiri'd-Dín Sháh], where, after the fetters of Our foes, We were afflicted with the perfidy of Our friends. God knoweth what befell Me thereafter! . . . I have borne what no man, be he of the past or of the future, hath borne or will bear.[26]

And in the *Kitáb-i-Íqán* (*The Book of Certitude*), Bahá'u'lláh refers to those who had risen so vehemently against Him:

> . . . a number of people who have never inhaled the fragrance of justice, have raised the standard of sedition, and have leagued themselves against Us. On every side We witness the menace of their spears, and in all directions We recognize the shafts of their arrows. This, although We have never gloried in any thing, nor did We seek preference over any soul. To everyone We have been a most kindly companion, a most forbearing and affectionate friend. In the company of the poor We have sought their fellowship, and amidst the exalted and learned We have been submissive and resigned. I swear by God, the one true God! grievous as have been the woes and sufferings which the hand of the enemy and the people of the Book inflicted upon Us, yet all these fade into utter nothingness when compared with that which hath befallen Us at the hand of those who profess to be Our friends.[27]

Eventually the forces of opposition became so fierce that in order to avoid any form of contention that might lead to a division within the community, and thus harm the integrity of

the religion of the Báb, Bahá'u'lláh decided to leave Baghdad and withdraw to a secluded area where He could not be reached by anyone. In the *Kitáb-i-Íqán*, composed some seven years later, Bahá'u'lláh describes the cause and the nature of His unexpected retirement in the following words:

> In the early days of Our arrival in this land [Baghdad], when We discerned the signs of impending events, We decided, ere they happened, to retire. We betook Ourselves to the wilderness, and there, separated and alone, led for two years a life of complete solitude. From Our eyes there rained tears of anguish, and in Our bleeding heart there surged an ocean of agonizing pain. Many a night We had no food for sustenance, and many a day Our body found no rest. By Him Who hath My being between His hands! notwithstanding these showers of afflictions and unceasing calamities, Our soul was wrapt in blissful joy, and Our whole being evinced an ineffable gladness. For in our solitude We were unaware of the harm or benefit, the health or ailment, of any soul. Alone, We communed with Our spirit, oblivious of the world and all that is therein. We knew not, however, that the mesh of divine destiny exceedeth the vastest of mortal conceptions, and the dart of His decree transcendeth the boldest of human designs. None can escape the snares He setteth, and no soul can find release except through submission to His will. By the righteousness of God! Our withdrawal contemplated no return, and Our separation hoped for no reunion. The one object of Our retirement was to avoid becoming a subject of discord among the faithful, a source of disturbance unto Our companions, the means of injury to any soul, or the cause of sorrow to any heart. Beyond these, We cherished no other intention, and apart from them, We had no end in view. And yet, each person schemed after his own desire, and pursued his own idle fancy, until the hour when, from the Mystic Source, there came the summons bidding Us return whence We came. Surrendering Our will to His, We submitted to His injunction.[28]

Bahá'u'lláh's unanticipated departure from Baghdad took place on April 10, 1854. On that day, without the knowledge of His family and friends, He left for the mountainous region of Kurdish Iraq. There in the vicinity of Sulaymáníyyih

Bahá'u'lláh began a life of complete isolation in a cave on top of a mountain named Sar Galú. Of His dwelling-place during this period, Bahá'u'lláh has remarked: "We sought shelter upon the summit of a remote mountain which lay at some three days' distance from the nearest human habitation. The comforts of life were completely lacking. We remained entirely isolated from Our fellow men . . . ."[29]

Towards the end of Bahá'u'lláh's retirement, a certain Shaykh of Sulaymáníyyih had a dream wherein he was directed to seek out the Prophet Muḥammad in the nearby mountains. The Shaykh accordingly proceeded in search of the Prophet and found Bahá'u'lláh at the location where his dream had bidden him to look. Shortly after this the leader of the Khálidíyyih[30] Order himself visited Bahá'u'lláh and became greatly affected by Him. The spiritually captivated sage, after repeated requests, succeeded in persuading Bahá'u'lláh to transfer His residence to Sulaymáníyyih and establish contact with the learned in the area. Within a short period of time, Bahá'u'lláh's reputation for piety and erudition spread through the region. Although no one knew of His real identity, for Bahá'u'lláh was living under the assumed name of Darvísh Muḥammad-i-Írání, those who came in contact with Him were immediately enamoured by His gentle character and abounding knowledge. Eventually Bahá'u'lláh's fame reached the learned circles in Baghdad and His family and friends recognized that Person to be none other than Bahá'u'lláh. They dispatched a messenger to Sulaymáníyyih to find Him and beg Him to return. Since Bahá'u'lláh had left Baghdad, the affairs of the Bábí community had fallen to an all time low and now more than ever His presence was desperately needed. The emissary found Bahá'u'lláh residing at one of the theological seminaries as an honoured guest surrounded by a large group of prominent admirers and devotees. Bahá'u'lláh acceded to the plea of His loved ones and a few days later set out for Baghdad. On His way, Bahá'u'lláh is known to have expressed to that same messenger: "these last days of My retirement would be the only days of peace and tranquillity left to Me, days which will

never again fall to My lot."[31]

After nearly a two year absence Bahá'u'lláh returned to Baghdad on March 19, 1856. On His arrival, He became so overwhelmed with sadness at the state of decadence of the Bábís that for some time He refused to leave His house and meet with anyone. Of this situation Bahá'u'lláh has written: "We found no more than a handful of souls, faint and dispirited, nay utterly lost and dead. The Cause of God had ceased to be on any one's lips, nor was any heart receptive to its message."[32] And again in the *Kitáb-i-Íqán* He writes:

> What pen can recount the things We beheld upon Our return! Two years have elapsed during which Our enemies have ceaselessly and assiduously contrived to exterminate Us, whereunto all witness. Nevertheless, none amongst the faithful hath risen to render Us any assistance, nor did any one feel inclined to help in Our deliverance. Nay, instead of assisting Us, what showers of continuous sorrows, their words and deeds have caused to rain upon Our soul.[33]

Once again, Bahá'u'lláh resumed His labours to resuscitate the withering body of the Bábí community. And once again, through His untiring efforts, the spiritual character and morale of the community was restored and its prestige greatly enhanced. Within a few years after Bahá'u'lláh's return from Kurdistán His new residence, the house of Sulaymán-i-Ghannám[34], which was situated near the western bank of the Tigris River, became a place sought and frequented by many people of various rank and file. Among the visitors who constantly thronged His house were such dignitaries as princes, high ranking government officials, religious leaders and scholars, but also there were many from humbler descent including the peasants and the poor, the sick and the needy. They would all gather at that sacred spot to unburden their souls and partake of the grace and bounty which was continually showered upon them by their loving and caring Host.

This period also witnessed a great expansion in the scope of Bahá'u'lláh's writings. During these years Bahá'u'lláh was frequently engaged in producing a variety of written

expressions to broaden the outlook and enlighten the minds of the Bábís. Indeed it was such a prolific time that, according to one eye witness, in a span of one day the equivalent of the *Qur'án*[35] would stream forth from the lips of Bahá'u'lláh! Yet as vast and numerous as these revelations were, countless were also the occasions when Bahá'u'lláh would order His amanuensis to cast the outpourings of His pen into the river, assuring him that no one was ready to set eyes on their soul-provoking contents.

It was in Baghdad that Bahá'u'lláh wrote some of His most celebrated writings.[36] Among them are such works as the *Hidden Words*, the *Seven Valleys*, the *Four Valleys* and *The Book of Certitude*[37].

With the composition of these and other prodigious volumes of writings, Bahá'u'lláh's prominence in the society of Baghdad and the surroundings was further enhanced. He was now regarded by all with great reverence as a holy and sanctified figure whose energy was constantly focused in bringing about moral and spiritual advancement to the generality of the population. This rising ascendancy of Bahá'u'lláh, however, invoked intense fear and hatred in the hearts of His enemies, especially the religious leaders who saw His popularity as a formidable threat to their own power and influence. They plotted persistently to destroy Bahá'u'lláh, even though He always stood ready to meet with them. This is Bahá'u'lláh's own testimony:

> For twelve years[38] We tarried in Baghdád. Much as We desired that a large gathering of divines and fair-minded men be convened, so that truth might be distinguished from falsehood, and be fully demonstrated, no action was taken . . . And likewise, while in 'Iráq, We wished to come together with the divines of Persia. No sooner did they hear of this, than they fled and said: "He indeed is a manifest sorcerer!" This is the word that proceeded aforetime out of the mouths of such as were like them. These (divines) objected to what they said, and yet, they themselves repeat, in this day, what was said before them, and understand not. By My life! They are even as ashes in the sight of thy Lord. If He be willing,

tempestuous gales will blow over them, and make them as dust. Thy Lord, verily, doth what He pleaseth.[39]

Finally, after years of unremitting endeavour, Bahá'u'lláh's enemies managed to persuade Náṣiri'd-Dín Sháh to convince the Turkish government to have Bahá'u'lláh removed from Baghdad. The Ottoman government concurred and orders were issued for Bahá'u'lláh's transfer from Baghdad to Istanbul (Constantinople), the capital city of the empire.

Five weeks before Bahá'u'lláh's departure from Baghdad, Námiq Páshá, the governor of Baghdad who was among His admirers, sent a message inviting Bahá'u'lláh to visit him at his headquarters. It was his intention to inform Bahá'u'lláh that the central government wanted Him to relocate to Istanbul. Bahá'u'lláh agreed to meet the governor but as He did not wish to visit government officials at their offices, He suggested that the meeting take place instead in the mosque opposite the government house. Námiq Páshá consented and a date was set. On that day, however, feeling ashamed to confront Bahá'u'lláh and relay to Him the news of His banishment, the governor sent his deputy to deliver the royal dispatch. At the mosque Bahá'u'lláh was presented with the prime minister's letter who, with utmost courtesy, had invited Him to come to Istanbul as the honoured guest of the Ottoman government. The letter had also provided Bahá'u'lláh with a substantial amount of money for His expenses and a mounted escort to accompany Him on the journey. Bahá'u'lláh readily accepted the invitation but refused to take the generous allowance. However, on the insistence of the deputy governor that rejection of the allocated sum would offend the authorities, Bahá'u'lláh reluctantly accepted it but later that same day distributed the sum among the poor.

The news of Bahá'u'lláh's forthcoming departure for Istanbul quickly spread throughout Baghdad and its neighbouring towns, bringing a multitude of anxious admirers who wished to pay their final respects to Him. Soon it was realized, however, that His house was too small to meet such a demand. It is said that when one of the notables of Baghdad heard of

this concern, he offered his garden-park (known as Najíbíyyih) to Bahá'u'lláh and placed it entirely at His disposal. This beautiful and enchanting garden, later designated by Bahá'ís as the Garden of Riḍván (Paradise), was situated in the proximity of Baghdad across the river from Bahá'u'lláh's house.

On the afternoon of April 22[40], 1863, Bahá'u'lláh left His house and set out for Najíbíyyih. From the account of those who were present, at the time of Bahá'u'lláh's departure the entire city was seized with an unprecedented commotion. People from all walks of life, including His own followers, had thronged outside His house and formed a procession along the route He was to take to the river. Tearful and heavy hearted, they waited anxiously to bid farewell to the One whose love, affection, kindness and generosity had touched so profoundly each and every one of them for a decade. In leaving His house, Bahá'u'lláh stood for some time among the disconsolate crowd speaking words of comfort and assuring them that later they would all be welcome to visit Him in the Garden. It is recorded that before crossing the river Bahá'u'lláh turned to His companions who had gathered around Him and addressed them in these words:

> O My companions, I entrust to your keeping this city of Baghdád, in the state ye now behold it, when from the eyes of friends and strangers alike, crowding its housetops, its streets and markets, tears like the rain of spring are flowing down, and I depart. With you it now rests to watch lest your deeds and conduct dim the flame of love that gloweth within the breasts of its inhabitants.[41]

Bahá'u'lláh then crossed the river in a small boat accompanied by His three sons and a number of His close companions. In the Garden as He prepared Himself to receive a large contingent of friends and admirers, Bahá'u'lláh made an historic declaration to a select group of His followers. To them He revealed His station as "Him Whom God Shall Make Manifest", the promised messenger of God foretold by the Báb and by sacred writings of earlier religions. We must bear in mind that the majority of Bahá'u'lláh's followers were for some time anticipating Him to openly reveal His divine identity. This

was due to Bahá'u'lláh's own remarks and allusions made both verbally and in His writings during the last few months of His stay in Baghdad. Also in this period there had been a noticeable change in Bahá'u'lláh's bearing and even in His appearance such as using a different type of head-dress, known as the táj (a tall felt hat) which He continued to wear for the remainder of His life.

With Bahá'u'lláh's momentous Announcement, the mood of sadness and grief was transformed into joy and delight and, as attested by Him, a new spirit of life was breathed into the soul of humanity.

> This is the Day whereon naught can be seen except the splendours of the Light that shineth from the face of Thy Lord, the Gracious, the Most Bountiful. Verily, We have caused every soul to expire by virtue of Our irresistible and all-subduing sovereignty. We have, then, called into being a new creation, as a token of Our grace unto men. . . . Say: He it is Who is the Manifestation of Him Who is the Unknowable, the Invisible of the Invisibles, could ye but perceive it. He it is Who hath laid bare before you the hidden and treasured Gem, were ye to seek it. He it is Who is the one Beloved of all things, whether of the past or of the future. Would that ye might set your hearts and hopes upon Him![42]

And in *Madínatu's-Ṣabr (The City of Patience)*, penned by Bahá'u'lláh on the very first day of His arrival in the Riḍván Garden, He writes:

> O present hour! Rejoice thou by virtue of this Hour which hath struck within thee through the power of God, and appreciate this eternal, this imperishable and celestial food which streameth down from the clouds of holiness from behind veils of light and descendeth from the heaven of glory upon Him Who beareth the Name of God.
>
> O present day! Shed thou illumination upon all created things through the advent of this radiant, this glorious Day which hath been manifested unto all the world from the horizon of 'Iráq. [43]

During the twelve days Bahá'u'lláh remained in the Garden of Najíbíyyih multitudes of people came to pay their respects. Among them were notables and high ranking officials of

Baghdad including the governor, Námiq Páshá, who came and visited Bahá'u'lláh in utmost humility.

Bahá'u'lláh left the Garden of Riḍván for the capital of the Turkish Empire at noon of May 3, 1863. Once again, He was accompanied by the members of His family and a number of His close followers. The convoy travelled overland for three months and reached the port of Samsun on the Black Sea in early August. They stayed in Samsun for a week and from there boarded a steamer which took them to Istanbul.

Istanbul (Constantinople)

The Ottoman steamer carrying the party of exiles anchored at the "Sublime Porte" on August 16, 1863. Upon their arrival, Bahá'u'lláh and His family were taken by two special carriages to the house of Shamsí Big in the vicinity of the Mosque of Khirqiy-i-Sharíf (the Exalted Cloak). Let Bahá'u'lláh Himself elaborate on the event of His entry into the "Great City":

> On the day of Our arrival the Government Official, whose duty it was to receive and entertain official visitors, met Us and escorted Us to the place he had been bidden to take Us. In truth, the Government showed these wronged ones the utmost kindness and consideration. The following day Prince Shujá'u'd-Dawlih, accompanied by Mírzá Ṣafá, acting as the representatives of the late Mushíru'd-Dawlih, the Minister (accredited to the Imperial Court) came to visit Us. Others, among whom were several Ministers of the Imperial Government, and including the late Kamál Páshá, likewise called on Us. Wholly reliant on God, and without any reference to any need He might have had, or to any other matter, this Wronged One sojourned for a period of four months in that city. His actions were known and evident unto all, and none can deny them except such as hate Him, and speak not the truth. He that hath recognized God, recognizeth none other but Him. We have never liked, nor like We, to make mention of such things.[44]

After one month of stay in the house of Shamsí Big, Bahá'u'lláh and His family were transferred to the more spacious house of Vísí Páshá near the Mosque of Sultan Muhammad the Conqueror. They dwelled at this residence

for the remainder of their sojourn in Istanbul.

As He Himself mentions, Bahá'u'lláh stood completely detached from the political scene of the capital. Although many high ranking officials came to visit and pay their respects, Bahá'u'lláh never reciprocated. In fact, the only places He visited in Istanbul were mosques and public baths. Bahá'u'lláh knew that it was customary for prominent figures visiting the capital to call upon the ministers of the royal court and through them arrange for an audience with the Sultan. He wrote:

> Whenever high dignitaries of Persia came to that city (Constantinople) they would exert themselves to the utmost soliciting at every door such allowances and gifts as they might obtain. This Wronged One, however, if He hath done nothing that would redound to the glory of Persia, hath at least acted in a manner that could in no wise disgrace it.[45]

Bahá'u'lláh had no favour to solicit. The only reason He had come to Istanbul was because He was invited by the Ottoman government. Nevertheless, the royal authorities were enraged by Bahá'u'lláh's attitude. They saw Him as a proud and arrogant man unwilling to comply with the common practice of the day and one who deserved to be banished to a remote location.

Having secured the approval of Sultan 'Abdu'l-'Azíz, the Turkish prime minister 'Álí Pá<u>sh</u>á sent an envoy to apprize Bahá'u'lláh of the decree for His banishment to the city of Edirne. Refusing to meet with the envoy, Bahá'u'lláh appointed His son 'Abdu'l-Bahá and His brother Mírzá Músá to receive the edict and tell its bearer that an answer would be forthcoming. Bahá'u'lláh was outraged. He had done nothing wrong to deserve such cruel treatment. He is reported to have said: "They called us here, as their guests, and innocent as we are, they turned on us with vengeance."[46]

That same day, a lengthy letter was penned by Bahá'u'lláh in which the Sultan and his ministers were censured in a scolding language. This document which has come to be known as the *Lawḥ-i-'Abdu'l-'Azíz-Va-Vukalá (Tablet to Sulṭán 'Abdu'l-'Azíz and his ministers)* was sealed in an envelope and sent to the royal court the following morning. The messenger who

delivered it was instructed by Bahá'u'lláh to deliver the package into the hands of the prime minister with the message that it was sent down from God. The courier is known to have reported that he did not know what was in the letter but as soon as the prime minister read it he became mortified, saying: "It is as if the King of Kings was addressing his humblest vassal and regulating his conduct."[47]

Pursuant to the orders of the Ottoman government, Bahá'u'lláh, accompanied by the same members of his family and the band of his close followers, left Istanbul on the morning of December 1, 1863. The journey to Edirne lasted twelve days and was very arduous for the outcast travellers. The weather was severely cold and proper means were completely lacking. Recalling their sufferings, as He addressed the same Ottoman Sultan three years later, in the *Súratu'l-Mulúk (The Epistle of the Kings)*, Bahá'u'lláh declares:

> We came unto thy city [Istanbul] at thine own behest, and entered therein with conspicuous honour. They ["thy ministers"] expelled Us, however, from thy city with an abasement with which no abasement on earth can compare. . . . They made Us journey until We reached the place [Edirne] which none entereth except such as have rebelled against the authority of the sovereign, and as are numbered with the transgressors. All this, notwithstanding that We had never disobeyed thee, though it be for a single moment, for when We heard thy bidding We obsereved it and submitted to thy will. In dealing with Us, however, thy ministers neither honoured the standards of God and His commandments, nor heeded that which hath been revealed to the Prophets and Messengers. They showed Us no mercy and committed against Us that which no one among the faithful hath ever wrought against his fellow, nor any believer inflicted upon an infidel. God knoweth and is a witness unto the truth of Our words.[48]

Expatiating on the condition of their journey and their arrival into the city of Edirne, Bahá'u'lláh, in the same document adds:

> When they expelled Us from thy city, they placed Us in such conveyances as the people use to carry baggage and the like. Such was the treatment We received at their hands, shouldst thou wish to know the truth. . . . Upon our arrival, We could

find no house in which to dwell, and perforce resided in a place where none would enter save the most indigent stranger. There We lodged for a time, after which, suffering increasingly from the confined space, We sought and rented houses which by reason of the extreme cold had been vacated by their occupants. Thus in the depth of winter we were constrained to make our abode in houses wherein none dwell except in the heat of summer. Neither My family, nor those who accompanied Me, had the necessary raiment to protect them from the cold in that freezing weather.[49]

Edirne (Adrianople)

Bahá'u'lláh and His weary fellow-exiles arrived in the ancient city of Hadrian (Hadrianopolis or Adrianople) on Saturday, December 12, 1863. On their arrival, they were all placed in a small and decrepit two-storey inn called Khán-i-'Arab. After a three night stay, Bahá'u'lláh and His family were moved to a small house in the Murádíyyih quarter, near the Takiyiy-i-Mawlaví (Mawlaví Seminary). A week later they were again transferred to another house in that same neighbourhood. The second house in the Murádíyyih quarter was occupied by Bahá'u'lláh and His family for about six months, after which they took up residence in a more spacious house known as the Khániyyih Amru'lláh (House of God's command). This house was located on the northern proximity of the Mosque of Sultan Salím.

The years of Bahá'u'lláh's exile in Edirne are marked by two momentous occurrences which, though calamitous and awe-inspiring in nature, were to establish Him as the supreme and undisputed Manifestation of God for the new age of humanity. These events were, namely, the traitorous rebellion of Bahá'u'lláh's half-brother Mírzá Yaḥyá and his diabolical accomplice Siyyid Muḥammad-i-Isfahání, whom the pen of Bahá'u'lláh denounced as the "quintessence of mischief"[50], and more significantly Bahá'u'lláh's open proclamation of His divine Mission to humanity and the rulers of the world.

The shameful behaviour of Mírzá Yaḥyá during this period plunged the community into severe crisis and tests. Such was

the extent of its impact on the fortunes of the Faith that Bahá'u'lláh Himself designated it as the *Ayyám-i-Shidád* (Days of Stress). It brought unimaginable sorrow to Bahá'u'lláh and made Him visibly age. Referring to this dreadful period and the effect of its intense grief on Him, Bahá'u'lláh writes: "The cruelties inflicted by My oppressors have bowed Me down, and turned My hair white. Shouldst thou present thyself before My throne, thou wouldst fail to recognize the Ancient Beauty, for the freshness of His countenance is altered, and its brightness hath faded, by the reason of the oppression of the infidels."[51]

About a year after Bahá'u'lláh's arrival in Edirne, Mírzá Yaḥyá began his malicious campaign to destroy his noble Brother whom he considered a barrier to his own leadership of the community. At this time he began to invite Bahá'u'lláh to his home, where one day he managed to poison Him by smearing His tea cup with a potent substance he had prepared. Bahá'u'lláh became so ill that there was no hope for His survival. A Bulgarian doctor was called to treat Him and diagnosed no chance for His recovery. But the Almighty willed otherwise. Eventually, after several weeks, Bahá'u'lláh's condition improved though the effect of the poisoning left Him with tremoring hands for the rest of His life. To this tragic outcome, Bahá'u'lláh Himself testifies in the following words: "Say: Verily the poison from them who have joined partners with God hath indeed penetrated the Most Holy Fingers and hath hindered them from writing."[52]

Having failed to bring about Bahá'u'lláh's death, Mírzá Yaḥyá attempted to kill his Brother two more times. On one occasion, trying to poison Him again, he contaminated the well of Bahá'u'lláh's household with a deadly toxin, causing many among His family members to fall ill. At another instance, he deceitfully tried to persuade one of Bahá'u'lláh's attendants to assassinate his Master. The humble servant was so enraged by this suggestion that he almost killed Mírzá Yaḥyá on the spot.

It was during the course of these events that Bahá'u'lláh,

through a momentous document known as the *Súriy-i-Amr (The Epistle of Command)*, formally announced His claim to Mírzá Yaḥyá as the Author of a divine Revelation. Written entirely in His own hand, which now suffered from trembling, Bahá'u'lláh arranged for the Tablet to be taken to Mírzá Yaḥyá and its contents to be read aloud to him. Mírzá Yaḥyá was then asked to reply. After one day of respite, which he requested to reflect on his answer, Yaḥyá shocked the community by claiming that he, rather than Bahá'u'lláh, was the One promised by the Báb.

Bahá'u'lláh's reaction to Yaḥyá's insolent response was firm and conclusive. The time had finally come for the Truth to be separated from falsehood. To allow each and every believer total freedom to choose between Him and His opponent, Bahá'u'lláh withdrew with His family to the rented house of Riḍá Big[53] and refused for two months to meet with anyone. Before leaving, He instructed His brother Mírzá Músá to divide all the household belongings found in His home and send half to the house of Mírzá Yaḥyá. In addition to this act of severance, Bahá'u'lláh also insured that Mírzá Yaḥyá would receive his entire share of the allowance allotted by the government for the subsistence of the exiles.

One may think that Bahá'u'lláh's voluntary seclusion would have allayed the animosity which raged so fiercely in Mírzá Yaḥyá and his partisans, but to the contrary, it only served to heighten their campaign of sedition. Eventually the situation became so grave that Bahá'u'lláh was impelled to come out of His retirement. It is reported that on His return, Bahá'u'lláh remarked: "We secluded ourselves that perchance the fire of hostility might be quenched, and such disgraceful acts be averted, but they have resorted to measures more extreme than before."[54]

Bahá'u'lláh stayed in the house of Riḍá Big for about one year and then returned to the house of Amru'lláh. After a three month stay, He moved again, this time to a new residence known as the house of 'Izzat Áqá, where He and His family continued to live until their departure from Edirne. It was

while in this house, in September of 1867, that an event of great importance took place. Although meant as another defamatory attack on Bahá'u'lláh, it completely destroyed Mírzá Yaḥyá's credibility in the eyes of friend and stranger alike.

A certain Mír Muḥammad, a Bábí of Shíráz, had requested Mírzá Yaḥyá to meet Bahá'u'lláh face to face for a public disputation. Thinking that his Brother would not respond to such a challenge, Mírzá Yaḥyá set a date and chose the Mosque of Sultán Salím as the place for their confrontation. To Yaḥyá's dismay, however, as soon as Bahá'u'lláh was informed of this arrangement, He gave His ready assent. On the appointed day, Bahá'u'lláh came out of His house with great power and majesty and set out on foot, and accompanied only by that same Mír Muhammad, for the designated place. On His way as He passed through the streets and markets, verses were continually pouring from His lips. The following are some of the words Bahá'u'lláh uttered on that historic occasion and which He later recorded in the *Lawḥ-i-Mubáhilih (Tablet of Confrontation)*:

> O Muhammad! He Who is the Spirit hath, verily, issued from His habitation, and with Him have come forth the souls of God's chosen ones and the realities of His Messengers. Behold, then, the dwellers of the realms on high above Mine head, and all the testimonies of the Prophets in My grasp. Say: Were all the divines, all the wise men, all the kings and rulers on earth to gather together, I, in very truth, would confront them, and would proclaim the verses of God, the Sovereign, the Almighty, the All-Wise. I am He Who feareth no one, though all who are in heaven and all who are on earth rise up against Me . . . . This is Mine hand which God hath turned white for all the worlds to behold. This is My staff; were We to cast it down, it would, of a truth, swallow up all created things.[55]

Bahá'u'lláh reached the mosque but there was no sign of Mírzá Yaḥyá. As He entered the mosque, the preacher delivering the sermon became completely speechless due to Bahá'u'lláh's overwhelming presence. He then went forward

and with unsurpassed authority seated Himself and graciously bade the preacher to continue his duty. Bahá'u'lláh remained in the mosque until nearly sunset, but Mírzá Yaḥyá never showed up. He sent some pitiful excuse for not attending and asked for the encounter to be postponed for a day or two. When Bahá'u'lláh returned to His house, He penned a letter, wherein He related what had occurred, fixed the time for the deferred meeting, stamped His seal on the letter, and entrusted it to one of His companions to deliver it to Yaḥyá's wretched deputy, Siyyid Muḥammad. It was then demanded from Siyyid Muḥammad to produce a sealed note pledging that should Mírzá Yaḥyá refuse to show up again, the latter would confess in writing that his claims were false. Siyyid Muḥammad agreed and promised to bring the required document the next day. But neither he nor Yaḥyá kept their word.

No pen can adequately describe the tremendous suffering and pain which the enormities of Yaḥyá and his supporters brought upon Bahá'u'lláh. "My Pen, verily, lamenteth over Mine own Self", declares the Wronged One of the world, "and my Tablet weepeth sore over what hath befallen Me at the hands of one (Mírzá Yaḥyá) over whom We watched for successive years, and who, day and night, served in My presence until he was made to err by one of My servants, named Siyyid Muḥammad. Unto this bear witness My believing servants who accompanied Me in My exile from Baghdad to this, the Most Great Prison. And there befell Me at the hands of both of them that which made every man of understanding to cry out, and he who is endued with insight to groan aloud, and tears of the fair-minded to flow."[56] And addressing Yaḥyá himself in another Tablet, Bahá'u'lláh has written: "By God! No spot is left on My body that hath not been touched by the spears of thy machinations." "Thou hast perpetrated against thy Brother what no man hath perpetrated against another."[57] Yet in the *Kitáb-i-Aqdas* (Bahá'u'lláh's *Most Holy Book*) a sin-covering Lord assures this same brother to "fear not because of thy deeds. . . . Return unto God, humble, submissive and lowly; verily, He will put away from thee thy sins for thy Lord,

of a certainty, is the Forgiving, the Mighty, the All-Merciful."[58] Thus, is the unconditional love of the ever-forgiving Lord.

Though surrounded by these and other hardships, Bahá'u'lláh never faltered in declaring to the world the Mission with which He had been entrusted. At all times and under all conditions, even in the midst of severe crisis, He produced numerous Tablets[59] to expound on the implications of His claim. There was, however, a dramatic increase in the outpourings of Bahá'u'lláh's writings towards the end of his sojourn in Edirne. During this period, especially after the severance of ties with Mírzá Yaḥyá, emanations from the pen of Bahá'u'lláh were so prolific that it truly staggers the imagination. According to eye-witness accounts, verses were streaming down in such profusion that it was impossible to record them. Nabíl, the renown Bahá'í chronicler, was personally privileged to observe this phenomenon and has left the following testimony: "A number of secretaries were busy day and night and yet they were unable to cope with the task. Among them was Mírzá Báqir-i-Shírází . . . He alone transcribed no less than two thousand verses every day. He laboured during six or seven months. Every month the equivalent of several volumes would be transcribed by him and sent to Persia. About twenty volumes in his fine penmanship, he left behind as a remembrance for Mírzá Áqá Ján[60]."[61] Bahá'u'lláh, Himself, referring to the copiousness of His writings during those years has written: "Such are the outpourings . . . from the clouds of Divine Bounty that within the space of an hour the equivalent of a thousand verses hath been revealed."[62] And again He writes: "I swear by God! In those days the equivalent of all that hath been sent down aforetime unto the Prophets hath been revealed." "That which hath already been revealed in this land (Edirne), secretaries are incapable of transcribing. It has, therefore, remained for the most part untranscribed."[63]

It was in the course of this period that Bahá'u'lláh began to address the kings and rulers of the world in a series of weighty epistles. He announced to them, both collectively and individually, that the long awaited age of world peace and

global unity was now at hand and that He Himself had been appointed by God so that humanity could attain this bountiful objective. Bahá'u'lláh also called upon these leaders of temporal power to unite under the banner of His Faith so that the spirit and form of the destined world order might be established. The following are excerpts from *Súratu'l-Mulúk*[64] *(The Epistle of the Kings),* a lengthy letter written in Edirne around 1866, in which Bahá'u'lláh for the first time summons collectively the entire body of the monarchs of the East and the West.

> O kings of the earth! Give ear unto the Voice of God, calling from this sublime, this fruit-laden Tree, that hath sprung out of the Crimson Hill, upon the holy Plain, intoning the words: 'There is none other God but He, the Mighty, the All-Powerful, the All-Wise.' . . . Fear God, O concourse of kings, and suffer not yourselves to be deprived of this most sublime grace. Fling away, then, the things ye possess, and take fast hold on the Handle of God, the Exalted, the Great. Set your hearts towards the Face of God, and abandon that which your desires have bidden you to follow, and be not of those who perish . . . Follow, therefore, that which I speak unto you, and hearken unto it with your hearts, and be not of such as have turned aside. For your glory consisteth not in your sovereignty, but rather in your nearness unto God and your observance of His command as sent down in His holy and preserved Tablets. Should any one of you rule over the whole earth, and over all that lieth within it and upon it, its seas, its lands, its mountains, and its plains, and yet be not remembered by God, all these would profit him not, could ye but know it . . . Arise, then, and make steadfast your feet, and make ye amends for that which hath escaped you, and set then yourselves towards His holy Court, on the shore of His mighty Ocean, so that the pearls of knowledge and wisdom which God hath stored up within the shell of His radiant heart, may be revealed unto you . . . Beware lest ye hinder the breeze of God from blowing over your hearts, the breeze through which the hearts of such as have turned unto Him can be quickened . . . .
>
> Be vigilant, that ye may not do injustice to anyone, be it to

the extent of a grain of mustard seed. Tread ye the path of justice, for this, verily, is the straight path.

Compose your differences, and reduce your armaments, that the burden of your expenditures may be lightened, and that your minds and hearts may be tranquillized. Heal the dissensions that divide you, and ye will no longer be in need of any armaments except what the protection of your cities and territories demandeth. Fear ye God, and take heed not to outstrip the bounds of moderation, and be numbered among the extravagant.

We have learned that you are increasing your outlay every year, and are laying the burden thereof on your subjects. This, verily, is more than they can bear, and is a grievous injustice. Decide justly between men, and be ye the emblems of justice amongst them. This, if ye judge fairly, is the thing that behoveth you, and beseemeth your station.

Beware not to deal unjustly with any one that appealeth to you, and entereth beneath your shadow. Walk ye in the fear of God, and be ye of them that lead a godly life. Rest not on your power, your armies, and treasures. Put your whole trust and confidence in God, Who hath created you, and seek ye His help in all your affairs. . . .

Know ye that the poor are the trust of God in your midst. Watch that ye betray not His trust, that ye deal not unjustly with them and that ye walk not in the ways of the treacherous. Ye will most certainly be called upon to answer for His trust on the day when the Balance of Justice shall be set, the day when unto every one shall be rendered his due, when the doings of all men, be they rich or poor, shall be weighed.

If ye pay no heed unto the counsels which, in peerless and unequivocal language, We have revealed in this Tablet, Divine chastisement shall assail you from every direction, and the sentence of His justice shall be pronounced against you. On that day ye shall have no power to resist Him, and shall recognize your own impotence. Have mercy on yourselves and on those beneath you, and judge ye between them according to the precepts prescribed by God in His most holy and exalted Tablet, a Tablet wherein He hath assigned to each and every thing its settled measure, in which He hath given, with distinctness, an explanation of all things, and which is in itself a monition unto them that believe in Him.

> Examine Our Cause, inquire into the things that have befallen Us, and decide justly between Us and our enemies, and be ye of them that act equitably towards their neighbours. If ye stay not the hand of the oppressor, if ye fail to safeguard the rights of the down-trodden, what right have ye then to vaunt yourselves among men? What is it of which ye can rightly boast? Is it on your food and your drink that ye pride yourselves, on the riches ye lay up in your treasuries, on the diversity and the cost of the ornaments with which ye deck yourselves? If true glory were to consist in the possession of such perishable things, then the earth on which ye walk must needs vaunt itself over you, because it supplieth you, and bestoweth upon you, these very things, by the decree of the Almighty. In its bowels are contained, according to what God hath ordained, all that ye possess. From it, as a sign of His mercy, ye derive your riches. Behold then your state, the thing in which ye glory! Would that ye could perceive it! Nay, By Him Who holdeth in His grasp the kingdom of the entire creation! Nowhere doth your true and abiding glory reside except in your firm adherence unto the precepts of God, your wholehearted observance of His laws, your resolution to see that they do not remain unenforced, and to pursue steadfastly the right course . . . .
>
> God hath committed into your hands the reins of the government of the people, that ye may rule with justice over them, safeguard the rights of the down-trodden, and punish the wrong-doers. If ye neglect the duty prescribed unto you by God in His Book, your names shall be numbered with those of the unjust in His sight. Grievous, indeed, will be your error. Cleave ye to that which your imaginations have devised, and cast behind your backs the commandments of God, the Most Exalted, the Inaccessible, the All-Compelling, the Almighty? Cast away the things ye possess, and cling to that which God hath bidden you observe. Seek ye His grace, for he that seeketh it treadeth His straight Path . . . .[65]

While in Edirne, Bahá'u'lláh also addressed two heads of state individually. They were the French emperor Napoleon III and Náṣiri'd-Dín Sh͟áh, the King of Persia. Although the Letter to the Sh͟áh was sent to him later from 'Akká, the Epistle to Napoleon III was forwarded to the Emperor shortly after its

composition through the French consulate in Edirne.

These proclamations had hardly begun when Yaḥyá and his small group of supporters unleashed another attack on Bahá'u'lláh, this time with serious political consequences. Having been abandoned by the entire community for his rejection of Bahá'u'lláh's claim, Yaḥyá sought another way to undermine the influence of his Brother. He sent anonymous letters to Istanbul warning the authorities that Bahá'u'lláh was engaged in a political conspiracy against the government. The officials in the capital were for some time aware of Bahá'u'lláh's growing popularity in the society of Edirne and were especially resentful of the esteem in which He was held by the authorities and representatives of foreign powers in that land. Thus, when they began receiving suspicious reports about Bahá'u'lláh, their apprehension toward Him and His followers grew more intense. For the Ottoman government, the question of the exiles had to be dealt with once and for all. It was, therefore, decided that Bahá'u'lláh should be removed to a remote and isolated colony where He could not exert His influence over anyone. They agreed that the fortress city of 'Akká, then in the province of Syria, would serve this purpose well. Hence, an imperial order was issued by the Sultan in which Bahá'u'lláh was condemned to life imprisonment within the walls of 'Akká.

Ironically, Yaḥyá and his accomplices became victims of their own evil scheme. Being suspected of political intrigues himself, Yaḥyá was sent as a prisoner to the island of Cyprus where he remained in isolation until the end of his life. A number of His supporters, including Siyyid Muḥammad, were also detained and deported with the Bahá'í exiles to 'Akká.

The decision for Bahá'u'lláh's banishment from Edirne came quite unexpectedly. One early summer morning, government soldiers surrounded the house of Bahá'u'lláh and would not allow anyone to enter or depart. Such was the restriction imposed by the sentinels that according to Bahá'u'lláh in the *Súriy-i-Ra'ís*[66] *(The Epistle of the Chief)*, on the first night His household was left without food as no one could leave the house to shop for provisions. "The loved ones of God and His kindred,"

He writes, "were left on the first night without food . . . The people surrounded the house, and Muslims and Christians wept over Us."[67] Next, Bahá'u'lláh's followers were rounded up by the government and told to prepare for departure from Edirne. No one was, however, informed of where they were going and what was going to happen to them. The news of the imminent removal of the exiles spread quickly throughout the city making many of the inhabitants disturbed and sorrowful at the plight of the ill-fated group. Even a number of foreign consuls went to Bahá'u'lláh and indicated that should He approve they were ready to intervene through their respective governments on His behalf. Bahá'u'lláh, however, courteously refused their offer of assistance and, as reported by one of His companions, said to them: "You wish me to give you the word to bring Me relief, but My relief lies in the hands of God. My focus is God, and to Him alone do I turn."[68] In one of His Tablets, Bahá'u'lláh recalls the assistance extended to Him by those representatives of foreign powers. He writes: "The consuls of that city (Edirne) gathered in the presence of this Youth at the hour of His departure and expressed their desire to aid Him. They, verily, evinced towards Us manifest affection."[69]

The last few days preceding Bahá'u'lláh's departure from Edirne was a period of great consternation for all the members of the community. No one knew what was going to happen to them or where they were being sent. They all knew their love for Bahá'u'lláh and were willing to sustain any hardship so long as they could accompany Him. But would they be deprived of this bounty? What was going to happen to their Beloved? Throughout these distressful times Bahá'u'lláh as always remained calm and serene. He continually addressed the believers with words of comfort and would lovingly direct them to put their trust in God and be content with His will. But there were still those to whom the thought of separation from Bahá'u'lláh was tantamount to death. One of these devotees by the name of Ḥájí Ja'far-i-Tabrízí, having realized that his name was not on the list of exiles who might accompany Bahá'u'lláh, became so despondent that he took a razor and

slit his own throat. His life, however, was saved by the other members of Bahá'u'lláh's retinue who immediately called a surgeon to attend his wounds. When Bahá'u'lláh was informed of this, He came to Ḥájí Ja'far's bedside and assured him with great affection that as soon as he got better He would summon him to His new place of exile. Bahá'u'lláh alludes to this episode in the *Súriy-i-Ra'ís* and describes it as an act "unheard of in bygone centuries," and which, "God hath set apart for this Revelation, as an evidence of the power of His might."[70]

Within a few days, on Wednesday August 12, 1868, Bahá'u'lláh and His family, escorted by a number of Turkish soldiers, left the city of Hadrian on another journey to exile. Four days later, the travellers reached the port of Gallipoli where they were to board ship for a destination as yet unknown to them. At this point, the military escort was changed. When the captain of the guards came to pay his respects and take his leave, Bahá'u'lláh addressed him in these words: "Tell the king that this territory will pass out of his hands, and his affairs will be thrown into confusion.[71] Not I speak these words, but God speaketh them."[72] One of Bahá'u'lláh's companions who was present that night has written that during those moments when Bahá'u'lláh was pronouncing these and other words, he and other believers could hear Him from downstairs. Bahá'u'lláh, he remembers, was speaking in such "vehemence and power" that it was as though "the foundation of the house trembled."[73] This same individual has further recorded in his memoirs some of the salient words spoken by Bahá'u'lláh during that meeting. He writes that Bahá'u'lláh said to the captain, who stood silent and submissive: "It would have been meet for His Majesty the Sultan to have gathered an assembly and called Us to be present, that he should have investigated the matter, and had he then found any portent of sedition, any sign of anything contrary to the Will of God, to have meted out this treatment to which he hath now resorted. He should have asked Us to present him proofs of what We profess. Should he have found Us wanting, then he could have subjected Us to whatever he wished. He should not have allowed such wrong-

doing, such enmity, such injuries, without reason, solely by following the behest of authors of mischief."[74] As reported, the captain promised to pass on what he had heard.

The Ottoman government had originally intended to banish Bahá'u'lláh, His two faithful brothers Mírzá Músá (Áqáy-i-Kalím) and Mírzá Muḥammad-Qulí, with a servant to 'Akká and send the rest of His family and retinue to Istanbul. This decision, as one can imagine, was the cause of great commotion and distress among Bahá'u'lláh's family and companions. Through the insistence of Bahá'u'lláh, however, and by the efforts of the official in charge of the escort, orders were changed and everyone was permitted to go with Him.

Before their departure from Gallipoli, Bahá'u'lláh being fully cognizant of the dangers and trials lying ahead, turned to His companions and addressed them in these words of warning: "This journey will be unlike any of the previous journeys"; whoever does not feel himself "man enough to face the future" would be best to "depart to whatever place he pleaseth, and be preserved from tests, for hereafter he will find himself unable to leave."[75] To this admonition, everyone listened attentively but not a single person chose to withdraw. How could they? They were all too in love to entertain any thought of separation from their Beloved.

Then came the hour of departure. On the morning of August 21, 1868, all the exiles, numbering about seventy, boarded an Austrian-Lloyd steamer bound for Alexandria. On the way the ship made two stops, one at Madelli for a few hours and another at Izmir for two days. In Alexandria, they were transferred to another Austrian-Lloyd steamer which, after brief stops in Port Said and Jaffa, arrived in Haifa on August 31. The exiles disembarked at Haifa and after a few hours were taken by a sailing vessel to 'Akká.

'Akká (Acre)

At the time of Bahá'u'lláh's arrival in 'Akká, the ancient city, once a Crusader stronghold, was a remote and pestilential place which under the Turks had become a penal colony. Within its

strongly fortified walls were consigned criminals from all around the empire, including felons, thugs and murderers. Its air was no better than its brutish prisoners. According to a local saying, if a bird flew over the city it would drop dead. In the Epistle to Náṣiri'd-Dín Sháh, Bahá'u'lláh refers to the condition of 'Akká. He writes: "According to what they say, it is the most desolate of the cities of the world, the most unsightly of them in appearance, the most detestable in climate, and the foulest in water. It is as though it were the metropolis of the owl."[76]

Bahá'u'lláh and the group of exiles entered 'Akká through its sea gate. At the point of entry, some of the inhabitants of the city had gathered near the landing site and scorned them with jeers and insults. Once all the captives had disembarked from the boat, they were conducted by the officials through narrow and filthy streets to the army barracks. There they were taken to the north-western wing of the citadel where, after being locked up, guards were posted at the doors. In the *Lawḥ-i-Ra'ís*[77] *(Tablet of the Chief)*, written soon after His incarceration at the barracks, Bahá'u'lláh describes vividly the circumstance of their arrival in 'Akká and the condition under which they were kept in the citadel.

> Upon our arrival, we were surrounded by guards and confined together, men and women, young and old alike, in the army barracks. The first night all were deprived of either food or drink, for the sentries were guarding the gate of the barracks and permitted no one to leave. No one gave a thought to the plight of these wronged ones. They even begged for water, and were refused. . . . The officials enforce every day a new decree, and no end is in sight to their tyranny. Night and day they conceive new schemes. They have assigned each prisoner, from the government storehouse, a daily allowance of three loaves of bread that no one can eat. From the foundation of the world until the present day a cruelty such as this hath neither been seen nor heard of.[78]

The cruelty of the officials coupled with the unsanitary condition of the prison created a truly intolerable situation for the innocent captives. Shortly after their arrival, they all

became ill except two who became responsible for attending to the needs of their ailing fellow prisoners. But they, too, eventually became sick. With malaria and dysentery raging among them, three of the exiles fell gravely ill and died. Two of these were brothers who, according to Bahá'u'lláh's testimony, died the same night "locked in each other's arms."[79] The guards, however, would not remove the bodies as they insisted on being paid before carrying out the burial. No money being available, Bahá'u'lláh gave the carpet He slept on to be sold and the money from that was given to the guards. In the *Lawḥ-i-Ra'ís*, Bahá'u'lláh recounts this episode in the following words:

> In the days following Our arrival, two of these servants hastened to the realms above. For an entire day the guards insisted that, until they were paid for the shrouds and burial, those blessed bodies could not be removed, although no one had requested any help from them. At that time we were devoid of earthly means, and pleaded that they leave the matter unto us and allow those present to carry the bodies, but they refused. Finally, a carpet was taken to the bazaar to be sold, and the sum obtained was delivered to the guards. Later, it was learned that they had merely dug a shallow grave into which they had placed both blessed bodies, although they had taken twice the amount required for shrouds and burial. The pen is powerless to depict and the tongue faileth to describe the trials which We have suffered.[80]

Such were the woes and afflictions of Bahá'u'lláh and His companions in the prison of 'Akká. Indeed the hardships sustained by Bahá'u'lláh had never been this severe and continuous in the past, not even when He was in the Síyáh Chál. "Know thou," Bahá'u'lláh Himself testifies, "that upon Our arrival at this Spot, We chose to designate it as the 'Most Great Prison'. Though previously subjected in another land (Ṭihrán) to chains and fetters, We yet refused to call it by that name. Say: Ponder thereon, O ye endued with understanding!"[81] Furthermore, He, referring to Himself, has recorded in one of His Tablets: "He hath, during the greater part of His life, been sore-tried in the clutches of His enemies. His sufferings have

now reached their culmination in this afflictive Prison, into which His oppressors have so unjustly thrown Him."[82]

A few days after Bahá'u'lláh's arrival in 'Akká the text of the farmán (royal edict) of Sultán 'Abdu'l-'Azíz was read out publicly in the principal mosque of the city. It was meant as a warning to the population. The farmán accused the exiles of having misled and corrupted the minds of the people and as a punishment had condemned them to life imprisonment. The document further stipulated that Bahá'u'lláh and His followers were to be confined within the walls of 'Akká and were prohibited from associating with anyone, even among themselves.

While engulfed in tribulations at the barracks, Bahá'u'lláh once again resumed His proclamation to the kings and rulers of the world. "Upon Our arrival at this Prison," He writes, "We purposed to transmit to the kings the messages of their Lord, the Mighty, the All-Praised. Though We have transmitted to them, in several Tablets, that which We were commanded, yet We do it once again, as a token of God's grace."[83] Having previously addressed the two major rulers of the Islamic world, Sultan 'Abdu'l-'Azíz and Náṣiri'd-Din Sháh, Bahá'u'lláh turned His attention to the crowned heads of state in Europe. Individual epistles were composed and sent to all the principal sovereigns of that powerful continent including Emperor Napoleon III, Queen Victoria, and Czar Alexander II.[84]

To the Emperor of France, Louis Napoleon Bonaparte, the most powerful European monarch of his day, who according to Bahá'u'lláh had "cast behind his back"[85] the Letter sent to him from Edirne, He the Prisoner of the army barracks wrote a second Tablet and dispatched it through the French consular agent in 'Akká. The following are excerpts from this second Tablet to Napoleon III:

> O King of Paris! Tell the priest to ring the bells no longer. By God, the True One! The Most Mighty Bell hath appeared in the form of Him Who is the Most Great Name, and the fingers of the will of Thy Lord, the Most Exalted, the Most High, toll it out in the heaven of Immortality, in His name, the All-Glorious. . . . Say: He Who is the Unconditioned is

come, in the clouds of light, that He may quicken all created things with the breezes of His Name, the Most Merciful, and unify the world, and gather all men around this Table which hath been sent down from heaven. . . .

O King! We heard the words thou didst utter in answer to the Czar of Russia, concerning the decision made regarding the war (Crimean War). Thy Lord, verily, knoweth, is informed of all. Thou didst say: "I lay asleep upon my couch, when the cry of the oppressed, who were drowned in the Black Sea, wakened me." This is what we heard thee say, and, verily, thy Lord is witness unto what I say. We testify that that which wakened thee was not their cry but the promptings of thine own passions, for We tested thee, and found thee wanting. Comprehend the meaning of My words, and be thou of the discerning. It is not Our wish to address thee words of condemnation, out of regard for the dignity We conferred upon thee in this mortal life. We, verily, have chosen courtesy, and made it the true mark of such as are nigh unto Him. Courtesy, is, in truth, a raiment which fitteth all men, whether young or old. Well is it with him that adorneth his temple therewith, and woe unto him who is deprived of this great bounty. Hadst thou been sincere in thy words, thou wouldst have not cast behind thy back the Book of God, when it was sent unto thee by Him Who is the Almighty, the All-Wise. We have proved thee through it, and found thee other than that which thou didst profess. Arise, and make amends for that which escaped thee. Ere long the world and all that thou possessest will perish, and the kingdom will remain unto God, thy Lord and the Lord of thy fathers of old. It behoveth thee not to conduct thine affairs according to the dictates of thy desires. Fear the sighs of this Wronged One, and shield Him from the darts of such as act unjustly.

For what thou hast done, thy kingdom shall be thrown into confusion, and thine empire shall pass from thine hands, as a punishment for that which thou hast wrought. Then wilt thou know how thou hast plainly erred. Commotions shall seize all the people in that land, unless thou arisest to help this Cause, and followest Him Who is the Spirit of God (Jesus Christ) in this, the Straight Path. Hath thy pomp made thee proud? By My Life! It shall not endure; nay, it shall soon pass away, unless thou holdest fast by this firm Cord. We

> see abasement hastening after thee, whilst thou art of the heedless. . . . Meditate on the world and the state of its people. He, for Whose sake the world was called into being, hath been imprisoned in the most desolate of cities ('Akká), by reason of that which the hands of the wayward have wrought. From the horizon of His prison-city He summoneth mankind unto the Dayspring of God, the Exalted, the Great. Exultest thou over the treasures thou dost possess, knowing they shall perish? Rejoicest thou in that thou rulest a span of earth, when the whole world, in the estimation of the people of Bahá, is worth as much as the black in the eye of a dead ant? Abandon it unto such as have set their affections upon it, and turn thou unto Him Who is the Desire of the world. Whither are gone the proud and their palaces? Gaze thou into their tombs, that thou mayest profit by this example, inasmuch as We made it a lesson unto every beholder. Were the breezes of Revelation to seize thee, thou wouldst flee the world, and turn unto the Kingdom, and wouldst expend all thou possessest, that thou mayest draw nigh unto this sublime Vision . . . .[86]

Also while immured in the citadel of 'Akká Bahá'u'lláh addressed a specific epistle to the renowned monarch of the British empire, Queen Victoria.

> O Queen in London! Incline thine ear unto the voice of thy Lord, the Lord of all mankind, calling from the Divine Lote-Tree: Verily, no God is there but Me, the Almighty, the All-Wise! Cast away all that is on earth, and attire the head of thy kingdom with the crown of the remembrance of thy Lord, the All-Glorious. He, in truth, hath come unto the world in His most great glory, and all that hath been mentioned in the Gospel hath been fulfilled. The land of Syria hath been honoured by the footsteps of its Lord, the Lord of all men, and North and South are both inebriated with the wine of His presence. Blessed is the man that inhaled the fragrance of the Most Merciful, and turned unto the Dawning-Place of His Beauty, in this resplendent Dawn . . . .
>
> Lay aside thy desire, and set then thine heart towards thy Lord, the Ancient of Days. We make mention of thee for the sake of God, and desire that thy name may be exalted through thy remembrance of God, the Creator of earth and heaven.

He, verily, is witness unto that which I say. We have been informed that thou hast forbidden the trading in slaves, both men and women. This, verily, is what God hath enjoined in this wondrous Revelation. God hath, truly, destined a reward for thee, because of this. He, verily, will pay the doer of good his due recompense, wert thou to follow what hath been sent unto thee by Him Who is the All-Knowing, the All-Informed. As to him who turneth aside, and swelleth with pride, after that the clear tokens have come unto him, from the Revealer of signs, his work shall God bring to naught. He, in truth, hath power over all things. Man's actions are acceptable after his having recognized (the Manifestation). He that turneth aside from the True One is indeed the most veiled amongst His creatures. Thus hath it been decreed by Him Who is the Almighty, the Most Powerful.

We have also heard that thou has entrusted the reins of counsel into the hands of the representatives of the people. Thou, indeed, hast done well, for thereby the foundations of the edifice of thine affairs will be strengthened, and the hearts of all that are beneath thy shadow, whether high or low, will be tranquillized. It behoveth them, however, to be trustworthy among His servants, and to regard themselves as the representatives of all that dwell on earth. This is what counselleth them, in this Tablet, He Who is the Ruler, the All-Wise . . . Blessed is he that entereth the assembly for the sake of God, and judgeth between men with pure justice. He, indeed, is of the blissful . . . [87]

The Czar of Russia, Alexander Nicolaevitch, was another European ruler whom Bahá'u'lláh called upon during that same period. To the mighty Czar, He, the chosen Manifestation of God, wrote:

O Czar of Russia! Incline thine ear unto the voice of God, the King, the Holy, and turn thou unto Paradise, the Spot wherein abideth He Who, among the Concourse on high, beareth the most excellent titles, and Who, in the kingdom of creation, is called by the name of God, the Effulgent, the All-Glorious. Beware lest thy desire deter thee from turning towards the face of thy Lord, the Compassionate, the Most Merciful. We, verily, have heard the thing for which thou didst supplicate thy Lord, whilst secretly communing with

> Him. Wherefore, the breeze of My loving-kindness wafted forth, and the sea of My mercy surged, and We answered thee in truth. Thy Lord, verily, is the All-Knowing, the All-Wise. Whilst I lay chained and fettered in the prison, one of thy ministers extended Me his aid. Wherefore hath God ordained for thee a station which the knowledge of none can comprehend except His knowledge. Beware lest thou barter away this sublime station . . . Beware lest thy sovereignty withhold thee from Him Who is the Supreme Sovereign . . .
>
> I, verily, have not sought to extol Mine Own Self, but rather God Himself were ye to judge fairly. Naught can be seen in Me except God and His Cause, could ye but perceive it. I am the One Whom the tongue of Isaiah hath extolled, the One with Whose name both the Torah and the Evangel were adorned . . . Blessed be the king whose sovereignty hath withheld him not from his Sovereign, and who hath turned unto God with his heart. He, verily, is accounted of those that have attained unto that which God, the Mighty, the All-Wise hath willed. Ere long will such a one find himself numbered with the monarchs of the realms of the Kingdom. Thy Lord is, in truth, potent over all things. He giveth what He willeth to whomsoever He willeth, and withholdeth what He pleaseth from whomsoever He willeth. He, verily, is the All-Powerful, the Almighty.[88]

Bahá'u'lláh continued to address other western potentates even after He was transferred from the army barracks. To Kaiser Wilhelm I, the King of Prussia and the recently declared emperor of the unified Germany, He wrote in the *Kitáb-i-Aqdas*:

> O King of Berlin! Give ear unto the Voice calling from this manifest Temple: Verily, there is none other God but Me, the Everlasting, the Peerless, the Ancient of Days. Take heed lest pride debar thee from recognizing the Dayspring of Divine Revelation, lest earthly desires shut thee out, as by a veil, from the Lord of the Throne above and of the earth below. Thus counselleth thee the Pen of the Most High. He, verily, is the Most Gracious, the All-Bountiful. Do thou remember the one whose power transcended thy power (Napoleon III), and whose station excelled thy station. Where is he? Whither are gone the things he possessed? Take warning, and be not of them that are fast asleep. He it was who cast the Tablet

> of God behind him, when We made known unto him what the hosts of tyranny had caused Us to suffer. Wherefore, disgrace assailed him from all sides, and he went down to dust in great loss. Think deeply, O King, concerning him, and concerning them who, like unto thee, have conquered cities and ruled over men. The All-Merciful brought them down from their palaces to their graves. Be warned, be of them who reflect.[89]

Another powerful ruler of Europe who was summoned by Bahá'u'lláh in the *Kitáb-i-Aqdas* was the Austro-Hungarian emperor and the acclaimed heir of the Holy Roman Empire, Franz Joseph Hapsburg. To him, the oppressed Prisoner of 'Akká wrote:

> O Emperor of Austria! He who is the Dayspring of God's Light dwelt in the prison of 'Akká, at the time when thou didst set forth to visit the Aqsá Mosque (Jerusalem). Thou passed Him by, and inquired not about Him, by Whom every house is exalted, and every lofty gate unlocked. We, verily, made it (Jerusalem) a place whereunto the world should turn, that they might remember Me, and yet thou hast rejected Him Who is the Object of this remembrance, when He appeared with the Kingdom of God, thy Lord and the Lord of the worlds. We have been with thee at all times, and found thee clinging unto the Branch and heedless of the Root. Thy Lord, verily, is a witness unto what I say. We grieved to see thee circle round Our Name, whilst unaware of Us, though We were before thy face. Open thine eyes, that thou mayest behold this glorious Vision, and recognize Him Whom thou invokest in the daytime and in the night-season, and gaze on the light that shineth above this luminous Horizon.[90]

In that same Book, Bahá'u'lláh also directs His words to the entire body of the ecclesiastical leaders of the world. To them He, whose Coming was the sole object of their practice, made this challenging pronouncement:

> O leaders of religion! Weigh not the Book of God with such standards and sciences as are current amongst you, for the Book itself is the unerring balance established amongst men. In this most perfect balance whatsoever the peoples and kindreds of the earth possess must be weighed, while the measure of its weight should be tested according to its own

standard, did ye but know it.

The eye of My loving-kindness weepeth sore over you, inasmuch as ye have failed to recognize the One upon Whom ye have been calling in the daytime and in the night season, at even and at morn. Advance, O people, with snow-white faces and radiant hearts, unto the blest and crimson Spot, wherein the Sadratu'l-Muntahá is calling: 'Verily, there is none other God beside Me, the Omnipotent Protector, the Self-Subsisting!'

O ye leaders of religion! Who is the man amongst you that can rival Me in vision or insight? Where is he to be found that dareth to claim to be My equal in utterance or wisdom? No, by My Lord, the All-Merciful! All on the earth shall pass away; and this is the face of your Lord, the Almighty, the Well-Beloved.

We have decreed, O people, that the highest and last end of all learning be the recognition of Him Who is the Object of all knowledge; and yet, behold how ye have allowed your learning to shut you out, as by a veil, from Him Who is the Dayspring of this Light, through Whom every hidden thing hath been revealed. Could ye but discover the source whence the splendour of this utterance is diffused, ye would cast away the peoples of the world and all that they possess, and would draw nigh unto this most blessed Seat of glory . . . .

We have not entered any school, nor read any of your dissertations. Incline your ears to the words of this unlettered One, wherewith He summoneth you unto God, the Ever-Abiding. Better is this for you than all the treasures of the earth, could ye but comprehend it.[91]

Among those religious leaders whom Bahá'u'lláh summoned individually was the supreme pontiff of the Roman Catholic Church. To Pope Pius IX, the longest reigning Pope in history, He, during His incarceration at the army barracks, addressed a weighty epistle in which He announced the following:

O Pope! Rend the veils asunder. He Who is the Lord of Lords is come overshadowed with clouds, and the decree hath been fulfilled by God, the Almighty, the Unrestrained . . . He, verily, hath again come down from Heaven even as He came down from it the first time. Beware that thou dispute not with Him even as the Pharisees disputed with Him (Jesus)

without a clear token or proof. On His right hand flow the living waters of grace, on His left the choice Wine of justice, whilst before Him march the angels of Paradise, bearing the banners of His signs. Beware lest any name debar thee from God, the Creator of earth and heaven. Leave thou the world behind thee, and turn towards thy Lord, through Whom the whole earth hath been illumined . . . . Dwellest thou in palaces whilst He Who is the King of Revelation liveth in the most desolate of abodes? Leave them unto such as desire them, and set thy face with joy and delight towards the Kingdom . . . Arise in the name of thy Lord, the God of Mercy, amidst the peoples of the earth, and seize thou the Cup of Life with the hands of confidence, and first drink thou therefrom, and proffer it then to such as turn towards it amongst the peoples of all faiths . . . .

Call thou to remembrance Him Who was the Spirit (Jesus), Who when He came, the most learned of His age pronounced judgment against Him in His own country, whilst he who was only a fisherman believed in Him. Take heed, then, ye men of understanding heart! Thou, in truth, art one of the suns of the heaven of His names. Guard thyself, lest darkness spread its veils over thee, and fold thee away from His light . . . . Consider those who opposed the Son (Jesus), when He came unto them with sovereignty and power. How many the Pharisees who were waiting to behold Him, and were lamenting over the separation from Him! And yet, when the fragrance of His coming was wafted over them, and His beauty was unveiled, they turned aside from Him and disputed with Him . . . . None save a very few, who were destitute of any power amongst men, turned towards His face. And yet, today, every man endowed with power and invested with sovereignty prideth himself on His Name! In like manner, consider how numerous, in these days, are the monks who, in My Name, have secluded themselves in their churches, and who, when the appointed time was fulfilled, and We unveiled Our beauty, knew us not, though they call upon Me at eventide and at dawn . . . .

The Word which the Son concealed is made manifest. It hath been sent down in the form of the human temple in this day. Blessed be the Lord Who is the Father! He, verily, is come unto the nations in His most great majesty. Turn your

> faces towards Him, O concourse of the righteous . . . This is the day whereon the Rock (Peter) crieth out and shouteth, and celebrateth the praise of its Lord, the All-Possessing, the Most High, saying: "Lo! The Father is come, and that which ye were promised in the Kingdom is fulfilled!" . . .
>
> O Supreme Pontiff! Incline thine ear unto that which the Fashioner of mouldering bones counselleth thee, as voiced by Him Who is His Most Great Name. Sell all the embellished ornaments thou dost possess, and expend them in the path of God, Who causeth the night to return upon the day, and the day to return upon the night. Abandon thy kingdom unto the kings, and emerge from thy habitation, with thy face set towards the Kingdom, and, detached from the world, then speak forth the praises of thy Lord betwixt earth and heaven. Thus hath bidden thee He Who is the Possessor of Names, on the part of thy Lord, the Almighty, the All-Knowing.[92]

Regrettably neither the Pope nor any of the other rulers and monarchs whom Bahá'u'lláh addressed responded to His call. Only Queen Victoria is reported to have made the following verbal statement upon reading Bahá'u'lláh's Tablet: "If this is of God, it will endure; if not, it can do no harm."[93]

Bahá'u'lláh and His companions were kept in the barracks for over two years. Four months before their transfer to other locations within the city, occurred a very tragic incident which brought profound sorrow to the already overburdened heart of Bahá'u'lláh. It was the premature death of His favoured and much loved son, Mírzá Mihdí. So pure and gentle was this son of Bahá'u'lláh that He, in His writings, had designated him as *Ghuṣnu'lláhu'l-Aṭhar* (The Purest Branch of God). Eyewitness accounts record that it was Mírzá Mihdí's custom to retire every evening to the roof-top of the citadel and spend hours in prayer and meditation. One evening as he was pacing the roof wrapped in thought and devotions, he did not notice an open skylight and fell through, landing on a wooden crate on the floor below. The crate pierced his chest, causing him to bleed profusely. An Italian doctor was called in but his treatment was ineffective. Twenty two hours after his fall the Purest Branch passed away. Before his death, Bahá'u'lláh, greatly distressed

by the accident, went to the bedside of His noble son and after dismissing everyone from the room remained with him for some time. One of the exiled believers recalls that he overheard Bahá'u'lláh asking the Purest Branch: "Áqá, what do you wish, tell Me." To which he replied, "I wish the people of Bahá to be able to attain Your presence." "And so it shall be," Bahá'u'lláh responded, "God will grant your wish."[94]

The death of Mírzá Mihdí left grave traces of sadness on the soul of Bahá'u'lláh. One of His attendants remembers hearing Bahá'u'lláh lamenting aloud: "Mihdí! O Mihdí!" But even the mournful loss of His beloved son could not deter Bahá'u'lláh from revealing the Words of God.

> At this very moment My son is being washed before My face, after Our having sacrificed him in the Most Great Prison. Thereat have the dwellers of the Abhá Tabernacle wept with a great weeping, and such as have suffered imprisonment with this Youth in the path of God, the Lord of the promised Day, lamented. Under such conditions My Pen hath not been prevented from remembering its Lord, the Lord of all nations. It summoneth the people unto God, the Almighty, the All-Bountiful."[95]

From the barracks Bahá'u'lláh and His family were moved to the house of Malik in the Christian south-western part of 'Akká. There they dwelled for three months and then relocated to the house of Manṣúr Khavvám situated across a narrow lane from the former house. Bahá'u'lláh's stay at this house was also short. About three months later the authorities moved Him again, this time to the house of Rábi'ih, in the Muslim section of the city. After four months in the house of Rábi'ih Bahá'u'lláh and His family were obliged once more to take up new residence. They were moved back to the Christian quarters and placed in the house of 'Údí Khammár. Although this house was more permanent than the others, it was still too small for Bahá'u'lláh's household. In fact so small was the house of 'Údí Khammár that in one of its rooms up to thirteen people of both sexes would sleep in rows.

With the passing of time Bahá'u'lláh's spiritual character began to display the same power of attraction it had wielded

in Baghdad and Edirne. Authorities became sympathetic towards Him and as a result the restrictions imposed on Him and His followers were somewhat mitigated. Then came a sudden catastrophe. Embittered by the improvement of the situation of the Bahá'í exiles, the scheming Siyyid Muḥammad-i-Iṣfahání and his small band of Azalís launched a fierce campaign of slander and resorted to disgraceful acts in the hope of instigating the already prejudiced and suspicious population of 'Akká to rise against the Bahá'ís. The conspirators even went so far as planning an attack on the house of Bahá'u'lláh with the intention of killing Him and His family.

As in the past, Bahá'u'lláh's reaction to this new assault by an obstinate enemy was complete detachment and utter submission to the Divine Will. To avoid any involvement in the brewing intrigues, He closed the door of His house to friend and stranger alike and refused to admit anyone to His presence. The seclusion of Bahá'u'lláh was a heavy and painful blow to the spirit of His companions. Like moths deprived of the flame they bitterly lamented their separation from their Beloved. It was during this intense period that the *Lawḥ-i-Iḥtiráq*[96] or *The Fire Tablet* was penned by Bahá'u'lláh. In this soul-stirring prayer, Bahá'u'lláh, in His communion with the Supreme Creator, expatiates on the grief and sufferings brought upon Him as a result of continuing attacks of His oppressors:

> . . . Bahá is drowning in a sea of tribulation: Where is the Ark of Thy salvation, O Saviour of the worlds? . . .
> The lamps of truth and purity, of loyalty and honour, have been put out: Where are the signs of Thine avenging wrath, O Mover of the worlds? . . .
> This Face is hidden in the dust of slander: Where are the breezes of Thy compassion, O Mercy of the worlds?
> The robe of sanctity is sullied by the people of deceit: Where is the vesture of Thy holiness, O Adorner of the worlds? . . .
> The door leading to the Divine Presence is locked through the tyranny of Thy foes: Where is the key of Thy bestowal, O Unlocker of the worlds?
> The leaves are yellowed by the poisoning winds of sedition: Where is the downpour of the clouds of Thy bounty, O Giver

> of the worlds? . . .
> This Youth is lonely in a desolate land: Where is the rain of Thy heavenly grace, O Bestower of the worlds?

Then comes a moving response from the Lord of the worlds:

> O Supreme Pen, We have heard Thy most sweet call in the eternal realm: Give Thou ear unto what the Tongue of Grandeur uttereth, O Wronged One of the worlds!
> Were it not for the cold, how would the heat of Thy words prevail, O Expounder of the worlds?
> Were it not for calamity, how would the sun of Thy patience shine, O Light of the worlds?
> Lament not because of the wicked. Thou wert created to bear and endure, O Patience of the worlds.
> How sweet was Thy dawning on the horizon of the Covenant among the stirrers of sedition, and Thy yearning after God, O Love of the worlds.
> By Thee the banner of independence was planted on the highest peaks, and the sea of bounty surged, O Rapture of the worlds.
> By Thine aloneness the Sun of Oneness shone, and by Thy banishment the land of Unity was adorned. Be patient, O Thou Exile of the worlds.
> We have made abasement the garment of Glory, and affliction the adornment of Thy temple, O Pride of the worlds.
> Thou seest the hearts are filled with hate, and to overlook it is Thine, O Thou Concealer of the sins of the worlds.
> When the swords flash, go forward! When the shafts fly, press onward! O Thou Sacrifice of the worlds.
> Dost Thou wail, or shall I wail? Rather shall I weep at the fewness of Thy champions, O Thou Who hast caused the wailing of the worlds.

And finally follows Bahá'u'lláh's acquiescence to the Call of the All-Glorious Beloved:

> Verily, I have heard Thy Call, O All-Glorious Beloved; and now is the face of Bahá flaming with the heat of tribulation and with the fire of Thy shining word, and He hath risen up in faithfulness at the place of sacrifice, looking toward Thy pleasure, O Ordainer of the worlds. . . .[97]

The revelation of *The Fire Tablet* brought further sorrow to the hearts of Bahá'u'lláh's companions who felt utterly helpless

to rescue their beloved Leader from the clutches of His enemies. Bahá'u'lláh had explicitly forbidden them to take retaliatory action against their tormentors and had even expelled an Arab believer from 'Akká who had expressed the desire to silence the Azalís. All they could do was to be patient and steadfast and follow the example of their Lord. Unfortunately, for some of Bahá'u'lláh's followers the harassment of their adversaries proved too intolerable to endure. Disregarding Bahá'u'lláh's stringent orders, seven of the Bahá'í exiles took the matter into their own hands and after intentionally starting a fight they killed Siyyid Muḥammad and two of his accomplices.

The shameful act of these men outraged and saddened Bahá'u'lláh beyond measure. In a Tablet written shortly after this episode He laments bitterly: "Were We to make mention of what befell Us, the heavens would be rent asunder and the mountains would crumble."[98] And at another occasion He writes: "My captivity cannot harm Me. That which can harm Me is the conduct of those who love Me, who claim to be related to Me, and yet perpetrate what causeth My heart and My pen to groan."[99]

The murder of the three Azalís created a violent uproar among the population of 'Akká. Discomposed and angry, they took to the streets demanding that the entire community of exiles be arrested and punished. Shortly after the crime, the governor, the chief of police and a large number of his men armed with swords and rifles set out for the house of Bahá'u'lláh and His companions, arresting whomever they met. It was an hour after sunset when the governor and his troops surrounded the house of Bahá'u'lláh. They arrested several of the exiles and demanded Bahá'u'lláh's presence at the government house. At the time of this intrusion, Bahá'u'lláh was engaged in dictating some verses to His secretary. When He was informed, however, of orders to appear before the governor, He readily complied. One of Bahá'u'lláh's attendants who accompanied Him to the courthouse recalls the majesty and power which emanated from Bahá'u'lláh that night. He writes that on their way, as Bahá'u'lláh walked through the streets, people were awed by

His presence. In fact so overwhelmed was one of the inhabitants of 'Akká that when he set eyes on that venerable Figure, he immediately confessed his belief in Him.

When Bahá'u'lláh entered the government house, the governor and all the other officials present rose to their feet at once. Bahá'u'lláh walked in and without uttering a word seated Himself at the top end of the room. For a few minutes there was an air of silence, then the military commandant turned to Bahá'u'lláh and said: "Is it proper that some of your followers should act in such a manner?" To which Bahá'u'lláh replied: "If one of your soldiers were to commit a reprehensible act, would you be held responsible, and punished in his place?"[100] Again there was complete silence. Bahá'u'lláh ended the interrogation by rising and walking out of the room. The authorities kept Bahá'u'lláh in custody for three days. In the afternoon of the third day, He was again summoned to the courthouse this time for a formal interrogation. The official in charge asked Bahá'u'lláh to state His name and the country of His origin. "It is more manifest than the sun," Bahá'u'lláh answered. He was again asked the same question, to which He promptly replied: "I deem it not proper to mention it. Refer to the farmán of the government which is in your possession." For the third time the official reiterated his question to Bahá'u'lláh, whereupon He spoke with great authority these words: "My name is Bahá'u'lláh and My country is Núr. Be ye apprized of it."[101] Bahá'u'lláh then turned to the entire gathering and addressed them in such fervid and imposing language that no one dared to answer Him. Afterwards He arose and left the assemblage. A short while later, the governor sent his apology to Bahá'u'lláh and informed Him that He was free to return to His home.

In time, a civil tribunal concluded that neither Bahá'u'lláh nor the majority of His followers were connected with the homicides, and only those who were guilty of the act were punished. This verdict along with the steady infiltration of the true spirit of Bahá'u'lláh's teachings gradually subdued the hatred of the populace, turning their animosity to

admiration and respect. Indeed such was the transformation in the attitude of the inhabitants of 'Akká, and such became their reverence towards Him whom they entitled as the "august leader", that they openly attributed the noticeable change in the climate and water of the city to the continued presence of Bahá'u'lláh in their midst.

It was about a year after this incident, while Bahá'u'lláh still occupied the house of 'Údí Khammár, that the "brightest emanation" of His Mind, the most important book of His Dispensation, the *Kitáb-i-Aqdas (The Most Holy Book)*, was composed. Of its contents and significance, Bahá'u'lláh Himself writes: "This Book is a heaven which We have adorned with the stars of Our commandments and prohibitions." "Blessed the man who will read it and ponder the verses sent down in it by God, the Lord of Power, the Almighty. Say, O men! Take hold of it with the hand of resignation. . . . By My life! It hath been sent down in a manner that amazeth the minds of men. Verily, it is My weightiest testimony unto all people, and the proof of the All-Merciful unto all who are in heaven and all who are on earth."[102] He states, furthermore: "In such a manner hath the *Kitáb-i-Aqdas* been revealed that it attracteth and embraceth all the divinely appointed Dispensations. . . . So vast is its range that it hath encompassed all men ere their recognition of it. Erelong will its sovereign power, its pervasive influence and the greatness of its might be manifested on earth."[103]

The composition of the *Kitáb-i-Aqdas* may be said to have inaugurated a new and final period of Bahá'u'lláh's ministry; a period marked by the triumph and fulfilment of His Cause. For the next two decades the condition of Bahá'u'lláh's stay in 'Akká progressively improved and His influence accordingly became stronger and more widespread.

Towards the end of 1873 Bahá'u'lláh moved from the house of 'Údí Khammár to the adjacent house of 'Abbúd. Shortly after His transfer, the two houses were joined together thus creating a more spacious residence for Him and His family. Bahá'u'lláh remained in these quarters until the last days of

His confinement within the walls of ‘Akká.

Eventually Bahá’u’lláh’s popularity became so pervasive that even the governor and the Muftí (the chief Muslim jurist) of ‘Akká joined the ranks of His staunch admirers. These men soon realized that it had been nearly a decade since Bahá’u’lláh, whom they so highly esteemed, had left the confines of His residence. Ashamed and remorseful they indicated to Bahá’u’lláh that should He wish He was free to leave the boundaries of the city and establish His residence in the countryside. Although Bahá’u’lláh had ever since His childhood loved the beauty and verdure of the country and had once even remarked that “the country is the world of the soul, the city is the world of bodies,”[104] He refused to leave ‘Akká, saying: “I am a prisoner.”[105] When the Muftí, who was very devoted to Bahá’u’lláh, heard that his Beloved was refusing to liberate Himself, he humbly went to the presence of Bahá’u’lláh and pleaded with Him: “God forbid! Who has the power to make you a prisoner? You have kept yourself in prison. It was your own will to be imprisoned, and now I beg you to come out.”[106] The Muftí is reported to have pleaded with Bahá’u’lláh for an hour before He finally gave His consent.

So ended Bahá’u’lláh’s incarceration within the cheerless walls of the “Most Great Prison.” In the early days of June 1877 He left behind the gates of ‘Akká and repaired to the summer residence of ‘Abdu’lláh Pá_sh_á at Mazra‘ih. This cottage house was at that time situated four miles north of the city. During the years of His stay at Mazra‘ih, Bahá’u’lláh frequently visited the exquisite and delightful garden of Na‘mayn[107] where He would relax and enjoy the peace and tranquillity that for many years had been denied Him.

After two years at Mazra‘ih, a much larger and spacious house was rented and later purchased for Bahá’u’lláh in the nearby estate of Bahjí. He moved to this location in September 1879 and continued to live there for the remainder of His life. Bahá’u’lláh’s years at Bahjí were spent in relative comfort and ease. He would occasionally visit the surrounding areas and enjoy the company of His faithful adherents and admirers who

had travelled from far off places such as Persia, India and Egypt, to have the blessing of attaining His presence. Bahá'u'lláh once during the darkest days of His confinement in the barracks had declared to those who bore Him company: "Fear not. These doors shall be opened. My tent shall be pitched on Mount Carmel, and the utmost joy shall be realized."[108] Bahá'u'lláh's prediction came true. On three separate occasions He travelled to Haifa and pitched His tent on the slopes of Mount Carmel. During the last of these visits, Bahá'u'lláh chose the site where the remains of the martyred Prophet and Herald of His Revelation, the Báb, were to be later interred, and also specified the area where the future world administrative centre of His religion would stand.

As in the past, most of Bahá'u'lláh's last years were devoted to the composition of a vast body of writings[109] that further refined His vision of humanity's future. In a Tablet written shortly before His passing, Bahá'u'lláh, surveying the entire range of His colossal and all-encompassing Revelation, writes:

> We, verily, have not fallen short of Our duty to exhort men, and to deliver that whereunto I was bidden by God, the Almighty, the All-praised . . . . Is there any excuse left for any one in this Revelation? No, by God, the Lord of the Mighty Throne! My signs have encompassed the earth, and my power enveloped all mankind.[110]

Bahá'u'lláh passed away in the early hours of the morning of May 29, 1892. About nine months earlier He had expressed to His eldest son 'Abdu'l-Bahá that His work was now finished and that it was time for Him to leave everything and "flee away."

In a telegram which began with the words "the Sun of Bahá has set,"[111] the reigning Sultan of Turkey, 'Abdu'l-Ḥamíd II, was informed of Bahá'u'lláh's ascension. The same communiqué also requested permission for interring His sacred remains in the precincts of His residence at Bahjí. The Sultan agreed and the body of Bahá'u'lláh was laid to rest shortly after sunset on the very day of His passing, where it remains today as a holy spot and a site of pilgrimage for His adherents.

Epilogue

After nearly forty years of uninterrupted exile and imprisonment, Bahá'u'lláh was no longer a prisoner. His spirit had been released from the shackles of this mortal world and winged its flight to that blissful abode to which He had so fervently longed to ascend.

In the days to come many were to gather near Bahá'u'lláh's residence and final resting place at Bahjí and, together with His family and close companions, mourn His loss. Among them were poets and writers who composed numerous elegies in His memory. Although the majority of them had never met Bahá'u'lláh, they felt profoundly moved by the mystical force of His being which permeated the area wherein He once dwelled.

Two years earlier, in the April of 1890, Bahá'u'lláh had similarly inspired a famous English orientalist by the name of Edward Granville Brown who was granted a rare audience with Him at Bahjí. Brown was so stirred when he attained the presence of Bahá'u'lláh that he decided to write a pen portrait of Him and have it published in one of his books. He writes:

> The face of Him on Whom I gazed, I can never forget, though I cannot describe it. Those piercing eyes seemed to read one's very soul; power and authority sat on that ample brow . . . . No need to ask in whose presence I stood, as I bowed myself before one who is the object of a devotion and love which kings might envy and emperors sigh for in vain!
>
> A mild dignified voice bade me be seated, and continued: "Praise be to God that thou hast attained! . . . Thou hast come to see a prisoner and an exile. . . . We desire but the good of the world and the happiness of the nations; yet they deem us a stirrer up of strife and sedition worthy of bondage and banishment. . . . That all nations should become one in faith and all men as brothers; that the bonds of affection

> and unity between the sons of men should be strengthened . . . and differences of race be annulled–what harm is there in this? . . . These strifes and this bloodshed and discord must cease, and all men be as one kindred and one family. . . . Let not a man glory in this, that he loves his country; let him rather glory in this, that he loves his kind. . . .[112]

Few, with the exception of the small group of His exiled followers who had immense love and adoration for Bahá'u'lláh, understood His true identity. The majority of those present knew Him only as a holy and sanctified personage, not as a divine Figure. Alas, if they only knew that the One to Whom they were so mysteriously drawn was none other than the chosen Manifestation of God for the new age of humanity.

Tragically history repeats itself! When Jesus Christ was crucified nearly two thousand years ago, those who grieved His passing were but a few, and even fewer understood the real loss they had suffered. It was not until many generations later that the true significance of His death was more profoundly realized. Now, over a hundred years after the passing of Bahá'u'lláh, the world is just beginning to glean the import of the life of He who passed amongst us. It is His life story we relate, and His suffering and sacrifice for the sake of humanity, we honor.

References

[1] In recent decades this district has come to be known as Mahalyih Arabhá (the Arab Quarters).

[2] For a more detailed description of Bahá'u'lláh's ancestry see H.M.Balyuzi, *Bahá'u'lláh the King of Glory* (Oxford, George Ronald, 1980), pp. 9-12 and *Eminent Bahá'ís in the time of Bahá'u'lláh* (Oxford, George Ronald, 1985), pp. 309-313.

[3] Shoghi Effendi confirms this fact in a letter written on his behalf to an individual Bahá'í dated 24 March 1943. See H.B.Hornby, *Lights of Guidance* (New Delhi, Bahá'í Publishing Trust, 1999), p. 474.

[4] Nabíl-i-Zarandí, *The Dawn Breakers* (Wilmette: BPT, 1974), p. 109.

[5] John E. Esslemont, *Bahá'u'lláh and the New Era* (Wilmette, Illinois: Bahá'í Publishing Trust, 1980), pp. 23-24.

[6] Bahá'u'lláh, *Epistle to the Son of the Wolf* (Wilmette: BPT, 1988), p. 11.

[7] Ibid.

[8] For more information on the life of the Báb and the circumstances leading to His claim as a divine Messenger see H.M. Balyuzi, *The Báb* (Oxford: George Ronald, 1973).

[9] Nabíl-i-Zarandí, *The Dawn Breakers*, p. 107.

[10] A customary corporal punishment for convicted criminals which involved beating the soles of the offender's feet with a whip or stick.

[11] Nabíl-i-Zarandí, *The Dawn Breakers*, p. 372.

[12] Bahá'u'lláh, *Epistle to the Son of the Wolf*, p. 77.

[13] Bahá'u'lláh, *Kitáb-i-Íqán*(Wilmette: BPT, 1983), pp. 230-34.

[14] Bahá'u'lláh, *Epistle to the Son of the Wolf*, p. 20.

[15] *Idem*, p. 20-21.

[16] Nabíl-i-Zarandí, *The Dawn-Breakers*, pp. 631-34.

[17] Bahá'u'lláh, *Epistle to the Son of the Wolf*, pp. 21-22.

[18] Shoghi Effendi, *God Passes By* (Wilmette: BPT, 1974), pp. 101-102.

[19] Prince Dimitri Ivanovich Dolgorukov was the chief representative of the Russian government in Tehran from January 1846 until May 1854.

[20] Shoghi Effendi, *God Passes By*, p. 106.

[21] Mírzá Riḍá-Qulí never recognized the station of his Brother. He always kept away from the cause of Bahá'u'lláh, even trying to hide the fact of their relationship. His wife Maryam, however, who also happened to be a cousin of Bahá'u'lláh, was completely and fervently devoted to Him.

[22] Bahá'u'lláh, *Tablets of Bahá'u'lláh revealed after the Kitáb-i-Aqdas* (Wilmette: BPT, 1988), p.40.

[23] Shoghi Effendi, *God Passes By*, p. 109.

[24] Káẓimayn was then situated three miles north of Baghdad. It derives its name from the fact that the two Káẓims, the seventh and the ninth Shí'a Imáms are buried there. For this reason, it is a place of pilgrimage for Shí'a Muslims.

[25] Mírzá Yaḥya was also known by the title of Ṣubḥ-i-Azal which literally means "morning of eternity". In later years his followers came to be known as "Azalís".

[26] Shoghi Effendi, *God Passes By*, p. 118.

[27] Bahá'u'lláh, *Kitáb-i-Íqán* (Wilmette: BPT, 1983), pp. 249-50.

[28] *Idem*, pp. 250-51.

[29] Nabíl-i-Zarandí, *The Dawn Breakers*, p. 585.

[30] A Súfí Order of Sunní Islam founded around the teachings of the eighteenth century Naqshbandí thinker Abú'l-Bahá Ḍíyá'u'd-Dín Khálid Shahrizúrí (d. 1827).

[31] Shoghi Effendi, *God Passes By*, p. 126.

[32] *Idem*, p. 125.

[33] Bahá'u'lláh, *Kitáb-i-Íqán*, pp. 251-52.

[34] This humble dwelling-place which the family of Bahá'u'lláh had moved to prior to His return from Sulaymáníyyih was known at the time as the house of Mírzá Músá Bábí. It is this house that Bahá'u'lláh in later years designated as the "Bayt-i-A'ẓam" (the Most Great House) and a future place of pilgrimage for His followers.

[35] The Holy Book of Islam revealed through the prophet Muhammad in the course of twenty-two years. It is a medium size book comprised of approximately six thousand three hundred verses.

[36] For a list of Bahá'u'lláh's major works during this period see Appendix I: Bahá'u'lláh's Best-Known Works.

[37] This Book is Bahá'u'lláh's second most important work. The English translation of *The Book of Certitude* is about two hundred and fifty pages.

[38] This is an approximation based on the Muslim lunar years.

[39] Shoghi Effendi, *The Promised Day is Come* (Wilmette: BPT, 1980), p. 85.

[40] This was thirty-one days after the Persian New Year, Naw-Rúz. Sometimes when the vernal equinox takes place after sunset Naw-Rúz is celebrated on March 22 rather than March 21. In such years, as in the year 1863, thirty-one days after Naw-Rúz falls on April 22.

[41] Shoghi Effendi, *God Passes By*, p. 149.

[42] Bahá'u'lláh, *Gleanings from the Writings of Bahá'u'lláh* (Wilmette: BPT, 1983), pp. 29-30.

[43] Cited in D. S. Ruhe, *Robe of Light*, p. 176.

[44] Bahá'u'lláh, *Epistle to the Son of the Wolf*, pp. 68-69.

[45] *Idem*, p. 69.

[46] From the unpublished narrative of Áqá Riḍáy-i-Qannád-i-Shírází, cited in H.M. Balyuzi, *Bahá'u'lláh the King of Glory*, p. 203.

[47] Shoghi Effendi, *God Passes By*, p. 160.

[48] Bahá'u'lláh, *The Summons of the Lord of Hosts*, pp. 215-16.

[49] *Idem*, pp. 216-17.

[50] Shoghi Effendi, *God Passes By*, p. 112.

[51] *Idem*, p. 169.

[52] 'Abdu'l-Ḥamíd Ishráq Khávarí, *Má'idiy-i-Ásamání* (Tehran: Mu'assasiy-i-Millíy-i-Matbú'át-i-Amrí, 129 B.E. [1972-73]), Vol. 8, p. 126. The English rendering of this passage is that made by the writer and unlike other excerpts in this book is provisional and not an official Bahá'í translation.

[53] This was on March 10, 1866.

[54] From the unpublished narrative of Áqá Riḍáy-i-Qannád-i-Shírází, cited in H.M. Balyuzi, *Bahá'u'lláh the King of Glory*, p. 233.

[55] Shoghi Effendi, *God Passes By*, pp. 168-69.

[56] Bahá'u'lláh, *Epistle to the Son of the Wolf*, p. 70.

[57] Shoghi Effendi, *God Passes By*, p. 170.

[58] Bahá'u'lláh, *The Kitáb-i-Aqdas The Most Holy Book,* (Haifa: Bahá'í World Centre, 1992), p. 87, ¶ 184.

[59] For a list of Bahá'u'lláh's major works during this period see Appendix I.

[60] A follower of Bahá'u'lláh who served Him as His main secretary.

[61] Shoghi Effendi, *God Passes By*, p. 171.

[62] *Ibid.*

[63] *Ibid.*

[64] Also known as *Súriy-i-Mulúk*.

[65] Shoghi Effendi, *The Promised Day is Come*, pp. 21-24.

[66] Bahá'u'lláh's first epistle addressed to the Turkish prime minister 'Álí Páshá. It was composed near the port of Gallipoli while Bahá'u'lláh was on His way to 'Akká.

[67] Shoghi Effendi, *God Passes By*, p. 179.

[68] From the unpublished narrative of Áqá Ḥusayn-i-Áshchí of Káshán, cited in H.M. Balyuzi, *Bahá'u'lláh the King of Glory*, p. 256.

[69] Shoghi Effendi, *God Passes By*, p. 180.

[70] *Ibid.*

[71] Bahá'u'lláh's prophecy indeed came true. For a detailed treatment of this subject, see Shoghi Effendi, *The Promised Day is Come* (Wilmette, Illinois: Bahá'í Publishing Trust, 1980).

[72] Shoghi Effendi, *God Passes By*, p. 181.

[73] *Ibid.*

[74] From the unpublished narrative of Áqá Riḍáy-i-Qannád-i-Shírází, cited in H.M. Balyuzi, *Bahá'u'lláh the King of Glory*, pp. 261-62. The words in this passage should not be taken as the exact utterances of Bahá'u'lláh but rather in the spirit of what He said.

[75] Shoghi Effendi, *God Passes By*, p. 182.

[76] *Idem*, p. 186.

[77] Bahá'u'lláh's second Tablet addressed to 'Álí Pá<u>sh</u>á, the Turkish prime minister.

[78] Bahá'u'lláh, *The Summons of the Lord of Hosts*, pp. 163-64.

[79] Shoghi Effendi, *God Passes By*, p. 187.

[80] Bahá'u'lláh, *The Summons of the Lord of Hosts*, p. 172.

[81] Shoghi Effendi, *God Passes By*, p. 185.

[82] *Idem*, p. 187.

[83] *Idem*, p. 206.

[84] According to Bahá'u'lláh's own testimoney, as recorded by Nabíl-i-Zarandí in his narrative, all these Tablets reached their recipients except the Letter to Alexander II, the Czar of Russia. See *The Dawn Breakers*, p. 586.

[85] Shoghi Effendi, *God Passes By*, p. 207.

[86] Bahá'u'lláh, *Epistle to the Son of the Wolf*, pp. 46-47, 50-51, 56.

[87] Shoghi Effendi, *The Promised Day is Come*, pp. 35-36.

[88] *Idem*, pp. 33-35.

[89] Bahá'u'lláh, *The Kitáb-i-Aqdas The Most Holy Book,* (Haifa: Bahá'í World Centre, 1992), p. 51, ¶ 86.

[90] *Idem*, pp. 50-51, ¶ 85.

[91] *Idem*, pp. 56-57, ¶ 99-104.

[92] Shoghi Effendi, *The Promised Day is Come*, pp. 31-33.

[93] *Idem*, p. 65.

[94] From the unpublished narrative of Áqá Ḥusayn-i-Á<u>sh</u>ch<u>í</u> of Ká<u>sh</u>án, cited in H.M. Balyuzi, *Bahá'u'lláh the King of Glory*, pp. 311-13.

[95] Shoghi Effendi, *Messages to America 1932-1946* (Wilmette: BPT, 1947), p. 33.

[96] Also known as the *Lawḥ-i-Qad Iḥtaraqa'l-Mukhlisún (Tablet of "Indeed the hearts of the sincere are consumed...")*.

[97] Bahá'u'lláh, *The Fire Tablet* in *Bahá'í Prayers* (Wilmette: BPT, 1985), pp. 217-220.

[98] Shoghi Effendi, *God Passes By*, pp. 189-190.

[99] *Idem*, p. 190.

[100] *Ibid.*

[101] *Ibid.*

[102] *Idem*, p. 216.

[103] *Ibid.*

[104] John E. Esslemont, *Bahá'u'lláh and the New Era*, p. 35.

[105] *Idem*, p. 36.

[106] *Ibid.*

[107] Bahá'u'lláh later honored this garden with the appellation of Riḍván (Paradise). Today it is a Bahá'í holy site and a place of pilgrimage for Bahá'ís.

[108] John E. Esslemont, *Bahá'u'lláh and the New Era*, p. 34.

[109] For a list of Bahá'u'lláh's major works during this period see Appendix I.

[110] Shoghi Effendi, *God Passes By*, p. 220.

[111] *Idem*, p. 222.

[112] Brown, Edward G., *A Traveller's Narrative*, (Cambridge University Press, 1891) Vol. 2, pp. xxxix-xl.

[113] Brown, Edward G., *A Traveller's Narrative*, (Cambridge University Press, 1891) Vol. 2, pp. xxxix-xl.

Left: The eldest son of Bahá'u'lláh, 'Abdu'l-Bahá was appointed by his Father to lead the Bahá'í Faith after His passing. Known as "the Master",'Abdu'l-Bahá played a crucial role in ensuring that the Bahá'í Faith would not fragment into different sects.
Reproduced with permission of the Bahá'í International Community.

'Abdu'l-Bahá as a young man.
Reproduced with permission of the Bahá'í International Community.

Bahá'u'lláh's eldest daughter, Bahíyyih Khánum.
Reproduced with permission of the Bahá'í International Community.

Bahá'u'lláh's second son, Mirzá Mihdi.
Reproduced with permission of the Bahá'í International Community.

Left: Historic photograph of the entrance to the House of Mirza Abbas Nuri, the father of Bahá'u'lláh, in Tehran, Iran (destroyed June 2004).
Reproduced with permission of the Bahá'í International Community.

Right: Entrance to the House of Bahá'u'lláh in Takur, Iran which was destroyed after the 1979 revolution.
Reproduced with permission of the Bahá'í International Community.

This house was Bahá'u'lláh's residence in Edirne, Turkey just before his final exile to the prison city of Acre.
Reproduced with permission of the Bahá'í International Community.

When He first arrived in 'Akká (Acre), Bahá'u'lláh and His family were confined in this prison on the edge of the Mediterranean Sea.
Reproduced with permission of the Bahá'í International Community.

Right: Historical photograph of the interior of Bahá'u'lláh's cell inside the citadel of 'Akká (Acre), Israel.
Reproduced with permission of the Bahá'í International Community.

Left: Historical photograph of the exterior of the House of 'Abbúd in 'Akká (Acre), Israel
Reproduced with permission of the Bahá'í International Community.

Sultan 'Abdu'l-'Azíz of the Ottoman Empire was the first monarch whom Bahá'u'lláh addressed individually.

French emperor Napoleon III was summoned by Bahá'ulláh in two separate letters.

Náṣiri'd-Dín Shah, the King of Persia was the recipient of Bahá'u'lláh's lengthiest letter to a single monarch.

Right: The Czar of Russia, Alexander Nicolaevitch II was another European ruler to whom Bahá'u'lláh wrote while imprisoned in 'Akká.

Left: Pope Pius IX was among the religious leaders to whom Bahá'u'lláh addressed a separate epistle while incarcerated in 'Akká.

Queen Victoria was also the receipient of a proclamatory letter from Bahá'u'lláh.

Bahá'u'lláh summoned the Austro-Hungarian emperor, Franz Joseph Hapsburg (above), and the King of Prussia, Kaiser Wilhelm I (right), in the *Kitáb-i-Aqdas*.

Left: Historical photograph of the house where Bahá'u'lláh often spent the night in the Riḍván Garden, 'Akká (Acre), Israel.
Reproduced with permission of the Bahá'í International Community.

Right: The site where Bahá'u'lláh's tent was pitched on one of His visits to Haifa
Reproduced with permission of the Bahá'í International Community.

Elevated view of the front (northwest side) of Bahá'u'lláh's residence at Mazra'ih.
Reproduced with permission of the Bahá'í International Community.

Bahá'u'lláh's final residence at Bahjí after restoration.
Reproduced with permission of the Bahá'í International Community.

Entrance to the Shrine of Bahá'u'lláh, in Bahjí, 'Akká (Acre), Israel.
Reproduced with permission of the Bahá'í International Community.

A Short Anthology of Bahá'u'lláh's Writings

Bahá'u'lláh's pen was remarkably copious during the course of His forty-year ministry (1852-1892) as the Spiritual Founder of the Bahá'í Faith (see Appendix I). The following is only a small selection from among His most prominent and well-known writings. All selections chosen are excerpts from each work with the exceptions of The Glad-Tidings *and* The Book of My Covenant, *which appear in their entirety.*

The Hidden Words (Kalamát-i-Maknúnih)

The Hidden Words *or the "Hidden Book of Fátimih", as it was originally known, is by far the most widely known and studied work among the writings of Bahá'u'lláh. It was reportedly composed about two years after His return from His solitary retirement to the mountains of Sulaymáníyyih (circa 1858), as He paced, wrapped in meditation, the banks of the Tigris River. Shoghi Effendi describes* The Hidden Words *as "the dynamic spiritual leaven cast into the life of the world for the reorientation of the minds of men, the edification of their souls and the rectification of their conduct"*[1] *and ranks it third in importance among the pre-eminent works of Bahá'u'lláh, after the* Kitáb-i-Aqdas (The Most Holy Book) *and the* Kitáb-i-Íqán (The Book of Certitude). The Hidden Words *is written in two parts, the first of which is in Arabic, the second in Persian. Although the theme of the two sections and the manner of their presentation is very similar, the tone of revelation is different in each part. The Irish scholar and theologian George Townshend writes that "the Author" in the Arabic section of* The Hidden Words *comes across as a "loving teacher" whereas the Author in the Persian part stands as a "teaching lover". He also adds:* "The Hidden Words *is not a digest, nor an ordered statement. It is a new creation. It is a distillation of Sacred Fragrances. It is a focus in which all Great Lights of the past are joined into one Light, and all of God's Yesterdays become today."*[2]

HE IS THE GLORY OF GLORIES

This is that which hath descended from the realm of glory, uttered by the tongue of power and might, and revealed unto the Prophets of old. We have taken the inner essence thereof and clothed it in the garment of brevity, as a token of grace

unto the righteous, that they may stand faithful unto the Covenant of God, may fulfill in their lives His trust, and in the realm of spirit obtain the gem of Divine virtue.

O SON OF SPIRIT! My first counsel is this: Possess a pure, kindly and radiant heart, that thine may be a sovereignty ancient, imperishable and everlasting.

O SON OF SPIRIT! The best beloved of all things in My sight is Justice; turn not away therefrom if thou desirest Me, and neglect it not that I may confide in thee. By its aid thou shalt see with thine own eyes and not through the eyes of others, and shalt know of thine own knowledge and not through the knowledge of thy neighbour. Ponder this in thy heart; how it behooveth thee to be. Verily justice is My gift to thee and the sign of My loving-kindness. Set it then before thine eyes.

O SON OF MAN! Veiled in My immemorial being and in the ancient eternity of My essence, I knew My love for thee; therefore I created thee, have engraved on thee Mine image and revealed to thee My beauty.

O SON OF MAN! I loved thy creation, hence I created thee. Wherefore, do thou love Me, that I may name thy name and fill thy soul with the spirit of life.

O SON OF BEING! Love Me, that I may love thee. If thou lovest Me not, My love can in no wise reach thee. Know this, O servant.

O SON OF BEING! Thy Paradise is My love; thy heavenly home, reunion with Me. Enter therein and tarry not. This is that which hath been destined for thee in Our kingdom above and Our exalted dominion.

O SON OF MAN! If thou lovest Me, turn away from thyself; and if thou seekest My pleasure, regard not thine own; that thou mayest die in Me and I may eternally live in thee.

O SON OF SPIRIT! There is no peace for thee save by renouncing thyself and turning unto Me; for it behooveth thee

to glory in My name, not in thine own; to put thy trust in Me and not in thyself, since I desire to be loved alone and above all that is.

O SON OF BEING! My love is My stronghold; he that entereth therein is safe and secure, and he that turneth away shall surely stray and perish. . . .

O SON OF SPIRIT! I created thee rich, why dost thou bring thyself down to poverty? Noble I made thee, wherewith dost thou abase thyself? Out of the essence of knowledge I gave thee being, why seekest thou enlightenment from anyone beside Me? Out of the clay of love I molded thee, how dost thou busy thyself with another? Turn thy sight unto thyself, that thou mayest find Me standing within thee, mighty, powerful and self-subsisting. . . .

O SON OF SPIRIT! Ask not of Me that which We desire not for thee, then be content with what We have ordained for thy sake, for this is that which profiteth thee, if therewith thou dost content thyself. . . .

O SON OF SPIRIT! Noble have I created thee, yet thou hast abased thyself. Rise then unto that for which thou wast created. . . .

O SON OF BEING! How couldst thou forget thine own faults and busy thyself with the faults of others? Whoso doeth this is accursed of Me. . . .

O SON OF SPIRIT! Know thou of a truth: He that biddeth men be just and himself committeth iniquity is not of Me, even though he bear My name. . . .

O SON OF BEING! Bring thyself to account each day ere thou art summoned to a reckoning; for death, unheralded, shall come upon thee and thou shalt be called to give account for thy deeds.

O SON OF THE SUPREME! I have made death a messenger of joy to thee. Wherefore dost thou grieve? I made the light to shed on thee its splendour. Why dost thou veil thyself

therefrom?. . .

O SON OF MAN! Magnify My cause that I may reveal unto thee the mysteries of My greatness and shine upon thee with the light of eternity. . . .

O SON OF MAN! For everything there is a sign. The sign of love is fortitude under My decree and patience under My trials. . . .

O SON OF BEING! If poverty overtake thee, be not sad; for in time the Lord of wealth shall visit thee. Fear not abasement, for glory shall one day rest on thee. . . .

O SON OF BEING! Busy not thyself with this world, for with fire We test the gold, and with gold We test Our servants. . . .

O YE PEOPLE THAT HAVE MINDS TO KNOW AND EARS TO HEAR! The first call of the Beloved is this: O mystic nightingale! Abide not but in the rose-garden of the spirit. O messenger of the Solomon of love! Seek thou no shelter except in the Sheba of the well-beloved, and O immortal phoenix! dwell not save on the mount of faithfulness. Therein is thy habitation, if on the wings of thy soul thou soarest to the realm of the infinite and seekest to attain thy goal.

O SON OF SPIRIT! The bird seeketh its nest; the nightingale the charm of the rose; whilst those birds, the hearts of men, content with transient dust, have strayed far from their eternal nest, and with eyes turned towards the slough of heedlessness are bereft of the glory of the divine presence. Alas! How strange and pitiful; for a mere cupful, they have turned away from the billowing seas of the Most High, and remained far from the most effulgent horizon.

O FRIEND! In the garden of thy heart plant naught but the rose of love, and from the nightingale of affection and desire loosen not thy hold. Treasure the companionship of the righteous and eschew all fellowship with the ungodly.

O SON OF JUSTICE! Whither can a lover go but to the land of

his beloved? and what seeker findeth rest away from his heart's desire? To the true lover reunion is life, and separation is death. His breast is void of patience and his heart hath no peace. A myriad lives he would forsake to hasten to the abode of his beloved.

O SON OF DUST! Verily I say unto thee: Of all men the most negligent is he that disputeth idly and seeketh to advance himself over his brother. Say, O brethren! Let deeds, not words, be your adorning. . . .

O MY SERVANTS! Ye are the trees of My garden; ye must give forth goodly and wondrous fruits, that ye yourselves and others may profit therefrom. Thus it is incumbent on every one to engage in crafts and professions, for therein lies the secret of wealth, O men of understanding! For results depend upon means, and the grace of God shall be all-sufficient unto you. Trees that yield no fruit have been and will ever be for the fire.

O MY SERVANT! The basest of men are they that yield no fruit on earth. Such men are verily counted as among the dead, nay better are the dead in the sight of God than those idle and worthless souls.

O MY SERVANT! The best of men are they that earn a livelihood by their calling and spend upon themselves and upon their kindred for the love of God, the Lord of all worlds.

The mystic and wondrous Bride, hidden ere this beneath the veiling of utterance, hath now, by the grace of God and His divine favour, been made manifest even as the resplendent light shed by the beauty of the Beloved. I bear witness, O friends! that the favour is complete, the argument fulfilled, the proof manifest and the evidence established. Let it now be seen what your endeavors in the path of detachment will reveal. In this wise hath the divine favour been fully vouchsafed unto you and unto them that are in heaven and on earth. All praise to God, the Lord of all Worlds.[3]

Notes

[1] Shoghi Effendi, *God Passes By*, p. 140.
[2] George Townshend, *Introduction to the Hidden Words*, 1932 Edition, pp. i-ii.
[3] Bahá'u'lláh, *The Hidden Words*, pp. 5-52 (U.K. edition)

The Seven Valleys (Haft Vádí)

Celebrated by Shoghi Effendi as "the greatest mystical composition"[4] *produced by the Pen of Bahá'u'lláh,* The Seven Valleys *is an uplifting and thought provoking commentary on the mystic path to spiritual union with God. It was written in1859/60, in response to the questions of a prominent magistrate from the city of Kháníqayn in northern Iraq, by the name of Shaykh Muḥyi'd-Dín, who himself was a leading Sufi Muslim. Shaykh Muḥyi'd-Dín, who had come to regard Bahá'u'lláh as an inspired holy savant, wrote to Him seeking enlightenment on the mystical journey of the human soul. By employing the seven progressive stages which the soul of a seeker must traverse in order to attain the object of its existence, Bahá'u'lláh unravels the true meaning and conditions of these seven stages originally proposed by the great Persian Sufi poet Shaykh Farídu'd-Dín Aṭṭár (d. 1230 C.E.) in his renowned work the* Mantiqu'ṭ-Tayr (The Conference of the Birds).

. . . .The stages that mark the wayfarer's journey from the abode of dust to the heavenly homeland are said to be seven. Some have called these Seven Valleys, and others, Seven Cities. And they say that until the wayfarer taketh leave of self, and traverseth these stages, he shall never reach to the ocean of nearness and union, nor drink of the peerless wine. The first is **The Valley of Search.** The steed of this Valley is patience; without patience the wayfarer on this journey will reach nowhere and attain no goal. Nor should he ever be downhearted; if he strive for a hundred thousand years and yet fail to behold the beauty of the Friend, he should not falter. . . .

In this journey the seeker reacheth a stage wherein he seeth all created things wandering distracted in search of the Friend. How many a Jacob will he see, hunting after his Joseph; he

will behold many a lover, hasting to seek the Beloved, he will witness a world of desiring ones searching after the One Desired. At every moment he findeth a weighty matter, in every hour he becometh aware of a mystery; for he hath taken his heart away from both worlds, and set out for the Ka'bih[5] of the Beloved. At every step, aid from the Invisible Realm will attend him and the heat of his search will grow. . . .

The true seeker hunteth naught but the object of his quest, and the lover hath no desire save union with his beloved. Nor shall the seeker reach his goal unless he sacrifice all things. That is, whatever he hath seen, and heard, and understood, all must he set at naught, that he may enter the realm of the spirit, which is the City of God. Labour is needed, if we are to seek Him; ardour is needed, if we are to drink of the honey of reunion with Him; and if we taste of this cup, we shall cast away the world.

On this journey the traveler abideth in every land and dwelleth in every region. In every face, he seeketh the beauty of the Friend; in every country he looketh for the Beloved. He joineth every company, and seeketh fellowship with every soul, that haply in some mind he may uncover the secret of the Friend, or in some face he may behold the beauty of the Loved One.

And if, by the help of God, he findeth on this journey a trace of the traceless Friend, and inhaleth the fragrance of the long-lost Joseph from the heavenly messenger,[6] he shall straightway step into **The Valley of Love** and be dissolved in the fire of love. In this city the heaven of ecstasy is upraised and the world-illuming sun of yearning shineth, and the fire of love is ablaze; and when the fire of love is ablaze, it burneth to ashes the harvest of reason.

Now is the traveler unaware of himself, and of aught besides himself. He seeth neither ignorance nor knowledge, neither doubt nor certitude; he knoweth not the morn of guidance from the night of error. He fleeth both from unbelief and faith, and deadly poison is a balm to him. . . .

The steed of this Valley is pain; and if there be no pain this journey will never end. In this station the lover hath no thought save the Beloved, and seeketh no refuge save the Friend. At every moment he offereth a hundred lives in the path of the Loved One, at every step he throweth a thousand heads at the feet of the Beloved. . . .

Love accepteth no existence and wisheth no life: He seeth life in death, and in shame seeketh glory. To merit the madness of love, man must abound in sanity; to merit the bonds of the Friend, he must be full of spirit. Blessed the neck that is caught in His noose, happy the head that falleth on the dust in the pathway of His love. Wherefore, O friend, give up thy self that thou mayest find the Peerless One, pass by this mortal earth that thou mayest seek a home in the nest of heaven. Be as naught, if thou wouldst kindle the fire of being and be fit for the pathway of love. . . .

And if, confirmed by the Creator, the lover escapes from the claws of the eagle of love, he will enter **The Valley of Knowledge** and come out of doubt into certitude, and turn from the darkness of illusion to the guiding light of the fear of God. His inner eyes will open and he will privily converse with his Beloved; he will set ajar the gate of truth and piety, and shut the doors of vain imaginings. He in this station is content with the decree of God, and seeth war as peace, and findeth in death the secrets of everlasting life. With inward and outward eyes he witnesseth the mysteries of resurrection in the realms of creation and the souls of men, and with a pure heart apprehendeth the divine wisdom in the endless Manifestations of God. In the ocean he findeth a drop, in a drop he beholdeth the secrets of the sea.

Split the atom's heart, and lo! Within it thou wilt find a sun.[7]

The wayfarer in this Valley seeth in the fashionings of the True One nothing save clear providence, and at every moment saith: "No defect canst thou see in the creation of the God of Mercy: Repeat the gaze: Seest thou a single flaw?"[8] He

beholdeth justice in injustice, and in justice, grace. In ignorance he findeth many a knowledge hidden, and in knowledge a myriad wisdoms manifest. He breaketh the cage of the body and the passions, and consorteth with the people of the immortal realm. He mounteth on the ladders of inner truth and hasteneth to the heaven of inner significance. . . . And if he meeteth with injustice he shall have patience, and if he cometh upon wrath he shall manifest love. . . .

After passing through the Valley of Knowledge, which is the last plane of limitation, the wayfarer cometh to **The Valley of Unity** and drinketh from the cup of the Absolute, and gazeth on the Manifestations of Oneness. In this station he pierceth the veils of plurality, fleeth from the worlds of the flesh, and ascendeth into the heaven of singleness. With the ear of God he heareth, with the eye of God he beholdeth the mysteries of divine creation. He steppeth into the sanctuary of the Friend, and shareth as an intimate the pavilion of the Loved One. He stretcheth out the hand of truth from the sleeve of the Absolute; he revealeth the secrets of power. He seeth in himself neither name nor fame nor rank, but findeth his own praise in praising God. He beholdeth in his own name the name of God; to him, "all songs are from the King,"[9] and every melody from Him. He sitteth on the throne of "Say, all is from God,"[10] and taketh his rest on the carpet of "There is no power or might but in God."[11] He looketh on all things with the eye of oneness, and seeth the brilliant rays of the divine sun shining from the dawning-point of Essence alike on all created things, and the lights of singleness reflected over all creation. . . .

And the wayfarer, after traversing the high planes of this supernal journey, entereth **The Valley of Contentment**.

In this Valley he feeleth the winds of divine contentment blowing from the plane of the spirit. He burneth away the veils of want, and with inward and outward eye, perceiveth within and without all things the day of: "God will compensate each one out of His abundance."[12] From sorrow he turneth to bliss,

from anguish to joy. His grief and mourning yield to delight and rapture.

Although to outward view, the wayfarers in this Valley may dwell upon the dust, yet inwardly they are throned in the heights of mystic meaning; they eat of the endless bounties of inner significances, and drink of the delicate wines of the spirit. . . .

After journeying through the planes of pure contentment, the traveller cometh to **The Valley of Wonderment** and is tossed in the oceans of grandeur, and at every moment his wonder groweth. Now he seeth the shape of wealth as poverty itself, and the essence of freedom as sheer impotence. Now is he struck dumb with the beauty of the All-Glorious; again is he wearied out with his own life. How many a mystic tree hath this whirlwind of wonderment snatched by the roots, how many a soul hath it exhausted. For in this Valley the traveler is flung into confusion, albeit, in the eye of him who hath attained, such marvels are esteemed and well beloved. At every moment he beholdeth a wondrous world, a new creation, and goeth from astonishment to astonishment, and is lost in awe at the works of the Lord of Oneness. . . .

O friend, the heart is the dwelling of eternal mysteries, make it not the home of fleeting fancies; waste not the treasure of thy precious life in employment with this swiftly passing world. Thou comest from the world of holiness—bind not thine heart to the earth; thou art a dweller in the court of nearness—choose not the homeland of the dust. . . .

After scaling the high summits of wonderment the wayfarer cometh to **The Valley of True Poverty and Absolute Nothingness**.

This station is the dying from self and the living in God, the being poor in self and rich in the Desired One. Poverty as here referred to signifieth being poor in the things of the created world, rich in the things of God's world. For when the true

lover and devoted friend reacheth to the presence of the Beloved, the sparkling beauty of the Loved One and the fire of the lover's heart will kindle a blaze and burn away all veils and wrappings. Yea, all he hath, from heart to skin, will be set aflame, so that nothing will remain save the Friend. . . .

He who hath attained this station is sanctified from all that pertaineth to the world. Wherefore, if those who have come to the sea of His presence are found to possess none of the limited things of this perishable world, whether it be outer wealth or personal opinions, it mattereth not. For whatever the creatures have is limited by their own limits, and whatever the True One hath is sanctified therefrom; this utterance must be deeply pondered that its purport may be clear. "Verily the righteous shall drink of a winecup tempered at the camphor fountain."[13] If the interpretation of "camphor" become known, the true intention will be evident. This state is that poverty of which it is said, "Poverty is My glory."[14] And of inward and outward poverty there is many a stage and many a meaning which I have not thought pertinent to mention here; hence I have reserved these for another time, dependent on what God may desire and fate may seal. . . .

In all these journeys the traveler must stray not the breadth of a hair from the "Law," for this is indeed the secret of the "Path" and the fruit of the Tree of "Truth"; and in all these stages he must cling to the robe of obedience to the commandments, and hold fast to the cord of shunning all forbidden things, that he may be nourished from the cup of the Law and informed of the mysteries of Truth.[15]. . .

These journeys have no visible ending in the world of time, but the severed wayfarer—if invisible confirmation descend upon him and the Guardian of the Cause assist him—may cross these seven stages in seven steps, nay rather in seven breaths, nay rather in a single breath, if God will and desire it. And this is of "His grace on such of His servants as He pleaseth."[16] . . .[17]

Notes

[4]Shoghi Effendi, *God Passes By*, p. 140.
[5]The holy Sanctuary at Mecca. Here the word means "goal."
[6]Refer to the story of Joesph in the Qur'án and the Old Testament.
[7]Persian mystic poem.
[8]Qur'án 67:3.
[9]The Mathnaví.
[10]Qur'án 4:80.
[11]Qur'án 18:37.
[12]Qur'án 4:129.
[13]Qur'án 76:5.
[14]Muhammad.
[15]This refers to the three stages of Súfí life: 1. Sharí'at, or Religious Laws; 2. Taríqat, or the Path on which the mystic wayfarer journeys in search of the True One; this stage also includes anchoretism. 3. Haqíqat, or the Truth which, to the Súfí, is the goal of the journey through all three stages. Here Bahá'u'lláh teaches that, contrary to the belief of certain Súfís who in their search for the Truth consider themselves above all law, obedience to the Laws of Religion is essential.
[16]Qur'án 2:84.
[17]Bahá'u'lláh, *The Seven Valleys and The Four Valleys*, pp. 4-41.

The Gems of Divine Mysteries
(Javáhiru'l-Asrár)

Another significant work, penned by Bahá'u'lláh during the same period as The Seven Valleys, *is a lengthy epistle in the Arabic language which its Author entitled* The Gems of Divine Mysteries. *According to Bahá'u'lláh, in a prefatory note of the original manuscript, the "treatise was written in reply to a seeker who had asked how the promised Mihdí [the Muslim Messiah] could have become transformed into 'Alí-Muḥammad (the Báb). The opportunity provided by this question was seized to elaborate on a number of subjects, all of which are of use and benefit both to them that seek and to those who have attained, could ye perceive with the eye of divine virtue."*[18] *The seeker referred to by Bahá'u'lláh in the note was an Iranian Shí'a Muslim by the name of Siyyid Yúsuf-i-Sihdihí who was then living in the city of Karbilá in Iraq. Siyyid Yúsuf sent his question to Bahá'u'lláh through a personal messenger who, after arriving at Bahá'u'lláh's residence, received from Him* The Gems of Divine Mysteries *on the same day.*

HE IS THE EXALTED, THE MOST HIGH!

O thou who treadest the path of justice and beholdest the countenance of mercy! Thine epistle was received, thy question was noted, and the sweet accents of thy soul were heard from the inmost chambers of thy heart. Whereupon the clouds of the Divine Will were raised to rain upon thee the outpourings of heavenly wisdom, to divest thee of all that thou hadst acquired aforetime, to draw thee from the realms of contradiction unto the retreats of oneness, and to lead thee to the sacred streams of His Law. Perchance thou mayest quaff therefrom, repose therein, quench thy thirst, refresh thy soul,

and be numbered with those whom the light of God hath guided aright in this day. . . .

But hear, O My brother, My plaint against them that claim to be associated with God and with the Manifestations of His knowledge, and yet follow their corrupt inclinations, consume the substance of their neighbour, are given to wine, commit murder, defraud and slander each other, hurl calumnies against God, and are wont to speak falsely. The people attribute all these deeds unto Us, whilst their perpetrators remain shameless before God. They cast aside that which He hath enjoined upon them and commit that which He hath forbidden. Yet it behoveth the people of truth that the signs of humility should shine upon their faces, that the light of sanctity should radiate from their countenances, that they should walk upon the earth as though they were in the presence of God and distinguish themselves in their deeds from all the dwellers of the earth. Such must be their state that their eyes should behold the evidences of His might, their tongues and hearts make mention of His name, their feet be set towards the lands of His nearness, and their hands take fast hold upon His precepts. And were they to pass through a valley of pure gold and mines of precious silver, they should regard them as wholly unworthy of their attention.

These people, however, have turned aside from all this and placed instead their affections upon that which accordeth with their own corrupt inclinations. Thus do they roam in the wilderness of arrogance and pride. I bear witness at this moment that God is wholly quit of them, and likewise are We. We beseech God to suffer Us not to associate with them either in this life or in the life to come. He, verily, is the Eternal Truth. No God is there but Him, and His might is equal to all things.

Quaff then, O My brother, from the living waters that We have caused to flow in the oceans of these words. Methinks the seas of grandeur are surging within them, and the gems of divine

virtue are shining within and upon them. Divest then thyself of that which debarreth thee from this fathomless crimson sea, and to the cry of "In the name of God and by His grace!" immerse thyself therein. Let the fear of no one dismay thee. Trust in the Lord, thy God, for He is sufficient unto whosoever trusteth in Him. He, verily, shall protect thee, and in Him shalt thou abide in safety.

Know thou, moreover, that in this most hallowed and resplendent city thou shalt find the wayfarer to be lowly before all men and humble before all things. For naught doth he behold save that he perceiveth God therein. He beholdeth the effulgent glories of God in the lights of His Revelation that have encompassed the Sinai of creation. In this station the wayfarer must not claim the seat of honour in any gathering or walk before others in the desire to vaunt and exalt himself. Rather must he regard himself as standing at all times in the presence of his Lord. He must not wish for anyone that which he doth not wish for himself, nor speak that which he would not bear to hear spoken by another, nor yet desire for any soul that which he would not have desired for himself. It befitteth him, rather, to walk upon the earth with undeviating steps in the kingdom of His new creation. . . .

Comprehend, in like manner, every station, sign, and allusion, that thou mayest perceive all things in their own place and consider all matters in their proper light. For in this station, the City of Divine Unity, are to be found those who have entered within the ark of divine guidance and journeyed through the heights of divine unity. Thou shalt behold the lights of beauty upon their faces and the mysteries of glory in their human temples. Thou shalt perceive the musk-laden fragrance of their words and behold the signs of His sovereignty in all their ways and doings. Nor wilt thou be veiled by the deeds of them that have failed to quaff from the crystal springs or to attain unto the cities of holiness, and who follow their selfish desires and spread disorder in the land, all the while believing themselves to be guided aright. . . .

Know then that all thou hast heard and witnessed that Daystar of Truth, the Primal Point, ascribe to Himself from the designations of former times is only on account of the weakness of men and the scheme of the world of creation. Otherwise, all names and attributes revolve round His Essence and circle about the threshold of His sanctuary. For He it is Who traineth all names, revealeth all attributes, conferreth life upon all beings, proclaimeth the divine verses, and arrayeth the heavenly signs. Nay, shouldst thou gaze with thine inner eye, thou wouldst find that all save Him fade into utter nothingness and are as a thing forgotten in His holy presence. "God was alone; there was none else besides Him. He remaineth now what He hath ever been." Since it hath been established that God—hallowed and glorified be He!—was alone and there was none besides Him, how can the law of change and transformation apply here? Shouldst thou reflect upon that which We have disclosed unto thee, the daystar of guidance would shine resplendent before thee in this everlasting morn, and thou wouldst be numbered therein with the pious.

Know, moreover, that all that We have mentioned concerning these journeys is intended for none but the elect amongst the righteous. And shouldst thou spur on the charger of the spirit and traverse the meads of heaven, thou wouldst complete all these journeys and discover every mystery in less than the twinkling of an eye.

O My brother! If thou be a champion of this arena, speed within the lands of certitude, that thy soul may be delivered in this day from the bondage of misbelief, and that thou mayest perceive the sweet savours that waft from this garden. Verily, the perfume-laden breezes that carry the fragrance of this city blow over all regions. Forfeit not thy portion thereof and be not of the heedless. How well hath it been said:

> His fragrant breaths diffused in Eastern lands could well
> To sick ones in the West restore their sense of smell![19]

Know, moreover, that should one who hath attained unto these

stations and embarked upon these journeys fall prey to pride and vainglory, he would at that very moment come to naught and return to the first step without realizing it. Indeed, they that seek and yearn after Him in these journeys are known by this sign, that they humbly defer to those who have believed in God and in His verses, that they are lowly before those who have drawn nigh unto Him and unto the Manifestations of His Beauty, and that they bow in submission to them that are firmly established upon the lofty heights of the Cause of God and before its majesty.

For were they to reach the ultimate object of their quest for God and their attainment unto Him, they would have but reached that abode which hath been raised up within their own hearts. How then could they ever hope to ascend unto such realms as have not been ordained for them or created for their station? Nay, though they journey from everlasting to everlasting, they will never attain unto Him Who is the midmost Heart of existence and the Axis of the entire creation, He on Whose right hand flow the seas of grandeur, on Whose left stream the rivers of might, and Whose court none can ever hope to reach, how much less His very abode! For He dwelleth in the ark of fire, speedeth, in the sphere of fire, through the ocean of fire, and moveth within the atmosphere of fire. How can he who hath been fashioned of contrary elements ever enter or even approach this fire? Were he to do so, he would be instantly consumed.

Know, moreover, that should the cord of assistance binding this mighty Pivot to the dwellers of earth and heaven be severed, they would all assuredly perish. Great God! How can the lowly dust ever reach unto Him Who is the Lord of lords? Immeasurably exalted is God above that which they conceive in their hearts, and immensely glorified is He beyond that which they attribute to Him. . . .[20]

Notes

[18] Bahá'u'lláh, *The Gems of Divine Mysteries*, pp. ii-iii.
[19]From the *Díván* of Ibn-i-Fáriḍ.
[20]Bahá'u'lláh, *The Gems of Divine Mysteries*, pp. 3-75.

The Book of Certitude (Kitáb-i-Íqán)

This highly acclaimed and widely studied book was composed by Bahá'u'lláh during the course of two days and two nights, in the early January of 1861. "A model of Persian prose," writes Shoghi Effendi, "of a style at once original, chaste and vigorous, and remarkably lucid, both cogent in argument and matchless in its irresistible eloquence, this Book, setting forth in outline the Grand Redemptive Scheme of God, occupies a position unequalled by any work in the entire range of Bahá'í literature, except the Kitáb-i-Aqdas, *Bahá'u'lláh's Most Holy Book."*[21] The Book of Certitude *was written as a reply to the questions put forth in writing to Bahá'u'lláh by an uncle of the Báb who was unclear about the position and significance of his illustrious Nephew in the context of Shí'a Islam.*

IN THE NAME OF OUR LORD, THE EXALTED, THE MOST HIGH.

No man shall attain the shores of the ocean of true understanding except he be detached from all that is in heaven and on earth. Sanctify your souls, O ye peoples of the world, that haply ye may attain that station which God hath destined for you and enter thus the tabernacle which, according to the dispensations of Providence, hath been raised in the firmament of the Bayán.

The essence of these words is this: they that tread the path of faith, they that thirst for the wine of certitude, must cleanse themselves of all that is earthly—their ears from idle talk, their minds from vain imaginings, their hearts from worldly affections, their eyes from that which perisheth. They should put their trust in God, and, holding fast unto Him, follow in His way. Then will they be made worthy of the effulgent glories

of the sun of divine knowledge and understanding, and become the recipients of a grace that is infinite and unseen, inasmuch as man can never hope to attain unto the knowledge of the All-Glorious, can never quaff from the stream of divine knowledge and wisdom, can never enter the abode of immortality, nor partake of the cup of divine nearness and favour, unless and until he ceases to regard the words and deeds of mortal men as a standard for the true understanding and recognition of God and His Prophets.

Consider the past. How many, both high and low, have, at all times, yearningly awaited the advent of the Manifestations of God in the sanctified persons of His chosen Ones. How often have they expected His coming, how frequently have they prayed that the breeze of divine mercy might blow, and the promised Beauty step forth from behind the veil of concealment, and be made manifest to all the world. And whensoever the portals of grace did open, and the clouds of divine bounty did rain upon mankind, and the light of the Unseen did shine above the horizon of celestial might, they all denied Him, and turned away from His face—the face of God Himself. Refer ye, to verify this truth, to that which hath been recorded in every sacred Book. . . .

The Bearers of the Trust of God are made manifest unto the peoples of the earth as the Exponents of a new Cause and the Revealers of a new Message. Inasmuch as these Birds of the celestial Throne are all sent down from the heaven of the Will of God, and as they all arise to proclaim His irresistible Faith, they, therefore, are regarded as one soul and the same person. For they all drink from the one Cup of the love of God, and all partake of the fruit of the same Tree of Oneness.

These Manifestations of God have each a twofold station. One is the station of pure abstraction and essential unity. In this respect, if thou callest them all by one name, and dost ascribe to them the same attributes, thou hast not erred from the truth. Even as He hath revealed: "No distinction do We make between

any of His Messengers." For they, one and all, summon the people of the earth to acknowledge the unity of God, and herald unto them the Kawthar of an infinite grace and bounty. They are all invested with the robe of prophethood, and are honored with the mantle of glory. Thus hath Muḥammad, the Point of the Qur'án, revealed: "I am all the Prophets." Likewise, He saith: "I am the first Adam, Noah, Moses, and Jesus." Similar statements have been made by Imám 'Alí. Sayings such as these, which indicate the essential unity of those Exponents of Oneness, have also emanated from the Channels of God's immortal utterance, and the Treasuries of the gems of Divine knowledge, and have been recorded in the Scriptures. These Countenances are the recipients of the Divine Command, and the Day Springs of His Revelation. This Revelation is exalted above the veils of plurality and the exigencies of number. Thus He saith: "Our Cause is but One." Inasmuch as the Cause is one and the same, the Exponents thereof also must needs be one and the same. Likewise, the Imáms of the Muḥammadan Faith, those lamps of certitude, have said: "Muḥammad is our first, Muḥammad is our last, Muḥammad our all."

It is clear and evident to thee that all the Prophets are the Temples of the Cause of God, Who have appeared clothed in divers attire. If thou wilt observe with discriminating eyes, thou wilt behold Them all abiding in the same tabernacle, soaring in the same heaven, seated upon the same throne, uttering the same speech, and proclaiming the same Faith. Such is the unity of those Essences of Being, those Luminaries of infinite and immeasurable splendor! Wherefore, should one of these Manifestations of Holiness proclaim saying: "I am the return of all the Prophets," He, verily, speaketh the truth. In like manner, in every subsequent Revelation, the return of the former Revelation is a fact, the truth of which is firmly established. . . .

The other station is the station of distinction, and pertaineth to the world of creation, and to the limitations thereof. In this respect, each Manifestation of God hath a distinct individuality,

a definitely prescribed mission, a predestined revelation, and specially designated limitations. Each one of them is known by a different name, is characterized by a special attribute, fulfils a definite mission, and is entrusted with a particular Revelation. Even as He saith: "Some of the Apostles We have caused to excel the others. To some God hath spoken, some He hath raised and exalted. And to Jesus, Son of Mary, We gave manifest signs, and We strengthened Him with the Holy Spirit."

It is because of this difference in their station and mission that the words and utterances flowing from these Well Springs of Divine knowledge appear to diverge and differ. Otherwise, in the eyes of them that are initiated into the mysteries of Divine wisdom, all their utterances are, in reality, but the expressions of one Truth. As most of the people have failed to appreciate those stations to which We have referred, they, therefore, feel perplexed and dismayed at the varying utterances pronounced by Manifestations that are essentially one and the same.

It hath ever been evident that all these divergencies of utterance are attributable to differences of station. Thus, viewed from the standpoint of their oneness and sublime detachment, the attributes of Godhead, Divinity, Supreme Singleness, and Inmost Essence, have been, and are applicable to those Essences of Being, inasmuch as they all abide on the throne of Divine Revelation, and are established upon the seat of Divine Concealment. Through their appearance the Revelation of God is made manifest, and by their countenance the Beauty of God is revealed. Thus it is that the accents of God Himself have been heard uttered by these Manifestations of the Divine Being.

Viewed in the light of their second station—the station of distinction, differentiation, temporal limitations, characteristics and standards—they manifest absolute servitude, utter destitution, and complete self-effacement. Even as He saith: "I am the servant of God. I am but a man

like you.”. . .

Were any of the all-embracing Manifestations of God to declare: “I am God,” He, verily, speaketh the truth, and no doubt attacheth thereto. For it hath been repeatedly demonstrated that through their Revelation, their attributes and names, the Revelation of God, His names and His attributes, are made manifest in the world. Thus, He hath revealed: “Those shafts were God’s, not Thine.” And also He saith: “In truth, they who plighted fealty unto Thee, really plighted that fealty unto God.” And were any of them to voice the utterance, “I am the Messenger of God,” He, also, speaketh the truth, the indubitable truth. Even as He saith: “Muḥammad is not the father of any man among you, but He is the Messenger of God.” Viewed in this light, they are all but Messengers of that ideal King, that unchangeable Essence. And were they all to proclaim, “I am the Seal of the Prophets,” they, verily, utter but the truth, beyond the faintest shadow of doubt. For they are all but one person, one soul, one spirit, one being, one revelation. They are all the manifestation of the “Beginning” and the “End,” the “First” and the “Last,” the “Seen” and the “Hidden”—all of which pertain to Him Who is the Innermost Spirit of Spirits and Eternal Essence of Essences. And were they to say, “We are the Servants of God,” this also is a manifest and indisputable fact. For they have been made manifest in the uttermost state of servitude, a servitude the like of which no man can possibly attain. Thus in moments in which these Essences of Being were deep immersed beneath the oceans of ancient and everlasting holiness, or when they soared to the loftiest summits of Divine mysteries, they claimed their utterances to be the Voice of Divinity, the Call of God Himself.

Were the eye of discernment to be opened, it would recognize that in this very state, they have considered themselves utterly effaced and non-existent in the face of Him Who is the All-Pervading, the Incorruptible. Methinks, they have regarded themselves as utter nothingness, and deemed their mention in that Court an act of blasphemy. For the slightest whispering

of self within such a Court is an evidence of self-assertion and independent existence. In the eyes of them that have attained unto that Court, such a suggestion is itself a grievous transgression. How much more grievous would it be, were aught else to be mentioned in that Presence, were man's heart, his tongue, his mind, or his soul, to be busied with any one but the Well-Beloved, were his eyes to behold any countenance other than His beauty, were his ear to be inclined to any melody but His Voice, and were his feet to tread any way but His way. . . .

By virtue of this station they have claimed for themselves the Voice of Divinity and the like, whilst by virtue of their station of Messengership, they have declared themselves the Messengers of God. In every instance they have voiced an utterance that would conform to the requirements of the occasion, and have ascribed all these declarations to Themselves, declarations ranging from the realm of Divine Revelation to the realm of creation, and from the domain of Divinity even unto the domain of earthly existence. Thus it is that whatsoever be their utterance, whether it pertain to the realm of Divinity, Lordship, Prophethood, Messengership, Guardianship, Apostleship, or Servitude, all is true, beyond the shadow of a doubt. Therefore these sayings which We have quoted in support of Our argument must be attentively considered, that the divergent utterances of the Manifestations of the Unseen and Day Springs of Holiness may cease to agitate the soul and perplex the mind. . . .

O My brother! When a true seeker determineth to take the step of search in the path leading unto the knowledge of the Ancient of Days, he must, before all else, cleanse and purify his heart, which is the seat of the revelation of the inner mysteries of God, from the obscuring dust of all acquired knowledge, and the allusions of the embodiments of satanic fancy. He must purge his breast, which is the sanctuary of the abiding love of the Beloved, of every defilement, and sanctify his soul from all that pertaineth to water and clay, from all shadowy and ephemeral attachments. He must so cleanse his

heart that no remnant of either love or hate may linger therein, lest that love blindly incline him to error, or that hate repel him away from the truth. Even as thou dost witness in this Day how most of the people, because of such love and hate, are bereft of the immortal Face, have strayed far from the Embodiments of the Divine mysteries, and, shepherdless, are roaming through the wilderness of oblivion and error.

That seeker must, at all times, put his trust in God, must renounce the peoples of the earth, must detach himself from the world of dust, and cleave unto Him Who is the Lord of Lords. He must never seek to exalt himself above any one, must wash away from the tablet of his heart every trace of pride and vain-glory, must cling unto patience and resignation, observe silence and refrain from idle talk. For the tongue is a smoldering fire, and excess of speech a deadly poison. Material fire consumeth the body, whereas the fire of the tongue devoureth both heart and soul. The force of the former lasteth but for a time, whilst the effects of the latter endureth a century.

That seeker should, also, regard backbiting as grievous error, and keep himself aloof from its dominion, inasmuch as backbiting quencheth the light of the heart, and extinguisheth the life of the soul. He should be content with little, and be freed from all inordinate desire. He should treasure the companionship of them that have renounced the world, and regard avoidance of boastful and worldly people a precious benefit. At the dawn of every day he should commune with God, and, with all his soul, persevere in the quest of his Beloved. He should consume every wayward thought with the flame of His loving mention, and, with the swiftness of lightning, pass by all else save Him. He should succor the dispossessed, and never withhold his favor from the destitute. He should show kindness to animals, how much more unto his fellow-man, to him who is endowed with the power of utterance. He should not hesitate to offer up his life for his Beloved, nor allow the censure of the people to turn him away from the Truth. He

should not wish for others that which he doth not wish for himself, nor promise that which he doth not fulfil. With all his heart he should avoid fellowship with evil-doers, and pray for the remission of their sins. He should forgive the sinful, and never despise his low estate, for none knoweth what his own end shall be. How often hath a sinner attained, at the hour of death, to the essence of faith, and, quaffing the immortal draught, hath taken his flight unto the Concourse on high! And how often hath a devout believer, at the hour of his soul's ascension, been so changed as to fall into the nethermost fire!

Our purpose in revealing these convincing and weighty utterances is to impress upon the seeker that he should regard all else beside God as transient, and count all things save Him, Who is the Object of all adoration, as utter nothingness.

These are among the attributes of the exalted, and constitute the hall-mark of the spiritually-minded. They have already been mentioned in connection with the requirements of the wayfarers that tread the path of Positive Knowledge. When the detached wayfarer and sincere seeker hath fulfilled these essential conditions, then and only then can he be called a true seeker. Whensoever he hath fulfilled the conditions implied in the verse: "Whoso maketh efforts for Us," he shall enjoy the blessings conferred by the words: "In Our Ways shall We assuredly guide him."

Only when the lamp of search, of earnest striving, of longing desire, of passionate devotion, of fervid love, of rapture, and ecstasy, is kindled within the seeker's heart, and the breeze of His loving-kindness is wafted upon his soul, will the darkness of error be dispelled, the mists of doubts and misgivings be dissipated, and the lights of knowledge and certitude envelop his being. At that hour will the Mystic Herald, bearing the joyful tidings of the Spirit, shine forth from the City of God resplendent as the morn, and, through the trumpet-blast of knowledge, will awaken the heart, the soul, and the spirit from the slumber of heedlessness. Then will the manifold favors

and outpouring grace of the holy and everlasting Spirit confer such new life upon the seeker that he will find himself endowed with a new eye, a new ear, a new heart, and a new mind. He will contemplate the manifest signs of the universe, and will penetrate the hidden mysteries of the soul. Gazing with the eye of God, he will perceive within every atom a door that leadeth him to the stations of absolute certitude. He will discover in all things the mysteries of Divine Revelation, and the evidences of an everlasting Manifestation.

I swear by God! Were he that treadeth the path of guidance and seeketh to scale the heights of righteousness to attain unto this glorious and exalted station, he would inhale, at a distance of a thousand leagues, the fragrance of God, and would perceive the resplendent morn of a Divine guidance rising above the Day Spring of all things. Each and every thing, however small, would be to him a revelation, leading him to his Beloved, the Object of his quest. So great shall be the discernment of this seeker that he will discriminate between truth and falsehood, even as he doth distinguish the sun from shadow. If in the uttermost corners of the East the sweet savors of God be wafted, he will assuredly recognize and inhale their fragrance, even though he be dwelling in the uttermost ends of the West. He will, likewise, clearly distinguish all the signs of God—His wondrous utterances, His great works, and mighty deeds—from the doings, the words and ways of men, even as the jeweler who knoweth the gem from the stone, or the man who distinguisheth the spring from autumn, and heat from cold. When the channel of the human soul is cleansed of all worldly and impeding attachments, it will unfailingly perceive the breath of the Beloved across immeasurable distances, and will, led by its perfume, attain and enter the City of Certitude.

Therein he will discern the wonders of His ancient Wisdom, and will perceive all the hidden teachings from the rustling leaves of the Tree that flourisheth in that City. With both his inner and outer ear, he will hear from its dust the hymns of glory and praise ascending unto the Lord of Lords, and with

his inner eye will he discover the mysteries of "return" and "revival."

How unspeakably glorious are the signs, the tokens, the revelations, and splendors which He, Who is the King of Names and Attributes, hath destined for that City! The attainment unto this City quencheth thirst without water, and kindleth the love of God without fire. Within every blade of grass are enshrined the mysteries of an inscrutable Wisdom, and upon every rose-bush a myriad nightingales pour out, in blissful rapture, their melody. Its wondrous tulips unfold the mystery of the undying Fire in the Burning Bush, and its sweet savors of holiness breathe the perfume of the Messianic Spirit. It bestoweth wealth without gold, and conferreth immortality without death. In each one of its leaves ineffable delights are treasured, and within every chamber unnumbered mysteries lie hidden.

They that valiantly labor in quest of God, will, when once they have renounced all else but Him, be so attached and wedded unto that City, that a moment's separation from it would to them be unthinkable. They will hearken unto infallible proofs from the Hyacinth of that assembly, and will receive the surest testimonies from the beauty of its Rose, and the melody of its Nightingale. Once in about a thousand years shall this City be renewed and readorned. . . .

That City is none other than the Word of God revealed in every age and dispensation. In the days of Moses it was the Pentateuch; in the days of Jesus, the Gospel; in the days of Muhammad, the Messenger of God, the Qur'án; in this day, the Bayán; and in the Dispensation of Him Whom God will make manifest, His own Book—the Book unto which all the Books of former Dispensations must needs be referred, the Book that standeth amongst them all transcendent and supreme. . . .[22]

Notes

[21]Shoghi Effendi, *God Passes By*, p. 138-39.
[22]Bahá'u'lláh, *Kitáb-i-Íqán The Book of Certitude*, pp. 3-200.

shedding the radiance of His Revelation upon the earth? Were ye to be fair in your judgment, ye would readily recognize how the realities of all created things are inebriated with the joy of this new and wondrous Revelation, how all the atoms of the earth have been illuminated through the brightness of its glory. Vain and wretched is that which ye have imagined and still imagine!

Retrace your steps, O My servants, and incline your hearts to Him Who is the Source of your creation. Deliver yourselves from your evil and corrupt affections, and hasten to embrace the light of the undying Fire that gloweth on the Sinai of this mysterious and transcendent Revelation. Corrupt not the holy, the all-embracing, and primal Word of God, and seek not to profane its sanctity or to debase its exalted character. O heedless ones! Though the wonders of My mercy have encompassed all created things, both visible and invisible, and though the revelations of My grace and bounty have permeated every atom of the universe, yet the rod with which I can chastise the wicked is grievous, and the fierceness of Mine anger against them terrible. With ears that are sanctified from vain-glory and worldly desires hearken unto the counsels which I, in My merciful kindness, have revealed unto you, and with your inner and outer eyes contemplate the evidences of My marvelous Revelation. . . .

O My servants! Deprive not yourselves of the unfading and resplendent Light that shineth within the Lamp of Divine glory. Let the flame of the love of God burn brightly within your radiant hearts. Feed it with the oil of Divine guidance, and protect it within the shelter of your constancy. Guard it within the globe of trust and detachment from all else but God, so that the evil whisperings of the ungodly may not extinguish its light. O My servants! My holy, My divinely ordained Revelation may be likened unto an ocean in whose depths are concealed innumerable pearls of great price, of surpassing luster. It is the duty of every seeker to bestir himself and strive to attain the shores of this ocean, so that he may, in proportion

to the eagerness of his search and the efforts he hath exerted, partake of such benefits as have been pre-ordained in God's irrevocable and hidden Tablets. If no one be willing to direct his steps towards its shores, if every one should fail to arise and find Him, can such a failure be said to have robbed this ocean of its power or to have lessened, to any degree, its treasures? How vain, how contemptible, are the imaginations which your hearts have devised, and are still devising! O My servants! The one true God is My witness! This most great, this fathomless and surging Ocean is near, astonishingly near, unto you. Behold it is closer to you than your life-vein! Swift as the twinkling of an eye ye can, if ye but wish it, reach and partake of this imperishable favor, this God-given grace, this incorruptible gift, this most potent and unspeakably glorious bounty.

O My servants! Could ye apprehend with what wonders of My munificence and bounty I have willed to entrust your souls, ye would, of a truth, rid yourselves of attachment to all created things, and would gain a true knowledge of your own selves—a knowledge which is the same as the comprehension of Mine own Being. Ye would find yourselves independent of all else but Me, and would perceive, with your inner and outer eye, and as manifest as the revelation of My effulgent Name, the seas of My loving-kindness and bounty moving within you. Suffer not your idle fancies, your evil passions, your insincerity and blindness of heart to dim the luster, or stain the sanctity, of so lofty a station. Ye are even as the bird which soareth, with the full force of its mighty wings and with complete and joyous confidence, through the immensity of the heavens, until, impelled to satisfy its hunger, it turneth longingly to the water and clay of the earth below it, and, having been entrapped in the mesh of its desire, findeth itself impotent to resume its flight to the realms whence it came. Powerless to shake off the burden weighing on its sullied wings, that bird, hitherto an inmate of the heavens, is now forced to seek a dwelling-place upon the dust. Wherefore, O My servants, defile not your wings

with the clay of waywardness and vain desires, and suffer them not to be stained with the dust of envy and hate, that ye may not be hindered from soaring in the heavens of My divine knowledge.

O My servants! Through the might of God and His power, and out of the treasury of His knowledge and wisdom, I have brought forth and revealed unto you the pearls that lay concealed in the depths of His everlasting ocean. I have summoned the Maids of Heaven to emerge from behind the veil of concealment, and have clothed them with these words of Mine—words of consummate power and wisdom. I have, moreover, with the hand of divine power, unsealed the choice wine of My Revelation, and have wafted its holy, its hidden, and musk-laden fragrance upon all created things. Who else but yourselves is to be blamed if ye choose to remain unendowed with so great an outpouring of God's transcendent and all-encompassing grace, with so bright a revelation of His resplendent mercy? . . .

O My servants! There shineth nothing else in Mine heart except the unfading light of the Morn of Divine guidance, and out of My mouth proceedeth naught but the essence of truth, which the Lord your God hath revealed. Follow not, therefore, your earthly desires, and violate not the Covenant of God, nor break your pledge to Him. With firm determination, with the whole affection of your heart, and with the full force of your words, turn ye unto Him, and walk not in the ways of the foolish. The world is but a show, vain and empty, a mere nothing, bearing the semblance of reality. Set not your affections upon it. Break not the bond that uniteth you with your Creator, and be not of those that have erred and strayed from His ways. Verily I say, the world is like the vapor in a desert, which the thirsty dreameth to be water and striveth after it with all his might, until when he cometh unto it, he findeth it to be mere illusion. It may, moreover, be likened unto the lifeless image of the beloved whom the lover hath sought and found, in the end, after long search and to his utmost regret, to be such as cannot

"fatten nor appease his hunger."

O My servants! Sorrow not if, in these days and on this earthly plane, things contrary to your wishes have been ordained and manifested by God, for days of blissful joy, of heavenly delight, are assuredly in store for you. Worlds, holy and spiritually glorious, will be unveiled to your eyes. You are destined by Him, in this world and hereafter, to partake of their benefits, to share in their joys, and to obtain a portion of their sustaining grace. To each and every one of them you will, no doubt, attain. . . .[23]

Notes

[23] Bahá'u'lláh, *Gleanings*, CLII, CLIII.

The Epistle of Utterance (Súratu'l-Bayán)

This highly eloquent and challenging treatise highlights some key spiritual verities from among Bahá'u'lláh's teachings. Written entirely in the Arabic language, its timeless message is primarily addressed to the generality of His faithful followers.

. . .O wayfarer in the path of God! Take thou thy portion of the ocean of His grace, and deprive not thyself of the things that lie hidden in its depths. Be thou of them that have partaken of its treasures. A dewdrop out of this ocean would, if shed upon all that are in the heavens and on the earth, suffice to enrich them with the bounty of God, the Almighty, the All-Knowing, the All-Wise. With the hands of renunciation draw forth from its life-giving waters, and sprinkle therewith all created things, that they may be cleansed from all man-made limitations and may approach the mighty seat of God, this hallowed and resplendent Spot.

Be not grieved if thou performest it thyself alone. Let God be all-sufficient for thee. Commune intimately with His Spirit, and be thou of the thankful. Proclaim the Cause of thy Lord unto all who are in the heavens and on the earth. Should any man respond to thy call, lay bare before him the pearls of the wisdom of the Lord, thy God, which His Spirit hath sent down unto thee, and be thou of them that truly believe. And should any one reject thine offer, turn thou away from him, and put thy trust and confidence in the Lord, thy God, the Lord of all worlds.

By the righteousness of God! Whoso openeth his lips in this Day and maketh mention of the name of his Lord, the hosts of Divine inspiration shall descend upon him from the heaven of My name, the All-Knowing, the All-Wise. On him shall also

descend the Concourse on high, each bearing aloft a chalice of pure light. Thus hath it been foreordained in the realm of God's Revelation, by the behest of Him Who is the All-Glorious, the Most Powerful.

There lay concealed within the Holy Veil, and prepared for the service of God, a company of His chosen ones who shall be manifested unto men, who shall aid His Cause, who shall be afraid of no one, though the entire human race rise up and war against them. These are the ones who, before the gaze of the dwellers on earth and the denizens of heaven, shall arise and, shouting aloud, acclaim the name of the Almighty, and summon the children of men to the path of God, the All-Glorious, the All-Praised. Walk thou in their way, and let no one dismay thee. Be of them whom the tumult of the world, however much it may agitate them in the path of their Creator, can never sadden, whose purpose the blame of the blamer will never defeat.

Go forth with the Tablet of God and His signs, and rejoin them that have believed in Me, and announce unto them tidings of Our most holy Paradise. Warn, then, those that have joined partners with Him. Say: I am come to you, O people, from the Throne of glory, and bear you an announcement from God, the Most Powerful, the Most Exalted, the Most Great. In mine hand I carry the testimony of God, your Lord and the Lord of your sires of old. Weigh it with the just Balance that ye possess, the Balance of the testimony of the Prophets and Messengers of God. If ye find it to be established in truth, if ye believe it to be of God, beware, then, lest ye cavil at it, and render your works vain, and be numbered with the infidels. It is indeed the sign of God that hath been sent down through the power of truth, through which the validity of His Cause hath been demonstrated unto His creatures, and the ensigns of purity lifted up betwixt earth and heaven.

Say: This is the sealed and mystic Scroll, the repository of God's irrevocable Decree, bearing the words which the Finger of

Holiness hath traced, that lay wrapt within the veil of impenetrable mystery, and hath now been sent down as a token of the grace of Him Who is the Almighty, the Ancient of Days. In it have We decreed the destinies of all the dwellers of the earth and the denizens of heaven, and written down the knowledge of all things from first to last. Nothing whatsoever can escape or frustrate Him, whether created in the past or to be created in the future, could ye but perceive it.

Say: The Revelation sent down by God hath most surely been repeated, and the outstretched Hand of Our power hath overshadowed all that are in the heavens and all that are on the earth. We have, through the power of truth, the very truth, manifested an infinitesimal glimmer of Our impenetrable Mystery, and lo, they that have recognized the radiance of the Sinaic splendor expired, as they caught a lightening glimpse of this Crimson Light enveloping the Sinai of Our Revelation. Thus hath He Who is the Beauty of the All-Merciful come down in the clouds of His testimony, and the decree accomplished by virtue of the Will of God, the All-Glorious, the All-Wise.

Say: Step out of Thy holy chamber, O Maid of Heaven, inmate of the Exalted Paradise! Drape thyself in whatever manner pleaseth Thee in the silken Vesture of Immortality, and put on, in the name of the All-Glorious, the broidered Robe of Light. Hear, then, the sweet, the wondrous accent of the Voice that cometh from the Throne of Thy Lord, the Inaccessible, the Most High. Unveil Thy face, and manifest the beauty of the black-eyed Damsel, and suffer not the servants of God to be deprived of the light of Thy shining countenance. Grieve not if Thou hearest the sighs of the dwellers of the earth, or the voice of the lamentation of the denizens of heaven. Leave them to perish on the dust of extinction. Let them be reduced to nothingness, inasmuch as the flame of hatred hath been kindled within their breasts. Intone, then, before the face of the peoples of earth and heaven, and in a most melodious voice, the anthem of praise, for a remembrance of Him Who is the King of the names and attributes of God. Thus have We decreed Thy destiny. Well

able are We to achieve Our purpose.

Beware that Thou divest not Thyself, Thou Who art the Essence of Purity, of Thy robe of effulgent glory. Nay, enrich Thyself increasingly, in the kingdom of creation, with the incorruptible vestures of Thy God, that the beauteous image of the Almighty may be reflected through Thee in all created things and the grace of Thy Lord be infused in the plenitude of its power into the entire creation.

If Thou smellest from any one the smell of the love of Thy Lord, offer up Thyself for him, for We have created Thee to this end, and have covenanted with Thee, from time immemorial, and in the presence of the congregation of Our well-favored ones, for this very purpose. Be not impatient if the blind in heart hurl down the shafts of their idle fancies upon Thee. Leave them to themselves, for they follow the promptings of the evil ones.

Cry out before the gaze of the dwellers of heaven and of earth: I am the Maid of Heaven, the Offspring begotten by the Spirit of Bahá. My habitation is the Mansion of His Name, the All-Glorious. Before the Concourse on high I was adorned with the ornament of His names. I was wrapt within the veil of an inviolable security, and lay hidden from the eyes of men. Methinks that I heard a Voice of divine and incomparable sweetness, proceeding from the right hand of the God of Mercy, and lo, the whole Paradise stirred and trembled before Me, in its longing to hear its accents, and gaze on the beauty of Him that uttered them. Thus have We revealed in this luminous Tablet, and in the sweetest of languages, the verses which the Tongue of Eternity was moved to utter in the Qayyúmu'l-Asmá.

Say: He ordaineth as He pleaseth, by virtue of His sovereignty, and doeth whatsoever He willeth at His own behest. He shall not be asked of the things it pleaseth Him to ordain. He, in truth, is the Unrestrained, the All-Powerful, the All-Wise.

They that have disbelieved in God and rebelled against His

sovereignty are the helpless victims of their corrupt inclinations and desires. These shall return to their abode in the fire of hell: wretched is the abode of the deniers! . . .

Say: Doth it beseem a man while claiming to be a follower of his Lord, the All-Merciful, he should yet in his heart do the very deeds of the Evil One? Nay, it ill beseemeth him, and to this He Who is the Beauty of the All-Glorious will bear Me witness. Would that ye could comprehend it!

Cleanse from your hearts the love of worldly things, from your tongues every remembrance except His remembrance, from your entire being whatsoever may deter you from beholding His face, or may tempt you to follow the promptings of your evil and corrupt inclinations. Let God be your fear, O people, and be ye of them that tread the path of righteousness.

Say: Should your conduct, O people, contradict your professions, how think ye, then, to be able to distinguish yourselves from them who, though professing their faith in the Lord their God, have, as soon as He came unto them in the cloud of holiness, refused to acknowledge Him, and repudiated His truth? Disencumber yourselves of all attachment to this world and the vanities thereof. Beware that ye approach them not, inasmuch as they prompt you to walk after your own lusts and covetous desires, and hinder you from entering the straight and glorious Path.

Know ye that by "the world" is meant your unawareness of Him Who is your Maker, and your absorption in aught else but Him. The "life to come," on the other hand, signifieth the things that give you a safe approach to God, the All-Glorious, the Incomparable. Whatsoever deterreth you, in this Day, from loving God is nothing but the world. Flee it, that ye may be numbered with the blest. Should a man wish to adorn himself with the ornaments of the earth, to wear its apparels, or partake of the benefits it can bestow, no harm can befall him, if he alloweth nothing whatever to intervene between him and God, for God hath ordained every good thing, whether created in

the heavens or in the earth, for such of His servants as truly believe in Him. Eat ye, O people, of the good things which God hath allowed you, and deprive not yourselves from His wondrous bounties. Render thanks and praise unto Him, and be of them that are truly thankful.

O thou that hast fled thy home and sought the presence of God! Proclaim unto men the Message of thy Lord, that it may haply deter them from following the promptings of their evil and corrupt desires, and bring them to the remembrance of God, the Most Exalted, the Most Great. Say: Fear God, O people, and refrain from shedding the blood of any one. Contend not with your neighbor, and be ye of them that do good. Beware that ye commit no disorders on the earth after it hath been well ordered, and follow not the footsteps of them that are gone astray.

Whoso ariseth among you to teach the Cause of his Lord, let him, before all else, teach his own self, that his speech may attract the hearts of them that hear him. Unless he teacheth his own self, the words of his mouth will not influence the heart of the seeker. Take heed, O people, lest ye be of them that give good counsel to others but forget to follow it themselves. The words of such as these, and beyond the words the realities of all things, and beyond these realities the angels that are nigh unto God, bring against them the accusation of falsehood.

Should such a man ever succeed in influencing any one, this success should be attributed not to him, but rather to the influence of the words of God, as decreed by Him Who is the Almighty, the All-Wise. In the sight of God he is regarded as a lamp that imparteth its light, and yet is all the while being consumed within itself.

Say: Commit not, O people, that which will bring shame upon you or dishonor the Cause of God in the eyes of men, and be not of the mischief-makers. Approach not the things which your minds condemn. Eschew all manner of wickedness, for such

things are forbidden unto you in the Book which none touch except such as God hath cleansed from every taint of guilt, and numbered among the purified.

Be fair to yourselves and to others, that the evidences of justice may be revealed, through your deeds, among Our faithful servants. Beware lest ye encroach upon the substance of your neighbor. Prove yourselves worthy of his trust and confidence in you, and withhold not from the poor the gifts which the grace of God hath bestowed upon you. He, verily, shall recompense the charitable, and doubly repay them for what they have bestowed. No God is there but Him. All creation and its empire are His. He bestoweth His gifts on whom He will, and from whom He will He withholdeth them. He is the Great Giver, the Most Generous, the Benevolent.

Say: Teach ye the Cause of God, O people of Bahá, for God hath prescribed unto every one the duty of proclaiming His Message, and regardeth it as the most meritorious of all deeds. Such a deed is acceptable only when he that teacheth the Cause is already a firm believer in God, the Supreme Protector, the Gracious, the Almighty. He hath, moreover, ordained that His Cause be taught through the power of men's utterance, and not through resort to violence. Thus hath His ordinance been sent down from the Kingdom of Him Who is the Most Exalted, the All-Wise. Beware lest ye contend with any one, nay, strive to make him aware of the truth with kindly manner and most convincing exhortation. If your hearer respond, he will have responded to his own behoof, and if not, turn ye away from him, and set your faces towards God's sacred Court, the seat of resplendent holiness.

Dispute not with any one concerning the things of this world and its affairs, for God hath abandoned them to such as have set their affection upon them. Out of the whole world He hath chosen for Himself the hearts of men—hearts which the hosts of revelation and of utterance can subdue. Thus hath it been ordained by the Fingers of Bahá, upon the Tablet of God's

irrevocable decree, by the behest of Him Who is the Supreme Ordainer, the All-Knowing. . . .

If ye meet the abased or the down-trodden, turn not away disdainfully from them, for the King of Glory ever watcheth over them and surroundeth them with such tenderness as none can fathom except them that have suffered their wishes and desires to be merged in the Will of your Lord, the Gracious, the All-Wise. O ye rich ones of the earth! Flee not from the face of the poor that lieth in the dust, nay rather befriend him and suffer him to recount the tale of the woes with which God's inscrutable Decree hath caused him to be afflicted. By the righteousness of God! Whilst ye consort with him, the Concourse on high will be looking upon you, will be interceding for you, will be extolling your names and glorifying your action. Blessed are the learned that pride not themselves on their attainments; and well is it with the righteous that mock not the sinful, but rather conceal their misdeeds, so that their own shortcomings may remain veiled to men's eyes. . . .[24]

Notes

[24] Bahá'u'lláh, *Gleanings*, CXXIX, CXXVIII, CXLV.

The Epistle of the Temple (Súratu'l-Haykal)

Ranked as "one of Bahá'u'lláh's most challenging works"[25]*,* The Súrih of the Temple *was composed sometime between March 1866 and August 1868, during the turbulent period which saw the formation of a schism within the rank and file of the Bábí community. This eloquent and incisive Arabic epistle combines a mystical and proclamatory style to enunciate Bahá'u'lláh's Mission to those among the Báb's followers who had failed to recognize His Revelation.*

This is the Súrih of the Temple which God hath ordained to be the Mirror of His Names between the heavens and the earth, and the Sign of His Remembrance amidst the peoples of the world.

HE IS THE MOST WONDROUS, THE ALL-GLORIOUS!

Glorified is He Who hath revealed His verses to those who understand. Glorified is He Who sendeth down His verses to those who perceive. Glorified is He Who guideth whomsoever He pleaseth unto His path. Say: I, verily, am the Path of God unto all who are in the heavens and all who are on the earth; well is it with them that hasten thereunto! . . .

O people of the Bayán! If ye aid Him not, God will assuredly assist Him with the powers of earth and heaven, and sustain Him with the hosts of the unseen through His command "Be", and it is! The day is approaching when God will have, by an act of His Will, raised up a race of men the nature of which is inscrutable to all save God, the All-Powerful, the Self-Subsisting. He shall purify them from the defilement of idle fancies and corrupt desires, shall lift them up to the heights of holiness, and shall cause them to manifest the signs of His sovereignty and might upon earth. Thus hath it been ordained

by God, the All-Glorious, the All-Loving. . . .

We, verily, have ordained this Temple to be the source of all existence in the new creation, that all may know of a certainty My power to accomplish that which I have purposed through My word "Be", and it is! Beneath the shadow of every letter of this Temple We shall raise up a people whose number none can reckon save God, the Help in Peril, the Self-Subsisting. Erelong shall God bring forth from His Temple such souls as will remain unswayed by the insinuations of the rebellious, and who will quaff at all times of the cup that is life indeed. These, truly, are of the blissful. . . .

O Living Temple! Through Thee have We gathered together all created things, whether in the heavens or on the earth, and called them to account for that which We had covenanted with them before the foundation of the world. And lo, but for a few radiant faces and eloquent tongues, We found most of the people dumbfounded, their eyes staring up in fear. From the former We brought forth the creation of all that hath been and all that shall be. These are they whose countenances God hath graciously turned away from the face of the unbelievers, and whom He hath sheltered beneath the shadow of the Tree of His own Being; they upon whose hearts He hath bestowed the gift of peace and tranquillity, and whom He hath strengthened and assisted through the hosts of the seen and the unseen. . . .

O Beauty of the All-Glorious! Shouldst Thou chance upon this people and enter their presence, recount unto them that which this Youth hath related unto Thee concerning Himself and the things that have befallen Him, that they may come to know what hath been inscribed upon the Preserved Tablet. Acquaint them with the tidings of this Youth, and with the trials and tribulations He hath suffered, that they may become mindful of Mine afflictions, and be of them that understand. Recount, then, unto them how We singled out for Our favour one of Our brothers [Mírzá Yaḥyá], how We imparted unto him a dewdrop from the fathomless ocean of knowledge, clothed him with the

garment of one of Our Names, and exalted him to such a station that all were moved to extol him, and how We so protected him from the harm of the malevolent as to disarm even the mightiest amongst them.

We arose before the peoples of earth and heaven at a time when all had determined to slay us. While dwelling in their midst, We continually made mention of the Lord, celebrated His praise, and stood firm in His Cause, until at last the Word of God was vindicated amongst His creatures, His signs were spread abroad, His power exalted, and His sovereignty revealed in its full splendour. To this bear witness all His honoured servants. Yet when My brother beheld the rising fame of the Cause, he became filled with arrogance and pride. Thereupon he emerged from behind the veil of concealment, rose up against Me, disputed My verses, denied My testimony, and repudiated My signs. Nor would his hunger be appeased unless he were to devour My flesh and drink My blood. To this testify such of God's servants as have accompanied Him in His exile, and they that enjoy near access unto Him.

To this end he conferred with one of My servants and sought to win him over to his own designs; whereupon the Lord despatched unto Mine assistance the hosts of the seen and the unseen, protected Me by the power of truth, and sent down upon Me that which thwarted his purpose. Thus were foiled the plots of those who disbelieve in the verses of the All-Merciful. They, truly, are a rejected people. When news spread of that which the promptings of self had impelled My brother to attempt, and Our companions in exile learned of his nefarious design, the voice of their indignation and grief was lifted up and threatened to spread throughout the city. We forbade, however, such recriminations, and enjoined upon them patience, that they might be of those that endure steadfastly.

By God, besides Whom is none other God! We withstood all these trials with forbearance, and enjoined upon God's servants to show forth patience and fortitude. Removing Ourself from

their midst, We took up residence in another house, that perchance the flame of envy might be quenched in Our brother's breast, and that he might be guided aright. We neither opposed him, nor saw him again thereafter, but remained in Our home, placing Our hopes in the bounty of God, the Help in Peril, the Self-Subsisting. When, however, he realized that his deed had been exposed, he seized the pen of calumny and wrote unto the servants of God, attributing what he had himself committed unto Mine own peerless and wronged Beauty. His purpose was none other than to inspire mischief amongst God's servants, and to instil hatred into the hearts of those who had believed in God, the All-Glorious, the All-Loving.

By the One in Whose hand is My soul! We were dismayed by his deceitfulness—nay, bewildered were all things visible and invisible. Nor did he find respite from what he harboured in his bosom until he had committed that which no pen dare describe, and by which he disgraced the dignity of My station and profaned the sanctity of God, the Almighty, the All-Glorious, the All-Praised. Were God to turn all the oceans of the earth into ink and all created things into pens, they would not suffice Me to exhaust the record of his wrongdoings. Thus do We recount that which befell Us, that haply ye may be of them that understand.

O Pen of Eternity! Grieve not at the things that have befallen Thee, for erelong shall God raise up a people who will see with their own eyes and will recall Thy tribulations. Withhold Thy pen from the mention of Thine enemies, and bestir it in the praise of the Eternal King. Renounce all created things, and quaff the sealed wine of My remembrance. Beware lest Thou become occupied with the mention of those from whom naught save the noisome savours of enmity can be perceived, those who are so enslaved by their lust for leadership that they would not hesitate to destroy themselves in their desire to emblazon their fame and perpetuate their names. God hath recorded such souls in the Preserved Tablet as mere worshippers of names. Recount then that which Thou hast purposed for this

Temple, that its signs and tokens may be made manifest upon earth, and that the brightness of this Light may illumine the horizons of the world and cleanse the earth from the defilement of those who have disbelieved in God. Thus have We set down the verses of God and made plain the matter unto those who understand. . . .

Beware lest ye shed the blood of anyone. Unsheathe the sword of your tongue from the scabbard of utterance, for therewith ye can conquer the citadels of men's hearts. We have abolished the law to wage holy war against each other. God's mercy, hath, verily, encompassed all created things, if ye do but understand. Aid ye your Lord, the God of Mercy, with the sword of understanding. Keener indeed is it, and more finely tempered, than the sword of utterance, were ye but to reflect upon the words of your Lord. Thus have the hosts of Divine Revelation been sent down by God, the Help in Peril, the Self-Subsisting, and thus have the armies of divine inspiration been made manifest from the Source of command, as bidden by God, the All-Glorious, the Best-Beloved.

Say: The measure of all created things hath been appointed in this concealed and manifest Temple, wherein lie enshrined the knowledge of the heavens and the earth, and of all things past and future. The finger of God's handiwork hath inscribed upon this Tablet that which the wisest and most learned of men are powerless to fathom, and hath created therein temples inscrutable to all save His own Self, could ye but apprehend this truth. Blessed be the one who readeth it, who pondereth its contents, and who is numbered with them that comprehend!

Say: Naught is seen in My temple but the Temple of God, and in My beauty but His Beauty, and in My being but His Being, and in My self but His Self, and in My movement but His Movement, and in My acquiescence but His Acquiescence, and in My pen but His Pen, the Mighty, the All-Praised. There hath not been in My soul but the Truth, and in Myself naught

could be seen but God. . . .

Say: O people! Fear ye God, and allow not your tongues to utter, in their deceitfulness, that which displeaseth Him. Stand abashed before the One Who, as ye well know, hath created you out of a drop of water. Say: We have created all that are in heaven and on earth in the nature made by God. Whosoever turneth unto this blessed Countenance shall manifest the potentialities of that inborn nature, and whosoever remaineth veiled therefrom shall be deprived of this invisible and all-encompassing grace. Verily, there is naught from which Our favour hath been withheld, inasmuch as We have dealt equitably in the fashioning of each and all, and by a word of Our mouth presented unto them the trust of Our love. They that have accepted it are indeed safe and secure, and are numbered among those who are immune from the terrors of this Day. Those, however, who have rejected it have, in truth, disbelieved in God, the Help in Peril, the Self-Subsisting. Thus do We distinguish between the people and pronounce judgement upon them. We, of a certainty, have the power to discern.

Say: The Word of God can never be confounded with the words of His creatures. It is, in truth, the King of words, even as He is Himself the sovereign Lord of all, and His Cause transcendeth all that was and all that shall be. Enter, O people, the City of Certitude wherein the throne of your Lord, the All-Merciful, hath been established. Thus biddeth you the Pen of the All-Glorious, as a token of His unfailing grace. Haply ye may not make His Revelation a cause of dissension amongst you. . . .

O Ancient Beauty! Turn aside from the unbelievers and that which they possess, and waft over all created things the sweet savours of the remembrance of Thy Beloved, the Exalted, the Great. This remembrance quickeneth the world of being and reneweth the temples of all created things. Say: He, verily, hath established Himself upon the Throne of might and glory. Whosoever desireth to gaze upon His countenance, lo, behold

Him standing before thee! Blessed be the Lord Who hath revealed Himself in this shining and luminous Beauty. Whosoever desireth to hearken unto His melodies, lo, hear them rising from His resplendent and wondrous lips! And unto whosoever desireth to be illumined by the splendours of His light, say: Seek the court of His presence, for God hath verily granted you leave to approach it, as a token of His grace unto all mankind.

Say: O people! We shall put to you a question in all truthfulness, taking God for a witness between you and Us. He, verily, is the Defender of the righteous. Appear, then, before His Throne of glory and make reply with justice and fair-mindedness. Is it God Who is potent to achieve His purpose, or is it ye who enjoy such authority? Is it He Who is truly unconstrained, as ye imply when ye say that He doeth what He pleaseth and shall not be asked of His doings, or is it ye who wield such power, and who merely make such assertions out of blind imitation, as did your forebears at the appearance of every other Messenger of God?

If He be truly unconstrained, behold then how He hath sent down the Manifestation of His Cause with verses which naught in the heavens or on the earth can withstand! Such hath been the manner of their revelation that they have neither peer nor likeness in the world of being, as ye yourselves beheld and heard when once the Daystar of the world shone forth above the horizon of 'Iráq with manifest dominion. All things attain their consummation in the divine verses, and these indeed are the verses of God, the Sovereign Lord, the Help in Peril, the All-Glorious, the Almighty. Beyond this, He hath been made manifest as the Bearer of a Cause whose sovereign might is acknowledged by all created things, and this none can deny save the sinners and the ungodly. . . .

Within the treasury of Our Wisdom there lieth unrevealed a knowledge, one word of which, if we chose to divulge it to mankind, would cause every human being to recognize the

Manifestation of God and to acknowledge His omniscience, would enable every one to discover the secrets of all the sciences, and to attain so high a station as to find himself wholly independent of all past and future learning. Other knowledges We do as well possess, not a single letter of which We can disclose, nor do We find humanity able to hear even the barest reference to their meaning. Thus have We informed you of the knowledge of God, the All-Knowing, the All-Wise. Were We to find worthy vessels, We would deposit within them the treasures of hidden meanings and impart unto them a knowledge, one letter of which would encompass all created things. . . .

Say: O people! We, verily, summoned you, in Our former Revelation, unto this Scene of transcendent glory, this Seat of stainless sanctity, and announced unto you the advent of the Days of God. Yet, when the most great veil was rent asunder, and the Ancient Beauty came unto you in the clouds of God's decree, ye repudiated Him in Whom ye had believed aforetime. Woe betide you, O company of infidels! Fear ye God, and nullify not the truth with the things ye possess. When the luminary of divine verses dawneth upon you from the horizon of the Pen of the King of all names and attributes, fall ye prostrate upon your faces before God, the Lord of the Worlds. For to bow down in adoration at the threshold of His door is indeed better for you than the worship of both worlds, and to submit to His Revelation is more profitable unto you than whatsoever hath been created in the heavens and on the earth. . . .

Take heed lest ye hesitate in recognizing this resplendent Beauty when once He hath appeared in the plenitude of His sovereign might and majesty. He, verily, is the True One, and all else besides Him is as naught before a single one of His servants, and paleth into nothingness when brought face to face with the revelation of His splendours. Hasten, then, to attain the living waters of His grace, and be not of the negligent. As to him who hesitateth, though it be for less than a moment, God shall verily bring his works to naught and return him to

the seat of wrath; wretched indeed is the abode of them that tarry![26]

Notes

[25] Bahá'u'lláh, *The Summons of the Lord of Hosts*, p. *i*.
[26] *Idem*, pp. 3-54.

The Epistle of the Chief (Súriy-i-Ra'ís)

Bahá'u'lláh penned this awe-inspiring epistle sometime between August 12 and August 17, 1868, during a short stop in the Turkish town of Káshánih on the way to the port-city of Gallipoli. At the time He and His family were being deported from the city of Edirne to the penal colony of 'Akká, situated then in the Ottoman Turkish province of Palestine. The Súrih is addressed to 'Álí Páshá, the crafty and highly influential Ottoman prime minister, who had helped secure Bahá'u'lláh's banishment to 'Akká. This is the first of two proclamatory letters that Bahá'u'lláh wrote to this high-ranking Turkish official.

IN HIS NAME, THE ALL-GLORIOUS!

Hearken, O Chief, to the voice of God, the Sovereign, the Help in Peril, the Self-Subsisting. He, verily, calleth aloud between heaven and earth, summoning all mankind unto the scene of transcendent glory. Neither thy grunting, nor the barking of those around thee, nor the opposition of the hosts of the world can withhold the Almighty from achieving His purpose. The whole world hath been set ablaze by the Word of thy Lord, the All-Glorious, a Word softer than the morning breeze. It hath been manifested in the form of the human temple, and through it God hath quickened the souls of the sincere among His servants. In its inner essence, this Word is the living water by which God hath purified the hearts of such as have turned unto Him and forgotten every other mention, and through which He draweth them nigh unto the seat of His mighty Name. We have sprinkled it upon the people of the graves, and lo, they have risen up, with their gaze fixed upon the shining and resplendent Beauty of their Lord.

Thou has, O Chief, committed that which hath caused

Muhammad, the Apostle of God, to lament in the most sublime Paradise. The world hath made thee proud, so much so that thou hast turned away from the Face through whose brightness the Concourse on high hath been illumined. Soon thou shalt find thyself in manifest loss! Thou didst conspire with the Persian Ambassador to harm Me, though I had come unto you from the source of majesty and grandeur with a Revelation that hath solaced the eyes of the favoured ones of God.

By God! This is the Day wherein the undying Fire crieth out from within all created things: "The Best-Beloved of the worlds is come!" And before all things there standeth a Moses, hearkening to the Word of thy Lord, the Almighty, the All-Knowing. Were We to divest Ourself of the mortal raiment which We have worn in consideration of your weakness, all that are in heaven and on earth would offer up their souls for My sake. To this thy Lord Himself doth testify. None, however, can perceive it save those who have detached themselves from all things for love of their Lord, the Almighty, the Most Powerful.

Hast thou imagined thyself capable of extinguishing the fire which God hath kindled in the heart of creation? Nay, by Him Who is the Eternal Truth, couldst thou but know it. Rather, on account of what thy hands have wrought, it blazed higher and burned more fiercely. Erelong will it encompass the earth and all that dwell therein. Thus hath it been decreed by God, and the powers of earth and heaven are unable to thwart His purpose. . . .

Was it in Pharaoh's power to stay the hand of God from exercising His sovereignty when he acted wantonly in the land and was of the transgressors? From within his own house and in spite of his will We brought forth Him Who conversed with God. Well able are We to achieve Our purpose. Recall, moreover, how Nimrod kindled the fire of impiety that its flames might consume Abraham, the Friend

of God; We delivered Him, however, through the power of truth and seized Nimrod with the fury of Our wrath. . . .

We, too, have revealed the Cause of God in His cities and raised aloft His remembrance amidst them that truly believe in Him. Say: This Youth hath come to quicken the world and unite all its peoples. The day is approaching when that which God hath purposed will have prevailed and thou shalt behold the earth transformed into the all-glorious paradise. Thus hath it been inscribed by the Pen of Revelation upon this weighty Tablet. . . .

Had Muhammad, the Apostle of God, attained this Day, He would have exclaimed: "I have truly recognized Thee, O Thou the Desire of the Divine Messengers!" Had Abraham attained it, He too, falling prostrate upon the ground, and in the utmost lowliness before the Lord thy God, would have cried: "Mine heart is filled with peace, O Thou Lord of all that is in heaven and on earth! I testify that Thou hast unveiled before mine eyes all the glory of Thy power and the full majesty of Thy law! I bear witness, moreover, that through Thy Revelation the hearts of the faithful are well assured and contented." Had Moses Himself attained it, He, likewise, would have raised His voice saying: "All praise be to Thee for having lifted upon me the light of Thy countenance and enrolled me among them that have been privileged to behold Thy face!"

Consider the people and their condition. Reflect upon the things that their mouths have uttered and that their hands have wrought in this blessed, this most holy and peerless Day. They that have tarnished the good name of the Cause of God and turned unto the Evil One are accursed of all created things and are numbered among the inmates of the fire. Verily, whosoever hath hearkened to My call shall remain unperturbed by the clamour of all that are on earth; and whosoever is influenced by the words of anyone beside Me hath never heard My call. By God! Such a man is

deprived of entering My Kingdom, is debarred from My realms of majesty and power, and is of them that are in utter loss. . . .[27]

Notes

[27] Bahá'u'lláh, *The Summons of the Lord of Hosts*, pp. 141-149.

The Most Holy Book (Kitáb-i-Aqdas)

Bahá'u'lláh wrote The Kitáb-i-Aqdas *around 1873, at a time when, according to Shoghi Effendi, "He was still encompassed by the tribulations that had afflicted Him, through the acts committed by His enemies and the professed adherents of His Faith."*[28] *Shoghi Effendi further adds that "this Book, this treasury enshrining the priceless gems of His Revelation, stands out, by virtue of the principles it inculcates, the administrative institutions it ordains and the function with which it invests the appointed successor of its Author, unique and incomparable among the world's sacred Scriptures."*[29] *Bahá'ís believe* The Kitáb-i-Aqdas *to be the most sacred book of Bahá'u'lláh's Dispensation and the Charter of His New World Order.*

IN THE NAME OF HIM WHO IS THE SUPREME RULER OVER ALL THAT HATH BEEN AND ALL THAT IS TO BE

1 The first duty prescribed by God for His servants is the recognition of Him Who is the Dayspring of His Revelation and the Fountain of His laws, Who representeth the Godhead in both the Kingdom of His Cause and the world of creation. Whoso achieveth this duty hath attained unto all good; and whoso is deprived thereof hath gone astray, though he be the author of every righteous deed. It behoveth every one who reacheth this most sublime station, this summit of transcendent glory, to observe every ordinance of Him Who is the Desire of the world. These twin duties are inseparable. Neither is acceptable without the other. Thus hath it been decreed by Him Who is the Source of Divine inspiration.

2 They whom God hath endued with insight will readily recognize that the precepts laid down by God constitute the highest means for the maintenance of order in the world and

the security of its peoples. He that turneth away from them is accounted among the abject and foolish. We, verily, have commanded you to refuse the dictates of your evil passions and corrupt desires, and not to transgress the bounds which the Pen of the Most High hath fixed, for these are the breath of life unto all created things. The seas of Divine wisdom and Divine utterance have risen under the breath of the breeze of the All-Merciful. Hasten to drink your fill, O men of understanding! They that have violated the Covenant of God by breaking His commandments, and have turned back on their heels, these have erred grievously in the sight of God, the All-Possessing, the Most High.

3 O ye peoples of the world! Know assuredly that My commandments are the lamps of My loving providence among My servants, and the keys of My mercy for My creatures. Thus hath it been sent down from the heaven of the Will of your Lord, the Lord of Revelation. Were any man to taste the sweetness of the words which the lips of the All-Merciful have willed to utter, he would, though the treasures of the earth be in his possession, renounce them one and all, that he might vindicate the truth of even one of His commandments, shining above the Dayspring of His bountiful care and loving-kindness.

4 Say: From My laws the sweet-smelling savour of My garment can be smelled, and by their aid the standards of Victory will be planted upon the highest peaks. The Tongue of My power hath, from the heaven of My omnipotent glory, addressed to My creation these words: "Observe My commandments, for the love of My beauty." Happy is the lover that hath inhaled the divine fragrance of his Best-Beloved from these words, laden with the perfume of a grace which no tongue can describe. By My life! He who hath drunk the choice wine of fairness from the hands of My bountiful favour will circle around My commandments that shine above the Dayspring of My creation.

5 Think not that We have revealed unto you a mere code of laws. Nay, rather, We have unsealed the choice Wine with the

fingers of might and power. To this beareth witness that which the Pen of Revelation hath revealed. Meditate upon this, O men of insight! . . .

30 The Lord hath ordained that in every city a House of Justice be established wherein shall gather counsellors to the number of Bahá, and should it exceed this number it doth not matter. They should consider themselves as entering the Court of the presence of God, the Exalted, the Most High, and as beholding Him Who is the Unseen. It behoveth them to be the trusted ones of the Merciful among men and to regard themselves as the guardians appointed of God for all that dwell on earth. It is incumbent upon them to take counsel together and to have regard for the interests of the servants of God, for His sake, even as they regard their own interests, and to choose that which is meet and seemly. Thus hath the Lord your God commanded you. Beware lest ye put away that which is clearly revealed in His Tablet. Fear God, O ye that perceive. . . .

37 Whoso layeth claim to a Revelation direct from God, ere the expiration of a full thousand years, such a man is assuredly a lying impostor. We pray God that He may graciously assist him to retract and repudiate such claim. Should he repent, God will, no doubt, forgive him. If, however, he persisteth in his error, God will, assuredly, send down one who will deal mercilessly with him. Terrible, indeed, is God in punishing! Whosoever interpreteth this verse otherwise than its obvious meaning is deprived of the Spirit of God and of His mercy which encompasseth all created things. Fear God, and follow not your idle fancies. Nay, rather, follow the bidding of your Lord, the Almighty, the All-Wise. Erelong shall clamorous voices be raised in most lands. Shun them, O My people, and follow not the iniquitous and evil-hearted. This is that of which We gave you forewarning when We were dwelling in 'Iráq, then later while in the Land of Mystery, and now from this Resplendent Spot. . . .

39 The peoples of the world are fast asleep. Were they to wake

from their slumber, they would hasten with eagerness unto God, the All-Knowing, the All-Wise. They would cast away everything they possess, be it all the treasures of the earth, that their Lord may remember them to the extent of addressing to them but one word. Such is the instruction given you by Him Who holdeth the knowledge of things hidden, in a Tablet which the eye of creation hath not seen, and which is revealed to none except His own Self, the omnipotent Protector of all worlds. So bewildered are they in the drunkenness of their evil desires, that they are powerless to recognize the Lord of all being, Whose voice calleth aloud from every direction: "There is none other God but Me, the Mighty, the All-Wise."

40 Say: Rejoice not in the things ye possess; tonight they are yours, tomorrow others will possess them. Thus warneth you He Who is the All-Knowing, the All-Informed. Say: Can ye claim that what ye own is lasting or secure? Nay! By Myself, the All-Merciful, ye cannot, if ye be of them who judge fairly. The days of your life flee away as a breath of wind, and all your pomp and glory shall be folded up as were the pomp and glory of those gone before you. Reflect, O people! What hath become of your bygone days, your lost centuries? Happy the days that have been consecrated to the remembrance of God, and blessed the hours which have been spent in praise of Him Who is the All-Wise. By My life! Neither the pomp of the mighty, nor the wealth of the rich, nor even the ascendancy of the ungodly will endure. All will perish, at a word from Him. He, verily, is the All-Powerful, the All-Compelling, the Almighty. What advantage is there in the earthly things which men possess? That which shall profit them, they have utterly neglected. Erelong, they will awake from their slumber, and find themselves unable to obtain that which hath escaped them in the days of their Lord, the Almighty, the All-Praised. Did they but know it, they would renounce their all, that their names may be mentioned before His throne. They, verily, are accounted among the dead. . . .

43 Lament not in your hours of trial, neither rejoice therein;

seek ye the Middle Way which is the remembrance of Me in your afflictions and reflection over that which may befall you in future. Thus informeth you He Who is the Omniscient, He Who is aware. . . .

51 We have made it lawful for you to listen to music and singing. Take heed, however, lest listening thereto should cause you to overstep the bounds of propriety and dignity. Let your joy be the joy born of My Most Great Name, a Name that bringeth rapture to the heart, and filleth with ecstasy the minds of all who have drawn nigh unto God. We, verily, have made music as a ladder for your souls, a means whereby they may be lifted up unto the realm on high; make it not, therefore, as wings to self and passion. Truly, We are loath to see you numbered with the foolish.

52 We have decreed that a third part of all fines shall go to the Seat of Justice, and We admonish its men to observe pure justice, that they may expend what is thus accumulated for such purposes as have been enjoined upon them by Him Who is the All-Knowing, the All-Wise. O ye Men of Justice! Be ye, in the realm of God, shepherds unto His sheep and guard them from the ravening wolves that have appeared in disguise, even as ye would guard your own sons. Thus exhorteth you the Counsellor, the Faithful.

53 Should differences arise amongst you over any matter, refer it to God while the Sun still shineth above the horizon of this Heaven and, when it hath set, refer ye to whatsoever hath been sent down by Him. This, verily, is sufficient unto the peoples of the world. Say: Let not your hearts be perturbed, O people, when the glory of My Presence is withdrawn, and the ocean of My utterance is stilled. In My presence amongst you there is a wisdom, and in My absence there is yet another, inscrutable to all but God, the Incomparable, the All-Knowing. Verily, We behold you from Our realm of glory, and shall aid whosoever will arise for the triumph of Our Cause with the hosts of the Concourse on high and a company of Our favoured angels.

54 O peoples of the earth! God, the Eternal Truth, is My witness that streams of fresh and soft-flowing waters have gushed from the rocks through the sweetness of the words uttered by your Lord, the Unconstrained; and still ye slumber. Cast away that which ye possess, and, on the wings of detachment, soar beyond all created things. Thus biddeth you the Lord of creation, the movement of Whose Pen hath revolutionized the soul of mankind. . . .

101 O ye leaders of religion! Who is the man amongst you that can rival Me in vision or insight? Where is he to be found that dareth to claim to be My equal in utterance or wisdom? No, by My Lord, the All-Merciful! All on the earth shall pass away; and this is the face of your Lord, the Almighty, the Well-Beloved.

102 We have decreed, O people, that the highest and last end of all learning be the recognition of Him Who is the Object of all knowledge; and yet, behold how ye have allowed your learning to shut you out, as by a veil, from Him Who is the Dayspring of this Light, through Whom every hidden thing hath been revealed. Could ye but discover the source whence the splendour of this utterance is diffused, ye would cast away the peoples of the world and all that they possess, and would draw nigh unto this most blessed Seat of glory.

103 Say: This, verily, is the heaven in which the Mother Book is treasured, could ye but comprehend it. He it is Who hath caused the Rock to shout, and the Burning Bush to lift up its voice, upon the Mount rising above the Holy Land, and proclaim: "The Kingdom is God's, the sovereign Lord of all, the All-Powerful, the Loving!"

104 We have not entered any school, nor read any of your dissertations. Incline your ears to the words of this unlettered One, wherewith He summoneth you unto God, the Ever-Abiding. Better is this for you than all the treasures of the earth, could ye but comprehend it. . . .

116 They who recite the verses of the All-Merciful in the most melodious of tones will perceive in them that with which the sovereignty of earth and heaven can never be compared. From them they will inhale the divine fragrance of My worlds—worlds which today none can discern save those who have been endowed with vision through this sublime, this beauteous Revelation. Say: These verses draw hearts that are pure unto those spiritual worlds that can neither be expressed in words nor intimated by allusion. Blessed be those who hearken.

117 Assist ye, O My people, My chosen servants who have arisen to make mention of Me among My creatures and to exalt My Word throughout My realm. These, truly, are the stars of the heaven of My loving providence and the lamps of My guidance unto all mankind. But he whose words conflict with that which hath been sent down in My Holy Tablets is not of Me. Beware lest ye follow any impious pretender. These Tablets are embellished with the seal of Him Who causeth the dawn to appear, Who lifteth up His voice between the heavens and the earth. Lay hold on this Sure Handle and on the Cord of My mighty and unassailable Cause.

118 The Lord hath granted leave to whosoever desireth it that he be instructed in the divers tongues of the world that he may deliver the Message of the Cause of God throughout the East and throughout the West, that he make mention of Him amidst the kindreds and peoples of the world in such wise that hearts may revive and the mouldering bone be quickened.

119 It is inadmissible that man, who hath been endowed with reason, should consume that which stealeth it away. Nay, rather it behoveth him to comport himself in a manner worthy of the human station, and not in accordance with the misdeeds of every heedless and wavering soul.

120 Adorn your heads with the garlands of trustworthiness and fidelity, your hearts with the attire of the fear of God, your tongues with absolute truthfulness, your bodies with the vesture of courtesy. These are in truth seemly adornings unto

the temple of man, if ye be of them that reflect. Cling, O ye people of Bahá, to the cord of servitude unto God, the True One, for thereby your stations shall be made manifest, your names written and preserved, your ranks raised and your memory exalted in the Preserved Tablet. Beware lest the dwellers on earth hinder you from this glorious and exalted station. Thus have We exhorted you in most of Our Epistles and now in this, Our Holy Tablet, above which hath beamed the Day-Star of the Laws of the Lord, your God, the Powerful, the All-Wise.

121 When the ocean of My presence hath ebbed and the Book of My Revelation is ended, turn your faces toward Him Whom God hath purposed, Who hath branched from this Ancient Root.

122 Consider the pettiness of men's minds. They ask for that which injureth them, and cast away the thing that profiteth them. They are, indeed, of those that are far astray. We find some men desiring liberty, and priding themselves therein. Such men are in the depths of ignorance.

123 Liberty must, in the end, lead to sedition, whose flames none can quench. Thus warneth you He Who is the Reckoner, the All-Knowing. Know ye that the embodiment of liberty and its symbol is the animal. That which beseemeth man is submission unto such restraints as will protect him from his own ignorance, and guard him against the harm of the mischief-maker. Liberty causeth man to overstep the bounds of propriety, and to infringe on the dignity of his station. It debaseth him to the level of extreme depravity and wickedness.

124 Regard men as a flock of sheep that need a shepherd for their protection. This, verily, is the truth, the certain truth. We approve of liberty in certain circumstances, and refuse to sanction it in others. We, verily, are the All-Knowing.

125 Say: True liberty consisteth in man's submission unto My commandments, little as ye know it. Were men to observe that which We have sent down unto them from the Heaven of

Revelation, they would, of a certainty, attain unto perfect liberty. Happy is the man that hath apprehended the Purpose of God in whatever He hath revealed from the Heaven of His Will that pervadeth all created things. Say: The liberty that profiteth you is to be found nowhere except in complete servitude unto God, the Eternal Truth. Whoso hath tasted of its sweetness will refuse to barter it for all the dominion of earth and heaven. . . .

144 Consort with all religions with amity and concord, that they may inhale from you the sweet fragrance of God. Beware lest amidst men the flame of foolish ignorance overpower you. All things proceed from God and unto Him they return. He is the source of all things and in Him all things are ended.

145 Take heed that ye enter no house in the absence of its owner, except with his permission. Comport yourselves with propriety under all conditions, and be not numbered with the wayward. . . .

149 Recite ye the verses of God every morn and eventide. Whoso faileth to recite them hath not been faithful to the Covenant of God and His Testament, and whoso turneth away from these holy verses in this Day is of those who throughout eternity have turned away from God. Fear ye God, O My servants, one and all. Pride not yourselves on much reading of the verses or on a multitude of pious acts by night and day; for were a man to read a single verse with joy and radiance it would be better for him than to read with lassitude all the Holy Books of God, the Help in Peril, the Self-Subsisting. Read ye the sacred verses in such measure that ye be not overcome by languor and despondency. Lay not upon your souls that which will weary them and weigh them down, but rather what will lighten and uplift them, so that they may soar on the wings of the Divine verses towards the Dawning-place of His manifest signs; this will draw you nearer to God, did ye but comprehend. . . .

153 Should anyone wax angry with you, respond to him with gentleness; and should anyone upbraid you, forbear to upbraid

him in return, but leave him to himself and put your trust in God, the omnipotent Avenger, the Lord of might and justice.

154 Ye have been prohibited from making use of pulpits. Whoso wisheth to recite unto you the verses of his Lord, let him sit on a chair placed upon a dais, that he may make mention of God, his Lord, and the Lord of all mankind. It is pleasing to God that ye should seat yourselves on chairs and benches as a mark of honour for the love ye bear for Him and for the Manifestation of His glorious and resplendent Cause.

155 Gambling and the use of opium have been forbidden unto you. Eschew them both, O people, and be not of those who transgress. Beware of using any substance that induceth sluggishness and torpor in the human temple and inflicteth harm upon the body. We, verily, desire for you naught save what shall profit you, and to this bear witness all created things, had ye but ears to hear. . . .

158 Blessed is the one who discovereth the fragrance of inner meanings from the traces of this Pen through whose movement the breezes of God are wafted over the entire creation, and through whose stillness the very essence of tranquillity appeareth in the realm of being. Glorified be the All-Merciful, the Revealer of so inestimable a bounty. Say: Because He bore injustice, justice hath appeared on earth, and because He accepted abasement, the majesty of God hath shone forth amidst mankind.

159 It hath been forbidden you to carry arms unless essential, and permitted you to attire yourselves in silk. The Lord hath relieved you, as a bounty on His part, of the restrictions that formerly applied to clothing and to the trim of the beard. He, verily, is the Ordainer, the Omniscient. Let there be naught in your demeanour of which sound and upright minds would disapprove, and make not yourselves the playthings of the ignorant. Well is it with him who hath adorned himself with the vesture of seemly conduct and a praiseworthy character. He is assuredly reckoned with those who aid their Lord through

distinctive and outstanding deeds.

160 Promote ye the development of the cities of God and His countries, and glorify Him therein in the joyous accents of His well-favoured ones. In truth, the hearts of men are edified through the power of the tongue, even as houses and cities are built up by the hand and other means. We have assigned to every end a means for its accomplishment; avail yourselves thereof, and place your trust and confidence in God, the Omniscient, the All-Wise.

161 Blessed is the man that hath acknowledged his belief in God and in His signs, and recognized that "He shall not be asked of His doings". Such a recognition hath been made by God the ornament of every belief and its very foundation. Upon it must depend the acceptance of every goodly deed. Fasten your eyes upon it, that haply the whisperings of the rebellious may not cause you to slip.

162 Were He to decree as lawful the thing which from time immemorial had been forbidden, and forbid that which had, at all times, been regarded as lawful, to none is given the right to question His authority. Whoso will hesitate, though it be for less than a moment, should be regarded as a transgressor.

163 Whoso hath not recognized this sublime and fundamental verity, and hath failed to attain this most exalted station, the winds of doubt will agitate him, and the sayings of the infidels will distract his soul. He that hath acknowledged this principle will be endowed with the most perfect constancy. All honour to this all-glorious station, the remembrance of which adorneth every exalted Tablet. Such is the teaching which God bestoweth on you, a teaching that will deliver you from all manner of doubt and perplexity, and enable you to attain unto salvation in both this world and in the next. He, verily, is the Ever-Forgiving, the Most Bountiful. He it is Who hath sent forth the Messengers, and sent down the Books to proclaim "There is none other God but Me, the Almighty, the All-Wise". . . .

172 We, of a certainty, have had no purpose in this earthly realm save to make God manifest and to reveal His sovereignty; sufficient unto Me is God for a witness. We, of a certainty, have had no intent in the celestial Kingdom but to exalt His Cause and glorify His praise; sufficient unto Me is God for a protector. We, of a certainty, have had no desire in the Dominion on high except to extol God and what hath been sent down by Him; sufficient unto Me is God for a helper. . . .

181 The world's equilibrium hath been upset through the vibrating influence of this most great, this new World Order. Mankind's ordered life hath been revolutionized through the agency of this unique, this wondrous System—the like of which mortal eyes have never witnessed.

182 Immerse yourselves in the ocean of My words, that ye may unravel its secrets, and discover all the pearls of wisdom that lie hid in its depths. Take heed that ye do not vacillate in your determination to embrace the truth of this Cause—a Cause through which the potentialities of the might of God have been revealed, and His sovereignty established. With faces beaming with joy, hasten ye unto Him. This is the changeless Faith of God, eternal in the past, eternal in the future. Let him that seeketh, attain it; and as to him that hath refused to seek it—verily, God is Self-Sufficient, above any need of His creatures.

183 Say: This is the infallible Balance which the Hand of God is holding, in which all who are in the heavens and all who are on the earth are weighed, and their fate determined, if ye be of them that believe and recognize this truth. Say: This is the Most Great Testimony, by which the validity of every proof throughout the ages hath been established, would that ye might be assured thereof. Say: Through it the poor have been enriched, the learned enlightened, and the seekers enabled to ascend unto the presence of God. Beware lest ye make it a cause of dissension amongst you. Be ye as firmly settled as the immovable mountain in the Cause of your Lord, the Mighty, the Loving. . . .

189 O members of parliaments throughout the world! Select ye a single language for the use of all on earth, and adopt ye likewise a common script. God, verily, maketh plain for you that which shall profit you and enable you to be independent of others. He, of a truth, is the Most Bountiful, the All-Knowing, the All-Informed. This will be the cause of unity, could ye but comprehend it, and the greatest instrument for promoting harmony and civilization, would that ye might understand! We have appointed two signs for the coming of age of the human race: the first, which is the most firm foundation, We have set down in other of Our Tablets, while the second hath been revealed in this wondrous Book. . . .[30]

Notes

[28] Shoghi Effendi, *God Passes By*, p. 213.
[29] Ibid.
[30] Bahá'u'lláh, *The Kitáb-i-Aqdas*, pp. 19-88.

The Glad-Tidings (Bis͟hárát)

In his assessment of Bahá'u'lláh's writings during the 'Akká period, Shoghi Effendi writes: "The formulation by Bahá'u'lláh, in His Kitáb-i-Aqdas, *of the fundamental laws of His Dispensation was followed, as His Mission drew to a close, by the enunciation of certain precepts and principles which lie at the very core of His Faith, by the reaffirmation of truths He had previously proclaimed, by the elaboration and elucidation of some of the laws He had already laid down, by the revelation of further prophecies and warnings, and by the establishment of subsidiary ordinances designed to supplement the provisions of His* Most Holy Book. *These were recorded in unnumbered Tablets, which He continued to reveal until the last days of His earthly life, among which . . . the* Bis͟hárát (Glad Tidings) . . . *the* Lawḥ-i-Maqṣúd (Tablet of Maqṣúd), *are the most noteworthy. These Tablets—mighty and final effusions of His indefatigable pen—must rank among the choicest fruits which His mind has yielded, and mark the consummation of His forty-year-long ministry."*[31]

This is the Call of the All-Glorious which is proclaimed from the Supreme Horizon in the Prison of Akká

HE IS THE EXPOUNDER, THE ALL-KNOWING, THE ALL-INFORMED.

GOD, the True One, testifieth and the Revealers of His names and attributes bear witness that Our sole purpose in raising the Call and in proclaiming His sublime Word is that the ear of the entire creation may, through the living waters of divine utterance, be purged from lying tales and become attuned to the holy, the glorious and exalted Word which hath issued forth from the repository of the knowledge of the Maker of the Heavens and the Creator of Names. Happy are they that judge

with fairness.

O people of the earth!

The first Glad-Tidings which the Mother Book hath, in this Most Great Revelation, imparted unto all the peoples of the world is that the law of holy war hath been blotted out from the Book. Glorified be the All-Merciful, the Lord of grace abounding, through Whom the door of heavenly bounty hath been flung open in the face of all that are in heaven and on earth.

The second Glad-Tidings

It is permitted that the peoples and kindreds of the world associate with one another with joy and radiance. O people! Consort with the followers of all religions in a spirit of friendliness and fellowship. Thus hath the day-star of His sanction and authority shone forth above the horizon of the decree of God, the Lord of the worlds.

The third Glad-Tidings concerneth the study of divers languages. This decree hath formerly streamed forth from the Pen of the Most High: It behoveth the sovereigns of the world—may God assist them—or the ministers of the earth to take counsel together and to adopt one of the existing languages or a new one to be taught to children in schools throughout the world, and likewise one script. Thus the whole earth will come to be regarded as one country. Well is it with him who hearkeneth unto His Call and observeth that whereunto he is bidden by God, the Lord of the Mighty Throne.

The fourth Glad-Tidings

Should any of the kings—may God aid them—arise to protect and help this oppressed people, all must vie with one another in loving and in serving him. This matter is incumbent upon everyone. Well is it with them that act accordingly.

The fifth Glad-Tidings

In every country where any of this people reside, they must behave towards the government of that country with loyalty, honesty and truthfulness. This is that which hath been revealed at the behest of Him Who is the Ordainer, the Ancient of Days.

It is binding and incumbent upon the peoples of the world, one and all, to extend aid unto this momentous Cause which is come from the heaven of the Will of the ever-abiding God, that perchance the fire of animosity which blazeth in the hearts of some of the peoples of the earth may, through the living waters of divine wisdom and by virtue of heavenly counsels and exhortations, be quenched, and the light of unity and concord may shine forth and shed its radiance upon the world.

We cherish the hope that through the earnest endeavours of such as are the exponents of the power of God—exalted be His glory—the weapons of war throughout the world may be converted into instruments of reconstruction and that strife and conflict may be removed from the midst of men.

The sixth Glad-Tidings is the establishment of the Lesser Peace, details of which have formerly been revealed from Our Most Exalted Pen. Great is the blessedness of him who upholdeth it and observeth whatsoever hath been ordained by God, the All-Knowing, the All-Wise.

The seventh Glad-Tidings

The choice of clothing and the cut of the beard and its dressing are left to the discretion of men. But beware, O people, lest ye make yourselves the playthings of the ignorant.

The eighth Glad-Tidings

The pious deeds of the monks and priests among the followers of the Spirit[Jesus]—upon Him be the peace of God—are remembered in His presence. In this Day, however, let them give up the life of seclusion and direct their steps towards the open world and busy themselves with that which will profit themselves and others. We have granted them leave to enter

into wedlock that they may bring forth one who will make mention of God, the Lord of the seen and the unseen, the Lord of the Exalted Throne.

The ninth Glad-Tidings

When the sinner findeth himself wholly detached and freed from all save God, he should beg forgiveness and pardon from Him. Confession of sins and transgressions before human beings is not permissible, as it hath never been nor will ever be conducive to divine forgiveness. Moreover such confession before people results in one's humiliation and abasement, and God—exalted be His glory—wisheth not the humiliation of His servants. Verily He is the Compassionate, the Merciful. The sinner should, between himself and God, implore mercy from the Ocean of mercy, beg forgiveness from the Heaven of generosity and say:

O God, my God! I implore Thee by the blood of Thy true lovers who were so enraptured by Thy sweet utterance that they hastened unto the Pinnacle of Glory, the site of the most glorious martyrdom, and I beseech Thee by the mysteries which lie enshrined in Thy knowledge and by the pearls that are treasured in the ocean of Thy bounty to grant forgiveness unto me and unto my father and my mother. Of those who show forth mercy, Thou art in truth the Most Merciful. No God is there but Thee, the Ever-Forgiving, the All-Bountiful.

O Lord! Thou seest this essence of sinfulness turning unto the ocean of Thy favour and this feeble one seeking the kingdom of Thy divine power and this poor creature inclining himself towards the day-star of Thy wealth. By Thy mercy and Thy grace, disappoint him not, O Lord, nor debar him from the revelations of Thy bounty in Thy days, nor cast him away from Thy door which Thou hast opened wide to all that dwell in Thy heaven and on Thine earth.

Alas! Alas! My sins have prevented me from approaching the Court of Thy holiness and my trespasses have caused me to

stray far from the Tabernacle of Thy majesty. I have committed that which Thou didst forbid me to do and have put away what Thou didst order me to observe.

I pray Thee by Him Who is the sovereign Lord of Names to write down for me with the Pen of Thy bounty that which will enable me to draw nigh unto Thee and will purge me from my trespasses which have intervened between me and Thy forgiveness and Thy pardon.

Verily, Thou art the Potent, the Bountiful. No God is there but Thee, the Mighty, the Gracious.

The tenth Glad-Tidings

As a token of grace from God, the Revealer of this Most Great Announcement, We have removed from the Holy Scriptures and Tablets the law prescribing the destruction of books.

The eleventh Glad-Tidings

It is permissible to study sciences and arts, but such sciences as are useful and would redound to the progress and advancement of the people. Thus hath it been decreed by Him Who is the Ordainer, the All-Wise.

The twelfth Glad-Tidings

It is enjoined upon every one of you to engage in some form of occupation, such as crafts, trades and the like. We have graciously exalted your engagement in such work to the rank of worship unto God, the True One. Ponder ye in your hearts the grace and the blessings of God and render thanks unto Him at eventide and at dawn. Waste not your time in idleness and sloth. Occupy yourselves with that which profiteth yourselves and others. Thus hath it been decreed in this Tablet from whose horizon the day-star of wisdom and utterance shineth resplendent.

The most despised of men in the sight of God are those who sit idly and beg. Hold ye fast unto the cord of material means,

placing your whole trust in God, the Provider of all means. When anyone occupieth himself in a craft or trade, such occupation itself is regarded in the estimation of God as an act of worship; and this is naught but a token of His infinite and all-pervasive bounty.

The thirteenth Glad-Tidings

The men of God's House of Justice have been charged with the affairs of the people. They, in truth, are the Trustees of God among His servants and the daysprings of authority in His countries.

O people of God! That which traineth the world is Justice, for it is upheld by two pillars, reward and punishment. These two pillars are the sources of life to the world. Inasmuch as for each day there is a new problem and for every problem an expedient solution, such affairs should be referred to the Ministers of the House of Justice that they may act according to the needs and requirements of the time. They that, for the sake of God, arise to serve His Cause, are the recipients of divine inspiration from the unseen Kingdom. It is incumbent upon all to be obedient unto them. All matters of State should be referred to the House of Justice, but acts of worship must be observed according to that which God hath revealed in His Book.

O people of Bahá! Ye are the dawning-places of the love of God and the daysprings of His loving-kindness. Defile not your tongues with the cursing and reviling of any soul, and guard your eyes against that which is not seemly. Set forth that which ye possess. If it be favourably received, your end is attained; if not, to protest is vain. Leave that soul to himself and turn unto the Lord, the Protector, the Self-Subsisting. Be not the cause of grief, much less of discord and strife. The hope is cherished that ye may obtain true education in the shelter of the tree of His tender mercies and act in accordance with that which God desireth. Ye are all the leaves of one tree and the drops of one ocean.

The fourteenth Glad-Tidings

It is not necessary to undertake special journeys to visit the resting-places of the dead. If people of substance and affluence offer the cost of such journeys to the House of Justice, it will be pleasing and acceptable in the presence of God. Happy are they that observe His precepts.

The fifteenth Glad-Tidings

Although a republican form of government profiteth all the peoples of the world, yet the majesty of kingship is one of the signs of God. We do not wish that the countries of the world should remain deprived thereof. If the sagacious combine the two forms into one, great will be their reward in the presence of God.

In former religions such ordinances as holy war, destruction of books, the ban on association and companionship with other peoples or on reading certain books had been laid down and affirmed according to the exigencies of the time; however, in this mighty Revelation, in this momentous Announcement, the manifold bestowals and favours of God have overshadowed all men, and from the horizon of the Will of the Ever-Abiding Lord, His infallible decree hath prescribed that which We have set forth above.

We yield praise unto God—hallowed and glorified be He—for whatsoever He hath graciously revealed in this blessed, this glorious and incomparable Day. Indeed if everyone on earth were endowed with a myriad tongues and were to continually praise God and magnify His Name to the end that knoweth no end, their thanksgiving would not prove adequate for even one of the gracious favours We have mentioned in this Tablet. Unto this beareth witness every man of wisdom and discernment, of understanding and knowledge.

We earnestly beseech God—exalted be His glory—to aid the rulers and sovereigns, who are the exponents of power and the daysprings of glory, to enforce His laws and ordinances. He is

in truth the Omnipotent, the All-Powerful, He Who is wont to answer the call of men.[32]

Notes

[31] Shoghi Effendi, *God Passes By*, p. 216.
[32] Bahá'u'lláh, *Tablet of Bahá'u'lláh revealed after the Kitáb-i-Aqdas*, pp. 21-29.

The Tablet of Maqṣúd (Lawḥ-i-Maqṣúd)

According to the colophon of the original manuscript, Bahá'u'lláh dictated this work on the 20th of January 1882.[33] *The Tablet was apparently written in response to two letters received by Bahá'u'lláh from one of His followers by the name of Mírzá Maqṣúd who was at that time residing in Damascus and Jerusalem.* The Lawḥ-i-Maqṣúd *is among those writings of Bahá'u'lláh that Shoghi Effendi has referred to as His "most noteworthy" works written after His* Most Holy Book (The Kitáb-i-Aqdas) *and prior to the end of His life.*

HE IS GOD, EXALTED IS HE,
THE LORD OF MAJESTY AND POWER

A PRAISE which is exalted above every mention or description beseemeth the Adored One, the Possessor of all things visible and invisible, Who hath enabled the Primal Point to reveal countless Books and Epistles and Who, through the potency of His sublime Word, hath called into being the entire creation, whether of the former or more recent generations. Moreover He hath in every age and cycle, in conformity with His transcendent wisdom, sent forth a divine Messenger to revive the dispirited and despondent souls with the living waters of His utterance, One Who is indeed the Expounder, the true Interpreter, inasmuch as man is unable to comprehend that which hath streamed forth from the Pen of Glory and is recorded in His heavenly Books. Men at all times and under all conditions stand in need of one to exhort them, guide them and to instruct and teach them. Therefore He hath sent forth His Messengers, His Prophets and chosen ones that they might acquaint the people with the divine purpose underlying the revelation of Books and the raising up of Messengers, and that everyone may become aware of the trust of God which is latent

in the reality of every soul.

Man is the supreme Talisman. Lack of a proper education hath, however, deprived him of that which he doth inherently possess. Through a word proceeding out of the mouth of God he was called into being; by one word more he was guided to recognize the Source of his education; by yet another word his station and destiny were safeguarded. The Great Being saith: Regard man as a mine rich in gems of inestimable value. Education can, alone, cause it to reveal its treasures, and enable mankind to benefit therefrom. If any man were to meditate on that which the Scriptures, sent down from the heaven of God's holy Will, have revealed, he would readily recognize that their purpose is that all men shall be regarded as one soul, so that the seal bearing the words 'The Kingdom shall be God's' may be stamped on every heart, and the light of Divine bounty, of grace, and mercy may envelop all mankind. The One true God, exalted be His glory, hath wished nothing for Himself. The allegiance of mankind profiteth Him not, neither doth its perversity harm Him. The Bird of the Realm of Utterance voiceth continually this call: 'All things have I willed for thee, and thee, too, for thine own sake.' If the learned and worldly-wise men of this age were to allow mankind to inhale the fragrance of fellowship and love, every understanding heart would apprehend the meaning of true liberty, and discover the secret of undisturbed peace and absolute composure. Were the earth to attain this station and be illumined with its light it could then be truly said of it: 'Thou shall see in it no hollows or rising hills.'[34]. . .

Behold the disturbances which, for many a long year, have afflicted the earth, and the perturbation that hath seized its peoples. It hath either been ravaged by war, or tormented by sudden and unforeseen calamities. Though the world is encompassed with misery and distress, yet no man hath paused to reflect what the cause or source of that may be. Whenever the True Counsellor uttered a word in admonishment, lo, they all denounced Him as a mover of mischief and rejected His claim. How bewildering, how confusing is such behavior! No

two men can be found who may be said to be outwardly and inwardly united. The evidences of discord and malice are apparent everywhere, though all were made for harmony and union. The Great Being saith: O well-beloved ones! The tabernacle of unity hath been raised; regard ye not one another as strangers. Ye are the fruits of one tree, and the leaves of one branch. We cherish the hope that the light of justice may shine upon the world and sanctify it from tyranny. If the rulers and kings of the earth, the symbols of the power of God, exalted be His glory, arise and resolve to dedicate themselves to whatever will promote the highest interests of the whole of humanity, the reign of justice will assuredly be established amongst the children of men, and the effulgence of its light will envelop the whole earth. The Great Being saith: The structure of world stability and order hath been reared upon, and will continue to be sustained by, the twin pillars of reward and punishment.... In another passage He hath written: Take heed, O concourse of the rulers of the world! There is no force on earth that can equal in its conquering power the force of justice and wisdom.... Blessed is the king who marcheth with the ensign of wisdom unfurled before him, and the battalions of justice massed in his rear. He verily is the ornament that adorneth the brow of peace and the countenance of security. There can be no doubt whatever that if the day star of justice, which the clouds of tyranny have obscured, were to shed its light upon men, the face of the earth would be completely transformed. . . .

The Great Being, wishing to reveal the prerequisites of the peace and tranquillity of the world and the advancement of its peoples, hath written: The time must come when the imperative necessity for the holding of a vast, an all-embracing assemblage of men will be universally realized. The rulers and kings of the earth must needs attend it, and, participating in its deliberations, must consider such ways and means as will lay the foundations of the world's Great Peace amongst men. Such a peace demandeth that the Great Powers should resolve, for

the sake of the tranquillity of the peoples of the earth, to be fully reconciled among themselves. Should any king take up arms against another, all should unitedly arise and prevent him. If this be done, the nations of the world will no longer require any armaments, except for the purpose of preserving the security of their realms and of maintaining internal order within their territories. This will ensure the peace and composure of every people, government and nation. We fain would hope that the kings and rulers of the earth, the mirrors of the gracious and almighty name of God, may attain unto this station, and shield mankind from the onslaught of tyranny. ...The day is approaching when all the peoples of the world will have adopted one universal language and one common script. When this is achieved, to whatsoever city a man may journey, it shall be as if he were entering his own home. These things are obligatory and absolutely essential. It is incumbent upon every man of insight and understanding to strive to translate that which hath been written into reality and action.... That one indeed is a man who, today, dedicateth himself to the service of the entire human race. The Great Being saith: Blessed and happy is he that ariseth to promote the best interests of the peoples and kindreds of the earth. In another passage He hath proclaimed: It is not for him to pride himself who loveth his own country, but rather for him who loveth the whole world. The earth is but one country, and mankind its citizens. . . .

The Great Being saith: O ye children of men! The fundamental purpose animating the Faith of God and His Religion is to safeguard the interests and promote the unity of the human race, and to foster the spirit of love and fellowship amongst men. Suffer it not to become a source of dissension and discord, of hate and enmity. This is the straight Path, the fixed and immovable foundation. Whatsoever is raised on this foundation, the changes and chances of the world can never impair its strength, nor will the revolution of countless centuries undermine its structure. Our hope is that the world's religious leaders and the rulers thereof will unitedly arise for the

reformation of this age and the rehabilitation of its fortunes. Let them, after meditating on its needs, take counsel together and, through anxious and full deliberation, administer to a diseased and sorely-afflicted world the remedy it requireth....

It is incumbent upon them who are in authority to exercise moderation in all things. Whatsoever passeth beyond the limits of moderation will cease to exert a beneficial influence. Consider for instance such things as liberty, civilization and the like. However much men of understanding may favorably regard them, they will, if carried to excess, exercise a pernicious influence upon men. . . . Please God, the peoples of the world may be led, as the result of the high endeavors exerted by their rulers and the wise and learned amongst men, to recognize their best interests. How long will humanity persist in its waywardness? How long will injustice continue? How long is chaos and confusion to reign amongst men? How long will discord agitate the face of society?. . . The winds of despair are, alas, blowing from every direction, and the strife that divideth and afflicteth the human race is daily increasing. The signs of impending convulsions and chaos can now be discerned, inasmuch as the prevailing order appeareth to be lamentably defective. I beseech God, exalted be His glory, that He may graciously awaken the peoples of the earth, may grant that the end of their conduct may be profitable unto them, and aid them to accomplish that which beseemeth their station. . . .[35]

Notes

[33] From a memorandum of the Research Department of the Universal House of Justice dated 1 May 2001 posted on http://bahai-library.com/index.php5?file=wilmette_lawh_maqsud_notes.

[34]Qur'án 20:106

[35] Bahá'u'lláh, *Tablet of Bahá'u'lláh revealed after the Kitáb-i-Aqdas*, pp. 161-72.

Epistle to the Son of the Wolf *(Lawḥ-i-Ibn-i-Dhi'b)*

This monumental book was penned by Bahá'u'lláh in the first half of 1891, about one year before He passed away. It is addressed to Shaykh Muḥammad-Taqí-i-Najafí, known as Áqá Najafí, a powerful Shí'a-Muslim priest from the city of Iṣfahán. For decades Áqá Najafí and his father, Shaykh Muḥammad-Báqir, also a high-ranking cleric whom Bahá'u'lláh denounced as "the Wolf" of His flock, tyrannized the members of the Bahá'í community in Iran through vicious and unrelenting attacks. In this weighty Epistle Bahá'u'lláh calls upon the notorious clergyman "to repent of his acts, quotes some of the most characteristic and celebrated passages of His own writings, and adduces proofs establishing the validity of His Cause."[36]

IN THE NAME OF GOD, THE ONE,
THE INCOMPARABLE, THE ALL-POWERFUL,
THE ALL-KNOWING, THE ALL-WISE.

Praise be to God, the Eternal that perisheth not, the Everlasting that declineth not, the Self-Subsisting that altereth not. He it is Who is transcendent in His sovereignty, Who is manifest through His signs, and is hidden through His mysteries. He it is at Whose bidding the standard of the Most Exalted Word hath been lifted up in the world of creation, and the banner of "He doeth whatsoever He willeth" raised amidst all peoples. He it is Who hath revealed His Cause for the guidance of His creatures, and sent down His verses to demonstrate His Proof and His Testimony, and embellished the preface of the Book of Man with the ornament of utterance through His saying: "The God of Mercy hath taught the Qur'án, hath created man, and taught him articulate speech." No God is there but Him, the One, the Peerless, the Powerful, the Mighty, the Beneficent.

The light that is shed from the heaven of bounty, and the benediction that shineth from the dawning-place of the will of God, the Lord of the Kingdom of Names, rest upon Him Who is the Supreme Mediator, the Most Exalted Pen, Him Whom God hath made the Dawning-Place of His most excellent names and the Dayspring of His most exalted attributes. Through Him the light of unity hath shone forth above the horizon of the world, and the law of oneness hath been revealed amidst the nations, who, with radiant faces, have turned towards the Supreme Horizon, and acknowledged that which the Tongue of Utterance hath spoken in the kingdom of His knowledge: "Earth and heaven, glory and dominion, are God's, the Omnipotent, the Almighty, the Lord of grace abounding!"

Give ear, O distinguished divine, unto the voice of this Wronged One. He verily, counselleth thee for the sake of God, and exhorteth thee unto that which will cause thee to draw nigh unto Him under all conditions. He, in truth, is the All-Possessing, the Exalted. Know thou that the ear of man hath been created that it may hearken unto the Divine Voice on this Day that hath been mentioned in all the Books, Scriptures, and Tablets. Purify thou, first, thy soul with the waters of renunciation, and adorn thine head with the crown of the fear of God, and thy temple with the ornament of reliance upon Him. Arise, then, and, with thy face set towards the Most Great House, the Spot round which, as decreed by the Eternal King, all that dwell on earth must circle, recite:

"O God, my God, and my Desire, and my Adored One, and my Master, and my Mainstay, and my utmost Hope, and my supreme Aspiration! Thou seest me turning towards Thee, holding fast unto the cord of Thy bounty, clinging to the hem of Thy generosity, acknowledging the sanctity of Thy Self and the purity of Thine Essence, and testifying to Thy unity and Thy oneness. I bear witness that Thou art the One, the Single, the Incomparable, the Ever-Abiding. Thou didst not take unto Thyself a partner in Thy dominion, nor didst Thou choose a peer for Thyself upon earth. All created things have borne

witness unto that which the Tongue of Thy grandeur hath testified ere their creation. Verily Thou art God; there is none other God but Thee! From everlasting Thou wast sanctified from the mention of Thy servants, and exalted above the description of Thy creatures. Thou beholdest, O Lord, the ignorant seeking the ocean of Thy knowledge, the sore athirst the living waters of Thine utterance, the abased the tabernacle of Thy glory, the poor the treasury of Thy riches, the suppliant the dawning-place of Thy wisdom, the weak the source of Thy strength, the wretched the heaven of Thy bounty, the dumb the kingdom of Thy mention.

"I testify, O my God, and my King, that Thou hast created me to remember Thee, to glorify Thee, and to aid Thy Cause. And yet, I have aided Thine enemies, who have broken Thy Covenant, who have cast away Thy Book, disbelieved in Thee, and repudiated Thy signs. Alas, alas, for my waywardness, and my shame, and my sinfulness, and my wrong-doing that have withheld me from the depths of the ocean of Thy unity and from fathoming the sea of Thy mercy. Wherefore, alas, alas! and again alas, alas! for my wretchedness and the grievousness of my transgressions! Thou didst call me into being, O my God, to exalt Thy Word, and to manifest Thy Cause. My heedlessness, however, hath deterred me and compassed me about, in such wise that I have arisen to blot out Thy signs, and to shed the blood of Thy loved ones, and of the dawning-places of Thy signs, and of the daysprings of Thy revelation, and of the repositories of Thy mysteries.

"O Lord, my Lord! and again, O Lord, my Lord! and yet again, O Lord, my Lord! I bear witness that by reason of mine iniquity the fruits of the tree of Thy justice have fallen, and through the fire of my rebelliousness the hearts of such of Thy creatures as enjoy near access to Thee were consumed, and the souls of the sincere among Thy servants have melted. O wretched, wretched that I am! O the cruelties, the glaring cruelties, I inflicted! Woe is me, woe is me, for my remoteness from Thee, and for my waywardness, and mine ignorance, and my

baseness, and my repudiation of Thee, and my protests against Thee! How many the days during which Thou didst bid Thy servants and Thy loved ones to protect me, whilst I commanded them to harm Thee and to harm them that Thou didst trust! And how numerous the nights during which Thou didst graciously remember me, and didst show me Thy path, whilst I turned away from Thee and from Thy signs! By Thy glory! O Thou Who art the Hope of such as have acknowledged Thy unity, and the Desire of the hearts of them that are rid of all attachment to any save Thee! I find no succorer except Thee, nor king, nor refuge, nor haven besides Thyself. Alas, alas! My turning away from Thee hath burnt up the veil of mine integrity, and my denial of Thee hath rent asunder the covering cast over mine honor. O would that I were beneath the depths of the earth, so that my evil deeds would remain unknown to Thy servants! Thou seest the sinner, O my Lord, who hath turned towards the dawning-place of Thy forgiveness and Thy bounty, and the mountain of iniquity that hath sought the heaven of Thy mercy and pardon. Alas, alas! My mighty sins have prevented me from approaching the court of Thy mercy, and my monstrous deeds have caused me to stray far from the sanctuary of Thy presence. Indeed, I am he that hath failed in duty towards Thee, and hath broken Thy Covenant and Thy Testament, and committed that which hath made the dwellers of the cities of Thy justice, and the dawning-places of Thy grace in Thy realms, to lament. I testify, O my God, that I have put away Thy commandments, and clung to the dictates of my passions, and have cast away the statutes of Thy Book, and seized the book of mine own desire. O misery, misery! As mine iniquities waxed greater and greater, Thy forbearance towards me augmented, and as the fire of my rebelliousness grew fiercer, the more did Thy forgiveness and Thy grace seek to smother up its flame. By the power of Thy might! O Thou Who art the desire of the world and the Best-Beloved of the nations! Thy long-suffering hath puffed me up, and Thy patience hath emboldened me. Thou beholdest, O my God, the tears that my shame hath caused to flow, and the sighs which my

heedlessness hath led me to utter. I swear by the greatness of Thy majesty! I can find for myself no habitation save beneath the shadow of the court of Thy bounty, nor any refuge except under the canopy of Thy mercy. Thou seest me in the midst of a sea of despair and of hopelessness, after Thou didst cause me to hear Thy words "Despair not." By Thy power! My sore injustice hath severed the cord of my hope, and my rebellion hath darkened my face before the throne of Thy justice. Thou beholdest, O my God, him who is as one dead fallen at the door of Thy favor, ashamed to seek from the hand of Thy loving-kindness the living waters of Thy pardon. Thou hast given me a tongue wherewith to remember and praise Thee, and yet it uttereth that which hath caused the souls of such of Thy chosen ones as are nigh unto Thee to melt, and the hearts of the sincere amongst the dwellers of the habitations of holiness to be consumed. Thou hast given me eyes to witness Thy signs, and to behold Thy verses, and to contemplate the revelations of Thine handiwork, but I have rejected Thy will, and have committed what hath caused the faithful among Thy creatures and the detached amidst Thy servants to groan. Thou hast given me ears that I may incline them unto Thy praise and Thy celebration, and unto that which Thou didst send down from the heaven of Thy bounty and the firmament of Thy will. And yet, alas, alas, I have forsaken Thy Cause, and have commanded Thy servants to blaspheme against Thy trusted ones and Thy loved ones, and have acted, before the throne of Thy justice, in such wise that those that have recognized Thy unity and are wholly devoted to Thee among the dwellers of Thy realm mourned with a sore lamentation. I know not, O my God, which among my evildoings to mention before the billowing ocean of Thy favor, nor which of my trespasses to declare when face to face with the splendors of the suns of Thy goodly gifts and bounties. . . .

O Shaykh! Know thou that neither the calumnies which men may utter, nor their denials, nor any cavils they may raise, can harm him that hath clung to the cord of the grace, and

seized the hem of the mercy, of the Lord of creation. By God! He, the Glory of God (Bahá), hath spoken not from mere impulse. He that hath given Him a voice is He that hath given a voice unto all things, that they may praise and glorify Him. There is none other God but Him, the One, the Incomparable, the Lord of strength, the Unconditioned. . . .

We beseech God to aid thee to be just and fair-minded, and to acquaint thee with the things that were hidden from the eyes of men. He, in truth, is the Mighty, the Unconstrained. We ask thee to reflect upon that which hath been revealed, and to be fair and just in thy speech, that perchance the splendors of the daystar of truthfulness and sincerity may shine forth, and may deliver thee from the darkness of ignorance, and illumine the world with the light of knowledge. This Wronged One hath frequented no school, neither hath He attended the controversies of the learned. By My life! Not of Mine own volition have I revealed Myself, but God, of His own choosing, hath manifested Me. In the Tablet, addressed to His Majesty the Sháh—may God, blessed and glorified be He, assist him—these words have streamed from the tongue of this Wronged One:

"O King! I was but a man like others, asleep upon My couch, when lo, the breezes of the All-Glorious were wafted over Me, and taught Me the knowledge of all that hath been. This thing is not from Me, but from One Who is Almighty and All-Knowing. And He bade Me lift up My voice between earth and heaven, and for this there befell Me what hath caused the tears of every man of understanding to flow. The learning current amongst men I studied not; their schools I entered not. Ask of the city wherein I dwelt, that thou mayest be well assured that I am not of them who speak falsely. This is but a leaf which the winds of the will of thy Lord, the Almighty, the All-Praised, have stirred. Can it be still when the tempestuous winds are blowing? Nay, by Him Who is the Lord of all Names and Attributes! They move it as they list. The evanescent is as nothing before Him Who is the Ever-Abiding. His all-compelling

summons hath reached Me, and caused Me to speak His praise amidst all people. I was indeed as one dead when His behest was uttered. The hand of the will of thy Lord, the Compassionate, the Merciful, transformed Me."

Now is the moment in which to cleanse thyself with the waters of detachment that have flowed out from the Supreme Pen, and to ponder, wholly for the sake of God, those things which, time and again, have been sent down or manifested, and then to strive, as much as lieth in thee, to quench, through the power of wisdom and the force of thy utterance, the fire of enmity and hatred which smouldereth in the hearts of the peoples of the world. The Divine Messengers have been sent down, and their Books were revealed, for the purpose of promoting the knowledge of God, and of furthering unity and fellowship amongst men. But now behold, how they have made the Law of God a cause and pretext for perversity and hatred. How pitiful, how regrettable, that most men are cleaving fast to, and have busied themselves with, the things they possess, and are unaware of, and shut out as by a veil from, the things God possesseth! . . .

Justice and equity are twin Guardians that watch over men. From them are revealed such blessed and perspicuous words as are the cause of the well-being of the world and the protection of the nations.

These words have streamed from the pen of this Wronged One in one of His Tablets: "The purpose of the one true God, exalted be His glory, hath been to bring forth the Mystic Gems out of the mine of man—they Who are the Dawning-Places of His Cause and the Repositories of the pearls of His knowledge; for, God Himself, glorified be He, is the Unseen, the One concealed and hidden from the eyes of men. Consider what the Merciful hath revealed in the Qur'án: No vision taketh in Him, but He taketh in all vision, and He is the Subtile, the All-Informed!"

That the divers communions of the earth, and the manifold

systems of religious belief, should never be allowed to foster the feelings of animosity among men, is, in this Day, of the essence of the Faith of God and His Religion. These principles and laws, these firmly-established and mighty systems, have proceeded from one Source, and are rays of one Light. That they differ one from another is to be attributed to the varying requirements of the ages in which they were promulgated. . . .

This Day, O Shaykh, hath never been, nor is it now, the Day whereon man-made arts and sciences can be regarded as a true standard for men, since it hath been recognized that He Who was wholly unversed in any of them hath ascended the throne of purest gold, and occupied the seat of honor in the council of knowledge, whilst the acknowledged exponent and repository of these arts and sciences remained utterly deprived. By "arts and sciences" is meant those which begin with words and end with words. Such arts and sciences, however, as are productive of good results, and bring forth their fruit, and are conducive to the well-being and tranquility of men have been, and will remain, acceptable before God. Wert thou to give ear to My voice, thou wouldst cast away all thy possessions, and wouldst set thy face towards the Spot wherein the ocean of wisdom and of utterance hath surged, and the sweet savors of the loving-kindness of thy Lord, the Compassionate, have wafted. . . .

In these days enemies have compassed Us about, and the fire of hatred is kindled. O peoples of the earth! By My life and by your own! This Wronged One hath never had, nor hath He now any desire for leadership. Mine aim hath ever been, and still is, to suppress whatever is the cause of contention amidst the peoples of the earth, and of separation amongst the nations, so that all men may be sanctified from every earthly attachment, and be set free to occupy themselves with their own interests. We entreat Our loved ones not to besmirch the hem of Our raiment with the dust of falsehood, neither to allow references to what they have regarded as miracles and prodigies to debase Our rank and station, or to mar the purity and sanctity of Our name.

Gracious God! This is the day whereon the wise should seek the advice of this Wronged One, and ask Him Who is the Truth what things are conducive to the glory and tranquillity of men. And yet, all are earnestly striving to put out this glorious and shining light, and are diligently seeking either to establish Our guilt, or to voice their protest against Us. Matters have come to such a pass, that the conduct of this Wronged One hath, in every way, been grossly misrepresented, and in a manner which it would be unseemly to mention. One of Our friends hath reported that among the residents of the Great City (Constantinople) he had heard with the greatest regret someone state that, each year, a sum of fifty thousand tumans was being despatched from his native land to Akká! It hath not, however, been made clear who had disbursed the sum, nor through whose hands it had passed!

Briefly, this Wronged One hath, in the face of all that hath befallen Him at their hands, and all that hath been said of Him, endured patiently, and held His peace, inasmuch as it is Our purpose, through the loving providence of God—exalted be His glory—and His surpassing mercy, to abolish, through the force of Our utterance, all disputes, war, and bloodshed, from the face of the earth. Under all conditions We have, in spite of what they have said, endured with seemly patience, and have left them to God. In answer to this particular imputation, however, We have replied, that if that which he affirmeth be true, it behooveth him to be thankful to Him Who is the Lord of all being, and the King of the seen and unseen, for having raised up in Persia One Who, though a prisoner and with none to help and assist Him, hath succeeded in establishing His ascendency over that land, and in drawing from it a yearly revenue. Such an achievement should be praised rather than censured, if he be of them that judge equitably. Should anyone seek to be acquainted with the condition of this Wronged One, let him be told that these captives whom the world hath persecuted and the nations wronged have, for days and nights, been entirely denied the

barest means of subsistence. We are loth to mention such things, neither have We had, nor do We have now, any desire to complain against Our accuser. Within the walls of this prison a highly esteemed man was for some time obliged to break stones that he might earn a living, whilst others had, at times, to nourish themselves with that Divine sustenance which is hunger! We entreat God—exalted and glorified be He—to aid all men to be just and fair-minded, and to graciously assist them to repent and return unto Him. He, verily, heareth, and is ready to answer. . . .

Either thou or someone else hath said: "Let the Súrih of Tawḥíd be translated, so that all may know and be fully persuaded that the one true God begetteth not, nor is He begotten. Moreover, the Bábís believe in his (Bahá'u'lláh's) Divinity and Godhood."

O Shaykh! This station is the station in which one dieth to himself and liveth in God. Divinity, whenever I mention it, indicateth My complete and absolute self-effacement. This is the station in which I have no control over mine own weal or woe nor over my life nor over my resurrection. . . .

Men have failed to perceive Our purpose in the references We have made to Divinity and Godhood. Were they to apprehend it, they would arise from their places, and cry out: "We, verily, ask pardon of God!" The Seal of the Prophets—may the souls of all else but Him be offered up for His sake—saith: "Manifold are Our relationships with God. At one time, We are He Himself, and He is We Ourself. At another He is that He is, and We are that We are."

Aside from this, why is it that thou didst not mention those other stations which the Abhá Pen hath disclosed? The tongue of this Wronged One hath, many a day and night, given utterance to these sublime words: "O God, my God! I bear witness to Thy unity and Thy oneness, and that Thou art God, and that there is none other God but Thee. Thou hast everlastingly been sanctified above the mention of any one but

Thee and the praise of all else except Thyself, and Thou wilt everlastingly continue to be the same as Thou wast from the beginning and hast ever been. I beseech Thee, O King of Eternity, by the Most Great Name, and by the effulgences of the Daystar of Thy Revelation upon the Sinai of Utterance, and by the billows of the Ocean of Thy knowledge among all created things, to graciously assist Me in that which will draw Me nigh unto Thee, and will detach Me from all except Thee. By Thy glory, O Lord of all being, and the Desire of all creation! I would love to lay My face upon every single spot of Thine earth, that perchance it might be honored by touching a spot ennobled by the footsteps of Thy loved ones!"

By the righteousness of God! Idle fancies have debarred men from the Horizon of Certitude, and vain imaginings withheld them from the Choice Sealed Wine. In truth I say, and for the sake of God I declare: This Servant, this Wronged One, is abashed to claim for Himself any existence whatever, how much more those exalted grades of being! Every man of discernment, while walking upon the earth, feeleth indeed abashed, inasmuch as he is fully aware that the thing which is the source of his prosperity, his wealth, his might, his exaltation, his advancement and power is, as ordained by God, the very earth which is trodden beneath the feet of all men. There can be no doubt that whoever is cognizant of this truth, is cleansed and sanctified from all pride, arrogance, and vainglory. Whatever hath been said hath come from God. Unto this, He, verily, hath borne, and beareth now, witness, and He, in truth, is the All-Knowing, the All-Informed. . . .

O Shaykh! My Pen is abashed to recount what actually took place. In the land of Ṣád (Iṣfahán) the fire of tyranny burned with such a hot flame that every fair-minded person groaned aloud. By thy life! The cities of knowledge and of understanding wept with such a weeping that the souls of the pious and of the God-fearing were melted. The twin shining lights, Ḥasan and Ḥusayn (The King of Martyrs and the Beloved of Martyrs) offered up spontaneously their lives in that city. Neither

fortune, nor wealth, nor glory, could deter them! God knoweth the things which befell them and yet the people are, for the most part, unaware!

Before them one named Káẓim and they who were with him, and after them, his honor Ashraf, all quaffed the draught of martyrdom with the utmost fervor and longing, and hastened unto the Supreme Companion. In like manner, at the time of Sardár Azíz Khán, that godly man, Mírzá Muṣṭafá, and his fellow martyrs, were arrested, and despatched unto the Supreme Friend in the All-Glorious Horizon. Briefly, in every city the evidences of a tyranny, beyond like or equal, were unmistakably clear and manifest, and yet none arose in self-defence! Call thou to mind his honor Badí, who was the bearer of the Tablet to His Majesty the Sháh, and reflect how he laid down his life. That knight, who spurred on his charger in the arena of renunciation, threw down the precious crown of life for the sake of Him Who is the Incomparable Friend.

O Shaykh! If things such as these are to be denied, what shall, then, be deemed worthy of credence? Set forth the truth, for the sake of God, and be not of them that hold their peace. They arrested his honor Najaf-'Alí, who hastened, with rapture and great longing, unto the field of martyrdom, uttering these words: "We have kept both Bahá and the khún-bahá (bloodmoney)!" With these words he yielded up his spirit. Meditate on the splendor and glory which the light of renunciation, shining from the upper chamber of the heart of Mullá 'Alí-Ján, hath shed. He was so carried away by the breezes of the Most Sublime Word and by the power of the Pen of Glory that to him the field of martyrdom equalled, nay outrivalled, the haunts of earthly delights. Ponder upon the conduct of 'Abá-Báṣir and Siyyid Ashraf-i-Zanjání. They sent for the mother of Ashraf to dissuade her son from his purpose. But she spurred him on until he suffered a most glorious martyrdom.

O Shaykh! This people have passed beyond the narrow straits

of names, and pitched their tents upon the shores of the sea of renunciation. They would willingly lay down a myriad lives, rather than breathe the word desired by their enemies. They have clung to that which pleaseth God, and are wholly detached and freed from the things which pertain unto men. They have preferred to have their heads cut off rather than utter one unseemly word. Ponder this in thine heart. Methinks they have quaffed their fill of the ocean of renunciation. The life of the present world hath failed to withhold them from suffering martyrdom in the path of God.

In Mázindarán a vast number of the servants of God were exterminated. The Governor, under the influence of calumniators, robbed a great many of all that they possessed. Among the charges he laid against them was that they had been laying up arms, whereas upon investigation it was found out that they had nothing but an unloaded rifle! Gracious God! This people need no weapons of destruction, inasmuch as they have girded themselves to reconstruct the world. Their hosts are the hosts of goodly deeds, and their arms the arms of upright conduct, and their commander the fear of God. Blessed that one that judgeth with fairness. By the righteousness of God! Such hath been the patience, the calm, the resignation and contentment of this people that they have become the exponents of justice, and so great hath been their forbearance, that they have suffered themselves to be killed rather than kill, and this notwithstanding that these whom the world hath wronged have endured tribulations the like of which the history of the world hath never recorded, nor the eyes of any nation witnessed. What is it that could have induced them to reconcile themselves to these grievous trials, and to refuse to put forth a hand to repel them? What could have caused such resignation and serenity? The true cause is to be found in the ban which the Pen of Glory hath, day and night, chosen to impose, and in Our assumption of the reins of authority, through the power and might of Him Who is the Lord of all mankind. . . .

In the Epistle to the Romans Saint Paul hath written: "Let

every soul be subject unto the higher powers. For there is no power but of God; the powers that be are ordained of God. Whosoever therefore resisteth the power, resisteth the ordinance of God." And further: "For he is the minister of God, a revenger to execute wrath upon him that doeth evil." He saith that the appearance of the kings, and their majesty and power are of God.

Moreover, in the traditions of old, references have been made which the divines have seen and heard. We beseech God—blessed and glorified be He—to aid thee, O Shaykh, to lay fast hold on that which hath been sent down from the heaven of the bounty of God, the Lord of the worlds. The divines must needs unite with His Majesty, the Sháh, and cleave unto that which will insure the protection, the security, the welfare and prosperity of men. A just king enjoyeth nearer access unto God than anyone. Unto this testifieth He Who speaketh in His Most Great Prison. God! There is none other God but Him, the One, the Incomparable, the Almighty, the All-Knowing, the All-Wise. . . .

At this moment the shrill voice of the Most Sublime Pen hath been raised, and hath addressed Me saying: "Admonish the Shaykh even as Thou hast admonished one of Thy Branches (sons), that haply the breezes of Thine utterance may attract and draw him nigh unto God, the Lord of the worlds."

"Be generous in prosperity, and thankful in adversity. Be worthy of the trust of thy neighbor, and look upon him with a bright and friendly face. Be a treasure to the poor, an admonisher to the rich, an answerer to the cry of the needy, a preserver of the sanctity of thy pledge. Be fair in thy judgment, and guarded in thy speech. Be unjust to no man, and show all meekness to all men. Be as a lamp unto them that walk in darkness, a joy to the sorrowful, a sea for the thirsty, a haven for the distressed, an upholder and defender of the victim of oppression. Let integrity and uprightness distinguish all thine acts. Be a home for the stranger, a balm to the suffering, a

tower of strength for the fugitive. Be eyes to the blind, and a guiding light unto the feet of the erring. Be an ornament to the countenance of truth, a crown to the brow of fidelity, a pillar of the temple of righteousness, a breath of life to the body of mankind, an ensign of the hosts of justice, a luminary above the horizon of virtue, a dew to the soil of the human heart, an ark on the ocean of knowledge, a sun in the heaven of bounty, a gem on the diadem of wisdom, a shining light in the firmament of thy generation, a fruit upon the tree of humility. We pray God to protect thee from the heat of jealousy and the cold of hatred. He verily is nigh, ready to answer." Thus hath My tongue spoken unto one of My Branches (sons), and We have mentioned it unto such of Our loved ones as have cast away their idle fancies, and clung unto that which hath been prescribed unto them in the day whereon the Daystar of Certitude hath shone forth above the horizon of the will of God, the Lord of the worlds. This is the day on which the Bird of Utterance hath warbled its melody upon the branches, in the name of its Lord, the God of Mercy. Blessed is the man that hath, on the wings of longing, soared towards God, the Lord of the Judgment Day. . . .

O Shaykh! The breezes of Revelation can never be confounded with other breezes. Now the Lote-Tree beyond which there is no passing standeth laden with countless fruits before thy face; besmirch not thyself with idle fancies, as have done the people aforetime. These utterances themselves proclaim the true nature of the Faith of God. He it is Who witnesseth unto all things. To demonstrate the truth of His Revelation He hath not been, nor is He, dependent upon any one. Well nigh a hundred volumes of luminous verses and perspicuous words have already been sent down from the heaven of the will of Him Who is the Revealer of signs, and are available unto all. It is for thee to direct thyself towards the Ultimate Goal, and the Supreme End, and the Most Sublime Pinnacle, that thou mayest hear and behold what hath been revealed by God, the Lord of the worlds. . . .[37]

Notes

[36] Shoghi Effendi, *God Passes By*, p. 219.
[37] Bahá'u'lláh, *The Epistle to the Son of the Wolf*, pp. 1-115.

The Book of My Covenant (Kitáb-u-'Ahdí)

This relatively short document, also known as The Book of the Covenant (Kitáb-i-'Ahd), *is Bahá'u'lláh's last will and testament. He apparently wrote it and sealed it away in a box about two years prior to His death. During His last illness, Bahá'u'lláh entrusted it to His eldest son, 'Abdu'l-Bahá, who had it unsealed and made public few days after Bahá'u'lláh's passing on 29 May 1892. Of the significance of the* Kitáb-u-'Ahdí, *Shoghi Effendi writes: "this unique and epoch-making Document, designated by Bahá'u'lláh as His "Most Great Tablet," and alluded to by Him as the "Crimson Book" in His* Epistle to the Son of the Wolf, *can find no parallel in the Scriptures of any previous Dispensation, not excluding that of the Báb Himself. For nowhere in the books pertaining to any of the world's religious systems, not even among the writings of the Author of the Bábí Revelation, do we find any single document establishing a Covenant endowed with an authority comparable to the Covenant which Bahá'u'lláh had Himself instituted."*[38]

ALTHOUGH the Realm of Glory hath none of the vanities of the world, yet within the treasury of trust and resignation We have bequeathed to Our heirs an excellent and priceless heritage. Earthly treasures We have not bequeathed, nor have We added such cares as they entail. By God! In earthly riches fear is hidden and peril is concealed. Consider ye and call to mind that which the All-Merciful hath revealed in the Qur'án: 'Woe betide every slanderer and defamer, him that layeth up riches and counteth them.'[104:1-2] Fleeting are the riches of the world; all that perisheth and changeth is not, and hath never been, worthy of attention, except to a recognized measure.

The aim of this Wronged One in sustaining woes and tribulations, in revealing the Holy Verses and in demonstrating

proofs hath been naught but to quench the flame of hate and enmity, that the horizon of the hearts of men may be illumined with the light of concord and attain real peace and tranquillity. From the dawning-place of the divine Tablet the day-star of this utterance shineth resplendent, and it behoveth everyone to fix his gaze upon it: We exhort you, O peoples of the world, to observe that which will elevate your station. Hold fast to the fear of God and firmly adhere to what is right. Verily I say, the tongue is for mentioning what is good, defile it not with unseemly talk. God hath forgiven what is past. Henceforward everyone should utter that which is meet and seemly, and should refrain from slander, abuse and whatever causeth sadness in men. Lofty is the station of man! Not long ago this exalted Word streamed forth from the treasury of Our Pen of Glory: Great and blessed is this Day—the Day in which all that lay latent in man hath been and will be made manifest. Lofty is the station of man, were he to hold fast to righteousness and truth and to remain firm and steadfast in the Cause. In the eyes of the All-Merciful a true man appeareth even as a firmament; its sun and moon are his sight and hearing, and his shining and resplendent character its stars. His is the loftiest station, and his influence educateth the world of being.

Every receptive soul who hath in this Day inhaled the fragrance of His garment and hath, with a pure heart, set his face towards the all-glorious Horizon is reckoned among the people of Bahá in the Crimson Book. Grasp ye, in My Name, the chalice of My loving-kindness, drink then your fill in My glorious and wondrous remembrance.

O ye that dwell on earth! The religion of God is for love and unity; make it not the cause of enmity or dissension. In the eyes of men of insight and the beholders of the Most Sublime Vision, whatsoever are the effective means for safeguarding and promoting the happiness and welfare of the children of men have already been revealed by the Pen of Glory. But the foolish ones of the earth, being nurtured in evil passions and desires, have remained heedless of the consummate wisdom

of Him Who is, in truth, the All-Wise, while their words and deeds are prompted by idle fancies and vain imaginings.

O ye the loved ones and the trustees of God! Kings are the manifestations of the power, and the daysprings of the might and riches, of God. Pray ye on their behalf. He hath invested them with the rulership of the earth and hath singled out the hearts of men as His Own domain.

Conflict and contention are categorically forbidden in His Book. This is a decree of God in this Most Great Revelation. It is divinely preserved from annulment and is invested by Him with the splendour of His confirmation. Verily He is the All-Knowing, the All-Wise.

It is incumbent upon everyone to aid those daysprings of authority and sources of command who are adorned with the ornament of equity and justice. Blessed are the rulers and the learned among the people of Bahá. They are My trustees among My servants and the manifestations of My commandments amidst My people. Upon them rest My glory, My blessings and My grace which have pervaded the world of being. In this connection the utterances revealed in the Kitáb-i-Aqdas are such that from the horizon of their words the light of divine grace shineth luminous and resplendent.

O ye My Branches! A mighty force, a consummate power lieth concealed in the world of being. Fix your gaze upon it and upon its unifying influence, and not upon the differences which appear from it.

The Will of the divine Testator is this: It is incumbent upon the Aghsán, the Afnán and My Kindred to turn, one and all, their faces towards the Most Mighty Branch. Consider that which We have revealed in Our Most Holy Book: 'When the ocean of My presence hath ebbed and the Book of My Revelation is ended, turn your faces toward Him Whom God hath purposed, Who hath branched from this Ancient Root.' The object of this sacred verse is none other except the Most Mighty Branch

['Abdu'l-Bahá]. Thus have We graciously revealed unto you Our potent Will, and I am verily the Gracious, the All-Powerful. Verily God hath ordained the station of the Greater Branch [Muhammad 'Alí] to be beneath that of the Most Great Branch ['Abdu'l-Bahá]. He is in truth the Ordainer, the All-Wise. We have chosen 'the Greater' after 'the Most Great', as decreed by Him Who is the All-Knowing, the All-Informed.

It is enjoined upon everyone to manifest love towards the Aghsán, but God hath not granted them any right to the property of others.

O ye My Aghsán, My Afnán and My Kindred! We exhort you to fear God, to perform praiseworthy deeds and to do that which is meet and seemly and serveth to exalt your station. Verily I say, fear of God is the greatest commander that can render the Cause of God victorious, and the hosts which best befit this commander have ever been and are an upright character and pure and goodly deeds.

Say: O servants! Let not the means of order be made the cause of confusion and the instrument of union an occasion for discord. We fain would hope that the people of Bahá may be guided by the blessed words: 'Say: all things are of God.' This exalted utterance is like unto water for quenching the fire of hate and enmity which smouldereth within the hearts and breasts of men. By this single utterance contending peoples and kindreds will attain the light of true unity. Verily He speaketh the truth and leadeth the way. He is the All-Powerful, the Exalted, the Gracious.

It is incumbent upon everyone to show courtesy to, and have regard for the Aghsán, that thereby the Cause of God may be glorified and His Word exalted. This injunction hath time and again been mentioned and recorded in the Holy Writ. Well is it with him who is enabled to achieve that which the Ordainer, the Ancient of Days hath prescribed for him. Ye are bidden moreover to respect the members of the Holy Household, the Afnán and the kindred. We further admonish you to serve all

nations and to strive for the betterment of the world.

That which is conducive to the regeneration of the world and the salvation of the peoples and kindreds of the earth hath been sent down from the heaven of the utterance of Him Who is the Desire of the world. Give ye a hearing ear to the counsels of the Pen of Glory. Better is this for you than all that is on the earth. Unto this beareth witness My glorious and wondrous Book.[39]

Notes

[38] Shoghi Effendi, *God Passes By*, p. 238.
[39] Bahá'u'lláh, *Tablet of Bahá'u'lláh revealed after the Kitáb-i-Aqdas*, pp. 219-23.

APPENDIX I

Bahá'u'lláh's Best-known Works

The following is a title-list of one hundred and fifty of Bahá'u'lláh's best-known works which has been arranged alphabetically and in accordance with the period of His ministry during which they were composed. It is by no means a complete representation of the entire range of Bahá'u'lláh's Creative Words. In many of His letters, generally known as "Tablets", Bahá'u'lláh Himself has made reference to the vastness of His writings and in the Epistle to the Son of the Wolf, *His last major work written a year before His passing, He maintains that if all His writings were gathered and arranged, the collection would exceed one hundred volumes.*

By the early 1990's some fifteen thousand separate works by Bahá'u'lláh were reportedly collected and catalogued at the archives of the Bahá'í World Centre in Haifa, Israel. Today the majority of this vast collection still remains unpublished. The following, therefore, is only a select listing of Bahá'u'lláh's published or widely-known writings which also bear a title.

The compiler of this list is most grateful to the Universal House of Justice, the Supreme Body of the Bahá'í World Community, for its assistance, through its research department, in preparing this list.

Prior to His Exile (TEHRAN)

1) Rashḥ-i-'Amá

BAGHDAD

2) Az-Bágh-i-Iláhí ("From the Divine Garden....")
3) Báz-Áv-u-Bidih-Jámí ("Come hither and proffer the Cup....")
4) Chihár-Vádí (The Four Valleys)
5) Haft-Vádí (The Seven Valleys)
6) Halih-Halih-Halih-Yá-Bishárat (Hallelújah! Hallelújah! Hallelújah! Glad-Tiding!)
7) Ḥúr-i-'Ujáb (The Wondrous Maiden)
8) Ḥurúfát-i-'Állín (The Exalted Letters)
9) Javáhiru'l-Asrár (The Gems of Divine Mysteries)
10) Kalimát-i-Maknúnih (The Hidden Words)
11) Kitáb-i-Íqán (The Book of Certitude)
12) Lawḥ-i-Bulbulu'l-Firáq (Tablet of the Nightingale of Bereavement)
13) Lawḥ-i-Fitnih (Tablet of the Test)
14) Lawḥ-i-Ghulámu'l-Khuld (Tablet of the Youth of Paradise)
15) Lawḥ-i-Ḥaq (Tablet of the Truth)
16) Lawḥ-i-Ḥúríyyih (Tablet of the Maid of Heaven)
17) Lawḥ-i-Kullu'ṭ-Ṭa'ám (Tablet of All Food)
18) Lawḥ-i-Malláḥu'l-Quds (Tablet of the Holy Mariner)
19) Madínatu'r-Riḍá (The City of Radiant Acquiescence)
20) Madínatu't-Tawḥíd (The City of Unity)
21) Qaṣídiy-i-Varqá'íyyih (Ode of the Dove)
22) Ṣaḥífiy-i-Shaṭṭíyyih (The Book of the River)
23) Sáqí-Az-Ghayb-i-Baqá
24) Shikkar-Shikan-Shavand
25) Subḥána-Rabbíya'l-A'lá (Praise be the Lord, the Most

Exalted)

26) Súriy-i-Dhikr (Súrih of Rememberance)

27) Súriy-i-Nuṣḥ (Súrih of Exhortation)

28) Súriy-i-Qadír (Súrih of the Omnipotent)

29) Súriy-i-Ṣabr (Súrih of Patience) **OR** Lawh-i-Ayyúb (Tablet of Job) **OR** Madínatu's-Ṣabr (The City of Patience)

30) Tafsír-i-Hú (Commentary on the pronoun "He")

31) Tafsír-i-Hurúfát-i-Muqaṭṭa'ih (Commentary on the Isolated Letters) **OR** Lawḥ-i-Áyiy-i-Núr (Tablet of the Verse of Light)

32) Zíyárat-Námiy-i-Awlíyá (The Visitation Prayer of the beloved ones)

ISTANBUL (Constantinople)

33) Lawḥ-i-Hawdaj (Tablet of the Howdah) **OR** Lawḥ-i-Sámsún (Tablet of Samsun)

34) Lawḥ-i-'Abdu'l-'Azíz-Va-Vukalá (Tablet to Sultan 'Abdu'l-'Azíz and his ministers)

35) Mathnaví-i-Mubárak

36) Subḥánika-Yá-Hú (Praise be to Him) **OR** Lawḥ-i-Náqús (Tablet of the Bell)

EDIRNE (Adrianople)

37) Kitáb-i-Badí' (The Wondrous New Book)

38) Lawḥ-i-Aḥmad (Tablet of Aḥmad-Arabic)

39) Lawḥ-i-Aḥmad-i-Fársí (Tablet of Aḥmad-Persian)

40) Lawḥ-i-Ashraf (Tablet of Ashraf)

41) Lawḥ-i-Bahá (Tablet of Bahá)

42) Lawḥ-i-Khalíl (Tablet of Khalíl)

43) Lawḥ-i-Mubáhilih (Tablet of Confrontation)

44) Lawḥ-i-Nápulyún (First Tablet to Napoleon III)

45) Lawḥ-i-Nuqṭih (Tablet of the Point)

46) Lawḥ-i-Naṣír (Tablet of Naṣír)
47) Lawḥu'r-Riḍván (Tablet of Riḍván)
48) Lawḥu'r-Rúḥ **OR** Lawḥ-i-Rúḥ (Tablet of the Spirit)
49) Lawḥ-i-Salmán I (First Tablet to Salmán)
50) Lawḥ-i-Sayyáḥ (Tablet of Sayyáh)
51) Lawḥ-i-Siráj (Tablet of Siráj)
52) Lawḥ-i-Sulṭán (Tablet to Násiri'd-Dín Sháh)
53) Lawḥu't-Tuqá **OR** Lawḥ-i-Tuqá (Tablet of the Fear of God)
54) Munáját háy-i-Ṣíyám (Prayers for Fasting)
55) Riḍvánu'l-Iqrár (The Paradise of Assurance)
56) Súratu'lláh (Súrih of God)
57) Súriy-i-Aḥzán (Súrih of Sorrows)
58) Súriy-i-Amr (Súrih of Command)
59) Súriy-i-Aṣḥáb (Súrih of Companions) **OR** Lawḥ-i-Ḥabíb (Tablet of Habíb)
60) Súriy-i-Damm (Súrih of Blood)
61) Súriy-i-Bayán (Súrih of Bayán)
62) Súriy-i-Dhibḥ (Súrih of Sacrifice)
63) Súriy-i-Ghusn (Súrih of the Branch)
64) Súriy-i-Ḥajj I (The First Súrih of Pilgrimage)
65) Súriy-i-Ḥajj II (The Second Súrih of Pilgrimage)
66) Súriy-i-Haykal **OR** Súratu'l-Haykal (Súrih of the Temple)
67) Súriy-i-Hijr (Súrih of Separation)
68) Súriy-i-'Ibád (Súrih of the Servants)
69) Súriy-i-Mulúk **OR** Súratu'l-Mulúk (Súrih of the Kings)
70) Súriy-i-Qalam (Súrih of the Pen)
71) Súriy-i-Qamís (Súrih of the Robe)
72) Súriy-i-Ra'ís (Súrih of the Chief)

73) Súriy-i-Vidád (Súrih of Love)

'AKKÁ

74) Alváḥ-i-Laylatu'l-Quds (Tablets of the Holy Night)
75) Aṣl-i-kullu'l-Khayr (Words of Wisdom)
76) Bishárát (Glad-Tidings)
77) Ishráqát (Splendours)
78) Kalimát-i-Firdawsíyyih (Words of Paradise)
79) Kitáb-i-'Ahd (The Book of Covenant) **OR** Kitáb-u-'Ahdí (The Book of My Covenant)
80) Kitáb-i-Aqdas (The Most Holy Book)
81) Lawḥ-i-'Abdu'l-Razzáq (Tablet of 'Abdu'l-Razzáq)
82) Lawḥ-i-'Abdu'l-Vahháb (Tablet of 'Abdu'l-Vahháb)
83) Lawḥ-i-Aḥbáb (Tablet of the loved ones of God)
84) Lawḥ-i-'Alí (Tablet of 'Alí)
85) Lawḥ-i-Amváj (Tablet of the Waves)
86) Lawḥ-i-Anta'l-Káfí (Tablet of "Thou the Sufficer" also known as The Long Healing Prayer)
87) Lawḥ-i-Aqdas (The Most Holy Tablet)
88) Lawḥ-i-Arḍ-i-Bá (Tablet of the Land of Bá-Beirut)
89) Lawḥ-i-Arḍ-i-Ṭá (Tablet of the Land of Ṭá-Ṭihrán)
90) Lawḥ-i-'Áshiq-va-Ma'shúq (Tablet of the Lover and the Beloved)
91) Lawḥ-i-Baqá (Tablet of Immortality)
92) Lawḥ-i-Basiṭatu'l-Ḥaqíqih (Tablet of Simple Truth)
93) Lawḥ-i-Bismilih (Tablet of "In the Name of God")
94) Lawḥ-i-Burhán (Tablet of the Proof)
95) Lawḥ-i-Dhabíḥ (Tablet of Dhabíh)
96) Lawḥ-i-Dunyá (Tablet of the World)
97) Lawḥ-i-Fu'ád (Tablet to Fu'ád Páshá)
98) Lawḥ-i-Hádíy-i-Qazvíní (Tablet to Hádíy-i-Qazvíní)
99) Lawḥ-i-Haft-Pursish (Tablet of Seven Questions) **OR**

Lawḥ-i-Shír-Mard (Tablet of the Lion-hearted One Amongst Men)

100) Lawḥ-i-Ḥikmat (Tablet of Wisdom)
101) Lawḥ-i-Hirtík (Tablet to G.D. Hardegg)
102) Lawḥ-i-Ḥusayn (Tablet of Ḥusayn)
103) Lawḥ-i-Ibn-i-Dhi'b (Epistle to the Son of the Wolf)
104) Lawḥ-i-Istintáq (Tablet of Interrogation)
105) Lawḥ-i-Ittiḥád (Tablet of Unity)
106) Lawḥ-i-Jamál (Tablet of Jamál)
107) Lawḥ-i-Javád (Tablet of Javád)
108) Lawḥ-i-Karím (Tablet of Karím)
109) Lawḥ-i-Karmil (Tablet of Carmil)
110) Lawḥ-i-Kitáb-aṣ-Ṣidq (Tablet of the Book of Truth)
111) Lawḥ-i-Malikih (Tablet to Queen Victoria)
112) Lawḥ-i-Malik-i-Rús (Tablet to the Czar of Russia)
113) Lawḥ-i-Mánikjí-Ṣáḥib (Tablet to Mánikjí-Ṣáḥib)
114) Lawḥ-i-Maqṣúd (Tablet of Maqsúd)
115) Lawḥ-i-Maryam (Tablet of Maryam)
116) Lawḥ-i-Mawlúd (Tablet of the Birthday)
117) Lawḥ-i-Nápulyún II (Second Tablet to Napoleon III)
118) Lawḥ-i-Páp (Tablet to Pope Pius IX)
119) Lawḥ-i-Pisar-'Amm (Tablet to the Cousin)
120) Lawḥ-i-Qad-Iḥtaraqa'l-Mukhliṣún (Tablet of "Indeed the hearts of the sincere are consumed..." also known as the Fire Tablet)
121) Lawḥ-i-Qiná (Tablet of the Veil)
122) Lawḥ-i-Ra'ís (Tablet of the Chief)
123) Lawḥ-i-Raqshá (Tablet of the She-Serpent)
124) Lawḥ-i-Ru'yá (Tablet of Vision)
125) Lawḥ-i-Saḥáb (Tablet of the Clouds)
126) Lawḥ-i-Salmán II (Tablet of Salmán II)

127) Lawḥ-i-Shaykh-Fání (Tablet to Shaykh-Fání)
128) Lawḥ-i-Siyyid Mihdíy-i-Dahají (Tablet to Siyyid Mihdíy-i-Dahajáí)
129) Lawḥ-i-Tawḥíd (Tablet of Oneness)
130) Lawḥ-i-Ṭibb (Tablet of Medicine)
131) Lawḥ-i-Times (Tablet to the Times of London)
132) Lawḥ-i-Yúsuf (Tablet of Yúsuf)
133) Lawḥ-i-Zaynu'l-Muqarrabín (Tablet of Zaynu'l-Muqarrabín)
134) Riḍvánu'l Adl (The Paradise of Justice)
135) Su-ál va Javáb (Questions and Answers)
136) Súriy-i-Amín (Súrih of Amín)
137) Súriy-i-A'ráb (Súrih of the Arabs)
138) Súriy-i-Haykal (Súrih of the Temple)
139) Súriy-i-Ismuna'l-Mursil (Súrih of "Our Name is the Sender")
140) Súriy-i-Nidá (Súrih of Proclamation)
141) Súriy-i-Sulṭán (Tablet to the believers of Sulṭán-Ábád)
142) Súriy-i-Vafá (Tablet of Vafá)
143) Súriy-i-Zíyárih (Súrih of Visitation)
144) Tafsír-i-Súriy-i-Va'sh-Shams (Commentary on the Qur'ánic Súrih of the Sun)
145) Tajallíyát (Effulgences)
146) Ṭarázát (Ornaments)
147) Zíyárat-Námih (Tablet of Visitation)
148) Zíyárat-Námiy-i-Bayt (The Visitation Tablet of the House)
149) Zíyárat-Námiy-i-Maryam (The Visitation Tablet of Maryam)
150) Zíyárat-Námiy-i-Siyyidu'sh-Shuhadá (The Visitation Tablet of the Prince of Martyrs-Imám Husayn)

APPENDIX II

A Chronology of Some Important Dates of Bahá'u'lláh's Life

12 November 1817	Birth in Tehran
October 1835	Marriage to Ásíyih Khánum (Navváb)
Late August to early September 1844	Acceptance of the Báb's Message and commencement of new life as a Bábí
Late 1847	First imprisonment - Tehran
Late June to early July 1848	Conference of Badasht
November and December 1848	Visits to the Fort of Shaykh Ṭabarsí
December 1848	Second imprisonment - Ámul and suffering the bastinado
June 1851	Journey to Karbilá
May 1852	Return from Iraq
Mid-late August 1852	Imprisonment in the Síyáh Chál
16-28 October 1852	Birth of the Bahá'í Revelation
12 December 1852	Release from the Síyáh Chál

12 January 1853	Departure from Tehran - exile to Iraq
8 April 1853	Arrival in Baghdad
10 April 1854	Retirement to the mountains of Sulaymáníyyih
19 March 1856	Return to Baghdad from Sulaymáníyyih
January 1861	Composition of the *Kitáb-i-Íqán*
22 April 1863	Open-private Declaration of His Mission at the garden of Najíbíyyih (Riḍván)
3 May 1863	Departure from Baghdad - invitation to Istanbul
16 August 1863	Arrival in Istanbul
1 December 1863	Departure from Istanbul - banishment to Edirne
12 December 1863	Arrival in Edirne
10 March 1866	"The Most Great Separation"
May to October 1866	Composition of *Súriy-i-Mulúk* - Open public Proclamation of His Mission
12 August 1868	Departure from Edirne - exile to 'Akká
31 August 1868	Arrival in 'Akká
23 June 1870	Death of His son Mírzá Mihdí

4 November 1870	Removal from the army barracks prison
September 1871	Occupation of the House of 'Udí Khammár
1873 *et seq.*	Composition of the *Kitáb-i-Aqdas*
Late 1873	Occupation of the House of 'Abbúd
Early June 1877	End of confinement within 'Akká and occupation of the House at Mazra'ih
September 1879	Occupation of the House at Bahjí
August 1883	Second visit to Haifa
April 1890	Third visit to Haifa
Summer 1891	Fourth visit to Haifa for three months
29 May 1892	Passing at Bahjí

To my dear spiritual brother

Hank

May the Light of Bahá

continues to illumine your

radiant heart!

Warmest love,

Shahrokh

July 20/2008